ANALYSIS AND DESIGN OF BUSINESS INFORMATION SYSTEMS

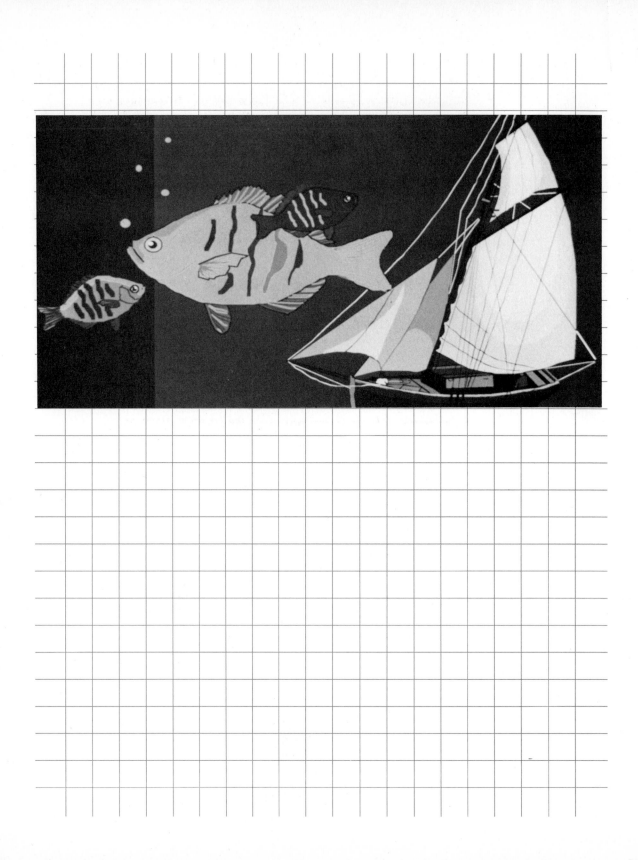

SECOND EDITION

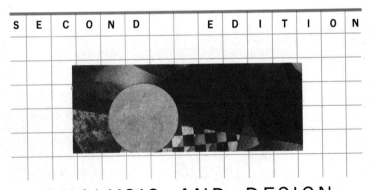

ANALYSIS AND DESIGN

OF BUSINESS

INFORMATION SYSTEMS

MERLE P. MARTIN

California State University
SACRAMENTO

PRENTICE HALL
Englewood Cliffs, New Jersey 07632

Library of Congress Cataloging-in-Publication Data

Martin, Merle P.
  Analysis and design of business information systems / Merle P.
Martin.—2nd ed.
    p.   cm.
  Includes bibliographical references and index.
  ISBN 0-02-376741-3
    1. Information storage and retrieval systems—Business.
2. Management information systems.   I. Title.
HF5548.2.M3436   1995
658.4′038′011—dc20   94-1357
                                                          CIP

Editor: P. J. Boardman
Production Supervisor: bookworks
Production Manager: Lynn Pearlman
Text Designer: Hothouse Designs
Cover Designer: Hothouse Designs
Cover Art: Slide Graphics

 Copyright © 1995 by Prentice-Hall, Inc.
A Simon & Schuster Company
Englewood Cliffs, New Jersey 07632

Previous edition copyright © 1991.

Printed in the United States of America

Printed in the United States of America
10 9 8 7 6 5 4 3 2

ISBN 0-02-376741-3

Prentice-Hall International (UK) Limited, *London*
Prentice-Hall of Australia Pty. Limited, *Sydney*
Prentice-Hall Canada Inc., *Toronto*
Prentice-Hall Hispanoamericana, S.A., *Mexico*
Prentice-Hall of India Private Limited, *New Delhi*
Prentice-Hall of Japan, Inc., *Tokyo*
Simon & Schuster Asia Pte. Ltd., *Singapore*
Editora Prentice-Hall do Brasil, Ltda., *Rio de Janeiro*

TO THE STUDENT

Welcome to the exciting world of information systems development. Analyzing and designing business information systems is hard work, but it is one of the most creative and fulfilling fields in the information systems discipline. This book introduces you to the field of business systems analysis and design through three views: the real world, your needs as a student, and the future.

REAL-WORLD ORIENTATION

I have designed large and small business information systems. I have designed some excellent systems and some that didn't work as well as they should have. You'll see my real-world experience in this textbook in several ways:

Coverage is comprehensive. Even if your instructor chooses to skip some of the topics because of time constraints, the full scope of the textbook will serve you in other courses and after graduation.

The book is accompanied by a computer-aided systems engineering (CASE) tool called Visible Analyst WORKBENCH, provided by Visible Systems Corporation of Waltham, Massachusetts. It will help you become part of the CASE revolution that will mark business systems development in the years to come.

Topics are presented realistically. Too often, recent graduates feel as if they have left one planet (academia) for another planet (the workplace). In this book, you will find examples of poorly designed systems, the impact of workplace politics, and the weaknesses as well as strengths of development tools and approaches. You'll come away prepared for the real world.

STUDENT ORIENTATION

In an effort to ease the difficulties I have had with some textbooks, I have used the following features to make *your* role as a student easier:

Planned redundancy is one of the design tactics you will study. It means that duplication is valuable if it serves a purpose. I have duplicated figures and examples in different parts of the book, so you won't have to search back to previous chapters. In addition, some material covered in earlier parts of the textbook is repeated later in summary format. This allows you to see how the material applies to different parts of the systems development life cycle.

Checklists are used throughout as an aid to learning and review and as a management guide in the workplace.

At the end of each chapter, Key Terms, Concepts Learned, and Review Questions are special checklists that will help you to learn the material and review for examinations.

Critical thinking opportunities at the end of each chapter encourage you to get out of the classroom and enter actual business settings.

There are twenty-four end-of-chapter cases, which add a real-world quality to the material.

You may have been introduced to some of the material in this book in earlier courses. We all get rusty, however, so review this material at your own pace.

FUTURE ORIENTATION

Analysis and design of business information systems is a rapidly changing field. This book offers you the skills you will need for today's jobs, plus the perspective and flexibility you will need to be tomorrow's manager. This mix of present and future is achieved in these ways:

Concepts and tools are brought together under a conceptual umbrella. Who knows what tools we will see ten years from now? The concepts, however, will remain.

Structured design is discussed but not overemphasized. Even though structured analysis and design approaches are evolving rapidly, nonstructured approaches are still prevalent in today's business workplaces.

There are chapters on process design reengineering and object-oriented analysis and design. These are topics that are just now taking shape in our field but will be established approaches by the year 2000.

The examples and many cases are directed to giving you a better understanding of how business applications operate. Recently, a vice president of information systems for a large aerospace company said, "We'd rather hire college graduates who know business and then teach them programming, than hire programmers and have to teach them business." This textbook will reinforce your knowledge of how business operates.

TO THE INSTRUCTOR

The primary thrust of the changes for this second edition has been to make the material flow more smoothly and directly through the systems development life cycle. The book has been redesigned to fit more closely the syllabus sequences for typical systems analysis and systems design courses. Following are the more important enhancements made to this edition.

1. Five new chapters have been added: Chapter 9, "Preliminary Design and the System Study"; Chapter 17, "Process Design/Reengineering;" Chapter 20, "System Evaluation"; Chapter 23, "Object-Oriented Analysis and Design"; and Chapter 24, "The Future."

2. The tool chapters (4, 5, and 6 in the first edition) have been separated and placed at more appropriate places within the SDLC. They include Chapter 6, "Structured Development Tools," and Chapter 11, "Data Dictionary and Other Design Tools."

3. There are now five rather than seven sections.

4. There are now twenty-four cases, which are placed behind the chapter pertaining to the topic of the case.

5. A glossary of terms has been added.

6. A total quality management (TQM) approach is emphasized; each chapter begins with a total quality approach to the topic.

7. Structured methodologies are emphasized more than in the first edition. Each chapter has an early section on a structured approach to the topic.

8. Each chapter concludes with a section on human aspects, which serves to remind us that analysis and design are not solely (or even largely) automated, structured processes. Humans are the most important elements.

9. Chapter 14, "Interactive Screen Design," has been derived from appendix and associated material in the first edition.

10. Chapter 16, "Database Design," has been expanded.

11. The instructor's manual has been updated and furnished with new, real-life case studies for instructor use.

12. There is no longer a need for an accompanying textbook devoted to Visible Analyst WORKBENCH (VAW) in conjunction with this book. All VAW instruction material is included in and can be copied from the instructor's manual.

13. There are now two running case studies. One, Goodbyte Pizza, is new in this edition.

14. There is a new running case on a class design project, which allows the instructor to assign a class project directly from the textbook.

WHO IS THE AUDIENCE FOR THIS BOOK?

This book has been designed in a modular fashion. Its flexibility allows it to be used in a one-semester or two-semester undergraduate course or a concentrated one-semester graduate course. Students in these courses are expected to have completed a computer concepts course. In addition, it is helpful if students have already taken several business core courses, such as management and marketing. Topics covered in this textbook are compatible with both the DPMA and ACM curriculum models.

WHY IS THIS BOOK AN EXCELLENT TOOL?

This book is comprehensive and modular enough to allow instructors to tailor it to particular classroom situations. It accomplishes the following goals:

- Places tools within an overall conceptual framework for development of business systems
- Provides equal emphasis on structured and conventional systems development
- Emphasizes a human factors approach to business systems development
- Concentrates on the decisions made rather than the tools used in the development process
- Stresses the realism of systems development in the typical business setting

HOW IS THIS BOOK ORGANIZED?

Section One, "The Role of Business Information Systems," provides a conceptual framework by describing the role of technology in business, the quality of information, and why new systems are developed.

Section Two, "Analysis of Information Systems," follows the analysis process from problem detection through preparation of the system study.

Section Three, "Design of Information Systems," includes quality design alternatives, a data dictionary, output and input design, interactive screen design, data storage and database design, and process design.

Section Four, "System Implementation," demonstrates program construction and testing, system changeover, and evaluation.

Section Five, "Advanced Topics," describes rapid prototyping, CASE and other automated aids, and object-oriented analysis and design. It also includes a chapter that reflects on what the future may look like for business sytem development.

WHAT AIDS ARE AVAILABLE FOR STUDENTS AND INSTRUCTORS?

Pedagogical elements that appear in each chapter assist students in the learning process:

- Chapter objectives
- Chapter outline

- Chapter setting that informally sets the scene
- Numerous real-world examples throughout
- Boldfaced key terms in the text and a list of key terms at the end of the chapter
- Review questions that students can use as checklists for material covered in the chapter
- Critical thinking exercises that students can use to hone skills
- Two continuous (running) case studies for course project development

INSTRUCTORS GUIDE

An instructor's guide provides suggested course syllabi, lesson planning outlines, textbook cross-references, transparency masters, additional case studies, and instructions on how to install and use the Visible Analyst WORKBENCH.

ACKNOWLEDGMENTS

Many people helped create this book—the word-processing team, contributors, the Macmillan staff, and reviewers.

The word-processing team was led by Dotty Martin, my extraordinary wife, who coordinated the word-processing efforts. She entered much of the material herself and supervised all other entry. Her considerable experience in the information systems field made her one of my most valuable editors. Two other family members also did extensive word processing for the book. I give my sincere love and gratitude to my daughter, Collette Gardner, of Sacramento, California, and my brother-in-law, Howard Best, of Canyon Lake, California. They jumped in when we really needed them and quickly became wily veterans.

I am grateful for the contribution of Dr. Jane Carey, Arizona State University, West Campus. Jane is responsible for part of the material in Chapters 6 and 11 on development tools and Chapter 21 on prototyping. She also added numerous real-life examples to the textbook.

Another acknowledgment is due to Don Sherwood of Visible Systems, Waltham, Massachusetts. Don provided many examples and case studies that enhanced the textbook's real-world flavor. His firm also rendered many of the illustrations.

Many Macmillan staff members deserve acknowledgment. Charles Stewart, as the editor supported and contributed to this book at every level. Karen Fortgang of *bookworks* was the remarkably efficient Production Editor. Aliza Greenblatt was the Production Manager. The book, including the cover, was designed by Hothouse Designs.

The reviewers of the first edition encouraged us on the one hand and on the other hand humbled us into making the book much better. They are Kirk Arnett, Mississippi State University; Kuriakose Athappilly, Western Michigan University; Yair Babad, University of Illinois; Emerson Bailey, Casper College; William Beidler, University of Southern Mississippi; Charles Bilbrey, James Madison University; Edwin Blanks, Virginia Commonwealth University; John Cary, George Washington University; H. Michael Chung, Texas A&M University; Carl Clavedetscher, California Polytechnic

State University-Pomona; Gordon Davis, University of Minnesota; Shepperd Gold, California Polytechnic State University-Pomona; P. J. Guinan, Boston University; Dale Gust, Central Michigan University; James Hansen, Brigham Young University; Thomas M. Harris, Ball State University; James Hearne, West Washington University; Dennis Hill, Moraine Park Technical Institute; Cary Hughes, Middle Tennessee State University; Jean Insinga, Middlesex Community College; Sheila Jacobs, Oakland University; Joe Jones, University of Arkansas; Connie Knapp, Pace University; Robert Keim, Arizona State University; Thomas Lutz, Baylor University; John McKinney; Ido Millet, Bentley College; Lorne Olfman, Claremont Graduate School; June Parsons, Northern Michigan University; William Pracht, Memphis State University; and Wanda Thies, University of North Carolina – Greensboro.

BRIEF CONTENTS

CONTENTS

ANALYSIS AND DESIGN
OF BUSINESS
INFORMATION SYSTEMS

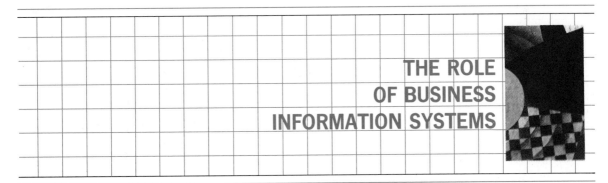

THE ROLE OF BUSINESS INFORMATION SYSTEMS

A doctor listens to her patient's description of his symptoms. Those symptoms show that the patient's health is deteriorating. The doctor draws on her knowledge of human anatomy to (1) determine the probable causes of the symptoms, (2) narrow down these alternative causes (through special tests) so she can select the most probable cause, and (3) design treatments for the most probable cause.

Systems analysts are the doctors of business information systems. They must measure the symptoms of ailing systems, select the most probable causes of system failings, and design new systems to cure the ills. So, if our analogy is to be complete, systems analysts must learn the anatomy of the business information systems they service. That is the purpose of this section.

Chapter 1, "Role of Technology in Business," explains the life flow of business and how information systems fit in. Chapter 2, "Quality of Information Systems," describes the structure of the different systems, designed for different purposes, that carry and deliver business information. Chapter 3, "Life and Death of Information Systems," discusses why information delivery systems must die and how to expect and plan for their replacements.

After studying this section of the book, you will have mastered the basic anatomy of business information systems. Then, as a doctor of such systems—that is, as an information systems analyst—you will be ready to receive your first patients.

In this chapter you will learn about:

WHAT: (Concepts) Approaches to integrating technology in a business firm.

WHY: Technology is expensive; it must be used only when it contributes to the
          profitability of the firm.

WHEN: Developing a corporate plan for information system development occurs
          before any individual systems are analyzed and designed.

WHO: These decisions are made by top-level (strategic) management and im-
          plemented by the chief information officer (CIO).

WHERE: The decisions take place at corporate headquarters. Actual implementa-
          tion of technology plans occurs in the field—at the operations level.

HOW: (Techniques) Business information planning
                       Critical success factors

OUTLINE

- Setting
- Information Technology Integration
- Business Information Planning
- Business Information Planning using IEF
- Information Systems Projects
- Information Systems Department
- Role of the Systems Analyst
- A Total Quality Management (TQM) Approach
- Human Aspects

THE ROLE OF TECHNOLOGY IN BUSINESS

You can never plan the future by the past.

— E D M U N D   B U R K E

SETTING

As you begin your study of systems analysis and design, it is important to place the discipline in its proper context—that is, the overall use of information technology in business firms. This chapter explains how systems analysis and design acts as a means of integrating and implementing information technology to support a firm's strategic missions.

Computer technology was introduced to business in the late 1950s. The first applications to be automated were accounting tasks such as payroll, accounts receivable, and accounts payable. During the 1960s, computer technology in business concentrated on manufacturing applications such as inventory, production control, customer order entry, and purchasing. Automation of these applications promised large savings in personnel costs. Nevertheless, by the end of the decade, the manufacturing industry in the United States had realized only a 2 percent decrease in jobs due to automation.

In the late 1960s and early 1970s, computers in business were considered a research and development (R&D) phenomenon. Often information systems costs were not monitored closely. Researchers were allowed to experiment to see how far business automation could stretch. Soon, however, this R&D period was over. In the middle to late 1970s, several events and conditions forced business managers to tighten

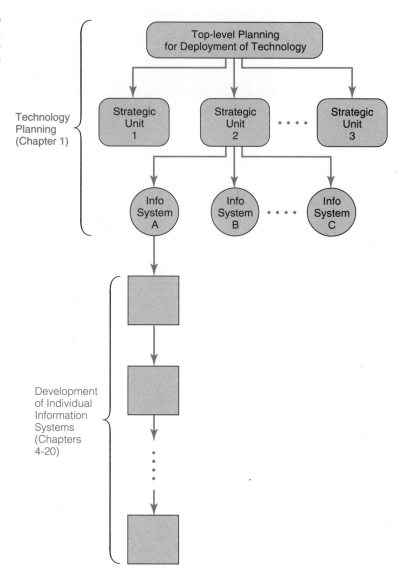

their belts. Some of these events were the OPEC oil embargo, deregulation of several industries, and the rise of international competition.

By the beginning of the 1980s, management was beginning to look closely at information systems costs, which had mushroomed in a relatively short time. Management began to investigate how to use information systems as a strategic tool rather than as a counter of nut and bolts. Information was considered as important a resource as money, material, and people. The terms **information resource management (IRM)** and **strategic computing** were coined to reflect a top-level management approach to computing.

Today, most business firms insist that the analysis and design of a business information system contribute directly to the firm's strategic goals. This requirement applies not only to use of computers but to other technologies as well. How can you be sure that a particular information system fits into a firm's overall business plans? This chapter answers the question by describing the planning process according to the top-down approach shown in Figure 1–1. This planning process occurs *before* individual systems are designed and implemented.

INFORMATION TECHNOLOGY INTEGRATION

There are two approaches to integrating information technology into a business firm. In the bottom-up approach, information technology is unsystematically implemented at lower levels of the organization by persons with technological interests, funds, or political influence. Information systems stack up until they become the firm's technological inventory. Such an inventory rarely has much relevance to overall firm strategies such as making profits. Alternatively, the top-down approach looks first at the firm's marketing strategy and determines what information technology is needed to enhance that strategy. Resources are allocated only to those projects that enhance strategic goals.

Consider the choice between two proposed information systems projects at Glorfeld Manufacturing Company. One system will keep statistics on the firm's vendors by tracking several important vendor performance characteristics: average material delivery time, percentage of material lost or defective, and freight costs. This proposed information system will help the purchasing department make better selections of vendors with whom to do business. The other proposed system will allow direct entry to the customer order entry system by salespeople in the field. Although the latter system is more expensive than the vendor system, it responds directly to the firm's strategic goal of doubling sales over the next five years. Management at Glorfeld Manufacturing rejects the vendor system and approves development of the remote order entry system because the latter system is *strategic* in nature.

Hence, development goals of information systems must be aligned with business marketing strategies. This must be done before beginning development of new, individual information systems.

Business Marketing Strategies

Four business marketing strategies are common for dealing with competitors: (1) produce the lowest cost product or service, (2) create a unique (differentiated) product for which there is no competition, (3) find a particular segment (niche) of the market to which a product or service has particular appeal, and (4) establish barriers to discourage entry of new competitors into the market. Each of these strategies requires different uses for information technology; therefore, the type of technology to be integrated into a firm will depend on that firm's marketing strategy.

Lowest Cost Strategy. The firm attempts to produce its product or service at a cost, and therefore at a price, lower than those of its competitors. Technological emphasis is on using computers for cost control—to develop planning and budgeting systems, cost control systems, process control systems, and inventory planning and control systems. Wal-Mart has been a consistent proponent of this strategy, as has Hyundai in the automotive industry.

Product Differentiation. The firm develops a product or service with a new twist—something that's unique in the market **(product differentiation).** Technological emphasis is on using computers to enhance sales. Product and service costs are not as important as making the product unique. Computers are used to develop customer sales support systems, systems that speed up customer order processing and product delivery, and product R&D systems.

American Hospital Supply (AHS) placed computer workstations in its customers' offices. The workstations were linked by telecommunication lines to the AHS computerized inventory and shipping system. Customers could order directly, with no delays; they also could make inquiries on the shipping status of the items they had ordered. AHS offered a service unmatched by any of its competitors. As a result, AHS's share of the medical supply market rose from a little over 10 percent to almost 70 percent.

Market Niche. The firm appeals to a specific customer segment (niche) of the market. This segment might be a particular group of businesses or a targeted demographic portion of the customer population. Technological emphasis is on studying the **market niche** and developing products or services that uniquely match that niche. Cost is important only when the market niche considers it important. The product need not be unique as long as it is delivered in a fashion that appeals to the market niche. Technological emphasis is on market research, customer service, and advertising.

Sears, Roebuck and Company has always targeted its products and services to middle-class, home-owning families. In the 1970s, market research indicated that these families were becoming interested in savings and investment opportunities. The company established the Sears Financial Network—a chain of one-stop financial shopping outlets where customers can perform all of their financial transactions: stocks, bonds, insurance, houses, IRAs. The Sears Financial Network consists of microcomputers located in retail stores. The microcomputers are tied by telecommunication lines to geographic databases containing financial information, thereby giving customers immediate access to the latest financial information.

Market Barriers. The firm uses technology to increase the level of customer service to the point where it becomes prohibitively expensive for a new firm to enter the market. The firm sets up **market barriers.** The emphasis is on use of new technologies to dramatically increase the cost of doing business. Two examples are AHS in the medical supply field and large supermarkets that introduced laser scanning checkout counters.

In both cases, a new firm entering the market is faced with a high level of initial technological costs.

In another example of market barriers, TRW's Information Systems Group (ISG) developed a national credit database with telecommunication access by thousands of lending institutions. ISG's database quickly delivers up-to-date credit reports. A new firm trying to enter the credit report market faces a large initial technological investment in order to be competitive.

In the face of these differing market strategies, a bottom-up approach to integrating information technology will most likely be unsuccessful. Emphasis on expensive technology can be counterproductive for a firm with a low-cost strategy. Conversely, emphasis on cost cutting can be counterproductive if the firm's marketing strategy is product differentiation, market niche, or entry barrier.

Businesses need a top-down approach that matches technology to a firm's marketing strategy. Yet, business information systems planning does not always fulfill the need for the top-down approach.

Management Levels

The type of information systems planning done by businesses falls within a broad spectrum. A firm's place in that spectrum is determined by where planning is done within the management structure. The structure of a firm's management can be portrayed by the triangle shown in Figure 1–2. There are three levels of management: strategic, tactical, and operational (Anthony, 1965).

At the **strategic** level, managers make decisions about the overall goals and direction of the firm. For example, managers decide the type of business to be in, geographical locations of operations, and the overall culture of the company. Such

FIGURE 1–2   **Organizational Levels of Decision Making**

strategic decisions are oriented to the future and apply to all of the firm's products, missions, and departments.

Managers at the **tactical** level are in charge of a specific product, mission, or department. Decisions are made within each specific tactical unit. For example, the tactical manager of product A may make a completely different advertising decision than the tactical manager of product B. However, both of these tactical managers may have to keep their advertising decisions within the strategic policy that all of the firm's advertising be done in good taste.

Managers at the **operational** level make the day-to-day decisions that keep the firm operating; they implement strategic and tactical decisions. Operational decisions include hiring workers, ordering materials, and scheduling work.

Top-down business planning starts at the strategic level with the determination of *what* is to be done. At the tactical level, planning is translated to *how* these strategic goals can be accomplished. Finally, at the operational level, the how is *implemented* according to tactical decisions. Here is an example. The strategic management group of Tsai's Oriental Food Distributors decides to use technology to erect market barriers and thereby discourage new competitors from entering the market (this is *what* is to be done). Tactical management decides that the best way to do this (the *how*) is by investing in laser scanning for checkout counters. Operational management then analyzes, selects, purchases, and puts into operation *(implements)* the laser scanning technology.

Unfortunately, business technological planning does not always follow this logical sequence. Reynolds (1988) suggests that technological efforts fall into a planning spectrum.

Planning Spectrum

Figure 1–3 presents Reynolds's spectrum for business technological planning in a modified format. The spectrum proceeds from left to right according to two dimensions. The first dimension is the extent of planning, which progresses from short to long

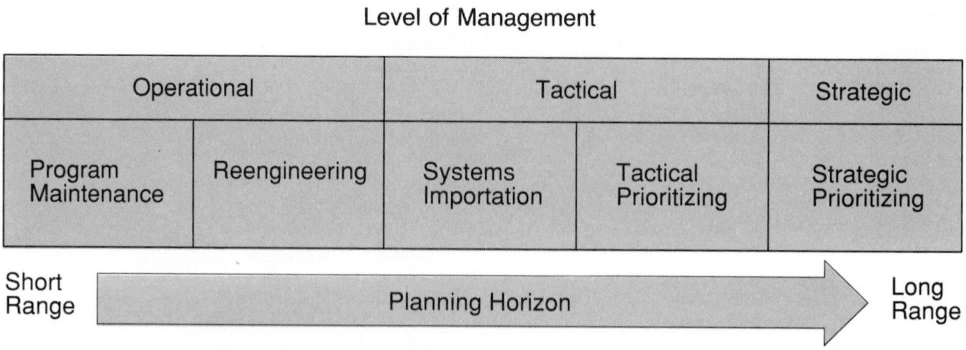

Level of Management

Operational		Tactical		Strategic
Program Maintenance	Reengineering	Systems Importation	Tactical Prioritizing	Strategic Prioritizing

Short Range → Planning Horizon → Long Range

FIGURE 1–3 **Spectrum for Business Technological Planning**

range. The second dimension is level of management involvement, which progresses from operational to strategic. Note the five stages in the spectrum: (1) program maintenance, (2) reengineering, (3) systems importation, (4) tactical prioritizing, and (5) strategic prioritizing.

Maintenance. In the maintenance stage, managers react to information systems problems. For example, program errors are corrected. McDonnell Douglas Corporation makes an average of almost 500 program maintenance changes each weekend. Unlike McDonnell Douglas, however, many firms *stop* at this end of the spectrum; they do not move into the planning stages.

Reengineering. The next stage in the spectrum—reengineering—is slightly more forward looking. Here managers look for ways to improve information systems before they begin to fail. Think of the maintenance work people do on cars to prevent them from breaking down. For example, during low-activity maintenance periods, Carey Contractors assigns programmers to analyze the program code of existing applications to improve the applications and make them more efficient.

Reengineering is a major goal of any information systems (IS) department. However, any firm that stops at this stage in the planning spectrum is still not really planning.

These first two phases in the planning spectrum occur at the operational level of management, where the focus is *how* to do information technology tasks rather than *what* tasks need to be done. The next two stages of the spectrum move information systems integration to the tactical management level.

Systems Importation. Tactical managers (e.g., product managers) look outside the firm for technological applications that have proved successful elsewhere. They then import the applications for implementation by operational management. Two examples follow. In the mid-1980s, two national insurance firms experimented successfully with expert systems to determine insurance policy types and rates. By the late 1980s, most other insurance carriers had imported versions of these expert systems for their own applications. Laser scanning technology for supermarket checkout counters was first introduced in the early 1980s. Now the technology is standard for all but the smallest supermarket chains.

Tactical Prioritizing. Each tactical manager (e.g., department head) looks at his or her unit goals and decides which information technologies will help secure the goals. The chosen projects are prioritized and the list of projects, by priority, is sent to the operational level for implementation.

A problem at this advanced stage of planning is that tactical managers must now compete with one another for the scarce resources of the firm. Often political infighting occurs.

The two stages of the planning spectrum just described were tactical in nature. The end of the spectrum is strategic planning.

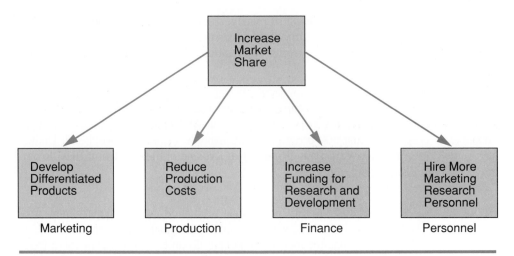

FIGURE 1−4   **Example of a Strategic Goal Passed Down for Tactical Prioritizing**

Strategic Prioritizing. At the strategic stage, information technology planning is truly top-down. Strategic managers set overall information technology goals based on the firm's overall goals. Then the goals are passed down to tactical units for tactical prioritizing (Figure 1–4). Tactical priorities are then transferred to operational managers for implementation.

This last, ideal phase of the planning spectrum can be reached only by a highly structured approach called business information planning.

BUSINESS INFORMATION PLANNING

Business information planning has seven steps: (1) develop mission statement, (2) identify strategic units, (3) define critical success factors, (4) identify information systems needed, (5) consider industry and technological trends, (6) categorize potential information systems projects, and (7) set information systems development strategy.

Develop Mission Statement

The **mission statement** sets forth the direction in which the organization wants to go. It is expressed in measurable terms—profit, market share, and so on. The mission statement allows individual business units (e.g., regional offices) to define their own goals for meeting the overall mission statement. Common objectives included in the mission statement might be:

- Achieve a 15 percent share of the market
- Increase sales volume by 10 percent per year for the next five years
- Expand international operations by 50 percent within two years

Identify Strategic Units

Eventually, the business information plan will move further and further down the organization until it is implemented at the operational level. Not all units in the firm are strategic in nature. In this sense, *strategic* is defined as contributing directly to the primary profit/nonprofit objectives of the firm. The Bulldog Maintenance department, for example, although it is essential, does not contribute directly to the profit margin of Gardner Plastics Company. Therefore, management at Gardner has not identified Bulldog Maintenance as a strategic unit. It is through strategic units that mission statements are passed, progressively refined and targeted, and then implemented at the operational level of management.

McKraklin Aerospace Company is organized into separate, almost autonomous, geographically separated divisions—aircraft, aerospace, industrial products, and so forth. Each division has been identified as a strategic business unit. Each unit separately contributes to the firm's overall profit picture. For each unit, a short description has been prepared that includes name, chief executive officer (CEO)/manager, organization chart with names of managers/supervisors, business activities (what the unit does), goals, and current information status (for example, systems automated, computers used). Figure 1–5 contains a shortened description for McKraklin's Industrial Products Division.

Define Critical Success Factors

Critical success factors (CSFs) are those essential activities that must go right if the business is to succeed. For example, a key success factor for the automotive industry is complying with government emission standards. A key success factor for large supermarket chains is volume sales; volume is critical because these supermarkets average less than one cent profit on each dollar of merchandise sold. The CSF methodology is described in the box on page 13.

Identify Information Systems Needed

Information systems need to be developed to facilitate and monitor the achievement of critical success factors. The focus is on delivering information systems that meet unfilled critical needs. McKraklin's Industrial Products Division identified the following information systems needs:

CSF	Information Systems Needs
Increase in division sales	Sales monitoring*
	Remote sales order entry and inquiry***
	Automated inventory and shipping**
Profit-to-sales ratio	Profit monitoring*
	Sales monitoring*
Hours of management ethics training	Training scheduling and information***

FIGURE 1–5   **Shortened Description of Strategic Business Unit: Industrial Products Division of McKraklin Aerospace Company**

McKRAKLIN AEROSPACE COMPANY
STRATEGIC BUSINESS UNIT DESCRIPTION

NAME: _Industrial Products Division_

MANAGER/
SUPERVISOR: _Paul Cronky_

TITLE: _Division Manager_

ORGANIZATION CHART: _See Attached_

LOCATION: _1600 Warehouse Drive, Sepulveda, Ca._

BUSINESS
ACTIVITIES: _Manufactures electronic and radar products for commercial customers_

GOALS: _1. Transform military to commercial products_
2. Increase share of commercial market

CURRENT   _Current accounting and manufacturing_
INFORMATION   _systems have been operating_
STATUS   _for several years. Few are real-_
time update. Batch reporting at
night and weekends. No use of higher
level systems such as expert systems.

Information systems marked with one asterisk are currently available and seem to be operating well. Systems with two asterisks are currently operating but seem to be in trouble; they need modification or replacement. Systems marked with three asterisks do not exist.

Consider Industry and Technological Trends

Before categorizing and setting priorities for identified information systems needs, a firm needs to forecast industry and technological trends. Sometimes these trends will change the costs and benefits for prospective information systems, which in turn will affect the priorities for information systems development and implementation. For example, the Alaska Court System delayed its planned revision of electronic court reporting in anticipation of cost-effective, voice-driven computers.

In the case of the McKraklin's Industrial Products Division, the dwindling size of laptop computers, which are needed in a remote sales order entry and inquiry system, may make that project (1) more cost-effective, (2) more amenable to the sales culture, or (3) a candidate for delay until the technology matures.

CRITICAL SUCCESS FACTORS

John Rockart is the director of the Center for Information Systems Research at the Sloan School of Management, Massachusetts Institute of Technology (MIT). In 1977, he and his colleagues began work on the development of critical success factors, or CSFs (Rockart, 1979). This approach allows strategic managers to translate strategic goals into progressively more detailed and measurable objectives. The measurable objectives become the basis for designing an executive information system (EIS), which allows chief executives to gauge the health of their companies.

The process begins with interviews of strategic managers to determine which are the key factors for success. For example, interviews at McKraklin Aerospace Company resulted in a list of six key success factors:

1. Maintain current share of aerospace market.
2. Increase share of government contracts awarded to aerospace firms.
3. Retain current profit level.
4. Decrease government project cost and time overruns.
5. Implement management ethics program.
6. Convert research output from military projects to profitable commercial ventures.

Key factors are then sent down to the strategic business units, which determine which of the factors are pertinent to their operations and what the local priorities should be. For example, McKraklin's Industrial Products Division determined that factors 3, 5, and 6 are pertinent to their operation. They prioritized them as follows:

1. Convert research output from military projects to profitable commercial ventures.
2. Retain current profit level.
3. Implement management ethics program.

The next step is to translate these key factors into measurable CSFs. Industrial Products Division managers were convened in a group session, where they arrived at the following CSFs:

Key Factor	CSF
Military research to profitable commercial ventures	Increase in division sales
Retain profit level	Profit-to-sales ratio
Management ethics program	Number of hours of management ethics training

Finally, the key and critical success factors are sent to operational managers, where they are implemented as day-by-day operational goals.

Categorize Potential Information Systems Projects

The next step in business information planning is to place potential projects into one or more of the following categories.

Hard-Dollar Savings. Some information systems projects reduce staff or cut costs, thereby saving actual dollars. For example, the proposed training system of McKraklin's Industrial Products Division is projected to reduce clerical positions and reduce paper costs.

Soft-Dollar Savings. Some projects show measurable improvements, but the improvements cannot be measured in dollars. For example, the Industrial Products Division's proposed remote order entry system will increase customer satisfaction, but it is difficult to translate increased customer satisfaction to actual sales increases or actual increased profit.

Improved Operational Control. Some projects provide on-line or off-line feedback, which allows managers to alter operations before they get out of control. For example, the Industrial Products Division would like to modify the current inventory and shipping system to provide more operational control (quick feedback) for quality inspection of incoming vendor shipments.

External Requirement. Some projects are favored because of factors outside the organization. For example, recently the aerospace industry has been the subject of several court cases and newspaper exposure dealing with alleged instances of aerospace executives bribing and taking kickbacks from government agencies. These external pressures may put a high priority on McKraklin Aerospace's key factor of implementing a management ethics program. In turn, the Industrial Products Division's need for training scheduling and information may become a higher priority.

Research and Development. Some proposed information systems projects cannot be justified by cost or control improvements. They are experimental in nature. For example, the Information Systems Department of the Industrial Products Division has proposed developing an experimental prototype of an expert system which would simulate what profits might be if current strategic policies were changed (what-if simulation). There are no direct cost savings or profit increases associated with this proposed system; it is experimental in nature.

Company Image. Some systems do not fall into any of the aforementioned categories but are viable because managers think they will enhance the overall company image. An example is a current proposal to allow free nationwide university telecommunication access to McKraklin's extensive computer literature database. Such a proposal can only be justified as increasing the overall national image of the company.

Set Information Systems Development Strategy

The strategy for developing information systems is a four-step sequence:

1. Eliminate potential information systems that do not contribute directly to critical business needs. For example, McKraklin Aerospace's proposal to allow free university access to its computer literature database will enhance the company's image. However, if enhancing company image is not a critical success factor, this proposed system enhancement should be eliminated.

2. Allocate resources to projects with excellent return on investment. For example, McKraklin has two proposed information systems that contribute directly to CSFs. The first is a remote sales order entry and inquiry system, which is projected to return 25 percent on the original development investment. The second system is a revised inventory and shipping system, which promises a 12 percent return on investment (ROI). The sales system should be given a higher priority.

3. Allocate resources to projects with a low level of risk. McKraklin's revised inventory and shipping system is fairly cut and dried. There is little risk associated with implementing this improved, not new, system. On the other hand, the remote sales order entry and inquiry system is a new concept for McKraklin. Information systems personnel have never attempted a system of this sort. Therefore, this proposed information project is risky.

Often you'll note a common phenomenon when prioritizing proposed information systems development projects. For one category, system A is preferable to system B. For another category, system B is preferable to system A. Which system is preferable overall? The answer depends on the culture of the individual firm establishing the business information plan. Some firms will consider return on investment more important than risk, whereas other firms will choose the riskier project. In our example, McKraklin Aerospace's culture calls for avoiding high-risk projects; therefore, the company will choose the revised inventory system.

4. Allocate a certain percentage of resources to exploration (R&D) projects that will extend the range of the firm's knowledge of information technology. McKraklin Aerospace may decide to allow the remote sales order and inquiry system, but as an exploratory R&D project.

BUSINESS INFORMATION PLANNING USING IEF

The planning process just described can be facilitated using computers. There are several software packages available that can lead management step by step through the top-down planning process. One such package is the **Information Engineering Facility (IEF)** produced by Texas Instruments Incorporated.

IEF belongs to a class of computer software called computer-aided systems engineering (CASE). You will be reading quite a bit about CASE throughout this book. Indeed, Chapter 22 is devoted to description of CASE and other automated aids. For the moment, we are concerned with one particular CASE tool (IEF), and with only that portion of the tool devoted to top-down, business technological planning. IEF has five

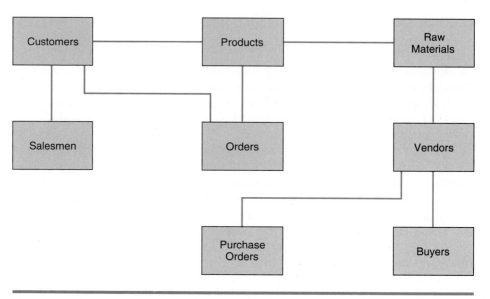

FIGURE 1–6   Subject Area Diagram

Adapted from *IEF Technical Description: Methodology and Technology Overview* (Texas Instruments Incorporated, 1992), p. 16.

layers: (1) architectural, (2) conceptual, (3) external, (4) implementation, and (5) execution. It is the architectural level with which we are concerned in this chapter.

The **architectural layer of IEF** is a high-level, nondetailed view of the organization to be automated. It is based on the assumption that information is a resource and that an organization enhances its profit potential by using that resource effectively. The architectural layer of IEF allows managers to structure the information resource more quickly and easily and to prioritize the means (information systems) by which the resource is to be used.

IEF deliverables applicable to top-level technological planning include the following:

1. *Enterprise facts:* This includes a mission statement; a list of objectives and critical success factors by strategic unit; and a number of supporting tables.
2. *Environment facts:* This is a list of the organization's current hardware and software.
3. *Information architecture:* The **information architecture of IEF** is a group of diagrams that show interrelationships between firm entities (strategic units) and information. Among these diagrams are the Subject Area Diagram (Figure 1–6) and the Function/Entity Type Matrix (Figure 1–7).
4. *Business systems architecture:* The **business systems architecture of IEF** deliverable presents a prioritized list of potential information system development projects. It does this in the form of an Implementation Plan.
5. *Technical architecture:* The **technical architecture of IEF** presents technical alternatives (e.g., laser scanning versus cash register) for implementing the business system architecture.

Key (Enter Highest Classification Only) C = Create D = Delete U = Update R = Read only Entity Types	Functions	Purchasing	Receiving	Scrap Disposal	Warehousing	Distribution Center	Shipping	Packing	Traffic Management	Marketing	Order Processing	General Accounting
Purchase Order		C	U	R	R	C	U	U	U	U	U	R
Purchase Order—Item		C	U	R	R	U	U	U	U	U	U	R
Supplier		C	U	R	R	U	R	R	U	U	U	R
Supplier—Sales—Order		C	U	R	R	R	R	R	R	R	R	R
Warehouse		R	R	R	C	U	U	U	R			

FIGURE 1–7   Function/Entity Type Matrix

Adapted from *IEF Technical Description: Methodology and Technology Overview* (Texas Instruments Incorporated, 1992), p. 16.

6. *Information Strategy Planning Report:* This is a formal report that documents all of the preceding to top management.

IEF represents a growing capability of extending computer software usage from technically trained persons to the entire organization. Computer programs such as IEF can facilitate the critical process of planning the integration of technology to the business firm.

The six steps of business information planning involve strategic planning. The steps prioritize technological integration across the entire firm, regardless of division, mission, or project. The plan decides *what* is to be done. Next, tactical management, taking the *what* as a given, determines *how* the chosen projects will be implemented. There are three components to the tactical development of information and other technological systems: (1) the project itself; (2) the information systems department, which is the organizational entity responsible for the actual integration of the technology into the firm; and (3) the systems analyst, the individual who makes the actual transition between the strategically planned and the operationally functioning information system.

INFORMATION SYSTEMS PROJECTS

Information systems projects fit into a range of complexity, as shown in Figure 1–8. From least to most complex, projects can be categorized as maintenance, modification, enhancement, replacement, or new capabilities. **Maintenance** involves fixing minor

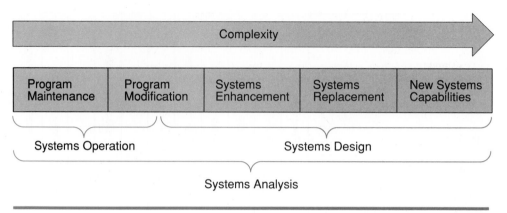

FIGURE 1–8   **Information Systems Complexity Spectrum**

system flaws, which may be the result of a design omission. For example, the design team may have neglected to consider a system condition that rarely occurs (e.g., order quantity equal to 10,000 in a small company). Flaws may also be the result of other factors, such as changing user expectations.

Modification involves more than simple program changes. For example, when the U.S. Postal Service changed the zip code from five to nine digits, many business firms had to make major modifications to their information systems programs. The difference between maintenance and modification is a matter of degree.

Enhancement means adding system capabilities that were not part of the original information system. For example, when the Industrial Products Division of McKraklin Aerospace implemented its inventory system five years ago, that system did not include a module for forecasting future demand for products and parts. The addition of such a sophisticated forecasting module would be considered a system enhancement.

Replacement occurs when existing information systems are becoming physically, technologically, or competitively obsolete. For example, a large supermarket chain may seek to replace its checkout system with one that uses laser scanning technology.

Finally, **new capabilities** are information systems for which there is currently no automated system. Palko Publishing Company is considering introducing an expert system (ES) that will allow the firm automatically to evaluate and rate textbook proposals submitted by prospective authors. Currently this capability is not computerized—it resides in the minds of Palko's acquisition editors.

A typical information systems department has a backlog of work that includes projects in all five categories of the spectrum. Unfortunately, rarely are there sufficient resources to accomplish all projects. How does the department decide which information systems projects to initiate and in what order? There are three sequential rules to follow in making such a determination:

1. Do not cheat on maintenance. Eighty-five percent of the dollars spent on business computer programming are spent for maintenance (minor repair) of current sys-

tems. If you borrow from maintenance to develop new or revised systems, your current systems will deteriorate rapidly.

2. Reject projects that do not contribute to the business plan. Requests for new or revised information systems must come from the top down, not from the bottom up. For example, the information systems department at Carey Contractors received a request from the personnel department for development of a decision support system for matching job applications to job openings. The request was denied because the proposed system was not aligned with the company's business information plan.

3. Consider resource constraints. There may be resource constraints that prevent immediate development of information systems projects which meet other criteria. Possible constraints are available analyst time, project funds that can be allocated, limits on information personnel skills, and current state of technology. For example, it may be difficult for McKraklin Aerospace to develop the remote sales order entry system if no one in the information systems department has knowledge of or experience with telecommunications.

At this point, the company has created a prioritized list of information systems and other technological projects to be integrated into the organization. The responsibility for development now lies with the information systems department.

INFORMATION SYSTEMS DEPARTMENT

The information systems (IS) department can be located at several different places in the organization, depending on the firm's emphasis on information processing. Many IS departments report to the vice president of a functional area; commonly, the IS manager reports to the vice president of finance, or comptroller.

In firms that put more emphasis on information processing, it is not unusual to see a vice president for information services. This position often is called the **chief information officer (CIO)**. When the IS department is at this level of the organization, IS personnel become more involved in strategic information planning (the *what*). When the IS department reports to the vice president of a functional area, IS personnel generally are restricted to an operational role (the *how*).

Many firms have both IS departments and an IRM department. In such firms, the IS department is operationally oriented, and the IRM department is strategically and tactically oriented. There are three essential differences between IRM and IS departments: staff orientation, role, and department orientation. First, the IRM staff is business trained; the IS staff is technically trained. Second, the IRM department is concerned with *what* technology needs to be integrated into the firm. After being given a prioritized list of technological projects, the IS department is concerned with *how* that technology should be implemented. Third, the IRM department's role is strategic; it looks at the overall use of technology to enhance the firm's critical goals. The IS department is concerned with developing one system at a time (tactical) and keeping all developed systems in working order (operational).

The remainder of this book deals with the role of the IS department. The IS department can be described in terms of its organization, the issues it faces, and how it develops information systems projects.

IS Department Organization

Figure 1–9 shows a typical organization of the IS department. There are four sections: systems development, systems maintenance, computer operations, and user services.

Systems Development. The systems development section develops the information systems that have been identified in the business information plan. It is the tactical arm of the IS department, and it makes decisions on a system-by-system basis. Nevertheless, decisions for any one system must be consistent with overall strategic goals. (We will be concentrating on the systems development section throughout much of the book.)

Systems Maintenance. The systems maintenance section is responsible for keeping current systems operating effectively. Across the United States, systems maintenance accounts for almost 85 percent of the dollars spent on business information processing. Recall that McDonnell Douglas makes an average of almost 500 maintenance changes each weekend.

Computer Operations. Computer operations is the technical support section of the IS department. It is responsible for functions such as computer room operations; computer and workstation maintenance; centralized data entry; the ordering, storage, and distribution of computer supplies; and distribution of computer output.

User Services. The user services section is responsible for operation of customer information centers, end-user training, evaluation of end-user satisfaction, and detection of information systems problems.

IS Department Issues

The typical IS department faces several issues:

- *Place of the IS department in the organization:* Should the IS department report to a functional area executive (e.g., comptroller), or should the head of the IS department be at the vice presidential level and report directly to the CEO?
- *Centralization versus decentralization:* Should technological resources be centralized in the IS department, or should they be decentralized in functional areas? There has been a significant trend toward decentralization and a rush toward end-user computing, where the means of computing (e.g., hardware and software) are owned by end-users rather than by a centralized IS department.
- *Alignment of IS department goals:* Can the goals of the IS department be aligned with the strategic goals of the organization? How to achieve that alignment has been the

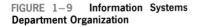

FIGURE 1–9   **Information Systems Department Organization**

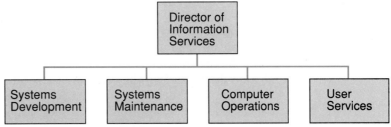

subject of this chapter. The key point is that no information systems project should be started unless it fits into the overall strategic goals of the firm.

■ *Linking disparate systems:* How can information systems running on different brands of computers under different operating systems be made to communicate with each other? The mixing of microcomputers and mainframes must be considered. This problem is sometimes referred to, almost poetically, as "merging islands of technology."

■ *Structured methodologies:* How can (or should) the IS staff be convinced to adopt structured analysis and design techniques? This book describes structured analysis and design methods, which have yet to be totally accepted in industry.

■ *Technology transfer:* How can the IS department lead the effort to find, sell, and implement new technologies in the organization? Technology transfer involves both personal skills and technical skills.

Project Development

The IS department must organize its efforts to develop information systems identified in the business information plan. There are several ways it can do so. Sometimes development is strictly an internal IS department function. A single systems analyst may be assigned to develop an information system. More often, analysts and programmers are formed into a project team. One of the members of the team is assigned as project leader.

It has become increasingly common for project teams to include members from outside the IS department. Often, prospective systems end-users are "drafted" to serve on the systems development team. Project teams also can be external to the IS department; such teams will be described later in the book.

Regardless of how the information systems development project is organized, the key actor in that development is the systems analyst.

ROLE OF THE SYSTEMS ANALYST

The **systems analyst** plays the key role in analysis and design of business information systems. The role can best be understood by looking at the roles of several information specialists and the skills required of the systems analyst.

Information Specialists

Several information specialists are involved in the development of business information systems. The **systems analyst** is a problem solver who compares performance of the current system with performance it should deliver and determines how to resolve any discrepancies. The systems analyst communicates with prospective system users and prepares technical specifications that will be translated into computer programming code. The **programmer** is a specialist who transfers the systems analyst's specifications into programming language code, much as the construction worker translates the architect's drawings into a building. The programmer tests the code to ensure that it works correctly. A **programmer/analyst** has the skills of both a systems analyst and a programmer and often serves as a **project leader** who supervises the entire development project.

Systems Analyst Skills

Successful systems analysts must meet the following requirements:

- *Oral and written communication skills:* Systems analysts continually communicate with end-users and occasionally are called on to brief top management.
- *Analytical and logical skills:* Systems analysts study complex problems and reduce them to simple terms. They must also be adept at using the many analytical tools available to them, tools that are described in this book.
- *Knowledge of business processes:* Systems analysts must be familiar with such business functions as payroll, inventory, and accounting.
- *Knowledge of technology:* Systems analysts must keep current on what technologies are emerging and are applicable to the business firm's environment.
- *Ability to work independently and in a team setting:* Systems analysts often work in project teams, but they must also be able to solve complex problems without much help.
- *An information systems education that is oriented toward the future:* Systems analysts need a rigorous education to prepare them for a rapidly changing future.

The career of a systems analyst is demanding but also rewarding. In the remainder of this book, you'll see how the systems analyst performs analysis and design tasks in the development of business information systems.

A TOTAL QUALITY MANAGEMENT (TQM) APPROACH

Total quality management (TQM) is a common term heard around most business firms these days. What is it? There are many definitions. Here is one from Joel Ross.

> [TQM is] the application of quality principles for the integration of all functions and processes of the organization. The ultimate goal is customer satisfaction. The way to achieve it is through continuous improvement. (Ross, 1993, p. 325)

In this context, **quality** is defined as fitness for use by customers (Juran, 1974). This book uniquely uses a TQM approach to information system development. It does so for two reasons. First, the goal of quality information systems has been given more lip service than serious attention during our short history of information processing. This textbook is based on the assumption that an information system's quality is at least as important as its cost.

The second aspect of TQM underlying this book is the perspective of customers, sometimes referred to as *clients*. The information system we develop must be customer-oriented. Otherwise, these information systems will fail. We will discuss this point further in the next section of this chapter.

There are many different approaches to TQM. This book uses an approach adapted from the works of Juran (see the References and Further Readings at the end of Section I).

This approach has the following steps:

1. Develop an overall mission statement applicable to all information systems in the firm.
2. Decompose this mission into specific information system objectives that lend themselves to measurement.
3. Determine what are the primary processes of each information system, the sequential transformation steps required to transform input to output.
4. For each process:
   a) Identify customers.
   b) Determine customer needs.
   c) Develop product (output) features that correspond to customer needs.
   d) Establish quality goals that meet the needs at minimum cost.
   e) Develop a process that can produce the needed product features.
   f) Test process capabilities.

This book describes development of information systems. We are then concerned with establishing total quality control of the development sequence. Following is a suggested mission (step 1) for the development of business information systems.

> *Development mission:* To design business information systems that satisfy the firm's information customers (both external and internal) while conforming to the overall mission and goals of the firm.

In Chapter 2, we will perform step 2—decomposing this mission statement into specific information system objectives. In Chapter 3, we will determine what are the primary processes of the typical information system (step 3). The remainder of the book will describe each of these processes (e.g., Output Design) in terms of step 4. This progression is shown in Figure 1–10.

Make no mistake about it! This textbook is about *quality* of information and *quality* of information systems.

FIGURE 1–10 **TQM Process in This Textbook**

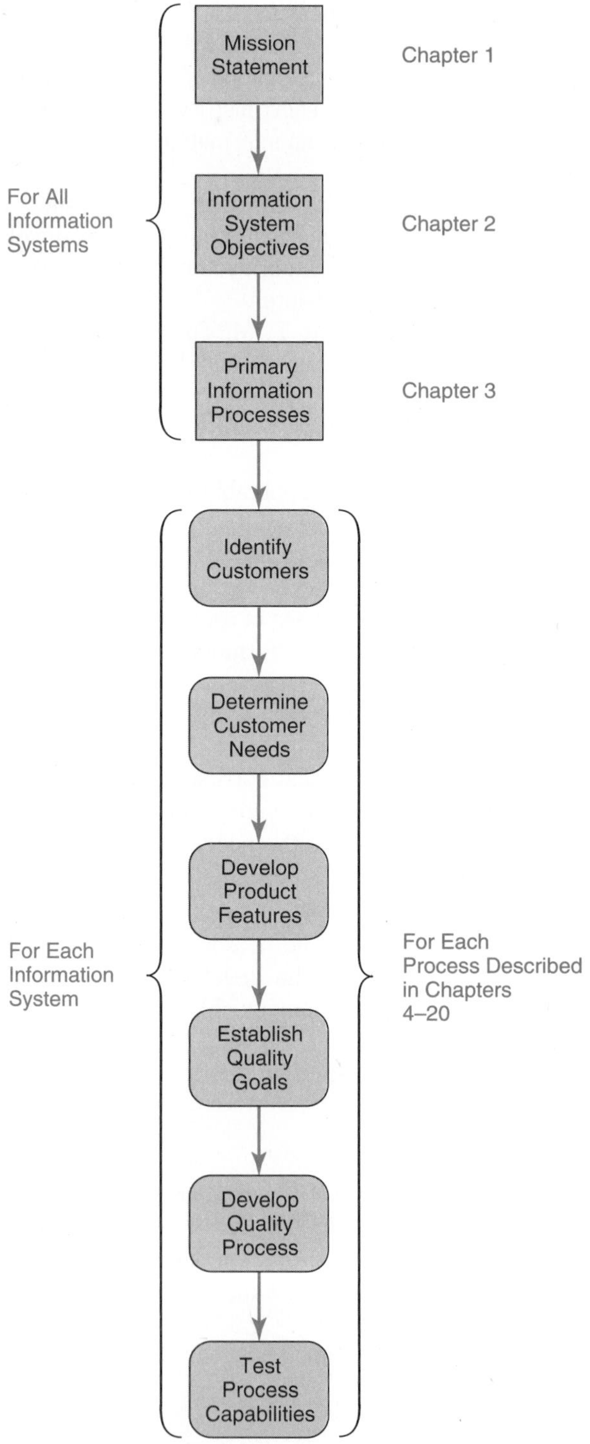

Mission Statement

Chapter 1

For All Information Systems

Information System Objectives

Chapter 2

Primary Information Processes

Chapter 3

Identify Customers

Determine Customer Needs

Develop Product Features

For Each Information System

For Each Process Described in Chapters 4–20

Establish Quality Goals

Develop Quality Process

Test Process Capabilities

HUMAN ASPECTS

People working in the information systems area often are accused of being mechanistic—concentrating on hardware and software at the exclusion of human workers. Too often those accusations have been close to the mark. That is why this book so emphasizes the perspective of the customer—the user of information systems. You will be reading a lot about the principle of *user ownership*—the feeling among information users that they own, rather than are captives of, information systems. The principle is simple. If you own a house, you are more tolerant of its flaws (e.g., a dripping faucet) than if you rent a house. The same is true of information systems.

One of the keys to effective management in general, and effective management of information systems in particular, is to instill a sense of ownership on the part of all members of the firm. The Japanese have retaught that lesson to us. In the case of technological planning, the topic of this chapter, this planning must start at the top of the firm and filter its way down. At every stage of the business information plan, however, all the actors/participants in the technology process—technicians and users alike—must be given their say. The entire firm must participate in long-range planning. Otherwise, there will be no sense of ownership, and the plans will likely fail.

User ownership—this will be a recurring theme in this book.

SUMMARY

Business information systems are not developed in a vacuum. Each information systems project should fit into the firm's overall business plan and goals. The top-down approach to planning begins at the strategic level of management, where what needs to be done is determined. The approach then proceeds to the tactical level of management, where the *what* is transformed into the *how*. Finally, at the operational level, information systems are implemented according to the overall business plan.

The top-down approach begins with identifying the firm's marketing strategy, which can include lowest cost, product differentiation, market niche, and market barriers. Each of these strategies requires a different set of technological and information systems tactics.

Information systems planning occurs along a spectrum that proceeds from maintenance to reengineering, to system importation, to tactical prioritizing, to strategic prioritizing. The last stage can be reached by a structured approach called business information planning. Seven steps are involved in business information planning: develop mission statement, identify strategic units, define critical success factors, identify information systems needed, consider industry and technological trends, categorize potential information systems projects, and set information systems development strategy. Automated tools can be used to enhance technological planning. The Information Engineering Facility (IEF) from Texas Instruments was briefly described.

The information systems projects identified as contributing to the overall business plan vary in complexity from maintenance to modification, to enhancement, to replacement, to new capabilities. Which of these projects commands immediate attention is determined by three guidelines: Do not cheat on maintenance; reject projects that do not contribute to the business plan; and consider the resource constraints of available analyst time, project funds, information personnel skills, and current state of technology.

The information systems department is responsible for developing targeted information systems. The IS department has decidedly different orientations and responsibilities than does the increasingly popular information resource management (IRM) department. The IS department typically includes four sections: systems development, systems maintenance, computer operations, and user services.

The IS department faces several important issues, including its place in the organization, centralization versus decentralization, alignment of IS department goals, linkage of disparate systems, structured methodologies, and technology transfer.

Development of information systems typically is organized into teams, which may include members from outside the IS department. The most important member of the development team is the systems analyst.

Top-down technological planning is consistent with Total Quality Management (TQM), which is the application of quality principles for the integration of all functions and processes of the organization. Quality is defined as fitness for use by customers. The TQM approach, described in this chapter, is one that will follow us throughout the book.

Finally, in this and subsequent chapters, the emphasis is not on the technical but on how human employees contribute to and fit into the scheme of the firm's technology. There is always a human side to the equation.

CONCEPTS LEARNED

- Four business marketing strategies
- Differences between strategic, tactical, and operational management
- Five stages of the business information planning spectrum
- Seven steps in business information planning
- Critical success factors
- Information Engineering Facility (IEF)

- How potential information systems projects are categorized
- Factors and prioritization of information systems projects
- Organization of IS department
- IS department issues
- Role of the systems analyst
- Total quality management (TQM)

KEY TERMS

architectural layer of IEF
business systems architecture of IEF
chief information officer (CIO)
critical success factor (CSF)
enhancement
information architecture of IEF
Information Engineering Facility (IEF)

information resource management (IRM)
maintenance
market barrier
market niche
mission statement
modification
new capabilities

operational management
product differentiation
programmer
programmer/analyst
project leader
quality
replacement

strategic computing
strategic management
systems analyst
tactical management
technical architecture of IEF
total quality management (TQM)

REVIEW QUESTIONS

1. What is meant by IRM, or strategic computing?
2. Describe the four business marketing strategies.
3. How do information systems needs differ among the four business marketing strategies?
4. What are the differences in decision making between the strategic, tactical, and operational levels of management?
5. What is reengineering?
6. Describe the seven steps of business information planning.
7. How can IEF help in the planning process?
8. What are critical success factors?
9. How are potential information systems projects categorized?
10. Describe the five stages of complexity into which information systems projects fall.
11. How is the typical IS department organized?
12. Describe four typical issues facing an IS department.
13. What skills should a systems analyst possess?
14. Describe the steps involved in TQM.

CRITICAL THINKING OPPORTUNITIES

1. Construct two examples where more than one marketing strategy may be used by the same firm.
2. Construct a mission and three CSFs for your business school.
3. Consider the skills that a systems analyst should possess. Describe how you will gain these skills in the curriculum (major) in which you are enrolled.
4. Draw a diagram that shows how this chapter is organized. *Note:* Figure 1–11 shows how such a diagram might look for a sandwich shop.

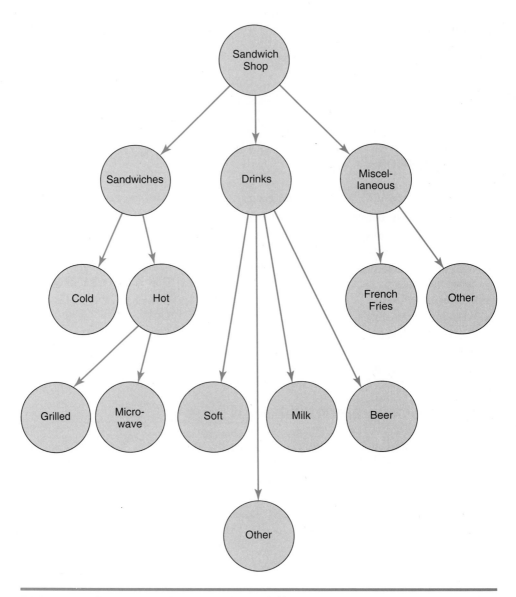

FIGURE 1–11   **Decomposition Diagram for Sandwich Shop**

MCKRAKLIN AEROSPACE COMPANY: OVERVIEW

SETTING

Dave Costner nervously opened the envelope marked "CONFIDENTIAL." He already knew what the memo inside was about. He had just finished a stormy telephone conversation with Mark Segford, the director for manufacturing. Dave's ears were still ringing as he pulled out the memo, placed the envelope in a drawer, and began to read.

The inventory system had been the cause of user complaints for some time. Dave, however, had not known that things were this bad. Why hadn't someone in the information systems department told him? His eyes locked on the last lines of the memo: "Perhaps your information systems group does not have the skills and enthusiasm to replace completely this atrocious inventory system. If that is the case, I have room in my budget to hire or contract the professionals required to cure this critical problem."

Dave Costner knew that his information systems department had "the skills and enthusiasm" to attack the problems with the inventory system. It had been merely a matter of priorities. "Well," he thought, as he tossed the memo on his desk, "there's no question of priorities now. The inventory system is this department's most critical project."

BACKGROUND

McKraklin is a large aerospace firm located in Southern California. It manufactures military electronics systems, satellite systems, and commercial by-products of these systems. The firm, which has more than 65,000 employees in sixteen locations throughout Southern California,

is organized into twelve major divisions. One of these is the Industrial Products Division.

The Industrial Products Division, located in Sepulveda, California, manufactures electronic and radar products for commercial rather than military use. The division has about 900 employees. Last year its revenue was $78 million. About one-third of this revenue was from exports outside the country.

The division is organized rather traditionally (Figure 1.1–1) into six departments. Our focus is on the interaction between Dave Costner's information systems department (Figure 1.1–2) and Mark Segford's manufacturing department (Figure 1.1–3). The beleaguered inventory system is owned by the manufacturing department.

MCKRAKLIN INVENTORY SYSTEM

The inventory system is a part of the materials control system (Figure 1.1–4). Dave Costner knew that the inventory system was largely dependent on the receiving system, so he decided to focus his department's investigation on the subsystem shown in Figure 1.1–5. Dave would assign this critical project to a skilled analyst team. Before he did so, however, he wanted to get a feel for the problem. He requested and received the following materials: (1) list of employees in inventory and receiving departments (Figure 1.1–6), (2) classification of inventory items stocked (Figure 1.1–7), and (3) the latest inventory performance report (Figure 1.1–8). Dave knew that his analyst team would need much more information than this. He also knew his team would analyze this particular information in more depth than he would. Still, he settled

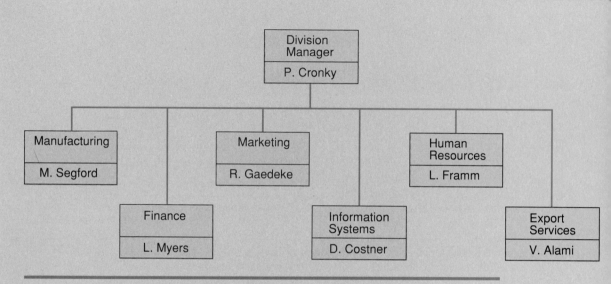

FIGURE 1.1–1   **Industrial Products Division's Organizational Chart**

down in his den's soft chair and studied the materials he had received.

REVIEW QUESTIONS

This is only the first part of the book, so don't expect to answer the following questions in a fully knowledgeable manner. Yet, your initial reactions are important. After proceeding further in this book, you can return to these questions and measure how your initial opinions may have changed.

1. Why did Dave Costner wait until he was threatened before he started looking at the inventory system?

FIGURE 1.1–2   **Information Systems Department's Organizational Chart**

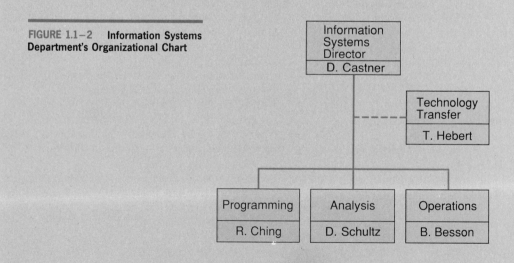

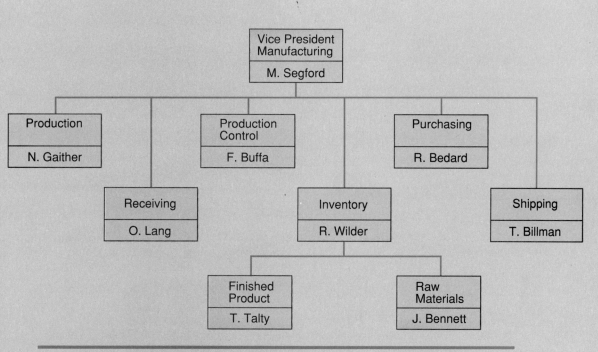

FIGURE 1.1-3   Manufacturing Department's Organizational Chart

2. Dave does not work for Mark Segford. Why did Dave respond so quickly to Segford's memorandum?

3. Why did Dave want to "get a feel for the problem" before assigning it to an analyst team?

4. Why did Dave request a list of section employees? Classification of inventory items? Inventory performance report?

5. After reading Chapter 1, comment on whether you think Dave Costner is correct in raising the inventory system to a high development priority.

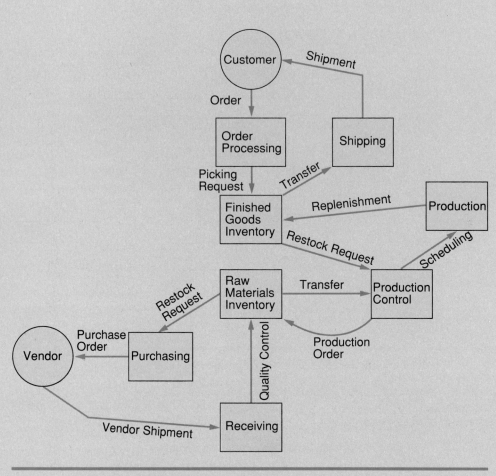

FIGURE 1.1–4   **McKraklin's Materials Control Systems**

FIGURE 1.1–5   **Dave Costner's Sub-system Focus**

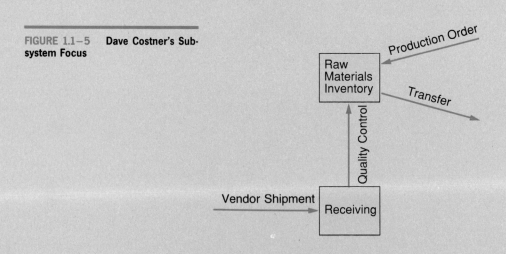

FIGURE 1.1–6   **Key Employees in Inventory and Receiving**

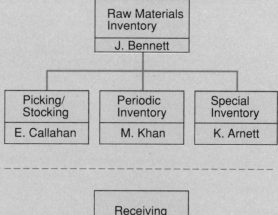

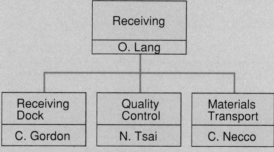

Classification Code	Raw Material Type
ELC	Electrical
MCH	Mechanical
HYD	Hydraulic
HRD	Pieceware
FIN	Finishing
TLS	Tools
WIR	Wiring
MSC	Miscellaneous

```
INDUSTRIAL PRODUCTS DIVISION                           MAY 199X

                    INVENTORY PERFORMANCE REPORT

            CATEGORY                    ITEMS              UNITS
1. Requested by Production              1,763             61,705
2. Delivered to Production              1,340             38,860
3. Fill Rate (2 ÷ 1)                    76.0%              63.0%
4. Received from Vendors                1,329             74,424
5. Vendor Delivery Times
   1 Month                                627             34,623
   2 Months                               144              8,123.
   3 Months                               315             17,175
   More than 3 Months                     243             14,503
6. Orders to Vendors                    1,524            100,584
7. Inventory Adjustments                  127                215
```

FIGURE 1.1−8   **Industrial Products Division's Monthly Inventory Performance Report**

GOODBYTE PIZZA COMPANY: OVERVIEW[1]

SETTING

Sam Nolte hadn't been able to sleep all night. In fact, he hadn't been sleeping well for some time now. Sam sighed, slowly rose from his bed, put on his bathrobe, and walked downstairs to the kitchen to pour himself a glass of milk and to think for a while.

He turned on the television as background noise, then concentrated on his business problems. As manager of Goodbyte Pizza Company, Sam Nolte knew that unless he did something drastic, his company would continue to lose business to Pizza Hut, Straw Hat, Round Table, and his many other pizza competitors. Goodbyte pizzas cost too much and they took too long to deliver. In addition, the whole operation was always in a state of confusion, and employees kept making errors. Goodbyte Pizza Company did not present a comfortable and trustworthy business atmosphere for its customers.

Sam Nolte had heard that several of his competitors had recently introduced computers to improve their operations. Sam suspected that automation might be the answer to his problem, but he had no computer expertise and didn't know where to start.

BACKGROUND

The Goodbyte Pizza Company is located in Daly City, California, just south of San Francisco. The company employs between 22 and 27 people, depending on the time of year. Most of the workers are part-time students ranging in age from 16 to 28 years. Employee turnover is high, ranging as high as 125 percent per year.[2] All current business operations are done manually and are very time consuming. This is a problem.

Goodbyte's location demands a fast and accurate order-processing system because it has many competing fast food franchises nearby. Fast service, especially during lunch hour, will cause customers to return, whereas slow service will result in loss of customers. The current manual system does not provide an efficient or accurate method of service and inventory. Little useful information can be extracted from the current system for management purposes. In a market as competitive as the fast food restaurant business, all information about sales and sales trends is crucial to a manager in order to retain a competitive edge.

Sam Nolte came into work the next morning with thoughts of computers dominating his mind. He waited until the slow customer time just before the noon rush hour, then went to his office, closed the door, and tried to structure his thoughts. Sam took out a notepad, labeled the top of a new page "Problems," and began to list the problems he believed he had with the current Goodbyte Pizza Company operation. He listed the following problems:

1. Hand-counting inventory once a week, as is now done, is too time consuming.
2. There is no easy method for determining how much of each inventory item (ingredient) should be on hand to anticipate sales for the day.

---

[1]This case study has been adapted from an actual study done by a CSUS student team. Members of this student team were Linda Alvarez, Jeff Dickenson, Jason Louie, Thomas Mink, and Tjong Ngoe.

[2]Annual employee turnover is computed by dividing the total number of employees leaving or terminated during a year by the number of authorized employee decisions (e.g., 25).

3. Converting order form data into useful management information is difficult.
4. Filling out order forms manually is time consuming and sometimes causes further delays when the writing is not legible.
5. Pilferage and waste are difficult to detect.
6. No thorough and quick method exists for verifying checks submitted by customers.

SEEKING HELP

Sam Nolte wondered how he could use computers to solve these problems. He knew that he had neither the knowledge nor the time to analyze the current system and design a new, automated system, but he certainly couldn't afford to hire a full-time information specialist. It also wasn't feasible to ask his competitors for help. Where would Sam Nolte get the help necessary to automate his pizza-processing system?

Sam reached into his desk drawer, pulled out the yellow pages from the Bay Area telephone directory, and flipped through the pages until he reached "computer consulting." There were a lot of firms listed. Starting at the top of the listing, Sam began making telephone calls. After only thirty minutes, he was completely frustrated. Of the six firms he had contacted, four were not interested in automating "such a small" firm, and the other two quoted hourly consulting rates far too high for Sam's comfort.

He was about to give up on the automation idea when he remembered that one of his employees, Linda Olvires, was studying management information systems at Bay Area State University. Maybe she would agree to work overtime to help him with his automation project. Sam looked at his worker schedule to see when Linda would be arriving at work. She was coming in at three o'clock that afternoon. He decided to talk with her then about the possibility of automating operations at Goodbyte Pizza Company.

At a little past three o'clock that afternoon, Sam Nolte asked Linda Olvires to step into his office for a talk. She was initially quite nervous until Sam explained that the talk had nothing to do with her job performance, that she was an excellent employee. Once Linda was more relaxed, Sam began to address the subject at hand:

Sam: I'm not too happy about how we're doing things around here. You've probably noticed that there's an awful lot of confusion and that customers have to wait too long for their orders.

Linda: Yes, I've noticed some problems, but I didn't think it was my place to say anything.

Sam: I understand, but I can use your help. I think the whole operation needs streamlining. Maybe we could use computers. What do you think?

Linda: Well, I'm learning that computers can be used for almost anything. Everything here is so manual. I've eaten at McDonalds, Taco Bell, and other places where their cash registers are automated.

Sam laughed to himself, imagining that Linda had probably also eaten at other pizza places with computers but that she was too polite to say so. He continued:

Sam: I understand that you're studying computers in college. Do you think you could put in some extra time to help me see if computers might help us?

Linda hesitated while she chose her answer carefully. She liked her job at Goodbyte Pizza and didn't want to make the boss unhappy.

Linda: I'm flattered at your offer, but I'm already working twenty hours a week and carrying a fifteen-hour course load, so I don't think I can afford to put in any more time here. I might have another solution for you, however.

I'm taking a Systems Analysis and Design course where they split the students into teams and have them study a real business firm for possible automation. Maybe my team could study Goodbyte.

Sam: That's a possibility. How can we check it out?

Linda: My professor has asked us to find a client and decide the scope of the automation project. Then we submit the proposed scope to my professor and she either concurs or recommends changes. We have to submit our proposal in graphic form. Do you have some sort of chart showing how everything works around here?

Sam laughed, then continued:

Sam: No, I don't have a chart like that. I'm not sure I know how things work around here. But I'll tell you what we can do. I'll get someone to cover for you this afternoon, and you can stay in here and draw the chart yourself.

Linda Olvires did just that. She produced the chart shown in Figure 1.2–1. She showed the

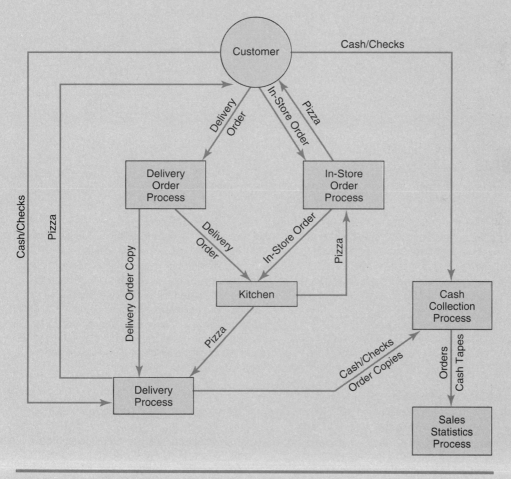

FIGURE 1.2–1   **How Things Work at GoodByte Pizza Company**

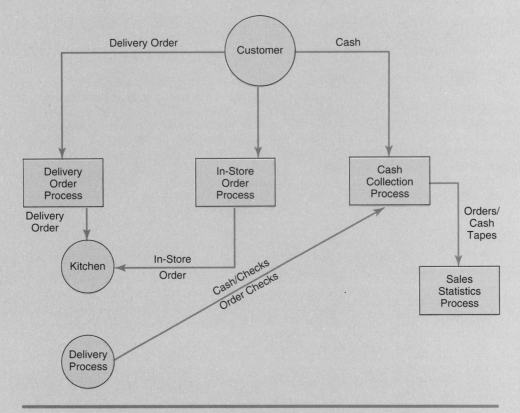

FIGURE 1.2–2   Scope of Goodbyte Pizza Company Study

chart to Sam Nolte, who reviewed it and agreed that it made sense. The next day, Linda showed it to her student team. The team members, delighted at having a design client, submitted the proposed scope to their professor at the end of the week.

PROJECT SCOPE

Linda Olvires hesitantly knocked at Sam Nolte's office door. Sam looked up, smiled, and said, "Come in, Linda, come in. How did your professor like our little project?"

Linda stepped into the office and replied, "She liked the project, but she thought it was too large for one semester's work. She suggested

that we narrow the scope to this." Linda showed Sam the revised project scope (Figure 1.2–2).

Sam studied the figure. His face showed some concern as he asked, "But won't it be a mess to automate only part of our operation? Shouldn't the operation be either computerized or noncomputerized, rather than a mishmash?"

Linda considered Sam's question and tried to remember what her professor had said when Linda had asked the same thing.

DISCUSSION QUESTIONS AND EXERCISES

1. From what you have learned in Chapter 1, what business marketing strategy does Goodbyte Pizza employ? Why do you think the firm is in trouble?

2. What are the advantages of using student teams to design actual business computer systems? The disadvantages?

3. What problems could Linda Olvires face as a student designing an information system for the firm for which she works?

4. Given the problems that Sam Nolte listed, why does he think that a computer might help?

5. Why do you think that the delivery and kitchen functions were eliminated from the scope of work? (Why not one of the other functions?)

6. What are the problems with automating only part of a business process?

7. Visit a pizza parlor and report on (a) how computers are used, and (b) how computers could be used.

In this chapter you will learn about:

WHAT: (Concepts) The Anatomy of information and information systems.

WHY: Before we can design automated systems that process and deliver infor-
          mation, we need to know just what is information.

WHEN: This chapter contains conceptual information that should be mastered
          before students are ready to design their first information system.

WHO: This conceptual material is essential to all students of systems analysis and
          design.

WHERE: The material in this chapter may have been covered in prerequisite
          courses. If not, it should be addressed early in the Systems Analysis and
          Design course.

HOW: (Techniques) Tests for information
                       Problem structure
                       Problem-solving cycle
                       Human factors techniques

OUTLINE

- Setting
- Data versus Information
- Information and Problems
- Characteristics of Information
- Information and Levels of an Organization
- Human Factors Considerations
- A Total Quality Management (TQM) Approach

THE QUALITY OF INFORMATION

He who holds information that someone else does not have is regarded to be "richer" than that other person and consequently is in a more powerful position.

—C. WEST CHURCHMAN, 1968

SETTING

Information systems often do not work well. One problem is that information systems may lack information; systems may be filled with data, but they may not contain useful information. Understanding the conceptual role of information is vital to the design of an effective business system. Preparing the way for quality information is the goal of designing new systems.

This chapter lays the foundation for succeeding chapters by defining *information* and *information systems*. The chapter establishes the framework for several conceptual models that are used throughout this book.

DATA VERSUS INFORMATION

The difference between *data* and *information* forms the essential framework for the design of business systems. **Data** is the description of things and events that we face. **Business data** is an organization's description of things (resources) and events (transactions) that it faces. **Information** is data organized to help choose some current or future action or nonaction. For **business information,** this choice is called **business**

decision making. Business information aids in choosing current or future ways to fulfill company goals.

For example, an employee submits a weekly time sheet. This time sheet is a business event (transaction) involving the labor resource. This sheet (resource event) includes fields of data such as number of hours worked. The information systems department uses this and other fields of data to produce payroll information. Managers use payroll information to decide if and how much to pay employees. Only when the data on time sheets is organized into business information can managers make proper payroll decisions. **Data processing** is the term used to describe changes performed on data to produce purposeful information.

Data Processing

Figure 2–1 shows how data is converted to information. Conversion requires one or more of the following data-processing operations:

1. Data input
   a) *Recording* transaction data onto a data-processing medium (e.g., punching numbers into a calculator)
   b) *Coding* transaction data into a different, easier to use mode (e.g., converting the sex attribute "female" to the letter F)
   c) *Storing* data or information for future decision making (potential information)
   d) *Selecting,* from among multiple data items, those with potential for decision making
2. Data transformation
   a) *Calculating* new amounts through arithmetic operation on data fields
   b) *Summarizing* by accumulating several data items (e.g., adding hours worked for each day of the week into a single total of hours worked per week)
   c) *Classifying* data into separate, identifiable groups
      (1) *Categorizing* data into groups according to one or more characteristics (e.g., distinguishing student data by a code for class standing)

FIGURE 2–1   Major Steps and Functions of Data Processing

	Data Input (Transaction)	Data Transformation	Information Output (Report)
Major Steps			
Functions	– Record	– Calculate	– Display
	– Code	– Summarize	– Reproduce
	– Store	– Classify	– Telecommunicate
	– Select		

(2) *Sorting* data into an identifiable sequence (e.g., in ascending customer number sequence)

(3) *Merging* two or more data sets based on the classified contents of one or more data fields (e.g., combining monthly sales data for January, February, and March into one quarterly group organized by regional office code)

(4) *Matching* a desired characteristic against a group of data to isolate individual data items that meet that characteristic (e.g., selecting all employees earning more than $30,000 per year)

3. Information output

a) *Displaying* results of data modification for information users (e.g., producing payroll totals on either a printed report or a video display terminal [VDT])

b) *Reproducing (copying)* stored data for use by multiple users (e.g., making a copy of sorted data in case the original data is destroyed or producing multiple copies for different users)

c) *Telecommunicating* stored data electronically over communication media

Here is an example of raw data that is transformed into information. A customer buys a pair of athletic shoes at a retail shoe store. The purchase is a transaction or an event, which is called *raw data*. The raw data alone has little meaning for the enterprise because it has not yet even been recorded. The first step is to record the sale. The salesperson enters the sale into the cash register. The sales transaction includes the following data: date (automatically stamped), type of sale (a number indicates athletic shoe—a coding process), product identification code (a number of significance for inventory processing), unit price, type of payment, quantity, tax, total price, amount tendered, and change.

When the transaction is completed, the information is transmitted to the on-site computer where the daily sales transaction file and the inventory master file are updated. This is a storage process. At the end of the sales day, the daily sales transaction file is sorted according to type of sale. A daily cash report is generated and is checked against the amount of money in the cash register. A bank deposit is created and any shortage or overage is noted. Sorting is a transformation process. The daily cash report requires summarization, which is another transformation process. The daily cash report is printed on paper and also sent via telecommunication to the regional office. The printing and telecommunication of the daily cash report are types of information output. Thus, a business event (sales transaction) is recorded, processed, aggregated, and output into meaningful information. Such information can be used for managerial decision making, such as identification of repeated cash register shortages or sales trends for various categories of goods.

Importance of Information to Management

Information has management purpose. Data does not. Receipt of nonpurposeful data is not only expensive but may be detrimental to the effectiveness of management's decision making. Adverse effects from too much data are referred to as **information overload** (Figure 2–2). The overload phenomenon exists for amoeba, animals,

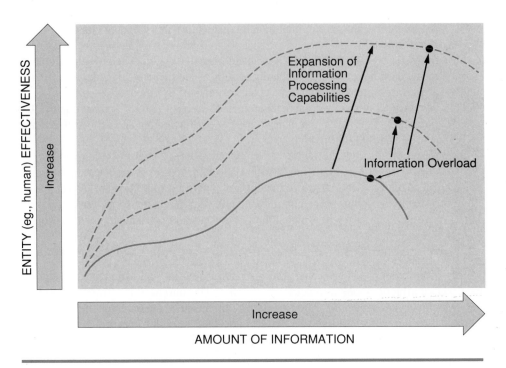

FIGURE 2-2   **Information Overload**

humans, and collections of humans (organizations). Although the effectiveness of any entity increases as it receives more messages about its environment, there is a point where the amount of information provided exceeds sensory capabilities. Effectiveness then not only slows but actually decreases.

When information systems designers fail to distinguish between purposeless data and important information, they saturate the receiver's perception capacity, and decision-making effectiveness decreases. Critical information becomes lost in heaps of useless data. As an experienced analyst once said, "I'm so busy squashing ants, the elephants are stomping me to death." For example, a user once insisted on a weekly sales report by division, territory, salesperson, product, and customer. After receiving a bulky report for two months, the user realized the value of summary and exception reports.

Too many information systems carry a lot of data but little information. Because of information overload, these systems impair, rather than aid, management decision making. Therefore, analysts test organization messages to see whether they are data or information. Data that is not converted to information is clutter.

One critical goal of information technology (computers, communications, software, and databases) is to expand human capacity and ability to handle information. We want to raise the height of the curve shown in Figure 2-2. This can be done by summarizing rather than presenting detailed data, providing management warnings only when an exceptional condition occurs, providing automatic trend and forecasting capabilities, and allowing electronic inquiry in addition to paper reports. Even with expansion of human information capabilities, however, at some point information overload occurs. It has just shifted to a higher point.

Managers must reject data from information systems when it has little chance of helping them make decisions. Think of doctors advising us to eliminate clogging cholesterol from our bloodstreams so that life-sustaining blood may flow. Analysts test an organization's messages for desired information versus cluttering data. Remember, when it comes to data, "More is *not* better!"

Tests for Information

There are four tests to determine whether or not a specific message (for example, an item on a printed report) is information:

1. To whom (which decision maker) is the message intended?
2. For what specific decision is the message intended?
3. How is the message used to detect or resolve the condition?
4. How often (when) is the decision made?

Who Is the Specific Decision Maker? Reports and copies of forms are often routed to departments, not to specific positions or individuals. Insist on learning who within the department needs the message. If a specific person cannot be identified, the message is *probably* data.

What Is the Specific Decision? Even if a message is tied to a specific person, that alone does not make the message information. As the noted author Ackoff (1967) states, "The manager who does not understand the phenomenon he controls plays it 'safe' and, with respect to information, wants 'everything.' " Therefore, ask problem solvers why they need the data. What is the specific decision to which the message belongs?

How Is the Decision Made? Even identification of a specific decision is not enough. Exactly how is the message used to make the identified decision? Decision makers unsure of the *what* and *how* of their decisions probably are using data rather than information.

When Is the Message Used? A message does not have to be used immediately for decision making in order to classify it as information. Many messages carry *potential* information—there is a chance that it will be used for future decision making. Nonspecific responses to the *when* question, such as "someday" or "I collect it just in case," point to collection of unnecessary data rather than meaningful information.

Valid information for one decision maker may be cluttering data for another. A monthly balance sheet may be critical information to an accountant. However, because that sheet contains figures in dollars rather than in physical units, it is cluttering to a warehouse manager.

In summary, the true test of whether a business message is information or not lies in its intended use for problem solving and decision making.

INFORMATION AND PROBLEMS

Managers use information for current or potential decision making. **Business decision making** is the selection of an action, from among two or more alternatives, to solve a business problem. The key to the definition is that problems drive decision making. If no problem exists, there is no need to consider alternatives and make a decision.

A **problem** is the gap between what we expect and our current status (Figure 2–3). Our expectations are goals, objectives, or standards. Status is a measurement of how the system is performing now. Not all problems defined in this manner deserve serious consideration. Suppose the goal for accuracy of data entry is 95 percent and the current level of performance is 94.7 percent. Should the operation be changed? Probably not. If we considered this small variance a problem, we might saturate scarce management resources and mask significant problems.

A problem detection structure must include a **tolerance filter** that determines whether expectation gaps are large enough to require management attention. Well-designed tolerance filters allow us to discard such problems as modest monthly rises and falls about an average that meets expectations, small expectation gaps surrounded by larger problems, and expectation gaps that have been decreasing at an acceptable rate.

Trend projection is another part of problem definition (or problem detection). Designing replacement information systems requires long development times, and of course the replacement system is desired before the current system collapses. Hence, the demise of the current system should be predicted well ahead of time. Figure 2–4 illustrates this point. Our goal for VDT response time is that no response time be longer than one second. Response time for the current month is faster than this standard; however, response time has been increasing steadily. We project that it will exceed the

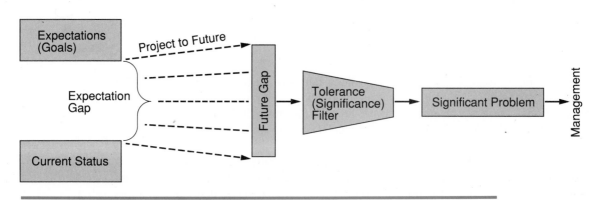

FIGURE 2–3   **Structure of Typical Problems**

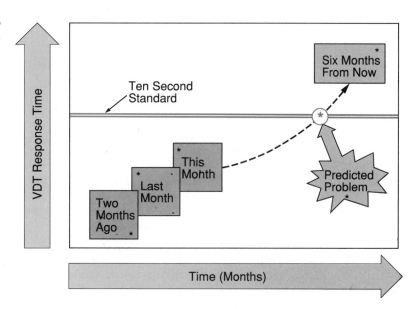

FIGURE 2–4   Trend Projection: Predicting VDT Response Time

standard four months from now, so we had better start working on this future (potential) problem now while there is still enough lead time.

Problem detection requires four identifiable parts:

1. Measurable expectations (goals, objectives, or standards)
2. Means for measuring current system performance
3. Tolerance filter to rank and separate the significant from insignificant problems
4. Forecasting unit to project performance trends

A simple example of an operational problem detection system is the home climate control unit (better known as a thermostat). The four components are as follows:

1. The measurable expectation is the desired temperature. (Let's say 80 degrees in the summer.)
2. The means for measuring current system performance is the thermometer within the thermostat.
3. The tolerance filter to separate significant from insignificant problems is the variance from the set amount that triggers the activation of the air conditioner. (Perhaps that's 2 degrees.)
4. The forecasting unit to project performance may be a timer that anticipates the need for cooling and activates the air conditioner before the measuring unit detects the need. (Of course, the real forecasting unit is the home owner.)

Good managers do not wait for problems to happen. They use forecasting systems, intelligence gathering, and other future-oriented techniques to detect potential problems. They reflect on what possible paths there may be in the firm's future. The problem model just described is an essential framework that is used throughout the book. This model is an essential part of the problem-solving cycle discussed in the next section.

Problem-Solving Cycle

Figure 2–5 shows one perspective of the manager's role as a problem solver. It is a simple perspective, yet it helps analyze just what information is. The **problem-solving cycle** is particularly valuable in analyzing and designing business information systems. Several components make up the problem-solving cycle:

- *Resource input (number 1 in Figure 2–5):* Resources input to any business process (production) include money, material, equipment, personnel, and information. A resource mix is critical to the effectiveness of the production process.
- *Production process (number 2 in Figure 2–5):* Management combines resources into teams to produce desired output. For example, a worker (personnel resource) is assigned to a specific machine (equipment resource) to produce a part (material resource) for a kitchen appliance (product output).
- *Product/service output (number 3 in Figure 2–5):* Product or service output is the intended result of the production process. Output can include multiple products, services, or by-products. For example, the lumber firm production of two-by-fours also results in a by-product of sawdust.
- *Goals/standards (number 4 in Figure 2–5):* The firm has expectations about what the product/service output should be when emerging from production processes. These goals are specific to each characteristic of output (e.g., size, weight, capacity).

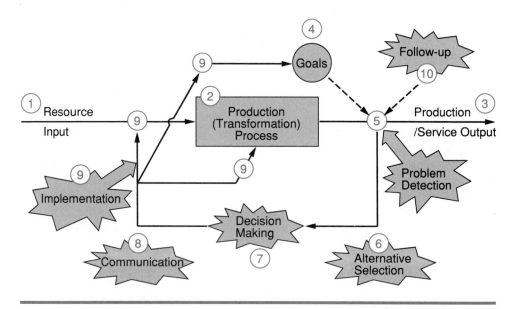

FIGURE 2–5   **Problem-solving Cycle**

- *Problem detection:* This mechanism, which was discussed earlier, includes analysis of causes of the problem. If we were able to peer within the circle marked number 5 in Figure 2–5, we would find the Problem Model described in the last section.
- *Generation of alternatives (number 6 in Figure 2–5):* When managers detect problems, they seek alternatives to correct (redesign) the system. They test these design alternatives for their contribution to goals and standards. One alternative is always "do not change."
- *Decision making (number 7 in Figure 2–5):* Managers select one alternative corrective action for implementation. Again, the alternative selected often is not to make any changes.
- *Decision communication (number 8 in Figure 2–5):* Managers communicate their decisions in a format understandable to those who must carry out that decision at the production level.
- *Decision implementation (number 9 in Figure 2–5):* Operational personnel carry out the decision by one of three methods:
  1. They change the resource mix; for example, they hire more people.
  2. They change the production processes by varying combinations of resources; for example, they assign a more experienced operator to a complex machine.
  3. They change the goals or standards to bring them more in line with reality; for example, they reduce product quality to that of their competitors.
- *Follow-up (number 10 in Figure 2–5):* Managers watch the process to be sure the problem is solved.

Managers decide only when they detect a significant problem. If no problem is present, there can be no decision. Therefore, the role of information is to serve problem detection and solving.

The problem-solving cycle is a simplistic model geared toward day-to-day management. Nonetheless, it is useful for binding together the various techniques and practices of systems analysis and design into a discipline.

CHARACTERISTICS OF INFORMATION

Data consists of unorganized messages for which there is no purpose. *Information* is data that has been processed for a management purpose. That purpose is to service the problem-solving cycle, including decision making. Information is the blood of management, because proper information flow is vital to management problem solving.

Just what is this resource called information? Does it have height or weight as material resources do? Does it have denominations, as monetary resources do? How can information be described so systems designers may judge, design, and fine-tune its management-sustaining flow?

Information is processed data; therefore, data and information have common characteristics. Some of these characteristics are described in the following list:

- **Relevancy:** How is the message used for problem solving (decision making)? Relevancy, of course, is the characteristic that separates information from data.

THE SOMETIMES DATA ENTRY OPERATOR

Ron is a data entry operator. His past performance has shown him to be very accurate. He averages less than 5 percent errors on entry (95 percent accuracy rate). However, Ron is absent an average of one and a half days each week. He is an unreliable employee because he fails to sustain his high accuracy rate.

- **Accuracy:**
  1. **Completeness:** Are necessary message items present?
  2. **Correctness:** Are message items correct?
  3. **Security:** Did the message reach all and only the intended system users?
- **Timeliness:** How quickly is input transformed to proper output?
- **Economy:** What level of resources is needed to move information through the problem-solving cycle?
- **Efficiency:** What level of resource is required for each unit of information output? Efficiency is measured in such terms as *accuracy per dollar* or *timeliness per dollar*.
- **Reliability:** Characteristics are reported as averages—for example, average error rate (correctness) or average VDT response time (timeliness). Reliability deals with how consistently a system maintains the averages—variances around the averages. Sometimes accuracy and reliability are confused. The example in the box on this page will help clear up that confusion.
- **Usability:** Information must be held or produced in a format that is usable. For example, information in a binary format is not very useful to human beings. Usability can be addressed from a machine (hardware) point of view. Nevertheless, the main thrust in this book is usability of information for humans. This need is often referred to as *human factors,* a topic discussed in some length later in this chapter.

INFORMATION AND LEVELS OF AN ORGANIZATION

One requirement of performance measurement for an information system is standards. What is expected for each characteristic of information? For example, should a standard be set at 95 percent accuracy or will 90 percent do? Should response time to user inquiries be less than ten seconds?

Managers set standards according to their information requirements. Yet, information requirements vary depending on the level of organization to which the problem solver belongs. This is so because different types of problems exist at each organizational level.

To assess differing information needs, we need to distinguish between levels of management (as we did briefly in Chapter 1). Anthony (1965) suggests a convenient organizational model consisting of three levels of decision making (Figure 2–6).

Managers make **strategic decisions** about the overall directions in which the firm should proceed. Such decisions influence all the firm's missions and products. For

FIGURE 2–6   **Structure and Types of Business Decisions**

example, a firm may strategically decide on a low-cost strategy to set prices lower than all competitors.

Managers make **tactical decisions** by mission, by product, by system, or by location. Decisions for one mission may be different from decisions for another mission, but decisions across all missions conform to the policy established by strategic decisions. Tactical decisions typically involve processes largely within the control of the organization (e.g., setting product price). So each product manager may set prices; however, these prices must be consistent with the strategic decision to have lower prices than all competitors.

Operational decisions include the everyday decisions required to carry out the overall firm and individual mission requirements determined by strategic and tactical management. For example, day-to-day advertising decisions will reflect *both* the strategic low-cost decision and the tactical price decision made by each product manager.

Information characteristics apply to all three levels of management. The requirements for the characteristics, however, differ as the level of management changes. Why? Because the nature of the decision changes at each management level. Figure 2–7 makes this point graphically.

Continuum of Information Systems

The problem-solving cycle is a conceptual framework that resurfaces throughout this book. Figure 2–8 shows the cycle in a different perspective—one that leads to a continuum of information systems. This figure combines the problem-solving cycle model (Figure 2–5) with the Anthony management model (Figure 2–6). Now let's look at the different types of information systems that form this continuum.

Transaction-Processing Systems

A **transaction-processing system (TPS)** keeps track of current and potential organizational resources such as people, funds, and materials. It services the top por-

Type Management Decision		
Operational	Tactical	Strategic
Medium ———————————	Relevancy ———————————	→ High
High ———————————	Completeness ———————————	→ Low
High ———————————	Correctness ———————————	→ Low
Low ———————————	Security ———————————	→ High
High ———————————	Timeliness ———————————	→ Low
High ———————————	Economy ———————————	→ Low
High ———————————	Efficiency ———————————	→ Low
High ———————————	Reliability ———————————	→ Low
High ———————————	Usability ———————————	→ High

Information
Characteristics

FIGURE 2–7   Differences in Information Needs at Different Management Levels

portion of the problem-solving cycle (see Figure 2–8). Transactions are entered to make changes in resource balances.

For example, a warehouse worker receives stock; this is a business event, or transaction. The source for data entered into the system is the receiving slip sent by the vendor with the stock. The warehouse clerk draws this source document across a laser scanner. The scanner reads the identity and quantity of the stock received and increases the balance on hand for each stock item received. The new balance on hand reflects the status of each specific resource (item of stock) involved in the transaction.

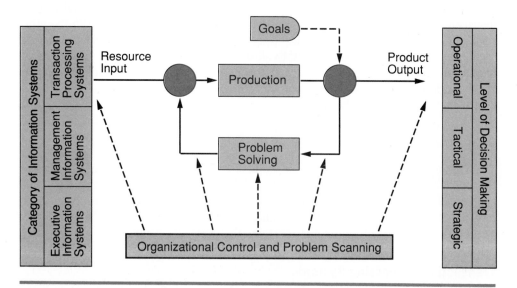

FIGURE 2–8   Problem-solving Cycle and Information Systems

Output from a transaction-processing system includes resource status reports such as physical and dollar inventory balances; detailed transaction listings, which are used by auditors to determine if the TPS is operating properly; resource status and change summaries (used by management); and action documents that trigger further changes in resources (e.g., purchase orders to trigger future stock receipt).

Management Information Systems

Experts disagree about the nature of management information systems. In this textbook, a **management information system (MIS)** is a system for providing information to meet problem-solving needs. We have already defined business decision making as the selection of a course of action from among two or more alternatives to solve a business problem. Therefore, MIS concerns problem solving; it services the middle portion of the problem-solving cycle of Figure 2–8. Three parts form this portion of the problem-solving cycle; thus, the ideal management information system contains three parts: problem detection, problem analysis, and decision making.

As a problem detection mechanism, the MIS contains the necessary elements of the problem structure (see Figure 2–3). As a problem analysis mechanism, the MIS provides data needed by managers to make decisions. Finally, the MIS decision-making mechanism includes structured methods (algorithms) for selecting the best from among several alternatives. Such structured methods strive to reach common goals, such as least cost, highest profit, or lowest risk.

An example of an MIS subsystem is a sales-monitoring system that alerts managers when sales are either above or below expected levels. The subsystem not only alerts managers but also offers logical explanations for the high or low levels by listing any potential causal actions that occurred prior to detection. In addition, the subsystem includes a what-if module that allows managers to raise and lower levels of contributing variables experimentally to determine if the variations could have contributed to the outcome.

Few existing MIS systems perform the problem analysis functions just described. This is particularly true in the case of generating alternatives. There are, however, two classes of systems that support the decision-making portion of the MIS: decision support systems and expert systems.

Decision Support Systems and Expert Systems

The **decision support system (DSS)** and the **expert system (ES)** support management decision processes, but each system supports a different decision setting. Three major features differentiate a DSS from an ES.

Problem Structure. Expert systems deal primarily with structured problems—problems that can be defined by a clear, consistent, and unambiguous series of steps to reach a solution. In contrast, the DSS is applied to semistructured problems in which there is some uncertainty. For example, a DSS can be used to design waiting-line facilities where the number of customers arriving is a probabilistic function. Arrivals cannot be predicted with precision at any specific point in time.

Level of Quantification. Decision support systems approach problem solving from a quantitative basis. Expert systems use some simple mathematical transformations, but primarily they deal with nonmathematical reasoning (for example, "If A then perform path 1; else perform path 2").

Purpose. The purpose of decision support systems is to provide information and suggestions to the manager. Expert systems often are designed not to assist but to partially replace human decision makers. Many times, expert systems are used when human decision experts are not readily available (e.g., the main chef for Campbell's Soup retires).

Executive Information Systems

The **executive information system (EIS),** which covers the bottom portion of Figure 2–8, is a special MIS dedicated to high-level (strategic) management. Such dedication is required because strategic managers require special methods of presentation (e.g., graphics) and draw much of their information from external, noncomputerized sources such as telephone calls, professional meetings, and personal conversations.

Figure 2–9 shows the relationships among transaction-processing systems, management information systems, decision support systems, expert systems, and executive information systems. The TPS feeds data into the MIS *when a potential problem is present.* All nine information characteristics apply to all of these delivery systems. Of particular importance is the characteristic of usability, a characteristic often referred to as human factors.

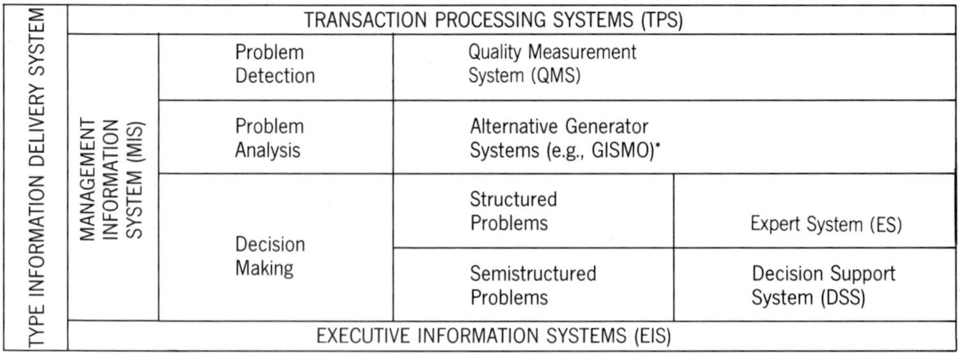

TYPE INFORMATION DELIVERY SYSTEM			TRANSACTION PROCESSING SYSTEMS (TPS)	
	MANAGEMENT INFORMATION SYSTEM (MIS)	Problem Detection	Quality Measurement System (QMS)	
		Problem Analysis	Alternative Generator Systems (e.g., GISMO)*	
		Decision Making	Structured Problems	Expert System (ES)
			Semistructured Problems	Decision Support System (DSS)
		EXECUTIVE INFORMATION SYSTEMS (EIS)		

*GISMO stands for graphic interactive structural modeling system. See W. Pracht, "GISMO: A Visual Problem Structuring and Knowledge Organization Tool," *IEEE Transactions in Systems, Man and Cybernetics* 14(1987):265–270.

FIGURE 2–9   **Relationships among Information Systems**

HUMAN FACTORS CONSIDERATIONS

Human factors, a frequently used term in the business information field, means the study of the welfare, satisfaction, and performance of people working with information systems. Some people also use the term *ergonomics.*

It seems obvious that users of information systems should be of major concern to the designers of such systems, but this has not always been the case. Until the 1980s, users of information systems were largely a captive audience, with few choices available to them other than subscribing to in-house design resources. Systems analysts presumably knew more about what users needed than did the users themselves. Few users dared to question their work just as few of Mozart's patrons would have had the audacity to question his musical masterpieces.

The 1980s saw the proliferation of microcomputers, end-user computing, and competitive, predesigned software packages. Despite the resulting stings to artistic integrity, systems analysts had to learn to cater to their patrons—to satisfy their customers.

Today, the user has indeed become a client, a customer—as integral a part of the systems domain as hardware, software, database structures, and telecommunications protocols. Designers of business information systems must know as much about the customer component as they do about the other, more predictable components. Let us start with trying to understand how our customers think.

A Simple Model of the Mind

The graphic model of the human mind (Figure 2–10) is intended only as a focus from which to discuss tactics for dealing with human factors. The model has eight parts.

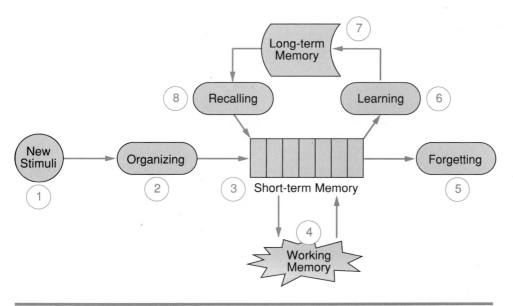

FIGURE 2–10   **Simple Model of the Human Mind**

New Stimuli (Number 1 in Figure 2–10). Our senses detect new **stimuli** to be processed by our minds. According to the computer analogy, the new stimuli are data ready to be processed.

Organizing (Number 2 in Figure 2–10). The mind has storage capacity **(memory capacity)** constraints. Thus, stimulus data must be summarized, classified, or otherwise reduced to separate chunks that working memory can manipulate. The computer analogy is conversion of human data into a computer-storable format such as EBCDIC.

Short-term Memory (Number 3 in Figure 2–10). Separate chunks are assimilated into **short-term memory (STM).** This element is similar to the arithmetic register through which computer data transfers are made. Short-term memory has limited capacity, which affects human perceptive abilities.

Working Memory (Number 4 in Figure 2–10). Short-term memory is used with **working memory** for processing data and for solving problems. "Short-term memory processes perceptual input whereas working memory is used to generate and implement solutions" (Shneiderman, 1987). The process is similar to the movement of data into a computer's functional circuits, where operations (e.g., comparison and arithmetic operations) are performed and results are returned to the arithmetic register (short-term memory).

Forgetting *(Number 5 in Figure 2–10).* Only two things can happen to chunks stored in short-term memory. Chunks are either learned (moved to long-term memory) or *forgotten* (lost from the mind entirely). If new chunks of stimuli are pushed into short-term memory, they displace the oldest chunks stored there. If these oldest chunks have not yet been learned, they will be forgotten. The computer analogy to forgetting is placement of new data into a storage location (e.g., a register). Data previously stored there are lost, unless they have been moved elsewhere.

Learning (Number 6 in Figure 2–10). **Learning** involves moving information chunks from short-term to long-term memory. The process is similar to moving computer data to more permanent, mass memory such as magnetic disk.

Long-term Memory (Number 7 in Figure 2–10). The mind's permanent storage is **long-term memory (LTM);** it has enormous capacity. Thus, chunks stored here are not replaced (forgotten) when new chunks are learned.

Recalling (Number 8 in Figure 2–10). Chunks of data stored in long-term memory are not erased (forgotten). However, if left idle (that is, not accessed), such chunks lose their retrieval keys. They are still there; we merely have forgotten the means to **recall** them. Think of a computer system where linkage between records is broken; there then remains no means to access a particular record.

This simple model of the human mind can be used to develop design tactics for the user interface. Before discussing these tactics, however, the nature and constraints of short-term memory and long-term memory must be explained further.

Short-Term Memory

Short-term memory (STM), the link between input stimuli and the mind, has a very restricted capacity. This capacity is related to the number of data chunks handled and acoustic (sound) interference between chunks. STM is also highly volatile.

Capacity

What is a chunk of memory? A **chunk** is a grouping of stimuli (data) distinguishable from other groupings but largely independent of stimulus size. For example, an individual's last name is distinguishable from his or her first name and middle initial. Each of these separate fields (parts of the name) is similar to a separate chunk of short-term memory; each field is a different length.

Actual chunk size is relative to the individual's familiarity with the stimulus. For example, a child hearing the new word *proboscis* may process it as three chunks, one per syllable *(pro-bos-cis)*. Yet, a commonly known name such as John Paul Jones may be handled as only one chunk in short-term memory.

Experts disagree over the number of chunks of short-term memory available to the typical human mind. One popular theory is Miller's 7 ± 2 chunks. Miller (1956) cites stimulus tests involving visual control panels, human separation of different tones, and experiments with taste intensities. He found that each stimulus has about seven categories (chunks). Miller thus suggests that, in a large number of human conditions, the number of categories consistently falls between 5 and 9. This is Miller's 7 ± 2 model for the capacity of short-term memory.

Some disagree with Miller's inductive conclusions regarding capacity. The following exceptions are of particular importance to the development of design tactics for dealing with human factors:

1. Capacity of short-term memory appears to increase with familiarity. For example, Shneiderman (1987) suggests that most Americans would have an easier time immediately recalling from short-term memory seven English words as opposed to seven Russian words. The reason may be that one unfamiliar Russian word might have to be broken into separate syllables, thus requiring more than one chunk of memory.
2. Capacity of short-term memory decreases with anxiety: Increased attention is demanded for the events producing the anxiety. Anxiety is distracting because it robs us of scarce short-term memory chunks. Anxiety poses a difficult design problem because often it is produced by the working environment, which is beyond the control of the systems designer. The designer does, however, have control over the amount of anxiety created at the user interface.

Congruence (Symmetry)

As stated, the capacity of short-term memory is a function not only of the number of chunks of data but of acoustic interference between chunks. If two separate data elements are similar in sound (the names *Smith* and *Smythe*), there is interference between these chunks. They are subsumed into one chunk and treated by the mind as one entity (Figure 2–11).

Chunks can be separated by making them opposite. Thus, the terms *black* and *white* are more congruent (separated) than *dark* and *white* or *black* and *clear*. In the same way, other congruent pairs of terms are *advance/retreat* and *right/left*. The lesson for designers is that design of codes (e.g., command codes) should follow the principle of **congruence (symmetry)** if users are to distinguish between separate commands such as GOTO/RETURN or SAVE/WITHDRAW.

Volatility (Instability)

Short-term memory is highly **volatile** because of its limited capacity and because it takes some effort to move chunks of data from short-term to long-term memory. New chunks of data push older stored chunks out, and the older chunks are forgotten.

Important chunks of data can disappear inadvertently through circumstances in the work environment or hardware that cannot be controlled by the systems designer. Common events causing such volatility are:

- Disruptions in concentration due to interruptions such as telephone calls
- Delays in processing such as long message response times

FIGURE 2–11   **Concept of Congruence (Symmetry)**

(a) Congruent Data Elements

Black — Chunk 1   White — Chunk 2

(b) Noncongruent Data Elements

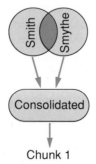

Smith   Smythe

Consolidated

Chunk 1

- Visual distractions (perhaps overuse of color on the terminal screen)
- Noisy work environments

Closure

Because of the limited capacity and high volatility of short-term memory, human tasks must be designed to be short in complexity (simple) and duration (quick). In this way, there is less chance that other new stimuli (either worthwhile data or disruptions) will push current task chunks out of memory before the task is successfully completed. This is the principle of **closure**—the completion of one task so the user can concentrate on the next.

In summary, short-term memory is acoustic (sound), has extremely limited capacity, and is highly volatile. To deal with STM constraints, humans combine similar chunks of data into a single chunk (some call this stereotyping). Because of the limitations to short-term memory, designers must make tasks short and simple. In this way, a task can be "in and out" of STM before it is displaced by new data or disruptive stimuli.

Long-Term Memory

Once chunks of data are pushed from short-term to long-term memory, they will not be forgotten. Long-term memory has low volatility. The pushing of chunks to long-term memory is called *learning*.

Learning takes a fair amount of time and several iterations (tries). Iterations are necessary because chunks do not remain in short-term memory long enough (only about fifteen seconds) to allow learning in one pass. Once learning takes place, however, the learned chunks are not forgotten.

How can we account for the common human foible of failing to remember (recall) some fact already learned? Chunks stored in memory have "access keys" through which they are retrieved. Such keys are similar to a record key (e.g., customer number) through which a record can be found in a file. If we lose track of access keys, we cannot retrieve facts, although they are still somewhere in long-term memory.

Unfortunately, it is easy to lose such access keys. As we collect (learn) new chunks in long-term memory, old chunks that are semantically (or pictorially) similar to the new chunks become more difficult to recall. Old access keys now lead to new chunks. It is more difficult to recall a chunk if there are other similar chunks in memory (discrimination principle).

So now the entire human mind has been condensed into a few textbook pages. (Please remember that this model was advertised as being simplistic.) What does this mean to the systems analyst? Many of our discipline's accepted rules of thumb have as their basis the human mind and how it works. If systems analysis and design is to become a discipline rather than a sporadic art, analysts and designers must demonstrate that their hunches and rules of thumb have a structured, logical base. The simplistic view of the human mind presents a powerful framework that explains why, for example, aesthetically designed screens work for most users. Let us now add to this model some additional principles based on how computer users often act.

User Attitudes

This section on user attitudes proceeds in an inductive manner. It does not state that, given the preceding model of the human mind, end-users must have certain attitudes. Instead, observed human patterns of behavior are presented. These patterns lead to insights about how and why an end-user acts in a certain manner.

Four models of user attitudes are discussed: (1) Zipf's principle of least effort, (2) planned redundancy, (3) goal reaching (closure), and (4) changing user expectations. Each of the models helps the designer better understand why users behave as they do. Such understanding allows designers to build systems that accommodate such behavior, that address human usability of information systems.

Zipf's Principle of Least Effort

In 1949, Zipf developed a model of human behavior that presumes humans have a desire to escape sustained effort. Zipf's formal hypothesis was that "as a task becomes more difficult, fewer humans attempt that task" (Figure 2–12). A suggested corollary to this hypothesis is that the more difficult the task (in effort and time), the greater the number of humans who will abandon that task after they start it. Zipf's **principle of least effort** demonstrates the principle of closure.

The lesson from Zipf's principle for designers of business systems is obvious: If you wish to reach most end-users, keep tasks simple and short.

Planned Redundancy

Throughout the short history of information systems, designers and programmers have been taught to seek efficiency. They have been taught to minimize storage space,

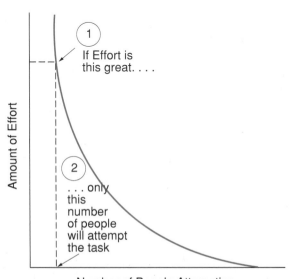

FIGURE 2–12   **Zipf's Principle of Least Effort**

lines of programming code, and data entry keystrokes. They have been told repeatedly that each character not critically needed is redundant. *Redundant* has become a synonym for inefficient. Times are changing, however.

Redundancy is an important dimension of the human repertoire. The English language is an example. If we used all letters of the alphabet with equal frequency, words of three equally likely letters could replace the entire English alphabet and convey the same amount of information. For example, all English words would look like XTV, AM3, or W?Z. Any noise in the system, however, would lead to misunderstanding. So the language has evolved with intentional redundancy to adjust for communication problems. It is 70 percent redundant.

In designing a business system, redundancy can be beneficial. It is only when the redundancy has not been planned that it is undesirable. When redundancy is planned to enhance communication or for protection, it is a viable design tactic called **planned redundancy.** For example, extra space is allowed in business records so new fields can be added at a later date. In addition, files are duplicated (backed up) periodically so if one file is destroyed, another is available for recovery. Highly redundant programming languages such as COBOL are tolerated so subsequent program modification is made easier. Planned redundancy is a proven systems tool.

Goal Reaching (Closure)

Humans are motivated to achieve goals only if these goals can be reached. Figure 2–13 shows the goal-reaching structure. First, expectations or goals are set by ourselves or by the environment. Second, we assess our current position. Third, we define the gap between expectations and current status as a problem. Fourth, we assess

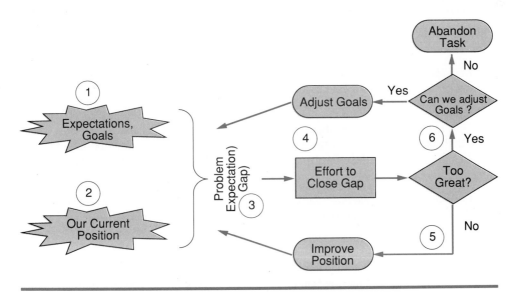

FIGURE 2–13   Goal-reaching Structure

efforts needed to close the gap—that is, to achieve our goals (to solve the problem). Fifth, if we do not judge closing efforts to be impossible, we begin efforts to improve performance and move to a point where we are closer to expectations. Sixth, if closing the effort is judged to be too great (Zipf's principle), we either try to lower expectations or abandon the task altogether. Given this model, systems designers must design tasks that users perceive as accomplishable without too much effort.

Changing User Expectations

There is still a further complicating dimension of human behavior: User expectations are a moving target. When performance is raised to reach expectations, the expectations are pushed upward and create a new challenge.

For example, the state of Alaska spent a considerable amount of funds and effort to change from batch to real-time computer applications. The results were impressive. The time it took for users to update or scan resource records decreased from days to an average of ten seconds. Within only a few months, however, users began to complain that the ten-second VDT response rate was far too slow. User expectations had changed again.

The designer must not set user expectations so high that users abandon the task. Likewise, the designer must not set task expectations so low that users will not have a challenge.

These, then, are the principles related to the important information characteristic of usability, described here in terms of human factors.

A TOTAL QUALITY MANAGEMENT (TQM) APPROACH

Recall that, in Chapter 1, we produced the following mission statement for designing information systems.

> *Development mission:* To design business information systems that satisfy the firm's information customers (both external and internal) while conforming to the overall mission and goals of the firms.

Our TQM task is to decompose this mission statement into specific system objectives that lend themselves to measurement. To do this, we will use the nine characteristics of information described earlier in this chapter. We then arrive at the following information objectives:

> *Information system objectives:* Each information system must, within the overall context of the development mission, demonstrate the following characteristics:

> 1. *Relevancy* to problem detection and solving
> 2. *Completeness,* in that all necessary message items are present
> 3. *Correctness* of all message items
> 4. *Security* of system messages in that all and only intended users receive these messages

5. *Timeliness* of information processing
6. *Economy,* so that, all other things being equal, information processing is performed with a minimum of resources
7. *Efficiency,* in that the ratio of characteristics 1 through 5 divided by characteristic 6 is maximized. For example, we want to maximize correctness per dollar or completeness per personnel hour
8. *Reliability* of all processes, so that the variances for all characteristics (e.g., timeliness) are minimized
9. *Usability,* in that human users can easily learn and use the system

In Chapter 3, we will show how these specific mission objectives can be used in every step of the process of analyzing and designing information systems.

SUMMARY

What is this entity called *information* for which businesses design, change, and replace systems? Information is observation of events (transaction data) converted, through data processing, to some intended use. That intended use is problem detection and solution. Decision making is an important part of the problem-solving cycle.

Information has characteristics that vary for different levels of an organization. Uses of information by a firm also vary. The continuum of information systems runs from transaction-processing systems (TPSs) to management information systems (MISs) to expert systems (ESs) and decision support systems (DSSs) to executive information systems (EISs). The structure for this continuum is the problem-solving cycle.

One characteristic of information that runs consistently throughout this textbook is that of *human usability.* Information systems must be easily usable by human users; or those systems will fail. A simple model of the human mind was presented, along with several attitude models that describe human characteristics. These principles give the systems analyst a better understanding of how to design information systems that are usable.

CONCEPTS LEARNED

- Differences between data and information
- How data is converted to information
- Information overload
- Tests for information
- Problem-solving cycle
- Problem detection
- Problem scanning
- Characteristics of information
- How information characteristics vary among organizational levels
- Transaction processing system (TPS)
- Management information system (MIS)
- Expert system (ES)
- Decision support system (DSS)
- Executive information system (EIS)
- Where each delivery system falls in the problem-solving cycle
- Human factors considerations

KEY TERMS

accuracy
business data
business decision making
business information
chunk
closure
completeness
congruence
correctness
data
data processing
decision support system (DSS)
economy
efficiency
executive information system (EIS)
expert system (ES)
forgetting
information
information overload
learning
long-term memory (LTM)
management information system (MIS)
memory capacity

operational decision
planned redundancy
principle of least effort
problem
problem detection
problem-solving cycle
recall
relevancy
reliability
security
short-term memory (STM)
stimuli
strategic decision
symmetry
tactical decision
timeliness
tolerance filter
transaction-processing system (TPS)
trend projection
usability
volatility
working memory

REVIEW QUESTIONS

1. What is the essential difference between data and information?

2. Describe four ways to convert data to information.

3. Describe information overload. What does it have to do with differences between data and information?

4. List the ten stages of the problem-solving cycle.

5. What is the difference between accuracy and reliability? Cite an example of this difference from your own experience.

6. How does the requirement for timeliness vary from strategic to operational levels of management? Why is there a difference?

7. What is the difference between problem finding and problem solving?

8. What is the purpose of a transaction-processing system?

9. Describe three primary parts of a management information system.

10. What are three essential differences between a decision support system and an expert system?

11. What is the difference between mental learning and forgetting?

12. What is a chunk of memory?

13. How many chunks are there in short-term memory?

14. Why is closure important?

15. What is Zipf's principle of least effort?

16. Why is planned redundancy important?

17. Why do user expectations of systems performance change?

CRITICAL THINKING OPPORTUNITIES

1. Draw a diagram that shows how this chapter is organized (refer to Figure 1–11 of Chapter 1).

2. Compare and contrast the terms *chunk, learning,* and *closure.*

3. Does the concept of planned redundancy agree or conflict with the information characteristic of *economy?* Defend your answer.

4. Most of a typical firm's development resources are devoted to transaction processing systems (TPSs). Explain why, using the problem-solving cycle model (Figure 2–6).

5. Find a copy of a computer-produced report from a firm in your geographic area. Select one page from the report. Interview a manager of the firm and, using the tests for information described in this chapter, determine if the elements presented on the report are data or information.

6. Select a software package such as word processing. Systematically evaluate the package to see how it agrees or conflicts with the human factors (usability) principles described in this chapter.

TRANSACTION PROCESSING SYSTEM TEMPLATES FOR CAREY CLOTHIERS

SETTING

Peggy Dramm is the new information systems manager for Carey Clothiers, Inc. She has recently completed her master's degree in MIS, taking classes at night while working as a systems analyst during the day. Peggy now wishes to apply some of her recently acquired knowledge to her new responsibilities.

By analyzing her firm's information system portfolio, Peggy discovers that 87 percent of the systems for which she is responsible are transaction processing systems (TPSs). She decides initially to concentrate on these systems. She remembers what one of her instructors had once emphasized in class:

> One aspect of a transaction-processing system differentiates it from other information systems. That aspect is commonality. The TPS is common to most business enterprises. All businesses have payroll, accounts payable, and purchasing systems. Such systems differ slightly from firm to firm, but they are similar in construction and means of processing. The MIS, DSS, ES, and EIS, on the other hand, are specific to the individual firm's decision-making setting. These models are more tailored than the TPS.

Peggy decides to begin her analysis by identifying the common structure of transaction-processing systems.

Common TPS Structure

Figure 2.1–1 shows the conceptual structure Peggy designed for transaction-processing systems. During the data entry phase (1.0), transactions are entered and verified. Purified transactions then change resource record balances during the record update phase (2.0). Finally, the report-processing phase (3.0) produces clerical reports and feeder information to higher level information systems (e.g., decision support systems). Each of these TPS phases contains several functions.

Data Entry Phase

Figure 2.1–2 shows the functions performed in the **data entry phase.**

Source Document. A TPS captures business transaction data as they enter the organization. Sometimes the capture is a clerk's recording of a business happening; for example, a clerk records the sale of a desk on a multipart sales form.

Often, parties outside the organization prepare **source documents.** Hence, a vendor receipt remains unchanged as it enters the organization from the vendor world.

Coding. **Coding** changes source (transaction) data to a more suitable storage format. At one time coding was done to save storage space; however, with recent decreases in hardware costs, storage space is no longer a major consideration.

An example of a code that is used to conserve storage space and data entry time is a marital status code for a personnel file. Using the letter S as the code for single and M for married allows data entry personnel to enter a one-digit code rather than several characters.

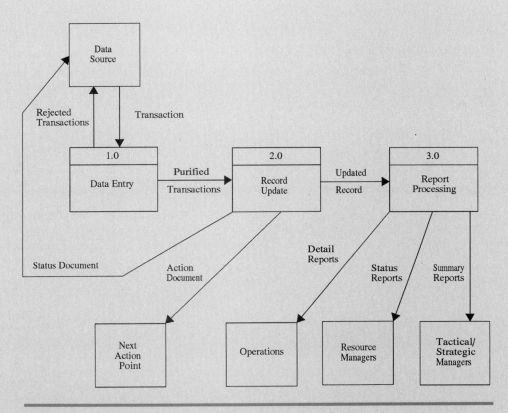

FIGURE 2.1–1 **Conceptual Structure of Transaction Processing Systems**

Batching (accumulation of transactions). **Real-time processing** refers to the immediate posting of a transaction to a resource record balance. In contrast, sometimes transactions are collected in a batch (group) before processing them further; record update is delayed. This delaying tactic is called **batch processing.**

Despite its reputation of being outdated, batch processing is an important design alternative. Many accounting applications such as payroll lend themselves to the process. It would be chaotic and inefficient to run a payroll on a real-time basis. Instead, time cards are collected on a weekly, biweekly, or monthly basis. The payroll is processed in batch mode, and all employees receive their paychecks at the same time.

Other applications, such as airline reservations, are well suited to real time. When a reservation is requested, it is immediately made and confirmed. In the days before real-time systems, passengers were required to "confirm" their reservations at least one day in advance to make sure they did indeed have a valid ticket. Now passengers know this immediately.

Transaction (Data) Entry. Operators enter transaction data (a business event) to update resource records. The entry can be **on-line,** which means it is entered directly to a computer system, often through a workstation. Entry can also be **off-line,** which is an intermediate stage between the data entry function and use of transaction data in the computer system.

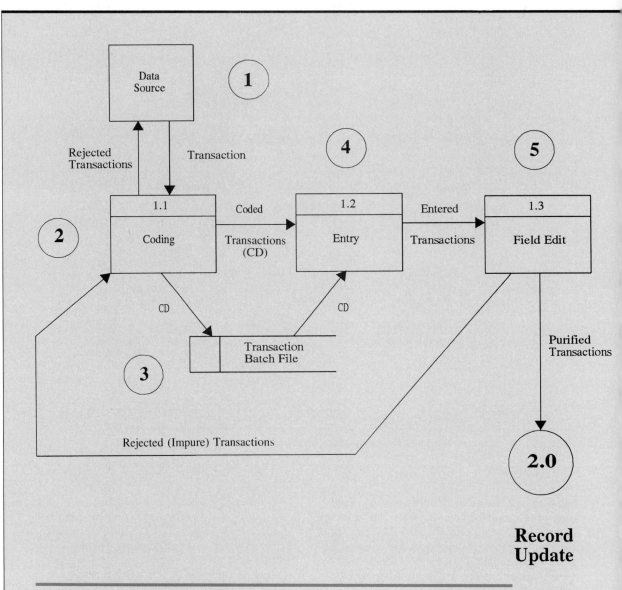

FIGURE 2.1–2   Data Entry Phase of TPS

Operators first key transactions into a key-to-disk or key-to-tape device. Later, the new data medium is input to the computer.

Many confuse the term *on-line* with real time. *On-line* refers to one method of entering transaction data to a computer system. *Real time* refers to one method of updating resource records.

Today, most retail stores have on-line data entry of sales transactions. A sale is entered into a cash register that is linked to a computer system. The computer system records and processes that information. The transaction may update a daily sales log that is part of the general ledger system. It may also update an inventory system. Such a setup is called a **point-of-sale (POS)** terminal. The cash register can also be off-line. Then, the cash register records the sale on paper tape. At the end of the day, a total is generated and printed at the bottom of the tape. The tape is used as a source document to enter total sales for each category of sale at each register.

Transaction Field Editing. A TPS must verify transactions before allowing them to alter important resource record balances. A TPS rigorously edits transaction entry fields for correctness. The field-editing module produces three products: (1) clean transactions passed to the record update phase, (2) error notices for faulty transactions, and (3) an error suspense file that keeps track of error rejects and their later reentry into the system.

Record Update

Figure 2.1–3 shows the **record update phase** of the TPS. This phase reads one purified transaction at a time and uses each transaction to update resource record fields. When all transactions are processed (batch mode), or a specific time is reached (end of day in a real-time mode), control is passed to the report-processing phase. The record update phase contains several modules.

Record Access. With the **record access method,** a program uses a key field on the transaction (e.g., inventory stock number) to search for and find the matching record to change. If the program cannot find a matching record, it produces an error message.

A mismatch between a transaction and a resource record can be due to two reasons. First, a data entry error can occur in the key field. For example, numbers in an inventory stock number could be transposed when being entered. The number 65379 may be entered as 63579. Notice

of a mismatch error prompts reentry of the key field. Second, a mismatch can occur because someone did not load a new resource record to the field before the TPS processed the first transaction change against that record. For example, a sale for new customer Martin was entered before Martin's customer record was established.

A mismatch causes an error transaction record to be written to the error suspense file. That error transaction record remains until someone resolves the transaction/record mismatch and reenters the purified transaction form.

Record Update. The TPS reads the found resource record (matched with transaction key field) from the particular file device (for example, magnetic disk). Then the TPS changes the resource record in one of these ways: (1) addition to resource balances (e.g., receipt of material), (2) subtraction from resource balances (e.g., sale causing withdrawal of material from warehouse), or (3) change to status fields (e.g., customer address change). Once a TPS has changed a resource record, it writes the new image to the resource file.

In an on-line, real-time order entry system, as the order is entered into the computer, stock availability is determined and credit is verified. If no problems occur, the balance due field of the customer is immediately increased. This increase, in turn, impacts the general ledger file as an addition to the resource balance (sales).

Action Document. Successful transaction update of a resource record leads to production of an **action document.** An action document is output that later becomes input into another or the same transaction-processing system.

When an action document becomes input (transaction) to the same TPS that produced it, that action document becomes a **turnaround document.** For example, an order entry system may produce customer invoices in an optical character reader (OCR) format. When customers pay the full amount of the invoice, they return

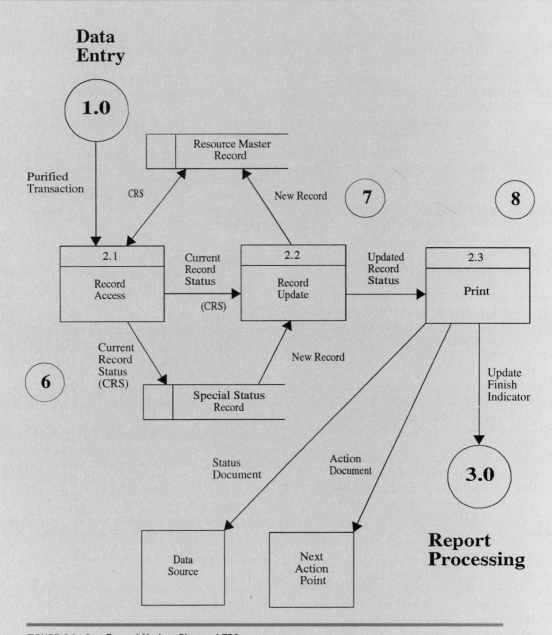

Data Entry

1.0

Purified
Transaction

CRS

Resource Master
Record

New Record

7

8

2.1
Record
Access

Current
Record
Status

(CRS)

2.2
Record
Update

Updated
Record
Status

2.3
Print

6

Current
Record
Status
(CRS)

Special Status
Record

New Record

Update
Finish
Indicator

Status
Document

Action
Document

3.0

Data
Source

Next
Action
Point

**Report
Processing**

FIGURE 2.1–3   **Record Update Phase of TPS**

that invoice with the payment. That returned invoice becomes a direct input transaction to the customer cash receipts program, with no keystroke entry required.

Examples of action documents are employee paychecks, picking slips for a warehouse, and customer billings.

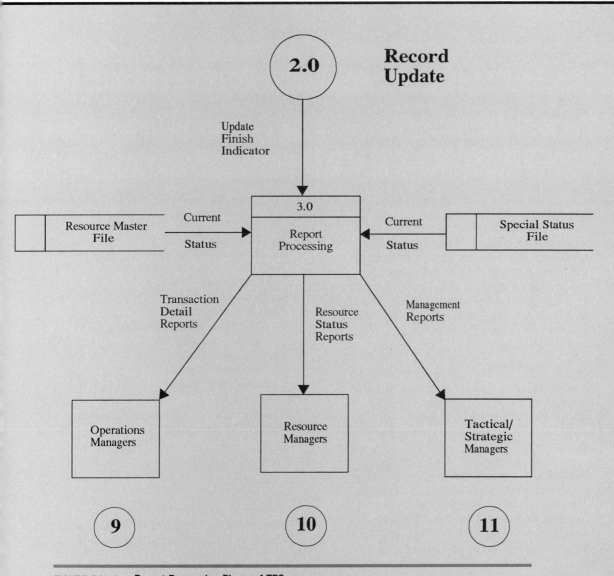

FIGURE 2.1–4   **Report Processing Phase of TPS**

Report Processing

Figure 2.1–4 shows the **report-processing phase.** This phase of the TPS begins when all batched transactions have been processed or when a natural time cutoff has been reached in a real-time record update mode (e.g., end of working day).

The system produces reports after, rather than during, the record update phase for three reasons. First, a report produced during record update competes for printer resources with action documents. Action documents require special printer forms; for example, customer billing may be done on a continuous form containing the firm's logo. Second, a printer's production is optimized when there are multiple (batch) rather than single messages waiting in the printer's buffer. Therefore, most report processing is in a batch mode. Third, managers rarely need reports on a minute-by-minute basis. They prefer to view them in a stabilizing period of a day, week, or month; this prevents temporary fluctuations in data or events from inducing panic reactions. Several types of reports are produced during the report processing phase.

Transaction Detail. Auditors use the **transaction detail report** to check that the system is functioning correctly. This report includes the transaction image, resource record data before the transaction was processed, and resource record image after update. An example is a purchase detail report that lists data from all purchase orders generated during the day. This report is sent to operations managers.

Resource Status. The **resource status report** is an as-requested inquiry report showing status (current and anticipated balances) for one or a group of resource items (for example, material in stock). This report is sent to resource managers.

Management. A **management report** is the output from a transaction system that is feeding into a management information system. Such a report shows potential problems, that is, variations from expected system outputs. Parts of the report include (1) expired triggering dates (e.g., date of last customer payment exceeds XX number of days), (2) information characteristics exceeding problem tolerances (e.g., transaction entry error rate greater than XX percent), (3) unfavorable information trends (e.g., increasing transaction entry backlog), and (4) resource status variances from standards (e.g., warehouse stock no one has ordered in the last X months).

This report is independent of report media: it can be produced as a traditional printed report or on a workstation. The report goes to tactical and strategic managers.

Peggy Dramm next decided to derive a taxonomy of TPS applications common to all business firms.

TAXONOMY OF TPS APPLICATIONS

There are generic TPS applications applicable to all business firms; they can be organized as follows:

- Materials applications:
  1. **Customer order entry**
  2. **Finished goods inventory**
  3. **Purchasing**
  4. **Receiving**
- Receivables applications:
  1. **Customer invoicing** (billing)
  2. **Accounts receivable**
- Payables applications:
  1. **Accounts payable**
  2. **Employee payroll**

Figure 2.1–5 illustrates the interactions among these eight TPS applications.

TPS Templates

Finally, Peggy Dramm constructed a processing template of each of these eight TPS applications using the common TPS structure she developed at the beginning of this case.

CUSTOMER ORDER ENTRY APPLICATION

Customer order entry is the heart of business systems. Without customer orders for goods or services, business organizations cease to exist. Figure 2.1–6 shows, in summary form, a TPS for entering customer orders. Note that the figure follows the TPS structure described at the beginning of this case.

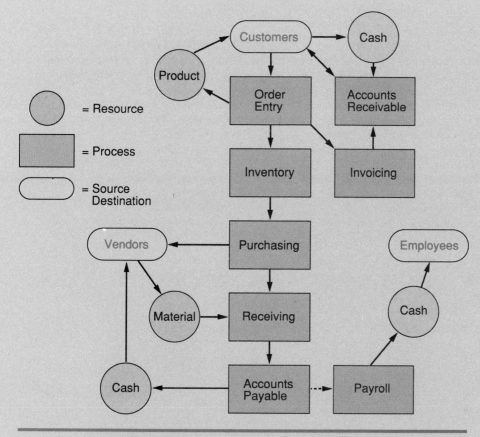

FIGURE 2.1–5   **Interaction of TPS Applications**

1. *Source document(s):*
   - Customer order
   - Credit memos for customer return of stock
   - Order adjustments to previously entered customer orders
   - Order cancellations (for orders in back-order status)
2. *Coding requirements:*
   - Customer ID
   - Salesperson ID
   - Stock ID
   - Store or retail location ID
   - Back-order code (for example, do or do not back order if item is not on hand)

3. *Batch or real-time decision:* Transactions update inventory records as received (real time) so inventory records are current as of the last transaction, and customer orders are processed quickly. Delayed customer orders lead to disgruntled customers and delayed cash flow.
4. *Transaction entry method:* Data entry is on-line regardless of whether file update is batch or real time. Operators enter transactions by VDT. If the method of update is batch, transactions are accumulated for record update after rather than before data entry.

On-line data entry is used to take immediate advantage of computer capability to detect transaction errors. The quicker the TPS detects and corrects errors, the more efficient is transaction processing. Thus, a TPS makes transactions subject to computer processing as quickly as possible.

5. *Transaction field editing:* A TPS checks for the following errors:
   - Date subfields in proper range (e.g., month is in ranges 1 through 12).
   - Data type proper (e.g., alphabetic character not present in numeric field)
   - Field size proper, neither too long nor too short (if minimum size specified)

- Coded items (e.g., method of shipment) checked to see if they are legitimate
- Required fields (e.g., quantity ordered) checked to be sure they have been entered (are not blank)
- Quantities (e.g., quantity shipped) checked for reasonableness that they do not exceed XXXX units

6. *Record access method:* The access method is direct so inventory record balances are quickly accessed and changed.

7. *Record update:*
   - **Master record:**
     a) Master inventory record updated from customer order:

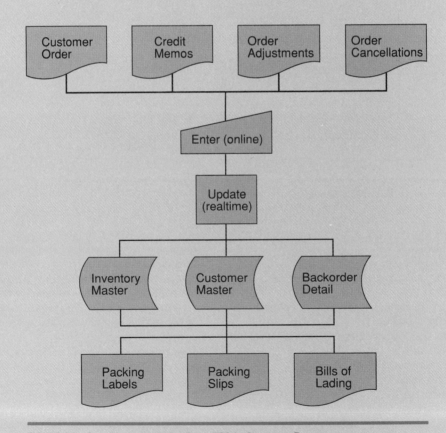

FIGURE 2.1–6   Customer Order Entry TPS in Summary Form

(1) On-hand balance reduced for filled customer orders

(2) Balance-owed field updated for customer balances that are back ordered

b) Master customer record updated for filled orders to reflect new amounts billed

- **Detail record**

a) TPS establishes a back-order detail record for each customer request back ordered

8. *Action documents:*
   - Picking slips for items to be removed from warehouse and shipped to customer
   - Packing slips listing items to be shipped to customer
   - Bill of lading designed for freight (transportation) information

9. *Transaction detail reports:* Auditors use these reports. There may be several permutations including detailed transaction listing and detailed listing of records changed.
   - Image of resource record before transaction processed (before record image)
   - Image of transaction changing resource record (transaction image)
   - Image of resource record after transaction processed (after record image)

10. *Resource status reports:*
    - Status of a special order for a customer
    - Balance available in warehouse for a particular inventory item
    - Estimated delivery dates for out-of-stock items

11. *Management reports:*
    - Back-order report—list of all customer orders not filled from stock, and expected delivery dates for stock to satisfy back orders. (Delayed fulfillment of back orders leads to customer order cancellation.)
    - Bin location report—list of fast- and slow-moving stock items. (Warehouse workers use this report to optimize physical stock storage; for example, they store fast-moving items close to the loading dock.)
    - Customer service report—report of fill-rate statistics. (Fill rate, or service rate, is the percent of customer orders filled directly from stock, not back ordered. Management uses the customer service report to review stockage and order policies.)

As Peggy then begins her inventory of the remaining seven TPSs, she finds that five (4, 5, 6, 9, and 10) of the eleven stages are the same as with the customer order application. A summary of the commonality she discovered follows:

- *Stage 4—Transaction entry:* Regardless of whether the method of file update is batch or real time, the data entry is on-line. Operators enter transactions to the computer by VDT. If the method of update is batch, transactions update records after, rather than before, data entry is completed. Carey Clothiers chose the on-line entry method to allow immediate computer editing of transaction input.

- *Stage 5—Transaction field editing:* Programs check for the following possible errors: (1) wrong data type (e.g., alphabetic rather than numeric entry), (2) incomplete field, (3) improper field length (either too long or too short), (4) unreasonable quantity (e.g., paycheck issued for $1 million), and (5) out-of-range entry.

- *Stage 6—Record:* The index sequential access method (ISAM) is used in all seven systems.

- *Stage 9—Transaction detail report:* For all systems, the report has the following elements: (1) image of resource record before update by transaction data, (2) image of transaction data, (3) image of resource record after update by transaction data, and (4) summary total of number of transactions successively entered by type and time of day.

- *Stage 10—Resource status report:* The parts of these reports are (1) resource ID (e.g., inventory stock number), (2) resource nomenclature (full name or description), (3) location (e.g., inventory bin number), (4) balance on hand, (5) balance due from vendor or source (e.g., number of items due from materials vendor), (6) estimated receipt date (for items due), (7) annual resource usage (e.g., number of units of this stock item ordered by customer the past year), and (8) special comments (specifically about this resource item).

For the remaining seven TPSs Peggy analyzed, these five stages were default values unless stated otherwise. The templates for the seven remaining TPSs follow.

INVENTORY

The purpose of the inventory application is to be sure that adequate but just enough stock is physically in storage (Figure 2.1–7). This is the most calculation-driven of all TPS applications; statistical formulas are used to compute such stock management fields as order quantity, forecast of customer demand, safety stock, and reorder point.

1. *Source document:* The inventory application is largely internally driven. Data is taken from master inventory records, stock management fields are computed, and these newly computed fields replace prior fields

FIGURE 2.1–7   **Finished Goods (Product) Inventory TPS**

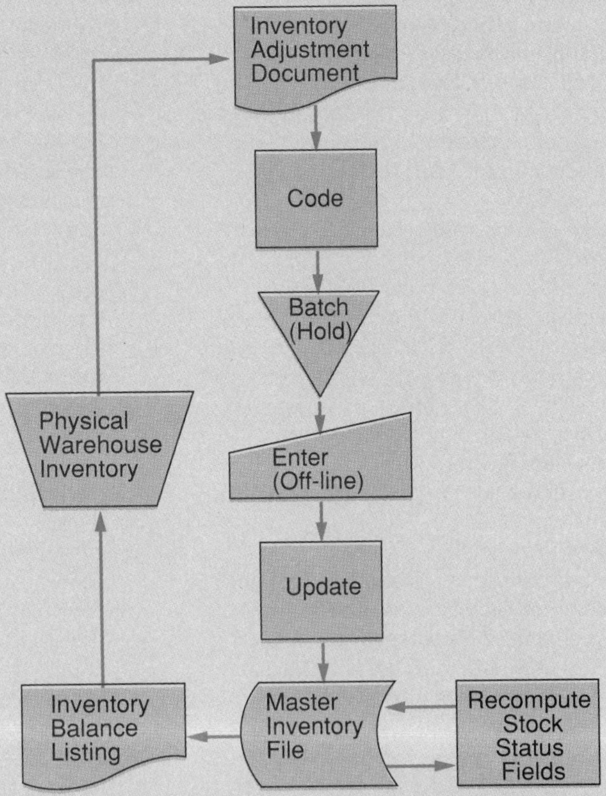

contained on the inventory record. The one source document used in this application is the inventory adjustment document (IAD), which records differences between inventory record balances and the amount of stock physically on hand in the warehouse.

2. *Coding requirements:* Inventory location is needed for IAD input.
3. *Batch or real-time decision:* The inventory application is typically a batch operation.
   - A portion of the inventory is selected each month for physical inventory (reconciliation of record with physical stock count). IADs are processed in a batch when the physical inventory is complete.
   - All inventory records are processed in a batch to update stock status (e.g., order quantity fields). The processing is typically done during slack computer processing times such as weekends.
4. *Transaction entry method (exception):* IAD transactions are often input to an off-line device such as a key-to-tape or key-to-disk device.
5. Stage 5 is standard.
6. Stage 6 is standard.
7. *Record types:* The single record used is the master inventory record. The stock status fields used include annual (or daily) demand rate, reorder point, order quantity, safety level, and vendor shipping time.
   Figure 2.1–8 shows the computation of and the interactions between the stock status fields.
8. *Action document:* None
9. Stage 9 is standard.
10. Stage 10 is standard.
11. *Management reports:*
    - The zero-balance report lists all active (i.e., customer demand highly probable) stock items for which there are no units on hand. The report also shows the status of pending stock receipts so management can follow up on outstanding purchase orders or produce rush orders for stock.

- The excess stock report lists all inventory items for which there has been no customer demand within a specified period (say, one year). Management must decide whether to salvage the stock or offer special sales to customers, so nonmoving stock will not occupy costly warehouse space.

PURCHASING

The purchasing application (Figure 2.1–9) allows timely ordering of inventory so, ideally, stock will always be available to satisfy all customer orders.

1. *Source documents:*
   - The purchasing parameters form allows the purchasing agent to specify what portion of the inventory file he or she wishes to work on (generate purchase orders). This portion may be a certain stock class, a specific vendor, or critical inventory items when purchasing funds are short. The output from processing the purchasing parameters input is a printed or screen report of computer-recommended order quantities by stock item.
   - The purchase order change document, which can be on paper or on screen, allows the purchasing agent to make changes to computer order quantities. The reasons for these changes are typically quantity discounts, economic freight considerations, or shortage of purchasing funds.
2. *Coding requirements:* The requirements for purchasing parameters input are vendor code, stock class code, and stock priority code.
3. *Batch or real-time decision:* Special requisitions to support customer back orders are processed on a real-time basis to reduce delays in satisfying customers. Normal stock replenishment purchasing is done on a batch basis.

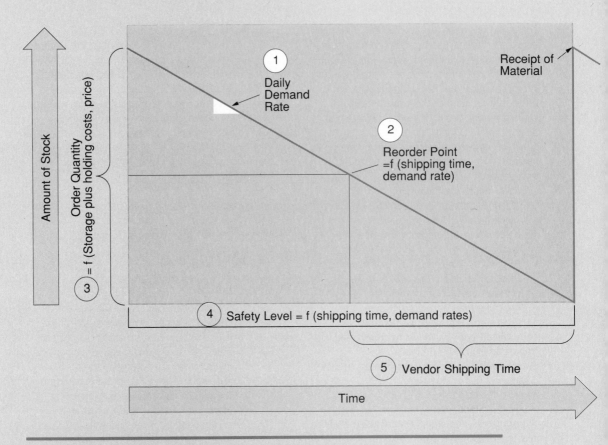

FIGURE 2.1—8   **Stock Status Fields**

4. Stage 4 is standard.
5. Stage 5 is standard.
6. Stage 6 is standard.
7. *Record types:*
    ■ The inventory master record is used. If
       the on-hand balance is less than or equal
       to the reorder point field, a purchase
       order is generated with the purchase
       order quantity equal to the order
       quantity of the inventory master record.
    ■ The purchase detail record, which is
       activated whenever a purchase order is
       produced, supports the on-order balance
       field in the inventory master record.
8. *Action document:* The vendor purchase
    order is produced.

9. Stage 9 is standard.
10. Stage 10 is standard.
11. *Management report:* A purchasing action
    report shows purchasing activity by vendor,
    by shipment mode, and by stock class. It
    also includes a summary of purchasing
    exceptions such as agent override of
    computer-recommended purchase items and
    quantities.

RECEIVING

The receiving application posts material receipts
from vendors to the inventory master record

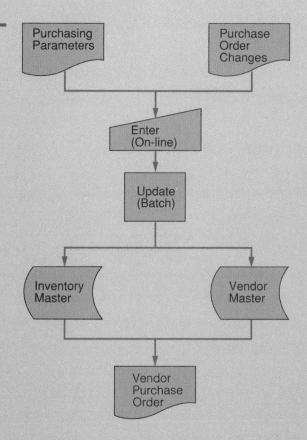

FIGURE 2.1–9   Purchasing TPS

Purchasing Parameters

Purchase Order Changes

Enter (On-line)

Update (Batch)

Inventory Master

Vendor Master

Vendor Purchase Order

(Figure 2.1–10). It also releases customer back orders.

1. *Source document:* The vendor packing slip is the source document. Only minimum information is entered since the purchasing application created a purchase detail record for each vendor order. The quantity received for each item on this source document is added to the balance-on-hand field on the inventory master record.

2. *Coding requirements:* All coding requirements are already included on the purchase detail record.

3. *Batch or real-time decision:* Receiving is typically a real-time process so stock is quickly available for customer orders and so back orders can be quickly released for shipment to the customer.

4. Stage 4 is standard.
5. Stage 5 is standard.
6. Stage 6 is standard.
7. *Record types:*
   - The inventory master record's balance on hand is increased.
   - The purchase order detail record is deleted if the vendor receipt is exactly the same quantity as ordered. Otherwise, the quantities in the detail record are decreased to reflect receipted quantities.
   - The back-order detail record is deleted. After receipted quantities are added to the inventory master record, any existing back orders are released. If the received quantity is not enough to satisfy all back orders, the older back orders are released first. When a back order is

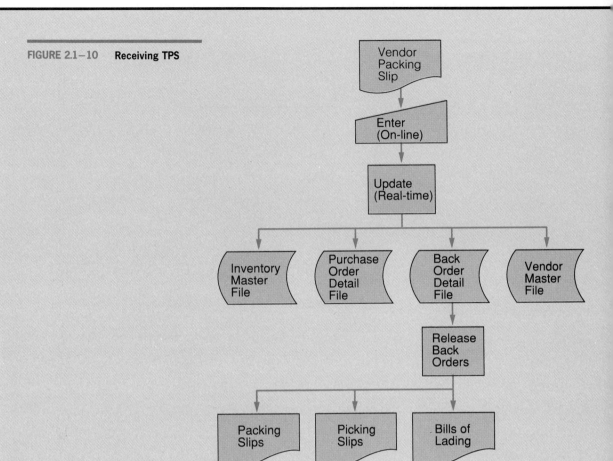

FIGURE 2.1–10   Receiving TPS

Vendor Packing Slip

Enter (On-line)

Update (Real-time)

Inventory Master File

Purchase Order Detail File

Back Order Detail File

Vendor Master File

Release Back Orders

Packing Slips

Picking Slips

Bills of Lading

released, the back-order detail record is deleted.

■ Vendor performance statistics are recorded on the vendor master record.

8. *Action documents:* Released back orders result in the generation of picking slips, packing slips, and bills of lading (see customer order entry applications).

9. Stage 9 is standard.

10. Stage 10 is standard.

11. *Management reports:*

■ The vendor evaluation report includes service statistics for each vendor, including delivery times, rate of material returned to vendor, and rate of short or damaged shipments.

■ The back-order satisfaction report lists customer service statistics about how long orders remain in back-order status. The report also contains customer order cancellation rates while in back-order status.

CUSTOMER INVOICING

The purpose of the customer invoicing application is to provide customer billing statements for each sale of goods and services (Figure 2.1–11). The quality of customer invoicing is related directly to rapid cash flow into the organization.

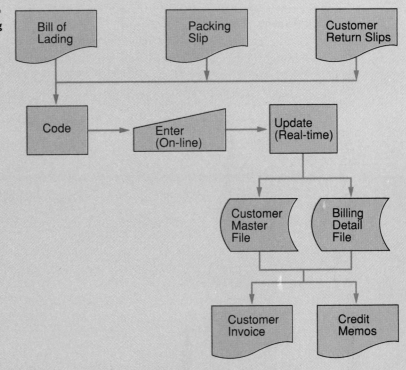

FIGURE 2.1–11 Customer Invoicing TPS

1. *Source documents:*
   - The bill of lading contains charges for shipment and insurance. This transaction will add to customer master record balances.
   - The packing slip contains the quantities of items actually shipped to the customer. This transaction will add to customer master record balances.
   - Customer return slips are for returned merchandise or merchandise not received by the customer (shipping discrepancies). This transaction will subtract from customer master record balances.
2. *Coding requirements:* The requirements are salesperson code, distribution (store) code, product (material) ID code, and customer ID code.
3. *Batch or real-time decision:* If it is the store's policy to send invoices and credit memos apart from the monthly billing statement, then this application is real time.

Otherwise, it is a batch application run just before the accounts receivable application.
4. Stage 4 is standard.
5. Stage 5 is standard.
6. Stage 6 is standard.
7. *Record types:*
   - In the customer master record, a change is made to the amount due field.
   - The billing detail record is set up for each customer shipment (combination of bill of lading and packing slip). This allows billings that show purchasing details to support the total customer amount due.
8. *Action documents:* These are the customer invoice document and credit memos (for returned merchandise).
9. Stage 9 is standard.
10. Stage 10 is standard.
11. *Management report:* An anticipated payments report is produced showing total customer billings and expected payments over time.

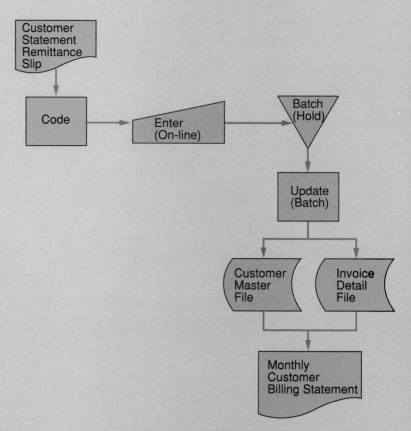

FIGURE 2.1–12 **Accounts Receivable TPS**

Managers use this report for cash flow management. A separate section of this report shows customer return rates by type of stock and customer class.

ACCOUNTS RECEIVABLE

The accounts receivable application posts customer payments and prepares the monthly customer billing statement (Figure 2.1–12).

1. *Source document:* A monthly statement remittance slip is prepared from the customer check and the returned portion of the monthly customer billing statement.
2. *Coding requirements:* A customer identification code is needed.

3. *Batch or real-time decision:* Accounts receivable is typically a batch application, for two reasons:
   - A clerk separates the customer check from the remittance slip and deposits the check immediately. Therefore, the money is immediately ready to use even though the transaction reflecting its receipt is not posted immediately to the customer master record.
   - The customer master record need not be current until the period (for example, end of month) when monthly customer billing statements are produced.
4. Stage 4 is standard.
5. Stage 5 is standard.
6. Stage 6 is standard.

7. *Record types:*
   - In the customer master record, the balance due field is decreased for each customer payment.
   - Some or all of the billing detail records will be deleted either upon production of the billing statement or upon customer payment.
8. *Action document:* This is the monthly customer billing statement.
9. Stage 9 is standard.
10. Stage 10 is standard.
11. *Management report:* An aging receivable report is produced showing customer balances unpaid over time. This report allows managers to determine the extent of payment follow-up or assignment of accounts to a collection agency. The report also provides data necessary to estimate future cash flow.

ACCOUNTS PAYABLE

The accounts payable application produces payments to vendors for material received in the receiving application (Figure 2.1–13).

1. *Source document:* The vendor billing document is the source document, as opposed to the vendor's monthly statement, because discounts are available for rapid payment of individual billings.
2. *Coding requirements:* The vendor code and material code are necessary.
3. *Batch or real-time decision:* Accounts payable is a real-time application, so payment discounts are taken before the allotted time expires.
4. Stage 4 is standard.
5. Stage 5 is standard.
6. Stage 6 is standard.
7. *Record types:*
   - Payment activity is recorded on the vendor master record.
   - Vendor billing is compared against the purchase order detail record for correctness. The detail record is deleted when a payment to the vendor is produced.
8. *Action document:* The document is a check for vendor payment.
9. Stage 9 is standard.

FIGURE 2.1–13 **Accounts Payable TPS**

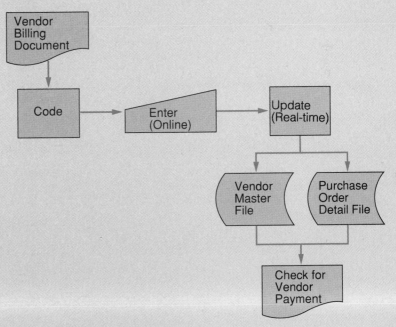

10. Stage 10 is standard.
11. *Management reports:* A cash outlay report is produced. Management uses this report to estimate negative cash flow and to make sure payment discounts are being taken when offered.

PAYROLL

The payroll application is a special version of the accounts payable application. It produces payroll checks for employees and updates employee tax, benefit, and other personnel information (Figure 2.1–14).

1. *Source document:* The employee time card is a machine-readable document.

2. *Coding requirements:* The employee ID number and job code (for job cost accounting purposes) are needed.
3. *Batch or real-time decision:* Payroll is almost always a batch application since paychecks are produced at specific periods (say, monthly).
4. *Transaction entry method (exception):* Time sheets are prerecorded, turnaround documents. They are entered directly to the computer, but in batches rather than one at a time.
5. Stage 5 is standard.
6. Stage 6 is standard.
7. *Record type:* The employee master record historical balance fields (for example, annual wages paid) are updated.

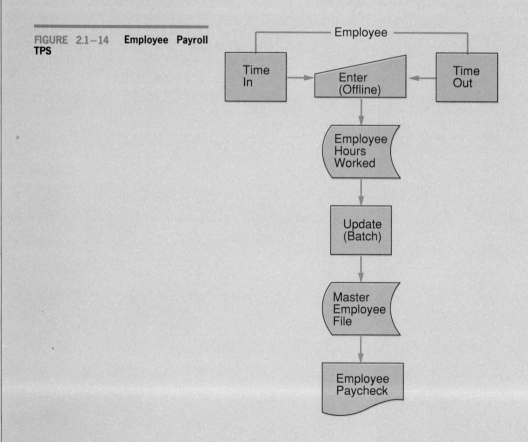

FIGURE 2.1–14 **Employee Payroll TPS**

8. *Action document:* The document is the employee paycheck.
9. Stage 9 is standard.
10. Stage 10 is standard.
11. *Management report:* Under job cost accounting systems, a job labor cost report might be produced.

Peggy Dramm was confident that the TPS templates described in this case worked for Carey Clothiers. However, she thought her applications descriptions were rather short and stilted. She wondered how she could change her descriptions so that nontechnical persons could understand how these operate.

KEY TERMS

accounts payable
accounts receivable
action document
batch processing
coding
customer invoicing•
customer order entry
data entry phase
employee payroll
finished goods inventory
management report
off-line

on-line
point-of-sale (POS)
purchasing
real-time processing
receiving
record access method
record update phase
report-processing phase
resource status report
source document
transaction detail report
turnaround document

EXERCISE

1. Select one of Peggy's TPS descriptions. Convert the description to a narrative form that can be better understood (1) by clerical personnel and then (2) by management.

In this chapter you will learn about:

WHAT: (Concepts) The structure and steps by which we analyze, design and implement information systems. The means by which we recognize deterioration of current information systems.

WHY: Development of information systems is an organized, structured process. We need to know what is the structure, and what is its logical basis: Moreover, we need to recognize when the current information system needs to be replaced.

WHEN: Planning the development stages for an information system is done at the very beginning of the project.

WHO: Systems analysts and information users form teams to plan and execute the development of an information system.

WHERE: Initial project planning typically is done in the Information Systems Department.

HOW: (Techniques) Piggybacking
Systems Development Life Cycle (SDLC)
Project Management Tools

- Setting
- General System Life Cycle (GSLC)
- Why and When Information Systems Die
- Piggybacking
- Information Systems Development Life Cycle (SDLC)
- Structured Life Cycles
- Project Management
- A Total Quality Management (TQM) Approach
- Human Aspects

C H A P T E R   3

THE LIFE AND DEATH OF INFORMATION SYSTEMS

It's cheaper to buy insurance when you're 25 than when you're 85.

—INSTANT ANALYST, 1990

SETTING

Information systems deteriorate. They cannot function forever without being replaced or extensively modified. Systems deterioration may not be physical, but it can show itself in ways such as increasing costs or decreasing user satisfaction. A basic principle of systems analysis and design is recognition of the need for replacement or modification. Another principle is preparation for system deterioration in an orderly manner. This chapter presents the concepts and principles involved in replacement of information systems.

GENERAL SYSTEM LIFE CYCLES (GSLC)

All systems—biological, physical, social, or otherwise—share a wide range of characteristics. This is important for the business discipline, because it means we can borrow concepts and principles from older, more thoroughly explored disciplines.

The **general systems life cycle (GSLC)** is one of the information field's most useful analogies. The model includes four distinct phases in the effective life of any system (Figure 3–1). The first phase is *development;* one example is formation of a new

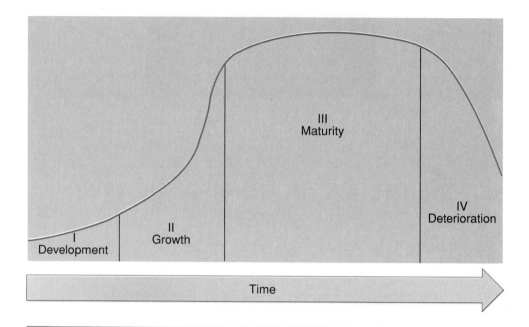

FIGURE 3−1   **General Systems Life Cycle**

company. The second phase is *growth;* an example is a new firm's increasing its share of product market sales. At some point, a system reaches the *maturity* phase. A firm's market share stops increasing and becomes stable. Finally, a system reaches its last stage, *deterioration;* the firm's market share steadily decreases.

UNIX-BASED SURROUND STRATEGY

Not all obsolete information systems need to be replaced. The UNIX-based surround strategy links multiple central processing units (CPUs) in a distributed system while appearing to the user to be a single system. The strategy allows dissimilar systems to be linked together without redesigning any of them. The responsibilities and rights of individual systems administrators can be preserved while usability for each end-user is enhanced.

A successful example of the UNIX-based surround strategy is AT&T's STARLAN, which was first implemented at the University of Wisconsin–Stevens Point (UW-SP). The goal of STARLAN was to link all students, faculty, and staff electronically. The computing environment at UW-SP prior to STARLAN included a single mainframe, many stand-alone microcomputers, and an outdated telephone system. Rather than redesign any of these systems, the surround strategy was used to link them together as if they were a single system. UW-SP envisioned a system that would consolidate voice and data communications while keeping the user interface as simple and consistent as possible. In addition, the university wanted flexibility, versatility, convenience, and compatibility. The solution, STARLAN, was developed jointly by AT&T and UW-SP.

Students, faculty, and staff have access to various applications via STARLAN for file transfers, communications, library access, on-line services such as registration, student record processing, financial applications, and database access. All activities can be accomplished from offices, dorm rooms, and laboratory environments through a simple, consistent, usable interface.

None of the existing systems had to be redesigned. The surround strategy thus becomes an alternative to full-systems design.

The GSLC is a useful model applicable to a wide range of nonbiological systems. Some common business applications are the product life cycle, organizational life cycle, and information systems life cycle.

Figure 3–2 shows the **information systems life cycle (ISLC).** It includes the four phases of systems development (design), systems implementation and fine-tuning, systems operation (maintenance), and systems obsolescence. There is a subtle but extremely important difference between the GSLC and the ISLC in the last phase of the cycle. Information systems rarely deteriorate physically. They become obsolete. They do not perform as well as newer, more technologically advanced designs. Often, obsolescence shows itself in increasing operational costs such as that of adding more personnel. Commonly, information systems are enhanced rather than replaced. Systems enhancements, or upgrades, are major modifications to an existing system. For example, a firm may add a statistical forecasting component to an inventory system so it can better predict customer demand.

For this book, a systems enhancement is considered a smaller version of a complete systems replacement. The steps of the systems development life cycle (SDLC), which are discussed later in this chapter, exist for both major modification and complete replacement. Although the steps are abbreviated for modification, they still are present. Another differentiation is between a major systems modification (e.g., adding a new capability) and a minor (maintenance) modification. Maintenance changes are more applicable to a textbook dealing with operations management (the management of existing information systems).

Our discussion of the information systems life cycle includes the following changes to existing business information systems: replacements (new system), upgrades (adding new capabilities), and major modifications (replacing system parts).

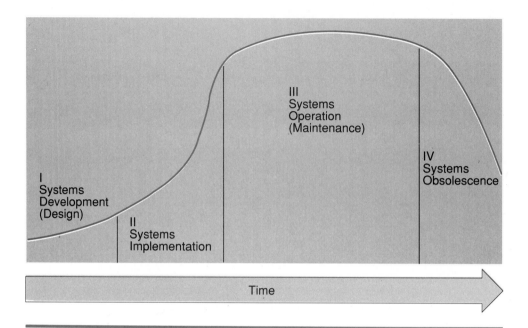

FIGURE 3—2   Information Systems Life Cycle

IS Life Cycles

Three levels of systems life cycles operate in a firm (Figure 3–3). The first is the strategic life cycle, which describes the firm's entire information-processing evolution. Within this **strategic life cycle,** at any one point in time, there is the aggregate life cycle of all business systems in development or operation. Finally, as a single part of this aggregate life cycle, there is the **tactical life cycle** for each system.

The firm's total IS strategic life cycle has been described by Nolan (Figure 3–4). As you can see, this strategic life cycle has six stages.

1. *Start-up (initiation):* The organization gets its first computer.
2. *Growth (expansion):* The computer system undergoes unanticipated and unplanned growth. Contagious enthusiasm occurs for the new system. Management allows decentralized control of the computer facility and application development in user departments.
3. *Control:* As the information processing budget becomes large, it becomes visible. Top management wants to gain control of that budget. Some centralization of resources and procedures occurs at this stage.
4. *Integration:* Information systems activity becomes sophisticated. Management distributes operational functions to users, but with centralized standards. Steering committees are formed to oversee overall organizational information priorities.

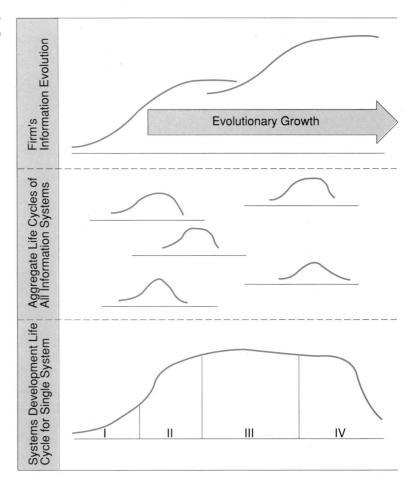

FIGURE 3–3   **Relationship of Three Levels of Systems Life Cycles**

5. *Data resource development (data administration):* The firm develops an integrated database. Management treats information as a resource equal in importance to material, personnel, capital, and money.

6. *Maturity:* The firm develops applications only when they fit into the total growth of the organization.

Nolan measured the organizational life cycle concept in dollars spent by an organization on information-processing resources. In this textbook, life cycle measurement is not restricted to dollars. Other measurements include number of workstations, telecommunications traffic, and percentage of automated applications.

Some of the literature dealing with the SDLC gives the mistaken impression that analysts work on only a single system at a time. This is not the case in the typical systems environment; rather, many systems are in differing stages of their individual

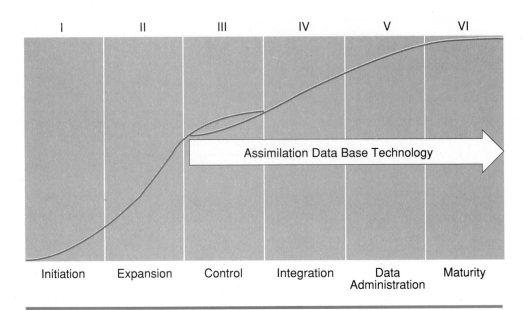

| I | II | III | IV | V | VI |

Assimilation Data Base Technology

| Initiation | Expansion | Control | Integration | Data Administration | Maturity |

FIGURE 3–4   Nolan's Life Cycles for an Information System

Adapted from R. L. Nolan, "Managing the Crisis in Data Processing," *Harvard Business Review* (March–April 1979).

life cycles at any time. Look at the aggregate life cycle in Figure 3–5. Systems B and C are mature systems. System D is in the middle of its growth cycle, while system E is in the initial development stage. System A is approaching its obsolescence. Will analyst resources be available to "save" system A, considering that systems D and E are still in development? The IS department cannot deal with one information system without considering all others.

An additional problem with managing multiple systems is **functional discontinuity**—the difficulty of operating several tasks that require different methods, procedures, and skills. It's like rubbing your stomach in a north–south direction with one hand, rubbing your head in an east–west direction with the other hand, and blowing bubble gum concurrently.

Functional discontinuity is a serious information systems problem when there are multiple applications. In Figure 3–5, system A may use terminal entry, whereas system E is using optical scanning for entry of transaction data. So both users and information specialists must deal with two technologically disparate systems.

Thus, the tactical life cycle nature of Figure 3–5 shows an environment filled with choices. Given a maximum amount of analyst resources, the IS department can develop one system only at the expense of the development or maintenance of other systems. It cannot consider the tactical development of a single business information system in isolation. When the IS department decides to develop a single business information system, that system proceeds according to its own life cycle, called the systems development life cycle.

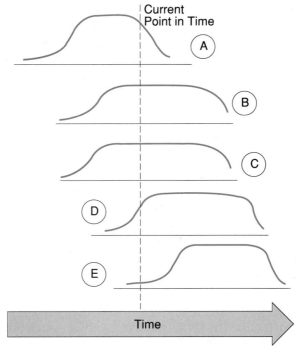

FIGURE 3–5   **Aggregate Systems Life Cycle Showing Five Systems at Different Stages**

Before exploring the systems development life cycle, it is important to discuss two topics: why and when information systems die and piggybacking a replacement system onto a deteriorating system.

WHY AND WHEN INFORMATION SYSTEMS DIE

Information systems deteriorate or become obsolete. Then, if they are not replaced in a timely manner, they die. Information systems analysts must recognize the imminent death of a system and plan accordingly.

✗Five Dimensions of IS Life

Why do information systems die? The life of an information system has five dimensions, and death can occur in any of them: accounting, technological, physical, user expectation, and outside influence.

Accounting. For tax purposes, profit-oriented organizations often write off capital equipment (e.g., computers) in a short period, such as five years. The accounting life of an information system is rarely correlated with the physical well-being of that system. Yet, the IS department can easily justify replacing a system that, from a bookkeeping perspective, no longer exists. Therefore, many information systems die accounting deaths.

Many commercial firms do not take advantage of this legal write-off; thus, their systems life cycles are longer than those of firms that do use the accounting tactic. Noncommercial firms, such as government agencies, cannot use this tactic at all. That is one reason that computer systems of noncommercial firms can last as much as three times longer than systems used by profit-making organizations.

Technological. An information system may be operating as intended, but the organization may be losing ground to competitors that are taking advantage of new technologies. For example, the Necco grocery chain, which still uses a cash register system, is losing customers to competitors using faster, more accurate bar code, optical scanning checkout systems.

Deterioration. Information systems do physically wear out. This author headed a conversion team where the old computer groaned, sighed, spit, and made other astounding noises. We held our breath, hoping we could implement the new computer before we had to bury the old one. We succeeded, but barely so.

Another example of hardware deterioration happened at a university where parallel conversion was taking place. In parallel conversion, the old and new systems are operated concurrently for a short period of time. Both the old CPU and new CPU were functional. The old system had a software patch that bypassed a temperature-triggered shutdown module. The analog connection that monitored room temperature had failed, and no replacement could be found. The system kept shutting down at times when the temperature was within tolerance; therefore, a decision was made to patch around the module that performed the shutdown. This repair presented no problems as long as human operators were around to keep the air temperature in line.

One day, during operatorless spring break hours, a rainstorm occurred. Leaves were blown into the air conditioning intake valve, and the air conditioning system shut down. The new CPU shut down, but the old one went right on processing as the room temperature reached 110 degrees. Major core meltdown occurred and the old system had to be scrapped. Users who had refused to migrate to the new system were extremely frustrated.

Luckily, files had been saved on backup tape the day before spring break, and most user files could be transferred to the new system with little effort.

User Expectations. An information system may be operating within its artificial accounting life, may not be technologically obsolete, and may show no signs of physical deterioration. Yet, it may be failing. Why? Because user expectations of the information system have changed. No matter how healthy a system may seem, if users tire of or are unhappy with it, the system is unhealthy.

Outside Influences. Occasionally, an information system must be replaced because forces external to the business firm exert pressure for replacement. For example, firm A acquires firm B. Firm A insists that firm B convert to the same hardware and software applications that it uses.

AN EXAMPLE OF TECHNOLOGICAL OBSOLESCENCE

Lee Henry is a statistician working with the marketing function at Startronics, a high-tech firm. He provides management with sales forecasting and performance analysis reports. Lee spends a lot of time writing mainframe SAS (statistical analysis system) code and generating graphics for presentation. Over time, more and more of his hours have been involved with computers. He interfaces with the IS group almost every day. Over the years, Lee has put together a menu-driven interface that integrates an SAS model base, the corporate database, and various graphics software and hardware. Lee calls his decision support system Stargaze and is very pleased with the output of his system.

Recently, the Startronics IS group was restructured. A decision was made to distribute some IS technical specialists to the functional areas to provide on-site support. A young MIT graduate named Hank Johnson has been assigned to Lee's unit. Hank has had extensive training in microcomputer-based, fourth-generation language (4GL), whiz-bang software. At first, Lee felt somewhat threatened by Hank's credentials, and there was some tension between the two. However, the stimulation of having someone who could speak "technese" with him and who understood what he was doing soon overcame the initial tensions. Hank was truly impressed with what Lee had managed to do with limited tools. It took many hours of analyses and coding to produce new products with Lee's system. Lee often spent late nights and weekends meeting deadlines. Hank quickly saw that the same flashy end products could be attained much faster with some of the new 4GL software and graphics capabilities.

Hank showed Lee some of his graduate projects. He took one of Lee's reports and generated the same output in about one-tenth of the time it had taken Lee. He let Lee experiment with the software, and Lee was soon convinced that he could be more productive with the newer technology. Together, Lee and Hank convinced marketing management to purchase two powerful workstations that were linked to the mainframe. IS sponsored the project by contributing some site-license software. Within two months, Lee and Hank replicated the capabilities of the old system and were able to produce new reports in hours rather than weeks. The old Stargaze system was dismantled, and parts of it were used to support the new environment. The old Stargaze system had died and had been replaced by a newer technology.

A second example is referred to as strategic computing. Strategic computing is the use of information processing to enhance the firm's financial posture directly. Suppose a firm is considering changing its purchasing transaction-processing system (TPS) so it produces purchase orders. The orders can be input automatically (without human intervention) to the information-processing system of one of the firm's primary vendors. Further suppose that the vendor will lower prices to the firm if it uses this means of placing orders. The firm would probably change or replace the current purchasing system even if it were still working.

Systems Success

A system is only as successful as users accept it to be. Indeed, systems success is defined in terms of user expectations. **Systems success** is a point along the continuum shown in Figure 3–6. Overall performance of a system runs from zero (no performance) to 100 percent (maximal system performance). No system is ideal—no system exhibits maximal performance. Too many practical constraints prevent the design of an ideal system. Such constraints include time, funds, skilled personnel, and political and environmental considerations. Even if we could design an ideal system, it would have flaws when completed. Technology and the business environment move too quickly to tolerate the lead times needed to design ideal information systems.

Somewhere along the performance continuum, there is an agreed-on point labeled "success." Parties to this agreement are the designer and user community. What is their point of agreement? A definition of a successful information system follows:

> A successful information system is one that, within tolerances,* meets a certain number or percentage* of measurable system goals,* such performance having been measured in some systematic manner.* (*Agreed on by the designer and the users.)

The definition contains a frustrating element. If users and the designer reach a measurable definition of success, that definition can only be temporary because the nature of users entering the agreement will change over time. Users are promoted from the ranks of those using the new system, transfer laterally to other applications in the organization, or leave the company. A year or two after the implementation of a new information system, the cast of users for the designed system will have changed. More surprisingly, the users who remain will have also changed. The remaining users have seen what the system can do, and they expand their focus to what the system could do. Now these users expect more than they expected when the new system was designed. Their business needs have changed.

Systems designers also change. They become more knowledgeable and dissatisfied with previously designed systems. They change their notions of what makes a successful system.

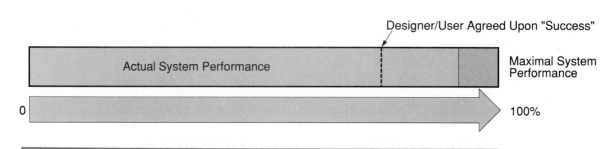

FIGURE 3–6   **Systems Performance Continuum**

Reprinted by permission from M. Martin and J. Trumbly, "Measuring Performance of Information Systems," *Journal of Systems Management* 37 (February 1986).

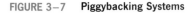

FIGURE 3–7   **Piggybacking Systems**

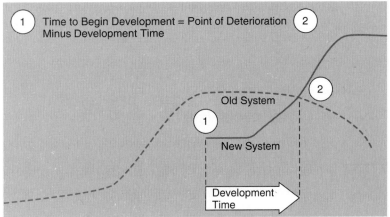

All information systems change and will eventually deteriorate in performance. All such systems need to be replaced or modified. The tactical approach to such replacement and modification is called piggybacking.

PIGGYBACKING

Piggybacking is not a sophisticated term, nor is it unique to the systems field. Yet, it presents an exact image: One system uses the previous system to leap forward to a more advanced status.

Figure 3–7 illustrates piggybacking. A replacement system is planned and started before the current system totally deteriorates. The development time for designing information systems is long. The new system should be designed so that it becomes operational just at the point when the old system begins to deteriorate (point 2 in Figure 3–7).

As you would expect, there is more than luck involved here. Point 2—when to implement the new system before the old system fails—must be predicted. Then the time to develop the new system can be estimated so that it can be implemented on time (at point 2). By subtracting the estimated development time from point 2, the designer arrives at point 1, which indicates when to begin developing the new system. What is surprising is how soon in the life of the existing system that new system development must begin.

The piggybacking concept is powerful. It forces designers and users to think of orderly system succession. It also demands the following estimates: (1) when the current system will die (estimated system life), (2) how long it will take to develop a replacement system, and (3) when to begin development of the replacement system.

Our discussion up to this point has been on life cycles in general and life cycles specific to the design of business information systems. By now, you should accept that all information systems have a defined life span. Your task as a systems analyst is to plan an orderly approach to the death and birth of systems. The remainder of this textbook is organized around the concept of the information systems development life cycle, which is our next topic.

INFORMATION SYSTEM DEVELOPMENT LIFE CYCLE (SDLC)

From the systems analyst's outlook, strategic life cycles cannot be controlled. They are dictated by the firm's environment, and analysts must work within that environment. Systems analysts do, however, have control of the systems development life cycle. This life cycle includes only the particular information system to which the analyst has been assigned.

Figure 3–8 illustrates the twelve stages of one version of the SDLC, segregated into the three modules of analysis, design, and implementation. Each stage of this SDLC can be described by its purpose and the specific product (**deliverable**) generated.

Analysis (Section Two of This Book). In the analysis phase, analysts determine if the current system is in trouble and what design remedies are appropriate. Many life cycles do not proceed beyond this phase because current systems are judged superior to new system alternatives. Analysis is conducted according to the following stages:

1. **Problem detection:**
   - *Purpose:* Detect if the current system is deteriorating.
   - *Deliverable:* Preliminary problem report
2. **Initial investigation:**
   - *Purpose:* Describe the current system, with emphasis on the detected problem area.
   - *Deliverable:* Current system description
3. **Requirements analysis** (determination of ideal system):
   - *Purpose:* Obtain a consensus from the user community on the ideal information system. A replacement system should fill the gap between the current and the ideal system.
   - *Deliverable:* Requirements analysis description
4. *System selection:*
   - *Purpose:* Explore different systems alternatives for narrowing the gap between the current and ideal system, and select the best system.
   - *Deliverable:* Cost–benefit analysis
5. *Preliminary design/system study:*
   - *Purpose:* Document proposed system at a preliminary level. Prepare system study.
   - *Deliverable:* System study

Design (Section Three). In this phase, the selected system is designed using the following stages:

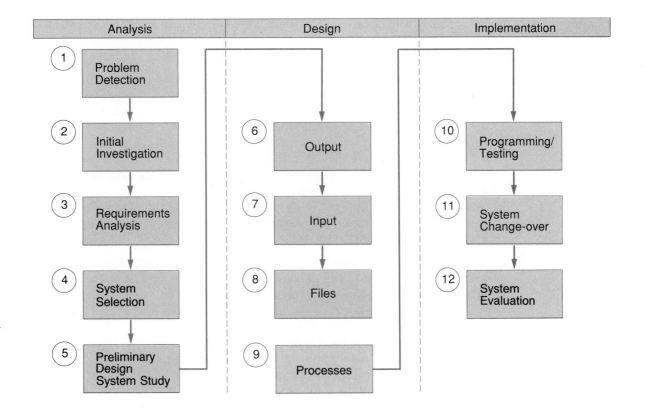

FIGURE 3–8   **Stages of the Problem-solving Systems Development Life Cycle (SDLC)**

6. *Output design:*
   - *Purpose:* Describe system reports and documents.
   - *Deliverable:* Output documentation forms
7. *Input design (including interactive screens):*
   - *Purpose:* Describe documents and screens entered to the information system.
   - *Deliverable:* Input documentation forms
8. *File design:*
   - *Purpose:* Describe information system files.
   - *Deliverable:* File documentation forms
9. *Process design:*
   - *Purpose:* Describe system processes in programmable terms.
   - *Deliverable:* Process descriptions

Implementation (Section Four). In this phase, logical design specifications are translated into the actual construction of the information system. The implementation phase includes the following stages:

10. *Programming and testing:*
    - *Purpose:* Convert logical design specifications to operating programming language code, and test all programs to be sure they operate correctly.
    - *Deliverable:* Program code and program specifications
11. *Systems changeover:*
    - *Purpose:* Change from the old to the new information system. Change responsibility of the new system from the designer team to the user organization.
    - *Deliverable:* Changeover contract
12. *System evaluation:*
    - *Purpose:* Establish means for measuring system success and problems.
    - *Deliverable:* Quality measurement specifications

One final, but critical, point must be made here. The systems development life cycle described here and shown in Figure 3–8 seems to be a purely sequential process. One step appears to always lead to the next. For example, requirements analysis (stage 3) seems *always* to flow into system selection (stage 4). This is rarely the case in a business information systems project.

The SDLC is highly iterative. Often analysts backtrack to previous stages because they discover something new in the current stage. Refer to Figure 3–9. Here, requirements analysis can proceed to generation of alternatives, but it can also return to the two preceding steps of the SDLC. Also, requirements analysis might have to be repeated if it is not done adequately the first time.

STRUCTURED LIFE CYCLES

There are other equally valid ways of breaking the development process into manageable chunks. No one version of an SDLC is inherently superior to another. Each version is applicable to different conditions and circumstances.

Suppose you are asked to take the common length of one foot and break it into meaningful parts. Tradition dictates that you separate the foot into twelve inches, but you are not sure how to subdivide each inch. You seek expert advice. Sara, an architect, suggests that you divide each inch into half, quarter, eighth, and sixteenth inches. Jeff, an engineer, prefers a division into tenths of an inch. Terry, a business executive, decides that measurement to the inch is precise enough.

A similar situation arises when trying to subdivide information systems development into manageable parts. Most analysts and designers agree on the major phases of analysis, design, and implementation; however, there is no such consensus about how to subdivide each of these phases. That division depends on how the SDLC will be used.

The problem-solving SDLC is used here because it allows the development process to be divided into cohesive and decoupled tasks. It is ideal for organizing a textbook.

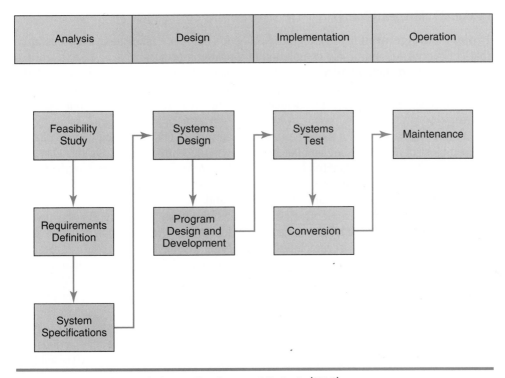

| Analysis | Design | Implementation | Operation |

FIGURE 3–9   **An Alternative System Development Life Cycle (SDLC)**

There is nothing wrong with any version of the life cycle as long as it is appropriately selected for a specific purpose or setting. Any SDLC version should be agreed on throughout a single firm and should produce specific products (deliverables) at each stage.

One important class of systems development life cycles are called *structured life cycles*. These are SDLCs focused on the particular methodology called the *structured approach*. This approach allows the analyst to define the information system first at a general, review level. Then each part of the general system undergoes successive refinement (more detail) until the bottom, most detailed functions are clearly defined. The structured approach and its associated structured life cycles are particularly important when we deal with computer-aided system engineering (CASE). We will discuss the structured approach and CASE in more detail as this book proceeds.

Figure 3–9 shows an SDLC developed by King (1984). This is included to demonstrate to you that there is no magic to the SDLC underlying this textbook (Figure 3–8). The problem-solving SDLC used here merely is convenient to our purposes. Any SDLC will work as long as it systematically breaks the development project into understandable chunks that can be controlled. The controlling of these chunks is referred to as project management.

PROJECT MANAGEMENT

Project management is the integrated collection of tools, techniques, and procedures that aid successful and timely completion of a systems project.

Project management is a comprehensive subject, much of which is beyond the scope of this book. Included here are the essentials you will need to control effectively small to medium-sized projects, including student projects required in your systems course.

Project management is implemented by a series of scheduling and control charts. The simplest of all scheduling and control charts is the **Gantt chart.** On this chart, all project activities are represented by horizontal bars on a time scale. The length of a bar indicates the duration of an activity. The chart shows interrelationships of all activities, including when they are scheduled to start and end.

Figure 3–10 shows a Gantt chart. Initially, the bars are open. As the project progresses, the bars gradually are shaded. By looking at a bar, you can estimate what percentage of an activity is completed at a specific instant of time. You can also see which activities are completed ahead of, behind, or on schedule. For example, activity d in Figure 3–10 is 50 percent complete as of the progress status date of March 15. Activities a, b, and c were completed on schedule. The status column contains a *C* if an activity is completed; otherwise, this column is blank.

The Gantt chart is updated periodically, and management reviews a project's progress from the updated chart. The review may reveal that corrective actions are necessary to meet a project schedule. If one activity is behind schedule while another

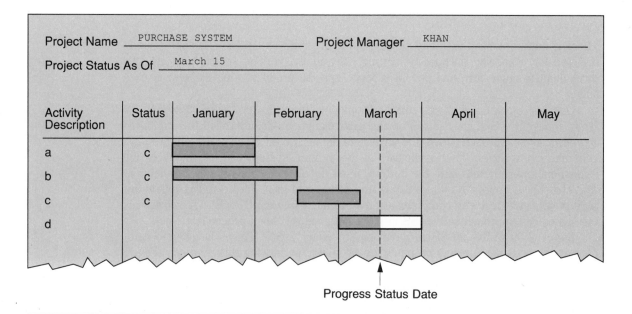

FIGURE 3–10   **Gantt Chart**

is ahead of schedule, management may reallocate resources from the latter activity to the former. The major advantage of a Gantt chart is that it is easy to understand. Its disadvantages include long preparation time and an unusually large number of charts for complex projects.

Figure 3–11 is the Gantt chart resulting from the following information:

Activities	Events	Planned Duration	Actual	Status
Preliminary study	1–2	14 days	10	Complete
Requirements definition	2–3	20 days	21	Complete
Logical design	3–4	30 days	45	Complete
Equipment specification	4–5	5 days	7	Complete
Equipment bid	5–6	30 days	30	Complete
Procedure preparation	5–7	14 days	11	Complete
Procedure walkthrough	7–9	3 days	2	Complete
Program preparation	5–8	45 days	60	Incomplete
Program testing	8–9	5 days	—	Incomplete
Equipment installation	6–9	2 days	4	Complete
Systems testing	9–19	5 days	—	Incomplete
User training	8–10	20 days	—	Incomplete
Final training	10–11	2 days	—	Incomplete
Systems conversion	11–12	10 days	—	Incomplete

A TOTAL QUALITY MANAGEMENT (TQM) APPROACH

Recall from chapters 1 and 2 the development mission and information systems objectives as follows:

> *Development mission:* To design business information systems that satisfy the firm's information customers (both external and internal) while conforming to the overall mission and goals of the firms

> *Information system objectives:* Each information system developed must, within the overall context of the development mission, demonstrate the characteristics of (a) relevancy, (b) completeness, (c) correctness, (d) security, (e) timeliness, (f) economy, (g) efficiency, (h) reliability, and (i) usability.

The system development life cycle shown in Figure 3–8 provides us with the means for implementing TQM throughout the entire development process. For each SDLC stage shown as a rectangle in Figure 3–8, we will apply the information system objectives. For example, when we are dealing with output design, we will be concerned with relevancy of output, completeness of output, and so on. We will revisit these TQM objectives in every chapter of this book.

HUMAN ASPECTS

The system development life cycle (SDLC) provides an excellent model for managing development of new information systems. However, do not let the SDLC become an

Project Status Report

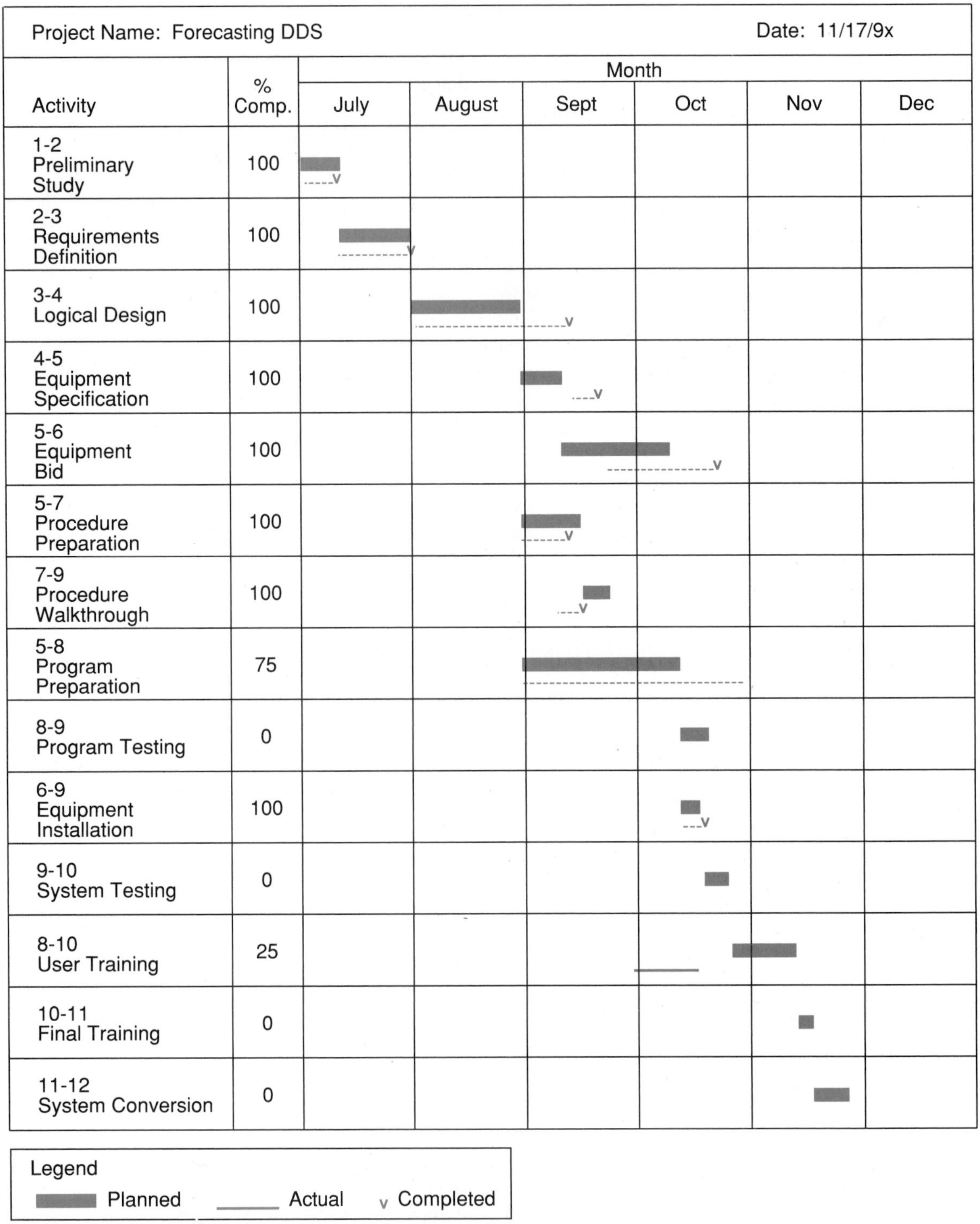

Project Name: Forecasting DDS						Date: 11/17/9x	
Activity	% Comp.	Month					
		July	August	Sept	Oct	Nov	Dec
1-2 Preliminary Study	100	▓▓ v					
2-3 Requirements Definition	100	▓▓▓ v					
3-4 Logical Design	100		▓▓▓▓ v				
4-5 Equipment Specification	100			▓ ...v			
5-6 Equipment Bid	100			▓▓▓▓ v			
5-7 Procedure Preparation	100			▓▓ ...v			
7-9 Procedure Walkthrough	100			▓ ..v			
5-8 Program Preparation	75			▓▓▓▓▓▓▓			
8-9 Program Testing	0				▓		
6-9 Equipment Installation	100				▓ _v		
9-10 System Testing	0				▓		
8-10 User Training	25				____	▓▓	
10-11 Final Training	0					▪	
11-12 System Conversion	0					▓▓	

Legend

▓▓▓ Planned   _____ Actual   v Completed

FIGURE 3-11   **Detailed Gantt Chart**

inflexible, ponderous giant that smothers analysts' creativity. The SDLC should be an overall outline of how the project should proceed. Nevertheless, time frames and sequence of steps should be easily modifiable if new circumstances are uncovered. Every system development is a new experience, regardless of the analyst's number of years of experience. Leave room for human creativity and flexibility.

SUMMARY

All systems—whether they are biological, organizational, or informational—must die. Therefore, all systems, including information systems, proceed through a predictable cycle of activity during their lives—a system's life cycle.

Organizations deal with two types of information systems life cycles. The *strategic life cycle* includes the entire organization's growth in its use of information resources. The *tactical life cycle* concerns the development and replacement of individual systems. This book is devoted to the tactical cycle.

Because information systems die naturally, eventually they must be replaced. Planning for replacements must begin early. Piggybacking, which emphasizes orderly replacement of information systems, must become a designer's mind set to avoid panic design of replacement systems.

Tactical design of a business information system proceeds according to the systems analysis, systems design, and systems implementation phases. This progression includes twelve separate stages. Circumstances uncovered at any one of these stages can lead to backtracking to one or more preceding stages of the SDLC.

There are many SDLC versions other than the one presented in this book. These include structured life cycles. Any SDLC version will work if (a) it is common throughout the firm, and (b) there are products delivered (deliverables) at each stage.

Information systems development is a complex process that must be controlled. This is the function of project management. A valuable project management tool is the Gantt chart, which allows project control of each SDLC stage.

The SDLC also provides the means for employing TQM throughout the entire project.

CONCEPTS LEARNED

- General systems life cycle (GSLC)
- Levels of information resource management: strategic, tactical, and operational
- Difference between strategic and tactical information systems life cycles
- Reasons that information systems must die
- How user expectations affect the life of an information system
- Definition of information systems success
- Concept of piggybacking
- Information systems development life cycle (SDLC)
- Project management (the Gantt chart)
- How TQM is used throughout the SDLC

KEY TERMS

deliverable
functional discontinuity
Gantt chart
general systems life cycle (GSLC)
information systems life cycle (ISLC)
initial investigation
piggybacking

problem detection
project management
requirements analysis
strategic life cycle
systems success
tactical life cycle

REVIEW QUESTIONS

1. What are the four stages of the information systems life cycle?

2. What is the relationship between the GSLC and the SDLC?

3. List four common strategic IS decisions.

4. What are the six stages of Nolan's strategic life cycle?

5. Describe the five different dimensions for measuring the life of an information system.

6. What is functional discontinuity? Why is it a problem in a business information systems environment?

7. What is tactical design of business information systems?

8. Define a successful information system.

9. Why is piggybacking important to the systems designer?

10. What occurs during the requirements analysis stage of the systems development life cycle?

11. What are the stages of SDLC implementation?

12. What does a Gantt chart do?

CRITICAL THINKING OPPORTUNITIES

1. Telephone ten managers of information-processing systems and ask them this question: How long do you estimate that the average business information system lasts before it is replaced? Draw a histogram of your survey results.

2. Ask the same ten managers how long it takes for an information system to proceed through the entire systems development life cycle. Draw a histogram of your survey results.

3. Ask the same managers to define a successful information system. Compare the definitions you receive with the one included in this chapter. How do they differ?

4. Contrast and compare the two SDLC models of Figure 3–8 and Figure 3–9.

5. Draw a diagram that shows how this chapter is organized (refer to Figure 1–11).

C A S E 3.1

CLASS DESIGN PROJECT: OVERVIEW

OVERVIEW

You and your project team are contracted by a local area client of your choice to perform the analysis and design phases of the system development life cycle (SDLC). You will conduct all activities and prepare all deliverable products associated with a structured systems study. You will use only the specific templates, reports, and conventions included in the Visible Analyst WORKBENCH. At the conclusion of your study, you will prepare a comprehensive, high-quality project team report containing your results.

PROJECT SCOPE CONSIDERATIONS

1. Locate a company or agency that is interested in either automating a manually based information system or enhancing its current computer-based system.
2. Explain to your client that your project team is willing to help them define their requirements for a new system. They can use your study for either custom development or software package selection. Your consulting services could easily cost your client $5,000. You are willing to provide this service free in return for the client's cooperation on the project.
3. You may choose any type or size company or agency. If you choose a small company, cover a fairly wide range of business functions. If you choose a medium- to large-sized company, confine your scope to a more narrowly defined business application (e.g., customer billing and collection). It is better to have a deeper, more comprehensive analysis of a narrow application scope.

4. The student version of the Visible Analyst WORKBENCH allows a maximum of 30 data flow diagrams (DFDs) for any project. Discounting the upper-level, control modules, this leaves only 20 to 25 DFDs at the primitive, or programmable level. This gives you a natural constraint on the size of your project.

MILESTONES

Your instructor will give you several deliverables to mark your progress on this project. All project deliverables will be (1) typed; (2) double spaced; (3) enclosed in a two- or three-ring folder; and (4) included in a folder labeled with team number, project deliverable number, due date, and names of *all* team members. Following are the deliverables pertinent to organization of the development project.

Team Composition (P1)

Names, phone numbers, class schedules, and work schedules of team numbers. Include agreed on weekly team meeting times.

Project Proposal (P2)

Your instructor will review it and either approve it or require changes and resubmittal by a specified time. The project proposal should include the following:

1. Name of company being reviewed, its line of business, a company contact, some indication of its size, and an organization chart.

2. Scope of proposed analysis in terms of business functions or activities to be evaluated.
3. A diagram of the project scope similar to that shown in Goodbyte Pizza (Case 1.2).

1. Narrative portion:
   a) Life cycle (e.g., problem detection)
   b) Task (e.g., interviewing)
   c) Name of analyst responsible
   d) Time allocated (e.g., one week)
   e) Completion date (e.g., sixth week)
2. Gantt chart (Martin, Chapter 3)

Your instructor will provide you with specific due dates for these milestones.

HINTS FOR A SUCCESSFUL PROJECT

- Try to obtain a client that has a manual process that your team may automate. The "proposed" automated system should be designed for a personal computer (PC) rather than a mainframe.
- The sooner the "proposed" system's description can be arrived at, the better. Try not to delay too long in arriving at a proposed system lest you run out of time to complete the data dictionary specifications for the proposed system.
- Try not to spend too much time on data flow diagrams at the expense of not completing the data dictionary specifications.
- The sooner you can complete the *information-gathering* phase of the analysis, the more time you will have to devote to the design phases of the project.
- The sooner a project schedule (Gantt chart) can be put together, the better.
- Doing everything as a whole team is often slow and inefficient. Use whole-team meetings primarily for brainstorming and coordinating sessions. Break the team up into smaller units of one or two members, and delegate specific tasks to each of these units. These smaller units are more efficient in completing the project's milestones than the whole team would be.
- Designate one member as quality control person. He or she should scrutinize the data dictionary specifications for completeness and should also check narrative pages using a spelling checker and a grammar package.
- Return to these hints as you progress through the project.

REFERENCES AND FURTHER READINGS

Ackoff, Russell. "Management Misinformation Systems." *Management Science* 14(December 1967):B147–B156.

Anthony, Robert. *Planning and Control Systems: A Framework for Analysis.* Cambridge, Mass.: Harvard University Graduate School, Business Administration, 1965.

Bryce, M. "Ten Myths of Data Processing." *Data Training* (1986):36–37.

DeLong, D. W., and J. F. Rockart. "Identifying Attributes of Successful Executive Information Systems." *Computer Information Systems Research Working Paper* 132(1986).

Eliason, Alan. *Online Business Computer Applications.* Chicago: Science Research Associates, 1987.

Fuerst, William, and Merle Martin. "Effective Design and Use of Computer Design Models." *MIS Quarterly* 8(March 1984):17–26.

Gory, G. Anthony, and Michael Scott Morton. "A Framework for Management Information Systems." *Sloan Management Review* 13(Fall 1971):55–70.

Holsapple, Clyde, and Andrew Whinston. *Business Expert Systems.* Homewood, Ill.: Irwin, 1987.

Juran, J. (Ed.). *Quality Control Handbook,* 3rd ed. New York: McGraw-Hill, 1974.

King, Donald. *Current Practices in Software Development.* New York: Yourdon Press, 1984.

Martin, Merle. "Problem Identification." *Journal of Systems Management* 29(September 1978): 36–39.

Martin, Merle. "The Human Connection in Systems Design: User Categories." *Journal of Systems Management* 37(October 1986):10–14.

McLeod, Raymond Jr. *Management Information Systems,* 4th ed. New York: Macmillan, 1990.

McNurlin, B., and R. Sprague. *Information Systems Management in Practice.* Englewood Cliffs, N.J.: Prentice-Hall, 1989.

Metzgar, Phillip, *Managing a Programming Project,* 2nd ed. Englewood Cliffs, N.J.: Prentice-Hall, 1981.

Miller, George. "The Miracle Number Seven, Plus or Minus Two." *Psychological Review* 63(March 1956):81–97.

Nauman, Justice, and A. Milton Jenkins. "Prototyping: The New Paradigm for Systems Development." *MIS Quarterly* 6(September 1982):29–44.

Nolan, Richard L. "Managing the Crisis in Data Processing." *Harvard Business Review* 60(July–August 1982):72–79.

Reynolds, George. *Information Systems for Managers.* St. Paul, Minn.: West, 1988.

Rockart, John. "Chief Executives Define Their Own Data Needs." *Harvard Business Review* (March–April 1979).

Ross, Joel. *Quality Management.* Delray Beach, Fla.: St. Lucie Press, 1993.

Shneiderman, Ben. *Designing the User Interface.* Reading, Mass.: Addison-Wesley, 1987.

Sprague, Ralph. "A Framework for the Development of Decision Support Systems." *MIS Quarterly* 4(December 1980):1–26.

Texas Instruments. *IEF Technical Description.* Texas Instruments, Inc., 1992.

Yourdon, Ed. *Managing the Structured Technique.* New York: Yourdon Press, 1976.

Zipf, George. *Human Behavior and the Principle of Least Effort.* New York: Hafner, 1949.

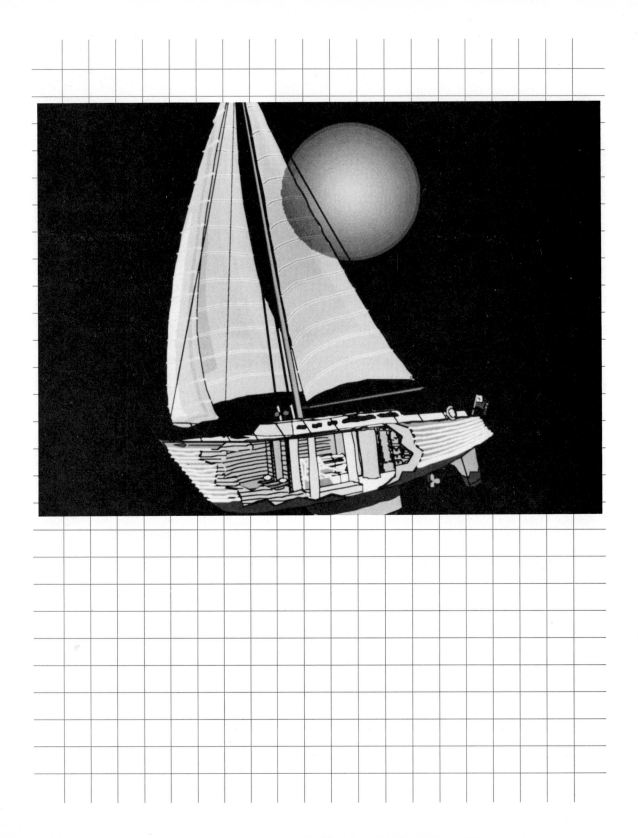

ANALYSIS OF INFORMATION SYSTEMS

Whatever the shape of a firm's systems design life cycle, certain functions and tasks must be done. Three phases are involved—analysis, design, and implementation—and they are described in the next three sections of this book.

Analysis is the most important of the three phases. If we do not analyze effectively, our work in the rest of the SDLC is questionable. Analysis can be faulty in two ways. If analysis signals a need for replacing a healthy system, such a false start commands scarce analyst resources and unnecessarily disrupts the end-user world. The other type of faulty analysis involves improper definition of information systems problems. Poor analysis lays the seeds for faulty design and implementation. Errors in analysis magnify as they flow through the remainder of the life cycle.

This section on analysis begins with Chapter 4, "Problem Detection." The discussion centers on types of information systems problems and how they may be detected.

Chapter 5, "Initial Investigation," explains the detective work that is done on problems. The deliverable product for this stage of the SDLC is the current system description. At this point, systems analysts decide whether to continue the SDLC or merely to patch the current information system.

Chapter 6 introduces several structured development tools primarily used in the systems analysis phase of the SDLC: hierarchy chart, data flow diagrams, HIPO charts, and the system flowchart.

The SDLC continues with requirements analysis, the subject of Chapter 7. Description of the current system is completed, and user expectations about an ideal information system are gathered. The gap between the ideal information system and the current system is reduced through identification of resource constraints.

The information systems department generates and analyzes the subset of potential information systems to decide which to recommend to top management. This is described in Chapter 8, "System Selection." Chapter 9 concludes this section by describing preliminary system design and the system study. This chapter concludes with the go/no-go decision, in which management decides whether or not to continue to the design stage of the SDLC.

In this chapter you will learn about:

WHAT: (Concepts) How to detect problems in current information systems.

WHY: We must detect information system problems early enough so that we have time to cure them before the patient dies.

WHEN: Problem detection is an ongoing process.

WHO: Problem detection is a joint responsibility of the information systems department and information system end-users.

WHERE: Problem detection largely occurs in the user area. Analysts must scout out information system problems.

HOW: (Techniques) Problem logs
                    User surveys
                    Preliminary problem report

OUTLINE

- Setting
- A Total Quality Approach
- Typical Information Systems Problems
- Information Systems Backlogs
- Detection Sources of Information Systems Problems
- Preliminary Problem Report
- Importance of the Current System
- Human Aspects

PROBLEM DETECTION

It has often been observed that we more frequently fail to face the right problem than fail to solve the problem we face.

—RUSSELL ACKOFF, 1978

SETTING

All information systems have problems, regardless of how well the systems are designed. There are several reasons for this. First, over time, incidents with a low probability of occurring are more likely to occur. For example, it is rare for a customer to make a payment after not doing so for a year or more. Yet, the older the accounts receivable system, the more likely it is that this unlikely event will occur. As the information system grows older, the probability increases that even low-probability flaws will show themselves. If you live to be 952 years old, you will have a better lifetime chance of winning the California lottery.

A second reason for operational problems in an information system is that the business environment surrounding the system is always changing, and that change necessitates change in systems. For example, suppose firm A acquires firm B. Firm A then requires firm B to reconfigure its information systems to make them compatible with firm A.

A third reason for operational problems is change in user expectations. As users become more experienced in using business information systems, they expect more from the systems. For example, users may accept a terminal response time of fifteen seconds during the first year of a system's operation. After that, fifteen seconds may be longer than the new, more sophisticated users desire or will tolerate.

For all these reasons, business information systems change constantly. Multiply any one system's changes by the number of such systems in any given firm and you'll find that the number of total systems changes is considerable. One aerospace firm in southern California makes an average of nearly five hundred program changes each weekend.

Day-to-day correction of information systems problems is called **maintenance programming.** It is equivalent to the periodic and sometimes unexpected minor maintenance and repairs given to a healthy automobile. Maintenance programming includes responding to minor information systems problems and adding minor new features to a system. A theme throughout this book is that systems analysts and designers must design new or replacement information systems to facilitate maintenance programming. Maintenance programming makes up 60 to 90 percent of business programming budget dollars. In addition, the maintenance programming function provides the clues that current information systems are deteriorating and may have to be replaced or enhanced. When your automobile is constantly in the shop being repaired, it may be time to think about a new set of wheels.

Maintenance and **development programming** are merely portions of the same spectrum, as Figure 4–1 demonstrates. Program changes proceed in seriousness and complexity from left to right, from minor repairs to major modifications to enhancements to replacement. Note that the last three types of changes are in the systems design or development programming area. You may be surprised to learn that systems design changes make up only 10 to 40 percent of dollars spent annually for business programming.

Systems analysis includes the critical decision of which type of program change, if any, to make in a given situation. Suppose you judge an information systems problem to be minor (maintenance programming), although it is really a symptom of a deteriorating system. You have lost valuable lead time in designing a replacement system. Figure 4–2 demonstrates this situation. At the same time, too quick a response to a

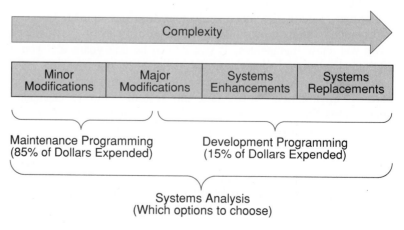

FIGURE 4–1   **Maintenance and Development Programming as Parts of the Programming Spectrum**

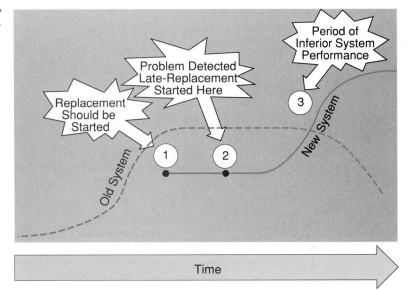

FIGURE 4–2   **Late Detection of Information Systems Problem**

false alarm will waste analyst resources. Consider the analogy to doctors as they find patient problems or police officers as they respond to citizen complaints. Systems analysts and designers need a problem detection structure to detect and classify information systems problems correctly.

A TOTAL QUALITY APPROACH

Recall the problem structure from Chapter 2. It is shown again, in a slightly different format, in Figure 4–3. We must determine the magnitude of any information system problem by:

- Determining current system performance status, or initial investigation (Chapter 5).
- Assessing what information system users feel would be the goals and objectives of the ideal information system, or requirements analysis (Chapter 7).
- Generating and evaluating alternatives to close the expectation gap, or system selection (Chapter 8).
- Moving toward the alternative selected as the new, replacement information system (Chapter 9).

This entire process cannot begin, however, until a potential problem is detected. In addition, problem detection must be a structured system that does not allow important information system problems to fall through the cracks. The problem detection structure used in this book is based on the nine characteristics of information described in Chapter 2: (1) relevancy, (2) completeness, (3) correctness, (4) security, (5) timeliness, (6) economy, (7) efficiency, (8) reliability, and (9) usability.

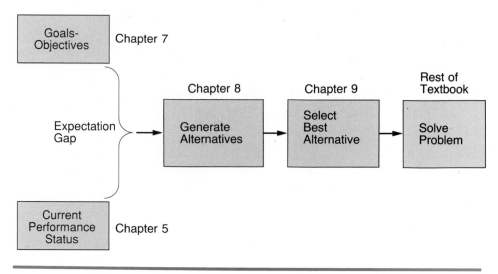

FIGURE 4–3   **Structure of Typical Business Problem**

TYPICAL INFORMATION SYSTEMS PROBLEMS

The first three chapters of this book showed that, regardless of the application, business information systems have similar structures. Hence, it should not be surprising that business information systems exhibit the same performance problems.

Common information system problems involve the characteristics of information described in Chapter 2:

- Relevancy to decision making
- Accuracy, comprising completeness, correctness, and security
- Timeliness to decision-making needs
- Economy (e.g., resources or costs)
- Efficiency, expressed as amount produced per economic unit
- Reliability, which measures the consistency (variance) of the other characteristics
- Usability, the human factors dimension.

Problems can occur in one, several, or all of these characteristic areas. Let's look at each of the characteristics and note the symptoms that indicate potential information systems problems.

Relevancy

Information systems output must be usable to operational, tactical, or strategic management. If it is not, the information is not worthwhile and may even obscure important information. Look for the following symptoms of information that are not relevant:

> ### THE REPORT CHECK
>
> A new information systems officer was alarmed at her operation's paper costs and the amount of overtime hours accrued on weekends to run batch reports. She ordered that her staff produce no weekend batch reports for the next two weekends. Only three users complained about not receiving the expected reports. The three complaints concerned the same inventory status report.
>
> The information systems officer restarted weekend production of the inventory status report but discontinued all other weekend batch reports. Paper and overtime costs plummeted. The user community did not complain.

- Many lengthy reports
- Reports not used by persons receiving them
- Requests for information not currently available in the information system
- As-required reports never requested
- Lack of user complaints when reports are not produced and distributed (see the box "The Report Check").

Completeness

Not only must data be entered correctly, they must be entered *completely*. An information system that is 95 percent accurate but captures only 80 percent of required information is ineffective. Look for the following symptoms of incompleteness:

- The data entry section returns to the user community a high percentage of source documents because forms are incomplete.
- Auditor analysis of data entry errors shows a high incidence of incomplete fields (e.g., customer address missing).
- The data entry section is making many phone calls to users for clarification of data on source documents.

Newly hired employees at Trumbly's Manufacturing must fill out a personnel action form for use by the data entry section. Many of the questions relate to items that the new employee may not know without some research (e.g., former employer's zip code and phone number, physician's phone number, phone number of person to contact in case of emergency). It has been Trumbly's policy to accept the incomplete forms and let the employee bring in the information later. Meanwhile, the incomplete forms go to data entry, which results in delays and problems.

Correctness

We usually think of accuracy as correctness. All fields of data entered must be entered correctly. Search for the following symptoms of problems with correctness:

- The total percentage of transactions with errors versus quality transactions is increasing.
- The number of *critical* errors is increasing (of course, someone will have to define a critical error). For example, errors on customer balances due a firm can reduce cash input and create customer dissatisfaction. This type of error is critical.
- The number of maintenance requests for program changes is increasing.
- Problems that occur after the normal workday are increasing.

Williams, Harcourt, and Slavanvich Investments, Inc., sent a dividend check to Harry Seal for the amount of $234,120.00. The amount due Harry was really $234.12. The mistake was finally isolated as a bounce problem on the zero key on a data entry keyboard. The mistake could have been eliminated by effective error-checking programming. Such an error is a symptom of an unhealthy information system.

Security

Often, information is transmitted to anybody who requires it; yet, information sent to a person who is not authorized to receive it is a security breach. Frequently, symptoms of security problems are discovered *after* security has been breached. This is like waiting for the first burglary to decide that your house needs protection.

Security audits are structured checks to determine if sensitive information is being disseminated to nonintended users. Audits must be periodic but irregular (unexpected) so that potential security problems are identified before they become a reality. Shared passwords and unattended workstations with screens left on are good clues to a lax security environment.

Timeliness

How quickly are resource records updated? How quickly does the system respond to user requests such as reports or program problems? A long list of symptoms indicates timeliness problems; among the most important, note:

- Throughput is decreasing. **Throughput** is the number of error-free transactions processed through the information system per unit of time (normally a day).
- Entry backlogs are increasing. An entry backlog occurs when transactions are not entered on the same day they are received.
- VDT response time is increasing.
- Complaints about late system-produced reports are increasing.
- The time required to correct maintenance programming problems is increasing.
- There are more complaints from users about difficulty in reaching maintenance programming and operations staff.

Stan Johnson runs performance statistics on a mainframe on the Friday of each week. He uses large data sets. Recently, Stan has had to wait as long as one hour for a job to run. Last year at this time, an average run was ten minutes. After complaining and doing some detective work, Stan discovered that payroll and billing had moved their runs from Mondays to Fridays because of other operational demands on the computer and the newly installed relational database. Stan finally solved his problem by switching to a powerful workstation that could accommodate his data sets, and changing his statistics run to Thursday afternoons. The throughput in payroll increased as a by-product.

Economy

Information systems costs increase over time. Although some costs may decrease, most will increase naturally. Figure 4–4 shows the pattern for natural, linear inflation. Thus, increasing costs are not necessarily a symptom of information systems problems. However, a deteriorating system exhibits cost increases that are not linear, but geometric (Figure 4–5). Such a pattern of increasing systems costs is a symptom of potential problems.

Some particularly revealing cost increases to look for are overtime, paper, hardware maintenance, consultants, and program maintenance.

Efficiency

Performance is increasing, but so are costs. Performance is decreasing, but costs are remaining reasonably constant. Is either information system in trouble? It is difficult to answer that question without computing some ratios that measure *unit performance per unit cost*. This is the definition of efficiency: how much production is gained for each additional unit of resource fed into the production process. For example, suppose a firm

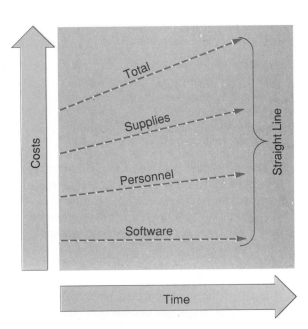

FIGURE 4–4   Natural Cost Inflation for Information Systems

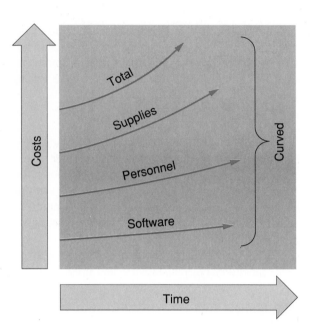

FIGURE 4–5   **Geometric Cost In-creases for Information Systems—A Pattern Indicating Problems**

spends $500,000 for a new inventory system. Sales increase $100,000 as a result of the new system. Efficiency of the new system is

$$\frac{100,000}{500,000} = 20\%$$

Unless a quality measurement system exists, there may not be any readily available efficiency ratios. You may have to generate them from scratch. Here are a few pertinent ratios you can calculate and analyze for increasing trends:

- Throughput/dollar
- Throughput/data entry hours worked
- Errorless transactions/hour
- Errors corrected/dollar
- Program changes/number of programmers
- Paper costs/transaction

The installation and use of an applications generator has dramatically increased the efficiency at KLM Food Products as measured by number of changes per programmer. All changes to new systems are performed by making high-level changes. The actual code is generated by the applications generator. The maintenance programming staff has virtually been eliminated for new systems.

Reliability

Most of the symptoms so far have been measured in averages—for example, average paper costs per transaction. An important indicator of information systems

---

PRODUCTIVITY AND INFORMATION SYSTEMS

Productivity is an issue that has received a great deal of attention. Young (1988) has stated that the ability of the United States to compete on a global basis has declined. Real wages are lower than they were a decade ago, and the goods and services that labor is producing are often unable to compete in the world market. Young sees information utilization as a critical aspect of competitive differentiation. Office productivity has decreased (about 7 percent) while productivity of production workers has increased. Technical barriers to progress such as inconsistent and difficult-to-use computer interfaces are seen as a major reason for lack of productivity in the office.

---

deterioration is lack of reliability. Reliability is the *variance* about symptom averages. As an example, Glorfeld Industry's total percentage of errors is only 5 percent, but the company's daily error rate varies from 0 to 15 percent. Glorfeld's information system is unreliable in the rate of errors it makes. Lack of reliability can be a serious problem because it makes planning difficult.

Note these critical symptoms of reliability problems:

- *Computer downtime:* The information system works well when the computer is up, but the computer is frequently down.
- *Employee turnover:* Employees perform well, but there is a high rate of people quitting and new employees being trained.
- *Workstation response time:* Times between 3:00 and 4:00 P.M. are tripled.
- *Program error correction time:* Users cannot predict how long it will take to correct an information problem. Sometimes it takes an hour, sometimes as long as four weeks. There seems to be little correlation between the size of the problem and the time needed to correct it.
- *Costs:* There is a high variance-to-mean ratio for monthly cost rate.
- *Backlogs:* The amount of unprocessed transactions bounces up and down.
- *Error rates:* The rate of errors never is predictable; it moves from too high to surprisingly low.

Information systems that are deteriorating often act irregularly. They become unreliable over a wide range of performance characteristics.

Usability

No matter how well a system has been designed according to other criteria, if the system is difficult to use, it is a problem system. Look for the following symptoms of poor usability:

- Long training times for novice users
- High error rates

- Increasing user complaints
- Increasing absenteeism on the part of computer users
- High turnover for users dealing directly with information

INFORMATION SYSTEMS BACKLOGS

One of the most pervasive problems in business information systems is a backlog. An **entry backlog** occurs when transactions arriving during a business day are not posted to business records by the beginning of the next day. The primary purpose of a business information system is to keep track of resources, so the failure to update resource records is a serious systems problem. An analyst needs to know what causes information system backlogs and what problems are caused by perpetual backlogs.

Causes of Backlogs

There are five reasons that an information systems backlog can occur.

1. *Transaction volume increase:* The level of transaction volume is increasing with no associated increase in personnel resources to process that volume. Personnel resources could be end-users who process source documents, data entry operators, or both.

Olney Savings and Loan recently acquired 23,000 new mortgage accounts as a result of the shake-up in the thrift industry, but the company did not change its number of data entry people. The result is a twelve-day backlog in payment processing.

2. *Decreasing performance:* Transaction volume is stable, but throughput rate is decreasing. Such a decrease can result from a variety of causes, including individual employee production deterioration, group production decreases, employee turnover, and computer system downtime.

3. *Employee turnover:* Data entry departments and end-user operations rarely are staffed with any margin to meet other than average situations. Therefore, when one employee leaves the firm before a new employee is trained, throughput decreases. This causes production to fall below transaction arrival rates; backlogs result.

LDS Systems recently converted from systems development with third-generation languages to a 4GL prototyping approach. Many of the existing staff members distrust the new environment and feel that the challenge of programming has been taken away. The turnover rate for the last four months has risen from 10 to 28 percent. Backlogs have increased.

4. *System downtime:* When the information system is not in operation, data entry production stops and backlogs occur.

5. *Transaction variances:* Even when transaction levels are not increasing and throughput remains steady, temporary backlogs occur. Why? Because transaction arrival rates are not steady; they vary widely about some average arrival rate. For example, assume transactions arrive at an average rate of 20,000 a day. Also assume there are enough data entry operators to enter those 20,000 average transactions properly. Everything appears to be in equilibrium. If 25,000 transactions arrive during one day, however, a temporary backlog occurs.

Problems of Perpetual Backlogs

Information systems backlogs are one of the most common problems systems analysts have to face. They can cause significant disruptions to a business operation. Several problems caused by backlogs are most disruptive.

Lack of Record Currency. Resource record balances that are not current can hurt business. For example, during a weekend, a Martin-Mart salesperson makes an inquiry to the information system to see how many executive chairs are on hand in the warehouse. The resource record shows a balance of zero on hand, and the sale is lost. Actually, five executive chairs were received on Friday, but the transaction was in the backlog that could not be processed by the end of the week. On Monday, the transaction will be processed, but the sale has already been lost.

Increased Error Rates. Production workers hate backlogs. They feel that management will interpret backlogs to mean that the workers are inefficient and are not getting their jobs done. Under this self-imposed pressure (and sometimes under actual management pressure), production workers attempt to speed up normal throughput rates. But an increased rate of entry causes more errors, and correction of the errors often slows the production rate to lower than it was before the speedup effort started. This frustrating cycle feeds upon itself until near chaos occurs.

Increased Costs. Under pressure to reduce transaction backlogs, data entry departments authorize operator overtime, hire temporary extra operators, or do both. Systems costs increase.

Increased Employee Turnover. When there is constant backlog pressure in a data entry department, it becomes an oppressive environment in which to work. Data entry operators look elsewhere for better atmospheres. Employee turnover increases, thus making the backlog situation even worse.

DETECTION SOURCES OF INFORMATION SYSTEMS PROBLEMS

Potential information systems problems can come to light from many sources. Six common sources are user complaints, top management concerns, scouting, user surveys, audits, and quality measurement systems.

User Complaints

Users sometimes communicate information problems to the information systems group, either by phone or by written memorandum. A reported problem should be logged immediately using a form like the one shown in Figure 4–6. The **problem log** becomes a checklist to ensure that each user complaint is investigated. Also, the log allows measurement of the time it takes to solve user problems.

```
+--------------------------------------------------------------------------+
|                                                                          |
|                               Control                                    |
|          Systems Problem Log        Number _____       |
|                                                                          |
|    Date Received: ___/___/___      Received By: _____  |
|    Time Received: _____                                           |
|    How Received: Telephone  Correspondence  Site Visit  Other _____  |
|                                                                          |
|    Who Reported: _____    Ext.: _____  |
|    Position: _____       |
|    Application System: _____  Component: _____  |
|    Problem Description: _____ |
|    _____ |
|    _____ |
|    _____                     |
|    _____ |
|                      (Use Other Side if Necessary)                       |
|                                                                          |
+--------------------------------------------------------------------------+
```

FIGURE 4–6   **Form for Logging Information Systems Problems Reported to the IS Department**

Top Management Concerns

Users are often reluctant to voice their dissatisfaction directly to the information systems group, particularly if they think IS personnel are unresponsive to user problems. In such cases, users complain to their supervisors, who then complain to top management. Problems detected in this manner become exaggerated and undermine the reputation of the IS group.

Scouting

Users who are reluctant to complain to the information systems group can be encouraged to report problems informally. Analysts can scout—that is, wander into user work areas and ask a simple question: "Is everything working all right?" Users become surprisingly open when the analyst is in *their* physical realm, their comfort zone. Nonetheless, scouting will work effectively only if users eventually see changes resulting from these informal interactions.

User Surveys

Periodic surveys should be sent to information systems users to detect undiscovered or emerging problems. Figure 4–7 shows portions of one such survey form. The **user survey** accomplishes three things. First, it detects problems and user attitudes. Second, it can track user attitudes over time to reveal important trends. Third, the survey is a marketing tactic, which shows users that the IS department really cares about doing an effective job. Of course, if nothing ever changes as a result of periodic surveys, users eventually will perceive them as merely a waste of their time.

Page 2

5. How would you rate the following services?

	5	4	3	2	1
	Excellent		Average		Poor
a. Terminal Response Time					
b. Computer Downtime					
c. Problem Resolution					
d. Report Delivery					
e. Staff Cooperation					
f. Computer Chargeback					

FIGURE 4–7   User Survey Form to Detect IS Problems

Audits

People who are not part of the IS group can detect systems problems by conducting formal audits. The audits can be performed by auditors within the firm or by consultants hired from outside the firm. Audit results are reported to the information systems department, to top management, or to both. If the information systems department has already detected and is working on identified problems, the impact of critical audit results can be reduced.

Quality Measurement Systems

In all the problem sources already discussed, detection occurs *after* the problem exists. It is preferable, of course, to spot potential problems before they become too serious and expensive to fix. Such early detection is the function of quality measurement systems, which will be discussed fully in Chapter 20.

Regardless of the detection source, problems should be entered into the correction process by a form like the one shown in Figure 4–6. Otherwise, problem symptoms will be lost in the press of everyday business, and the reputation of the information systems department will suffer.

PRELIMINARY PROBLEM REPORT

Any entry on the problem log report should be assigned to an individual systems analyst for preliminary study. This study determines if the reported or detected problem is serious enough to warrant further attention and what that further attention should be. This is similar to the type of report that a doctor prepares after preliminary investigation of a patient's complaint. The analyst prepares a **preliminary problem report** that includes the following four elements:

1. *Source:* where the problem information originated
2. *Nature:* a brief description in terms described by the source
3. *Detailed analysis:* expansion in technical detail of the problem nature
4. *Recommendation:* how further resolution of the reported problem should proceed. Typical recommendations include:
   - The problem is minor and requires Band-Aid maintenance.
   - The problem requires additional systems capabilities; in this case, the problem is placed in the future file for a time when replacement of the information system is more appropriate.
   - The problem seems serious enough to warrant more detailed analysis. This recommendation starts the systems development life cycle. Detailed analysis determines whether or not the current system should be replaced by a new information system. As with the doctor or the police officer, not every complaint that the systems analyst receives is legitimate — is indicative of real system problems.

The information systems department requires the preliminary problem report for several reasons. First, it represents closure to a reported information systems problem. Closure is completion of a user-started task. If an IS department does not require a formal report for referred problems, it invites the danger that reported problems will be ignored or misplaced, leading to erosion of user confidence in the information systems department.

Second, the report allows information systems management to decide how to allocate scarce analyst resources. What if there are only enough analyst resources to tackle two systems problems? The preliminary problem report allows management to determine the two most important problems.

Third, the file of reports allows detection of trends in systems performance. One clue to a deteriorating system is an increase in reported problems for that system. Certainly this is the case for those systems we call automobiles.

Starting the path of the SDLC will be expensive and time consuming. It also will be traumatic to clerical personnel who have become used to the current business information system. Therefore, before you choose to follow the SDLC path, you would be wise to consider the merits of the current system.

IMPORTANCE OF THE CURRENT SYSTEM

Systems caretaking is dull when compared to systems development. Who would choose to polish an old statue when he or she could sculpt a new one? The nature of the IS profession is such that potential improvements over current ways of doing things can always be spotted. Our natural tendency is to demolish the old system so we can be free to build a loftier version. Information systems professionals like to experiment with new technology. They have sometimes been criticized for being more interested in experimenting than in solving problems.

Yet, any massive change is traumatic to the firm and may at least temporarily decrease profits. Certainly change is unsettling to people. As a result, creative instincts must be tempered. Only suggest major surgery when you must breathe new life into the information system. In the trite words of a seasoned systems analyst, "If it ain't broke, don't fix it!"

Once a systems development life cycle is started, it gains momentum and becomes difficult to stop. Problem detection is the start of a SDLC that is costly, time consuming, and disruptive to the end-user community. Do not pursue the SDLC unless evidence clearly suggests it is necessary. If that evidence strongly suggests that the current information system is deteriorating, more detailed analysis of the situation is needed. This detailed analysis is the topic of the next few chapters.

HUMAN ASPECTS

No one likes to be criticized, particularly in front of others. Nevertheless, when the systems analyst is scouting for problems in user work areas, that analyst often is seen as a troublemaker whose only function is to point out other people's mistakes. As an analyst seeking problems, be polite and explain that you are not searching for user problems, but for problems with the information system they must use. When you have finished preparing the preliminary problem report, perform this revealing exercise: Pretend you are an end-user, and then read the report. Does the report seem accusatory when you are wearing the hat of the end-user? If it does, reword the report so it is positive (stressing opportunities) rather than negative (stressing faults).

SUMMARY

Regardless of how well an information system has been designed, problems will occur. Even low-probability problems will surface after the system has been in operation for any length of time.

Day-to-day correction of problems is called systems maintenance. When information systems begin to deteriorate, problems become more frequent, complex, and costly. Then systems analysts need to consider developing a replacement information system.

The transition between systems maintenance and development requires a structured approach to detecting information systems problems. The beginning of such an approach is classification of typical information problems and their associated symptoms. Be alert to problems in these areas: relevancy, completeness, correctness, security, timeliness, economy, efficiency, reliability, and usability.

Transaction backlogs are a common and frustrating problem. They can be the result of increasing transactions, decreasing entry performance, employee turnover, system downtime, and variance in transaction arrival rates. Backlogs cause lack of record currency, increased error rates, and increased costs. Transaction backlogs are difficult to cure because typical personnel policies gear staffing to average rather than extreme transaction volumes.

IS personnel detect information systems problems through several sources: user complaints, top management concerns, scouting, user surveys, audits, and quality measurement systems. Quality measurement systems are structured approaches for early and comprehensive detection of information systems problems. They are composed of several elements: goals/performance objectives, current performance status, performance tolerances, trend analysis, and problem notification.

Whatever the source of information systems problems, they must first be logged in the IS department. Then, an analyst is assigned to further investigate and produce the preliminary problem report. This report contains the detection source, a description of the problem in the source's terms, a detailed analysis, and recommendations for how to deal with the problem.

Do not initiate the process of developing a new information system unless you are certain the current system is deteriorating beyond the point of recovery. Development of a system is costly, time consuming, and disconcerting to users.

If systems problems are serious, however, possible system replacement must be investigated. This investigation continues in the next chapters.

CONCEPTS LEARNED

- Why business information systems have problems
- Differences between maintenance and development programming
- Typical information systems problems
- Causes of information systems backlogs, problems caused by backlogs, and why backlogs are difficult to cure
- How to detect information systems problems
- Contents of the preliminary problem report
- Why not to take the current system lightly

KEY TERMS

development programming
entry backlog
maintenance programming
preliminary problem report

problem log
security audit
throughput
user survey

REVIEW QUESTIONS

1. Explain why even low-probability flaws in a system will show up as the information system grows older.

2. What is maintenance programming? How is it different from development programming?

3. List the categories of information systems problems.

4. Give three symptoms of relevancy problems.

5. What are the differences between problems of completeness and problems of correctness?

6. How can security problems be detected?

7. List four symptoms of timeliness problems.

8. What are the differences between efficiency and economy problems?

9. How do reliability problems differ from correctness problems?

10. How do systems backlogs occur? What problems do they cause?

11. Why are backlog problems difficult to correct?

12. What are the various sources by which information systems problems are detected?

13. What are the components of the preliminary problem report?

CRITICAL THINKING OPPORTUNITIES

1. Consider typical information system problems. Explain how these same problem categories exist when the analyst is a doctor; a detective.

2. Consider the ways in which information system problems are detected. Explain how the same detection sources exist for a doctor; for a detective.

3. Draw a diagram to show how this chapter is organized.

4. Select an information-processing facility to determine daily volumes of throughput, errors, and backlog. From this facility, gather any reports produced about problem detection. Analyze the reports according to the structures presented in this chapter.

In this chapter you will learn about:

WHAT: (Concepts) How to conduct the initial investigation of a detected information system problem.

WHY: We must determine the status of the current information system so we can see how large the information system problem is.

WHEN: This stage of the SDLC is initiated only for those problems deemed to be serious during the problem detection stage.

WHO: Systems analyst assigned to the investigation.

WHERE: This study is conducted mostly in the user workplace.

HOW: (Techniques) Direct investigative probes
Indirect probes
Synthesis investigative probes
Current system description

OUTLINE

- Setting
- A Total Quality Approach
- Pragmatics of Systems Investigation
- Investigative Tactics
- Investigative Techniques
- Focusing the Investigation
- Initial Feasibility Analysis
- Current System Description
- Human Aspects

INITIAL INVESTIGATION

Whenever it is not necessary to change, it is necessary not to change.

—WRITING ON WALL OF FACULTY CLUB
AT THE UNIVERSITY OF CALIFORNIA, BERKELEY

SETTING

In the previous chapter, you learned that information systems problems are detected from a variety of sources. A preliminary problem report includes a recommendation about how to deal with detected problems. The recommendation may be to (1) assign the problem to the maintenance programming backlog, (2) place it in a future file for subsequent systems enhancement, or (3) begin the process of designing a replacement or enhancement to the current information delivery system.

If you give a detected problem one of the first two recommendations, it never reaches the procedures and tactics described in this chapter. At this point, it might seem that the investigative work described in Chapter 4 is irrelevant. This is not so, however, for by doing the work you record valuable performance data in the preliminary problem report and provide closure to the end-users who report systems flaws. '

Problems that receive the third recommendation enter the next stage of the systems development life cycle (SDLC): initial investigation. Three types of information systems problems reach this stage. The first type of problem is one that shows a current major gap between performance and expectations (e.g., an engine failing in an automobile). The second type of problem is one that is not yet critical but is projected to be, analogous to an automobile engine that is predicted to fail within six months.

The third type of problem is one in which the gap between goals and current status is not major, but where the current problem is only the latest of many problems. One symptom of a deteriorating information system is an increase in the frequency of minor and moderate flaws in the system. For example, your car may have no major repair problems, but frequently it is in the garage for minor or moderate repairs. Replacement of that automobile begins to seem attractive from the perspectives of cost savings and avoiding disruption of service.

Movement to the initial investigation stage of the SDLC is a serious commitment for the information systems department. Development of new or replacement systems generates disruptions to normal end-user operations. In addition, the information skills and resources required to design a new system are not plentiful. Where do these systems resources come from? Are they taken from the maintenance programming function, thereby creating delays in customer service? Are outside consultants hired or do systems personnel work overtime?

Systems analysts cannot casually recommend design of a new system. They proceed to the initial investigation stage of the SDLC only when detected problems are significant. The initial stage requires a thorough investigation of the current system. This chapter describes why this investigation is necessary and how it proceeds.

A TOTAL QUALITY APPROACH

The goal in this stage is to describe the current information system. We established in Chapter 3 that we will use at each stage of SDLC a task structure consisting of the nine characteristics of information systems. These same characteristics were used in Chapter 4 to systematically detect information problems. Now the nine characteristics will be used to serve as a checklist for investigating current information systems.

PRAGMATICS OF SYSTEMS INVESTIGATION

In deciding if a potential problem is serious enough to require further, expensive movement along the SDLC, systems analysts face several investigative constraints. They then must choose one of a limited number of recommendations.

Constraints

The initial investigation is not an endless endeavor. The following factors place limits on it:

- *Time:* Analysts are a scarce resource, and only part of their time can be spent on investigation.
- *Cost:* Sometimes the cost of analyst time is charged back to the user community reporting the problem. Naturally, users may limit charge-back costs.

- *Knowledge:* IS managers sometimes assign junior analysts with limited technical knowledge to investigations. Their inexperience can constrain them from investigating the problem in sufficient depth.
- *Politics:* Management may designate certain potential areas of investigation as off limits. For example, the accounting manager may place his favorite report outside the realm of investigation.
- *Interference:* What analysts measure changes because of their measurement. The box entitled "Measurement Experiment" illustrates this point. Analysts may have to limit their on-site presence because it is disruptive to user operations.

MEASUREMENT EXPERIMENT

When we measure an entity directly, we change it, for we become part of its immediate environment and all entities react to their environment. If this sounds academic, conduct the following experiment to place the concept in a real-world context.

1. Select a large department store. Schedule two one-hour visits to the store, with one day between visits.
2. On the first visit, select one department.
3. Scout that department without being noticed by the salesclerks. Mentally record observations such as:
   - How fast the clerks move
   - How long it takes them to acknowledge a customer
   - How much the clerks talk to each other
   - How often the clerks are on the phone
   - How often clerks leave the department for what seem to be activities other than work (e.g., coffee breaks).
4. If you must take written notes, do so without being seen by the clerks. Move around and try to be invisible. If you are spotted by any of the clerks, start over at another department.
5. Make your second visit to the store and the same department. Wear formal clothes and carry a notepad and a stopwatch.
6. Position yourself where the salesclerks can see you.
7. Simulate a department investigation. Use the stopwatch to time events such as phone calls. Exhaustively and openly record the entries of step 3 on the notepad.
8. Note differences in the levels, frequencies, and types of activities during the two visits.

This experiment will show that your measurement of the department changed the way salesclerks performed. More important, had you not made your first visit, you would have assumed that the performance seen on the second visit was the norm. You would have recorded as normal the unusual activities caused by your presence. The presence of an observer always changes things.

Recommendations

The product of the initial investigation is a recommendation. One of several is possible:

1. Take no action. The problem is not a valid one.
2. Conduct systems maintenance for this minor problem. Recall that systems maintenance is the day-to-day smoothing of minor problems.
3. Improve user training. Users are not trained adequately to operate the information system. (Be careful! This recommendation can easily become a convenient excuse when constraints prevent a more thorough analysis of the true causes of the problem.)
4. Place the problem in the future file. The problem is real, but it is more a user wish than a deficiency in the system. For example, new capabilities need to be added to the current system, but the need is not so pronounced that development of a replacement system must begin now. A future file is useful because it accumulates desired changes before the current system's replacement is to be developed.
5. Consider major modification to the system. The detected problem is real and serious. Further investigation is needed to determine if and how the current system can be modified or replaced. (This recommendation leads to further steps in the SDLC.)

As you have seen, the nature of the investigative mission has limits. Nevertheless, systems analysts can use several tactics and techniques to assist them.

INVESTIGATIVE TACTICS

Analysts who are investigating problems are outsiders—welcomed by some users but distrusted by others. Nobody is really comfortable with people who ask embarrassing questions. Doctors, detectives, and systems analysts are all investigators and evaluators of a particular aspect of life.

Look at systems investigation from a detective's perspective. Here are some tactics that you can use.

Listen—Do Not Lecture. If you knew all the answers, you would not be investigating. People love to talk; when not interrupted, they tell more than they originally intended.

> Joe Liston is a new systems analyst for Sportsworld Info. He has been given the job of interviewing managers for needs assessment during systems development. At Joe's last job, the computer architecture was quite different. Instead of adapting to the new environment, Joe wants to change the environment to fit his prior mental model. He sees the interview as a chance to convert management to his way of thinking. Consequently, he dominates the interview and does not give managers a chance to talk about anything, let alone the project at hand.

Do Not Pre-solve the Problem. Your technical and systems knowledge is not nearly as important as the objectivity you bring to the situation. You are not part of any politics, disputes, or controversies. You lose that objectivity if you show up in the user area with preconceived ideas of what the problem is and how to solve it.

> The data entry backlog is out of control at Sunnyslope Insurance. All phases of the business are being affected by the backlog. Helen Gather believes the solution is to install scanners and replace all human data entry. She has done a poor job of interviewing because she tends to tune out any responses that do not correspond with her solution.

Compare Stories. Different people have different views of the same situation. Compare witness accounts. Make sure that an opinion of a single user is not the only version you hear. Ask both clerks and supervisors about their views of the problem. Investigate an inventory problem in both the warehouse and purchasing sections. Gain a wide range of possible viewpoints. Search for different opinions. When users have different opinions, look for areas of agreement between them. This is the concept of opinion triangulation, shown in Figure 5–1.

Look for Reluctant Responses. Reluctant responses sometimes indicate people with something to hide. More commonly, such responses show a lack of knowledge of how things should be done. Many information systems problems are caused by a disguised lack of knowledge.

Probe for Logical Inconsistencies. Logical inconsistencies are interrupted data flows — points where data disappear, then magically resurface. Some common logical inconsistencies are:

- Multiple inputs into a clerical area with no outputs (black hole)
- Outputs from a clerical area with no identifiable inputs (miracles)
- Inputs to a clerical area leading to delayed outputs from that area (laboratory)

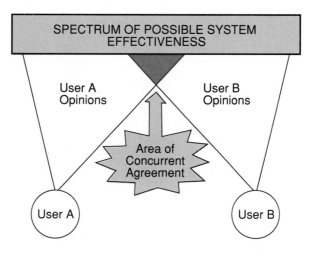

FIGURE 5–1   Concept of Opinion Triangulation

Observe Your Effect. Your measurement changes what you measure. Measure the differences in the user setting between the times you are absent and the times you are present. Measuring the setting directly, when you are present, is an **internal probe.** Internal probes can change the setting being measured much as an unskillful surgeon's exploring can lead the patient to develop a staph infection.

Balance your use of internal probes with external probes. An **external probe** is a measurement conducted without anyone knowing. A detective does this by searching external material such as a newspaper file or a criminal history. A systems analyst does this by reviewing reports, past problem history, and other secondary investigative sources. A consultant for Palko Publishing reviewed file drawers of communications between the company and textbook authors. She recorded numerous instances of letters with complaints of late payments of advances and royalties. Her research led her to suspect a serious deficiency in Palko's author payments system. She acquired this knowledge before her first interview with Palko employees.

Expect Hard, Boring Work. Problem patterns rarely leap at you; instead, you painstakingly uncover them through step-by-step fact finding. Eventually, when you have gathered enough pieces of the puzzle, the overall problem picture starts to surface. Be patient. Be a detective.

Avoid Politics. Your mission is *fact,* not *judgment.* Let management interpret your facts by using whatever microscopes they wish. Never lose your objectivity; it is the pact you have with systems users. You won't be able to avoid exposure to politics, but do not let politics disrupt your objective investigation of the problem.

INFORMATION POLITICS

We avoided looking at our watches as we listened to the associate supreme court justice for almost two hours. Justice Jestrom complained about the current information system. He complained about his fellow justices, about the legislature, about the court administrators who had commissioned us to design a new statewide information system. He said he could never support a new information system unless it included an attorney reference system, something he had been promoting for years.

Over lunch, I said, "That attorney reference system is easy. If we include it in our requirements analysis, we can add Jestrom to the list of those who support our proposal."

Talty shook his head immediately. "No," he said. "Justice Jestrom's too political. If we back his idea, his enemies will consider us Jestrom's allies. They'll fight whatever we propose."

"So what do we do with the attorney reference system?" I asked.

Talty replied: "We'll document it in an appendix. If a lot of people ask us why we didn't include it in our specifications, we'll add it. Otherwise, we'll forget it."

Question: Was Talty handling politics correctly?

Be Systematic. Plan your investigation so that no potential parts of the problem are left uncovered. You can do this by ensuring that all problems address all information characteristics: relevancy, completeness, correctness, security, timeliness, economy, efficiency, reliability, and usability.

Systems analysts combine these investigative tactics with an array of investigative techniques, which are described next. The sequence is important. Select techniques to carry out tactics, not the other way around. Thus, in the discussion that follows, ask yourself how a particular investigative technique will enhance or detract from the tactics just discussed.

INVESTIGATIVE TECHNIQUES

Investigative techniques include direct (internal) probes, indirect (external) probes, and synthesis, where the results of all probes are drawn together.

Direct (Internal) Probes

Internal probes are used to invade the user community to see what is happening. They allow you to see the setting directly, with no interpreters in between. Internal probes are disruptive. You cannot be sure that what you measure is not affected by your presence. People act differently when others are watching. Three commonly used direct investigative techniques are questionnaires, interviews, and observations.

Questionnaires. The **questionnaire** is appropriate when there are critical time and cost constraints. Although you reach many respondents with a single mailing, you have no opportunity to change the questionnaire format as you do through face-to-face interview.

In the initial investigation phase, the best use of questionnaires is for documentation of controversial findings. For example, evidence exists that a report supported by top management is useless. That evidence is more binding when it is supported by the results of a user questionnaire than when only an analyst's opinions back it up.

Interviews. The **interview** takes time and requires skill. Not everyone can interview successfully. The interview allows you to adapt a series of questions to the specific person being interviewed and to adjust to specific responses.

The initial investigation stage of the SDLC has time and skill constraints. Therefore, formal interviewing is usually restricted at this stage. What passes as interviewing is often no more than a courtesy visit designed to let end-users know you are there and working on their problems. If the problem detected is stated in vague terms, however, the interview can be used to clarify the problem. (Interviewing is discussed in more detail in Chapter 7.)

Observation. **Observation** is a powerful internal probe. Sit with the end-user and ask questions such as "Why are you doing this?" or "Where does this document go from here?" Such questions unravel systems mysteries.

Indirect (External) Probes

Systems analysts do not use internal probes to the exclusion of external probes, or vice versa. Internal probes gather a richer, truer group of facts, but they are expensive and intrusive. By contrast, external probes are quick and invisible to operating personnel. The sources of these probes are outside of the user community and hidden from it. But external probes are secondhand; the data collected is often not as directly relevant as that from internal probes.

A proper mix of internal and external probes differs depending on the stage of the systems development life cycle. Figure 5–2 shows that external probes dominate the earlier stages of the SDLC, whereas internal probes are the key to later stages. The initial investigation stage is almost entirely dependent on external probes because of time and cost constraints.

Four common external probes are procedure flow, document review, sampling, and tabular analysis.

Procedure Flow. Operational procedures are the vehicles by which new employees learn their jobs and experienced employees discover how to handle infrequent problems. If the **procedure flow** is not correct, information systems cannot be expected to operate without problems.

Use one of the structured tools described in Chapter 6 to trace the information flow that is described in operating procedures. When there are gaps in the procedures, gaps are likely to occur in actual operation.

Document Review. Collect critical documents for **document review.** For example, if the problem is a large backlog of customer orders, collect the original customer order source document, the document used for data entry, interactive screen formats, transaction detail and summary reports, and error reports. Documents are often the cause of problems. In addition, you gain user confidence by learning more about their operations.

FIGURE 5–2   Mix of Internal and External Investigative Probes at Different Stages of the SDLC

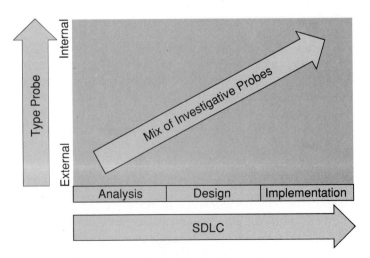

Chart the flow of documents between workstations, using a form like the one shown in Figure 5–3. By sorting collected data into different sequences, answer the following questions:

- Which workstations receive more information than they send (field 3 greater than field 2)? These workstations are often trouble spots that delay transaction throughput.
- Which workstations send more information than they receive (field 2 greater than field 3)? Such workstations are often in a position of inferior control. Fulfilling information requests for other departments gets in the way of information throughput.
- What are the major information backlogs (field 6)?
- What are the most unreliable workstations (field 7 divided by field 6)?
- What are the high-volume workstations (field 3)? There is a high probability that systems problems start in these workstations.
- Which workstations have the highest throughput variance (field 4 divided by field 3)? Variance in transaction arrival rates causes transaction backlogs.

Sampling. Another external probe is **sampling.** Suppose you need to determine what percentage of vendor billings the firm pays after the time allowed for payment discounts. The firm loses money for each discount not taken because of delayed payment.

You could get the information by consulting the thousands of daily transaction listings for customer payments. Or, instead, you can sample the data in the listing by (1) randomly selecting one day from the last week, (2) randomly selecting twenty pages from the daily transaction listing produced for that day, (3) selecting every fifth item from each page selected, (4) recording information for every fifth item, and (5) computing means and variances for this sample of all payment transactions.

Samples save time and, if you plan them correctly, produce results close to what you would get by reviewing the entire transaction population. Sources for more information on sampling are listed in the references and further readings at the end of this section.

Tabular Tools. Tabular tools, called matrices, are checklists for discovering discrepancies in transaction flow. A **matrix** is a graphic tool that has rows, columns, and cells. There is one cell for each combination of row and column.

FIGURE 5–3 Form to Chart Flow of Documents between Workstations	Field Number	Field Name	Field Position
	1	Document ID	1–4
	2	Sending Workstation	5–8
	3	Receiving Workstation	9–12
	4	Monthly Volume (Mean)	13–15
	5	Monthly Volume (Range)	16–17
	6	Processing Days (Mean)	18–19
	7	Processing Days (Range)	20–21

Record Fields	Output Reports				
	Order Detail	Backorder	Customer Service	Shipping Status	Salesperson Summary
Customer Number	✓	✓	✓	✓	
Order Date	✓				
Inventory Item Number	✓	✓			
Quantity Ordered	✓	✓	✓	✓	✓
Warehouse Location					
Shipping Code	✓			✓	
Substitute Code	✓	✓			
Backorder Code	✓		✓		

FIGURE 5–4   Input-to-Output Matrix for an Order Entry System

Figure 5–4 is a matrix relating fields on a customer order source document to output reports. The rows of the matrix include all the fields on the customer order. The columns include all documents and reports produced in the order entry TPS. Cells include check marks when the customer order field is included in a particular output. Even this simple matrix contains a wealth of clues. Look at the warehouse location field of the customer order (row 5). This field is not included on any of the documents or reports. Why do we need this field on the input document if it is not output? Look at the salesperson summary (column 6). Only one of the customer order input fields is included in this report. Where does the report gather the rest of its information?

Tabular techniques generate investigative questions rather than answers. Therefore, they are particularly important in the initial investigation stage of the SDLC. The following matrices are commonly used in this stage:

- *Input to file:* What files include which input?
- *File to output:* What reports and documents contain fields from which files?
- *Decision tables* (described in Chapter 6). What decisions do managers make for combinations of decision information? Figure 5–5 is an example of decision analysis using a decision table.

FIGURE 5–5   Decision Table for Evaluation of Input Fields

Input Field Also Found On	Condition			
	1	2	3	4
Record	Y	Y	N	N
Output	Y	N	Y	N
Critical Input Field	*			
Computes Other Field		*		
Copied from Input			*	

At this point in the investigation, data from both internal and external probes have been gathered. Now it's time to compare and combine the data using methods of synthesis.

Synthesis

Two **synthesis techniques** are available to tie things together. The first is the data flow diagram. Figure 5–6 is a DFD expanded to include monthly transaction volume (in parentheses) and workstation processing times (in brackets). This is an example of combining data gathered from both internal and external probes. The DFD is constructed during on-site observation. The volumes and times are gathered from an external review of records.

The second synthesis technique is comparing data gathered from internal and external probes. When data from the two sources are compared, discrepancies often appear. Review these three examples:

1. Maria charted information flow by on-site observation (internal probe). Then she charted flow using written procedures (external probe). She compared her two flowcharts and found they did not agree. When flowcharts do not agree, there are discrepancies between what *should be* done and what *is* done.
2. Steven interviewed a department head and noted her ideas about how managers use information in her department, what is wrong with the current information system, and what are the major problems facing the department. This is an external probe, since it was done away from the department's clerical activities. He then conducted an internal probe by asking the same questions of clerks in the work area. He compared the responses. Any discrepancies he found in the answers point to uncoordinated user efforts and communication problems between levels of the organization.
3. Kim asked users how often they used certain reports (internal probe). She compared their responses against the IS department's statistics on report request and distribution frequencies (external probe). The differences she found indicated user unsureness.

Problems with Technique-Oriented Investigation

The references and further readings at the end of this section expand on this chapter's discussion of investigative techniques. Whatever investigative techniques you choose to use, be aware of the important defects inherent in each:

- *Time:* Unless you confine these techniques to a narrow area of operations, you will need a lot of time to complete them.
- *Cost:* Considerable analyst resources and user time are involved.
- *History:* Business systems change rapidly. When you finally finish recording the problem area in detail, the system has changed. You have recorded the system's history, rather than its current state.

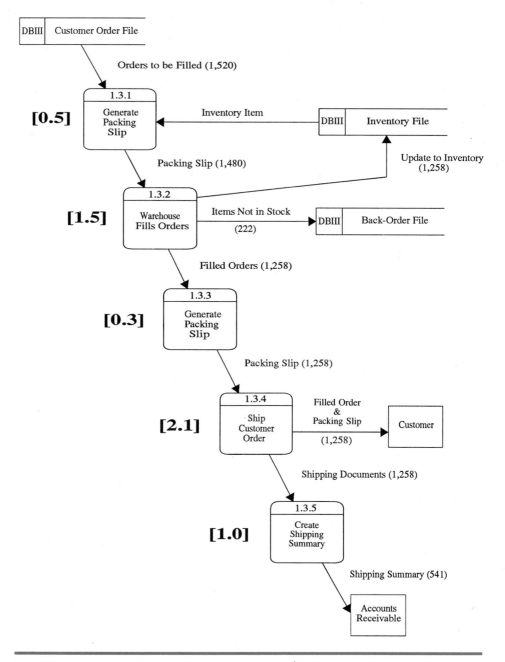

FIGURE 5–6   **Data Flow Diagram Expanded by Synthesis (Monthly transaction volume is shown in parentheses and workstation processing times are shown in brackets.)**

- *Interruption:* Whenever you directly investigate a user setting, you interrupt it. The longer the investigation, the more significant are the effects of your interruption.
- *Lack of communication:* Analysts are familiar with the structured, graphic forms of investigative techniques. These forms are often alien to the user community; they have little relationship to the clerical or management world.

Successful analysts recognize these defects. They adjust to them by first narrowing the problem area so that they can apply investigative techniques more quickly and less expensively.

FOCUSING THE INVESTIGATION

Sometimes information systems problems are narrow. If a manager does not like a specific report, the investigation of the problem is straightforward. Unfortunately, such well-focused problems are rare. More often, the reported problem is something like this: "Transactions are stacked up." There could be a thousand causes for a fuzzy problem such as this one.

Successful analysts narrow the search for a cause to the most probable sources. They quickly focus their investigations, following a logical rule: *Most problems occur in complex tasks that have high user impact.* Things go wrong more frequently in complex operations. In addition, users in high-impact areas are less tolerant of flaws in a system.

One helpful tactic for focusing the investigation uses a matrix of application complexity and user impact. The matrix includes complexity rows, user impact columns, and a cell-focusing tactic.

Application Complexity. Complexity can be gauged in several ways, including (1) number of different types of input transactions, (2) number of different types of output products, (3) number of lines of program code, (4) page length of system and program documentation, and (5) number of hours devoted to user training. Elements can be ranked in order of relative complexity for every task or application. A group of experienced analysts and programmers can assign the ranks.

User Impact. User impact for each application can be measured with indicators such as (1) the degree to which the application connects to other applications, (2) the costs of operating the system, (3) the visibility of systems outside the applications area, and (4) the speed required for managers to make decisions. A user group can rank all applications by their relative impact on clerical and management operations.

Focusing Tactic. The problem description established by measuring application complexity and user impact allows narrowing of the problem scope. Each task or application is plotted by the intersection of application complexity and user impact (Figure 5–7). System C is an inventory control system with a forecasting module. It is very complex in its logic and use of subprograms. In addition, it is critical to customer sales, and thus to profit. System E, on the other hand, is an annual report application that is not complex and has no impact on day-to-day operations.

FIGURE 5–7 **Narrowing Problem Scope by Plotting Application Complexity and User Input**

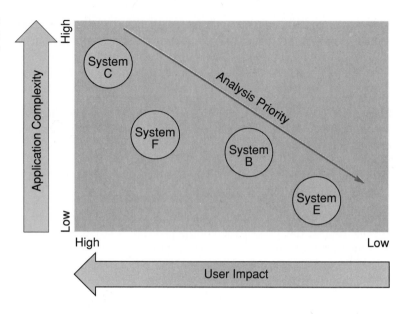

Detailed analysis then proceeds from top left to bottom right. Hence, in this example, analyze C, then F, then B, then E. Probabilities of finding problem sources are greatest for the applications that are attacked first—those that are complex and affect users.

INITIAL FEASIBILITY ANALYSIS

Project feasibility is defined as the degree to which a project is worth doing and possible to do. Eliason (1990) has identified six different aspects of feasibility with respect to an information systems project:

1. ***Economic feasibility:*** Will anticipated project costs be within management's expectations, capabilities, or both?
2. ***Technical feasibility:*** Is the technology available and suitable for this firm?

> The Alaska Court System wanted to replace its tape-oriented electronic courtroom reporting equipment with voice-activated, computer-driven recorders. That technology was still experimental and very costly. Hence, the court system's goals were technically infeasible.

3. ***Social feasibility:*** Will the new system be accepted by the people using the system? Implementing artificial intelligence systems in a setting where computers have yet to be introduced probably is a mistake because it is socially infeasible.
4. ***Management feasibility:*** Will the project be accepted and supported by management? For example, a firm characterized by considerable management infighting will present risks to new information systems implementation.

PROFILING THE INFORMATION SYSTEMS PROFESSIONAL

In the early days of computing, there was only one type of computer professional—the programmer. Programmers coded programs in assembler language, machine language, or a procedural language such as COBOL. They also wired plug boards, punched cards, and operated the computer. Since that time, however, the role of the computer professional has diversified dramatically.

The task of analysis was separated from that of programming early in the history of computing. Analysis requires conceptual skills, whereas coding requires a fairly strict and mechanical grasp of logic. Also, the various phases of the software development life cycle led to the separation of duties. Systems analysts, designers, programmers, test programmers, and maintenance programmers are all specifically performing some phase of the development life cycle. In addition, such tasks as operations, management, and technical support have been separated from the earlier orientation where the programmer was a jack-of-all-trades.

Specialists require specific and different skills to perform their jobs. Studies have determined that most systems professionals, regardless of specialization, have low needs for social interaction. Managers, on the other hand, are much more gregarious and skilled at interpersonal communication. Systems professionals who interact with managers to accomplish the system investigation phase for a new information system are often perceived by managers as antisocial and unresponsive.

In addition, systems professionals seem to have as much or more loyalty to their profession than to the organization for which they work. They may advocate courses of action that managers view as contrary to the best interests of the firm. A typical example is the desire to acquire the latest hardware and software even when there are no clear benefits to the firm from the acquisitions. The underlying motivation of the IS professionals may be concern for their careers rather than concern for organizational well-being.

This profile seems less than positive in many aspects. To ensure longevity in a firm, individual systems professionals should consider trying to combat the stereotypical image by enhancing interpersonal skills and proving loyalty to the organization whenever possible. The system professional's image can be enhanced by smooth interaction with end-users during the early stages of analysis.

---

5. *Legal feasibility:* Does the project infringe on federal, state, or local laws? A key concern in determining legal feasibility is whether the project violates individual privacy due to storage of sensitive personal information.
6. *Time feasibility:* Can the project be implemented within the proposed time frame? Projects with implementation periods exceeding one and a half to two years are likely to be rejected.

Determining project feasibility is a tricky business. You want to spot infeasible conditions early enough in the project so that you do not waste resources. At the same time, you don't always have sufficient information available early in the project to determine accurately whether or not the project is feasible. Therefore, feasibility analysis may be done at several points in the system development life cycle.

For simplicity, this book has two points of feasibility determination. *Initial feasibility analysis* is done during the initial investigation stage. Its purpose is to weed out those information projects that obviously have serious feasibility concerns.

The second feasibility point is during systems selection (Chapter 8), when much more detailed information is available to allow more refined feasibility analysis.

CURRENT SYSTEM DESCRIPTION

The systems cycle is driven by the definition of an information systems problem. An information systems problem is the difference between user expectations and current system performance. At the initial investigation stage of the SDLC, analysts have two means of viewing user expectations. First, there should be a document called the changeover contract, which was developed for the current system when it was implemented. This contract specifies how the information system is expected to perform on such dimensions such as speed, accuracy, and security. Second, changes in user expectations are documented in the future file. These two types of documentation allow analysts to determine what users expect from their information system.

Determining current system performance can be difficult if the firm does not have a formal quality measurement system. Unfortunately, firms tend not to update documentation of current systems. They view such update as being too time consuming. Therefore, the analyst should update the current system description while investigating system problems. An analogy is to a surgeon who inspects general body conditions while performing exploratory surgery. The updated system description is necessary for comparing current system conditions to the ideal.

The current system description includes the following specifications:

- Inputs
- Outputs
- Files
- Data elements
- Transaction and action document volume
- Costs
- Flow (data flow diagrams)

At this point, the investigative portion of the systems development life cycle is complete. If the systems analyst judges the problem to be within the correction capabilities of the current system, the SDLC is terminated. Otherwise, the SDLC continues with requirements analysis, the subject of the next chapter.

HUMAN ASPECTS

Throughout this book, information systems analysis has been compared to a doctor's examination of a patient or a policeman's investigation of a criminal complaint. Are you totally comfortable when a doctor examines you, even when you requested the appointment? Would you be perfectly calm if a police officer started asking you questions about an alleged crime? Of course not.

Your presence as a systems investigative analyst may be perceived in the same light as a doctor's probe or a police officer's investigation. Sometimes, there is not much you can do about that negative perception on the part of end-users. If you are aware of this human aspect, however, you probably will make greater efforts to relax your investigative subjects as much as possible. Be aware of the effects of your intrusive presence in the end-user world!

SUMMARY

An analyst is assigned to conduct an initial investigation of serious information systems problems. The problems can be current or projected major problems, or they can be minor problems that recur with some frequency. The purpose of the initial investigation is to determine whether or not to continue the SDLC.

A decision to proceed further in the development process is a serious commitment of IS department resources. Often, management borrows the resources required to design a new system from maintenance of current systems. Therefore, the initial investigation stage of the systems development life cycle is important to the IS department and the firm as a whole.

The problem structure discussed in Chapter 2 is the basis for the concepts underlying the initial investigation of an information system. A problem is the gap between the ideal and current information systems. Gaps reported in the earlier problem detection stage of the SDLC may not be real or solvable. The initial investigation stage determines the validity and feasibility of alleged problems.

In the initial investigation, systems analysts face several constraints: time, cost, analyst knowledge, organizational politics, and self-interference in the operations being observed. Analysts must be certain they are investigating the true situation, not one changed by their presence.

Systems analysts are also limited in the recommendations they can make: (1) take no action because the problem is not a valid one, (2) conduct systems maintenance for this minor problem, (3) improve user training, (4) include the problem in a future file for systems replacement, or (5) consider major modifications to the system. Modification may include complete replacement.

When conducting the initial investigation, adopt several tactics similar to those used by doctors and detectives:

- Listen; do not lecture.
- Do not pre-solve the problem.
- Compare stories.
- Look for reluctant responses.
- Probe for logical inconsistencies.
- Notice your effect on the setting.

- Expect hard, boring work.
- Avoid politics.

Combine these tactics with an array of investigative techniques that can be grouped into three categories: internal probes, external probes, and synthesis. Internal (direct) probes include questionnaires, interviews, and direct observations. External (indirect) probes allow investigation without disturbing the system's operation. External probes include procedure flow, document review, sampling, and tabular analysis. Synthesis techniques tie together results of internal and external probes.

Technique-oriented approaches have several problems: time to complete, cost, system change during investigation, interruption of the system while it's being measured, and formats not easily communicated to end-users.

Costs and time allotted to investigation are often depleted before technique-oriented fact finding is complete. Analysts need a method that focuses on probable sources of systems problems and presents the highest probability of quickly isolating the real problem. One such method describes systems applications in terms of a matrix of application complexity and user impact. Applications high in both dimensions (complexity and impact) are investigated first. Applications low in both dimensions are investigated last.

Analysts must determine the initial feasibility of designing a new information system. This feasibility has six dimensions: economic, technical, social, management, legal, and time.

Solving an information systems problem requires documenting the status of the current system. This documentation is called the current system description. While investigating information problems, analysts usually update the description of the current system. Hence, if a problem is serious, the analyst is ready to begin the next stage of the SDLC.

The current system description includes specifications of inputs, outputs, files, data elements, transaction and action document volume, costs, and data flow diagrams. If the problem can be handled within the current system, the current system description has been updated and the SDLC is halted. Otherwise, the SDLC proceeds to the requirements analysis stage.

CONCEPTS LEARNED

- Why initial investigation is important
- The problem structure as the framework for analysis of information systems problems
- Investigative constraints
- Concept of analyst interference
- Investigative recommendations
- Investigative tactics
- Direct (internal) probe techniques

- Indirect (external) probe techniques
- Synthesis techniques
- Problems with technique-oriented investigation
- A method for focusing the investigation
- Initial feasibility concerns
- Reason for and components of the current system description

KEY TERMS

document review
economic feasibility
external probe
internal probe
interview
legal feasibility
management feasibility
matrix
observation

procedure flow
project feasibility
questionnaire
sampling
social feasibility
synthesis techniques
technical feasibility
time feasibility

REVIEW QUESTIONS

1. Why may detected problems not be real or solvable?

2. Why is the initial investigation so important to the information systems department?

3. Describe five factors that constrain investigation of information systems problems.

4. Explain how investigation of a problem may change things.

5. List possible recommendations resulting from the initial investigation.

6. Describe eight investigative tactics that systems analysts might use.

7. What are differences between internal and external probes?

8. Discuss the relative advantages and disadvantages of questionnaires and interviews.

9. Describe how procedure flow operates.

10. Why is sampling important?

11. Describe the three tabular techniques commonly used in the initial investigation.

12. How can you compare data gathered from internal and external probes?

13. What defects are associated with technique-oriented investigation?

14. How do systems analysts gauge application complexity?

15. How is user impact measured?

16. Describe how complexity and impact are combined to focus an investigation.

17. Describe the six types of project feasibility.

18. Why is it difficult to determine project feasibility?

19. Why is a current system description necessary?

20. List the contents of the current system description.

CRITICAL THINKING OPPORTUNITIES

1. Draw a diagram of the organization of this chapter.

2. Compare and contrast interviews with questionnaires.

3. Perform the experiment described in the box "Measurement Experiment." Describe your results.

4. Describe the internal and external probes you would use to investigate a library information system. Include name of probe, how applied, frequency of application, and unit of measurement.

5. Describe how you would use sampling to investigate an alleged information systems problem of late reports.

OBJECTIVES

In this chapter you will learn about:

WHAT: (Concepts) Use of structured development tools.

WHY: Structured development tools allow the analyst systematically to define
            the existing and proposed information system starting from the conceptual
            level down to the detailed, programmable level.

WHEN: Through all stages of system implementation, but especially the analysis
            portion.

WHO: Systems analyst in conjunction with end-user.

WHERE: Charting is done in the analysts' office after fact-gathering in the end-user
            work area.

HOW: (Techniques) Hierarchy chart
                         Data flow diagram
                         HIPO charts
                         System flowcharts

OUTLINE

- Setting
- History of Development Tools
- Structured Development
- Hierarchy Chart
- Data Flow Diagram
- HIPO Charts
- System Flowcharts
- Which Tool Should I Use?

STRUCTURED DEVELOPMENT TOOLS

Irrationality is usually in the mind of the beholder, not in the mind of the beheld.

— RUSSELL ACKOFF, 1978

SETTING

Ours is a tool-oriented profession. We fill our toolboxes with a wide variety of systems development tools. Some of these tools are simple, others complex. Some of these tools are commonly used; others are not. Some of these tools have been around for a long time; others are new to business information systems development.

    James Martin (1987) suggests that the following development tools are part of basic literacy for systems analysts:

- Decomposition diagrams
- Dependency diagrams
- Data flow diagrams
- Action diagrams (a replacement for structure charts)
- Data analysis diagrams
- Data structure diagrams
- Entity relationship diagrams
- Data navigation diagrams
- Decision trees and tables
- State transition diagrams
- Dialogue design diagrams

Many surveys have shown that most business firms use only a small subset of development tools from this impressive list. It is the subset that is included in this book. This chapter contains four development tools most commonly used in the systems analysis portion of the SDLC: (1) the hierarchy chart, (2) the data flow diagram, (3) the HIPO chart, and (4) the system flowchart.

HISTORY OF DEVELOPMENT TOOLS

Traditional Approach

Early systems development included a long, narrative, technical specification document as a product of the systems specification phase. The user was expected to read this document, make any necessary changes, and then sign off. Most users did not have the time, capability, or desire to read such a document and would simply sign off without understanding how the systems specifications had been defined. Other users would try to read the document and then spend hours trying to understand and adjust the system. Neither approach was effective.

Because user understanding of the proposed system was inaccurate or partial, the resulting system was frequently far from what the user wanted or expected. The incorrect system was then subjected to many undocumented alterations, which led to difficulty in maintaining the system. Indeed, many systems never made it into production because of grossly incorrect specifications.

Structured Approach

Systems became more complex. They required thousands of lines of code, dozens of programmers to produce the code, and input from several different end-users. Communication problems compounded. Maintenance of complex systems consumed 50 to 85 percent of the total cost of the system. By the 1970s, many graphic-oriented tools became available to combat problems associated with these earlier approaches.

Introduction of these tools has been called the **structured revolution.** The first structured tools were oriented toward programming. Other systems-oriented tools appeared later to complement them. The goals of structured tools are to allow a **top-down approach** to systems development, enhance communication, and simplify the maintenance process. In the top-down approach, the system is defined first at a general, overview level. Then it undergoes successive refinement until the bottom, primitive-level functions are clearly defined. **Primitive level** is the point where specifications can be translated on a one-per-one basis to lines of programming code. Thus, a system is decomposed into small, loosely coupled program modules that perform simple, understandable tasks. These modules should be as independent as possible so that maintenance programmers can make changes to a single simple module and not have to worry about creating errors in other modules.

Radical Top-Down Approach

At first, the introduction of structured tools did little to alter the sequence of phases followed in the traditional SDLC. The phases of the life cycle were still adhered to in a sequential fashion: A later phase would not be entered until the previous phase had been completed. For example, once the systems analysis phase had been completed, then and only then could the systems design phase begin. The full system would then be designed from the top down to the lowest level modules. The next step would be coding the full system, which would then be tested. Finally, implementation and maintenance would occur.

Introduction of top-down, successive refinement of the system allowed a different approach to the SDLC. The initial phases of the SDLC still had to be completed in a sequential fashion. Once the systems analysis phase was finished, however, it was possible to begin an iterative cycling through the next phases. The top level (executive module) could be designed, coded, tested, and implemented without developing the full system. Then the next level could go through the cycle, and so on until the entire system was completed.

This **radical top-down approach** allowed for partial development of the system. Lower level (detail) modules with high priority could be selected for early completion; the lower priority modules could be completed at a later time. So a *portion* of the system can be functional before the total system is developed. This approach includes "stubbing out" any module that is not yet functional. A **program stub** is an incomplete program that merely passes control back to the call module. Usually some kind of message is flashed on the screen or printer to show that the program is not yet functional. For example, suppose a menu selection of "print paychecks" is called but is not fully functional. Control passes to the printer, which prints a message reading, "This module is not yet completed." Control then is passed back to the call program. Thus, interfaces are tested without requiring full functionality of the *entire* system.

The radical top-down approach allows delivery of a partial, not yet fully functional, system to the user group. As time allows, the less important modules can be added. For example, all the routine payroll modules in a payroll system could be functional, but the less critical modules (e.g., reports) may be added later. A partial, well-tested system, delivered on time to the user, is usually preferable to no delivery due to incompleteness.

Prototyping as an Alternative

As time passed, sophisticated, fourth-generation languages were introduced to the systems development environment. The 4GLs allow rapid code generation on the computer as opposed to hand coding in a third-generation language like COBOL. Screens, reports, and menus (the system–user interfaces) can be altered quickly based on user input. Fourth-generation languages also allow a prototype, or model, of the final system to be built as a communication tool. The IS professional and the end-user sit down together and focus on a hands-on version of the final system. Instead of reading narrative text about the proposed system or studying a series of layout charts, the end-user sees a mockup of the interfaces of the actual system on the user's workstation. Necessary changes can be identified, made, and refined until both the IS professional and the end-user are satisfied with the interfaces.

Prototyping has become very popular. Many organizations have taken advantage of powerful prototyping tools. Newest releases of CASE software combine automated design tools with prototyping tools, forming an integrated package that allows systems development to proceed in a more rapid fashion. The rapidity with which changes can be made and the enhanced communication between IS professionals and end-users has lead to the delivery of correct systems in a timely manner. We discuss prototyping and CASE in more detail in chapters 21 and 22.

STRUCTURED DEVELOPMENT

During the past several years, there have been moderately successful attempts to make systems development less artistic and more engineering oriented. Such attempts are called structured development. **Structured development** refers to the systematic and integrated use of tools and techniques to aid the analysis and design of information systems.

Structured methodologies use one or more tools to define information flow and processes. Definition is from top to bottom in increasing levels of detail. Major flows and processes are identified and then exploded into subprocesses, which are exploded into even further detail. Ideally, this process continues to the primitive level, where programming begins directly from the exploded diagram.

Now, let's look at structured development in the following sequence: (1) benefits of structured development, (2) four commonly used approaches, (3) basic terms, (4) a typical structured development sequence, (5) use of CASE, and (6) problems with structured development approaches.

Benefits of Structured Development

Structured development provides a concise but complete, nonredundant systems specification that is developed in a logical, replicable sequence.

Structured development provides five benefits over traditional approaches:

1. *Reduction of complexity:* The top-down, explosion approach partitions large problems into smaller ones. Individuals or development teams can handle these smaller problems more easily.
2. *Focus on ideal:* Structured methodologies allow designers first to develop an ideal (logical) model of the information system without the constraints of physical considerations such as mainframe, printers, workstations, and so on. After they develop the ideal model, they then add physical realities.
3. *Standardization:* Standard definitions, tools, and approaches allow designers to work both separately and concurrently on various subsystems without jeopardizing integration of the separate parts later in the project.

4. *Future orientation:* The focus on a complete systems specification allows changes to be made easily once the new system is operational.
5. *Less reliance on artistry:* Artists never build bridges. Engineers do. Structured development imposes engineering principles and discipline on a development task too often dominated by artistic design.

Commonly Used Approaches

The four commonly used approaches to structured development are known by the names of their developers:

Gane and Sarson. The **Gane and Sarson approach** uses the data flow diagram and includes (1) data dictionaries with precise definitions for each data element; (2) process descriptions using structured English, decision trees, or decision tables; and (3) file layouts to describe data stores.

Warnier and Orr. The **Warnier and Orr approach** also uses a hierarchical approach. However, the Warnier/Orr diagram is read from left to right rather than from top to bottom (Figure 6–1). The approach starts with the desired output and works backward to the required input.

Yourdon and DeMarco. The **Yourdon and DeMarco approach** is similar to the Gane and Sarson methodology, although there are some differences in DFD symbols. The

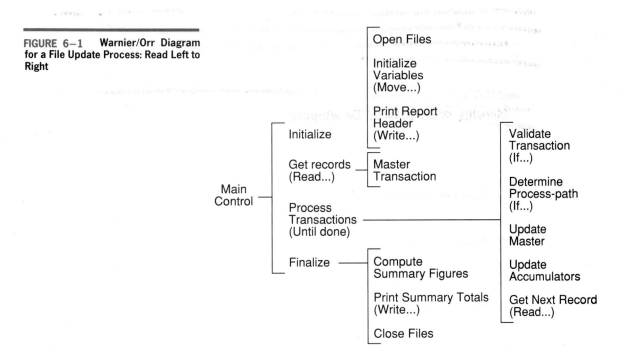

FIGURE 6–1   Warnier/Orr Diagram for a File Update Process: Read Left to Right

Yourdon and DeMarco approach adds tools to bridge the gap between the DFD and computer programming. Recent enhancements of this approach introduce state transition diagrams for modeling time-dependent systems (Figure 6–2).

Jackson. The **Jackson approach** uses a version of the hierarchy chart. The legs of the chart are expanded further and further until the level of detail is enough to begin programming.

All four of these structured approaches share the same basic terms.

Structured Terms

Data and information can be described in different manners. **Physical data** consist of the resources you can see and count—for example, insurance policies, vendors, and finished goods. Physical data are represented by data stores in data flow diagrams, entities in data modeling, and files and records in conventional file design.

Informational data (logical data) consist of the values, characteristics, and labels associated with physical data. For example, insurance policies have premiums, vendors have addresses, and finished goods have warehouse locations. Informational data are represented by data flows in data flow diagrams, attributes in modeling, and record fields in traditional file design.

Data elements form the lowest level of information on which a process can act. Examples of data elements (record fields) are product-number, unit-price, and zip code. **Group data** are collections of data elements; another term is **data structure. Data stores** (files) are groupings of data structures held temporarily until needed.

Data flows (forms and reports) consist of the data input and output to system processes that manipulate data. **Process specifications** are definitions of how processes work.

The **data dictionary** is the document containing definitions of all system data. The dictionary includes data elements, data structures, data stores, data flows, and process specifications.

Figure 6–3 shows the relationships of these structured terms.

Structured Development Sequence

Designers implement the structured development approach in the following stages:

1. Development of physical data flow diagram for current system (initial investigation)
2. Translation to logical DFD for the current system (requirements analysis)
3. Redesign to logical DFD of proposed system (logical design)
4. Amplification to physical DFD of proposed system (physical design)

At each of these stages, explosion, or decomposition, occurs. Case 6.1 will take you through this entire process for Mega Video, a video rental firm.

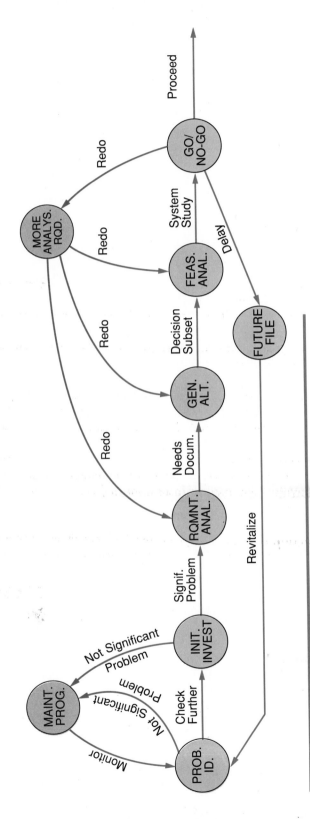

FIGURE 6–2   State Transition Diagram for Analysis Phase of Systems Development Life Cycle

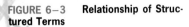

FIGURE 6–3   **Relationship of Structured Terms**

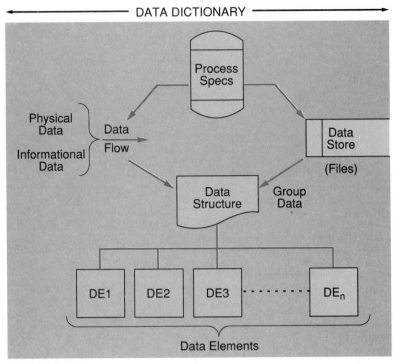

Problems with Structured Methodologies

The shortcomings of structured methodologies are discussed in this section.

Tool Orientation. The method of Gane and Sarson was the first widely accepted structured design approach. These authors tried to deliver a methodology that was simple and easy for users to understand. Nevertheless, their methodology includes a large set of complex tools. Other methodologies have added tools such as transform analysis and state transition diagrams. The abundance of structured tools is beyond the understanding of most end-users and even many analysts.

Lack of Breadth. These technique-driven methodologies do not cover the entire systems development life cycle (Figure 6–4). They do not address all of the systems analysis phase. In the implementation phase, they address only the programming portion.

Illusion of Automatic Design. The designers of structured methodologies did not intend their approaches to be self-inclusive. They did not want to exclude analyst judgment, intuition, or inspiration. Yet, presentation of these methodologies often leaves the

SDLC Phases	Structured Development Methodology			
	Gane & Sarson	Yourdon & DeMarco	Jackson	Warnier & Orr
1. Problem Detection				
2. Initial Investigation				
3. Requirements Analysis	•	•	•	•
4. Generation of Systems Alternatives				
5. Selection of Proper System				
6. Output Design				
7. Input Design				
8. File Design	•	•	•	•
9. Programming and Testing		•		
10. Training and Other Preparations				
11. Systems Changeover				

*Specific structured tool available

FIGURE 6–4   **Coverage of Structured Development Tools across the Systems Development Life Cycle**

mistaken impression that systems development is an automatic process with little room for human intellect. This is simply not the case. The human designer and the human user are the most potent parts of the development equation.

Despite these problems, structured tools are commonly in use in business information system development. For the remainder of this chapter, we will explore those structured development tools most applicable to the analysis phase of the SDLC.

HIERARCHY CHART

A **hierarchy chart** is a graphic tool that identifies all the tasks or processes in a system and also groups them into various hierarchical levels. The hierarchy chart is organized in a treelike manner, with a one-to-many relationship between the upper and lower levels of the chart. Each node in the chart has a single **parent node** and may have zero or more **children nodes.** All **sibling nodes** (children at the same chart level) have the same amount of detail. The bottommost nodes are called functional primitives. These nodes will eventually be translated into program code, which performs the work of a system. Any module or task directly above the **functional primitive** level is a **control module** and will serve to drive or call the functional primitives. Figure 6–5 is a generic hierarchy chart that includes tasks that could be performed by almost any system. The topmost process in the hierarchy chart is, by definition, a single process. It ties together the whole system. In a menu-driven system, this process (or node) is the main menu.

The following scenario describes a rental-processing system for an apartment complex. The scenario will be used throughout this chapter to illustrate various tools as they are presented.

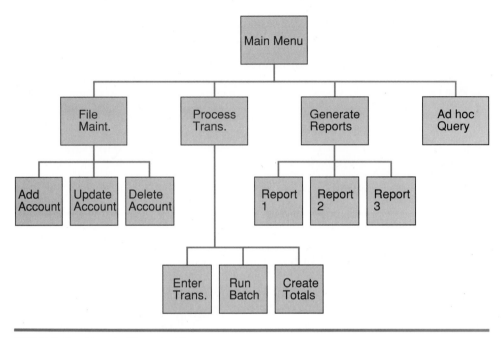

FIGURE 6—5   Generic Hierarchy Chart

Colonial Heights Apartment Rental System

The Colonial Heights apartment complex uses the following system for processing security deposits and rental payments:

When a tenant signs a lease and pays a security deposit, the manager creates a data sheet on the tenant that includes name, apartment number, phone number, permanent address (if other than the new apartment), amount of rent, amount of security deposit, move-in date, length of lease, pet deposit (if any), and person to notify in case of an emergency. The manager sends this form to the data-processing (DP) department to be entered via terminal into the accounts receivable (A/R) file. The manager also gives a receipt and a copy of the lease to the tenant.

A card is created with the tenant's name, apartment number, amount due, and amount paid from the A/R file and sent back to the manager. The manager then attaches the security deposit check to the card.

This card and check are sent to the A/R department, where daily deposits are batched and the checks are deposited into the proper bank account. The cards that came with the checks are sorted by name alphabetically and become data entry for a card reader. The cards are read, a daily cash report is generated, and the A/R file is updated. At the end of the month, new cards are generated for each tenant. As the tenants pay the rent due, a card is pulled for each tenant and attached to the check or money order payment. The same procedure (from ** to **) is followed for the rent payment as the security deposit.

On the tenth day of the month, a delinquent list is generated by the A/R department from the A/R file. The list includes all tenants who have some balance due on their account. The manager sends a notice to each delinquent tenant along with an overdue charge.

In order to construct a hierarchy chart for Colonial Heights, the first step is to list all the processes that occur in the order that they occur:

1. Sign lease.
2. Create data sheet.
3. Send form to DP.
4. Enter data to create tenant file.
5. Create card.
6. Send card to manager.
7. Attach card to check and send to A/R.
8. Batch cards and checks.
9. Deposit checks in bank.
10. Pull cards and sort.
11. Read cards.
12. Generate daily cash report.
13. Update A/R file.
14. Generate new cards for all tenants.
15. Repeat steps 6 through 13 for rent processing.
16. Generate delinquent list.
17. Generate notices and overdue charges.
18. Notify tenants.

All these processes are at the primitive level. An upper tree structure needs to be built to tie these functional primitives together. Thus, the next step is to group these primitive processes into functionally related groups. The first four processes can be grouped as new tenant processing. The next eleven processes encompass collection processing (both security deposit processing and rental payment processing). The last three processes are related to delinquent accounts processing.

The hierarchy chart begins with a single rectangle at the top level. In this example, it is named Colonial Heights and is numbered as level 0, consistent with the Gane and Sarson (1982) methodology. The next hierarchy level contains the grouping to which the functional primitives new tenant processing, collection processing, and delinquent accounts processing were assigned. The third level contains some functional primitives. Because collection processing includes both security deposit processing and rental payment processing, it requires a fourth level to reach other functional primitives. See Figure 6–6 for the resultant hierarchy chart. The hierarchy chart is useful as a base for building data flow diagrams.

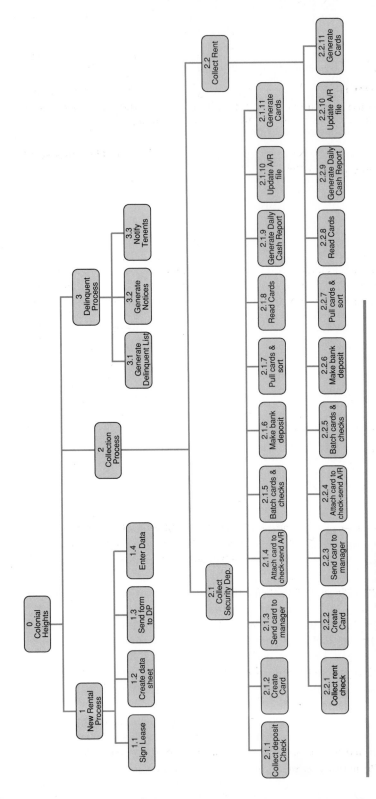

FIGURE 6–6   Hierarchy Chart for Colonial Heights

DATA FLOW DIAGRAM

Data flow diagrams (DFDs) are a graphic representation of the flow of data through a system. They can be physical data flow diagrams, in which case the physical locations and details are reflected in the diagram, or they can be logical only.

Data flow diagrams are useful for communication between analysts and users because they contain only four symbols, which are easy to understand. The purpose of DFDs is to track the flow of data through an *entire* system. Data and processes are critical to the understanding of a system.

DFD Components (Gane and Sarson Methodology)

External Entities. **External entities** are people or groups of people who interact with the current system but are not internal to the system. External entities are also called **sources** or **sinks,** depending on whether the entity generates or receives data. An example of an external entity in an order entry system would be customers. An example of an external entity in an inventory system would be suppliers. Sometimes external entities can be members of the business organization but still external to the specific system (for example, an indirect manager who receives a report). Often, it is difficult to determine whether an entity is external or internal. The key question is: Does this person or group of people perform the processes that are part of this system on which I am concentrating? If the answer is no, that entity is external.

The symbol for an external entity is a square (Figure 6–7). The most common convention for identifying the external entity is to place a unique, lower-case alphabetic character in the upper-left-hand corner of the square. Then the entity is given a single, descriptive noun as a name. The first identified or drawn entity would be a, the second b, and so forth.

Processes. **Processes** are actions performed on data flowing through the system; they may be simple or complex. An example of a simple process is recording an order on an order form. An example of a complex process is screening an order for customer credit, item availability, and so on.

The symbol for a process is a rounded rectangle (see Figure 6–7), although some methodologies use a circle (Yourdon, 1988). It is easier to find a rectangle in existing templates. It is also easier to write information in a rectangle than in a circle. Each process is identified by a number corresponding to the level of the process on the hierarchy chart.

Each process is named with a simple verb–object pair. Examples of process names are screen customer-order and record customer-order. In a physical DFD, the actual location or computer program in which a process occurs is identified on the bottom of the process; in a logical DFD, physical location is not referenced.

Data Stores. A **data store** is a repository for data. In a physical DFD, a data store could be as simple as an in/out box or as complex as a database.

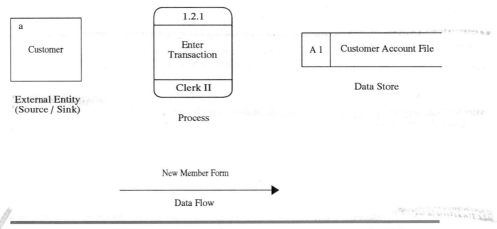

FIGURE 6–7 **Data Flow Diagram Symbols**

The symbol for a data store is an open-ended rectangle (see Figure 6–7). The open end is on the right side. The name of the store should be descriptive. If the store is a manual file such as a file cabinet or an in/out box, it should be labeled so. Data stores are identified by a unique combination of an upper-case alphabetic character and a digit. Each data store in a system has the same upper-case alphabetic character used with different digits. The first drawn or identified store would be identified as A1, the second as A2, and so on.

Data Flows. A **data flow** represents the movement of data through a system. Frequently, data move through a system as a form or report. Data flows are very important to DFDs (as the name suggests). Data move out of sources (external entities), between processes, into and out of data stores, and into sinks (external entities).

The symbol for a data flow is a solid line with an arrowhead showing flow direction (see Figure 6–7). Each data flow must be identified with a descriptive name. If the data are flowing on a form, all the data are flowing as a **data packet.** The name of the flow is placed above the flow line. Flow lines are not identified with specific numbers or characters.

DFD Levels

One feature of the DFD is that it fits nicely into the top-down approach to systems analysis and design. The first DFD that is drawn is the context-level DFD, which lays out the sources and sinks and a single process with a generic name representing the entire system. Then a first-level **explosion** is formed by expanding the single high-level process into multiple processes.

One mental model that may help you understand the relationship between the different levels is a menu-driven system. The top-level node is analogous to the main menu. The first-level explosion contains all the options of the main menu. In a payroll system, these options may be: Manage files, compute pay, generate paychecks, generate reports. None of the nodes at this level is functional. Selecting any of these menu options will result in a submenu with more options. For example, selecting file management as an option may result in the following choices: Add a record, delete a record, edit a record. Choosing any of these options will actually get you into a detail level where the work is done. Each successive level of a DFD is a stepwise refinement that allows more and more detail to be determined and illustrated. The lowest level DFDs are called functional primitives. At this level, the processes perform the actual (programmed) functions of the system. A leveled set of DFDs has a one-to-one correspondence with the levels on the hierarchy chart. Figure 6–8 illustrates a leveled set of

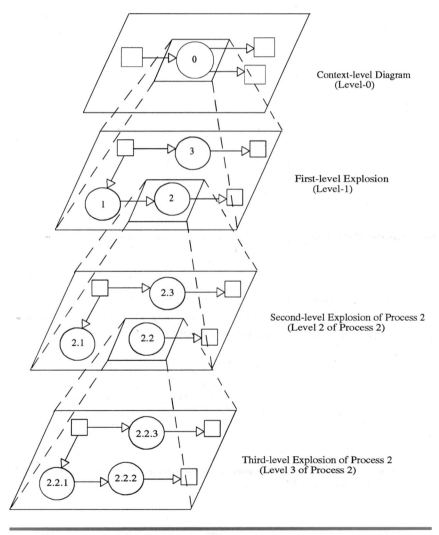

Context-level Diagram
(Level-0)

First-level Explosion
(Level-1)

Second-level Explosion of Process 2
(Level 2 of Process 2)

Third-level Explosion of Process 2
(Level 3 of Process 2)

FIGURE 6–8   Leveled Sets of DFDs (Other diagrams for each process exist but are not illustrated here.)

DFDs and how each diagram is related to the others in the set. Several general guidelines are important for constructing DFDs:

1. Draw a hierarchy chart to determine the levels of the DFDs.
2. List all the processes that occur in a system.
3. For each process, identify data that flows into and out of it and the source of that data.
4. Group the processes in the sequence shown in the hierarchy chart.
5. Identify data that must be retained by the system (stores).
6. Draw the leveled set of diagrams beginning at the context level and working down the hierarchy chart from general to specific or context to primitive. Each DFD should be drawn from left to right. The sources should be drawn on the left and the sinks on the right. When a source is also a sink, repeat the entity on the right rather than draw a flow line that returns to the source. In other words, all data should flow from left to right. Remember that the DFD is not sequential and that processes can occur either simultaneously or in parallel. They do not have to follow one after the other unless the output from one process is needed as input to another process.
7. Make your first attempt at drawing a set of DFDs freehand. It is more important to get all the components into the DFDs accurately than to make them look attractive.
8. Once you have constructed a rough draft of the DFDs, walk through them with a user or a colleague to ensure that they are comprehensive and comprehensible. Make corrections as you go.
9. Use a template or a computerized tool to render the next draft.
10. Keep refining the diagrams until they are correct, legible, and usable.

To illustrate the construction of a leveled set of physical DFDs, let's refer to the Colonial Heights example. The hierarchy chart constructed earlier contains three primitive-level branches related to (1) new tenant processing, (2) collection processing, and (3) delinquent accounts processing. Siblings (nodes at the same level with the same parent) make up one DFD. As you inspect the hierarchy chart, note the six separate sets of siblings plus the 0, or context-level, node. Figure 6–9 contains circles around each sibling set and around the context level. Therefore, there will be seven separate DFDs.

To construct the leveled set of DFDs, begin at the top level and work down. The first DFD, the context-level DFD, is fairly simple to construct. The only process is the generic Colonial Heights rental system process. Add sources and sinks (external entities). The primary external entity is the tenant. The other external entities in this system are the bank, the external manager, and the tenant. The tenant is both a source of data (information and payment) and a data sink (receipt and delinquent notice). Figure 6–10 is the context-level DFD for Colonial Heights.

The next step is to create the first-level DFD from the context-level DFD, then the second-level DFD, and so on. Explosion of this context-level DFD occurs in the following sequence:

1. Figure 6–11 creates the three main processes from the second level of the hierarchy chart (labeled as the circled 2 in Figure 6–10).

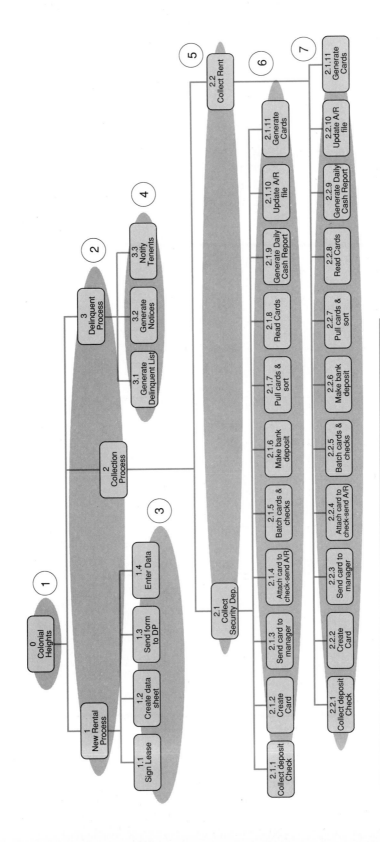

FIGURE 6–9   Hierarchy Chart for Colonial Heights Indicating Seven DFDs

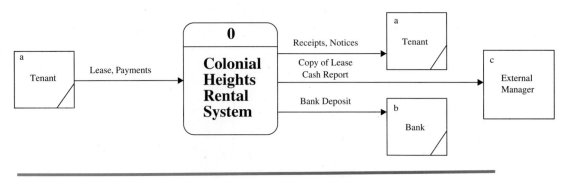

FIGURE 6–10   Context-level DFO (Level 0) for Colonial Heights

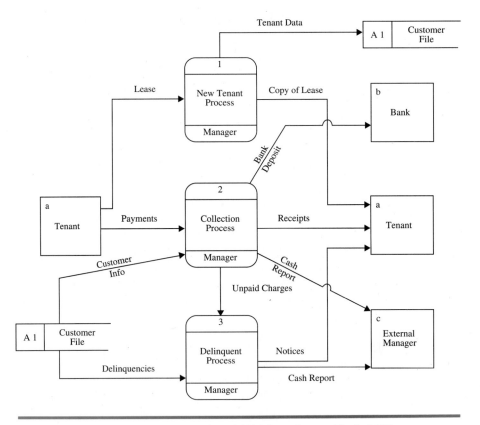

FIGURE 6–11   First-level Explosion for Colonial Heights—Current Physical DFD

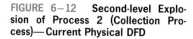

FIGURE 6–12   Second-level Explosion of Process 2 (Collection Process)—Current Physical DFD

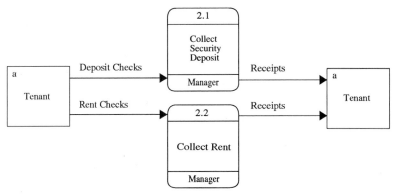

FIGURE 6–12   Second-level Explosion of Process 2 (Collection Process)—Current Physical DFD

2. Figure 6–12 is an explosion of process 2, collection process, of Figure 6–11 (labeled as the circled 5 in Figure 6–10).
3. Figure 6–13 explodes further process 2.1 of Figure 6–12 (equivalent to the level labeled 6 in the hierarchy chart of Figure 6–10).

Figures 6–11 through 6–13 represent only three of the seven DFDs required to level (explode) the Colonial Heights Rental System according to the Hierarchy chart of Figure 6–9. The other DFDs are not included in this explanation.

Physical DFDs

The diagrams used to illustrate the construction of the leveled set of DFDs for Colonial Heights are current physical DFDs. They include physical attributes such as the location where a process occurs, the person who performs the process, the device used to perform the process, and routing details. Physical DFD's contain not only *what* processes are in the system, but also *how* the processes operate.

Data stores may also contain physical details. For example, an in/out box, a file cabinet, or an accounts receivable master file is a physically specific detail about a store rather than what is logically contained in the store. Flows may consist of particular printed forms, documents, and reports.

Physical DFDs are important tools that allow us to understand how the current system works; this is usually a first step in the analysis process. However, physical details can be restrictive in the design process. Thinking about possibilities of new design is more important than being tied to physical details. The first step in becoming free of physical constraints is to derive the logical equivalent of the current physical set of DFDs.

Logical DFDs

When a new system is going to be designed, users will describe the current system in terms of its physical implementation (who performs a task, what forms flow through

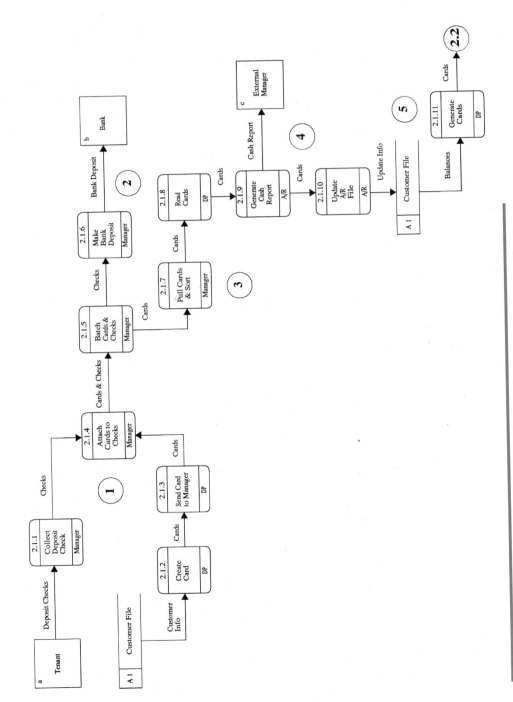

FIGURE 6–13 Third-level (Primitive) Explosion of Process 2.1 (Collect Security Deposit)—Current Physical DFD (Note circled numbers for comparison with Figure 6–14.)

the system, when the processing occurs, and where the processing takes place). It is easier for them to describe these physical details than to give an abstract equivalent. However, these physical details are limiting. It is important for system designers to develop a new system that solves the problems of the old system.

To begin the design process, designers need to derive the logical equivalent of the current physical diagram, which strips away the *how* from the physical DFD. In forming logical DFDs, designers follow these steps:

1. Identify the actual data that a process needs rather than the forms or documents that carry the data.
2. Remove any routing information and processes that do not alter the data. Routing does not change the data; it merely moves the data from place to place. It is especially important to remove implementation-specific processes (e.g., read cards, sort cards, scan tags).
3. Remove any reference to physical devices or programs.
4. Remove any control information.
5. Look for redundant data stores and consolidate them.

A logical DFD contains only the minimal data that flow through the system, independent of any devices, persons, forms, or specific physical implementations. In other words, logical DFDs are implementation free—the *what* of the system.

When naming data flows, processes, and stores in a logical DFD, it is important to eliminate any references to physical implementation. A data flow named "form 900b" should be changed to reflect the nature of the form and even to eliminate any reference to forms. "Work request" is a better label for this form than "form 900b" or even "work request form."

Figure 6–14 is a logical DFD derived from the physical DFD of Figure 6–13. Compare Figures 6–13 and 6–14 to see how a physical DFD is transformed to a logical DFD. The numbers in circles on the figures are to be used for the following comparisons:

1. Note that processes 2.1.1, 2.1.2, and 2.1.3 on Figure 6–13 do not appear on Figure 6–14. These are physical processes that do not belong on a logical DFD.
2. On Figure 6–13, the processes have a bottom entry indicating who does the process. These are implementation-oriented entries that do not belong on the logical DFD of Figure 6–14.
3. Processes 2.1.5 and 2.1.7 on Figure 6–13 do not appear on Figure 6–14. These are automated operations that merely rearrange data. Batching and sorting are specific to the current method of data processing; they do not belong on a logical DFD.
4. Process 2.1.9 in Figure 6–13 has an output data flow labeled "cards." This is changed in Figure 6–14 (renumbered process 2.1.3) to a more generic, less implementation-oriented label: "deposit info."
5. Process 2.1.11 in Figure 6–13 does not appear in Figure 6–14 since it is implementation oriented. It applies to how things are currently done, rather than what is done.

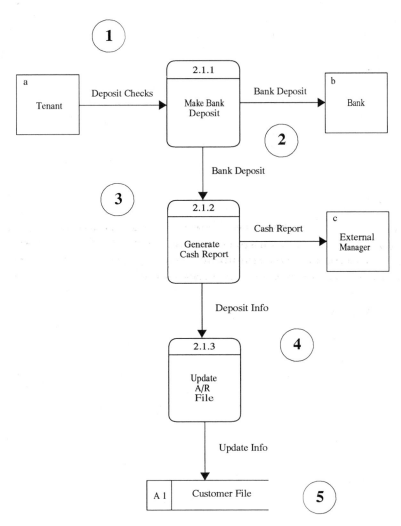

This conversion from physical to logical would be done for all seven DFDs emanating from the hierarchy chart of Figure 6–6. Case 6.1 takes you through an entire DFD leveling process for Mega Video.

HIPO CHARTS

The two tools just described are tools associated with structured analysis and design. The next two tools predate the "structured revolution." They are traditional tools still used by many business firms that do not yet use structured design methodologies. It is interesting to note, however, that both HIPO charts and system flow charts emanate naturally from the hierarchy chart.

Most programmers are familiar with the IBM flowchart template, which includes symbols required for both systems flowcharts and **HIPO charts.** All processes have inputs and outputs. The HIPO system uses this commonality to lay out the requirements for an information system using two distinct means. The first is the hierarchy chart just discussed (Figure 6–6). The second is the **input-process-output (IPO) chart,** which delineates the input files and output files or reports associated with processes. The level of detail is quite general, so the IPO is not particularly useful for conveying primitive-level logic to the programmer. It does, however, give an overview of the system. It also shows how individual processes relate to each other and to data files.

The IPO chart has three distinct rectangles (Figure 6–15) containing inputs (leftmost), processes (middle), and outputs (rightmost). In the middle rectangle, processes are listed in the order of the hierarchy chart. Numbers in the hierarchy chart correspond to numbered processes. Input files are connected to appropriate processes by large vector-like arrows. When two or more arrows flow from one file into two or more processes, it is called a **dispersion flow.** When one process receives input from two or more input files, it is a **confluence flow.** When files are output from one process and input into another process, it is a **feedback flow** (designated by a return arrow).

Follow these steps when creating HIPO charts:

1. Create the hierarchy chart. Do not go into too much detail. The hierarchy chart should be no more than three levels deep, including the root (top) node.
2. Begin at the highest level of abstraction—one level below the root (uppermost) process.
3. Identify basic inputs and outputs associated with the system.
4. Identify major processes that transform inputs into outputs. Associate which inputs and outputs belong with which processes.

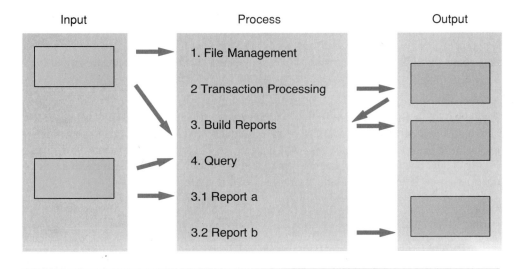

FIGURE 6–15   **Generic IPO Chart**

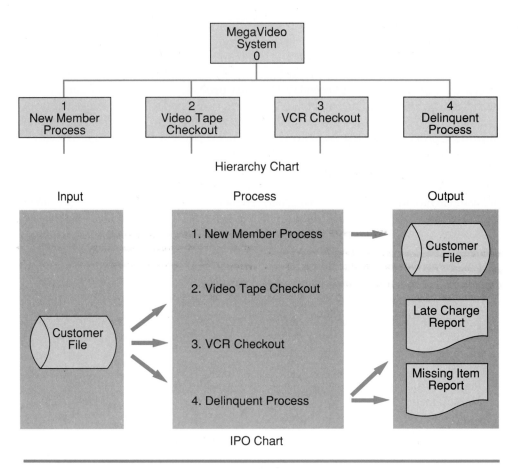

FIGURE 6–16   **HIPO Chart for Mega Video System**

5. Create the IPO chart. List each process in sequence. Link the associated input files and output to individual processes via arrows.

You can repeat these steps and move down into the primitive levels of abstraction. However, other tools accomplish this task more effectively. Hence, HIPOs should stop at a high level of abstraction and give an overview of the system. You can continue explosion into detail by continuing with another tool, such as the system flow chart. Figure 6–16 illustrates a hierarchy chart and an IPO chart for the highest level of abstraction of the Mega Video system described in Case 6.1.

SYSTEM FLOWCHARTS

System flowcharts are used primarily to document physical or hardware interfaces within a system. Symbols are physically oriented. Many—for example, punched cards, magnetic tape, and punched tape—relate to batch processing. The advent of database technologies and interactive, real-time systems has outdated many symbols in the systems flowchart set.

A systems flowchart is divided into three vertical portions (Figure 6–17). The left side is reserved for input symbols, the right side for output symbols, and the center for process symbols. Figure 6–17 was derived from the following description of a batch system for the Colonial Heights apartment complex.

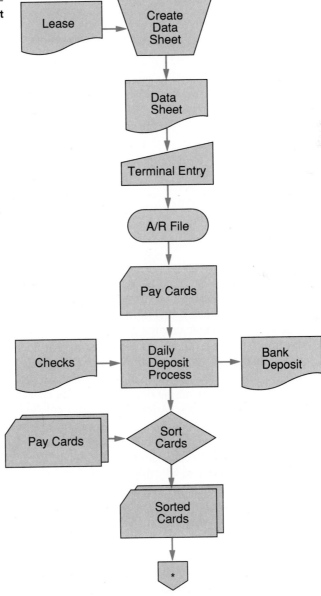

FIGURE 6–17(a)   Systems Flowchart for Colonial Heights

FIGURE 6−17(b)   **Systems Flowchart
for Colonial Heights**

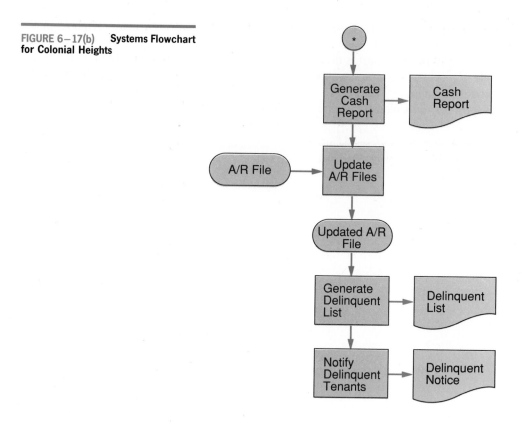

The Colonial Heights apartment complex uses the following system for processing security deposits and rental payments: When a tenant signs a lease and pays a security deposit, the manager creates a data sheet on the tenant. This sheet includes name, apartment number, phone number, permanent address (if other than the new apartment), amount of rent, amount of security deposit, move-in date, length of lease, pet deposit (if any), and person to notify in case of an emergency. The manager sends this form to the data-processing department. Data operators enter the data via terminal into the accounts receivable (A/R) file.

The computer produces a card with the tenant's name, apartment number, amount due, and amount paid from the A/R file. The card is sent back to the manager, who attaches the security deposit check to the card.

The manager sends this card and check to the A/R department, where daily deposits are batched. Checks are deposited into the proper bank account. Cards that came in with the checks are sorted by name alphabetically and become data entry for a card reader. The computer reads the cards and produces a daily cash report. The A/R file is updated. At the end of the month, the computer generates new cards for each tenant. As the tenants pay the rent due, a card is pulled for each tenant and is attached to the check or money order payment. The same procedure (from ** to **) is followed for the rent payment.

AUTOMATIC PROGRAM DOCUMENTATION GENERATORS

One of the most difficult tasks in information systems support is that of maintaining an old, poorly documented program in a third-generation language (usually CO-BOL). In order to simplify the maintenance task in newly created programs, automatic documentation generators have been created. The documentation generators are particularly helpful in documenting unstructured (spaghetti) code.

Automatic documentation generators (ADGs) perform the following functions:

- Produce lists of arrays.
- Generate exception output.
- List files.
- List indicators.
- List labels.
- List subroutines (often in an indented, nested manner that aids in determining structure).
- List variables.
- List all statements that alter indicators.
- Generate cross-reference lists with statements.
- Produce screen images.
- Produce print chart images.
- Produce field information.

ADGs also have been created for systems-level documentation. Products such as REMDOC from REM Associates produce as many as thirty documentation reports that indicate all systems in a distributed environment, including up to thirty libraries. REM-DOC's features include automatic generation of systems flowcharts, locations of inconsistencies in files, displays of file usage, and general documentation production.

Documentation is important for users as well as for data-processing staff. A recent study at IBM Human Factors Laboratory determined that users were approximately 41 percent more productive using task-oriented *(how)* documentation versus product-oriented *(what)* documentation. Writing task-oriented user documentation is time consuming and has not yet been automated. With the status of artificial intelligence and natural language advancing all the time, however, fully automated user documentation may be possible within the near future.

On the tenth day of the month, the A/R department generates a delinquent list from the A/R file. This list includes all tenants who have some balance due on their account. The manager sends a notice to each delinquent tenant along with an overdue charge.

WHICH TOOL SHOULD I USE?

The data flow diagram, HIPO, and system flowchart (in conjunction with the hierarchy chart) all get the job done. They start with an information system at a high level of abstraction and allow you to refine system processes successively to the lowest, primitive level of detail. Which tool is best for you to use? The answer to that question depends on several factors.

1. The DFD has been designed for ease of end-user understanding. This user understanding is critical during the analysis portion of the SDLC. Therefore, at the early stages of the information systems project, consider using the DFD. You can switch the other tools as the level of refined detail becomes greater—goes beyond what you would show most nontechnical end-users.
2. DFDs are the basis for most graphic components included in CASE products. Hence, if your firm is CASE driven, you may not have the choice of using HIPO charts or system flowcharts.
3. Most firms have documentation standards. The tools you choose should be consistent with those standards.
4. HIPO charts and systems flowcharts are old standards. Their use is decreasing. Even if you choose or must use them now, be prepared to use DFDs in the future.
5. Command of all five tools described in this chapter is considered to constitute basic literacy for information system specialists.

SUMMARY

Structured development—the systematic and integrated use of tools and techniques to aid analysis and design of information systems—allows definition of a system from general to specific (top to bottom) in increasing levels of detail. A recent innovation of the structured approach is radical top-down design, which allows on-time delivery of partial, effective systems.

The most commonly used structured approaches are those of Gane and Sarson, Warnier and Orr, Yourdon and DeMarco, and Jackson. Structured approaches have several advantages, including reduction of complexity, focus on the ideal system, standardization, future orientation, and less reliance on artistry. Problems with structured methodologies include tendency to adapt a tool orientation, lack of breadth across the SDLC, and illusion of automatic design.

This chapter described four tools: hierarchy chart, data flow diagram, HIPO, and system flowchart. The hierarchy chart works as a partner with the other three tools. Choice of tool depends on (1) ease of end-user understanding, (2) whether or not CASE is used, (3) individual firm documentation standards, and (4) future as well as current use. Facility with all four tools is considered requisite knowledge for systems analysts.

CONCEPTS LEARNED

- History of development tools
- What structured development is
- How to design a hierarchy chart
- How to design DFDs
- How to design an HIPO
- How to design a system flowchart
- Which of these tools is best to use

KEY TERMS

children nodes
confluence flow
control module
data dictionary
data elements
data flow
data flow diagram (DFD)
data packet
data store
data structure
dispersion flow
explosion
external entity
feedback flow
functional primitive
Gane and Sarson approach
group data
hierarchy chart
HIPO charts
informational data

input-process-output (IPO) chart
Jackson approach
logical data
parent node
physical data
primitive level
process
process specifications
program stub
radical top-down approach
sibling node
sink
source
structured development
structured revolution
system flowcharts
top-down approach
Warnier and Orr approach
Yourdon and DeMarco approach

REVIEW QUESTIONS

1. What is structured development? How does it work?

2. Explain how the radical top-down approach works.

3. What are the advantages of prototyping?

4. What are the benefits of structured development?

5. Describe the problems associated with structured development.

6. Describe the four commonly used structured approaches.

7. How is the hierarchy chart organized?

8. Draw and label the four symbols used in the data flow diagram.

9. What is meant by "a leveled set of DFDs"?

10. What are the differences between logical and physical DFDs?

11. How does the HIPO chart differ from the DFD?

12. Explain the differences between a dispersion flow, a confluence flow, and a feedback flow.

13. How is a system flowchart organized?

14. How would you determine which of the tools described in this chapter to use in a given design opportunity?

MEISTER AUTO PARTS*

Meister Auto Parts is a distributor of new and used automobile parts and accessories. This dealer buys parts such as transmissions, engines, and drive shafts from a variety of vendors and inventories them for resale to retailers such as Western Auto, Pep Boys, and Kragen Auto Stores.

The owner of Meister Auto Parts believes that computerization is needed in a variety of areas, particularly in the processing of customer orders. An on-line, real-time customer order processing system is desired to automate the following manual processes and procedures.

A customer usually calls Meister requesting an order for parts. Meister's customer service representative prepares a customer order form by first looking up the customer's name, address, and account number in a customer card file and then posting this data to the top of the order form.

Next, a customer order number is assigned. This is done by looking up the last assigned number in a log book, adding one to this number, assigning this number to the customer order, and posting the customer's name and order date, with the assigned customer order number, to the log book (so this number is not used again).

Unless overridden by the customer service representative, the customer order is given today's date as the order date.

The customer service representative notes the parts desired by the customer. Specifically, he or she jots down each part's stock number, unit price quotation, and quantity requested. Next, the parts inventory file is checked to verify that the desired part number is still stocked by Meister and that the customer's price quotation is still valid—that is, within 10 percent of the current sales price for the corresponding part. This process is performed for all parts ordered by the customer. Finally, the customer order is stored in an open customer order file.

Sometimes, customers send in a purchase order in writing with no price quotation information on it. When this happens, the customer's purchase order is placed temporarily in the customer order file, to be replaced by a customer order form, which is completed from the purchase order rather than from telephone communication with the customer. (The customer order file is in customer account number and date sequence, so it is easy to find a corresponding purchase order if one has been received.) The purchase order is then disregarded.

The person responsible for generating the customer order also prepares a customer shipment/price confirmation and sends the confirmation to the customer.

*This case was prepared by David Schultz, MIS Department, California State University, Sacramento.

CRITICAL THINKING OPPORTUNITIES

1. Draw a diagram that illustrates the organization of this chapter.

2. Reference the hierarchy chart of Figure 6–9 and the first level DFD explosion of Figure 6–11:
   a) Explode process 1 into a third-level DFD.
   b) Explode process 3 into a third-level DFD.

3. Refer to the preceding description of Meister Auto Parts and do these exercises:

   a) Draw a hierarchy chart for the process.
   b) Convert the hierarchy chart into a leveled set of physical data flow diagrams.
   c) Convert the physical DFDs to logical DFDs.
   d) Prepare an IPO from the hierarchy chart.
   e) Prepare a system flowchart from the hierarchy chart.

MEGA VIDEO: STRUCTURED TOOLS AND THE SDLC

SETTING

As explained in Chapter 3, there are many different versions of the system development life cycle (SDLC). Each version is most appropriate in certain situations. In this case, you will proceed quickly through the complete development of an automated video rental store. A commonly used SDLC, which will allow this rapid journey and will demonstrate the use of common development tools, is adapted from Yourdon (1988). Its analysis and design phases are described next.

The following steps, which are consistent with the **Yourdon methodology** (Yourdon, 1988), make up the analysis and design phases of the SDLC.

1. Describe the current physical systems:
   - Identify the system's components (external entities, outflows, inflows, processes, and stores).

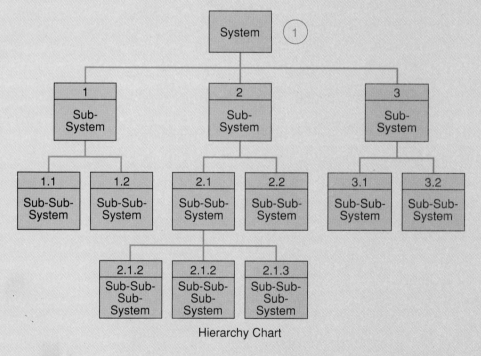

Hierarchy Chart

FIGURE 6.1–1   The Structured Analysis and Design Process

■ Develop a hierarchy chart.
■ Construct a leveled set of data flow diagrams (DFDs).

2. Derive the current logical system (leveled set of logical DFDs).
3. Specify the new system:
   ■ Needs requirements statement
   ■ Management constraints
   ■ Project definition statement
   ■ Proposed logical DFD
4. Develop the data dictionary.
5. Package the proposed system.

STRUCTURED DEVELOPMENT PROCESS

From a graphic perspective, the process proceeds as shown in Figure 6.1–1:

■ A hierarchy chart is developed for the application (number 1 in Figure 6.1–1).
■ The hierarchy chart is converted line by line into a leveled set of data flow diagrams (number 2 in Figure 6.1–1).
■ The first set of DFDs describes the current physical system—how things are done as well

	WHAT/HOW	WHAT	WHAT	WHAT/HOW
Data Flow Diagram Level	Physical Current System	Logical Current System	Logical Proposed System	Physical Proposed System
Context Diagram		N/A	N/A	N/A
(2) Level 0		N/A	N/A (7)	N/A
Level 1				
Level 2	(3)	(4)	(5)	(6)
Lower Levels				

Data Flow Diagrams

FIGURE 6.1–1 **(continued)**

as what processes are performed (number 3 in Figure 6.1–1).

- Implementation features (how things will be done) are eliminated from the physical DFD; the result is the logical DFD of the current system (number 4 in Figure 6.1–1).
- The pure processes remaining are rearranged, combined, or deleted; the result is the logical DFD of the proposed (new) system (number 5 in Figure 6.1–1).
- Implementation features (how things are done) are added; the result is the physical DFD of the proposed system (number 6 in Figure 6.1–1).
- Only the lower level DFDs need to be changed; the upper, control-level DFDs will remain constant during the design process (number 7 in Figure 6.1–1).

Before the development team can model the current system, it conducts a fact-finding process. Fact finding was described in Chapter 5; for this chapter, it is assumed the fact-finding phase has been done. The development team has gathered the information necessary to model the current physical system. The following descriptive scenario synthesizes knowledge about a simple current system for a video tape rental store. In reality, of course, such a concise scenario is rarely available.

MEGA VIDEO'S CURRENT SYSTEM

Mega Video (MV) rents video tapes and VCRs. To rent a movie or a VCR, the customer must become a member of Mega Video. Membership is free, but each customer must hold a major credit card in his or her own name to be eligible to join.

The first time a customer comes into MV, he or she fills out a membership application form. The form contains the following information:

- First name
- Last name
- Date of birth
- Current date
- Street address
- City
- State

- Zip code
- Phone number
- Major credit card type
- Credit card number
- Driver's license number
- Age

The customer fills out the membership form. The cashier verifies the credit card and then enters the new information into the computer to create a customer account. The computer assigns a sequential account number to the account. The cashier places a sticker with this number on a blank member card and types the new member's name onto the card. After the new member signs the card, the card is laminated and given to him or her. Now the customer may check out video tapes and VCRs.

Customers are limited to three video tapes per visit. To check out a tape, the customer browses the shelves, which contain empty boxes for all the videos not checked out. The boxes contain descriptions of the movies (they are the original boxes in which the tapes were packaged). The customer selects up to three empty boxes and takes them to the checkout point, along with the membership card. The cashier enters the member's number into the computer. A screen is pulled up containing that customer's information, including balance due. If there are any late charges, they must be paid before any additional tapes may be checked out. The screen also prompts for up to three videos to be checked out. The cashier enters the transaction (name, number, and rental price) for each tape. The computer program automatically arrives at the balance due.

As soon as the customer has paid, the tapes are retrieved from long shelves behind the counter, where they are stored by number. The cashier takes the tapes, which are stored in hard plastic boxes, replaces each one with the correct empty box, and gives the tapes to the customer along with a receipt.

When the customer returns the tapes, they are placed in a return bin. At a convenient time, the cashier removes the tapes from the return bin and enters them into the computer system as returned so the customer will not be charged for additional time. If the tapes are late, a late charge is determined and entered into the customer's account. Later, the cashier returns the tapes to the storage shelves and removes the corresponding boxes, which are returned to the display shelves.

The checkout procedure for VCRs is exactly the same, except that the customer has to sign a contract (because of the high cost of the VCR). The cashier enters the member number from the member card into the computer, and the customer record is pulled up. Then the cashier enters the number of the VCR and a charge is generated. The customer signs a contract, which is stored in a hard copy active file until the VCR is returned. The VCR is retrieved from storage and given to the customer. When the VCR is returned, the return is noted on the contract and the contract is moved to an inactive file. The customer account is updated with the return information, and any late charges are added to the customer balance.

Each week Mega Video generates two reports. The first report lists all the unreturned tapes and VCRs alphabetically by customer name. The second report contains unpaid charges resulting from late returns. The first report is used to send letters manually to customers who have not returned items; the letter urges them to return the items and spells out current and future charges and actions. If the items have not been returned after two weeks from the due date, the account is forwarded to a collection agency, the customer is dropped as a member, and a report is filed with the credit bureau (this affects the customer's credit record). The second report is an internal one, used only for records. Any long-term late charges are due to the fact that the customer has returned the items but has never come into the store to check anything else out.

MODEL THE CURRENT PHYSICAL SYSTEM

Note that the description of Mega Video included physical details (e.g., moving actual video tapes). At this initial stage, the physical details are of interest, even though we are designing an information (not a physical) system. Once the current physical system is understood and described (modeled) via data flow diagrams, the physical details will be removed. Physical details limit the creativity and optimality of proposed information systems solutions because they clutter the basic nature of the information flow.

Identify the System's Components

The first step toward developing a leveled set of data flow diagrams for Mega Video is to read the description of the current system. Next, identify the sources and destinations of data, data flows, data stores, and processes. An easy way to accomplish this is to underline any potential processes as you read through the description and then make a list for each process. Look at all the verbs—they may be processes in the system. First, list the processes and number them sequentially. Second, read the description again and identify the inflows and outflows related to each process. A list of the processes and corresponding inflows and outflows for Mega Video's current system follows:

Inflow	Process	Outflow
member information	1. Fill out membership form	membership form
credit card	2. Verify credit card	credit status
membership form	3. Enter new customer information	computer account
sticker	4. Place sticker on card	
membership form	5. Type name on card	
card	6. Laminate card	card
card	7. Enter member number	account on screen
late charge	8. Collect late charges	OK status
tape information	9. Enter rental information	balance due
money	10. Collect fee	receipt
boxes	11. Retrieve tapes	tapes
tapes	12. Remove tapes from bins	tapes
tapes	13. Enter returns	altered account

due information	14. Determine late charges	altered account
tapes	15. Return tapes to storage	
boxes	16. Return boxes to display area	
card	17. Enter member number	account on screen
late charges	18. Collect late charges	OK status
contract	19. Enter transaction	updated account
money	20. Collect fee	receipt
contract	21. Store active contract	
VCR storage	22. Retrieve VCR	VCR
VCR	23. Update account with return	updated account
time and date	24. Determine any late charges	updated account
contracts	25. Move contract to inactive file	
accounts	26. Generate late charge report	report 1
accounts	27. Generate delinquent list	report 2
report 1	28. Send out letters to customers	letters
report 2	29. Drop customer	deleted accounts

Note: Some of the processes do not have outflows because they are physically oriented. They do not alter the data; they merely move data from one point to another.

After listing the processes, inflows, and outflows, identify external entities and stores. The four external entities involved in Mega Video are the customers, collection agency, external manager, and credit bureau. The data stores include the customer account file, display shelves for video tape boxes, storage shelves for video tapes, return bin, active contract file for VCRs, and inactive contract file for VCRs.

Develop a Hierarchy Chart

The next step is to create a hierarchy chart with these processes. Figure 6.1–2 is the hierarchy chart for Mega Video.

Construct Data Flow Diagrams

There are twenty-nine separate processes in the Mega Video system. Many of them can be lumped together because they are subprocesses that form a general task group. There is a relationship between the paragraph structure in the description and tasks; each paragraph concerns a single concept. Looking at each paragraph and identifying its subject gives clues to the organization of tasks. The first three paragraphs (processes 1–6) are all concerned with getting a membership. The next three paragraphs (processes 7–16) describe renting and returning video tapes. The next paragraph (processes 17–25) describes renting a VCR. The last paragraph describes various processes (26–29) involved with delinquency procedures (see Figure 6.1–2).

Context-level DFDs. Context-level (or 0-level) DFDs illustrate external entities and major data flows associated with a system. No data stores are identified at the context level. Essentially, the purpose is to present the context within which the system operates. First, draw the 0-level process in the center of a piece of paper. In a menu-driven system, this would be the main menu, which provides direct or indirect access to all functions of the system. A general name like Mega Video System will suffice. On the left of the paper, draw any external entities that are sources of information. On the right draw any external entities that are sinks (receivers) for information. Draw flow lines connecting the external entities to the process, and label the flow lines with appropriate names (Figure 6.1–3).

First-level Explosion DFD. The next level of the DFD is called the first-level explosion. The first-

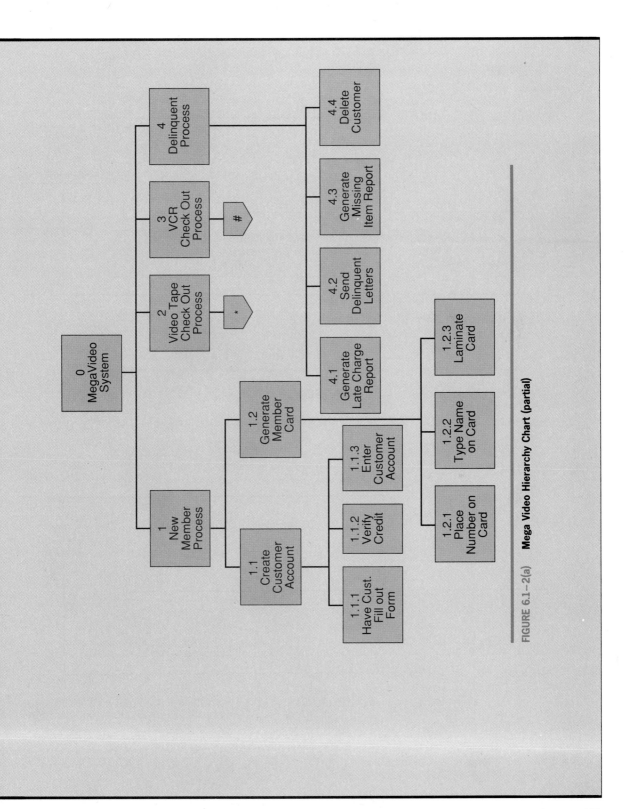

FIGURE 6.1–2(a)   Mega Video Hierarchy Chart (partial)

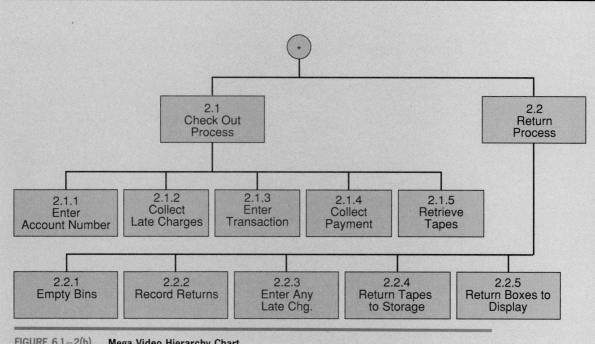

FIGURE 6.1–2(b)   **Mega Video Hierarchy Chart**

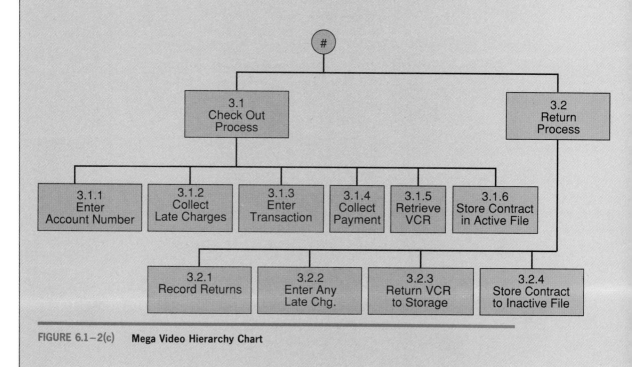

FIGURE 6.1–2(c)   **Mega Video Hierarchy Chart**

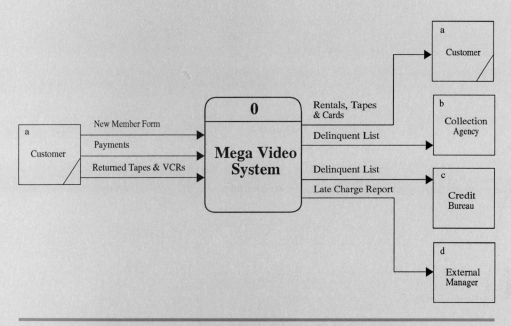

Context-level DFD (Level 0) for Mega Video

level DFD includes all functions of the system at a higher level than primitive (Figure 6.1–4). It is probably the most informative of all the DFDs because the context DFD gives us little information about what the system can do and the primitive levels give us detailed information about only part of the system.

It is almost impossible to get this diagram right the first time you draw it, so be prepared to redo it several times. In general, data should flow from left to right and from top to bottom—the same sequence as the hierarchy chart. One of the best qualities of a DFD is that, unlike the systems flowchart, it is not sequential in nature. Many processes may occur simultaneously. To show simultaneous processing, processes are drawn on top of one another. To show sequential processing, processes are drawn in a sequence from left to right.

This first-level explosion gives us an overview of the entire system. It is helpful for the analyst to sit down with the user and walk through this diagram; this enhances understanding of the various parts of the target system. As a

student, you can gain greater understanding by walking through the system yourself. Try explaining the system to someone else.

Note the following in Figure 6.1–4:

1. The processes are numbered with single digits.
2. The symbol for the external entity named "customer" is repeated several times, even though each duplication is the same entity (the slash to show graphically that these customers are the same).
3. The flow is from left to right (the source is on the left and the sinks are on the right.
4. The store named "customer file" is introduced at this level (it is needed as a source for process 4).
5. There are no overlapping flow lines (this is achieved by duplication of symbols).
6. All flow lines are labeled.

Second-level Explosion DFD. Note the simplicity of this DFD (Figure 6.1–5). Not much detail is learned by inspecting it. Leaving out this level may not eliminate much information; however,

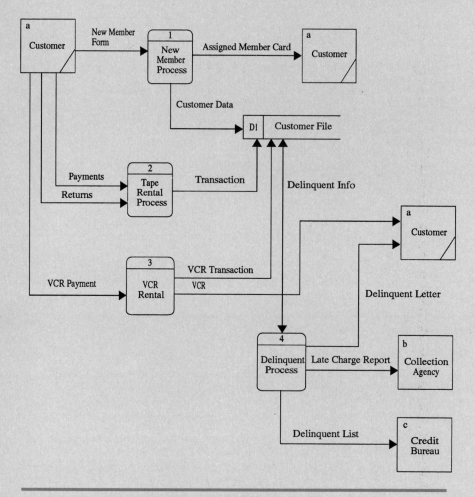

FIGURE 6.1—4   **First-level Explosion for Mega Video**

while you are learning the task, you should complete all portions of constructing the current physical system.

Figures 6.1–6 through 6.1–14 present the rest of the physical DFDs for Mega Video's current system.

DERIVE THE CURRENT LOGICAL SYSTEM

Deriving the current logical system is relatively easy. The first step is to remove any mention of physical location or devices. The next step is to remove processes that are required because of an imperfect world; for example, credit card verification is required only because of dishonest or careless people. The last step is to remove any processes that do not actually transform the data. If the data flow into a process and out of a process without any changes, that process should be removed. The set of logical DFDs for Mega Video (Figures 6.1–15 through 6.1–19) illustrates that there are significantly fewer processes in a logical DFD than in a physical DFD. Only the

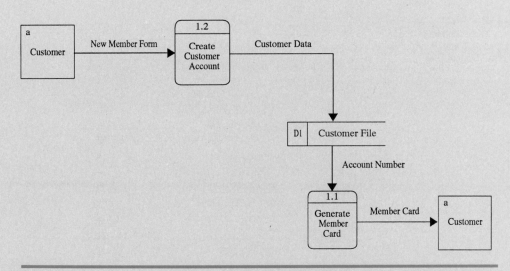

Second-level Explosion of Process 1 (New Member Process)—Current Physical DFD

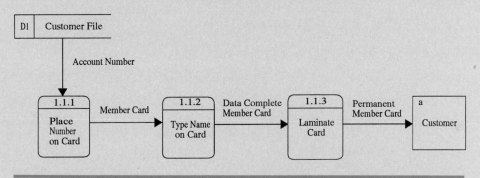

FIGURE 6.1−6 **Third-level Explosion of Process 1 (Generate Member Card)—Current Physical DFD**

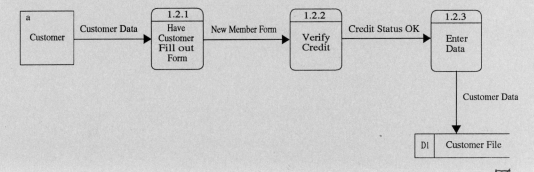

FIGURE 6.1−7 **Second Third-level Explosion of Process 1 (Create Customer Account)—Current Physical DFD**

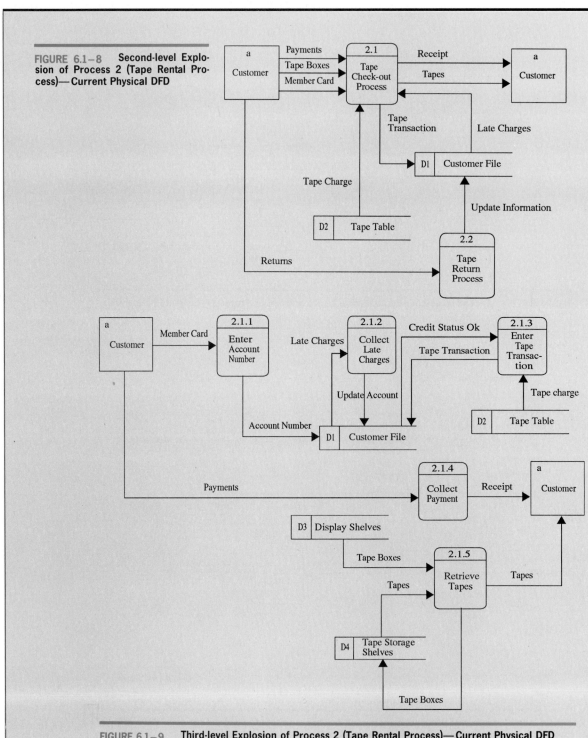

FIGURE 6.1–8   Second-level Explosion of Process 2 (Tape Rental Process)—Current Physical DFD

FIGURE 6.1–9   Third-level Explosion of Process 2 (Tape Rental Process)—Current Physical DFD

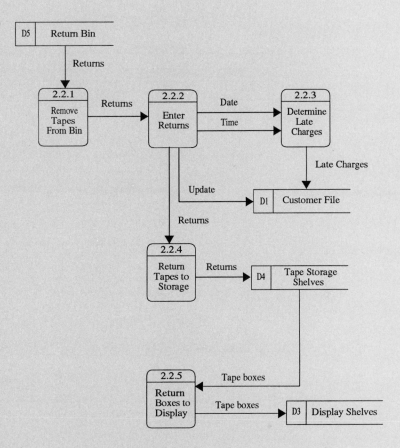

FIGURE 6.1—10 Second Third-level Explosion of Process 2 (Tape Return Process)—Current Physical DFD

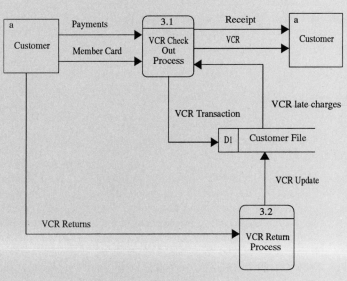

FIGURE 6.1—11 Second-level Explosion of Process 3 (VCR Rental Process)—Current Physical DFD

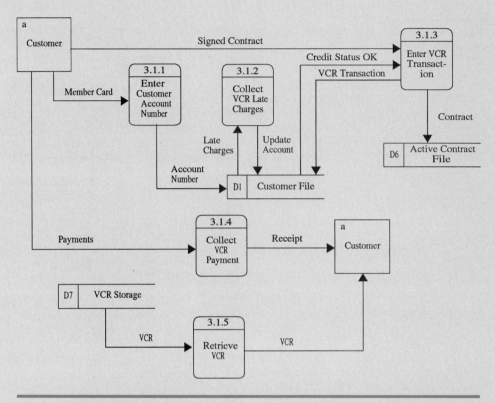

FIGURE 6.1−12   **Third-level Explosion of Process 3 (VCR Rental Process)—Current Physical DFD**

primitive-level DFDs are shown because the higher level DFDs *are* basically unchanged.

SPECIFY THE NEW SYSTEM

Needs Requirements for Mega Video

A simple list of needs requirements was compiled by the manager of Mega Video (with staff input):

1. In general, the current system is too slow. Customers have to wait in line at both the new member point and the cashier line. We need a method to speed up checkout and location of the actual tapes.
2. Using tape boxes to show tapes available is rather cumbersome. Also, when we remove boxes from the display shelf, we eliminate advertising. If the boxes were to remain on the shelf, customers could see our complete selection more readily. They then would come back more often to get the tapes that are now checked out.
3. Waiting for credit card verification is time consuming. Several customers have walked out because of long lines at the new member processing point.
4. The computer is too slow in retrieving customer information.
5. Some of the cashiers are poor typists, who cannot enter the customer number and the tape information fast enough. This causes long lines at the checkout point.
6. Customers who are returning tapes complain about having to park their cars in a crowded

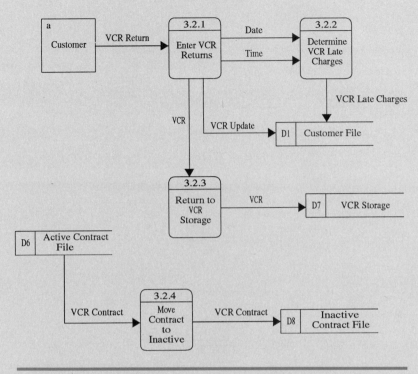

FIGURE 6.1–13 **Second Third-level Explosion of Process 3 (VCR Rental Process)— Current Physical DFD**

parking lot and walk to the back of the store to return tapes. We need to find a way to streamline this process.

7. Our hours are from 10:00 A.M. to 10:00 P.M. Customers complain about not being able to return tapes in the early morning or late at night when we are not open.

8. We often lose sales because popular tapes are sitting in the return bins. The busiest time for checking tapes out is also the same time as the return deadline.

9. As a manager, I do not feel I have adequate access to my customer data. I would like to extract information from the data to help me increase business. For example, if I could organize my customers by zip code, I could send out targeted advertising. Right now, I have to print out all the customers alphabetically and use this printed list to build separate mailing lists on a word processor. This takes time and labor. In the end, I have spent more money on advertising than I have gained from it.

There are other reports I would like to have to increase my control and understanding of my financial position. The reports I want are not part of the system, and my needs change from day to day.

Management Constraints

A good information system must be cost-effective. Small businesses such as Mega Video have limited budgets. When exploring alternative systems solutions, cost considerations are paramount. The optimal technical solution may not

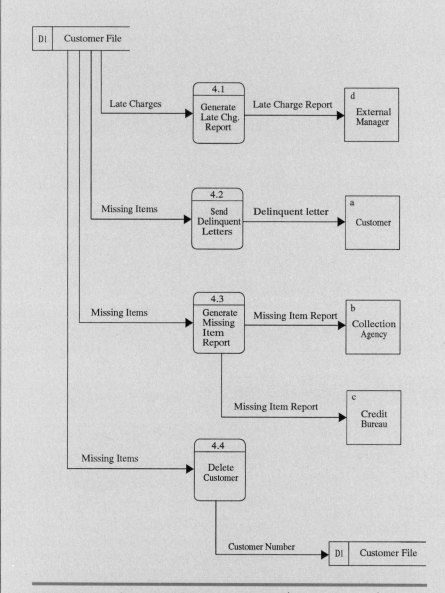

FIGURE 6.1—14 **Second-level Explosion of Process 4 (Delinquent Process)—Current Physical DFD**

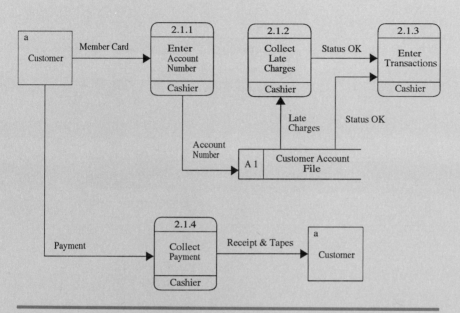

FIGURE 6.1—15   **Third-level Explosion of Process 2—Logical DFD (Note that process 2.1.5 is a physical process eliminated from the logical DFD.)**

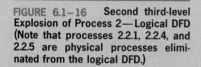

FIGURE 6.1—16   **Second third-level Explosion of Process 2—Logical DFD (Note that processes 2.2.1, 2.2.4, and 2.2.5 are physical processes eliminated from the logical DFD.)**

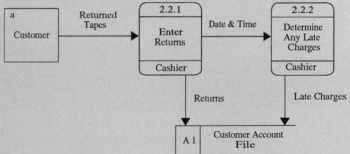

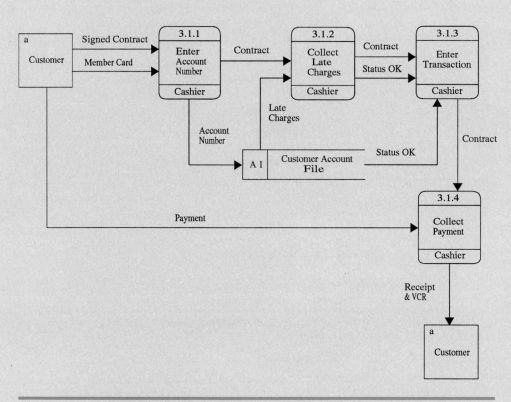

FIGURE 6.1—17   Third-level Explosion of Process 3—Logical DFD (Note that process 3.1.5 is a physical process eliminated from the logical DFD.)

FIGURE 6.1—18   Second Third-level Explosion of Process 3—Logical DFD (Note that processes 3.2.3 and 3.2.4 are physical processes eliminated from the logical DFD.)

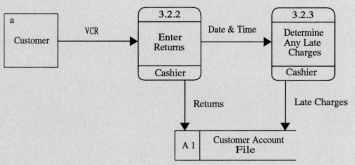

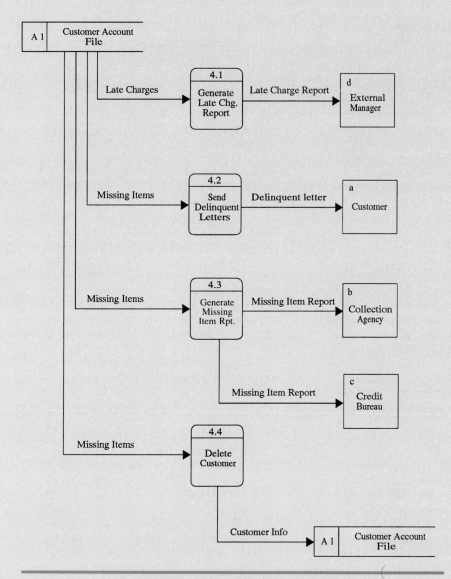

FIGURE 6.1–19   **Second-level Explosion of Process 4—Logical DFD**

be feasible because of the expense involved. All solutions must be evaluated economically, operationally, and technically.

Project Definition Statement

We have analyzed Mega Video's current system through the physical and logical DFDs, and we have analyzed needs requirements. Now we are ready to develop the project definition statement for Mega Video. Where possible, objectives should be stated in quantified terms. This facilitates evaluation once the system is in place. Qualitative objectives are vague and difficult to assess.

Mega Video Project Definition Statement. The progress of Mega Video is being stifled by an outdated information system. The current system is operating close to capacity. If the customer base grows much larger, the system will not be able to handle it. A new information system is needed to accomplish the following objectives:

- The new system must meet current and future storage capacity needs. The number of customers is estimated to increase at a rate of 10 percent per year. Now there are 2,050 customers who check out an average of 3.1 tapes per month.
- The new system must speed up the processing of transactions to satisfy customer needs. The average transaction time to process tapes with no late charges is 5.5 minutes. This time must be decreased to 3.5 minutes. The time it takes to process new members averages 12.5 minutes; this time must be decreased to 9.5 minutes.
- The new system must provide access to data for managerial control and marketing needs.
- The new system should have an initial startup cost of no more than $75,000. It should be paid out over five years for a total annual cost of $15,000. An additional $5,000 per year may be spent to support the system.
- The new system must be supported adequately. If the computer system is down, the store will be out of business. Support

must always be available when the store is open. A manual backup system should be in place in case of system failure.
- Cashiers, new member assistants, and the manager must be trained when the new system is delivered.
- The new system should be easy to use. As much as possible, the new computer screens should be similar to the current screens.

In addition to attaining these objectives, the new system should fulfill the needs listed in the needs requirements statement.

Mega Video System Solution. At this point it is possible to explore alternative solutions. Creative input is important so that many possibilities will be explored. Some of the needs stated in the needs requirements statement can be solved without technical assistance. For example, need 6 can be solved by placing a drop box in the parking lot—a box that can be reached without getting out of the car.

After careful consideration of all the needs and objectives, we determine the following system components as necessary for the new system:

1. To increase the speed of customer service and to eliminate the keystroking task for the cashiers, scanning wands and universal product code (UPC) stickers will replace data entry by hand.
2. To allow the boxes to remain on the display shelves, a hard plastic card (4 by 8 inches) will be attached to each box by a rubber band. The customer will know a tape is available if there is a plastic card attached to the box. The customer will remove the plastic card and take it to the register. The card will have the title of the movie and a UPC sticker with the movie identification number on it. It will be easier to return tapes to the shelves, because twenty cards are much easier to alphabetize and carry than twenty boxes.
3. To speed up validation of the credit card, an automatic card reader will be attached to a

phone line. The clerk at the new member point will draw the credit card through the machine, which will read the magnetic strip. The machine will dial the right number and verify the credit status in an average of sixty seconds.

4. Since the computer hardware is outdated, is too slow, and lacks storage capacity, it will be replaced with a newer, hard-drive microcomputer. A tape backup system will be purchased.

5. A drop box for tapes will be placed in the parking lot. This will allow customers to return tapes during off hours. During business hours, customers who use the drop box do not leave their cars in the parking lot, so there is more parking space for customers who wish to rent tapes.

6. Tapes checked out any time during one day will be due at 8:00 P.M. the following day. In this way, the returned tapes can be processed and the cards put on the shelves before the beginning of the next business day.

7. A relational database with query language capabilities will be installed on hard disk. This will be more efficient for daily transaction processing and will allow the manager to generate reports without programmer intervention and with minimal training.

Proposed Logical DFD

The leveled set of proposed logical DFDs is based on the proposed system changes just listed. They are almost identical to the current logical DFDs because most of the changes are not logical but technical. The only real logical change is that the store called A1—Customer File will be changed to A1—Customer Database.

Data Modeling

The structure of data within a system is integral to systems design. Most modern systems are architecturally tied to a database of either the relational, hierarchical, or network type. Understanding the structure of the existing or proposed database package and the general schema of the data housed in that database is essential to the successful completion of systems design and production.

DEVELOP THE DATA DICTIONARY

Figures 6.1–20 through 6.1–23 illustrate how the data dictionary is used to catalog all the data within Mega Video. This is just the tip of the iceberg—hundreds of entries are needed to document the complete system. Chapter 11 will describe how to construct these data dictionary entries. It is sufficient now to realize that all parts of DFDs ultimately must be defined in programmable detail in the data dictionary.

PACKAGE THE PROPOSED SYSTEM

The final step in the analysis and design process is physically packaging the proposed system. At this point, the hardware and specific software such as database packages and the language in which the software will be coded are selected. To do this, we need to evaluate vendor products. In large organizations, requests for proposals are sent out to vendors so the organization can select the best product for the money. In small organizations (with small budgets), it is up to the staff to evaluate potential products and make choices.

This step should be the last one. Ideally, hardware selection is based on logical requirements. In many cases, however, hardware and database systems are already in place. Unfortunately, this places limitations on software solution.

The leveled set of physical DFDs shown as Figures 6.1–24 through 6.1–30 is the last set of DFDs in the design process. These DFDs are used to communicate the proposed system to the end-users who must approve the design. After approval, the logical and physical sets of DFDs,

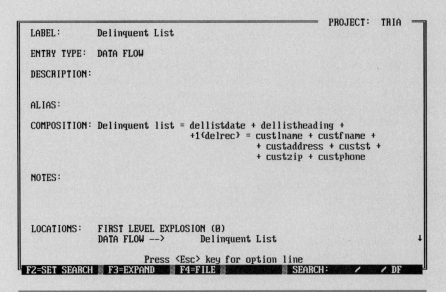

```
                                        ———————— PROJECT:  TRIA ———
    LABEL:        Delinquent List

    ENTRY TYPE:  DATA FLOW

    DESCRIPTION:


    ALIAS:

    COMPOSITION: Delinquent list = dellistdate + dellistheading +
                              +1{delrec} = custlname + custfname +
                                          + custaddress + custst +
                                          + custzip + custphone

    NOTES:



    LOCATIONS:   FIRST LEVEL EXPLOSION (0)
                 DATA FLOW -->        Delinquent List              ↓

                       Press <Esc> key for option line
   F2=SET SEARCH   F3=EXPAND   F4=FILE            SEARCH:    /   / DF
```

FIGURE 6.1-20   Data Flow Entry for Mega Video's Data Dictionary

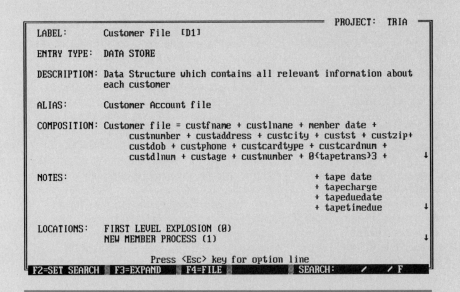

```
                                        ———————— PROJECT:  TRIA ———
    LABEL:        Customer File  [D1]

    ENTRY TYPE:  DATA STORE

    DESCRIPTION: Data Structure which contains all relevant information about
                 each customer

    ALIAS:       Customer Account file

    COMPOSITION: Customer file = custfname + custlname + member date +
                    custnumber + custaddress + custcity + custst + custzip+
                    custdob + custphone + custcardtype + custcardnum +
                    custdlnum + custage + custnumber + 0{tapetrans}3 +    ↓

    NOTES:                                        + tape date
                                                  + tapecharge
                                                  + tapeduedate
                                                  + tapetimedue        ↓

    LOCATIONS:   FIRST LEVEL EXPLOSION (0)
                 NEW MEMBER PROCESS (1)                                ↓

                       Press <Esc> key for option line
   F2=SET SEARCH   F3=EXPAND   F4=FILE            SEARCH:    /   / F
```

FIGURE 6.1-21   Data Store Entry for Mega Video's Data Dictionary

LABEL: Customer File [D1]

ENTRY TYPE: DATA STORE

```
NOTES:                                              + tape date
                                                    + tapecharge
                                                    + tapeduedate
                                                    + tapetimedue
                      + custbal + latecharges + creditstatus
                      + activestatus + 0{VCRtrans}1 = VCRID +VCRdate
                                                        + VCRcharge
                                                        + VCRduedate
                                                        + VCRtimedue
```

Press <Esc> key for option line

F2=SET SEARCH   F3=CONTRACT   F4=FILE   SEARCH: /   / F

PROJECT: TRIA

LABEL: Customer File [D1]

ENTRY TYPE: DATA STORE

```
LOCATIONS:    FIRST LEVEL EXPLOSION (0)
              NEW MEMBER PROCESS (1)
              CREATE CUSTOMER ACCOUNT (1.2)
              GENERATE MEMBER CARD (1.1)
              TAPE RENTAL PROCESS (2)
              TAPE CHECK-OUT PROCESS (2.1)
              TAPE RETURN PROCESS (2.2)
              VIDEO RENTAL PROCESS (3)
              VCR CHECK OUT PROCESS (3.1)
              VCR RETURN PROCESS (3.2)
```

Press <Esc> key for option line

F2=SET SEARCH   F3=CONTRACT   F4=FILE   SEARCH: /   / F

FIGURE 6.1-21   (continued)

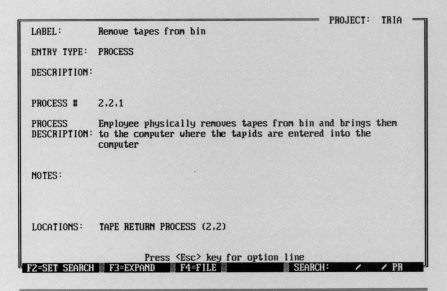

```
                                                     PROJECT:  TRIA
  LABEL:        Remove tapes from bin

  ENTRY TYPE:  PROCESS

  DESCRIPTION:


  PROCESS #    2.2.1

  PROCESS      Employee physically removes tapes from bin and brings them
  DESCRIPTION: to the computer where the tapids are entered into the
               computer


  NOTES:




  LOCATIONS:   TAPE RETURN PROCESS (2.2)

                    Press <Esc> key for option line
  F2=SET SEARCH   F3=EXPAND   F4=FILE          SEARCH:      /    / PR
```

FIGURE 6.1-22   **Data Process Entry for Mega Video's Data Dictionary**

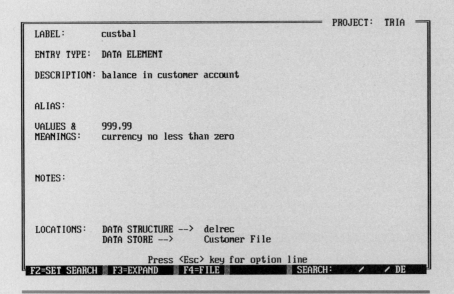

```
                                                     PROJECT:  TRIA
  LABEL:        custbal

  ENTRY TYPE:  DATA ELEMENT

  DESCRIPTION: balance in customer account


  ALIAS:

  VALUES &     999.99
  MEANINGS:    currency no less than zero




  NOTES:




  LOCATIONS:   DATA STRUCTURE --> delrec
               DATA STORE -->     Customer File

                    Press <Esc> key for option line
  F2=SET SEARCH   F3=EXPAND   F4=FILE          SEARCH:      /    / DE
```

FIGURE 6.1-23   **Data Element for Mega Video's Data Dictionary**

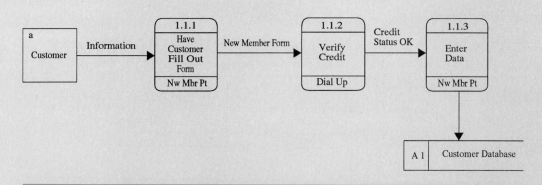

FIGURE 6.1–24 **Third-level Explosion of Process 1—Proposed Physical DFD**

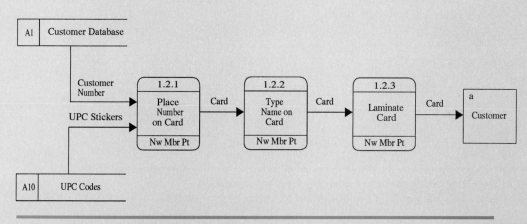

FIGURE 6.1–25 **Second Third-level Explosion of Process 1—Proposed Physical DFD**

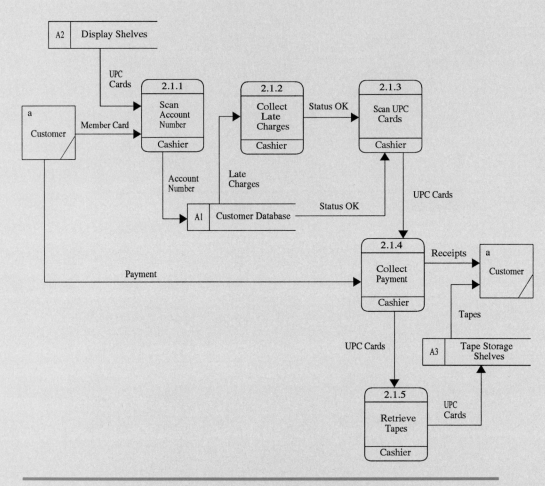

FIGURE 6.1–26   **Third-level Explosion of Process 2—Proposed Physical DFD**

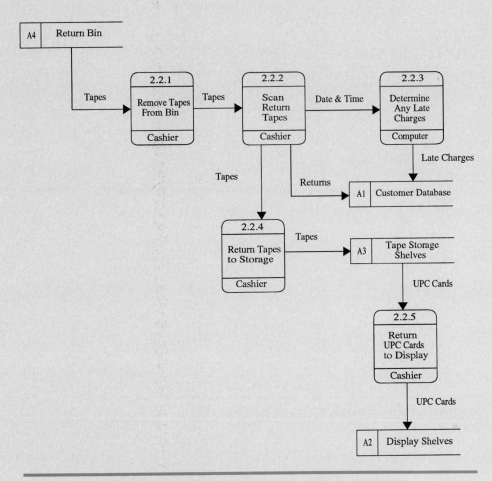

FIGURE 6.1–27   **Second-level Explosion of Process 2—Proposed Physical DFD**

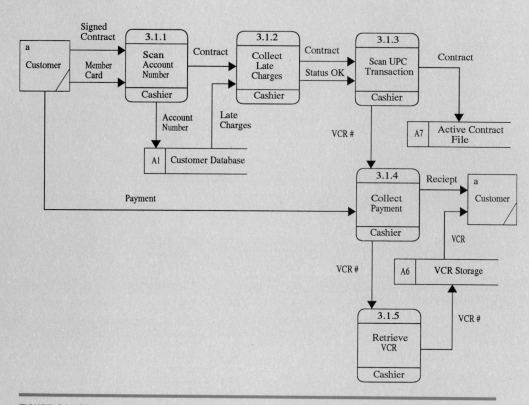

FIGURE 6.1–28   **Third-level Explosion of Process 3—Proposed Physical DFD**

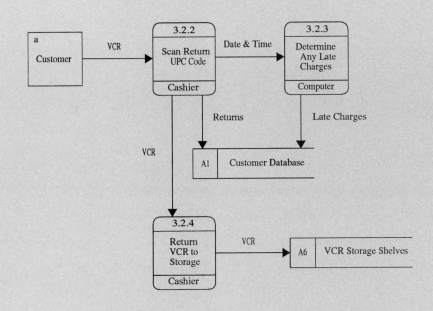

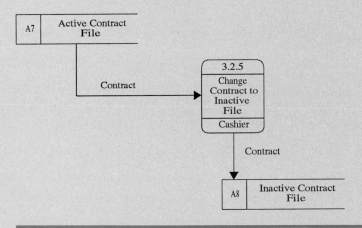

FIGURE 6.1–29   **Second Third-level Explosion of Process 3—Proposed Physical DFD**

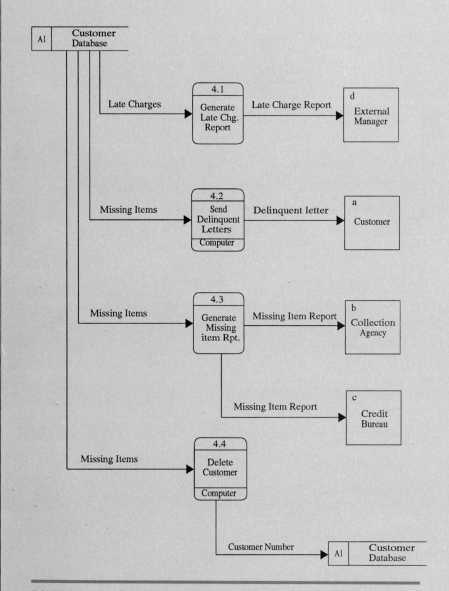

FIGURE 6.1–30   Second-level Explosion of Process 4—Proposed Physical DFD

the hierarchy chart, and the complete data dictionary are sent to the programming staff for coding the new system.

SUMMARY

In this case you saw how to use development tools within the systems development life cycle of a specific system—Mega Video. The analysis and design phases of systems development follow these steps:

1. Model the current physical system.
   - Identify the system's components (external entities, outflows, inflows, processes, and stores).
   - Develop a hierarchy chart.
   - Construct a leveled set of physical data flow diagrams.
2. Derive the current logical system (leveled set of logical DFDs).

3. Specify the new system.
   - Needs requirements statement
   - Management constraints
   - Project definition statement
   - Proposed logical DFD
4. Develop the data dictionary.
5. Package the proposed system.

CRITICAL THINKING OPPORTUNITIES

Read the following description of an inventory system and do these exercises.

1. List the inflows, processes, outflows, stores, and entities involved in the system.
2. Draw a hierarchy chart.
3. Draw a leveled set of physical data flow diagrams for the current system.
4. Draw a system flowchart.

THE FOOTLOOSE FOOTGEAR INVENTORY SYSTEM

Vendors deliver goods to the back door of Footloose Footgear. A clerk who works in the stockroom checks the physical goods against the packing slip and, if they match, signs the receipt. If they don't match, the clerk makes a note on the packing slip, signs the slip, and completes a separate missing item report. As soon as possible, the packages are opened and the items are checked against the stock-out list. If an item is on the stock-out list, it is priced and goes to the front of the store to be displayed. If the item is not on the stock-out list, it is priced and stored in the appropriate section of the stockroom. Price is based on the following markup list:

Category Code	Description	Markup (%)
101	Men's dress shoes	35
102	Men's casual shoes	30
103	Men's boots	40
104	Men's slippers	15
105	Men's athletic shoes	35
201	Women's dress shoes (follow men's scheme)	35 :
301	Children's dress shoes (follow men's scheme)	35 :

400	Hosiery	15
500	Handbags	20
600	Miscellaneous	

The packing slips are batched on a daily basis, and the inventory items received that day are entered into the computer every night after the store closes. New items are added to the inventory file and repeat items are updated. The inventory record has the following fields:

```
CATEGORY CODE = 999999999 (THREE-DIGIT
                           CATEGORY CODE,
                           THREE-DIGIT
                           MANUFACTURER ITEM
                           ID, THREE-DIGIT
                           VENDOR ID)
DESCRIPTION   = 30A
COST          = 999.99
MARKUP        = 99
AUTOCOUNT     = 9999 (COMPUTER-GENERATED
                      COUNT)
PHYSCOUNT     = 9999 (ACTUAL COUNT)
```

When a sale is rung up on the cash register, the inventory levels are adjusted automatically. Therefore, the inventory counts should be accurate every morning before business begins.

Occasionally, customers return goods that cannot be resold because they are defective or damaged. Such goods are stored in the stockroom and once a week are packed up and returned to the appropriate vendors. A list of returned goods is generated and entered into the computer at this time.

On the last Sunday of each month, a physical inventory count is taken. Inventory sheets correspond to the physical layout of the stockroom so that the people who are taking physical inventory can walk around the room counting stocks in the same sequential order in which inventory file records are stored. A physical count of the display room is also made and the two lists are added together.

As the two lists are added, the total item counts are entered into the inventory file. When all the items have been entered, the following tasks are performed by a menu-driven set of computer programs:

- Total wholesale value of the inventory is calculated on the basis of physical counts (sum of count × wholesale price). This is done for tax and accounting purposes.
- Total retail value of inventory is calculated on the basis of physical counts (sum of count × wholesale price × markup). This is done for calculating insurance rates.

CASE 6.2

GOODBYTE PIZZA COMPANY: DOCUMENTATION

SETTING

Linda Alvires and her fellow university students began their study of the Goodbyte operation. They recognized that their first step was to describe the current system in detail. With approval from Sam Nolte, they spent one entire afternoon observing operations and interviewing key personnel. They produced the following manual description of the Goodbyte Pizza Company process.

DESCRIPTION OF CURRENT SYSTEM

All sales information is contained on a three-copy Customer Order form. A yellow copy goes to the kitchen for use as an order menu. If the order is for delivery, the pink copy is used for the delivery driver. The original copy is kept by the manager for his records. In-store orders are processed differently from delivery orders.

In-Store Orders

1. The customer places an order with the cashier.
2. The order is written on the Customer Order form, along with the current date and time.
3. A price list is consulted, and the appropriate price is entered to the cash register.
4. If the customer has a coupon, it is given to the cashier, who deducts the coupon amount from the total order price.
5. If the customer is paying by check, the cashier compares the check's name and address fields against the Bad Check List. If the customer's name is on that list, the current sale is aborted. Otherwise, it continues.

6. The cashier gives the customer the cash register receipt annotated with the order number and the table number where the customer will be sitting.
7. The cashier sends a copy of the Customer Order to the kitchen.
8. The original white copy is placed in the cash register drawer.
9. At the end of each night, the manager collects the white copies from the register drawer.
10. The manager compiles total sales information from the white order copies.

Delivery Orders

1. The customer phones in the order.
2. The order is written on the Customer Order form.
3. The following additional information is written on the order form:
   a) Price (from price list)
   b) Delivery fee (constant from price list)
   c) Customer's name, phone number, address, and nearest cross street
4. One copy of the order is sent to the kitchen.
5. Two copies of the order are sent to the driver; one will be given to the customer. The second copy is used for driving directions and is returned to the manager after each delivery run.
6. At the end of each night, all delivery orders are entered into the cash register at one time. The collected money is counted and any excess is returned to the driver as tips.
7. The manager uses the returned Customer Order copies (white) for compiling total delivery sales information.

1. Why was it important for the student design team to describe the current system before the proposed automated system?
2. Briefly describe three ways to improve the current system *without automation*.
3. Draw a hierarchy chart for the current system.
4. Draw a context diagram for the current system.
5. Draw a set of exploded physical data flow diagrams for the current system.
6. Draw a system flowchart for the current system.
7. Draw a HIPO chart for the current system.

C A S E   6.3

MCKRAKLIN AEROSPACE: DOCUMENTATION

SETTING

Dave Costner, the head of McKraklin's Informations System Department, reduced the area of investigation to the inventory system shown in Figure 6.3–1. He assigned a senior analyst (Susan Willebe) and a new analyst (Ron Sauter) as a team to analyze the current system. The team started with a manual description of the system.

DESCRIPTION OF CURRENT INVENTORY SYSTEM

Receiving

1. Stock is received from vendor with copy of the purchase order.
2. Materials are counted and inspected.

3. If there are any discrepancies in count or material quality:
   - An inspection discrepancy form is completed and sent to the purchasing department.
   - Any faulty material is set aside for return to the vendor.
4. A receiving slip is completed and sent to the warehouse with the accepted material.
5. Warehouse personnel:
   - Check a manual listing to find the warehouse location for the material to be stocked.
   - Place the material in that warehouse location.
   - Stamp the receiving slip to show that the material was stocked.
   - Send the receiving slip to the data entry department.
6. At the end of each day, data entry personnel

FIGURE 6.3–1   **Dave Costner's Subsystem Focus on McKraklin's Inventory System**

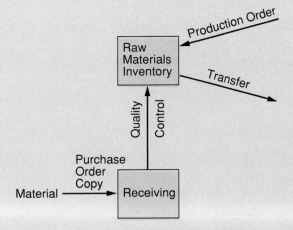

217

FIGURE 6.3–2 **Data Elements for Receiving Slip**

```
Receiving Slip  =  Purchase-Order-Number
               +  Purchase-Order-Date
               +  Vendor-Shipping-Date
               +  Vendor-Code
               +  Shipment-Mode-Code
               +  1 {Order-Item} 15 = Stock-Number
                  +  Short-Description
                  +  Quantity-Ordered
                  +  Quantity-Shipped
                  +  Unit-Price
                  +  Extended-Amount
                  +  Total-Billing-Amount
```

enter receiving slip data. Figure 6.3–2 shows the data elements entered.

Inventory

1. Each production control order is sent to the data entry department.
2. As each order is received, data entry personnel enter the data shown in Figure 6.3–3.
3. The computer produces two products:
   - Picking slip, which includes warehouse locations where ordered items are stored
   - Packing slip, to be included with shipment of material to production control
4. The packet of forms is sent to the warehouse department.
5. Warehouse personnel use the packing slip to:
   - Find the warehouse location where ordered items are stored.
   - Extract from the location the number of units ordered.
   - Mark on the packing slip and picking slip any units ordered that cannot be shipped because not enough stock is on hand.
   - Send insufficient stock picking slips to the data entry department.
   - Send the picked material and packing slip to production control.
6. At the end of each day, data entry personnel enter data from insufficient stock picking slips to inventory records.

REVIEW QUESTIONS

1. Why does the data entry department enter customer orders immediately, whereas all other entries are done at the end of each day?

FIGURE 6.3–3 **Data Elements for Production Order**

```
Production Order  =  Order-Number
                 +  Order-Date
                 +  Production-Job-Number
                 +  1 {Order-Item} 30 = Stock-Number
                    + Quantity
                 +  Authorizing-Initials
```

2. Could the picking and packing slips be combined? How?
3. Provide three ways to improve the described system *without changing the automated system*.

1. Draw a hierarchy chart for the current inventory system.
2. Draw a context diagram for the current system.
3. Draw a set of exploded physical data flow diagrams for the current system.
4. Draw a systems flowchart of the current system.
5. Draw a HIPO chart for the current system.

In this chapter you will learn about:

WHAT: (Concepts) Performing a requirements analysis to determine what type of information system is desired and required by end-users.

WHY: An information systems problem is defined as the gap between what exists and what is needed. Requirements analysis is the process that defines this gap.

WHEN: The initial investigation stage has determined that an alleged information systems problem requires further analysis.

WHO: Systems analyst team.

WHERE: End-user work area.

HOW: (Techniques) Interviews
Questionnaires
Observation
Requirements analysis document

OUTLINE

- Setting
- A Total Quality Approach
- A Structured Approach
- Describing the Current System
- User Expectations
- Requirements Analysis Methods
- Interviewing
- Questionnaire and Observation Guidelines
- Resource Constraints
- Requirements Analysis Document
- Human Aspects

C H A P T E R 7

REQUIREMENTS ANALYSIS

You can observe a lot by just watching.

—YOGI BERRA

SETTING

An information systems problem is the gap between the ideal and current system. The current system was defined in Chapter 5, but only in an abbreviated form. The next stage in the systems development life cycle is requirements analysis; this stage has four goals:

1. Describe the current system completely.
2. Determine the ideal information system.
3. Bring the ideal system into realistic range by identifying resource constraints.
4. Inspire user confidence in the systems development team.

In the requirements analysis stage, there is maximum interaction between systems personnel and the end-user community. Sometimes, end-users are skeptical of systems people—not of their skills but of their ability to understand real-world, user-oriented problems. The requirements analysis stage allows the IS development team to sell their qualifications to and secure the respect and trust of end-users. This is also the stage for making end-user participation an underlying theme of the entire systems development life cycle.

On the other hand, some systems professionals are skeptical of end-users. Often end-users remember incidents of systems failure and forget the day-by-day, month-by-month examples of systems success. In addition, it is difficult for a group of end-users to reach a consensus about what they need (want) from a business information system.

So end-users are sometimes skeptical of systems people, and systems people are sometimes skeptical of end-users. Requirements analysis, if done well, can serve as a communication and confidence builder for end-users and systems people alike. Both groups are talented, but they speak different languages. The requirements analysis stage establishes a common language for analyst and users.

Performing requirements analysis can be tricky. Analysts would like to narrow down possible new systems options so that choosing the best system is not an enormous task. Yet, they do not want to exclude new ideas by broadcasting preconceived solutions and constraints.

It is easy to enter this stage with preconceived ideas. After all, the preliminary problem report and the current system description have already been completed. Nevertheless, preconceptions can be avoided by performing requirements analysis in the following sequence:

1. Determine from users what they want in an information system.
2. Narrow down this desired system through introduction of systems resource constraints.
3. Sell the narrowed system to users.

A TOTAL QUALITY APPROACH

Remember that our analysis, and later design, is focused on the nine information characteristics: (1) relevancy, (2) completeness, (3) correctness, (4) security, (5) timeliness, (6) economy, (7) efficiency, (8) reliability, and (9) usability. When we interview end-users, our questions must systemically include these characteristics. When we observe processes, these characteristics must be part of our checklists. Only in this manner can we be sure that we do not miss something, that some vital element does not "fall between the cracks." This is one of the basic precepts of total quality management.

A STRUCTURED APPROACH

The physical data flow diagram (DFD) has been used as a checklist for many of the analysis techniques discussed in this chapter. Many advocates of structured development suggest that the physical DFD is not required. Indeed, many suggest that the entire requirements analysis stage could be eliminated from the SDLC. This is an important contention. As stated throughout this chapter, fact gathering is expensive and takes considerable time. If the requirements analysis stage could be eliminated, business information systems could be designed more quickly and less expensively. The possibility deserves discussion.

Structured development advocates rest their position on the assumption that many business information systems are similar from firm to firm. This point was stressed in

Section One, where a standard template was described for transaction-processing systems. The template was used to show standard versions of such common TPS applications as purchasing, receiving, and order entry. Although there may be some unique features, such systems are largely the same from one firm to another. For such relatively standard systems, why do systems analysts need to determine what end-users consider to be the desired system or develop a physical data flow diagram? Remember the sequence of DFD development:

1. The physical DFD of the current system describes what is done and how it is done.
2. The logical DFD of the current system is developed by stripping from the physical DFD all implementation features *(how)*.
3. The remaining features *(what)* are redesigned to form the logical DFD of the proposed system.
4. Implementation features *(how)* are added to form the physical DFD of the proposed system.

If analysts know what the new receiving TPS will look like—that is, a standard system—why not start with the logical data flow diagram of the proposed system? This would decrease dramatically the time and effort required in the systems analysis phase of the SDLC.

As with all development tactics, disadvantages counter the advantages. Consider these disadvantages:

- Although many business applications are similar, many more are not. This is particularly true for management information systems, decision support systems, expert systems, and executive information systems.
- The requirements analysis stage contains maximum opportunities for interaction and communication between designers and users. Eliminating this stage may lead to a decrease in user involvement.
- When end-user involvement is not emphasized, the developed system is not perceived as *our* (the users') information system. The users do not assume ownership of the new information system and are less tolerant of subsequent system flaws.

Structured development approaches are a significant addition to the development of business information systems. However, proponents of structured development must guard against an approach that relegates end-users to a minor role. An information system is only as successful as end-users perceive it to be. Elimination of the physical DFD and the requirements analysis stage should be considered carefully.

DESCRIBING THE CURRENT SYSTEM

Chapter 5 explained the current system description—the end product of the initial investigation. The description is done through review of documentation, limited observation, and limited interviewing. The current system description is not detailed enough to be the basis for an extensive analysis.

Hence, the current system is not described *extensively* until the requirements analysis stage of the SDLC. In conducting the requirements analysis stage, ask two questions about the current system.

First, are there differences between the way the system was designed to be used and actual usage? Often, actual usage varies from the design's intentions. If you continually drive your car faster than it was designed to be driven, why should you be surprised if your gasoline mileage is less than advertised?

McLeod Plumbing's inventory system was designed to accommodate a maximum of 50 concurrent users. Now there are 120 workstations linked to the inventory system. Users are complaining about slow interactive response time. The problem exists because users are exceeding the design's expectations.

Second, how does the current system perform? The answer to this question is critical to learning what users want in an information system. Analysts must gather current performance statistics, such as averages, highs, lows, and most frequently occurring values (statistical mode), for all nine information characteristics (e.g., accuracy).

End-users remember single events rather than a stream of happenings, so systems analysts face the so-called supply officer's dilemma. People remember the one item the supply officer delivered late; they tend to forget the 999 items that were delivered on time. Users of business information systems seem to remember the two hours the computer was down while taking for granted the twenty-nine days during the month when the computer was operating at full capacity.

When end-users are presented statistics about how the current system is operating, a common reaction is, "Oh, I didn't know that. I must have remembered one of the bad times." Do not try to justify the current system; just try to identify the real gap between current and desired systems.

The data flow diagram can serve as a guide to the necessary performance statistics. Figure 7–1 is a data flow diagram of a receiving system. Note these performance statistics on the DFD:

- *Data flows (e.g., forms and reports):* Minimum, average, and maximum volume of incoming data flows
- *Data stores (files):* Minimum, average, and maximum items stored
- *Processes:* Minimum, average, and maximum number of days to process incoming data flows

Simplicity of the data flow diagram is crucial if it is to be used as a tool for communication between analysts and end-users. The purpose of a figure such as Figure 7–1 is to stir end-user memories of the current system's performance.

A data flow diagram such as Figure 7–1 also provides analysts with a requirements analysis checklist for the parts of the system that must be analyzed. The DFD indicates that the following tasks must be performed:

1. Collect and analyze all forms (incoming data flows).
2. Collect and analyze all reports (outgoing data flows).

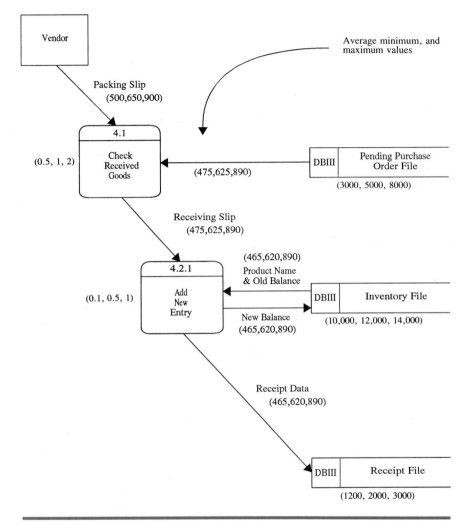

FIGURE 7–1   Data Flow Diagram for a Receiving System

3. Collect and analyze all data elements stored in records (data stores).
4. Obtain a list of end-users in each process as potential interviewees.
5. Consider each process as a target for on-site observation.
6. Collect all procedures (process workings) for documentation analysis.
7. Collect minimum, average, and maximum throughput volumes and times for all data flows and processes.

With the checklist and description of the current system in hand, we are poised as Don Quixote to seek the user's ideal information system.

USER EXPECTATIONS

The next step of requirements analysis is to survey user expectations and determine the desired, ideal information system. The term *ideal* is used in a conceptual rather than a realistic sense. There really is no ideal system. Even if it were possible to reach an ideal, the user community probably could not agree on what that ideal is. The term *ideal* is too subjective. Instead, systems analysts speak of an information system that *satisfices*. **Satisficing** means selecting an alternative that is better than others but not necessarily the best. Think about what is possible rather than what is perfect.

At the same time, systems analysts cannot afford to raise user expectations so high that a practically selected new system will be an immediate disappointment. Requirements analysis is a balancing act. It is much like asking a child what he or she wants for Christmas when you have a tight budget.

Four issues are important in obtaining information from users: problems with user expectations, problems with analyst bias, products generated, and documentation of user expectations.

Problems with User Expectations

Information systems expectations provided by the user community cannot always be taken at face value, for several reasons:

- User expectations change over time, and the cast of users changes. Individual users learn more and then increase their needs and expectations.
- After implementation of a new information system, users understandably forget the expectations they had that guided design of the new system. Are your expectations the same now as they were when you began your college career?
- Users have both perceptions and opinions. Perceptions are based on actual observation of the situation; often, opinions are not based on facts or observations. Users base their information systems expectations on perceptions, on opinions, and sometimes on both. The analyst must separate requirements based on perception from those based on opinion.
- Sometimes users are unsure. Users who are unsure of how to perform their jobs typically ask for all the information they can get. They do not know enough to determine what information they really need. The information they actually require differs from their stated expectations.
- There will be a considerable range of user opinions on what is the desired, or ideal, information system. The analyst tries to narrow the range to some consensus. For example, interviews with users of Palko Publishing's order entry system included this question: What would be ideal workstation response time? Answers ranged from one second to three minutes. Analysts reduced this range to a consensus: median desired response time—10.5 seconds; mean desired response time—7.2 seconds; and mode desired response time—10.0 seconds (33 percent of respondents). In this case, Palko Publishing's analysts established a new goal that workstation response time should be less than 10 seconds (the mode).

■ The desired system may be only a moderate step above the current system. Given data and time to think, most users will agree that the current system really is better than they thought, that many of the features of the current system are quite satisfactory, and that a modest increase in performance will be "good enough."

Given these problems with user expectations, it is not an easy task to combine them into a single picture of the user community's *ideal* information system. It is even more difficult to convince end-users that the single picture is what the user community wanted, rather than what the analyst decided. This second task can be made easier by guarding against analyst bias.

Problems with Analyst Bias

Analysts must collect user ideas without being constrained by their own ideas, experiences, or feelings. Later in the SDLC, there is an appropriate place for analysts to whittle the system to personal perceptions. Now is not the time for that.

Analysts must enter end-user interviews guarding against biases that could influence those interviews. Analyst biases include:

■ Preconceived solutions to information problems ("Well, Mr. End-user, let me run this idea by you.")
■ Constraints inhibiting implementation of user-desired features ("That's a nice idea, Ms. End-user, but it would cost too much.")
■ Relative importance of end-user ("That's an interesting idea, Mr. End-user. Are you aware that your superiors are not thinking along that line?")

Keep information options open. Do not hide innovative approaches by flaunting preconceived biases.

Products Generated

Solicitation of end-user expectations produces the following five products:

1. *Specific objectives* (e.g., workstation response time will be no more than 30 seconds)
2. *Report type and frequency* (e.g., a Delayed Shipments report is used once a week)
3. *Training needs:* the interviews with end-users will uncover cases of users who are unsure of their tasks or of how to use the computer systems. This leads to identification of user training needs.
4. *Documented versus reported system use:* External probes (e.g., usage logs) can reveal how often and to what extent users actually use the system. Compare this with what users say.
5. *Feel for organization politics:* Politics is rarely documented. Nevertheless, you can learn to identify the power players, troublemakers, and information spreaders (gossips). All organizations have such people, including the IS department. A feel for organization politics will prove invaluable throughout the SDLC. Do not get involved with these politics—just note them!

Documentation of User Expectations

As analysts interview end-users, they should keep records of the expectations voiced. Such documentation can be used to (1) arrive at a consensus of user expectations, (2) help convince end-users that *they* actually generated the resulting description of the desired system, and (3) provide a structured interview format that helps reduce the influence of analyst bias.

Figure 7–2 is an example of such documentation. It is a form for recording user requirements and preferences and can be completed easily during each end-user interview.

REQUIREMENTS ANALYSIS METHODS

Common data-gathering methods used during the requirements analysis stage are *interviews, questionnaires, observation, procedure analysis,* and *document survey.* Each method will be described now according to the following checklist:

1. How the method is used
2. Target for the method (using symbols of the data flow diagram: data flows, data stores, processes, and entities)
3. Advantages of the method
4. Disadvantages of the method
5. When the method is best used

Sampling is a technique that can be used to save time in all the methods.

Later, interviews, questionnaires, and observation will be discussed in more detail. At the end of this section of the book, References and Further Readings provide sources for obtaining more information on each method.

Interviews

1. How the method is used:
   - Potential interviewees are selected.
   - Appointments are made with those selected.
   - Structured questions are designed for interview sessions.
   - Selected persons are interviewed personally and their responses are recorded.
2. Target for the method:
   - Key personnel in DFD processes
   - Sometimes outside personnel, such as customers or vendors
3. Advantages of the method:
   - Allows interviewer to gauge responses to questions and adjust questions accordingly.
   - Good for probing, nonstructured questions, such as, "Why do you think this is happening?"
   - Shows interviewee's personal presence.
   - Response rate is high, since there is an actual scheduled meeting.

USER REQUIREMENTS AND PREFERENCES

User (Individual's Name) *Sara Bendright*

Organization Unit *Purchasing Department*

Title or Position *Purchasing Clerk*

Required or Preferred System Characteristic *Daily Report on Purchase orders not cleared after 180 days*

Reason for Need *Follow-up to venders on delayed Purchase orders*

Does Current System Provide This? *No*

If Not, Reason (if known) *No program to scan file and select aged Purchase orders*

If Characteristic Involves Information, Specify source (if known) *Pending Purchase order file*

FIGURE 7–2   **Form for Recording User Requirements and Preferences**

From R. Carlsen and J. Lewis, *The Systems Analysis Workbook* (1973), p. 95. Used by permission of the publisher, Prentice Hall, a division of Simon and Schuster, Englewood Cliffs, N.J.

4. Disadvantages of the method:
   - It is time consuming (thus costly)
   - Requires training and experience on the part of the interviewers.
   - It is difficult to compare interview results because of interview's tailored, subjective nature.
   - It is difficult to select only a few to be interviewed without hurting feelings of others.
5. When the method is best used:
   - Eliciting opinions from key personnel
   - Testing credibility of interviewees
   - Looking for interviewee unsureness or contradictions
   - Establishing credibility of design team

QUESTIONNAIRES

1. How the method is used:
   - Standard questionnaire is designed.
   - Questionnaire is sent to a broad range of end-users.
   - Structured responses are summarized into statistical distributions.
2. Target for the method:
   - All end-users with possible insights into potential solutions to systems problems
   - End-users associated with the process symbols on the data flow diagram
3. Advantages of the method:
   - Cheaper and faster than interviews
   - Does not need as many trained investigators (only one expert need design a questionnaire used by all selected end-users).
   - Is easy to synthesize results since the questionnaire is structured.
   - Can easily reach all end-users with minimum costs.
4. Disadvantages of the method:
   - Cannot tailor questions to specific end-users.
   - Analyst involvement seems impersonal to end-users.
   - Low response rates because there are few means to force end-users to return questionnaires.
   - Cannot adjust questions to specific end-user responses.
5. When the method is best used:
   - Simple, nonambiguous questions (e.g., usage frequency, ranking of desired features)
   - Broad coverage of end-users needed
   - Time and funds scarce

Observation

1. How the method is used:
   - Analyst personally visits observation area.
   - Analyst records happenings in area, including volumes and processing speeds.

2. Target for the method:
   - Geographic process locations as shown in the DFD
3. Advantages of the method:
   - Records facts rather than opinions.
   - Does not require question construction.
   - Can be unobtrusive or hidden (end-users do not know they are being observed).
   - Analyst does not have to rely on oral responses of end-users.
4. Disadvantages of the method:
   - If seen, analyst may affect operation.
   - Unless observation is over a long period, facts gathered during any one observation may not be representative of typical day or week.
   - Requires experience and skill on part of the analyst.
5. When the method is best used:
   - Need to gather quantitative figures such as times, volumes, and so on (such figures cannot be gathered dependably through interview or questionnaire, since respondents must rely on fallible memory).
   - Suspicion that what people say is happening is really not happening

Procedure Analysis

1. How the method is used:
   - In **procedure analysis,** operating procedures are studied to identify key documents flowing through the information system. These should be the data flows of the physical data flow diagram.
   - The flow of each key document is charted as described in the system's operating procedures.
   - Through observation, the analyst studies *actual* rather than described document flow to determine volume distributions (high, low, mean), where actual document flow differs from procedural document flow, and what is done with different copies of the document.

NEW MEXICO SUPREME COURT

Court rules (procedures) were used to diagram appeals from the trial courts to the New Mexico Supreme Court. Then, observations were made of what actually happened with the appeals. One observed task varied notably from procedures. Law clerks were supposed to screen all appeals and summarize their key facts. The summaries were intended to save the justices time when they studied the appeals. Because of a shortage and overburdening of law clerks, this step had been eliminated in practice (but not in procedure). As a result, appeal processing times had increased considerably.

2. Target for the method:
   - Key data flows in DFD
   - Processes in DFD
3. Advantages of the method:
   - Evaluation of procedures can be done with minimum interference of and influence on operating personnel.
   - Procedural flows become a structured checklist for observation. Thus, such observation is quicker, which reduces analyst interference with operating functions.
4. Disadvantages of the method:
   - Procedures may not be complete or up to date.
   - Charting of procedural document flow takes time and skilled analysis.
5. When the method is best used:
   - Deciding whether problem is faulty systems design or failure of personnel to follow good design.
   - Analysis team is not totally familiar with document flow.

Document Survey

1. How the method is used:
   - Key documents and reports are identified.
   - Copies of actual documents and reports are collected.
   - For each document or report, the following types of data are recorded: fields included, field format (e.g., size and type), frequency of use (e.g., special instructions field used on only 3 percent of customer orders surveyed), and coding structures.
2. Target for the method:
   - Key data flows as shown on the DFD.
3. Advantages of the method:
   - Minimum interruption of operational functions
   - Often leads to considerable improvements without major procedural modifications to current system
4. Disadvantages of the method:
   - Time consuming (the typical business organization is inundated with documents and reports)
5. When the method is best used:
   - Eventually must be done if a new system is being designed (if, during the analysis stage, it becomes clear that new systems design is necessary, document analysis can aid the analysis effort and later design tasks).

The different analysis methods just described have two points in common. First, each method is targeted to specific components of the physical data flow diagram. Hence, the physical DFD is not only a communication medium between users and analysts but also a structured checklist for analysis.

Second, all the methods require an investment of analyst time, and there will always be constraints on this time. For example, top management may exert pressure to perform the analysis and solve the information problem quickly. Another constraint may be a shortage of analyst resources. Whatever the reason, analyst time is at a premium, and efforts must be made to reduce the time required to use the methods described. One method of reducing the time requirement is sampling.

Sampling

Sampling can help reduce the time to analyze a problem and costs. Carefully chosen, a small subset (sample) of a population can yield almost the same insight as the entire population (census). Because you are not reading a statistics textbook, it would be inappropriate to present a full treatment of the subject. However, some suggestions may help you when you need to use sampling in analysis of business information systems.

First, beware of **convenience sampling.** The subset that is easy to reach rarely is typical of the total population. For example, one analyst looked at a sample of purchasing forms to determine how often clerks did not fill in the field called Date Received. She entered the room containing purchase orders, selected the first two filing cabinets near the door, and inspected every tenth purchase order. She found a high rate of orders with the Date Received field missing. The senior analyst patiently explained that the filing cabinets were arranged in date sequence. The most recent purchase orders were in the cabinets nearest the door (the ones selected so conveniently). The more recent the date of the purchase order, the greater the probability that the material ordered is still in transit. If the material has not yet been received, how can clerks have completed the Date Received field?

Second, realize that sophisticated sampling is not necessary. Remember, you are not trying to arrive at critical, undeniable conclusions. You merely are trying to gain insight into information systems problems. Therefore, sophisticated sampling is not needed if it significantly increases analysis cost and effort—unless, of course, the sophisticated methods improve knowledge significantly.

Formal statistical sampling requires establishment of parameters such as sample size, confidence intervals, randomization of starts, and so on. Yet, systems analysts are detectives seeking clues, not researchers seeking definitive solutions. Strive for what works approximately, quickly, and accurately.

Third, use sampling only when appropriate (when you can justify it). Choosing a sample of 100 from 10,000 receiving documents is appropriate if that sample is chosen correctly. By contrast, do not select a 20 percent sample of managers to interview. Even a single manager not interviewed may bias your sample and cause political problems. A good rule of thumb is: Sample facts but never opinions. The facts in documents, procedures, and reports do not get their feelings hurt or complain as people do. From a DFD perspective, sample data flows and data stores. Do not sample processes.

Fourth, use **systematic random sampling.** For example, select every *n*th (say, third) filing cabinet, two drawers in each cabinet, and every *k*th (say, fifth) record in each drawer selected.

Fifth, do not be afraid to re-sample. Unsophisticated sampling may produce results that are startling, difficult to sell to management, or politically explosive. Repeat the

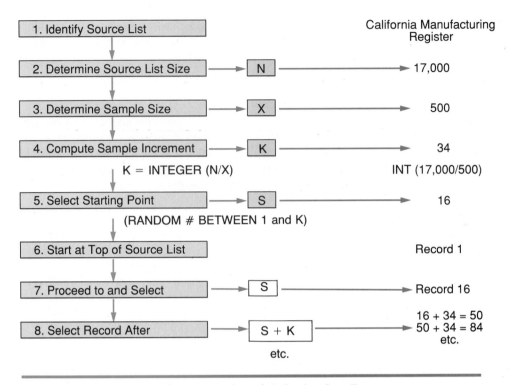

FIGURE 7–3   **Recommended Approach for Systematic Random Sampling**

analysis using the most sophisticated and correct sampling techniques available. In short, in matters of establishing credibility, dot all sampling i's and cross all sampling t's.

Figure 7–3 portrays the recommended sampling approach.

The most commonly used requirements analysis methods will now be discussed more thoroughly, beginning with interviewing.

INTERVIEWING

Several factors are important to conducting good interviews: objectives, audience, format, weighting and combining responses, and documentation.

Objectives

Interviews are performed to:

1. Obtain user responses to key questions and follow up on the questions accordingly.
2. Seek opinions about questions such as, "How do you feel about the support you get from the information systems department?"
3. Make sure key end-users feel someone is listening to their opinions.

4. Gauge unsureness of and contradictions from key end-users.
5. Present a "show of force" for the credibility of the analysis team.

Audience

Any end-user can be interviewed. Since interviewing is time-consuming and requires skill, however, it is best to restrict the interviewing audience to those who are in positions of power and can politically derail or push forward the proposal for a new information system, are systems knowledgeable, are workers totally involved with the system, have asked to be interviewed, and have reported the problem that started the SDLC. Even this may seem a large list. Yet, most candidates you select will fit into two to four of these groups.

Format

Positive or negative results can occur in an interview. Positively, you learn more about the problem through end-users' responses. If you are not careful, however, you can cause two negative results.

First, you can influence the end-users with your own opinions so that end-users express your idea, not their own. Second, you can induce negative end-user reactions to your interviewing style. Arrogance or ineptitude may influence an end-user not to support your recommended changes.

Interviews are not training events for junior analysts; they are crucial to analyzing information systems problems. Interviews also establish credibility among users.

There are no casual interviews. Interviews must be carefully designed, staged, and performed. Ask these questions before every interview.

■ *Who should interview?* Interviewing requires communication skills and knowledge of information systems in general, this information system in particular, and the political environment. Inexperienced analysts should interview only if they are teamed with experienced analysts.

■ *Should I take notes?* The justice system in the United States rarely has allowed jurors to take notes during trials. Of the many reasons for this, one is germane to the systems analysis setting: Jurors taking notes are not paying full attention to the witness and may miss crucial testimony.

Taking detailed notes detracts from your concentration on what end-users are saying. It also prevents you from noticing their body language. In addition, the presence of an analyst taking notes discourages the end-user from being totally open. (Never tape record the session!) Taking notes in outline form and filling in details later is suggested.

Then how can you possibly remember the interview? Here are three tips:

1. Make the interview short so you do not overtax your memory.
2. Immediately after leaving the interview, find a quiet place where you can record your recollections.
3. If, during the interview, a detailed point comes up, ask the end-user, "Do you mind if I take notes on *this* point so I remember it correctly?"

■ *How many interviewers should there be?* There should be at least two but no more than three analysts at an interview. Two or three analysts aid after-the-fact note taking and provide a basis for discussion of and consensus on what the end-user "really said" or "really meant." An interview group of more than three can be threatening to a single end-user. (This is referred to as a gang interview.)

■ *Should structured or unstructured questions be used?* Structured questions are predefined. They are asked in exactly the same way in different interview sessions. An example of a structured question is, "Which of the following reports do you use?" Unstructured questions are tailored to end-user responses and the specific interview setting. An example of an unstructured question might be (in response to an end-user opinion), "Why are you so dissatisfied with the attitudes of information systems personnel?"

Structured questions require less interviewing skill—they are checklists. They are also easier to collate into a consensus, because there is a limited range of interviewee responses. Unstructured questions require detective skills. The analyst senses a potential area of knowledge and probes deeper within that area. It is difficult to construct systematically a composite of responses to unstructured questions, because the posing of each question is unique to the particular interview situation.

The interview includes a mixture of structured and unstructured questions. That mix depends upon several characteristics: the analyst's interview skills, management level of the interviewee, and type of knowledge gleaned from the interview. Figure 7–4 shows the spectrum of structured and unstructured questions.

Structured questions are also called **closed questions,** while unstructured questions are called **open questions.** A follow-up question such as, Why do you think that? is called a **probe.** Only the most experienced analysts should try probes during an interview.

■ *How long should the interview last?* Once more scan the audience list for the interviews. That list includes busy people to whom time is a valuable commodity. Manage the interview time according to the following guidelines:

1. If you are not taking notes, an interview of more than 30 minutes will tax your memory.
2. Never exceed the time the interviewee has scheduled. Five minutes before the scheduled end, the interviewee's interest decreases rapidly. If you exceed scheduled time because of your enthusiasm, those being interviewed begin to resent the interview and the interview team.

FIGURE 7–4   Spectrum of Structured and Unstructured Interview Questions

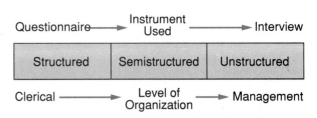

3. If possible, conclude the interview before the allotted time. You will have gained an end-user supporter because you respected important time constraints.
4. If the interviewee causes the interview to extend beyond the allotted time, do not look at your watch and act fidgety.

Weighing and Combining Responses

Typically, analysts conduct several interviews and then combine interview results to detect consensus opinions and requirements. Yet, not all interview results are exactly the same. Some interviews may be more revealing and some interview subjects may be more trustworthy than others.

When combining interviews, the analyst is like a member of a trial jury, who listens to various witnesses and weighs the testimony on the basis of each witness's perceived credibility. In the analysis situation, relative credibility is based on factors such as decision-making (approving) influence, presence of contradictions in answering questions, unsureness when answering questions, and perceived lack of openness.

Having more than one interviewer is important here. Multiple interviewers can discuss interview experiences and arrive at consensus evaluations—similar to jury deliberations. In this way, an interviewer's personal bias can be revealed and adjusted for. For example, one interviewer may give more credence to those end-users who support his or her preconceived notions of how to design a new system. Two fellow interviewers can filter out this analyst bias.

Documentation

A **synopsis of interviews** is the deliverable product from the interviewing process. The synopsis includes:

- Names, dates, and times of interview sessions
- Structured question formats used
- Names and positions of interviewees
- Synopsis of results
- Individual interview documentation
- Analysis of facts discovered and further analysis suggested as a result of the interview process

Interviewing Tips

These ten tips are based on this analyst's successes and failures in interviewing:

1. Watch the time. Do not cause the interview to proceed beyond its scheduled time.
2. If the end-user causes the interview to last longer than scheduled, do not keep looking at your watch.

3. Avoid questions such as, "Don't you think this is the way the system should work?"
4. Listen. Do not talk except to ask questions (briefly).
5. Do not use body language to show either approval or disapproval of what the end-user is saying. Do not grimace or shift uncomfortably.
6. Make the end-user feel that this interview is the most important one of the entire project.
7. Be courteous and professional. Remember, you are also selling the competence of your design team.
8. Do not take exhaustive notes during the interview. Record detailed observations immediately after the interview.
9. Use a structured set of interview questions. This allows easier consolidation of results from multiple interviews. It also decreases reliance on memory.
10. Do not ask questions that require the user to remember many details (e.g., How many? How often? When?).

Interviewing is costly and requires interactive skills. Restrict the interview method to situations that are quite important to the analysis effort. When in doubt, do not interview. Instead, use the questionnaire or observation methods discussed next.

QUESTIONNAIRE AND OBSERVATION GUIDELINES

Two alternatives to interviewing are questionnaires and observation.

Questionnaires

The questionnaire method is appropriate when questions are simple and unambiguous. Use the questionnaire when you need to gather facts rather than opinions or when the costs and time required to interview a large range of end-users are excessive.

Questionnaires are relatively inexpensive. The cost of sending a set of questions to a group of subjects is only the cost of questionnaire copying and mailing. Therefore, the audience for questionnaires is almost unlimited.

Administration of questionnaires is easy. Mail the questionnaires and wait for them to return. Analysis of returned questionnaires is a little more difficult. Nevertheless, guidelines and tools are available (see the References and Further Readings at the end of this section).

Questionnaire response rate is typically low. **Response rate** is the percentage of questionnaires sent out and returned completed. A good response rate is 15 to 20 percent. With poorly designed questionnaires, response rates decrease rapidly. The lower the response rate, the harder it is to justify that responses received represent the total population of end-users.

COMPUTERIZED OPINION GATHERING

In today's business organizations, electronic mail systems are fairly commonplace. If the analysis team has determined that questionnaires need to be completed for requirements analysis, why not use the computer to collect the data via an electronic mail system? Computers have been used in a variety of data collection applications. Marketing companies use computers to poll campuses and shopping malls. The benefits of computer use include control of interviewer bias, savings in data collection costs, elimination of coding and data entry errors, and the ability to track data on a day-to-day or week-to-week basis. In one instance, UPI ASK (a survey branch of United Press International) was able to collect 10,000 responses in a three-week period. Traditional data collection techniques would have gathered only 500 responses in that time.

The following problems common to manual surveys can be eliminated with electronic surveys:

- Incomplete forms
- Illegible forms
- Biased sample of users
- Low response rate
- Long time between program execution and evaluation
- Data coding errors
- Keying errors
- High error rate in data transcription
- User resentment of excessive paperwork

Most studies report that respondents either enjoy or, at worst, are indifferent to the computerized survey. Studies have also found that cooperation rates increase when personal computers are used to perform interviews. Response rates can be improved by minimizing the cost of responding, maximizing the reward for responding, and establishing trust that the reward will be delivered.

The use of computers to present information and perform personal interviews does not present any barriers to cooperation. There are, however, some differences between computerized and noncomputerized methods that have been determined through empirical studies:

1. The interactive nature of computer interviewing encourages greater cooperation and higher response rates than traditional methods.
2. Computer interviewing reduces the amount of "social desirability" in responses; that is, respondents are likely to give their real views, not what they think the interviewer expects to hear.
3. The means selected for computer dialogue affects distribution of responses in answers to scale questions. Using the arrow keys results in a range of responses narrower than normal, and using the number keys results in a wider than normal range.
4. Computer interviewing puts the respondent in a better mood, which in turn generates more positive scores for attitude questions.
5. Computer interviews generate more effort from a respondent than traditional noncomputerized interviews.

PROTOTYPING PROFILE

The information you provide will help us decide just how prototyping should be taught in an MIS curriculum. All responses are confidential. If you wish a copy of the results of this study, please include your mailing address.

1. *Do you use prototyping?* _____ _____ (If no, go to
                      (Yes) (No) question 10)

2. *How often do you
   use prototyping?* _____ _____ _____ _____ _____
            (Often)   (Sometimes)   (Rarely)

3. *Do you use a microcomputer for prototyping?*
   _____ _____ _____ _____ _____ _____ _____
   (Almost always)   (Sometimes)   (Never)

4. *What do you think are the benefits of prototyping?*

Scale	Quite Important		Important		Not Important
User Designer Communications	_____	_____	_____	_____	_____
User Involvement	_____	_____	_____	_____	_____
Short Development Time	_____	_____	_____	_____	_____
User Training	_____	_____	_____	_____	_____
Decreased Costs	_____	_____	_____	_____	_____
Fewer Maintenance Problems	_____	_____	_____	_____	_____

5. *How long does it take to develop a prototype (weeks)?*
   Minimum _____ Average _____ Maximum _____

6. *What types of applications do you prototype?*
   Transaction Processing _____ MIS _____
   Decision Support _____ Expert Systems _____
   Other (Specify) _____

FIGURE 7–5   Sample Questionnaire

Your response rate will increase if you follow these tips for designing a questionnaire:

1. In the first item on the questionnaire, state the purpose of the questionnaire and state that all responses are confidential. Figure 7–5, a sample questionnaire, includes such a statement. It also includes examples for all the remaining tips.
2. Reduce questionnaire length. The person to whom you are sending the questionnaire is important. Otherwise, why bother with the questionnaire? That person's time is valuable. Ask only for the information you need. The longer the questionnaire, the lower the response rate. The sample questionnaire (see Figure 7–5) is two pages (front and back of one sheet).

7. *What prototyping languages do you use?*

_____

8. *What production programming languages do you use for daily applications processing?*
   COBOL _____   C _____   PL/I _____   FORTRAN _____
   Other (Specify) _____

9. *What do you do with prototypes after the new system is operational?*
   Discard _____   Training _____   Demonstration _____
   Becomes operational system _____   Other (Specify) _____

10. *If you don't use prototyping very often, why not?*

_____
_____

- -

INDUSTRY DATA
We need the following data to ensure responses we receive are representative of the community as a whole.

   Your Position
      Title _____
   Your Firm's Major Product(s) or Service(s) _____
   Number Firm Total Employees (estimated) _____
   Number Information Department Employees _____

- -

SURVEY RESULTS
If you wish to receive a copy of survey results, please provide your name and mailing address.

_____
_____
_____
_____

THANK YOU FOR YOUR TIME AND ASSISTANCE!

3. Concentrate on closed questions where respondents can check blocks or write short answers. Note that Figure 7–5 has only one open question—number 10.
4. Do not ask the user to recall exact facts (e.g., "How many times a day do you use your telephone?"). When you need numeric estimates, try to assist users by asking for minimums, averages, and maximums (see question 5 in Figure 7–5).
5. Do not include **loaded questions.** An example of a loaded question is, "Don't you agree that prototyping is a very effective technique?"
6. Use a **Likert scale** to gather opinions. Note question 4 in Figure 7–5. Respondents check their opinions along a continuum of choices. Likert scales should have no more than nine and no fewer than five choices.
7. Conduct a **pilot test** with the questionnaire. Use colleagues, a small sample of end-users, or any other small group. Ask them to complete the questionnaire and

inform you of questions that were difficult to answer. Reconstruct your questionnaire on the basis of their responses.

So far, interviews and questionnaires have been described as fact-finding ventures. There is another side to these methods that may be just as important. Interviews and questionnaires generate clues about where to dig deeper, where to analyze further. Consider the following example.

An analyst for Casitrin Bottling Company investigated a complaint that the information-processing department delivered daily sales reports too late the next day to be useful to the marketing analysis staff. On interviewing the information processing manager, the analyst recorded the following comment: "I don't know what marketing analysis would do with the report if they received it on time. They're 20 percent understaffed and have low morale. You should visit them sometime." Given this clue, the analyst decided to observe operations of the marketing analysis staff.

Observation

People observe all the time. We look at an event and record, often in our memory, what we see. In the systems analysis setting, observation is far more structured. Analysts decide what specific events they wish to record (narrowing), observe these events as benignly as possible (passive observation), and record observations in a durable format (e.g., on paper or tape).

Observation is appropriate for gathering quantitative factors—volumes, processing speeds, length of lines, and so forth. Using interviews and questionnaires to elicit such facts requires end-user memory, and human memory is not reliable. Observation is also important when you suspect that what end-users are saying is not really what is happening.

Observation always must be a structured event. Analysts predesign a series of statistics and observations they wish to gather based on the nine information characteristics (e.g., accuracy). Real-life events move too fast for us to record what we see unless we know what we are looking for. Without structured observation, we are subject to **selective perception**—the tendency to notice events that fit a preconceived notion of the world. For example, the Casitrin Bottling Company analyst mentioned earlier now visits the marketing analysis section already believing the section's operation is faulty. It is human nature for the analyst to place more weight on observations that confirm her opinion that the section has problems and to discard evidence that counters this opinion.

Follow these practical tips when making observations:

1. Do not observe for long periods of time. Instead, schedule several shorter sessions, for two reasons. First, the longer you are in a place observing, the more chance you will disrupt the operation you are observing. Second, an observation for a full day will

be specific to that particular day, whereas an observation of one hour a day over eight days will reflect an average of a typical day rather than a selected day.

2. Take only minimal notes. Suppose someone approached you while you were preparing a flowchart for a program and began to take extensive notes. Would your speed and accuracy change? They probably would.

3. Before your observation, tell the supervisor and other end-users what you are doing and why. This will lessen the effect of your intrusion.

4. Use a short, specific checklist of the information you need to gather. Never observe without planning.

The requirements analysis stage of the SDLC result in two deliverable products: a description of resource constraints and the requirements analysis document.

RESOURCE CONSTRAINTS

At this point in the requirements analysis, the current system has been described fully. Also, the system desired by users has been determined. In most cases, user consensus about the desired system will be evolutionary, not revolutionary; it will be only a moderate step up from the current system.

Regardless of how moderate is the change from the current system to the desired system, there will be resource constraints prohibiting delivery of the ideal system. These constraints narrow down end-user expectations to a smaller number of practical alternatives.

Constraints are faced *after* rather than before the gathering of user expectations. If you started with constraints, you might squelch ideas with such statements as, "Well, that won't work because. . . ." Gather end-user ideas first, no matter how wild they may seem. Then bring those expectations down to reality by considering resource constraints.

Five constraints can prohibit delivery of an ideal information system: time, funds, skills, technology, and external factors. These constraints relate to the types of project feasibility discussed in Chapter 5.

Time

A replacement system must be delivered in a prescribed time frame because the current system may be deteriorating rapidly. This time constraint may prevent the analyst from considering technological innovations that will not be operationally possible within the allotted time.

The DASD (direct-access storage device) at Old U has reached saturation. The management team had originally intended to move to a relational database system with the next purchase of a DASD. However, because there is little time for software and file migration before total degradation of the system occurs, the short-term solution—staying with the old technology while increasing storage capacity—must suffice. The ideal, relational database system is not time feasible. The short-term solution is.

Funds

Some ideal systems alternatives may be too expensive for available funds. Any proposed information system must compete with other company alternatives for investing funds. For any information system, there is an upper limit to the funds that can be invested before that system can no longer compete against other investment alternatives.

Old U has decided to set up three new microcomputer laboratories on campus. The original proposal called for computers with 486 microprocessors. The state budget was cut drastically and the laboratory budget was cut by 40 percent. A decision was made to buy cheaper, less powerful, obsolete 286 microcomputers so that the same number of students could be served. Another possibility would have been to stay with the same quality of machine but to outfit only two of the three labs. The 486 proposal was not economically feasible. The obsolete microcomputer option is.

Skills

Information systems staff may not have the knowledge or experience to deal with complex enhancements such as telecommunications, integrated databases, and multimedia settings. The firm can contract with outside consulting services to augment internal design skills. Yet, such consulting services may be so expensive that the firm exceeds fund constraints.

Old U has been anxious to become a fully networked computing facility. IS managers read about the advances made at Stevens Point University and were able to obtain the software that AT&T and the Stevens Point staff created to support the campus environment. The software and cabling the managers thought was necessary have been installed. Now that the network is implemented, the IS staff receives problem calls every hour from students, faculty, and administrators. The problem does not lie in the software but in the lack of proper support from the untrained IS group to users. The new system is not operationally feasible because there are skill shortages among IS personnel.

Technology

The desired system may not be technologically ripe. For example, users may desire voice input; however, the information systems department judges the current state of that technology to be too restricted, too costly, or both.

Old U wants to initiate a dial-up registration system so students can access the system from their dorms. Two problems exist: lack of sufficient capacity on the host computer and lack of sophisticated telephone equipment at the campus level. The proposed new system will not be technologically feasible until campus technology is updated.

External Factors

Often, there are constraints imposed from outside the design setting. For example, audit considerations may prevent use of exotic technologies. A centralized database management system may prevent end-users from maintaining local, decentralized databases. Often, there are reports and other current systems functions favored by influential end-users.

Old U has a branch campus located seventy miles from the main campus. The branch campus would like to maintain a distributed local database containing student records. The state legislature views this desire as an attempt to attain separate status and refuses to allow the creation of such a database. The proposed system lacks management feasibility because of external factors.

Fact and opinion gathering for the requirements analysis stage of the SDLC is now complete. The one remaining task is preparation of the deliverable product—the requirements analysis document.

REQUIREMENTS ANALYSIS DOCUMENT

The **requirements analysis document** has two purposes. First, it serves as a record of extensive analysis efforts. Just as a detective's investigative report may later be searched for facts that did not seem important at the time but now fit into a pattern, this also is the case with the requirements analysis document. Second, the requirements analysis document allows narrowing down of the possible information systems alternatives.

Use this checklist when preparing the requirements analysis document. Make sure all elements are included in your final document.

1. Conduct of analysis:
   - End-users contacted
   - Records, forms, and reports analyzed
   - Processes observed
   - Analysis methods used
   - Problems encountered in data collection
   - Entity relationship diagrams

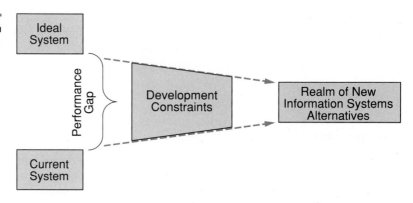

FIGURE 7–6   Reduced Information System Expectations

2. User requirements:
   - Unfettered systems objectives (what users really want) oriented around the nine information characteristics (e.g., accuracy)
   - Report requirements (type and frequency)
   - User training needs
   - Effect any new system will have on different end-users
3. Systems constraints:
   - Description of time, funds, skills, technology, and external factors
   - Realistic systems objectives (unfettered systems objectives adjusted to reflect resource constraints) by information characteristics
4. Documentation:
   - Data collection instruments (e.g., questionnaires used)
   - Consensus statistics (for example, synopsis of interviews)
   - Physical and logical data flow diagrams

At this point, we have come quite a way in the systems analysis phase of the SDLC. We have described the current information system. We have also documented the consensus about the ideal information system to service user requirements. Finally, we have brought the ideal system into a practical range by considering constraints on resources such as time, funds, and designers' skills. Now we are ready to find information systems alternatives for filling the gap between the current system and realistic user expectations. Figure 7–6 illustrates our position.

HUMAN ASPECTS

In this stage of the SDLC, you are dealing with people, not with computers, flowcharts, or file layouts. People can be inconsistent, vague, frustrating, and time-consuming. Nevertheless, people are fun—and people are what true information systems development is all about. Polish up your people skills. They will prove far more important to you at this stage than your technical skills. Also, do most of your work in end-user work areas, not in your isolated office. Get down there to where the action is!

SUMMARY

In the requirements analysis stage of the SDLC, there is maximum interaction between systems personnel and end-users. The purposes of this stage are to complete documentation of the current system, gather users' ideas about an ideal information system, and narrow down new systems options by considering resource constraints.

In describing the current system, analysts ask two questions. First, are there differences between the way the system was designed to be used and actual use? Many information systems are designed adequately but are not used as intended. Second, how does the current system perform? Analysts look for specifics—highs, lows, means, and modes. Often, end-users are pleasantly surprised by statistics on how the current system is really operating. A checklist helps analysts document the current system.

User expectations about an ideal information system cannot always be taken at face value. Several problems can arise: User expectations change over time, or users forget what they originally wanted. Also, not all users are sufficiently aware or certain of what they really need, and users' opinions vary considerably and must be made into a consensus.

In documenting user expectations, analysts must guard against personal bias, which may lead users to conclusions that are really not their own. Products generated from assessing user expectations include specific objectives for a system, desired report types and frequencies, user training needs, documented versus reported system use, and a feel for organization politics.

Analysts use five common methods for requirements analysis: interviews, questionnaires, observation, procedure analysis, and document survey. Each method has its own targets, advantages, and disadvantages. Interviews, questionnaires, and observation are particularly important because they are the most frequently used.

Requirements analysis leads to an end-user consensus about an ideal business information system. This consensus must be tempered, however, with realistic systems constraints such as time, funds, skills, technology, and external conditions and policies.

The deliverable product for this stage of the SDLC is the requirements analysis document. It is a reference document that justifies the analysis performed and prepares the way for systems design. The requirements analysis document includes a description of how the analysis was conducted, user requirements, systems constraints, and proper documentation.

Now you have seen how to narrow the gap between user expectations and the current system to a reasonable distance. In the next chapter, you'll learn how to determine which alternative types of information systems can fill that gap, and how to compare these alternatives.

CONCEPTS LEARNED

- How to furnish descriptions of the current system
- The physical data flow diagram as a checklist to generate current systems performance statistics
- Problems with assessing user expectations about information systems
- Relative advantages, disadvantages, and targets of interviews, questionnaires, observation, procedure analysis, and document survey

- The value of sampling in requirements analysis
- How and with whom to conduct interviews
- How to construct and administer questionnaires
- When and how to use observation
- Types of resource constraints
- Parts of the requirements analysis document

KEY TERMS

closed question
convenience sampling
document survey
interview
Likert scale
loaded question
observation
open question
pilot test
probe

procedure analysis
questionnaire
requirements analysis document
response rate
sampling
satisficing
selective perception
synopsis of interviews
systematic random sampling

REVIEW QUESTIONS

1. What performance statistics should be gathered for the current information system?

2. What are the seven steps of the requirements analysis checklist?

3. State four problems analysts face in describing user expectations about information systems.

4. How can analyst bias distort collection of user expectations?

5. What products are generated by soliciting end-user expectations about information systems?

6. Briefly discuss the targets, advantages, and disadvantages of the five methods of requirements analysis.

7. Describe the process of document analysis.

8. What are the advantages of sampling in requirements analysis?

9. Describe the use of systematic random sampling.

10. Why should you avoid taking notes while interviewing?

11. What is the difference between structured and unstructured interview questions?

12. What is a probe? Provide an example.

13. Explain the term *response rate*. Why is it important?

14. Describe the Likert scale. Why is it important?

15. Why should observation be restricted to short periods?

16. What are the five resource constraints that prohibit delivery of an ideal information system?

17. Why are resource constraints considered after, rather than before, gathering user expectations?

18. Describe the contents of the requirements analysis document.

CRITICAL THINKING OPPORTUNITIES

1. Draw a diagram to show how this chapter is organized.

2. Conduct a structured interview with an instructor on how he or she could improve a specific course in the curriculum.

3. Design a questionnaire to assess how firms in your zip code area are using 4GLs.

4. You are asked to analyze how your business school could perform more effectively.
   a) Whom would you interview, and why?
   b) How might you use questionnaires?
   c) What might you observe, and why?
   d) What constraints might you find that would prevent your school from implementing an ideal educational system?

OBJECTIVES

In this chapter you will learn about:

WHAT: (Concepts) Generating information system alternatives and selecting the best of these alternatives.

WHY: We must search for the best alternative information systems to fill the gap between current status and ideal information needs.

WHEN: After requirements analysis stage.

WHO: System analyst in conjunction with end-users.

WHERE: IS department and end-user work area.

HOW: (Techniques) Payoff diagram
                      Feasibility matrix
                      Breakeven analysis
                      Payback period analysis
                      Discounted payback period analysis

OUTLINE

- Setting
- A Total Quality Approach
- Generating System Alternatives
- Comparing System Alternatives
- Information Systems Costs
- Estimating Costs
- Methods for Comparing Systems
- Fortyne Dairy Case
- Qualitative Factors
- Human Aspects

SYSTEM SELECTION

In most cases, getting rid of what one doesn't want is not equivalent to obtaining what one does want.

— RUSSELL ACKOFF, 1978

SETTING

Analysis of an information system proceeds according to the problem structure discussed in Chapter 2. Figure 8–1 is a modified version of this basic structure. The structure includes:

- Current system performance as recorded in the current system description (Chapter 5)
- Systems expectations as captured in the requirements analysis document (Chapter 7)
- The problem—that is, the gap between systems expectations and performance (Chapter 8)

This chapter addresses the question: How is the performance gap closed? First, alternatives need to be generated for solving the information systems problems. Then, the alternatives should be evaluated to determine which is best or most expedient.

Practical evaluation of systems alternatives requires that the alternatives be reduced to a small subset. However, there seem to be an infinite number of ways to design a new information system. Several factors, however, limit the number of alternatives to a manageable group. These factors include:

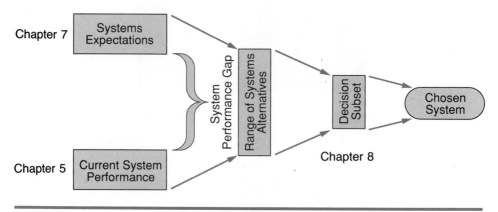

FIGURE 8–1   Modified Version of Problem Structure

1. Technical feasibility (Is the required technology available?)
2. Social feasibility (Will the new system be accepted?)
3. Management feasibility (Will the new system be acceptable to management?)
4. Legal feasibility (Does the new system infringe on laws?)
5. Time feasibility (Can the new system be implemented on time?)
6. Economic feasibility (Will the new system be cost-effective?)

Economic feasibility typically is applied only to the few system alternatives that remain after the other five feasibility tests have been used to narrow down the alternatives. This chapter includes material to guide you first in generating alternative information systems and then in narrowing this set to a workable subset. Then material is presented on how to perform a **feasibility analysis:** an economic comparison of two or more alternative information systems.

A TOTAL QUALITY APPROACH

Our TQM approach throughout this book has been to concentrate on the nine characteristics of information: relevancy, completeness, correctness, security, timeliness, economy, efficiency, reliability, and usability. Some of these characteristics can be measured quantitatively—with numbers. Other characteristics can be measured only qualitatively—in nonnumeric terms. For example, you cannot place a number on security. You can only judge whether or not a system has reached a certain requisite level of security.

Many quantitative measures cannot be measured in dollars, the common unit of measurement of the business firm. Correctness, for example, can be measured by a ratio such as

$$\text{Correctness} = \frac{\text{Number of correct entries}}{\text{Total entries}}$$

It is difficult, however, to translate this ratio into dollars saved in order to compare expenditures on information systems with other competing alternatives in the typical business firm. If we increase correctness by 20 percent, how many dollars will be returned to the firm? This is a difficult question to answer.

We will discuss this dilemma in more detail later in this chapter and will suggest an approach to resolving it.

GENERATING SYSTEM ALTERNATIVES

Continuum of System Choices

At first glance, the number of different information systems that can be designed seems infinite. Actually, designers have limited choices of information systems alternatives. Four constraints limit designers:

1. Higher level decisions within which the current system operates
2. Level of the current system (e.g., a designer does not move backward from real-time to batch record update)
3. Interface requirements with other information systems (e.g., receiving with purchasing)
4. Available resources (e.g., funds, time, and skilled personnel)

In generating information system alternatives, there are always higher level decision constraints and a continuum of systems choices remaining after these constraints are faced. The terms *alternatives* and *choices* are used interchangeably.

Levels of Choices

Recall Anthony's decision-making hierarchy and its relevance to information processing (Chapter 1). The decision-making levels (strategic, tactical, and operational) place constraints on what systems alternatives can be generated. For example, assume you must design a better method of servicing a bank's customers. Your choices are constrained by existing bank walk-up facilities, automatic teller machine (ATM) stations, and teller hiring policy. Without these preestablished constraints, the system you might have designed may be quite different from the one you actually design.

Design decisions about business information systems are made at the strategic, tactical, and operational levels. Strategic and tactical decisions set the overall constraints within which systems designers must operate. Designers control operational decisions, although they may personally influence tactical and even strategic decisions.

Strategic decisions encompass all information systems. They are umbrellas under which all individual information systems gather. For instance, a strategic decision to decentralize the firm's information processing will limit options for developing a new customer order entry system. Strategic decisions regarding business information systems are normally covered under the topic of information resource management.

Management makes tactical information decisions system by system. Decisions for one system are relatively independent of decisions for other systems. For example, the choice of batch record update for a payroll system has little effect on how the inventory system is updated. Normally, the designer of a specific information system has some control over such tactical decisions. However, tactical decisions are often the purview of information management; individual designers have a voice but not a vote. An example of a tactical information decision is whether to replace the current system now or later.

Operational information decisions dictate how a business information system functions day by day, week by week, month by month for the life of that system. Operational decisions are within the control of the systems designer. An example of an operational decision is whether record update should be real time or batch for this particular system.

Now, consider briefly the information systems choices made at each management level.

Strategic Choices

Top management makes strategic choices, which are then an overall constraint to the choices a systems designer makes. The most common strategic choices are distributed versus centralized processing, integrated versus dispersed databases, and the surround strategy of systems development.

Distributed versus Centralized Processing. Currently, there is a tendency to move information decisions from the information systems department (**centralized data processing**) to decentralized end-user responsibility centers. In a **distributed data processing** environment, end-users decide equipment, implementation, and development priorities.

The situation that results is this: Top management makes the choice of a distributed information setting. The systems designer lives with that choice and then deals with operational choices that are a compromise between users who are conservative and those who are almost rash.

Top management at Trustee Savings and Loan decided to move from a centralized, highly controlled processing environment to a distributed environment. As a result, loose and inconsistent standards were applied to data entry, depending on management at local sites. After about nine months, customers were starting to complain about incorrect balances. A federal regulatory board determined that the new systems architecture had uncontrolled risk exposures and put the S&L on probation. Management determined that the best solution was to go back to the more controlled albeit less responsive centralized system. Thousands of dollars in hardware, software, and labor were lost, to say nothing of the frustration of the employees and customers during the changeover period. However, this was not the fault of system designers, who had been forced to accept the system constraints imposed by local management.

Integrated versus Dispersed Databases. When an organization uses **dispersed databases,** the systems designer has considerable choice of what files to include in the database and what to include in the files. A top management decision to use a centralized, integrated database removes such choices from the systems designer. **Integrated databases** are managed by a database administrator who maintains overall control of data storage, access, and modification. The systems designer exercises choices only within this overall constraint.

During the time that Trustee Savings and Loan went to decentralized data processing, local databases were maintained that uploaded into the central database on a periodic basis. Again, the standards and controls at the branch locations were loose and not consistent. That meant that not only were the local databases corrupted, but so was the corporate database. If management had distributed the data processing and left the database centralized, control could have been maintained and many problems could have been avoided. In this centralized mode, all local system designers would have lost many of their independent file design choices. This is one case where local autonomy (decentralized choices) did not work.

Surround Strategy of Systems Development. Throughout the United States, there is considerable investment in information systems that operate well enough but are outdated. Many of these information systems cannot communicate with others. For example, Roesact Department Stores has a product file that is on one brand of computer in Chicago. A customer file is on another brand of computer in Phoenix. The two brands of computers do not communicate with each other, so product and customer files cannot be matched easily. Sales at Roesact are suffering because of this incompatibility.

A classic solution to the problem is to convert one of the disparate systems to a new system that is consistent with the other. This is expensive and time-consuming. Now, however, a new solution has been developed, called the **surround strategy.** It uses a telecommunications (UNIX) environment to let each disparate system operate independently and to design a supersystem that allows communication between many disparate systems. Figure 8–2 shows how the surround strategy works.

The surround strategy is important because many firms have a backlog of new systems to be designed and current systems to be modified. This strategy allows

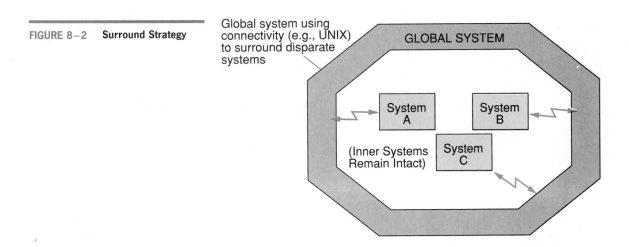

FIGURE 8–2   **Surround Strategy**

systems designed in different languages and run on different brands of computers to exist in a totally compatible system. The surround strategy is particularly important in cases of corporate takeovers, where one firm acquires another firm and, most likely, another information system that is incompatible with its own.

Borden-Mom buys and sells subsidiaries quite frequently. It is impossible and meaningless to try to standardize systems across these companies. The one function that Borden-Mom has tried to implement across all companies is payroll. It has done this using a UNIX system that communicates between many brands of computers.

Top management decides whether or not to adopt the **surround strategy.** Once the strategy is adopted, systems designers are limited to patching and making minor modifications to the current system. Replacement choices are removed to top management. Their strategic choices are discussed in more detail in later chapters. For now, recognize that systems designers do not make strategic choices. Yet, these choices limit designers' options. Figure 8–3 illustrates the constraining nature of strategic information systems choices.

Tactical and Operational Choices

The information systems department makes tactical choices within the framework of the strategic decisions already made. IS managers answer the following questions:

- Should the new system be designed now or later?
- Should the current system be replaced or modified?
- How shall the systems development life cycle be configured?

FIGURE 8–3   **Constraining Nature of Strategic System Decisions**

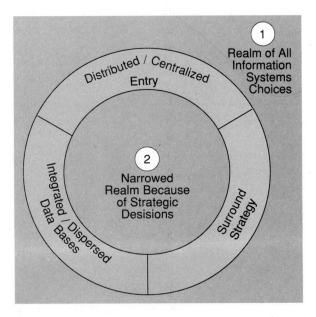

Tactical choices constrain the systems designer's selection of operational choices. For example, if the information systems department decides to modify rather than replace an inventory system, the designer's options are restricted.

Operational choices are choices the systems designer can control. Operational design choices include:

1. Input:
   - On-line or off-line data entry
   - Key or machine-readable data entry
   - Centralized or decentralized entry
2. Processing:
   - Batch or real-time record update
   - Type of record access
   - Security and restriction of access
3. Output:
   - Traditional or turnaround documents
   - Structured or inquiry-based reports

COMPARING SYSTEM ALTERNATIVES

The strategic and tactical decisions just discussed limit the operational choices that you as a systems analyst can make. Even the operational choices you generate are limited by this one essential fact. You do not implement a new information system that is not technologically better than the current system. Hence, there is a natural movement from

- Off-line to on-line data entry
- Keyed to machine-readable data entry
- Centralized to decentralized data entry
- Batch to real-time record update
- Sequential to direct record access
- Low to high security
- Traditional to turnaround documents
- Structured to inquiry-based reports

In addition, certain of these choices must be used in combination. Readable data entry is necessary to support turnaround documents. Real-time record update requires both on-line data entry and direct record access. As a result, the seeming unlimited number of choices available to the analyst narrows down to two or three alternatives, including retaining the current system. Figure 8–4 illustrates this point. Eight typical systems are shown, separated by a small and large systems track. Whenever the current system is, say, System B, progression to a higher level system proceeds down the alphabet (e.g., to system C or D). It is unusual for systems to progress more than two letters (e.g., from A to C, or from F to H) in a single systems development life cycle.

FIGURE 8–4   Eight Typical Business Information Systems

Small Firm Track	Large Firm Track
System A	**System E**
1 On-line Data Entry	1 On-line Data Entry
2 Keyed Entry	2 Keyed Entry
3 Centralized Entry	3 Decentralized Entry
4 Batch Update	4 Real-time Update
5 Sequential Access	5 Direct Access
6 Single User	6 Multiple Users
7 Traditional Documents	7 Traditional Documents
8 Structured Reports	8 Structured Reports
System B	**System F**
1 On-line Data Entry	1 On-line Data Entry
2 Keyed Entry	2 Keyed Entry
3 Decentralized Entry	3 Decentralized Entry
4 Batch Update	4 Real-time Update
5 Sequential Access	5 Direct Access
6 Single User	6 Multiple Users
7 Traditional Documents	7 Traditional Documents
8 Structured Reports	8 Inquiry Reporting
System C	**System G**
1 On-line Data Entry	1 On-line Data Entry
2 Keyed Entry	2 Machine-readable Entry
3 Decentralized Entry	3 Decentralized Entry
4 Real-time Update	4 Real-time Update
5 Direct Access	5 Direct Access
6 Single User	6 Multiple Users
7 Traditional Documents	7 Turnaround Documents
8 Structured Reports	8 Structured Reports
System D	**System H**
1 On-line Data Entry	1 On-line Data Entry
2 Keyed Entry	2 Machine-readable Entry
3 Decentralized Entry	3 Decentralized Entry
4 Real-time Update	4 Real-time Update
5 Direct Access	5 Direct Access
6 Single User	6 Multiple Users
7 Traditional Documents	7 Turnaround Documents
8 Inquiry Reporting	8 Inquiry Reporting

Systems are compared according to relative costs and benefits. *Costs* are the payments required to design and operate an information system. *Benefits* are values or conditions added as the result of implementing information systems. Benefits that are quantitative can be measured. They include reduced error rates, increased customer sales, and faster VDT response time. Other benefits are difficult to measure; they are qualitative. Increased customer satisfaction and decreased end-user resistance are qualitative benefits. Benefits are opportunities for improving the firm's profit status.

Firms often justify new information systems on the basis of increased benefits rather than decreased costs. The first uses of ATM cards were justified by *projected* increases in bank customers due to this added service. The first uses of laser scanning for supermarket checkout were partially justified by decreasing the length of checkout lines, which was translated into a *projected* increase in market share of customers.

More and more, emphasis is being placed on automation as a means to increase sales and profit rather than to reduce costs. Yet, selling an information system to management on projected benefits has two problems.

First, it is often difficult to quantify benefits. How many new bank customers will be attracted by ATM machines? What will be the average new customer's loan, checking, and savings balance? Some have tried to resolve such questions through use of future probabilities. Such approaches add the problem of estimating future probabilities to the problem of estimating future revenues.

Second, even when benefits can be quantified, often this cannot be done in dollars. How do you translate shorter customer waiting time into profit dollars? How can you translate decreased error rates into either reduced costs or increased revenue? It has been done, but it is a difficult, imprecise task.

Why is it important to translate benefits to measurable dollars? There are three reasons.

1. Firms keep track of dollars with traditional accounting systems. Therefore, it is possible to project cost or revenue changes from past performance. Firms do not collect other measurables, such as error rates, as frequently or as formally as they do dollar measures.
2. Information systems alternatives compete with alternatives from other areas of the firm. Perhaps a new information system has to compete with a production retooling plan or the marketing of a new product. It is difficult to compare benefits across different functional areas. The common unit of measurement throughout the firm is the dollar.
3. Top management decides whether or not to proceed with development of a new information system. Many of these managers are dollar oriented. The marketing vice president will ask, "How will this increase sales revenue?" The finance vice president will ask, "How will this decrease operating costs?" The chief executive officer will ask, "How will this increase profit?" The responses to all three questions are in dollars.

Therefore, this chapter presents a practical rule for comparing alternative information systems: *Choose one system over another based on dollars. When two alternatives are nearly equal in dollars, select the system with more nondollar benefits.* In using this rule, or tactic, the systems analyst should be aware of the following considerations:

■ Only a systems person with superior communication skills and considerable influence can sell to management a system with higher measurable costs but better unmeasurable benefits. This is sad, but still true.
■ Dollar figures imply more accuracy than they deserve. A firm can predict its market share twenty years from now. The forecast figure containing three decimal points seems highly accurate. The true accuracy of the figure is highly questionable, as are all twenty-year forecasts.

INFORMATION SYSTEMS COSTS

Benefits included in the analysis model only matter when they can be expressed in dollars. When they can be expressed in dollars, however, they are shown as negative costs:

Additional systems costs	$49,357
Additional systems benefits	(16,423)
Net additional systems costs	$32,934

Information systems costs can be described in three ways: categories, nature, and when they occur.

Cost Categories

Typical costs fall into these categories:

- *Hardware:* Mainframe, minicomputers, microcomputers, and peripheral equipment
- *Software:* Systems, utility, and applications software
- *People:* Analysts, programmers, operators, data entry personnel, and so on
- *Supplies:* Paper, tapes, disks, and so on
- *Telecommunications:* Modems, local area network cabling, multiplexors, front-end processors, and so on
- *Physical site:* Air conditioning, humidity control, security, and so on

Figure 8–5 shows relative costs for McGriff Sporting Goods, but these costs will vary by type of business.

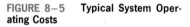

FIGURE 8–5   **Typical System Operating Costs**

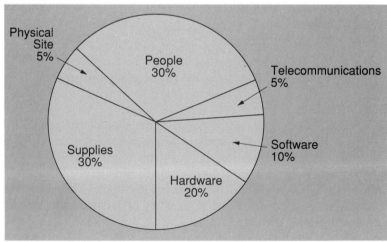

Nature of Costs

To compare information systems costs over the lives of systems, analysts project how costs will change in the future. To do that, they must have some idea (some models) of how information systems costs operate. There are three common models.

Linear. **Linear costs** (Figure 8–6) increase or decrease in a straight line. For example, information personnel costs may increase 5 percent per year as a result of inflation.

Exponential. **Exponential costs** (Figure 8–7) change at a steadily increasing or decreasing rate. Repair costs for an old system's hardware rise at an exponential rate. For example, they may rise 7 percent in year 1, 8 percent in year 2, 10 percent in year 3, and so on. Hardware storage costs have decreased exponentially over the past decade. Paper costs have increased exponentially.

Step Function. **Step functions** (Figure 8–8) involve costs that remain relatively stable until some event occurs that causes costs to rise suddenly and sharply. For example, one programmer may be enough to maintain systems during the initial stages of a firm's automation. Then volume increases to a point where the firm hires a second and then a third programmer.

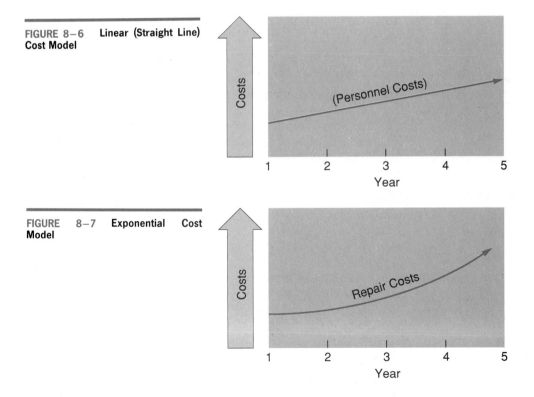

FIGURE 8–6   Linear (Straight Line) Cost Model

FIGURE   8–7   Exponential   Cost Model

FIGURE 8–8   Step Function Cost Model

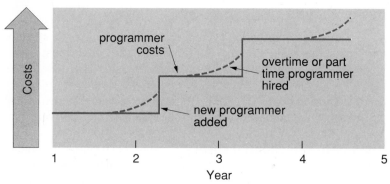

Often step functions are not as precise as shown by the solid line in Figure 8–8. The first programmer may have incurred overtime costs; or perhaps contract programmers were hired until management decided to hire the second programmer. Therefore, typical step functions for business information systems look more like the dashed line in Figure 8–8.

When Costs Occur

Information systems costs can occur once or on a continuing basis. **One-time costs** or **development costs** are associated with systems development, and **recurring costs** or **operational costs** are related to the day-to-day operation of information systems.

The payoff diagram of Figure 8–9 separates these costs. The bulging curve on the left represents one-time development costs. The straight line on the right represents operational costs. Operational costs often rise over time because of factors such as inflation and systems deterioration.

The difference between one-time (development) and recurring (operational) costs is often a matter of choice. For instance, a computer purchase is a one-time development cost. Yet, rental of the same computer is a recurring operational cost. Use this checklist for determining when common systems costs occur:

- One-time (development) costs:
  1. Hardware purchase
  2. Software purchase
  3. Personnel hours for analysis, design, programming, and testing
  4. Preparation of computer site
  5. Initial training and orientation of users
  6. Documentation for new system
  7. Changeover from old to new system
  8. Conversion from old to new system file format
- Recurring (operational) costs:
  1. Hardware and software lease
  2. Hardware and software maintenance contracts

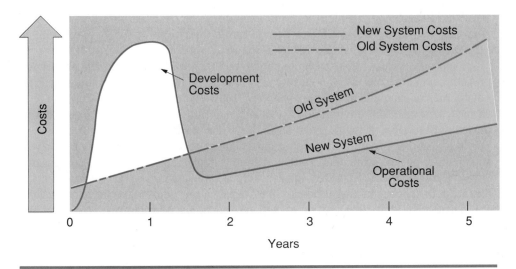

3. Day-to-day personnel costs, including analysts and programmers, computer operations, data entry operators, and end-user costs
4. Computer supplies
5. Telecommunications costs
6. Computer site rental or lease
7. Ongoing training

There is a third way included in cost comparisons—indirect costs.

Indirect Costs

Indirect costs are expense categories that cannot be credited directly to a specific computer system. Accountants distribute these costs across all computer systems according to some measurable criteria. Often they refer to these as **overhead costs.** Here is an example.

Palko Publishing Company incurs monthly utility costs for air conditioning and humidity control for a central mainframe computer site. Accounting assigns these costs to each applications area on the basis of that area's relative use of computer time. Palko's information systems department proposed a new decision support system. Part of the costs accounting projected for that system is a portion of utility costs based on projected computer usage. Yet, the new DSS will not require any additional computer hardware, and there will be no out-of-pocket new utility payments. Why should the new DSS be assigned such nonexistent costs?

Overhead costs include items such as utilities, management, security, and building rental. Whether overhead costs should be assigned to a new system's projected costs is questionable. The answer lies in marginal costs. **Marginal costs** are the actual additional out-of-pocket costs of implementing a new business information system. In the Palko Publishing example, there were no utility costs for the proposed DSS. Marginal utility costs were zero. Hence, when considering the costs of the new DSS, the firm should not have included utility costs.

Suppose, though, that implementation of the new DSS would exceed Palko's present computer capacity. The firm would have to buy new computer equipment and environmental surroundings. Then, the new DSS would be assigned the full charge for all new hardware and environmental equipment. This is so because if Palko did not implement the DSS, it would avoid all of these new costs.

Marginal costs require that any proposed information system be assigned only the actual out-of-pocket costs added if that system is implemented. It must be emphasized that this marginal cost approach applies only to evaluating potential information systems, not to cost accounting procedures that apply after the new system is operational. It is permissible to assign a portion of hardware costs to a new information system after it is implemented. It may not be advisable to assign those hardware costs to the new system when its economic feasibility is being examined.

ESTIMATING COSTS

Your job is to estimate costs for the current system, which already exists, and for a proposed information system, which exists only in the minds of you and your design team. In addition, you must estimate not only current costs, but costs that will occur five or more years into the future. This is not an easy task, but there are certain rules you can use to make your job easier.

1. *Keep it simple.* Forecasting the future with a detailed model rarely increases the accuracy of the projections. For example, you wish to forecast programmer costs for the next three years. You are tempted to break down these costs into separate programming tasks: program design, coding, testing, and recoding. This seems clever, but it is unlikely that forecasts broken down to this level of detail will be any more accurate than forecasts simply based on total programming hours, regardless of task.

2. *Explain your logic.* You will have to make assumptions. Your assumptions probably will be no less valid than those of another analyst who might have been assigned to this task, but you must demonstrate how your assumptions led to your estimated costs. Otherwise, it will seem that you merely pulled your figures out of the air.

3. *Rely on credible sources.* Few will question your estimates if they are based on such credible sources as accounting records or vendor specifications. Such credible sources are not always available for all cost elements. However, use credible sources as much as possible. Reference these sources in your feasibility study through the use of footnotes.

4. *Downplay intuition.* There is a systems theory precept called the **Law of Insufficient Reason.** Simply stated, this law prescribes that unless you have evidence to support the contention that data follow a certain pattern, you must assume that the data follow no pattern. For example, an analyst feels intuitively that programmer costs will rise during the next five years. Inspection of accounting records reveals that there has been no change in programming costs over the past two years. The analyst has no

credible source to support the hunch that programming costs will increase. That analyst had better use programming costs that do not increase—that reflect a flat cost line over time. Otherwise, the analyst's hunch may well be challenged by management or by other analysts who have different hunches.

5. *Use other people.* Run your assumptions and estimated costs by other analysts to determine if they are logical. Better yet, have a small team of analysts make the estimates (There is always safety in numbers!).

The following example will give you a better feel for how we estimate information systems costs.

NITRAM Inventory System Costs

Martin Manufacturing Company is considering replacing its current system, which keeps track of the number of nitrams it stocks and sells. Tiffany Gardner is the analyst assigned the task of preparing a feasibility analysis to compare estimated costs for the current system with the proposed replacement system. Her first task is to find a basis (source) for estimating costs. She breaks this task into three parts: (1) one-time development costs for the proposed inventory system, (2) recurring operational costs over a five-year estimated life for the proposed system, and (3) recurring operational costs for the current nitram system.

One-time Development Costs. Hardware purchase: Tiffany secures a written commitment from the UNIFAX hardware vendor on what exact hardware purchase costs will be and the expected payment schedule.

Software Purchase. Tiffany determines which of the required software is a part of the hardware package being purchased from UNIFAX. She also determines what additional software must be purchased. She then secures selected bids from software vendors on what would be their purchase price for this software. Tiffany uses the lowest vendor figure (*Note:* Formal software and selection is described in Case 8.1).

Analysis, Design, Programming, and Testing Personnel Hours. Tiffany researches the number of such hours spent in information projects occurring during the past two years. She feels that the nitram inventory system replacement project will be about 20 percent larger than the largest project occurring during the past two years. She adds 20 percent to the figures for this largest project.

Preparation of Computer Site. Tiffany consults with her operations personnel to determine if any changes will be required to the computer sites with purchase of the new hardware. The operating personnel provide her with an estimate of additional expenditures that will be required for (1) air conditioning, (2) wiring, and (3) security control.

Remaining One-Time Costs. Tiffany again researches the accounting records for the largest information system project occurring during the part two years. She computes several cost ratios, including the following.

$$\frac{\text{Training cost}}{\text{ratio}} = \frac{\text{Training costs for old project}}{\text{Analysis, design, etc., personnel hours for old project}}$$

Tiffany then multiplies this training cost ratio by the personnel hours she estimated for the nitram inventory system. This gives her a training cost estimate for the proposed inventory system. Tiffany follows the same procedure for (1) training costs, (2) documentation for new system, (3) changeover from new to old system, and (4) conversion from old to new file format.

Recurring Operational Costs for Current System. Tiffany researches cost accounting records to determine what costs have been assigned to the current nitram inventory system in the cost categories of (1) hardware and software lease, (2) hardware and software maintenance contracts, (3) day-to-day personnel costs, (4) computer supplies, (5) telecommunications costs, (6) computer site rental, and (7) ongoing training. Tiffany finds, to her horror, that the cost accounting system does not break these costs down by individual information system. Undaunted, Tiffany goes to the computer operations center and consults the computer usage log. She calculates that, over the past three months, the current nitram inventory system has used 6.4 percent of computer run time hours. Tiffany then multiplies total system costs in each category (from cost accounting records) by 0.064 to arrive at estimated nitram in each category costs. For example:

$$\frac{\text{Estimated nitram}}{\text{system computer}} = \frac{\text{Total computer}}{\text{supplies costs}} * 0.064$$
supplies cost

or

$$\$97,633 * 0.064 = \$6,248.5$$
$$\$6,250 \text{ rounded}$$

Three examples follow of how estimated nitram costs for the first year can now be projected to the next five years.

Example 1. Tiffany returns to the cost accounting records to determine the pattern of operating costs over time so she can project what these costs will be over the next five years. She finds, for example, that total computer personnel costs have been increasing approximately 3 percent each year for the past three years. This is a linear cost. She projects her five-year nitram system personnel costs in the following manner.

$$\frac{\text{Year } i + 1}{\text{personnel costs}} = \frac{\text{Year } i}{\text{personnel costs}} * 1.03$$

Estimated Nitram Systems Personnel Costs

Year 0 (last year)	Year 1 Estimated	Year 2 Estimated	Year 3 Estimated	Year 4 Estimated	Year 5 Estimated
$132,753	136.7*	140.8*	145.1*	149.4*	153.9*

*In thousands of dollars, rounded.

Example 2. Tiffany discovers not only that past computer supplies expenditures for all information systems have increased, but that the *rate* of increase has increased, as follows.

Rate of increase 3 years ago:	Rate of increase 2 years ago:	Rate of increase 1 year ago:
1.5	1.7	1.9

This pattern can be described as an exponential cost increase of $(1 + i)^n$ or 1.02^n. However, Tiffany and her colleagues feel that the nitram inventory system is deteriorating and that its computer supplies costs will increase at a higher rate than other information systems. Therefore, Tiffany assumes an exponential function of $(1.03)^n$. She then computes projected supplies costs using the following formula.

$$\frac{\text{Year } (i + 1)}{\text{Supplies costs}} = \frac{\text{Year 0 (last year)}}{\text{Supplies costs}} * \frac{(i + 1)}{(1.03)}$$

Her ensuing five-year pattern then looks like this:

Last year assigned computer supplies costs	Year 1*	Year 2*	Year 3*	Year 4*	Year 5*
$6,248.5	6.4	6.6	6.8	7.0	7.3

*In thousands of dollars, rounded.

Example 3. Tiffany's inspection of cost accounting records indicates that telecommunication costs for all systems show a pattern of remaining constant for two years, then exhibiting a 5 percent increase. Tiffany's cost pattern for projected telecommunications costs becomes:

Last year assigned telecommunications costs	Year 1*	Year 2*	Year 3*	Year 4*	Year 5*
$5,348	5.3	5.3	5.6	5.6	5.9

*In thousands of dollars, rounded.

Recurring Operational Costs for Proposed System. If Tiffany has no reason to assume (no facts) that new system costs will be different from old system costs, then she must assume the same costs for both system scenarios. This is the law of insufficient reason. However, Tiffany does find several cost categories where there is evidence to support new system projected costs that are lower than current system projected costs. Among those categories are the following.

1. Since Tiffany knows exactly what software is to be purchased for the new system, she can determine exactly what yearly renewal and software maintenance contract costs will be. She obtains these figures from software vendors.
2. Management estimates that the new nitram inventory system will reduce day-to-day personnel costs by 10 percent. However, this reduction will take four years to take effect through retirements and normal personnel transfers. No layoffs will be made.

Tiffany then reduces current system day-to-day personnel costs for the current system by 2.5 percent for each of the first four years of the projected five-year period.

3. No costs for the new system are expected to increase exponentially, but only linearly. Thus, supplies costs will increase only 3 percent a year (1.03) rather than at a geometric power.

This abbreviated case study is intended only to give you a feel for how to approach cost estimation. This study also should convince you that such cost estimation is, at best, structured guessing.

METHODS FOR COMPARING SYSTEMS

Three methods are commonly used for comparing two or more information systems: breakeven analysis, payback period, and discounted payback period. For simplicity, each method is presented here as a comparison between a current and a proposed replacement system.

Three important variables recur throughout these methods: system life, return on investment, and alternative views of the future. **System life** is the length of time you can expect a new information system to operate before it begins to deteriorate. In the descriptions that follow, system life is not always the actual physical life of an information system. Often, it is an arbitrary value set by top management. For example, the comptroller for Palko Publishing has decreed, "We will not consider any proposed investment that does not pay for itself in five years." Hence, while a proposed information system may last ten years, it must return a profit within five years. Otherwise, the comptroller will not consider it. System life has arbitrarily been set at five years.

Return on investment (ROI) is the percentage of profit the firm expects to garner through investing its resources. Suppose Palko Publishing placed all of its cash resources in a savings account. The firm would expect these resources to generate 4 to 6 percent interest per year, so ROI would be 4 to 6 percent. Most healthy businesses realize a return of 15 to 50 percent or more on their investments. Management will rarely accept a proposed new information system if it cannot generate the firm's expected ROI. This is particularly true if investment in a new information system is being compared to investment in some other proposed firm project, such as a new product.

The third variable, alternative views of the future, is more subtle. Palko Publishing is comparing the current accounts receivable system with a proposed replacement system. Palko cannot afford to design the new system, then operate it beside the current system to see which is preferable. Palko must make its decision on the proposed replacement system *before* design and implementation costs are incurred.

Therefore, Palko Publishing must forecast two different alternative views of the future. The first view is what will happen if the replacement system proposal is scrapped and the current system continues to operate. The second view is one where the current system is allowed to operate while the replacement system is being designed. Then the current system is discarded and the replacement system begins

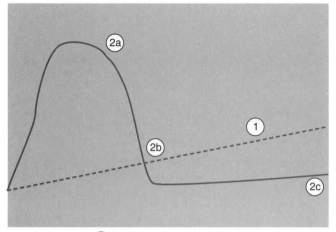

Alternative view (1): Current system continues to operate

Alternative view (2): New system developed

(2a): Development occurs while current system still operating

(2b): New system implemented; current system discontinued

(2c): New system operates at lower cost level than discontinued system

operation. Figure 8–10 contrasts these two alternative views for Palko Publishing's accounts receivable system.

Feasibility analysis includes assigning costs to each of these alternative views over selected systems life. Systems analysts, then, must also be forecasters.

Breakeven Analysis

Breakeven analysis is the simplest form of cost comparison (see Figure 8–11). Note that at year 1.5, the costs of the proposed new system (solid line) intersect the costs of the old system (dashed line). At this point of intersection, the proposed new system begins to generate a positive monetary return in comparison with the old system. From now on, the amount invested in the new system will be offset by the savings the new system allows.

The period to the left of the intersection point in Figure 8–11 is called the **investment period** (when funds go out). The period to the right is referred to as the **return period** (when funds come in). The **breakeven point** is the exact point in time (e.g., 1.5 years) that separates investment and return periods.

Firms that use breakeven analysis typically have surplus funds to be invested but also want to realize a positive cash flow within a given period. For instance, Gannon

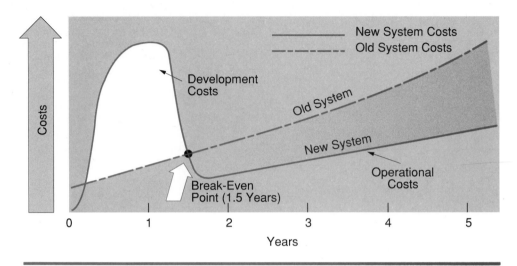

FIGURE 8–11   Break-even Point Separating the Investment and Return Periods of a New Information System

Trucking finds itself with a large amount of immediate cash due to a temporary tax windfall that will last only two years. The firm wants to invest in new information systems, but only if it will begin showing a profit in less than two years. After two years, the firm will not have the surplus funds to invest. In Figure 8–11, the breakeven point of 1.5 years is less than Gannon Trucking's two-year criterion. Hence, Gannon's comptroller will approve development of the new system.

Payback Period

Breakeven analysis ignores an important concern. Will the new system *fully* recover its investment costs before the end of its life? Examine Figure 8–12, which is an extension of Figure 8–11. Note the arrow at 4.5 years—the point when the geometric area of the return period is exactly equal to that of the investment period. This is a physical description of the payback period.

Figure 8–13 presents a more accounting-oriented description of the **payback period.** The tool used is the feasibility matrix. Note the following elements:

1. Incremental years of systems development and operation (along the horizontal axis)
2. Systems costs for each year broken down by cost category:
   - Current system
   - New system alternative (including old system operating while the new system is being developed)
   - Difference (new system minus current system)

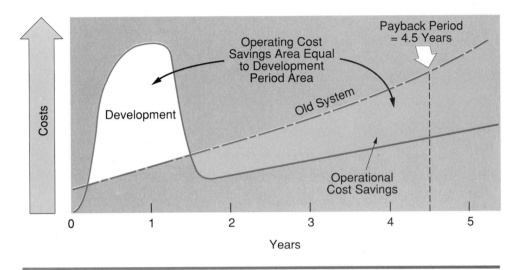

FIGURE 8–12   **Payback Period: When Area of Return Period (Operational Period) is Exactly Equal to Area of the Investment Period (Development)**

- *Cumulative difference:* The sum of all differences from the far left column to the current column. For example, in year 3 the cumulative difference figure is computed by adding the difference columns figures for years 1, 2, and 3, as follows:

1	−40
2	−14
3	+23
Total	−31

Let's examine how we arrived at the costs included in this matrix.

1. *Number 1 in Figure 8–13:* Current system costs are projected to increase at an exponential rate. This means the rate of increase is itself increasing, rather than remaining at a fixed percentage increase per year. Exponential rates of cost increases often are associated with deteriorating systems.
2. *Number 2 in Figure 8–13:* Development costs are spread over the first year and the *first half* of the second year. At that point, the new system is ready to start operating.
3. *Number 3 in Figure 8–13:* The current system must still be operated while we are developing the old system. Therefore, current system operating costs associated with the new system proposed are first-year costs plus one-half of second-year costs (i.e., one-half of 28). At that time, the new system takes over.
4. *Number 4 in Figure 8–13:* New system operating costs begin taking place when the new system design is completed and the current system is deactivated (at year 1.5).

FIGURE 8–13   **Feasibility Matrix**

System Costs*	End-of-year Period				
	1	2	3	4	5
Current System	22	28	37	49	62 (1)
New System					
(2) Development	40	21	–	–	–
Operating (current system)	22	14	–	–	– (3)
(4) Operating (new system)	–	7	14	15	16
Total new system	62	42	14	15	16
Difference	-40	-14	+23	+34	+46
Cumulative Difference	-40	-54	-31	+3	+49

*Thousands of dollars (k).

Therefore, second-year operating costs for the new system are estimated at one-half of full year operating costs in year 3 (0.5 times 14, or 7).

Notice in Figure 8–13 that the cumulative difference changes from a negative value in year 3 to a positive value in year 4. Somewhere between years 3 and 4, the new system will recover all of its initial investment costs and will begin making a profit. The exact point at which that happens is the payback period, defined as the point in time when initial investment costs are recovered completely and new system savings begin. Compute the payback period as follows:

$$\text{Payback period} = \begin{array}{c}\text{Last year of}\\ \text{negative cash flow}\\ \text{difference}\end{array} + \frac{\begin{array}{c}\text{Cumulative difference}\\ \text{last negative year}\end{array}}{\begin{array}{c}\text{Absolute value of}\\ \text{cumulative difference}\\ \text{(last negative plus}\\ \text{first positive year)}\end{array}}$$

For Figure 8–13, this computation is

$$\text{Payback period} = 3 + \frac{31,000}{31,000 + 3,000} = 3.91, \text{ or 3 years 11 months}$$

For Palko Publishing, the payback period is less than the five-year maximum set by the comptroller. Thus, this new system is eligible for investment consideration.

The payback method ignores the critical fact that profit-making firms strive to invest their resources to make a profit. Nonprofit firms commonly use this method because they cannot invest available funds to gain profit. Profit-making firms expect a return on any investment they make on new products, production methods, or information systems. Therefore, for profit-seeking firms, systems analysts need a more profit-oriented comparison method. This is the discounted payback period.

Discounted Payback Period

Discounted payback period is based on the fact that a dollar you earn today is more valuable than a dollar you earn a year from now. Having earned the dollar today, you can invest it in a savings account. At the end of a year, that dollar will have gained interest. This concept is called the **present value** of money, and Figure 8–14 illustrates it.

Profit-taking firms invest available funds in profit-making activities. The amount of profit earned by such investment is the ROI. Commonly, firms expect an ROI in the

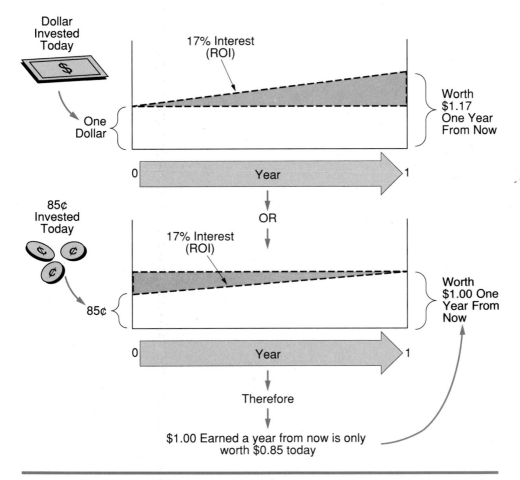

FIGURE 8–14   **Concept of Present Value of Money (Assumed Return on Investment of 17 Percent)**

range of 15 to 50 percent. A dollar invested today gains interest and is worth $1.15 to $1.50 a year from now.

Here is an example of how ROI comes into play. Palko Publishing's proposed new information system would pay itself off in 3.91 years, according to payback period analysis (see Figure 8–13). The first positive return on the initial investment, however, would not occur until sometime in year 3 when the difference row in Figure 8–13 becomes positive. But the present value of money is more than the value of future dollars earned. Future dollars earned are not as valuable as present dollars earned. Hence, Palko will discount any future returns from its new information system to reflect the lesser value of future savings versus present savings.

The **present value** of a dollar at any time in the future is equal to

$$\frac{1}{(1+ROI)^n}$$

where ROI = the firm's expected return on investment, and n = the number of years into the future.

Inspect Figure 8–13 again. Here, the payback years are 3.91. However, this calculation ignores the time value of money. Palko Publishing has averaged a 17 percent return on investment. When Palko inserts this ROI figure into the present-value formula, it arrives at a discount rate by which it can *devalue* dollars earned in the future.

Year Since Project Start	Discount Rate (future value of dollar)
1	.85
2	.73
3	.62
4	.53
5	.46

Therefore, if Palko projects its new information system to earn $10,000 in year 5, those earnings are worth only ($10,000 × .46) or $4,600 in today's money. This is so because Palko could invest $4,600 today at its expected ROI of 17 percent, and that investment would accrue to $10,000 by year 5. Figure 8–15 adds to Figure 8–13 to account for the time value of money. Note the new row that includes the discount rates. The payback period of 3.91 now increases to 4.44 years. This is still within the acceptable time frame dictated by Palko Publishing's comptroller.

Suppose the comptroller is also considering a proposal to retool the production line. The production proposal has a discounted payback period of 3.6 years. How do you think Palko's information systems proposal will fare against this production proposal? Probably not very well. Figure 8–16 lists some discount values associated with common ROIs.

Each of the comparison models described can be used to compare alternative information systems. The methods are combined in the Fortyne Dairy case described next.

FIGURE 8–15   Discounted Payback Matrix

System Costs*	End-of-year Period				
	1	2	3	4	5
1. Current	22	28	37	49	62
2. New	62	42	14	15	16
3. Difference (1-2)	-40	-14	+23	+34	+46
4. Discount (ROI = .17)	.85	.73	.62	.53	.46
5. Discounted Difference (3*4)	-34.0	-10.2	+14.3	+18.0	+21.2
6. Cumulative Discounted Difference	-34.0	-44.2	-29.9	-11.9	+9.3

*Thousands of dollars (k).

$$\text{Discounted Payback Period} = 4 + \frac{9.3}{11.9 + 9.3} = 4.44 \text{ years}$$

ROI	End-of-year Period				
	1	2	3	4	5
15%	.87	.76	.66	.57	.50
20%	.83	.69	.58	.48	.40
25%	.80	.64	.51	.41	.33
30%	.77	.59	.46	.35	.27
35%	.74	.55	.41	.30	.22
40%	.71	.51	.36	.26	.19

FIGURE 8–16   Common Return on Investment (Discount) Rates

FORTYNE DAIRY CASE

Fortyne Dairy Products is a firm located in Sacramento, California; it has about 1,500 employees. The data-processing department has 75 employees, and outside contractors (job shoppers) are employed during peak development periods.

Fortyne is now using batch processing for order entry. Customer orders received one day are entered the next day. Picking slips, packing slips, and customer billings are produced at the end of each working day.

Volume of customer orders has increased over several years. It is becoming more and more difficult to enter all customer orders to the computer within one day after receipt. The marketing manager has proposed an on-line, real-time update system. The information systems department prepared a cost evaluation comparing the proposed system with the current system. The evaluation includes a synopsis of current system costs, new system costs, breakeven analysis, payback period analysis, and discounted payback period analysis.

Current System Costs. Figure 8–17 shows current system costs for the past year and projected annual increases in these costs per year during the analysis period of five years. Note that some of these costs are projected to increase exponentially: $(1 + a)^n$. This is because the current system is deteriorating.

New System Costs. Figure 8–18 shows estimated development costs for the proposed new system. Figure 8–19 shows projected recurring costs for the new system. Figure 8–20 is a complete feasibility matrix for this analysis.

Cost Category	Current Year Costs*	Projected Cost Pattern	Cost Model	Projected Annual Increase
Hardware†	$ 75	Increase	Exponential	$(1 + .03)^n$
Software	18	Stable	Linear	–0–
People	70	Increase	Linear	.10
Supplies	55	Increase	Exponential	$(1 + .05)^n$
Telecommunications	25	Increase	Linear	.05
Physical Site‡	15	Increase	Step	.10 Every Third Year
Total	$258			

*Thousands of dollars
†Including maintenance
‡Utility increase every three years

FIGURE 8–17   Fortyne Dairy—Projected Annual Costs for the Current System

Development Cost Category	Basis for Estimate*	Estimated Costs†
Hardware	Purchase	$120.0
Software	Purchase	20.0
Analyst/Programmer	1200 Hours	135.0
Computer Site Preparation	Expansion	8.5
User Training/Orientation	100 Hours	5.0
Documentation	70 Hours	3.5
Changeover to New System	Parallel	4.0
File Conversion	80 Hours	4.0
		$300.0

*Personnel costs at $50 per hour
†Thousands of dollars

FIGURE 8–18   Fortyne Dairy—Estimated Development Costs for the New System

Cost Category	Year Costs*	Projected Cost Pattern	Cost Model	Projected Annual Increase
Hardware†	14	Stable	Linear	0
Software	10	Stable	Linear	0
People	40	Increase	Linear	.10
Supplies	35	Increase	Linear	.05
Telecommunications	5	Increase	Linear	.05
Physical Site‡	6	Increase	Step	.05 Every Third Year
Total	$110			

*Thousands of dollars
†Maintenance
‡Utility increase every three years

FIGURE 8−19   Fortyne Dairy—Projected Annual Costs for the New System

Systems Costs*	End-of-year Period				
	1	2	3	4	5
Current	271	291	320	358	411
New	618†	375‡	116	123	130
Difference	−347	− 84	+204	+235	+281
Cumulative Difference	−347	−431	−227	+8	+289

*Thousands of dollars.
†Two-thirds development costs ($347 K) plus current system operating costs ($271 K)
‡One-third development costs ($174 K), one-half year current system costs ($146 K), and one-half year new system costs ($55 K)

FIGURE 8−20   Fortyne Dairy—Complete Feasibility Matrix

Breakeven Analysis. Figure 8−21 presents the breakeven analysis. The new system will start making a profit at year 2.29.

Payback Period Analysis. Figure 8−22 shows the payback period analysis. It will take 3.97 years for the new system to recover its development costs. After that time, all cost savings will be pure profit for the new system.

Discounted Payback Period Analysis. Fortyne Dairy is a profit-taking firm. Over the past three years, the firm's average return on investment has been 18 percent. However, Fortyne's optimistic vice president for finance has decided that he will not consider any new investment proposal unless it yields at least an annual 20 percent ROI over the investment's first five years.

Neither the breakeven nor the payback period analysis for the order entry systems addresses this condition. So now present-value analysis must be done with discount

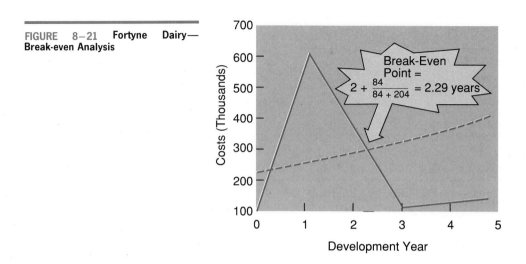

FIGURE 8–21   Fortyne Dairy—Break-even Analysis

Systems Costs	End-of-year Period				
	1	2	3	4	5
Cumulative Difference	−347	−431	−227	+8	+289

Change from negative to positive

$$\text{Payback years} = 3 + \frac{227}{227 + 8}$$

$$= 3.97 \text{ years}$$

FIGURE 8–22   Fortyne Dairy—Payback Period Analysis

rates set at a 20 percent ROI expectation. Figure 8–23 shows the discount computations. Using present-value calculations, the payback period is increased from 3.21 to over 5 years. (The last row is still at −3 at year 5.) This is beyond the comptroller's payoff year limit.

Now the information systems manager of Fortyne Dairy can present to management the following cost comparisons of the proposed new system versus the current system:

$$\begin{aligned}
\text{Breakeven years} &= 2.29 \text{ years} \\
\text{Payback period} &= 3.97 \text{ years} \\
\text{Discounted payback period} &= \text{more than 5 years}
\end{aligned}$$

Management's decision is unclear. The payback period looks good, but the other indicators do not. It is time to introduce qualitative, nonmeasurable factors so the IS department can sell the new system to management.

Systems Costs*	End-of-year Period				
	1	2	3	4	5
Current	271	291	320	358	411
New	618	375	116	123	130
Difference (Table 14.8)	−347	−84	+204	+235	+281
Discount (ROI = .20; Table 14.5)	.83	.69	.58	.48	.40
Discounted Difference	−288	−58	+118	+113	+112
Cumulative Discounted Difference	−288	−346	−228	−115	−3

*Thousands of dollars

Discounted Payoff Years beyond 5 Years _____

FIGURE 8−23   Fortyne Dairy—Discounted Payback Analysis (ROI = 20%)

QUALITATIVE FACTORS

Only the most charismatic systems person can sell to top management a new system that does not show increased profits. Sometime you may be in the enviable position of being able to sell a new information system to management on anticipated benefits rather than cost savings. You likely will be aided in your endeavor by a high-level manager whose operation will be enhanced. Perhaps you will sell a capability that currently does not exist. In such a case, there is no current information system with which to compare the costs of the proposed new system.

Fortyne Dairy recently implemented a marketing analysis decision support system. It was a new rather than replacement system. The information systems department and the marketing department made a joint presentation recommending the new system to top management. The presentation was a success. Top management agreed to allow design and implementation of this innovative DSS.

Unfortunately, such exciting scenarios of selling new systems based on qualitative benefits rather than quantitative costs are not common. More often, you have to show some cost differentiation before top management will even consider your recommendation for design of a new information system.

In cases of ties between systems that have been compared on costs, nonmeasurable and noncost factors enter the comparison. Such qualitative factors as information systems performance and strategic competitive advantages become relevant.

Information Systems Factors

Several qualitative factors are tied to specific performance of information systems:

- Decreased error rate (increased accuracy)
- Decreased time for correcting errors
- Decreased interactive (workstation) response time
- Faster report delivery time
- Increased level of systems security

- More current updating of resource records
- Increased user satisfaction through increased system usability

Some of these factors are measurable, but not in dollars. For example, Fortyne Dairy can claim a new error reduction rate of 16 to 12 percent for the proposed system. However, because this error reduction rate is difficult to translate into dollars, it never shows up in the important cost comparison figures.

Strategic Firm Factors

Information systems can create competitive advantages for a firm. The increase in actual profits, however, is difficult to estimate. In addition, such profit increases are often not immediate but occur several years after implementation of the new system.

When two alternative information systems are close in cost comparisons, the window opens for considering strategic qualitative factors. Consider these four common factors:

1. *Customer satisfaction:* A new information system may cause quicker product delivery and more efficient customer inquiries. Increased customer satisfaction will undoubtedly lead to increased sales. Such increased sales are, however, difficult to predict and quantify.
2. *Increased sales:* Colby Computer Company's new point-of-sale order entry system frees salespeople from record-keeping tasks. Management expects the sales staff to devote more time to marketing efforts and thus increase sales. Just how much sales will increase is difficult to predict in dollars.
3. *Customer and vendor commitments:* Consider the classic case of American Hospital Supply. The company designed an on-line order entry system and then allowed its customers direct access to that system. Customers were now locked in; AHS even bought workstations for them. AHS's market share leaped to over 60 percent. Such a gain in sales and customer commitment would have been difficult to predict when justifying the new information system.
4. *Information product marketing:* Often, a new information system is applicable to other firms. Arthur Andersen and Company developed an internal CASE tool called Foundation and now is marketing this package as a generic CASE product. When the firm justified development of Foundation, it would have been difficult to predict the package's market potential or translate it to dollar benefits. American Airlines provides another example of information product marketing. During the 1970s, the company developed a reservation system called SABRE and then marketed the system to other airlines. SABRE became one of American Airlines' most profitable products.

These four qualitative strategic factors can break quantitative (cost) ties when two alternative information systems are being compared.

After proceeding through the cost analysis already described, Fortyne's information systems department narrowed the choices down to two information systems. The systems had the following statistics:

	System A	System B
Breakeven years	1.9	2.3
Discounted payback period (years)	3.9	4.2

COMPETITIVE STRATEGY AND INFORMATION SYSTEMS

Technological advances may enable a firm to gain a competitive advantage by introducing products with improved performance and price characteristics and by changing the manufacturing economics of the product or process.

In addition to using information systems to assess and augment technological advances, companies are using IS to establish strategic advantages in human resources management (HRM). HRM systems enhance competitiveness by helping to restructure and organize the firm's personnel. They reduce unnecessary movement of information, eliminate bureaucratic processes and layers of middle management, and simplify the organization.

Sprague and McNurlin (1986) identify three types of strategic information systems: competitive systems, cooperative systems, and systems that change how organizations work.

Competitive systems can be outwardly oriented (dealing with customers, suppliers, and competitors) or inwardly oriented (dealing with productivity and pricing). Competitive systems increase the firm's competitive position by adding to the firm's value chain. The term value chain comes from the work of Porter (1985). The primary activities in the value chain are inbound logistics, operations, outbound logistics, marketing and sales, and service. Support factors include the firm's infrastructure, HRM, technological development, and procurement. Any value added to the value chain can give rise to competitive advantage.

Cooperative systems are interorganizational systems, composed of two or more organizations working together to achieve strategic goals. Cooperative systems have the following characteristics:

- Partners are willing participants.
- Standards exist to make the systems portable.
- Education is important.
- Third parties may be involved.
- Work is synchronized.
- Work processes are reevaluated often.
- Technical aspects are not a major issue.
- Efforts are not secretive.

Systems that offer strategic value by changing the way the organization works include the HRM systems mentioned previously. These systems may change the way in which decisions are made, may offer more communication options, and may provide tools for coordination. Streamlining the organization and providing efficient and effective management tools allow organizations to function more productively.

System A is better in every statistic. Nevertheless, the figures are close. To declare system A the better system would place an accuracy level on cost estimation that is not warranted. A small error in estimating costs for either system A or system B could change comparative advantages. Therefore, these two alternative information systems are too close to call. They are tied.

The tie may be broken using qualitative factors. A senior analyst argues that system B is less specialized than system A. Hence, system B has the potential for tying into customer and vendor systems. It also has potential as a marketable information product. Both of these characteristics are strategic factors that have potential, but they do not translate to direct dollar benefits. However, in this close cost comparison, these qualitative advantages for system B are persuasive. The information systems department agrees to recommend system B to Fortyne Dairy's top management.

In summary, systems analysts rarely recommend or choose a higher cost system because it has superior qualitative characteristics. Qualitative characteristics usually become important only when two or more systems have similar cost profiles.

The comparison task is now completed. One alternative information system has emerged as the favorite of the information systems department. Now, the department must sell its choice to top management before design can begin. This is the topic of the next chapter.

HUMAN ASPECTS

There are a lot of tables and computations in this chapter. Do not let them fool you. We must place the comparison of information systems into a format compatible with the top-level executives that make the decision of whether or not to proceed with the development of a proposed information system. However, we should never forget that our analysis is, at best, structured guessing. We are projecting to a future we do not know, costs we are not sure of. This must be done. It is properly done. Still, we must not let our ensuing stack of accurate-looking figures dominate our thinking. These figures are not reality; they are our best estimate of an uncertain future.

Did you ever hear about the statistician who drowned in a river that *averaged* three feet deep?

SUMMARY

The systems designer generates system alternatives to close the gap between current system performance and performance expectations. The number of different business information systems that can be designed seems infinite, but there are practical constraints that ultimately limit the analyst's comparison to two or three alternative information system configurations.

To compare alternative information systems, follow this practical rule: First, compare systems costs. Then, if two or more systems are close in costs, use qualitative, noncost factors to select the most appropriate system.

Dollars are important as a measurable unit for three reasons:

1. Traditionally, firms use dollars to keep track and forecast. Accounting systems have extensive historical cost data on which to base estimates and forecasts.
2. Information systems compete against a firm's other alternatives. The dollar is a common measurement unit for comparing alternatives across departments.
3. Top managers decide whether or not to proceed with development of the new information system. Such managers often are most comfortable in dealing with dollar comparisons.

The tools used for cost comparisons are the feasibility matrix and the payoff diagram.

Information systems costs involve hardware, software, people, supplies, telecommunications, and the physical computer site. Costs are one-time or recurring. One-time costs, incurred during development of the new system, include hardware purchase, programming, preparation of the computer site, and installation. Recurring costs are the day-to-day operational costs of an information system. They include hardware and software leasing, supplies, and leasing of telecommunications lines. A new information system should be assigned only those out-of-pocket costs actually incurred; it should not be assigned overhead costs that do not actually increase cash outlays. This is the concept of marginal costs.

Three methods are commonly used for comparing systems: breakeven analysis, payback period, and discounted payback period. When, after cost comparisons, two or more information systems alternatives compare equally, qualitative factors are used to break ties.

Qualitative factors are benefits or savings that cannot be easily converted into dollars. Some qualitative factors involve information systems performance; these include reduced errors, increased speed, improved accuracy, improved security, and improved record currency. Other qualitative factors are strategic in nature; they affect the firm's profit posture. These include customer satisfaction, increased sales, customer and vendor commitment, and information product marketing.

CONCEPTS LEARNED

- The nature of strategic and tactical decisions that constrain choices of operational information systems
- Types of information systems costs
- Guidelines for estimating costs.
- Difference between one-time (development) and recurring (operational) costs
- Common one-time and recurring information systems costs

- Concept of marginal costs and its application to information systems alternatives
- Three methods of comparing information systems alternatives: breakeven analysis, payback period, and discounted payback period.
- What qualitative factors are and how they are used to compare information systems

KEY TERMS

breakeven analysis
breakeven point
centralized data processing
development costs
discounted payback period
dispersed databases
distributed data processing
exponential costs
feasibility analysis
indirect costs
integrated databases
investment period
Law of Insufficient Reason

linear costs
marginal costs
one-time costs
operational costs
overhead costs
payback period
present value
recurring costs
return on investment (ROI)
return period
step function
surround strategy
system life

REVIEW QUESTIONS

1. Explain the relationships among strategic, tactical, and operational system choices.

2. Why should an analyst consider noncost items after comparing the costs of alternative information systems?

3. What are the six categories of information systems costs?

4. Give an example of an exponential cost.

5. Explain the step function and give an example.

6. How can a new computer be either a one-time or a continuous cost?

7. List guidelines for estimating computer system costs.

8. Accounting charges a portion of building heating costs to the development costs of a proposed new information system. Is this proper? Why or why not?

9. Briefly describe the difference between the breakeven and payback methods of comparing information systems.

10. What is the difference between the payback period method and discounted payback period method?

11. List four qualitative factors of information systems.

12. Describe two strategic qualitative factors.

CRITICAL THINKING OPPORTUNITIES

1. Draw a diagram of how this chapter is organized.

Cost Category	Last Year's Costs	Type of Cost	Annual Increase
Personnel	$35,000	Exponential	10%
Supplies	10,000	Exponential	3%
Other	5,000	Linear	5%
Total	$50,000		

FIGURE 8–24   **Arnett Sportswear Manufacturers—Projection of Operating Costs for Old System**

Cost Category	Costs First Year	Costs Second Year*	Total Costs
Personnel	$ 50,000	$20,000	$ 70,000
Hardware	—	50,000	50,000
Software Package	40,000	—	40,000
Supplies	5,000	—	5,000
Other	5,000	5,000	10,000
Total	$100,000	$75,000	$175,000

*New system projected to be completed in twenty months

FIGURE 8–25   Arnett Sportswear Manufacturers—Estimated Development (One-time) Costs

Cost Category	First-Year Costs	Type of Cost	Annual Increase
Personnel	$10,000	Linear	5%
Computer Maintenance	5,000	Stable	N/A
Software Maintenance	1,000	Stable	N/A
Supplies	2,000	Linear	5%
Other	2,000	Linear	3%
Total	$20,000		

FIGURE 8–26   Arnett Sportswear Manufacturers—Projection of Operating Costs for New System

Refer to Figures 8–24 through 8–26 for all remaining exercises.

2. Project old system and new system costs over a five-year period.

3. Construct a feasibility matrix.

4. Perform breakeven analysis.

5. Perform payback period analysis.

6. Arnett Sportswear Manufacturers had the following return on investments over the past five years:

−4	−3	−2	−1	Last Year
15%	19%	17%	19%	22%

Perform a discounted payback period analysis.

7. Given all of your analyses, should the new information system be developed? Why or why not?

CASE 8.1

CAREY CLOTHIERS: ACQUISITION OF COMPUTER RESOURCES

SETTING

Peggy Dramm found another problem at Carey Clothiers that required use of her systems education. Periodically, different vendor brands of computer hardware must be evaluated to determine which brand to purchase. There are no written procedures for this. There are on file past complaints from computer vendors complaining about arbitrary decisions made by Carey Clothiers relative to acquisition of computer resources.

Peggy decides to construct a procedures manual for computer resource acquisition. She journeys to the library at her local university to perform literature research in this area. She focuses her research on the following areas:

- Factors to be used in comparing vendors and products
- A method for showing comparative data
- A method for assigning different weights for the different factors

- Some way of selecting the best computer resource

FACTORS TO BE USED

Peggy segregated computer resource selection into three parts: (1) vendor evaluation, regardless of the product; (2) hardware product evaluation; and (3) software product evaluation. After considerable research, she constructed three tables. Each table has three columns. The first column contains the major factors of evaluation. The second column contains several subfactors within each major factor. The third column lists common units of measurement for each subfactor. The "rate" unit assumes use of a user questionnaire where the quality of the subfactor is rated on a scale from 1 (poor) to 10 (outstanding). The three tables Peggy constructed are:

1. Vendor evaluation factors, regardless of the nature of the product (Figure 8.1–1)

Factor	Name	Unit of Measurement
Vendor Reliability	Years in Business	Number
	Geographic Coverage	Rate (1–10)
	Profitability	Dollars
	Customer Base	Number
	Similar Systems	Number
	User Satisfaction	Rate (1–10)
Vendor Services	Training	Rate (1–10)
	Implementation Support	Rate (1–10)
	Problem Response Time	Hours
	Hot-line Services	Rate (1–10)
	Technical Personnel	Number
	Technical Library	Rate (1–10)

FIGURE 8.1–1 Vendor Evaluation Factors and Their Subfactors

2. Hardware selection factors (Figure 8.1–2)
3. Software selection factors (Figure 8.1–3)

A METHOD FOR SHOWING COMPARATIVE DATA

Peggy came across the acquisition matrix shown in Figure 8.1–4. This matrix is comprised of (1) the various resource alternatives evaluated (columns), (2) the subfactors used in discriminating between alternatives (rows), (3) subfactor weights for differences in importance (rows), and (4) measurements of performance for each resource alternative for each subfactor (cells).

ASSIGNING DIFFERENT SUBFACTOR WEIGHTS

Peggy found that the use of subfactor weights in resource selection allows the computation of a weighted average as follows:

$$\text{Weighted average} = \Sigma_i(w_1)(f_1) + (w_2)(f_2) + (w)(f) + \ldots + (w_n)(f_n)$$

| Factor | Subfactor | |
	Name	Unit of Measurement
Costs	Mainframe	Dollars
	Peripherals	Dollars
	Data Communications	Dollars
	Maintenance	Dollars
	Personnel	Dollars
	Software	Dollars
	Installation	Dollars
	Training	Dollars
Hardware Capabilities	Physical Space	Square Feet
	Warranty Period	Months
	Maintenance Coverage	Rank (1–10)
	Upgrade Capacity	Rank (1–10)
	Site Requirements	Rank (1–10)
	Processing Speed	MIPS
	Memory Capacity	Megabytes
	Reliability	MTBF
	Backup Equipment	Rank (1–10)
	Repair History	MTTR
Software Capabilities	Documentation Availability	Rank (1–10)
	Documentation Quality	Rank (1–10)
	Applications Program Scope	Rank (1–10)
	Applications Program Performance	MIPS
	Utility Program Scope	Rank (1–10)
	Utility Program Performance	MIPS
	Modification Capability	Rank (1–10)
Vendor Services	Training Available	Rank (1–10)
	Delivery Time	Days
	Maintenance Response Time	Hours
	Special Support	Rank (1–10)

FIGURE 8.1–2   Hardware Selection Factors and Subfactors

Factor	Subfactor Name	Subfactor Unit of Measurement
Costs	Single-site License	Dollars
	Multiple-site License	Dollars
	Documentation	Dollars
	Training	Dollars
	Hot-line Services	Dollars
	Copy Permission	Dollars
Design Features	Human Factors	Rank (1–10)
	Tutorials	Rank (1–10)
	Help Functions	Rank (1–10)
	User-tailoring Capabilities	Rank (1–10)
	Access Control	Rank (1–10)
	Report Generators	Rank (1–10)
	On-line Inquiry	Rank (1–10)
	Audit Trails	Rank (1–10)
	Performance Speed	MIPS
Vendor Support	Documentation	Rank (1–10)
	Source Code Availability	Rank (1–10)
	Right to Modify	Rank (1–10)
	Hot-line Services	Rank (1–10)
	Delivery Time	Months

FIGURE 8.1–3 **Software Evaluation Factors and Subfactors**

Factors	Subfactors Name	Subfactors Weight	Resource Alternatives 1	2	3	C−1	C
F_1	SF_{11}	W_{11}					
	SF_{12}	W_{12}					
	SF_{13}	W_{13}					
F_r	SF_{r1}	W_{r1}					
	SF_{r2}	W_{r2}					
	SF_{r3}	W_{r3}					
	SF_{r4}	W_{r4}					

Measurement of alternative for subfactor SF_{r4}

FIGURE 8.1–4 **Resource Acquisition Matrix**

where

> w = weight for subfactor i; (Σw_i = 1.0)
> f_i = subfactor value
> n = number of subfactors

By using a weighted average, subfactors of different degrees of importance can be combined into a total performance score.

The practical problem Peggy found with the use of a weighted average is that it is difficult to assign relative subfactor weights, particularly so when the weights must sum to 1.0 (100 percent). It is easy for most people, though, to rank subfactors according to their relative importance. For example, if there are five subfactors, a rank of 5 can be assigned to the most important subfactor, a rank of 4 to the next most important, and so on. Peggy found that once these ranks are assigned, they can be converted to weights summing to 1.00 by the following algorithm (Figure 8.1–5):

1. Add up the individual ranks for each subfactor to arrive at the total rank.
2. Divide each rank by this total rank to determine the individual subfactor weight. The total of these weights should be 1.0.
3. Make subjective adjustments to the weights as desired in order to bring two subfactors closer together or to make them farther apart.

These derived weights are used as the w variables in the weighted average computation.

Peggy discovered that three methods are available for combining subfactor measurements into a total performance score for each resource alternative. Two of the methods are used routinely. The third, dimensional ranking, requires the use of a computer and is not used as frequently.

Each of the three methods begins with the acquisition matrix shown in Figure 8.1–4. The matrix includes (1) resource alternatives (matrix columns), (2) criteria subfactors (matrix rows), and (3) measurement of the performance of each alternative for each subfactor (matrix cells). The three methods produce a total performance score for each resource alternative. This score is the total of measurements across all subfactors for a particular resource alternative.

The first method is the additive rank procedure (Figure 8.1–6). Resource alternatives are given relative ranks for each performance subfactor. The ranks are summed across all subfactors to produce the total performance score for each alternative. This is the simplest of the three combining methods. It often is used to reduce a large number of vendor alternatives to a few that undergo more extensive analysis.

The second method is the weighted rank procedure (Figure 8.1–7). Relative subfactor weights are entered to the selection matrix. Each alternative's rank for a subfactor is multiplied by that subfactor's weight. The resulting subfactor rank/weight products are added to produce the total performance score for each alternative. This

---

FIGURE 8.1–5 Converting Ranks to Weights

Item	Rank (Highest Is Best)	Weight (Rank ÷ 28)
A	3	.107 (3 ÷ 28)
B	4	.143
C	1	.036
D	6	.214
E	7	.250
F	2	.071
G	5	.179
Total	28	1.000

FIGURE 8.1–6   **Additive Rank Procedure**

Factor	Ranking (1–10)
A	6
B	2
C	5
D	8
E	2
Total	23
Average	4.6

Total Performance Score for This Vendor

approach is preferable to the additive rank procedure because it considers different degrees of importance among the performance subfactors. On the other hand, the weighted rank procedure requires more calculations and therefore may require use of a computer for all but the simplest selection matrices.

The final method is called dimensional ranking procedure, but it first converts natural interval measurements (e.g., time or MIPS) into ordinal rankings required by that procedure. This allows use of natural units of measurement, which are automatically converted to ranks. The procedure requires the use of a computer.

Whichever of these methods is selected to combine subfactor ranks, the result is a total performance score for each resource alternative. The resource alternative with the highest score is preferred. It is this resource product that is purchased.

Peggy was somewhat concerned that the evaluation method she had pieced together was too quantitative. It seemed to her that the structure of the approach and the quantitative nature of this total performance score might mask

(1) Factor	(2) Ranking (1–10)	(3) Factor Weight	(4) Weighted Ranking (2) × (3)
A	6	.21	1.26
B	2	.32	.64
C	5	.17	.85
D	8	.09	.72
E	2	.21	.42
Total	23	1.00	3.89

Total Performance Score for This Vendor

FIGURE 8.1–7   **Weighted Rank Procedure**

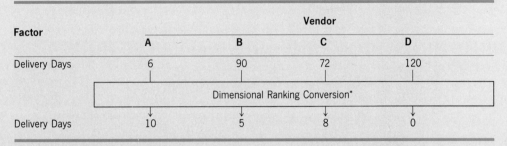

Factor	Vendor			
	A	B	C	D
Delivery Days	6	90	72	120
	Dimensional Ranking Conversion*			
Delivery Days	10	5	8	0

$$^{*}\text{Ranking} = 10 - \left(\left(\frac{\text{Vendor value} - \text{Minimum value}}{\text{Maximum value} - \text{Minimum value}} \right) \cdot 10 \right)$$

For vendor B:

$$\text{Ranking} = 10 - \left(\left(\frac{90 - 60}{120 - 60} \right) \cdot 10 \right) = 5$$

FIGURE 8.1—8 **Dimensional Ranking to a Scale of 0 to 10**

the subjective nature of the entire selection process.

She knew that the assignment of relative subfactor weights is subjective. In addition, the measurement of performance on certain subfactors can be subjective, particularly if the performance unit of measurement is in rankings rather than natural units of measurement. Thus, a vendor alternative's ranking of 4 on a documentation quality subfactor with a weight of .05 appears more accurate than the entirely subjective estimate creating these numbers.

Therefore, Peggy recognized that slight differences between total performance scores of vendor resource alternatives should be viewed with skepticism. Indeed, she decided that the structured evaluation methodology would be more appropriate to narrowing the range of resource competitors than to selecting the one best alternative. Despite the subjective weaknesses of this structured approach, Peggy decided that it would provide Carey Clothiers with a more objective selection method than was currently used.

CASE 8.2

GOODBYTE PIZZA COMPANY: SYSTEM SELECTION

SETTING

Two-thirds of the university semester has passed. Linda Alvires and her student team have been busy. They have proceeded through the following stages of the systems development life cycle:

- Initial investigation
- Requirements analysis
- Generation of system alternatives

They have narrowed the search for an effective order-processing system for Goodbyte Pizza Company to two alternatives: (1) the current manual system and (2) the automated system with characteristics summarized in Figure 8.2-1.

Now the student team must conduct a feasibility study to see which alternative Sam Nolte, Goodbyte's manager, will accept. Linda and her team conduct the feasibility analysis in the following parts:

- Recurring costs for the current system (Figures 8.2-2 and 8.2-3)
- One-time costs for the new system (Figure 8.2-4)
- Recurring costs for the new system (Figures 8.2-5 and 8.2-6)

FEASIBILITY STUDY ASSUMPTIONS

The student analysis team has derived the following four assumptions about the feasibility study:

investment is 20 percent.
2. All development costs must be recovered by the end of five years.
3. Only out-of-pocket costs are to be used in project justification.

```
1. Inventory processed on real-time system.

2. Orders entered to computer—costs automatically computed.

3. Four management reports generated.

4. Registers would have keys for entry of many order characteristics such
   as size ('SMALL', 'MEDIUM', and 'LARGE').

5. Keyboard entry of orders will reduce order-taking time.

6. In-store order and delivery order functions combined.
```

FIGURE 8.2-1   **Characteristics of New Order Processing System**

Cost Category	Annual Costs (Thousands of Dollars)	Note
Hardware	0	
Software	0	
Personnel	72.0	1
Supplies	1.9	
Management	31.0	
Maintenance	0.5	2
Total	105.4	
Notes:		
1. Clerical as opposed to management.		
2. Janitorial, etc.		

FIGURE 8.2—2   Current System Costs for Last Year

Cost Category	Type of Cost Function	Projected Increase per Year
Personnel	Linear	10%
Supplies	Exponential	4%
Management	Linear	10%
Maintenance	Linear	5%

FIGURE 8.2—3   Projected Change in Costs for Current System

Cost Category	Annual Costs (Thousands of Dollars)	Note
Hardware Purchase	8.3	1
Software Purchase	7.5	
Personnel	42.3	2
Supplies	0.9	
User Training	5.4	
Documentation	4.6	
File Conversion	3.8	3
Total	72.8	

Notes:

1. IBM 486 with cash registers and printer.

2. Analysts/programmers (assuming contracted to outside firm).

3. Conversion of current manual records.

FIGURE 8.2−4   **Estimated Implementation Cost of New System**

Cost Category	Annual Costs (Thousands of Dollars)	Note
Hardware	0	1
Software	0	1
Personnel	65.0	2
Supplies	2.5	
Management	27.5	
Maintenance	0.8	3
Total	95.8	

Notes:

1. Purchased, not leased.

2. Cost avoidance—not hire replacements.

3. Added computer maintenance.

FIGURE 8.2—5   Estimated Operational Costs for First Year for New System

Cost Category	Type of Cost Function	Projected Increase per Year
Personnel	Linear	6%
Supplies	Linear	2%
Management	Linear	6%
Maintenance	Linear	3%

FIGURE 8.2—6   Projected Change in Costs for New System

4. The new system promises to realize some noncost benefits, including:
    a) There will be quicker and more useful management data available.
    b) Pilferage and waste will be easier to detect.
    c) The quantity of ingredients needed each day will be easier to predict.

CRITICAL THINKING OPPORTUNITIES

1. How do you think the student team gathered the data just shown?

2. Explain the concept of cost avoidance in the context of Goodbyte's personnel costs.
3. Perform a breakeven analysis on these alternatives.
4. Perform a payback period analysis.
5. Perform a discounted payback period analysis.
6. How will the noncost benefits enter the cost analysis?
7. Prepare an outline for Linda Alvires to use in presenting her team's results to Sam Nolte.

MCKRAKLIN AEROSPACE: SYSTEM SELECTION

SETTING

Dave Costner picked up the telephone and said, "Hello. This is Dave. How may I help you?"

"Hi, Dave. This is Steve Langford of Application Packages in Topeka, Kansas. I understand that you're having problems with your current inventory system. They tell me you're planning to develop a new one in house. Is that right?"

"Yes, that's right," Dave said carefully.

"I've got an alternative for you," Steve said. "We've got a packaged inventory system that's being used successfully by more than twenty firms of your size. One of your main competitors has been using it for three years now. Would you be interested in a demonstration?"

"No," Dave said, "but if you'll send us the complete specifications and a sample version, we'll consider it."

"Fine," Steve said, "I'll send it next-day mail this afternoon. I hope to talk to you soon."

"I'll be waiting for your material," Dave said while hanging up the phone.

Dave thought, "I wonder how he found out about our inventory system problems? Oh well, it won't hurt to look at an alternative to developing the system in house. I'm short of analysts and programmers right now."

The material arrived from Application Packages on Monday. Dave assigned Sharon Bisby to perform an analysis of the most cost-effective means of replacing the inventory system. The alternatives were in-house development or purchase from Application Packages.

A COMPARISON MODEL

Sharon Bisby studied the proposal from Application Packages. She also studied the feasibility study provided to her by the inventory analysis team. Then she began constructing a model for comparing the package with the in-house development alternative. Sharon began by listing the key factors desired of the resulting software product. She then arranged the list from most to least important. Figure 8.3–1 shows her prioritized key factors. Sharon decided to use a weighting model to compare the two software alternatives.

SOFTWARE EVALUATION

Sharon studied the submission from Application Packages again. She rated the inventory package for each of the key factors shown in Figure 8.3–1. Figure 8.3–2 shows her evaluation of the packaged inventory system. Sharon then restudied the feasibility study for the proposed in-house development of the inventory system. Figure 8.3–3 presents her evaluation of the in-house system.

Now Sharon was prepared to construct her comparison model. She would then use it to recommend one of the two alternatives to Dave Costner.

REVIEW QUESTIONS

1. Why did Dave Costner refuse Steve Langford's offer of a demonstration of the packaged inventory system?
2. Why did Dave select Sharon Bisby to evaluate the software alternatives rather than the inventory system design team?
3. How can Sharon provide weights for the key factors shown in Figure 8.3–1?
4. Are there any factors missing from Sharon's list?

Factor		Subfactor	
Name	**Rank**	**Name**	**Rank**
System Cost	1	N/A	N/A
Design Features	3	Human Factors	4
		Tutorials	2
		Help Functions	3
		User-tailoring Capabilities	6
		Access Control	7
		Report Generators	5
		On-line Inquiry	1
Vendor Support	2	Documentation	2
		Source Code Availability	5
		Right to Modify	4
		Hot-line Services	3
		Delivery Time	1

FIGURE 8.3–1   **Prioritized Selection Factors for Choosing Software Alternatives (Lowest number is preferred.)**

Factor	Subfactor		
Name	**Name**	**Dimension**	**Value**
System Cost	System Cost	Dollars	$125 K
Design Features	Human Factors	Rank (1–10)	5
	Tutorials	Rank (1–10)	8
	Help Functions	Rank (1–10)	6
	User-tailoring Capability	Rank (1–10)	7
	Access Control	Rank (1–10)	2
	Report Generators	Rank (1–10)	8
	On-line Inquiry	Rank (1–10)	6
Vendor Support	Documentation	Rank (1–10)	—
	Source Code Availability	Rank (1–10)	2
	Right to Modify	YES/NO	NO
	Hot-line Services	Rank (1–10)	9
	Delivery Time	Months	1

FIGURE 8.3–2   **Evaluation of Packaged Inventory System**

Factor	Subfactor		
Name	Name	Dimension	Value
System Cost	System Cost	Dollars	$150 K
Design Features	Human Factors	Rank (1–10)	6
	Tutorials	Rank (1–10)	5
	Help Functions	Rank (1–10)	6
	User-tailoring Capability	Rank (1–10)	10
	Access Control	Rank (1–10)	8
	Report Generators	Rank (1–10)	6
	On-line Inquiry	Rank (1–10)	4
Vendor Support	Documentation	Rank (1–10)	6
	Source Code Availability	Rank (1–10)	10
	Right to Modify	YES/NO	YES
	Hot-line Services	Rank (1–10)	7
	Delivery Time	Months	15

FIGURE 8.3–3   **Evaluation of In-house Inventory System**

CRITICAL THINKING OPPORTUNITIES

1. Assign weights to the key factors shown in Figure 8.3–2.
2. Solve this resource acquisition problem.
3. Write a short memorandum to Dave Costner explaining the comparison method used, results of the comparison, and reliability of the analysis.

In this chapter you will learn about:

WHAT: (Concepts) How to accomplish preliminary design and produce the system
               study.

WHY: A decision must be made of whether or not to continue the SDLC beyond
               the analysis phase. The system study provides management decision mak-
               ers with the information necessary to make that decision.

WHEN: This is the last part of the system analysis phase.

WHO: ...   ... for review by manage-
               ment.

WHERE: The decision to proceed or not with the SDLC occurs at the management
               level of the organization.

HOW: (Techniques) System study
                             Print layout sheet
                             Screen layout sheet
                             Entity-relationship diagram

OUTLINE

- Setting
- A Total Quality Approach
- A Structured Approach
- Preliminary Design Checklists
- Entity-Relationship Diagram
- The System Study
- The System Presentation
- Go/No-go Decision
- Human Aspects

C H A P T E R 9

PRELIMINARY DESIGN AND THE SYSTEM STUDY

Show me!

— THE STATE OF MISSOURI'S UNOFFICIAL MOTTO

SETTING

We arrive now at a major milestone in the analysis and design of a business information system: the end of the analysis stage. Not all proposed business information systems proceed into the design stage. The resources required to design the new system may be judged too costly. Alternatively, management may feel that the analysis team has not done a detailed enough job or has not considered all relevant information system alternatives. In some cases, detailed analysis of the current information system may show that it is not as bad as we thought it was.

The decision whether or not to allow the proposed information systems project to continue into the costly design phase typically is made by management-level personnel. This decision is commonly referred to as the **go/no-go decision.** The analyst team must present their findings in a clear, concise, and (as much as possible) nontechnical manner amenable to management decision making. In addition, the details gathered during the analysis stage must be organized into a comprehensive, easily referenced document that allows systems design to begin without missing a beat.

Both types of documentation are included in the deliverable called the **system study.** This chapter describes how to put together this important study and how to present the results of that study to management.

A TOTAL QUALITY APPROACH

In a firm and an information systems department using the total quality approach, missions and objectives will have been established encompassing all information systems. A proposed new information system naturally is expected to conform to these missions and objectives. Therefore, the systems study is expected to include the following TQM elements.

1. How this proposed information system conforms with the overall firm mission statement for information systems (Chapter 1)
2. How the proposed information system corresponds with objectives related to the information characteristics of:
   - Relevancy
   - Completeness
   - Correctness
   - Security
   - Timeliness
   - Economy
   - Efficiency
   - Reliability
   - Usability

Note that these elements are included in the system study format described later in this chapter.

A STRUCTURED APPROACH

No matter what version of the systems development life cycle your firm uses, the step-by-step process appears graphically to be sequential in nature. In addition, each of the steps seems distinct. Analysis is completed, then design begins; design is completed, then implementation begins. This appearance of distinctness, however, is misleading. You will find that you may be performing some design tasks while your project is still in the analysis stage. Conversely, you may have to repeat some analysis tasks after beginning the design stage. The different stages overlap and continually flow back and forth into each other, although the graphic SDLC appears as a discrete, serial process.

This is true particularly when we are employing a structured development approach using a leveled set of data flow diagrams (Chapter 6). Recall the sequence for this approach.

1. The *what* and *how* of the current system are described using a leveled set of *physical* DFDs.
2. The *how* is stripped away, leaving only the *what* in a leveled set of *logical* DFDs for the current system.
3. The processes *(what),* unencumbered by implementation details, are made more efficient by deletion, resequencing, consolidating, and changing sequence. This results in a leveled set of *logical* DFDs for the proposed information system.

4. New ways of implementing this information system (*hows* such as laser scanning) are added resulting in a leveled set of *physical* DFDs for the proposed system.
5. This final set of DFDs is used to create the data dictionary.

The first three steps in this sequence clearly are accomplished in the Analysis stage of the SDLC. The fifth step clearly is done in the design stage. The fourth step, creation of physical DFDs for the proposed system is done in a two-part sequence that starts in the Analysis stage and ends in the Design stage.

The two parts of the sequence typically are called logical design and physical design. **Logical design** produces a systems blueprint. Much like the architect's blueprint, the systems blueprint contains an overview, with minimum detail, of the outputs, inputs, screens, files, and processes comprising the information. The level of detail of the logical design is sufficient only to allow (1) meaningful cost–benefit analysis and (2) management determination of the suitability of continuing the SDLC.

Physical design converts the system blueprint into the specific detail required for programmers to construct computer code. Physical design is expensive and time consuming. You do not want to embark on it when the decision has yet to be made on whether to continue the SDLC or to abort the project at the end of the analysis stage. Therefore, there is a fine line between what is logical and what is physical design. This line differs with every design situation; each analyst must decide how he or she will walk this line.

Two final points must be made on this subject. First, the terms *logical design* and *physical design* should not be confused with logical and physical data flow diagrams. Logical and physical designs are SDLC stages. Logical and physical DFDs are tool techniques used within the construct we call *structured development*.

The second point is that, in the terminology of the U.S. government, logical design is referred to as **conceptual design** whereas detailed design is referred to as **detailed design**.

PRELIMINARY DESIGN CHECKLISTS

To reduce confusion, we refer to logical design as preliminary design. **Preliminary design** is the development of general design specifications to a level of detail sufficient to (1) perform feasibility analysis and (2) allow the decision of whether or not to continue the information system development project. This presents a minor dilemma in constructing a textbook. For example, should a chapter on output design be placed in the analysis or the design section?

We resolve this dilemma by including in the analysis section enough detail to allow you to design output, input, files, and processes only in the most general manner. Concise design checklists are provided, which explains to you *what* should be done. The conceptual reasons *why* design should proceed in this manner are left to the more detailed chapters included in the design section.

Output Checklist. Output includes forms and reports that are provided by the information system. It is important that end-users see exactly what reports will look like.

Reports are the products that end-users will receive and work with. Following are some general guidelines for designing system output.

1. Make the report look good. It should be aesthetically balanced, with equal spacing on both sides and at the top and bottom.
2. Include only fields that are really needed. Do not clutter the report with "nice-to-have" fields. (Remember the concept of information overload?)
3. Stay with an 80-position format so that reports can be easily communicated to workstation screens and remote printers.
4. Use a print layout form like the one shown in Figure 9–1.

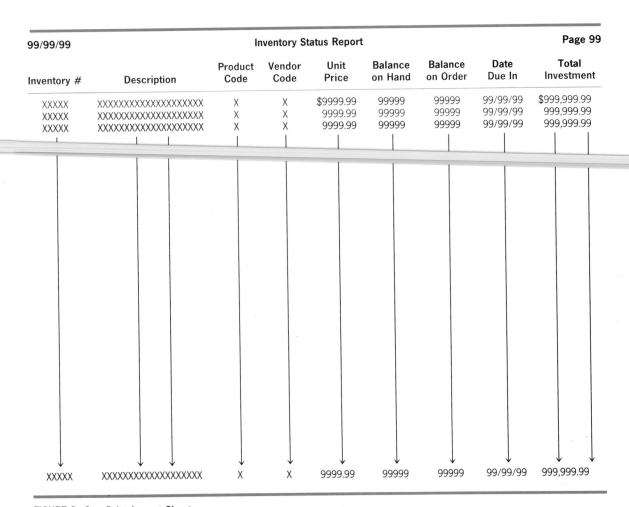

FIGURE 9–1   **Print Layout Sheet**

Input Checklist. Input includes forms primarily used as source documents for entry to the computer system. Following are some general guidelines for designing computer input.

1. Make the form easy to use, so that there is a low rate of incomplete and erroneous fields. Field labels should be clear and there should be sufficient space to easily allow written or typed entries.
2. Make the form concise, including only those fields absolutely required.
3. Make the form aesthetically pleasing, prompting users to be more careful in its preparation.
4. Try to make the form machine-readable, thereby reducing data entry requirements.

Figure 9–2 is an example of a well-designed form.

Interactive Screens. In an on-line data entry system, data is entered to user workstations by interactive screens. Following are some general guidelines for these screens.

1. Screen layouts should be well balanced (e.g., equal spacing at top and bottom).
2. Screens should not be cluttered. A rule of thumb is that no more than 20 percent of the screen should be filled with information.
3. Minimize use of color. Too much color is distracting.
4. Use highlighting (e.g., reverse video) for parts of the screen requiring user input. However, too much highlighting is distracting. A rule of thumb is that no more than 10 percent of the characters on the screen should be highlighted.

Figure 9–3 is an example of a well-designed screen.

Processes. Processes accept data, transform it through a series of tasks, and produce refined information. Processes can be identified, of course, through the data flow diagram. They are first described exactly as they exist (physical and logical DFDs of current system). They are then reengineered to arrive at a more effective process mix (logical DFD of proposed system). Following are some general guidelines for preliminary process design.

1. Eliminate processes that do not alter data (e.g., Process 2.15 of Figure 9–4).
2. Look for consolidation of similar processes, particularly if they are done in the same geographic area (perhaps processes 2.1.7 and 2.1.8 of Figure 9–4).
3. Make serial processes parallel. Serial processes are those where the first must be completed before the second can start. One excellent method for making two processes parallel is to make multiple copies of forms. These multiple copies can flow simultaneously to multiple processes which then can process at the same time. (Two candidates for making parallel are processes 2.1.9 and 2.1.10 in Figure 9–4.)
4. Decouple processes. Have the output from one process flow to a file (data store) rather than directly to a second process. This allows the two processes to work at different speeds, each with minimum effect on the other. (Process 2.1.3 of Figure 9–4 could send cards to a data store instead of directly to process 2.1.4. This would decouple the two processes.)

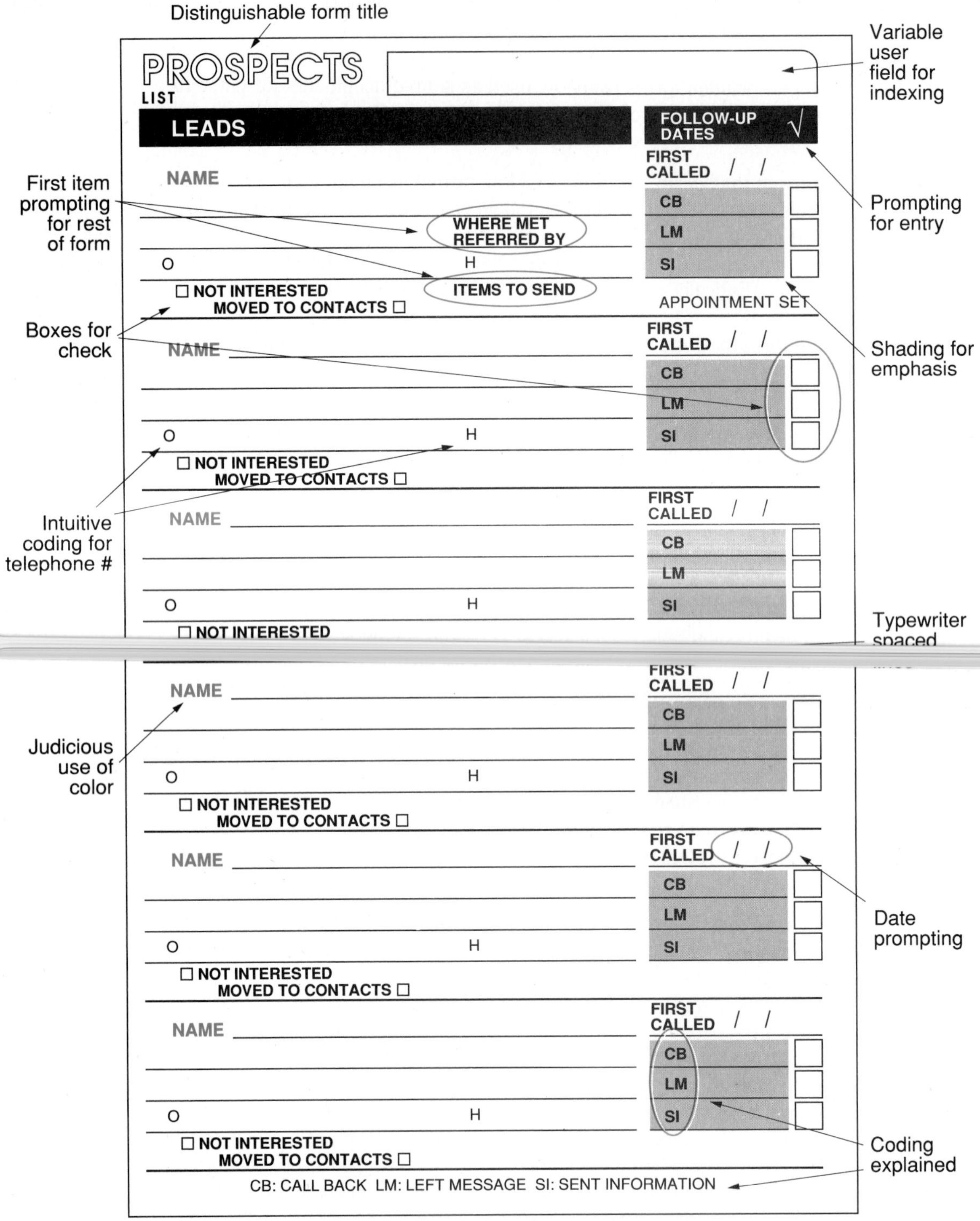

FIGURE 9-2   Example of a Well-designed Form

306

FIGURE   9–3   **Interactive   Report Menu**

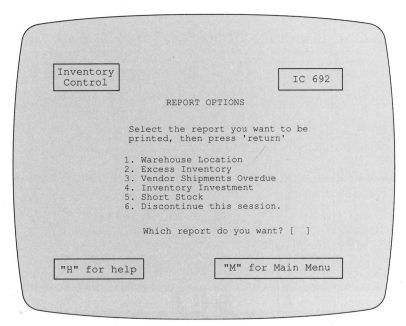

```
┌─────────────┐                              ┌──────────┐
│ Inventory   │                              │  IC 692  │
│ Control     │                              └──────────┘
└─────────────┘           REPORT OPTIONS

                   Select the report you want to be
                   printed, then press 'return'

                   1. Warehouse Location
                   2. Excess Inventory
                   3. Vendor Shipments Overdue
                   4. Inventory Investment
                   5. Short Stock
                   6. Discontinue this session.

                   Which report do you want? [   ]


  ┌──────────────────┐            ┌────────────────────┐
  │ "H" for help     │            │ "M" for Main Menu  │
  └──────────────────┘            └────────────────────┘
```

Files. Files, also referred to as data stores, temporarily hold data over time until it is ready to feed to a process. Following are some general guidelines for preliminary file design:

1. Look for possible consolidation of files with similar names. In Figure 9–4, the Customer Order file and Customer Backorder file are candidates for merging into a single file.
2. Do not strive for too much file detail at this time. Decisions on details such as field sequence, file access method, file retention/recovery, and file space requirements can be deferred until the design stage of the SDLC.
3. Determine the relationship of entities, files, and data elements by constructing entity-relationship diagrams as described next.
4. Construct a data-element-to-file table as shown in Figure 9–5.

ENTITY-RELATIONSHIP DIAGRAM

It may be too early to have decided whether or not your proposal system will include traditional files or databases. However, it is useful to employ here a descriptive tool used in data modeling.

Data modeling is a critical aspect of requirements definition and design of systems. The origins of data modeling are in database design. Understanding data requirements and how the application view of the database must be constructed is crucial to the design and successful implementation of an information system.

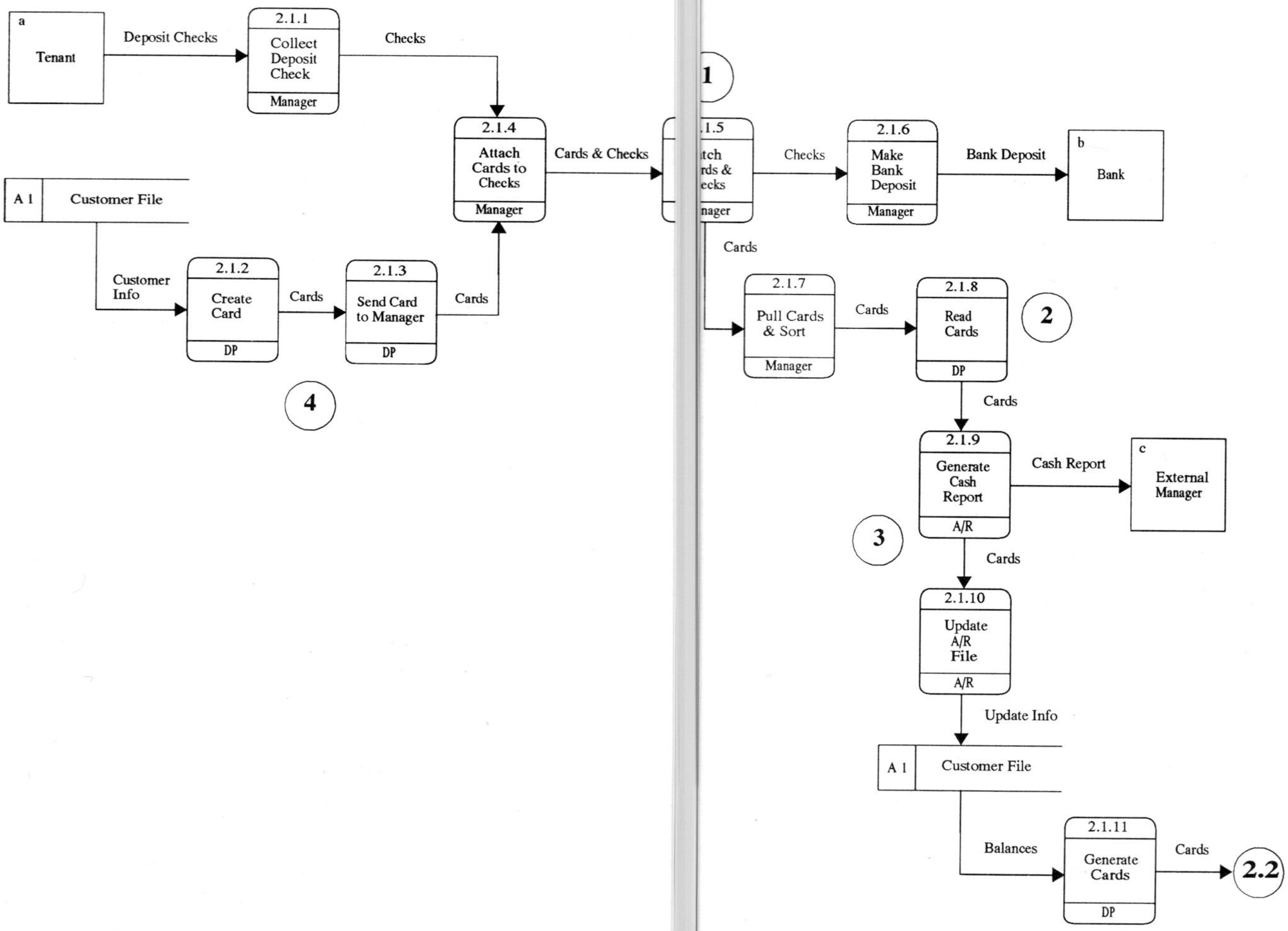

FIGURE 9–4 Preliminary Process Design

FIGURE   9–5   Data-Element-to-File Table

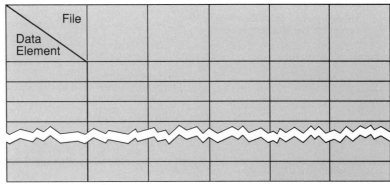

A popular approach to modeling data is the **Chen entity-relationship approach,** which uses the **entity-relationship diagram (ERD)** to illustrate the logical design of a database **schema** (complete enterprise data) or **subschema** (application view of the data). The ERD contains three classes of things: entities, relationships, and attributes.

Entities are objects (persons, places, things, or events) that make up the data of the database. Entities must be unique. An example of an entity is a customer order. **Relationships** are conceptual links or ties that exist between or among entities. An example of a relationship between customers and customer orders is placement (i.e., customers *place* orders). The customers are entities, the customer orders are entities, and *place* describes one relationship between customers and customer orders. **Attributes** modify or describe both entities and relationships. Attributes are the information about an entity that we are interested in capturing and processing. Examples of attributes of a customer are name, address, account number, and balance due. An example of an attribute of the place relationship is date of order placement.

Specific symbols are used in ERDs. Rectangles represent entities and diamonds represent relationships. Lines connect the entities and the relationships. The number 1 or the letter m or n on a line represents the entity occurrence. Entity occurrences can be one to one (1 to 1), one to many (1 to m), and many to many (m to n). The 1's, m's, and n's are placed on straight lines between the diamonds and the rectangles. Figure 9–6 illustrates a generic ERD. Figure 9–7 illustrates an ERD for a mortgage lender; read it as follows: Each customer is the titled owner of one home. The mortgage lender holds mortgages on many homes. The mortgage lender has a creditor relationship with many customers. The customers have a debtor relationship with many lending institutions.

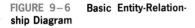

FIGURE 9–6   Basic Entity-Relation-ship Diagram

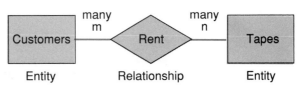

FIGURE 9–7   Entity-Relationship Diagram for Lending Institutions

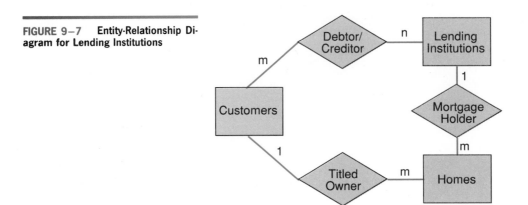

In addition to entities, relationships, and entity occurrences, the attributes associated with each entity may be added to the ERD. Figure 9–8 adds attributes to the original ERD in Figure 9–7. Interpret it as follows: The entity customers contains three attributes: customer-ID, customer name, and customer address. The primary key is customer-ID, and it is underlined to show that it is primary. The entity lending institutions contains three attributes: Savings-and-Loan (S&L) ID, S&L name, and S&L

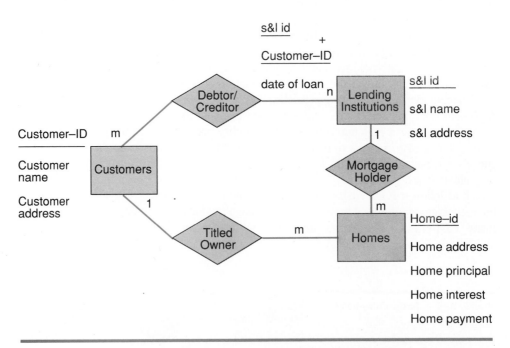

FIGURE 9–8   Entity-Relationship Diagram for Lending Institutions with Attributes

address. The primary key is S&L ID and is underlined. The primary key is the field that will be used to find a specific record in a file (sometimes called record ID). The entity homes contains six attributes: home-ID, home address, home principal, home interest, home payment. The primary key is home-ID and is underlined.

The relationship debtor/creditor is a many-to-many relationship and therefore must be contained in a separate file. The primary keys of the two files that it is relating are necessary as attributes (called a composite key), as is the date of the first loan. The date of the first loan is a secondary key because it is not unique (other customers may take out loans on that same date).

In summary, ERDs are important tools for the logical modeling of systems requirements. Deriving the logical data model using the ERD will dictate physical file requirements such as the number of files, the primary keys, and attributes. The ERD is an excellent tool for showing file and data element relationships during preliminary design.

THE SYSTEM STUDY

The system study is a synopsis of all analysis efforts, from original detection of the information systems problem (Chapter 4) to comparison of alternative information systems (Chapter 8). It contains sections for problem statement, existing system description, problem correction alternatives, recommended solution, and documentation. Case 9.1 is a system study for Fortyne Dairy. Follow this outline when preparing a system study.

Problem Statement

1. Nature of the problem detected (e.g., increasing data entry backlogs)
2. How problem was detected (e.g., customer complaints or performance measurement system)
3. Impact of problem on organizational goals (e.g., delays in processing of customer orders or reduces cash flow)
4. Departments and functions involved (e.g., marketing department and order-processing section of production department)

Existing System Documentation

1. System functions and interrelationships (This should be done with a physical data flow diagram, accompanied by a step-by-step narrative description.)
2. Processing volumes by type of document
3. Processing times by type of document
4. Bottlenecks (distribution of backlogs)
5. Organization policies affecting processing (e.g., a policy requiring that clerks process all commercial orders before residential orders)

6. Processing constraints:
   - People (e.g., an average 20 percent vacancy rate among data entry operators)
   - Hardware
   - Software
   - Development funds
7. Organization of involved departments and functions (e.g., an organizational chart)

Problem Correction Alternatives

1. Procedure for generating information systems alternatives
2. Cost determination for different alternatives
3. Feasibility analysis:
   - Breakeven years
   - Payback years or discounted payback years
4. Qualitative factors
5. Alternative recommended and why
6. Alternative comparison with firm's goals (e.g., ROI)

Recommended Solution

1. Overall system description for recommended alternative
2. New system functions and relationships (data flow diagram)
3. Expected new system results:
   - Costs
   - Benefits
   - TQM elements (e.g., usability)
4. Proposed development schedule
5. Development resource needs

Documentation

1. Physical and logical data flow diagrams
2. Processing flow statistics (volume, timing, etc.)
3. Organizational charts
4. Feasibility analysis details
5. Development project schedule chart
6. Development project proposed cost schedule
7. Sample output reports
8. Sample input forms
9. Sample screen formats
10. Data-element-to-file table
11. Entity-relationship diagram

The information systems department sends its proposals to the person or group in the firm responsible for rating and approving potential investments. Management then sets a date for the IS department to present a synopsis of its study.

THE SYSTEM PRESENTATION

The IS department presents its system study in a specific business setting. First, the audience consists of middle- and top-level managers. They are short of time, relatively unsophisticated in computer knowledge, and often present by organizational demand (policy) rather than by choice. Second, most will only glance at the system study, because that study tends to be long and complicated. Third, the presentation has a set time limit. Even if the presentation is allowed to exceed that time limit, audience attention drops sharply the longer it lasts. Fourth, managers at the presentation may have investment alternatives in their own departments. They may lose funding if they approve this proposed new information system.

Given this setting, here are some guidelines for presenting the system study successfully:

1. Practice the presentation to reduce dangers of exceeding allotted times.
2. Reduce technical detail to a minimum. It is better to present technical details in response to specific questions than to offer them unsolicited.
3. Use clear, uncluttered visual aids.
4. If you have used prototyping, bring a portable workstation. A hands-on demonstration is far more informative and interesting than inactive visual aids.
5. Stress advantages of the proposed information system over other alternatives available to the firm. Do not restrict comparison to other information systems. Use financial comparative figures such as ROI.

GO/NO-GO DECISION

Top management must now decide to proceed (go) with development of the new information system or to delay or disapprove that development (no-go decision). If top management's decision is to proceed with development, the information systems department begins the design process described in the next section of this book. If top management disapproves entirely the proposed new information system, then the systems development life cycle is abandoned at this stage. Rarely are decisions as straightforward as this.

Often, top management finds problems with the system study that are not serious enough to cause abandonment of the project but require rework of the system study. This decision is the basis for the waterfall model of systems analysis shown in Figure 9–9. The model indicates that any part of the system study may be repeated. Sometimes, the information systems department makes the decision to repeat stages before it presents the system study. Alternatively, the decision to repeat a previous SDLC stage results from management's go/no-go decision.

If top management approves development of the proposed new information system, the next phase in the systems development life cycle is systems design—the topic of Section Three of this book.

These checklists will allow you to perform a preliminary design of system input, output, screens, processes, and files. This design may be modified and made more

FIGURE 9–9 **Waterfall Model of Systems Analysis**

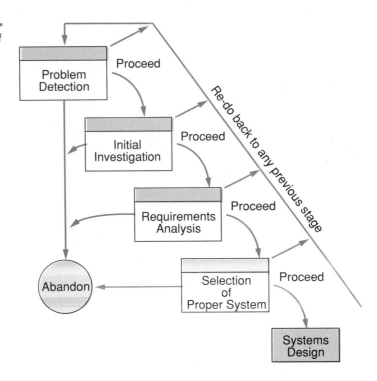

sophisticated in the design phase of the proposal project. That is, detailed design will occur *if* management approves continuation of the project beyond the analysis phase.

HUMAN ASPECTS

At this point, you have put a lot of work into the proposed information system. You have built in yourself a lot of pride, a lot of ownership in the idea of a new system. Now that ownership is in danger. If your proposal does not receive management approval (the go/no-go decision), your pet project likely will be scrapped. This is a nervewracking time.

Remember, an idea is more important than your ego. Prepare for your presentation by first curbing your zeal—not your enthusiasm, but your zeal. Approach the presentation in a cool, logical, and fair manner. All investment proposals are based on assumptions. Do not hide those assumptions or try to defend them when some manager has spotted a critical flaw. One day before the presentation, have one of your colleagues make the presentation before you. Pretend you are one of those nontechnical managers who tomorrow will be listening to you.

At this point in the SDLC, you are a salesperson. Do not oversell—do not appear as a pesky, door-to-door salesperson. You have a quality product, which will help your firm. Sell your system from that point of view.

MEISTER AUTO PARTS*

Meister Auto Parts is a distributor of new and used automobile parts and accessories. This so-called aftermarket dealer buys parts such as transmissions, engines, and drive shafts from a variety of vendors and inventories them for resale to retailers such as Western Auto, Pep Boys, and Kragen Auto Stores.

The owner of Meister Auto Parts believes that computerization is needed in a variety of areas, most particularly, in the processing of customer orders. An on-line, real-time customer order-processing system is desired to automate the following manual processes and procedures.

A customer usually calls Meister requisitioning an order for parts. Meister's customer service representative prepares a customer order form by first looking up the customer's name, address, and account number in a customer card file and then posting this data to the top of the order form. (The future computer system will have to allow the customer service representative to key in a customer name and account number so such data can be first checked for syntax errors. If not in error, the computer will have to validate the account number against a customer master file. Then, if the account number is not found, or if the first four characters of the customer's name do not correspond to the name in the customer record matched on account number, an error message would have to be displayed. If a successful match is made, the customer's name, address, account number, and credit status would then be displayed for confirmation purposes.)

Next, a customer order number is assigned. This is done by looking up the last assigned number in a log book, adding one to this number, assigning this number to the customer order, and posting the customer's name and order date, with the assigned customer order number, to the log book (so this number is not used again).

Unless overridden by the customer service representative, the customer order is given today's date as the order date.

The customer service representative notes the parts desired by the customer. Specifically, he or she jots down each part's stock number, unit price quotation, and quantity requested. (In the computer system, if such data are not syntactically correct, an error message would have to be displayed.) Next, the parts inventory file is checked to verify that the desired part number is still stocked by Meister and that the customer's price quotation is still valid—that is, within 10 percent of the current sales price for the corresponding part. (The computer system would have to display the part number, part description, quantity desired, quantity in stock, and the lower of price quotation or current sales price if successfully matched on part number and with a satisfactory price quotation; otherwise, an error message would have to be displayed.) This process is performed for all parts ordered by the customer.

Finally, the customer order is stored in an open customer order file.

Sometimes, customers send in a purchase order in writing with no price quotation information on it. When this happens, the customer's purchase order is placed temporarily in the customer order file, to be replaced by a customer order form, which is completed from the purchase order rather than from telephone communication with the customer. (The customer order file is in customer account number and date sequence, so it is easy to find a corresponding purchase order if one has been received.) The purchase order is then disregarded.

The same person responsible for generating the customer order also prepares a customer shipment/price confirmation and sends the confirmation to the customer.

*This case was prepared by David Schultz, MIS Department, California State University, Sacramento.

SUMMARY

We are at the end of the analysis phase of the system development life cycle. If management assesses the proposed information system as worthwhile, your project will continue to the design phase. Otherwise, you may have to repeat some analysis stages, or your project will be scrapped without proceeding further.

The deliverable that culminates this phase is the system study, which documents all work that has been done in the analysis phase. Included is preliminary design of proposed system outputs, inputs, interactive screens, processes, and files. This chapter has presented brief checklists of what should make up this preliminary design. Described also was a system tool that can aid in preliminary design description: the entity-relationship (ER) diagram.

The system study is accompanied by a system presentation before management. Here the analyst briefly presents the advantages of the proposed system and reasons that the SDLC should be continued for this project. If the go/no-go decision is made in favor of continuing the project, then the system design phase will begin. This phase is discussed in the next section of this book.

CONCEPTS LEARNED

- Why preliminary design
- Preliminary design checklists
- Entity-relationship diagram

- The system study
- The go/no-go decision

KEY TERMS

attributes
Chen entity-relationship approach
conceptual design
detailed design
entities
entity-relationship diagram (ERD)
go/no-go decision
logical design

physical design
preliminary design
relationships
schema
subschemas
system study
waterfall model of systems analysis

REVIEW QUESTIONS

1. What are the differences between logical and physical design?

2. Why do we need preliminary design?

3. Describe three guidelines for designing output.

4. Describe three guidelines for designing input.

5. Describe three guidelines for designing interactive screens.

6. Describe three guidelines for improving processes.

7. Describe three guidelines for designing files.

8. What are the differences between entities, relationships, and attributes?

9. What are the main elements of a system study?

10. Cite three guidelines for presenting the system study.

11. Describe the possible results of the go/no-go decision.

CRITICAL THINKING OPPORTUNITIES

1. Draw a diagram of the organization of this chapter.

2. Compare and contrast what comprises logical and physical (preliminary) design.

The remaining exercises refer to the description of Meister Auto Parts on page 315.

3. Identify the inputs in this system. Select one input and design an input form using the guidelines discussed in this chapter.

4. Identify the outputs in this system. Select one output and design a report using the guidelines discussed in this chapter.

5. Design a preliminary interactive screen for use by the customer service representative, using the guidelines offered in this chapter.

6. How can the process described here be redesigned?

7. Draw an entity-relationship diagram for Meister Auto Parts.

8. Construct a data-element-to-file table.

(*Note:* You may better be able to perform these exercises if you first construct a DFD.)

CASE 9.1

SYSTEM STUDY FOR FORTYNE DAIRY

SETTING

This system study has the following components:

- Cover letter
- System study
- Problem statement
- Existing system documentation
- Problem correction alternatives
- Recommended solution
- Documentation

COVER LETTER

6/27/95

Mr. Samuel Barber
Executive Vice President
Fortyne Dairy Corporation
1620 J Street
Sacramento, CA 95826

RE: Proposed Order Entry System

Dear Mr. Barber:

Enclosed is our study and proposal on the subject system (Exhibit 1). We will present a management overview of this study at 1 P.M. Friday, July 6, as arranged by your office. Please feel free to contact me before this time if you have questions on this study. I look forward to meeting with you on July 6.

Sincerely,

Merle P. Martin
President
University Consultants

SYSTEM STUDY

Problem Statement

Nature of Problem Detected. There is an increasing backlog of customer orders to be entered to the current order entry system. This backlog is causing delays in filling customer orders. The backlog seems to be caused by:

1. Increasing volume of customer orders
2. Batch processing nature of current system
3. High turnover rate of data entry employees

How Problem Was Detected. Problems with the current system surfaced from two sources. First, the marketing department was receiving an increasing number of customer complaints about late delivery of orders. Several customers cancelled their accounts. Second, the information systems department had sent memos indicating increased data entry backlog due to increasing employee turnover (see memos attached as Exhibit 1).

Impact on Organization. These problems with the current order entry system have the following impact on Fortyne Dairy:

1. Increasing customer dissatisfaction, which will ultimately lead to lost sales and lost customer accounts.
2. Decreasing morale in the information systems department's entry section (if not checked, this may lead to increased employee turnover, larger backups, and decreasing entry quality).

Departments and Functions Involved. Problems with the current system directly affect the marketing department and information systems department. There are indirect implications for the picking and shipping sections of the production department.

Existing System Documentation

Documentation of the current system is included in exhibits located in the appendix. These include:

1. System functions and relationships (Exhibit 2)
2. Processing volumes by document type (Exhibit 3)
3. Processing times by document type (Exhibit 4)
4. Distribution of data entry backlogs (Exhibit 5)
5. Physical and logical data flow diagrams for the current system (Exhibit 7)
6. Current organizational chart (Exhibit 8)
7. Sample output records (Exhibit 9)
8. Sample input forms (Exhibit 10)
9. Sample interactive screen formats (Exhibit 11)
10. Data-element-to-file table (Exhibit 12)
11. Entity-relationship diagrams (Exhibit 13)

Organizational Policies. One organizational policy affects the processing of customer orders. This is the policy communicated by your memorandum of February 10, 1995 (Exhibit 6). The policy calls for servicing all commercial customers before residential customers. The policy has created the following order entry problems:

1. Data entry personnel take one hour each morning to separate commercial customers from residential customers. This requirement decreases order entry time by one hour per day, thus contributing to part of the backlog problem.

2. Residential customers bear the brunt of the late delivery problem (see Exhibit 5). Marketing personnel state that Fortyne Dairy's competition is in the residential more than the commercial sector. Therefore, lost customer sales and accounts are more likely in the residential sector.

Processing Constraints. Several constraints affect the performance of the current order entry system. Unless relieved, these constraints will also affect any newly designed order entry system. These constraints include:

1. *Personnel:* The number of data entry positions in the information systems department has not been increased in three years. During these three years, there have been transaction increases for customer orders (25 percent), purchase orders (20 percent), receipts (18 percent), and customer billings (12 percent). On average, data entry workload has increased 19.3 percent over the past three years, with no increase in data entry positions.
2. *Hardware:* The current Honeybun 1699 computer was introduced twenty years ago. It is slow and has limited storage capacity. However, this hardware will probably be adequate for the proposed new customer order system.
3. *Software:* None.
4. *Development funds:* The comptroller's policy is that no new development projects will be considered unless they show at least a 20 percent return on investment (ROI) within five years of project initiation. In addition, there is always a limit on development funds available. Therefore, development projects must compete against each other for limited funds available.

Problem Correction Alternatives

We evaluated several alternatives in the following sequence:

1. *System goals:*
   a) Reduce customer order backlog to an average of 10 percent of daily transactions received.
   b) Update records on a real-time basis.
   c) Employ a human-factors-designed interactive system oriented to novice entry operators.
   d) Reduce entry clerk turnover rate by 40 percent.
2. *Alternatives generated:* We initially considered the systems alternatives shown in Exhibit 14. All but two of the alternatives were eliminated because of cost or technical feasibility considerations. The two alternatives remaining were the current system and the proposed interactive system described in this proposal.
3. *Alternative costs:* Costs of the current system are shown in Exhibit 15. Projected costs of the new system are shown in Exhibit 16. Comparison of these costs is shown in Exhibit 17 over the five-year planning horizon for this development project.
4. *Feasibility analysis:* We performed two levels of cost comparison:
   a) Breakeven years (Exhibit 18)
   b) Discounted payback period (Exhibit 19)
5. *Qualitative factors:* Several qualitative factors could not be included in the feasibility analysis:
   a) *Future expansion:* The proposed system will have greater capacity to deal with the still increasing volume of customer orders.
   b) *Employee turnover:* The proposed system includes human-factors-designed screens, which will be easier for data entry operators to use. This should reduce employee turnover by an unspecified amount.
   c) *Customer satisfaction:* The proposed system will speed up processing of customer orders. This will increase customer satisfaction, which in turn should ensure continued increases in customer orders.
6. *Recommendation:* We recommend development of the proposed new customer order system. We base this recommendation on the following analysis.
   a) The proposed system will begin generating a positive cash flow in less than two years (see Exhibit 18).
   b) Using a 20 percent ROI present value criterion (see Exhibit 19), the proposed new system will recover development costs in four years. This falls well within the comptroller's guidelines.
   c) The proposed customer order system will show qualitative benefits for future expansion, employee turnover, and customer satisfaction.

Recommended Solution

The proposed new order system we recommend has the following features:

1. System description (Exhibit 20)
2. Functions and relationships (Exhibit 21)
3. System outcomes:
   a) Costs (Exhibit 22)
   b) Benefits (Exhibit 23)
   c) Total quality management considerations (Exhibit 24)
   d) Development schedule (Exhibit 25)
   e) Resources required (Exhibit 26)

Documentation

Exhibit 1. Information Systems Memorandum
Exhibit 2. Current System Functions and Relationships
Exhibit 3. Current System Volumes by Document Type
Exhibit 4. Current System Processing Times by Document Type
Exhibit 5. Current System Description of Data Entry Backlogs
Exhibit 6. Customer Order Policy Memorandum
Exhibit 7. Physical and Logical Data Flow Diagram for Current System
Exhibit 8. Current Organizational Chart

CLASS DESIGN PROJECT: ANALYSIS PHASE

In this phase, you will produce three deliverables for your class project: (1) current system description, (2) requirements analysis, and (3) system study.

CURRENT SYSTEM DESCRIPTION CONTENTS

1. Company overview:
   a) Product/services
   b) Transaction/sales volume
   c) Geographical locations
   d) Personnel (by type)
   e) Organization chart
2. Current system description:
   a) Narrative description (using Level 1 DFD)
   b) Physical DFD current system
   c) Processing volumes/times by type of document/report
3. Problem statement:
   a) Nature of problems detected
   b) Impact on organizational goals
   c) Departments/functions involved

REQUIREMENTS ANALYSIS CONTENTS

1. Conduct of analysis
2. User requirements
3. System constraints
4. Logical DFDs current/proposed systems
5. Problem correction alternatives:
   a) Hardware
   b) Software
   c) Processing (e.g., batch versus real-time)

SYSTEM STUDY CONTENTS

1. Executive overview
2. Current system description (corrected)
3. Requirements analysis (corrected)
4. Proposed system (using Level 1 DFD as guide)
5. Physical DFDs for proposed system
6. Hardware/software requirements
7. Cost–benefit analysis
8. Development project schedule chart
9. Preliminary design specifications

REFERENCES AND FURTHER READINGS

Benham, Harry, Leon Price, and Jennifer Wagner. "Comparison of Structured Development Methodologies." *Information Executive* (Spring 1989):18–23.

Bratton, G. R., and P. R. Newsted. "Response Effects in Computerized Data Collection: An Explanatory Model." In *Proceedings of Second Symposium on Human Factors in Management Information Systems.* Sacramento, Calif., 1989.

Brose, M. "Technology Factor in Corporate Planning." *Planning Review* 12(April 1984):10–15.

Chen, Peter. "Optimal File Allocation in Multi-Level Storage Systems." *In Proceedings* 1973 NCC, AFIPS, Vol. 42, pp. 227–282.

DeMarco, Tom. *Structured Analysis and System Specification.* Englewood Cliffs, N.J.: Prentice-Hall, 1979.

Eliason, Alan. *System Development.* Glenview, Ill.: Scott, Foresman/Little Brown, 1990.

Emory, C. William. *Business Research Methods,* 3rd ed. Homewood, Ill.: Irwin, 1985.

Gane, C., and T. Sarson. *Structured Systems Analysis: Tools and Techniques.* Englewood Cliffs, N.J.: Prentice-Hall, 1979.

Gildersleeve, Thomas. *Successful Data Processing Systems Analysts,* 2nd ed. Englewood Cliffs, N.J.: Prentice-Hall, 1985.

Hare, Van Court. *Systems Analysis: A Diagnostic Approach.* New York: Harcourt, Brace & World, 1967.

Kendall, Kenneth, and Julie Kendall. *Systems Analysis and Design.* Englewood Cliffs, N.J.: Prentice-Hall, 1988.

King, O. *Current Practices in Software Development.* New York, Yourdon Press, 1977.

Markus, L. *Systems in Organizations.* Boston: Pittman, 1984.

Martin, James. *Recommended Diagramming Standards for Analysts and Programmers.* Englewood Cliffs, N.J.: Prentice-Hall, 1987.

Martin, Merle. "Decision Making: The Payoff Matrix." *Journal of Systems Management* 30(January 1979):14–18.

Martin, Merle, and James Trumbly. "Measuring Performance of Computer Systems." *Journal of Systems Management* 37(February 1986):7–17.

Newbold, Paul. *Statistics for Business and Economics.* Englewood Cliffs, N.J.: Prentice-Hall, 1984.

Orr, K. T. *Structured Systems Development.* New York: Yourdon Press, 1977.

Porter, M. *Competitive Strategy Technique for Analyzing Industries and Competitors.* New York: Free Press, 1985.

Semprevivo, Philip. *Systems Analysis: Definition, Process, and Design.* Chicago: Science Research Associates, 1982.

Solman, P. "Shoshana Zuboff—Smart Computers: The Challenge to Smart Managers." *Business Month* 133(1989):61–62.

Sprague, R., and B. McNurlin. *Information Systems Management in Practice.* Englewood Cliffs, N.J.: Prentice-Hall, 1986.

Wetherbe, James. *Systems Analysis and Design,* 3rd ed. St. Paul, MN: West, 1988.

Young, J. "Productivity: Comment." *Computerworld* (Supplement 7, 1988).

Yourdon, E. *Managing the Structure Techniques.* New York: Yourdon Press, 1988.

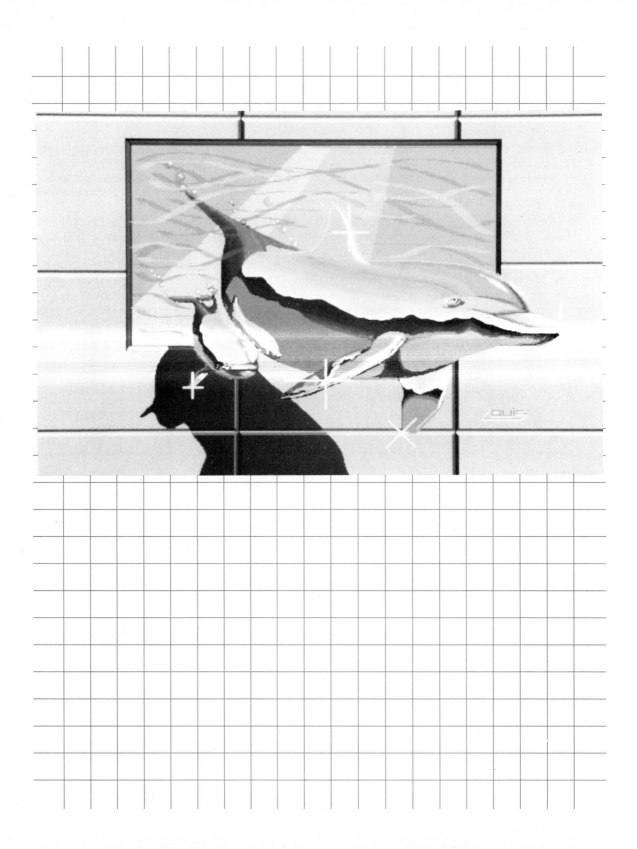

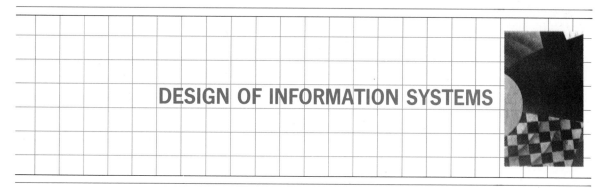

DESIGN OF INFORMATION SYSTEMS

At this point in the SDLC, you have detected and investigated an information systems problem. You have examined alternative solutions and recommended one solution: design of a replacement information system. Fortunately, you sold that solution to top management and have received an O.K. to proceed with the design of the new system. Now it is time to design that system. That is the focus of this section.

Chapter 10, "Quality Design Alternatives," describes the principles, coordination, and politics that are part of the design process. The chapter emphasizes designing systems to make future changes easier.

Chapter 11, "Data Dictionary and Other Design Tools," presents you with a toolbox of techniques to choose from when designing information systems.

Chapter 12, "Output Design," explains the modes and principles for designing the output of business information systems. Future user output requirements are stressed, and well-designed business reports are compared to those that are poorly designed.

Chapter 13, "Input Design," introduces considerations such as form design, coding, and error checking (validation). Again, the emphasis is on the future; the topics of paperless transaction systems and voice input medium are included.

Chapter 14, "Interactive Screen Design," concentrates on input and output design principles as they relate to interactive screens.

Chapter 15, "Data Storage Design," reviews the different methods of file organization in a conventional, non-database environment. The chapter presents standard record structures and discusses alternatives for designing fields and records. A critical discussion of how to design files for the future concludes the chapter.

Chapter 16, "Database Design," describes file design in an integrated database environment. It includes a checklist for constructing a database using a bottom-up design approach. The chapter highlights the role of the systems analyst in a database environment.

Chapter 17, "Process Design/Reengineering," presents approaches to improving old information processes and designing new ones.

OBJECTIVES

In this chapter you will learn about:

WHAT: (Concepts) General considerations for designing quality information systems.

WHY: Certain design principles apply to all new information systems—in different firms, across different business applications, and with different tasks such as output design and input design.

WHEN: These principles apply to all stages in the SDLC design phase.

WHO: Systems analyst now playing the role of system designer.

WHERE: Information systems department and end-user work area.

HOW: (Techniques) Systems blueprint
                      Structured walkthroughs
                      Joint Application Design

OUTLINE

- Setting
- A Total Quality Approach
- A Structured Approach
- Principles of Well-Designed Systems
- Profile of a Poorly Designed System
- Design Stages
- Design Coordination
- Joint Application Design
- Automated Design Tools (CASE)
- Design across Different Types of Information Systems
- Human Aspects

C H A P T E R 10

QUALITY DESIGN ALTERNATIVES

Established technology tends to persist in the face of new technology.

— GERRIT A. BLAAUW

SETTING

It takes only moderate skills to design an information systems report or an input document. It takes only a slightly higher level of skill to design an information systems file or an information process. It takes considerable talent, however, to tie together outputs, inputs, files, and processes into a cohesive, effective information system.

The systems design phase of the SDLC is completely different in nature from the systems analysis phase. The analysis phase was exploratory, allowing at least initial consideration of all possible systems alternatives. Only in the last stages of analysis were alternatives reduced to the most viable. Finally, one new information system was proposed and then accepted by management.

The systems design phase is constrained by decisions made during systems analysis. The new system must be designed within specified costs, in an agreed-on time, and within accepted processing alternatives. In addition, certain management and user expectations are preestablished, and managers and users will find it difficult to accept anything less.

Given such constraints, the design process must be a tightly coordinated effort. There is little room for variance from established procedures. This chapter describes several principles for coordinating the varied and separate tasks that are part of the design of business information systems.

A TOTAL QUALITY APPROACH

In Chapter 3 we established the nine quality objectives of relevancy, completeness, correctness, security, timeliness, economy, efficiency, reliability, and usability. For each stage in the SDLC (each chapter in this section of the book), these quality objectives are used as design criteria. Thus, these objectives apply to design of output, input, files, and processes.

A STRUCTURED APPROACH

The systems blueprint includes one or more data flow diagrams, which show the linkage between files, input documents, output documents and reports, and processes. You can see the role of the DFD as a unifying force behind the systems blueprint by examining the DFD of a customer order process, shown in Figure 10–1. Note the following elements:

- Three files are shown: product file, customer file, and order file. Design of each of these files will be documented using the techniques described in Chapters 15 and 16. Several documents are used in this system: packing slip, picking slip, and invoice. Design of such documents will be described using the techniques included in Chapter 13.
- Three reports are produced by the system: activity, exception, and resource status. Each of these reports is described in Chapter 12.
- Several input documents or messages are required by the system: customer order, customer status, product status, and order status. Design of each of these inputs is described in Chapters 13 and 14.
- Three processes are shown: order processing, shipping, and report generation. Each of these processes will be reengineered using the techniques described in Chapter 17.

The data flow diagram is not only a graphic technique to show system flow (linkage) but also a checklist to ensure that all specifications are included in the systems blueprint.

PRINCIPLES OF WELL-DESIGNED SYSTEMS

Several principles are essential to the design of any system in general and of business information systems in particular: modularity, cohesion, decoupling, user involvement, satisficing, human interface, and orientation toward the future.

Cohesion

Cohesion refers to how well activities within a single module are related to one another. This characteristic reveals how well the system has been divided into modules. Of the several types of cohesion, **functional cohesion** concerns systems designers most. A module has complete functional cohesion if it contains all—and only—those tasks contributing to the generation of a single information function or product.

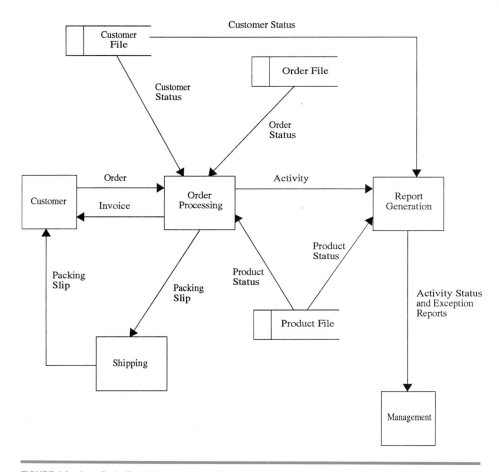

FIGURE 10–1   **Data Flow Diagram for a Customer Order Process**

For example, you are assigned to produce a purchase order form. You design a purchase order module that includes *all* the tasks needed to produce the form. You *do not* include any tasks in this module that do not contribute to the generation of the purchase order.

Functional cohesion allows effective systems maintenance because malfunctioning modules are easy to understand, separate, and repair.

Decoupling

Decoupling calls for separate modules to be relatively independent; often this is called **loose coupling.** Loosely coupled modules allow one module to be repaired with minimum disruption to other modules. One way to decouple modules is by planned redundancy, the deliberate inclusion of overlapping or duplicate functions to protect the system against disruptions. For example, a designer includes procedures in a receiving

TPS so it can operate manually should the automated purchasing TPS it depends on fail. In this way, the receiving system is decoupled from the purchasing system. Use of planned redundancy and other decoupling methods lead to the achievement of relatively fail-safe systems, systems that can operate effectively despite disruptive events.

Modularity

Systems are designed in relatively small sections using organizational tools such as the hierarchy chart. **Modularity** is useful for three reasons:

1. It allows assignment of different programmers and analysts to separate tasks. The project leader links all the separate activities together through the hierarchy chart, which becomes the master plan.
2. Modularity allows designers to develop small sections of a system independently. They do not have to wait for completion of another module.
3. Maintenance programmers can repair small modules of program code with minimal disruption to other modules. Automobile engines are designed modularly so a mechanic can replace or repair one part without having to extract the entire engine.

The design of a stereo system is an example of the concepts of cohesion, decoupling, and modularity. A "boom box" (self-contained small radio and tape player) is tightly coupled and lacks both cohesion and modularity. All the parts are packaged in one box and hard-wired. If any one part breaks, the whole system is affected. The alternative design is a component system, in which speakers, receiver, tape player, and radio are all separate and connected by removable jacks. If any one part breaks, the other parts are not affected. One part performs one function. The result is a system with parts that work well together but are independent. Thus, maintenance and upgrading are easy.

User Involvement

An information system is only as successful as its users believe it to be. Early and active involvement in the systems analysis and design phases gives users a sense of ownership. This increases the chance of systems success, because users imbued with a sense of system ownership are more tolerant of minor and even moderate flaws. Think about the difference between renting and owning a house. When you rent, you tend to call the landlord to fix the smallest problems. When you own the house, you are more tolerant of these small problems.

User involvement must be real rather than decorative. Otherwise, users think they have contributed to the design only to face a working system bearing little or no resemblance to what they expected. Often, systems designers fail to emphasize user involvement in the design phase because of the more technical nature of the tasks.

Richmond Manufacturing, Inc., is a small company that produces different types of plastic hair-care products (barrettes, hair ties, brushes, combs, etc.). When a retail outlet orders from Richmond, it orders small quantities of many items. Traditionally, the order entry forms have been filled out and batched on a daily basis for data entry. Management has determined that an on-line data entry system that allows data entry at the time of receiving phone orders (75 percent of all orders) and written orders would be highly feasible. Richmond has no in-house programmers or analysts. Outside consultants have been hired to design and construct the new system.

The consultants made a wise decision to involve Mary West, head of data entry, fully in the analysis and design of the new system. Her participation resulted in the following benefits:

- The computer screens were easy and efficient for her staff to use.
- The staff had a feeling of ownership and commitment to the new system.
- The normal resistance to change that a new system brings did not occur.
- Training took less time.

Another means of effectively involving users is prototyping.

Satisficing

It is difficult to design the perfect information system. There are too many constraints: time, costs, personnel skills, politics. Therefore, designers try to design a system that is better than the current one, rather than the best possible one. The process of seeking the best possible choice is called **optimizing. Satisficing,** by contrast, is the process of seeking a better, but not necessarily the best, solution to a problem. It is unrealistic for systems designers to try to optimize, so they satisfice.

If users are not aware that satisficing is the true goal, the realities of the new system may not match their expectations. Users view the smallest flaws as poor design rather than as conditions they should expect in any new product—particularly a product as complex as a business information system. For example, Palko Publishing Company's new order-processing system has an order summary report. When the first report was issued, the summary totals page had erroneous figures. Some users immediately distrusted the entire new system because of this one problem.

Users can be conditioned to the satisficing principle by making them aware of the types of systems flaws expected to occur. Figure 10–2 shows one classification of information systems flaws. Flaws are classified by how serious they are and by whether or not they were expected.

Impact On Users	Predicted Occurrence	
	Unanticipated	Anticipated
Minor	Systems Maintenance	Empty Set
Major	Contingency Management	Future File

FIGURE 10–2   **Classification of Information Systems Flaws**

Major Anticipated Flaws. Major anticipated flaws are systems functions that were not included in the design because of constraints such as time or cost. For example, a firm implements an inventory system without a forecasting module because it decided that the module is too expensive for available funds.

This type of systems flaw is placed in a **future file.** When constraints are relaxed (e.g., more funds are available), the missing function can be added as an enhancement to the system.

Major Unanticipated Flaws. The major unanticipated flaw is the most serious type of systems shortcoming. It exposes major design and testing deficiencies. An *intended* fulfillment of user needs has failed. Prompt, calm action must be planned jointly by the designer and users and quickly initiated. This planning for major flaws is called **contingency management.**

An example of a major unanticipated flaw is a payroll system that is implemented midyear without the capability of storing year-to-date and quarter-to-date totals. Payroll checks can be generated, but the stored amounts are inaccurate. These inaccuracies affect quarterly summary totals and IRS reports. The main payroll system cannot wait for development of the module that would store these figures.

Minor Unanticipated Flaws. Minor unanticipated flaws are the most prevalent type of systems shortcoming. Detecting and correcting such flaws falls under the function referred to as systems maintenance. Users must be prepared to expect such minor flaws.

In that same new payroll system, the program that generates time cards does not sort the cards by department. The result of the flaw is the minor inconvenience of separating and sorting the time cards by hand. The program can be fixed overnight, with no long-term ramifications.

Minor Anticipated Flaws. This category should be an empty set. It serves no legitimate or professional purpose to plan for intentional, minor flaws in the final design of an information system. The principle of satisficing requires that systems designers inform users that implemented systems will not be perfect and that flaws will be corrected within a planned and predictable structure.

Human Interface

Recall the human factors principles described in Chapter 2. Human usability is an important criteria for judging the quality of an information system. It is particularly important at the seams where users directly interface with the information systems— for example, output reports and interactive screens.

Systems analysts are technically trained and tend to view the world in a mechanical rather than a human context. This can be dangerous to the eventual success of the new information system, for an information system is only as successful as human users judge it to be. When designing output reports and interactive screens, analysts must temporarily throw off their technical glasses and put on the less elaborately framed glasses of the nontechnical and often minimally computer trained end-user.

IBM Corporation has a clever motto that: "if the automotive industry had progressed as rapidly as the computer industry, then a Cadillac would cost one dollar, get one million miles per gallon of gas, and could sit on your thumb. The obvious question that should occur to any systems analyst is: "But how could a human being drive a car that was that small?" IBM's Cadillac ignores the human interface. We analysts should not make the same mistake.

Orientation toward the Future

New information systems are rarely ideal. As stated before, there are always constraints on funds, time, and skills. In addition, users often change their minds while the new system is being developed. At some time during the project, there must be a **design freeze.** From then on, no new changes to specifications are allowed. For all these reasons, newly implemented systems are always less than ideal.

Even when a system is new, designers are already thinking about the design of its replacement. We know we will have to change today's systems, so why not design new systems so they can be changed easily and economically? Use these three tactics to design systems for future modification:

1. Build some redundancy into the current system to ease future expansion. Put extra space in resource records so you can add fields without redesigning the total record. Design forms and screens with unused space to accommodate future changes. Develop dummy subprogram modules so that when new functions are added to the information system, you need not recompile existing programs.
2. Maintain a future file for every information system. The future file contains all desired changes to the current system. After you freeze a design, place all newly requested changes in the future file. After you implement the new system, place all suggested modifications in the future file. Then, when management relaxes resource constraints, you are prepared to enhance the system.
3. Develop solid documentation. Systems designers tend to be artistic and to document their thoughts briskly or as an afterthought. Yet, good systems documentation, however tedious, allows you to modify or enhance an information system quickly and correctly. Would you trust a mechanic who did not own an up-to-date and accurate schematic of your automobile?

The principle of orientation toward the future, as well as the other six principles discussed, are prevalent in most successful information systems.

PROFILE OF A POORLY DESIGNED SYSTEM

If the six principles just discussed describe well-designed systems, what would a poorly designed system look like? What characteristics might you find (or look for) in a poorly designed system? It is likely that a poorly designed system:

- Is one extremely large block of intertangled code that defies the analyst to make a small change without changing steps and links throughout the entire system.
- Has no one person who knows how the massive block works.
- Creates continuous problems for other applications systems by providing late, incomplete, and inaccurate feeder information.
- Shuts down or limps along when other applications systems have problems.
- Has no user steering committee, has one that meets infrequently, or has one that listens but does not speak.
- Has a cast of users who become upset at the most minor flaws.
- Exhibits delay between detection and correction of flaws.
- Has interactive screens and output reports that are difficult for many users to learn and use.
- Has no contingency plan.
- Has no future file.
- Includes records and forms fully packed, with no room for expansion.
- Has poor, incomplete, or outdated documentation.

In the parlance of popular self-analysis tests, if your system has six of these symptoms, it is probably poorly designed. It needs help.

DESIGN STAGES

Structured development methodologies divide the systems design phase into two parts—logical design and physical design. **Logical design** is development of architectural plans for the new information system. **Physical design** is adding sufficient details to the logical design to allow the information system to be constructed. The U.S. government often refers to these as **conceptual design** and **detailed design.**

Logical Design

All logical design tasks are planned carefully because the remainder of the stages in the SDLC are dependent on this stage. Even the smallest errors here are magnified throughout the SDLC and become major problems when the new system is implemented.

The logical design phase produces a systems blueprint. Much like an architect's blueprint, the **systems blueprint** is a series of charts, graphs, and data layouts that describe output documents and reports; input documents that the system will process; computer records required to store processed data; and the sequence and method by which output, input, and storage are linked. All descriptions are in a general rather than technical format.

In a structured approach, logical design is transformation of the logical data flow diagram from the current system to the logical DFD for the proposed system. Recall that, in Chapter 9, we also referred to logical design as preliminary design, and that we placed it in the analysis phase of the SDLC.

Physical Design

The physical design stage of the SDLC converts the systems blueprint into the specific detail required for programmers to construct computer code. The code transforms logical design into a working, day-to-day business information system.

Physical design includes specifying complete descriptions of file, input, and output formats. It also involves describing information processes (e.g., producing the payroll report) to a primitive level easily translated to program code.

In a structured approach, physical design is transformation of the logical DFD of the proposed system into the physical DFD of the proposed system.

Design Sequence

The primary reason for information systems is output. Output is what users need, and their needs are the primary purpose of any information system. Therefore, designers look at output first; then they determine what types of data should be entered into and stored within the computer to produce that output. For example, structured methodologies focus on the logical DFD as the pivotal point for systems design. As designers enter the systems design stage, they have already identified outputs and inputs on this DFD. Also, they have already established the names if not the contents of files.

Designing output first is similar to choosing the automobile you wish to buy, then finding ways to get the funds to afford it. First, design output that the user ideally needs; then, find ways of acquiring data to feed this output. To design input first would limit the potential of what output could really be because output would then be based only on the designed input, rather than the opposite.

Ideal output may have to be condensed later to meet real-life considerations, such as inability to collect the input data required economically. On the other hand, output requirements sometimes force designers to find new ways of collecting input—ways they didn't recognize before.

Design proceeds by first defining output, then defining input, and finally defining file and process (record) requirements. The design phase also includes another task: linking input, output, and storage. This is often described as systems flow.

Systems Flow

Several graphic techniques record the linkage between input, files, and output. The two most commonly used are the systems flowchart (SFC) and data flow diagram. Details about these graphic linkage tools were presented in Chapter 6. Opinions differ about which of these two techniques is most effective. The controversy assumes that the two techniques compete with each other. In fact, many industrial firms use both the SFC and DFD.

The data flow diagram is essentially a picture of how data links together different parts of a system (files, reports, source documents, etc.). The DFD is an excellent communication medium between the designer and the user because it is something that

FIGURE 10–3   **Use of Graphic Techniques in the Systems Development Life Cycle**

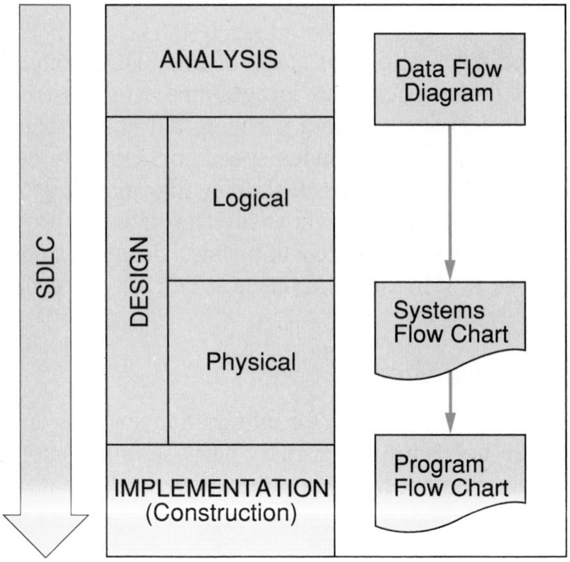

both can understand. However, as various levels of the DFD become more detailed, its advantage deteriorates. The systems flowchart takes over. Consider this analogy. An artist's sketch of what a new house will look like is important for securing the approval of the home buyer. As construction engineers focus on the details of smaller and smaller chunks (modules) of the house, the sketch becomes ineffective. It cannot be used for actual construction of the house. Construction workers require more detailed descriptive techniques.

The data flow diagram is the artist's sketch. It is used in the systems analysis and logical design phases of the SDLC. The systems flowchart is the construction worker's medium. It is used in the physical design phase of the SDLC. Figure 10–3 shows the relationship between these and other commonly used techniques within the systems development life cycle.

DESIGN COORDINATION

Several factors contribute to proper coordination of systems design efforts: project scheduling, user participation, design teams, structured walkthroughs, and politics.

Project Scheduling

The design project is broken down into small modules. Each module is assigned to specific persons for completion. Module tasks must be coordinated because (1) many people are involved, (2) some tasks must be completed before others can start, and (3) there are fixed limits on the time and funds to be expended on the systems design phase of the SDLC.

Project scheduling and coordination are done by a senior systems analyst on small design projects. They are done by project leaders for large projects. Formal project management often is required on very large projects.

User Participation

People who use the information system should have a say in its design. Otherwise, they will have no sense of ownership when the system is working. Lack of user ownership often leads to failure of the system. Generally, we are more tolerant of flaws in homes we own than in apartments we rent.

The way users participate is critical. Users who feel they are being consulted for appearance's sake will refuse ownership and may fight the system as well. Insincere user involvement is worse than no user involvement at all. Few guidelines are available as to what form user participation should take. The sociotechnical systems literature has specified stringent guidelines for user involvement. However, these guidelines focus on fairly large organizations that are converting from manual to automated technology.

Here are three general questions that need to be asked in any design situation.

When Should Users Participate? This question has two parts. The first relates to the point in the systems development life cycle at which users participate. Traditionally, users are quite active in the requirements analysis stage when the systems analyst is trying to discover the ideal system in the eyes of users. Use of prototyping, however, can extend user involvement throughout the SDLC.

The second part of the question involves the frequency of user involvement, which can range from ad hoc meetings, through once a week meetings, to assigning users to the design team on a full-time basis. The answer depends on what class of user (who) is participating. Managers will not be willing to spend as much time as clerical personnel.

Who (Which Users) Should Participate? Supervisors and managers hold the power to delay the implementation of a system. Yet, the underlying success of an information system rests with clerical users, and they should be involved in the design of business information systems. At periodic intervals, managers and supervisors should give their stamp of approval to what has been done up to that point.

How (in What Format) Should Users Participate? User participation can take several different formats, including prototyping, steering committees, checkoff groups, and temporary assignment. Prototyping is one of the more exciting methods of user participation. **Steering committees** are made up of managers or supervisors who have the power to stop the implementation of a system. These groups are more active in the systems analysis phase. **Checkoff groups** include persons lower in the organizational hierarchy than managers and supervisors. They meet more frequently than steering groups and act as a fail-safe mechanism to prevent fatal design errors. **Temporary assignment** to the design team of a knowledgeable, energetic clerk from the applications area has two advantages. First, systems designers are forced to think about what is happening in the working area. Second, the clerical member of the design team returns to the working area when the new system is implemented. That clerk can sell the system to his or her colleagues and will strive to make the new system work, regardless of the problems encountered.

Design Teams

The information systems field used to be characterized by analysts and programmers who were flamboyant individualists, each doing his or her own artistic thing. Personal creativity was encouraged. In the present era, the **design team** predominates. Team members sacrifice personal egos to build systems that are easy to modify or replace by someone else. Except for small systems, design is typically done in teams. A control group sets the overall standards, procedures, and time frames. The remainder of the team members design assigned modules according to these global policies.

Therefore, the systems analyst of today must be able to communicate and work with others. In addition, the senior analyst or project leader must closely coordinate the efforts of many talented analysts and programmers. Often, this coordination involves compromising divergent views expressed by team members.

Structured Walkthroughs

At specific points in the design process, analysts present design details before a group of peers. This **structured walkthrough** accomplishes several things. First, it forces analysts to explain the step-by-step logic of their designs. Second, design colleagues provide new ideas or spot flaws that the analyst, being too close to the project,

---

STRUCTURED WALKTHROUGH CHECKLIST

1. *Objective:* Peer review of development activity to pinpoint errors and omissions that can still be corrected within project scope.
2. *Audience:* One or more peers of the designer or programmer whose work is to be reviewed.
3. *Procedure:*
   - Programming supervisor identifies participants.
   - Sixty- to ninety-minute walkthrough is scheduled.
   - Before the meeting, each reviewer is sent at least the following materials: program overview, program documentation (e.g., hierarchy chart), and clean compilation listing (no more than 200 lines of code).
   - Reviewers study material before meeting.
   - Author describes product.
   - Reviewers ask questions and make comments.
   - Reviewers take notes.
   - Author changes product accordingly.

has not noticed. The third benefit of structured walkthroughs is more subtle, but important. The structured walkthrough presents another opportunity for the analyst to practice explaining the features and benefits of the new system before facing users and managers.

Structured walkthroughs have become a traditional part of the SDLC. When design flaws are detected early in the project, they are still easy to correct. In addition, analysts, aware that walkthroughs are ahead, double-check their design efforts. Structured walkthroughs are also an excellent medium for the sharing of ideas and techniques among the design team.

JOINT APPLICATION DESIGN

Joint application design (JAD) is a highly structured form of user participation, consisting of sessions where users and analysts interact to develop higher level (logical) systems specifications. JAD has been used primarily in the requirements analysis stage of the SDLC but also has been found to be useful in the design of user interfaces such as interactive screens.

All JAD sessions include the following elements:

- *Participants:* Users, IS analysts, observers, scribes, a session leader, and an executive sponsor
- *Structured session preplanning:* Audiovisual aids, agenda, and a presession orientation meeting
- *Structured session:* What topics should be covered and how the sessions should be conducted
- *Documentation:* A dozen or more session deliverables such as management objectives, issues, data element definitions, and operating procedures.

Joint application design involves putting the end-users and the systems analysts on the same development team. JAD is an accelerated systems development approach that shortens the applications development cycle, improves design quality, and increases productivity. The three separate phases of JAD are customization, design, and wrap-up, including documentation and prototyping. Each organization must adapt JAD to its own culture and managerial and technical ability level. As always, top management commitment is critical to the success of any project.

One of the key features of JAD is that group design sessions improve systems usability by decreasing maintenance costs and increasing productivity. The CNA Insurance Company of Chicago has been using IBM's JAD since the early 1980s with success. CNA suggests that the following steps be followed when attempting to introduce group design methodology into an organization:

1. Set up an advisory group of project managers to evaluate JAD software.
2. Obtain vendor references.
3. Interview user groups.
4. Survey the systems methodology to ensure that the technique fits the systems development culture.

5. Select a small project that can be measured against a control project as a pilot project.
6. Lead the pilot project with a member from the vendor's staff.
7. Develop an implementation plan.
8. Select session leaders.
9. Train the development staff.
10. Train the session leaders.

A specific JAD session is like a workshop. Eight types of work are identified for each development application: (1) planned work, (2) received work, (3) initial processing and tracking work, (4) monitoring and assigning work, (5) processing work, (6) recording results, (7) sending work, and (8) management reports. The JAD session consists of four phases: project selection, application familiarization, materials preparation, and the workshop itself.

The preworkshop phases take three to four days, and the workshop itself takes about the same amount of time. At the end of the workshop, the JAD team will have studied the eight types of work, discussed current practices within the organization, explored alternatives, and made certain design decisions.

Most JAD techniques focus on the design phase of the systems development cycle. Because JAD is a team technique, however, communication facilitation can be an important aspect of JAD success. Martin (Buckler, 1987) has listed four problem areas in data processing today: the lack of quality code, the excessive length of time it takes to develop applications, the cost of development, and the resources required to maintain systems. James Martin believes that JAD can solve some of these problems by involving the end-users in the design process, meeting end-user needs, producing more usable and useful systems, and encouraging computer literacy among users.

Joint application design has shown some success. It has been criticized, however, for its highly structured format and its failure to give individual end-users a sense of owning the system.

AUTOMATED DESIGN TOOLS (CASE)

Until the last few years, the way systems were designed was quite embarrassing. The creators of automated business systems were using pencil and paper to perform their miracles. Finally, systems design has entered the modern era by using computers as an aid in designing automated systems.

Automated help for systems designers is organized under the topic of CASE—a subject covered in detail in Chapter 22. CASE products offer the following design aids:

- *Graphics:* Data flow diagrams, systems flowcharts, and other design tools
- *Screen and document design:* Design of systems input and output
- *File design:* Creating an automated data element dictionary and design changes to that DED
- *Rapid prototyping:* Easy and quick generation of prototype models for user experimentation

- *Code generator:* Automatic generation of operational language code (e.g., COBOL or C) from flowcharts

DESIGN ACROSS DIFFERENT TYPES OF INFORMATION SYSTEMS

The next two sections of this book will take you step by step through the design and implementation phases of the systems development life cycle. An important question must be answered before that trek begins: Is the development process the same for different types of information systems?

The term *different* can be measured in at least two ways. The first is a system's size. Is a smaller system designed in the same way as a larger system? The answer is both yes and no. All SDLC steps occur regardless of the size of a system. All development tasks must be accomplished no matter how large the system. However, the effort and time spent on SDLC tasks varies given the size of the information system under development.

One example is project management. A lot of time and resources are spent on formal management of large-scale information systems projects. Indeed, an analyst's full-time position may be designated as project leader or project manager. On the other hand, project management is informal for a small system. Often, the task is an added responsibility for the senior analyst on the project.

Second, the term *different* can also deal with the types of information systems. The question then becomes, Are transaction-processing systems designed in the same way that management information systems, decision support systems, expert systems, or executive information systems are designed? Again, the answer is both yes and no.

The life cycles are the same for all these delivery systems. The design principles just discussed also apply to all types of delivery systems. Again, however, the distribution of effort on development tasks and stages may vary. It is convenient to divide the spectrum of information systems into standard information systems and tailored information systems.

A **standard information system** is one that is applicable across a wide spectrum of industries, firms, and agencies. As described in Chapter 2, transaction-processing systems can be considered as standard. For example, purchasing systems do not vary considerably from one firm to the next.

A **tailored information system** is one that must be matched to the specific characteristics of a firm or individual decision makers within that firm. This category generally includes MIS, DSS, ES, and EIS. For each of these systems, it is difficult to transfer the system from one specific setting to another.

Design of standard information systems can be done by a **top-down approach.** The designer starts with a clear concept (logical DFD of proposed system) of what the new information system should be. Then, the designer explodes that concept to further and further detail (physical DFD of proposed system). The analysis phase of the SDLC is not emphasized.

Design of tailored information systems cannot follow this path. The designer has no prior knowledge of what specific decision makers require to solve specific problems in specific settings. Therefore, a **bottom-up approach** must be used. The designer must build the system by gathering elementary data and descriptions of how decisions are currently made (physical DFD of current system). Then, the designer can synthesize the elements into the overall system (logical DFD of current system). In this approach, the analysis stage of the SDLC is elongated.

So, the conceptual development approach varies for different types of information delivery systems. However, the SDLC stages and development tasks apply regardless of the type of system being designed.

HUMAN ASPECTS

Systems analysts do not create information systems in a vacuum. An important constraint is the organizational environment. Analysts must be (1) aware of the politics that can influence design choices, (2) able to sell the system to all sides of a political setting, (3) willing to make noncritical design compromises to placate the political environment, and (4) willing to tackle political problems that jeopardize the design of an effective information system.

In summary, design of business information systems requires coordination with all parties to the design effort. The effective systems designer can no longer be merely a technician. That designer must also have the necessary people skills to coordinate the various design players. Design cannot be done effectively in the designer's office.

SUMMARY

Design of any business information system is a complex endeavor. Design cannot be sporadic; it must be carefully planned. Common design tactics act as an umbrella under which all systems modules are designed.

Adherence to certain principles separates successful from unsuccessful business information systems. These principles are modularity, cohesion, decoupling, user involvement, satisficing, human interfaces, and orientation toward the future.

Business information systems are designed in two stages: logical design and physical design. Logical design is the preparation of a systems blueprint. This blueprint is a graphic description of inputs, files, and outputs, along with a procedural mechanism that links these elements together. It is equivalent to an architect's rendering of a building. Physical design adds details necessary for system construction. It explodes the logical description of a system to a level of primitive detail at which construction workers (programmers) can actually build the system.

Design proceeds in the sequence of output, then input, resource files, and processes. This sequence forces designers to determine first what product users really require, then to find input and storage means to satisfy these requirements. The mechanism linking this design sequence is the data flow diagram.

Design of a business information system requires coordination within and outside the boundaries of the immediate applications area. Such coordination includes the considerations of project scheduling, user participation, design teams, Joint Application Development, and structured walkthroughs.

Recently developed automated tools (CASE) can help the systems designer. CASE techniques include graphics, screen and document design, file design, rapid prototyping, and program code generation.

Although the design approach may vary among different types of information systems, the SDLC stages and tasks remain the same.

CONCEPTS LEARNED

- Conditions (constraints) under which systems design takes place
- Principles of well-designed systems
- Differences between logical and physical design of business information systems
- Concept and contents of a systems blueprint
- Values and alternatives of user participation

- Use of design teams
- Joint application design (JAD)
- Use of structured walkthroughs
- General features of CASE
- How design varies among different types of information systems

KEY TERMS

bottom-up approach
checkoff group
cohesion
conceptual design
contingency management
decoupling
design freeze
design team
detailed design
functional cohesion
future file
joint application design (JAD)
logical design

loose coupling
modularity
optimizing
physical design
satisficing
standard information system
steering committee
structured walkthrough
systems blueprint
tailored information system
temporary assignment
top-down approach

REVIEW QUESTIONS

1. Why is modularity important in the design of business information systems?

2. What is the principle of cohesion?

3. How does satisficing differ from optimizing?

4. Describe the four categories of systems flaws.

5. Explain the three tactics to use for giving a systems design a future orientation.

6. What is the difference between logical and physical systems design?

7. Describe the contents of the systems blueprint.

8. Why is output designed before input?

9. Who is in charge of project scheduling for systems design?

10. When should users participate in the design phase?

11. What types of users should participate?

12. What are the advantages of design teams?

13. Why are structured walkthroughs valuable?

14. Describe four characteristics of JAD.

15. Describe five CASE design aids.

16. Explain the difference between standard and tailored information systems.

17. How do the top-down and bottom-up approaches to information systems design differ? To what types of systems do they apply?

CRITICAL THINKING OPPORTUNITIES

1. Draw a diagram of the organization of this chapter.

2. Compare and contrast JAD and structured walk-throughs.

STUFFIT TICKET COMPANY*

The Stuffit Ticket Company operates eighteen ticket-selling outlets in selected Sears stores in the Sacramento Valley between Modesto and Chico. The company is in business to sell tickets to plays, concerts, sporting events, and other events.

A ticket outlet consists of a counter, the Stuffit Ticket sign, one telephone, and two to three ticket clerks assigned to ticket booths located behind the counter.

The Stuffit operation works as follows: Stuffit's owner, Mr. Yormy Mark, enters into an agreement with event promoters to buy a designated number of tickets (unsold tickets are not refundable). Customers desiring tickets to an event go to the nearest Stuffit ticket location and queue up. When it is his or her turn, the customer requests a ticket (or tickets) for an event on a specified date. The ticket clerk checks availability of the desired ticket from a master ticket inventory prepared each night by Mr. Mark at Stuffit's headquarters. If the ticket is shown available on the master ticket inventory, the clerk prepares a ticket voucher, calculates the ticket price (equal to face value of the ticket plus $0.50 per ticket commission), and collects payment from the customer.

One copy of the ticket voucher is given to the customer, one copy is sent to the event's box office, and the last copy is sent at day's end to Stuffit headquarters. The customer presents his or her copy of the ticket voucher at the "will call" window of the event's box office to redeem the ticket on the day of the event. The ticket clerk also posts the number of tickets sold to the master ticket inventory and computes a new balance of available tickets for the event.

If the ticket desired by the customer is shown as unavailable, the ticket clerk tries to persuade the customer to buy a ticket for an alternative date or event. If that fails, the ticket clerk is instructed to call Stuffit headquarters to see if additional tickets have been purchased that day by Stuffit that might be available for sale.

Each evening, Mr. Mark receives the just concluded day's ticket vouchers from the ticket outlets. He subtracts the number of tickets sold from the event and event–date available counts shown on the master ticket inventory and produces a new ticket inventory for the next day.

*This case was prepared by Professor David Schultz, MIS Department, California State University, Sacramento.

Refer to the following description of the Stuffit Ticket Company and do the remaining exercises.

3. Using a hierarchy chart, translate the current Stuffit Ticket Company system to cohesive, decoupled modules.

4. Convert the hierarchy chart to a first-level explosion data flow diagram.

5. Is this a well- or poorly designed system? Why?

In this chapter you will learn about:

WHAT: (Concepts) Tools used during the design phase of the SDLC.

WHY: Tools selected for design often are different from those selected for analysis.

WHEN: Design phase of the SDLC.

WHO: Systems analyst in conjunction with end-users.

WHERE: Information system department and end-user work areas.

HOW: (Techniques) Data dictionary
            Decision tables
            Decision trees
            Structured English

OUTLINE

- Setting
- A Total Quality Approach
- A Structured Approach
- Data Dictionary
- Decision Tables
- Decision Trees
- Structured English and Structure Charts
- Computer-Aided Systems Engineering (CASE)
- Human Aspects

DATA DICTIONARY AND OTHER DESIGN TOOLS

*With reflection it becomes apparent that there is more than
one way to look at a problem.*

— RUSSELL ACKOFF, 1978

SETTING

There is an essential difference in development tools used in the design phase as compared to those used in the analysis phase. Most of the analysis tools discussed in Chapter 6 had as their primary objective communication with users — with non–technically trained people. There the emphasis was on using graphic tools that conveyed to end-users a picture of what they might expect with the proposed new information system.

The audience is different in the design phase. Here, the audience to which the analyst seeks to communicate includes the technical programmers who must convert system specifications to computer code. The analyst can afford to, indeed must, become more technical when using design tools than when using analysis tools. One analogy is development of a new house.

In the early (analysis) phase of house development, the architect builds scale models and draws pictures which will show the home buyer what the house will look like. After the buyer has agreed to the architect's vision, these nontechnical renderings must be converted to sufficient detail to allow construction experts to build the house physically. The resulting blueprints are undecipherable to the home buyer but absolutely necessary to construction workers. Programmers are the construction workers in development of information systems.

This chapter presents a structured approach to the use of tools in the design phase of the system development life cycle. These tools are intended to allow information system programmers to begin the translation between textual/graphic system specifications to computer language code.

A TOTAL QUALITY APPROACH

One underlying precept of TQM is the use of systematic approaches that guarantee that (1) all required tasks are done and (2) only required tasks are done. TQM is a highly structured approach. Similarly, the structured approach to design tool use described in this chapter is systematic. It lends itself well to a TQM approach. Use of this structured tool approach ensures you that your ensuing design specifications will be thorough but only as detailed as they need to be.

A STRUCTURED APPROACH

A structured approach to development tool usage follows a rather predictable path as shown in Figure 11–1.

1. A hierarchy chart is developed for the current system.
2. Each level of the hierarchy chart is transferred to a leveled set of physical data flow diagrams for the current system.
3. This leveled set of DFDs is translated in turn to a leveled set of:
   a) logical DFDs for the current system
   b) logical DFDs for the proposed system
   c) physical DFDs for the proposed system
4. The DFDs for the current system are used to generate a **data dictionary,** which is a repository for all the data structure and data elements within an information system. In some structured design approaches, the data dictionary is derived from the logical DFD of the current system.
5. Data flow and data store descriptions in the data dictionary lead to development of specific output, input and file specifications. These specifications are described in Chapters 12 through 15.
6. Process descriptions in the data dictionary are exploded into decision tables, decision trees, structured English, and structure charts. Decision tables and decision trees are described in this chapter. Structured English and structure charts are described in Chapter 17.

This structured approach to use of design documents ensures that the ensuing specifications are complete but not redundant.

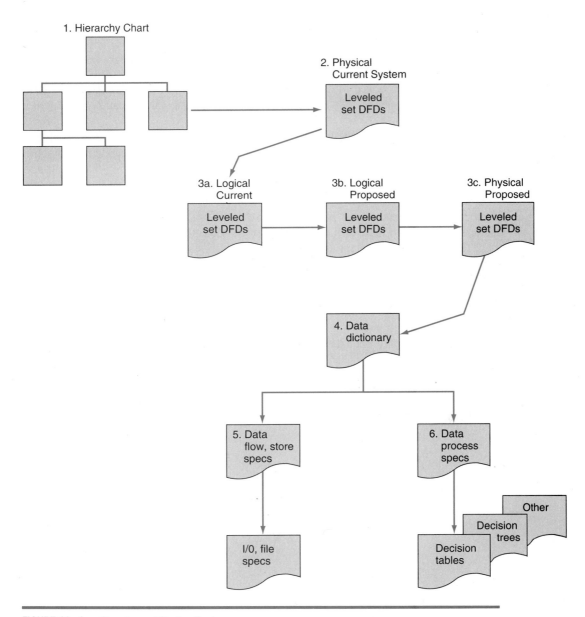

FIGURE 11–1   **Structure of Design Tools**

DATA DICTIONARY

A data dictionary is a repository for all the primitive-level data structures and data elements within a system. As its name suggests, it is a catalog of everything we want to know about the nature of data within a system. Such detail as data type (numeric, alphanumeric, alphabetic, etc.), length, range, and specific values, can be cataloged in the data dictionary.

The data dictionary combined with a leveled set of DFDs gives the detail-level specifications for a system. The data dictionary fully describes the data in many (sometimes hundreds) of separate entries. The data dictionary may exist on-line or off-line. The most effective way to enforce consistent use of data among the members of a software development team is to use an integrated, on-line data dictionary (repository). In fact, many organizations have adapted the data dictionary to their environments independently from or with the use of other structured tools.

The relationship of data dictionary entries is shown in Figure 11–2. Refer to the circled numbers as you read the following explanation:

1. One process entry is made for each process shown in the hierarchy chart.
2. A data flow entry is made for each packet of data (e.g., form) flowing into or out of each process.
3. A data store entry is made for each file that feeds or is updated by a process.

FIGURE 11–2   Relationship of Data Dictionary Entries

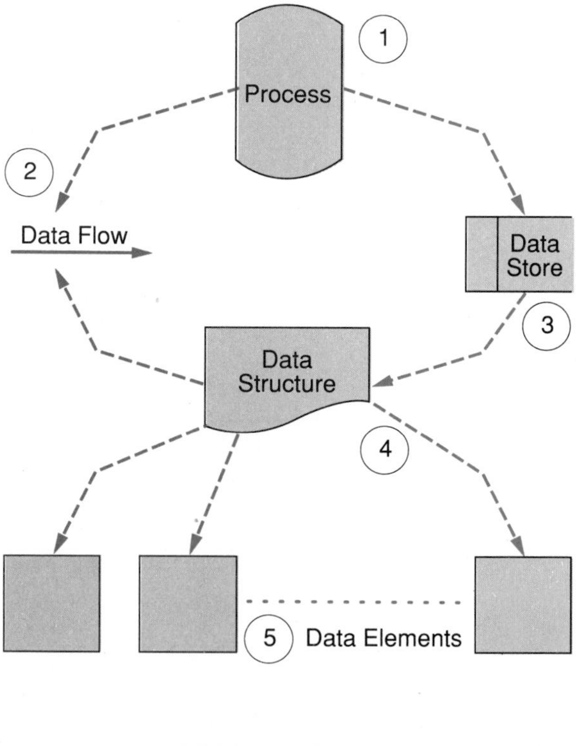

4. A data structure entry is made for each data flow and data store entry. The data structure entry contains, in part, a listing of all data elements contained in the data flow or data store.
5. A data element entry is made for each data element listed in a data structure entry.

The forms and notation of data dictionary entries vary from system to system. The notation and forms discussed and illustrated here follow the conventions and format of Visible Analyst, a computerized tool developed by Visible Systems Corporation. These formats are fairly common and representative of most methodologies.

Notation

Figure 11–3 is the shell of a data dictionary entry form from Visible Analyst. This form is used for entering data structures (flows and stores), data processes, and the data elements that make up the data structures. Refer to the figure as you read the following explanation of the fields in the form.

Project. This field identifies the **project root** of the currently selected project. It is an automatically generated field. Here the project name is CPO.

FIGURE 11–3 **Typical Dictionary Screen from Visible Analyst**

Reprinted by permission of Visible Systems Corporation, Waltham, Mass.

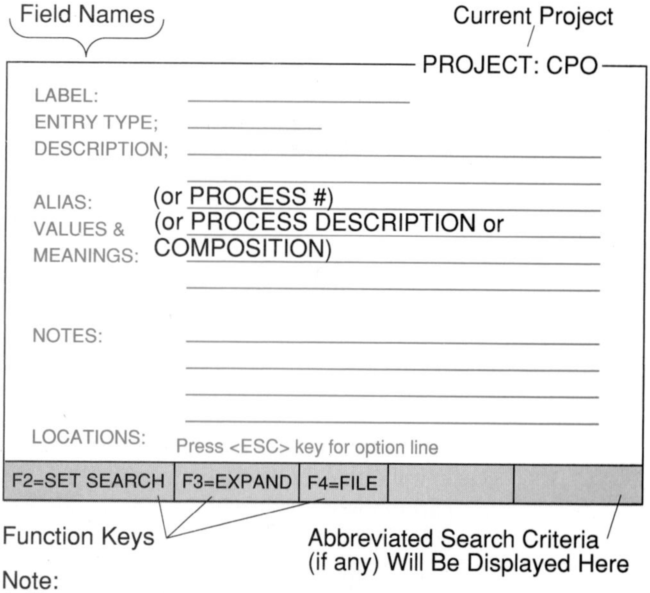

Field Names

Current Project

PROJECT: CPO

LABEL:
ENTRY TYPE;
DESCRIPTION;

ALIAS: (or PROCESS #)
VALUES &   (or PROCESS DESCRIPTION or
MEANINGS: COMPOSITION)

NOTES:

LOCATIONS: Press <ESC> key for option line

F2=SET SEARCH | F3=EXPAND | F4=FILE

Function Keys

Abbreviated Search Criteria
(if any) Will Be Displayed Here

Note:
1. The screen for a process displays PROCESS # and PROCESS DESCRIPTION fields instead of Alias and Values & Meanings.

2. The screen for a data flow, data structure, or files uses a COMPOSITION field instead of Values & Meanings.

Label. **Label** is another term for data name. The data name, or label, should be unique and meaningful. Because the name is used to refer to a particular data item throughout the system, all the members of the development team and the users must understand and recognize the name. Care should be taken to select data names that prevent confusion. In the Visible Analyst data names are limited to forty characters, must begin with an alphabetic character, and constitute the primary search key.

Entry Type. Data **entry types** include data element, file, process, data store, external entity, source/sink, data flow, and alias. These are common terms from data flow diagrams. Dictionary records may be automatically entered from some other function like creating a DFD or they may be manually entered. If they are automatically entered by Visible Analyst, they cannot be changed manually.

Description. This field allows for a more complete description of the data entity (up to sixty characters). It is particularly useful if the label is not self-explanatory.

Alias. Users and other IS staff members may have different names for the data entity. For example, one department may call a field "Age," whereas another department may refer to the same field as "CUSTOMER AGE." The **alias** field allows searching on the alternate name to reach the specified name. When a name is placed in the alias field, Visible Analyst automatically creates a new dictionary entry that is cross-referenced to the original data entry.

Values & Meanings or Process Description or Composition. This field changes depending on the entry type. If the entry type is defined as a process, the field is called process description. The analyst then enters a logic summary in the field. If the entry type is defined as a data structure, data flow, or data file, the field is called composition. The analyst then enters the data elements that compose the data structure using the notation defined in Figure 11–4. If the entry type is a data element, then the field is called values & meanings. The analyst enters such details as length of data element, type (alphabetic, numeric, and so on), and values that the element can take on.

Notes. This field is used primarily for describing editing details such as range.

Locations. This is another automatically generated, and therefore unchangeable, field. It will either be the label of the DFD in which the entity is located, with its number in parentheses, or it will reference other entities that contain this entity in their composition field. Up to ten locations may be generated.

Additional fields are software-specific operational fields and will not be explained.

Because there is limited space in the data dictionary and there are hundreds of entries, a shorthand notation is useful for cutting down on required storage space. Additionally, the notation may trigger certain actions in a CASE tool. For example, the + between data elements may signal the CASE tool that a data element is present, and in turn the CASE tool may automatically create a **shadow entry** in the data dictionary for that data element. The analyst must then go into the entry and add the details.

```
                                    Data Dictionary Notation

Symbol                                        Operation (English Equivalent)
  =                                           IS COMPOSED OF (CONSISTS OF or IS EQUIVALENT TO)
  +                                           AND (separates data elements)
  []                                          EITHER—OR (i.e., selection)
  X{  }Y                                      ITERATIONS OF (ranging from x to y)
  (  )                                        OPTIONAL


- - - - - - - - - - - - - - - - - - - - - - - - - - - - - - - - - - - - - - - - - - - - - -

                                       For Example:

  CUSTOMER_ORDER  =    CUSTOMER_NAME  +
                       CUSTOMER_NAME  +
                       CUSTOMER_ADDRESS  +
                       1{ORDER_ITEM}10  =  ITEM_ID+
                                           ITEM_DESC  +
                                           ITEM_PRICE  +
                       (SALESPERSON)  +
                       ORDER_TYPE = [``phone''|``mail'']
                       ORDER_SUBTOTAL  +
                       ORDER_TAX  +
                       ORDER_TOTAL
```

(To be read as: Customer order consists of data elements customer ID plus customer name plus customer address plus from one to ten order items each of which consist of item ID plus item description plus item price plus an optional sales person plus order type which is either phone or mail plus order subtotal plus order tax plus order total.)

FIGURE 11–4   **Data Structure Notation**

Data Process

The entry form for a data process includes a summary of primitive-level logic (e.g., Structured English) in the process description field. Figure 11–5 is an example of data dictionary entry for a process.

Data Flow

The data dictionary entry for a data flow includes all the data elements that make up the flow listed in notational form in the composition field. Figure 11–6 is an example of the data dictionary entry for a data flow.

Data Store

The data dictionary entry for a data store includes all the data elements (fields) that make up the data store listed in notational form in the composition field. Figure 11–7 is an example of the data dictionary entry for a data store.

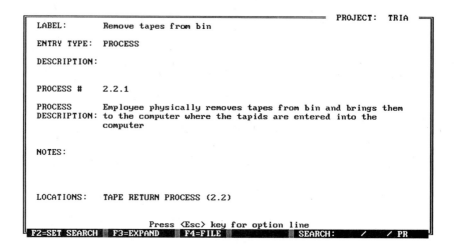

FIGURE 11—5   Data Dictionary Entry for Data Process

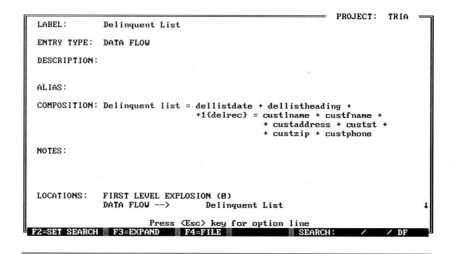

FIGURE 11—6   Data Dictionary Entry for Data Flow

Data Element

The data dictionary entry for a data element includes meanings and values associated with each particular data element. It represents the smallest level of detail in the system. Figure 11–8 is an example of the data dictionary entry for a data element.

The detailed descriptions for the data flow, data store, and data element entries will automatically generate or will allow a programmer to generate record descriptions in

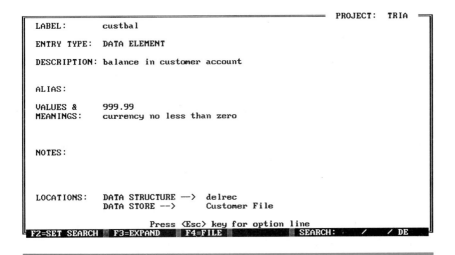

```
                                          ═ PROJECT:   TRIA ═┐
│ LABEL:       Customer File  [D1]                            │
│                                                             │
│ ENTRY TYPE:  DATA STORE                                     │
│                                                             │
│ DESCRIPTION: Data Structure which contains all relevant information about │
│             each customer                                   │
│                                                             │
│ ALIAS:       Customer Account file                          │
│                                                             │
│ COMPOSITION: Customer file = custfname + custlname + member date + │
│                 custnumber+custaddress + custcity + custst + custzip + │
│                 custdob + custphone + custcardtype + custcardnum + │
│                 custdlnum + custage + custnumber + 0{tapetrans}3 +     ↓ │
│                                                             │
│ NOTES:                                    + tape date       │
│                                           + tapecharge      │
│                                           + tapeduedate     │
│                                           + tapetimedue     ↓ │
│                                                             │
│ LOCATIONS:   FIRST LEVEL EXPLOSION (0)                      │
│              NEW MEMBER PROCESS (1)                         ↓ │
│                                                             │
│                  Press <Esc> key for option line           │
│ F2=SET SEARCH  F3=EXPAND   F4=FILE        SEARCH:    /   / F │
```

FIGURE 11−7   **Data Dictionary Entry for Data Store**

```
                                          ═ PROJECT:   TRIA ═┐
│ LABEL:       custbal                                        │
│                                                             │
│ ENTRY TYPE:  DATA ELEMENT                                   │
│                                                             │
│ DESCRIPTION: balance in customer account                    │
│                                                             │
│                                                             │
│ ALIAS:                                                      │
│                                                             │
│ VALUES &     999.99                                         │
│ MEANINGS:    currency no less than zero                     │
│                                                             │
│                                                             │
│                                                             │
│ NOTES:                                                      │
│                                                             │
│                                                             │
│                                                             │
│ LOCATIONS:   DATA STRUCTURE ─>  delrec                      │
│              DATA STORE ─>      Customer File               │
│                                                             │
│                  Press <Esc> key for option line           │
│ F2=SET SEARCH  F3=EXPAND   F4=FILE        SEARCH:   /   / DE │
```

FIGURE 11−8   **Data Dictionary Entry for Data Element**

programming language code. For example, suppose the new information system is to be programmed in COBOL. The data flow, data store, and data element entries will translate to DATA DIVISION entries at the 01 and lower levels.

The description in the data process entry will need to be described in sufficient details to allow translation to specific lines of program instructions. This will occur in the PROCEDURE DIVISION of COBOL language. Hence, the data process entry commonly is augmented by one or more design tools providing this required level of detail.

Design tools commonly used for this purpose are (1) decision tables, (2) decision trees, (3) structured English, and (4) structure charts. A description follows for each of these techniques.

DECISION TABLES

A **decision table** is a textual tool that lays out the logic of complex problems where there are multiple actions based on multiple conditions. Decision tables have four separate components: **conditions, decision rules, actions,** and **action entries.** The main reason for constructing a decision table is to be sure we consider all possible combinations of conditions and actions. Figure 11–9 is a decision table in generic form.

The number of conditions and their possible values determine the number of decision rules. Rules are formed in a systematic way. The total possible number of decision rules represents the total possible combinations, or permutations, of the condition values. The rule for determining the number of decision rules when the values are simply yes or no is

$$\text{Number of decision rules} = 2^n$$

where n = the number of conditions.

For example, if there are three conditions with yes or no values, the maximum number of decision rules is eight ($2^n = 2^3 = 8$).

Not all conditions have yes or no values; a condition may have multiple values. An example is a credit policy decision table in which a range of values for gross income yields the credit policy. The range of values might be: 1 = $0–$19,999, 2 = $20,000–$39,999, 3 = $40,000–$59,999, 4 = $60,000–$79,999, 5 = $80,000 or over. Now

Conditions	Decision Rules							
	1	2	3	4	5	6	7	8
Condition 1	Y	Y	Y	Y	N	N	N	N
Condition 2	Y	Y	N	N	Y	Y	N	N
Condition 3	Y	N	Y	N	Y	N	Y	N
Actions	Action Entries							
Action	X						X	
Action 2		X				X		
Action 3			X		X			
Action 4				X				X

FIGURE 11–9   **Generic Decision Table**

there are five values for this condition. In the case of multiple values, determining the number of decision rules is different. Here the guideline is to multiply the number of values for each condition times each other. For example, in a decision table with three conditions where the first condition has yes or no values, the second condition has three values, and the third condition has five values, the number of decision rules is $2 \times 3 \times 5$, or 30 possible decision rules.

Follow this procedure for entering decision rules in the table (refer to Figure 11–9). Divide the first row of decision rules in half. In the example, half of eight is four. Enter Y's for yes (one of two values) in the first half—the first four boxes in the first row. Enter N's for no (the second of two values) into the second half—the last four boxes in the first row. In the next row, divide the first half in half again. That gives two boxes for Y's and two for N's. Then complete the second half of the row in the same way. In this example, the second row is YYNNYYNN. Repeat this algorithm until the last row of decision rules contains YNYNYNYN. If you follow this algorithm, you'll take all combinations of rules into consideration.

The next step is to define actions for each rule. The correct action for a decision rule is marked with an X in that column. If you are not sure about the resultant action for a combination of conditions, place a question mark in all boxes in that column during the first iteration (rather than an X). Now go out into the end-user work area and ask people what action they take when this combination of conditions occurs. When you resolve the issue, indicate the correct entry and remove the question mark.

A decision table can grow quickly to an unmanageable size. Four conditions with yes or no values require sixteen decision rules. The number of decision rules should be reduced to make the final decision table more readable. So the next step is to cull out unnecessary rules from the table; this is called simplifying the decision table. Frequently, a combination of conditions is not permissible due to mutual exclusivity or other reasons. **Mutual exclusivity** is a situation in which the existence of one condition precludes the existence of another (day precludes night and vice versa). The systems analyst considers all combinations of conditions and drops those that cannot exist (for example, a compact car with a 3.0-liter engine).

The following examples show how to build a decision table. The first example concerns the collection policy for overdue accounts at a video rental store. The second example is the grading policy of a university professor.

Example 1: Collection Policy. Mega Video rents video tapes and VCRs. All tapes and VCRs are due back in the store twenty-four hours after checkout. There is a late charge of $2 per day per tape up to the value of the tape (all tapes are valued at $80). There is a late charge of $10 per day per VCR up to the value of the VCR (all VCRs are valued at $400).

Reports are generated on Fridays of each week. At that time, if any customer has accrued late charges of $10 or more (any combination of late tapes and VCRs), the customer is sent a letter of notification that outlines charges due and actions that will be taken. Any charges of less than $10 are simply carried on the customer's account and must be paid before any other tapes or VCRs can be checked out. If the charges remain unpaid for two weeks after the first letter is sent and are $100 or more, the account is sent to a collection agency. If the charges are unpaid for two weeks after the first letter is sent and are $50 or more, the customer's name is sent to the credit bureau. In both cases, the customer is dropped as a member and barred from checking out any more tapes.

The following steps are necessary to translate this credit policy into a decision table (Refer to Figure 11–10).

1. *Identify all the conditions affecting the actions of the policy and their respective values.* Each of these conditions must be data elements stored in the data dictionary. Enter these conditions in the decision table:

Conditions	Values	
1. Letter sent (LETTER-SENT)	Y = yes,	N = no
2. Two weeks elapsed since letter sent (TWO-WEEKS-ELAPSED)	Y = yes,	N = no
3. Amount of late charges (LATE-CHARGE-AMOUNT)	1 = $0–$10.00	
	2 = $10.01–$49.99	
	3 = $50.00–$99.99	
	4 = $100.00 or greater	

		Decision Rules														
Conditions	1	2	3	4	5	6	7	8	9	10	11	12	13	14	15	16
1. Letter sent	Y	Y	Y	Y	Y	Y	Y	Y	N	N	N	N	N	N	N	N
2. Two weeks elapsed	Y	Y	Y	Y	N	N	N	N	Y	Y	Y	Y	N	N	N	N
3. Amount of late charges	1	2	3	4	1	2	3	4	1	2	3	4	1	2	3	4
Actions																
1. Send notification letter														X	X	X
2. Drop customer			X	X												
3. Send account to collection agency			X	X												
4. Send name to credit bureau		X	X	X												
5. Do nothing	X					X	X	X					X			
6. Impossible				X				X	X	X	X					

FIGURE 11–10   Decision Table for Mega Video's Late Charge Policy

2. *Determine the maximum number of rules.* Multiply the number of values for each condition together. Condition 1 has two values, condition 2 has two values and condition 3 has four values. Two times two times four equals sixteen. Therefore, there can be no more than sixteen decision rules. Note that there are 16 rules listed across the top of Figure 11–10.
3. *Identify possible actions.* Enter these actions in the decision table:
   - Send notification letter.
   - Drop customer as member.
   - Send account to the collection agency.
   - Send name and amount owed to credit bureau.
   - Also enter two more actions: do nothing and impossible. These entries will help later during the simplification process.
4. *Enter all possible rules (sixteen) in the decision table according to the following algorithm:*
   - For condition 1, which has two values, divide the 16 rules in half. Place Y's in the first eight entries and N's in the last eight entries of the table.
   - For condition 2, which has two values, first divide the eight entries in both halves of the table (see condition 1) in half again. For the four parts containing four rules, alternate placing Y's and N's, giving a pattern of YYYYNNNNYYYYNNNN.
   - Condition 3 has 4 values. As a result of condition 2, the table has been divided in sets of 4 rules each. Divide the 4 rules by the four conditions; the result is 1. That means that, from left to right, you place one value in a rule, followed by the next value. This continues until the 16 rules are filled in.
5. *Mark the action entries for each rule.* If the action is unknown for a rule, place a question mark in all the boxes in that column. If the rule cannot exist (is mutually exclusive), place an X in the impossible box of that column. If any rule results in no action, place an X in the do nothing box. Clarify any rules with question marks by consulting end-users.
6. *Simplify the decision table by eliminating impossible rules, combining any rules that result in the same action, and eliminating any do nothing columns.* Figure 11–11 is the simplified decision table for this example. Note:
   - Impossible rules were eliminated by not copying decision rules from the decision table in Figure 11–10 to the decision table in Figure 11–11.
   - Rules were eliminated in Figure 11–10 because the action was do nothing.

So ten of the sixteen decision rules of Figure 11–10 were eliminated, leaving the six decision rules of Figure 11–11. A programmer can now generate code from this simplified table.

Example 2: Grading Policy. Professor Fuerst has a fairly complex grading policy consisting of three conditions and five actions. The three conditions are average exam score, individual project, and homework assignments. The five actions are the assignment of A, B, C, D, or F as grades. The grading policy includes the following points. The average exam score is determined by summing the exam scores and dividing by the number of exams. The grading scale is as follows: 90–100 = A, 80–89 = B, 70–79 = C, 60–69 = D, and below 60 = F. To receive the grade in the range corresponding to

Conditions	Decision Rules					
	1	2	3	4	5	6
1. Letter sent	Y	Y	Y	N	N	N
2. Two weeks elapsed	Y	Y	Y	N	N	N
3. Amount of late charges	2	3	4	2	3	4
Actions						
1. Send notification letter				X	X	X
2. Drop customer	X	X	X			
3. Send account to collection agency		X	X			
4. Send name to credit bureau	X	X	X			

FIGURE 11–11   Simplified Decision Table for Mega Video's Late Charge Policy

the average exam score, the student must turn in all homework assignments and receive a "pass" on the individual project. If the student receives a "fail" on the individual project and turns in all the homework, the student receives one grade lower than the average exam score. If the student does not turn in all the homework, the student fails the class, regardless of the average exam score and the grade on the individual project. Refer to Figure 11–12.

The following steps are necessary to translate this grading policy into a decision table.

1. Identify all the conditions affecting the actions of the policy and their respective values. Each of these conditions must be elements stored in the data dictionary. Enter these conditions in the decision table.

Condition	Values	
Average exam score (EXAM)	90–100 = A,	80–89 = B,
	70–79 = C,	60–69 = D,
	below 60 = F	
Individual project (PROJECT)	P = pass,	F = fail
Homework assignments (HOMEWORK)	Y = yes (turned in),	
	N = no (not turned in)	

2. Determine maximum number of rules. Multiply the number of values for each condition together. Condition 1 has five values, condition 2 has two values, and condition

Conditions	Decision Rules																			
	1	2	3	4	5	6	7	8	9	10	11	12	13	14	15	16	17	18	19	20
Average Exam score	A	A	A	A	B	B	B	B	C	C	C	C	D	D	D	D	F	F	F	F
Individual project	P	P	F	F	P	P	F	F	P	P	F	F	P	P	F	F	P	P	F	F
Homework assignments	Y	N	Y	N	Y	N	Y	N	Y	N	Y	N	Y	N	Y	N	Y	N	Y	N
Actions	Action Entries																			
Assign A	X																			
Assign B			X		X															
Assign C							X		X											
Assign D											X		X							
Assign F		X		X		X		X		X		X		X	X	X	X	X	X	X
Impossible																				

FIGURE 11–12   **Decision Table for Grading Policy**

3 has two values. Five times two times two equals twenty. Therefore, there can be no more than twenty decision rules.

3. Identify possible actions. Enter these actions in the decision table.
   - Assign grade A.
   - Assign grade B.
   - Assign grade C.
   - Assign grade D.
   - Assign grade F.

4. Enter all possible rules (twenty) in the decision table according to the following algorithm:
   - For condition 1, which has five values, divide twenty (total number of rules) by five (number of values), which yields four. In order to include all combinations of all rules, four iterations of each grade are needed. Therefore, place four A's, four B's, four C's, four D's, and four F's in row 1 for condition 1 in that order.
   - For condition 2, which has two values, repeat two P's and two F's ten times across the second row. This is determined by dividing the number of occurrences of each value of the previous condition by two (i.e., four divided by two is two).
   - For condition 3, which has two values, alternate Y's and N's across the third row. Again, divide the number of values for the previous condition (two) by two, yielding one.

5. Mark the action entries for each rule. If the action is unknown for a rule, place a question mark in all the boxes in that column. If the rule cannot exist, place an X in

	Decision Rules									
Conditions	1	2	3	4	5	6	7	8	9	10
Average exam score	A	A	B	B	C	C	D	D	F	—
Individual project	P	F	P	F	P	F	P	F	—	—
Homework assignments	Y	Y	Y	Y	Y	Y	Y	Y	—	N
Actions	**Action Entries**									
Assign A	X									
Assign B		X	X							
Assign C				X	X					
Assign D							X	X		
Assign F									X	X

FIGURE 11–13   **Simplified Decision Table for Grading Policy**

the impossible box of that column. Clarify any rules with question marks by consulting Professor Fuerst.

6. Simplify the decision table by eliminating impossible rules and combining any rules that result in the same action. Figure 11–13 is the simplified decision table for the example.

The decision table has been simplified by collapsing all the N's for condition 2 (did not turn in homework assignments) into one rule. In addition the F value for condition 1 was collapsed into one decision rule, because if the exam average score is F, the student will earn an F regardless of whether the homework was turned in or the project received a "pass." Therefore, this decision table was simplified from twenty rules to ten. The table is ready to be converted to program code.

DECISION TREES

A **decision tree** is a graphic representation of a decision structure. For decision structures that are not too complex, a decision tree is a graphic alternative to the decision table. When the decision structure becomes too complex, however, the graphic decision tree becomes so cluttered that it loses its communication value. Construction of a decision tree will be illustrated using the decision table for Mega Video's Late Charge Policy (Figure 11–11).

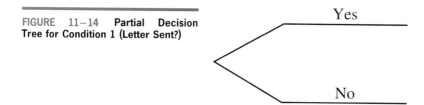

FIGURE   11–14   **Partial   Decision Tree for Condition 1 (Letter Sent?)**

1. *Condition 1 (Letter Sent):* Figure 11–14 shows a partial decision tree with the simple yes/no split for this condition.
2. *Condition 2 (Two Weeks Elapsed):* Figure 11–15 provides additional branches for the two Y/N branches of Figure 11–14.
3. *Condition 3 (Amount of Late Charges):* Figure 11–16 completes the partial decision tree of Figure 11–15 by adding branches for Condition 3. Figure 11–16 also adds appropriate actions for the expanded decision tree.

Decision trees are particularly useful in describing process logic associated with expert systems and decision support systems.

STRUCTURED ENGLISH AND STRUCTURE CHARTS

Two other tools used to expand data process entries are **Structured English** and **structure charts.** These tools are described in some detail in Chapter 17, "Process Design/Reengineering." For now it is sufficient to show you examples of what these tools look like.

Figure 11–17 is a Visible Analyst data dictionary description for the process called "End of Month Processing." Note that logic statements resemble programming code, but do not seem to be tied to a specific programming language. These statements are coded in Structured English which will allow (a) automatic creation of specific code, or (b) programmer translation to specific code, in more than one programming language.

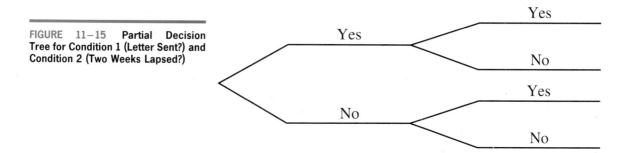

FIGURE   11–15   **Partial   Decision Tree for Condition 1 (Letter Sent?) and Condition 2 (Two Weeks Lapsed?)**

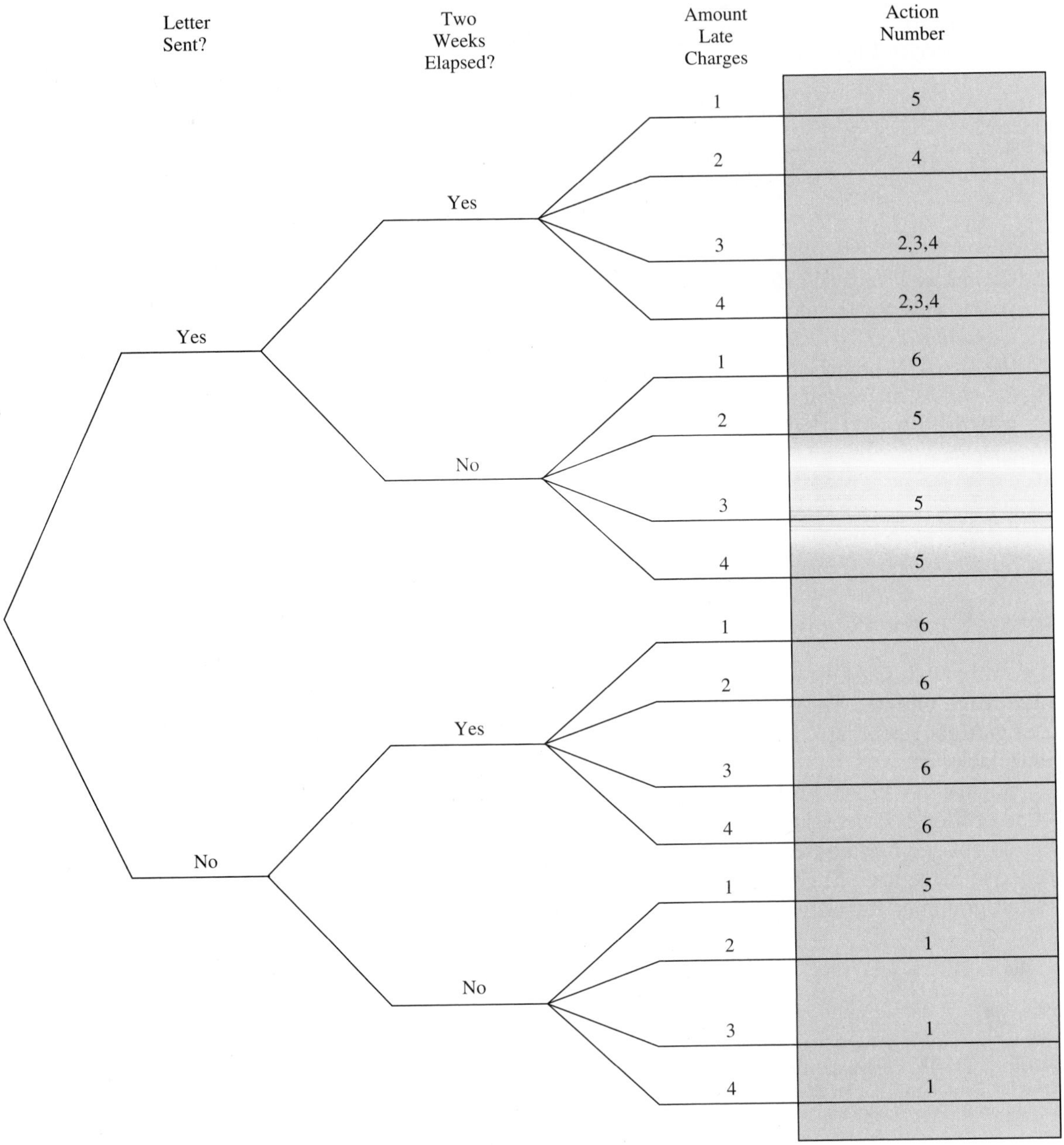

Letter Sent?	Two Weeks Elapsed?	Amount Late Charges	Action Number
Yes	Yes	1	5
		2	4
		3	2,3,4
		4	2,3,4
	No	1	6
		2	5
		3	5
		4	5
No	Yes	1	6
		2	6
		3	6
		4	6
	No	1	5
		2	1
		3	1
		4	1

FIGURE 11–16   **Full Decision Tree**

LABEL:	4.1.1
ENTRY TYPE:	PROCESS
DESCRIPTION:	END OF MONTH PROCESSING
ALIAS:	NONE

VALUES AND
MEANINGS:
(COMPOSITION
AND LOGIC
SUMMARY)

```
DO FOR EACH INVENTORY ITEM
        COUNT STOCK IN STOCK ROOM
        ENTER COUNT ON INVENTORY SHEET
END DO

DO FOR EACH INVENTORY ITEM
        COUNT STOCK IN DISPLAY ROOM
        ENTER COUNT ON INVENTORY SHEET
END DO

DO FOR EACH INVENTORY ITEM
        READ ITEM FROM INVENTORY FILE
        ADD DISPLAY ROOM COUNT TO STOCK ROOM COUNT
        ENTER AMOUNT IN RECORD
END DO

SELECT CASE
CASE 1:        (CONDITION 1-CALCULATE WHOLESALE)
                    INITIALIZE TOTALWSVALUE
                    DO FOR EACH INVENTORY ITEM
                            READ PHYSCOUNT, WSPRICE
                            MULTIPLY PHYSCOUNT TIMES WSPRICE
                                GIVING WSVALUE
                            ACCUMULATE TOTALWSVALUE
                    END DO
                            WRITE TOTALWSVALUE
END CASE 1

CASE 2:        (CONDITION 2-CALCULATE RETAIL)
                    INITIALIZE TOTALRETAIL
                    DO FOR EACH INVENTORY ITEM
                            READ PHYSCOUNT, WSPRICE, MARKON
                            MULTIPLY PHYSCOUNT TIMES WSPRICE
                                    TIMES MARKON GIVING RETAIL
                            ACCUMULATE TOTALRETAIL
                    END DO
                            WRITE TOTALRETAIL
END CASE 2

CASE 3:        (CONDITION 3-CALCULATE SHRINK)
                    INITIALIZE TOTALAUTOCOUNT
                            AND TOTALPHYSCOUNT
                    DO FOR EACH INVENTORY ITEM
                            READ PHYSCOUNT, AUTOCOUNT
                            ACCUMULATE TOTALPHYSCOUNT
                            ACCUMULATE TOTALAUTOCOUNT
                    END DO
                    SUBTRACT TOTALPHYSCOUNT FROM
                            TOTALAUTOCOUNT GIVING SHRINKCOUNT
                            WRITE SHRINKCOUNT
                    DO FOR EACH INVENTORY ITEM
```

FIGURE 11–17   Data Dictionary Entry for End-of-Month Inventory Processing

```
                              READ AUTOCOUNT, PHYSCOUNT, WSPRICE
                              TOTAL SHRINKBUCKS = TOTAL
                                    SHRINKBUCKS + (AUTOCOUNT *
                                        WSPRICE) — (PHYSCOUNT *
                                            WSPRICE))
                       END DO
                       WRITE TOTALSHRINKBUCKS
        END CASE 3

        CASE 4:      (CONDITION 4 — BEGINNING BALANCE)
                       DO FOR EACH INVENTORY ITEM
                           READ RECORD
                           PLACE AUTOCOUNT WITH PHYSCOUNT
                           SET PHYSCOUNT TO ZERO
                       END DO
        END CASE 4

                              DO FOR EACH INVENTORY ITEM
                              READ PHYSCOUNT, WSPRICE
                              MULTIPLY PHYSCOUNT TIMES WSPRICE
                                    GIVING WSVALUE
                              ACCUMULATE TOTALWSVALUE
                       END DO

                              WRITE TOTALWSVALUE

        END
```

NOTES:
LOCATIONS: THIRD LEVEL EXPLOSION OF INVENTORY PROCESSING

FIGURE 11–17   **(continued)**

Figure 11–18 is a structure chart. Diamond symbols are decisions (yes or no); rectangles are tasks to be performed. The truncated rectangles with the arrow-like bottom are off-page connectors; they refer us to another page of the chart. Chapter 17 describes the structure chart in more detail.

COMPUTER-AIDED SYSTEMS ENGINEERING (CASE)

The structured tool approach discussed in this chapter can be enhanced by use of a CASE software package. A CASE tool can:

1. Aid in graphic construction of hierarchy charts and data flow diagrams.
2. Automatically generate shadow entries for data dictionary specifications. For example, if you draw a data flow connection, the CASE tool can automatically generate a shadow specification for a data flow entry. The analyst then can complete this entry at a later time.
3. Provide quality control. For example, if the analyst fails to complete the shadow data flow entry, the CASE software can provide a warning message.

FIGURE 11-18   **Partial Program Flowchart**

4. From process entries containing Structured English, generate actual program code in languages such as COBOL and PL/1.

CASE capabilities will be described in more detail in Chapter 22.

HUMAN ASPECTS

The entire approach described in this chapter may seem too structured—too automatic. This is particularly true if a CASE product is used to generate program code, thus bypassing human programmers. Nevertheless, this or any other structured approach merely is an aid to, not a substitution for, human deduction and instinct. For example, CASE may generate automatically shadow data dictionary entries, and then keep reminding you to complete them. Nevertheless, you determine the *what, why,* and *when* of what will be included in those data dictionary entries. Structured design strengthens human analysts; it does not replace them. Try this test to show the role of the human mind in fashioning design tools. Note how the decision table of Figure 11–10 was simplified to the decision table of Figure 11–11. Could you write a program (in any language) that would include the logic of this simplification? Try it. The exercise will give you considerable appreciation for the human mind.

SUMMARY

A structured approach to design tool use follows a path from the hierarchy chart, through data flow diagrams, through the data dictionary, through detailed specifications such as decision tables, to program code. The tools used in the design phase are intended for communication with technical programmers.

The data dictionary is a repository for all data structures and data elements within an information system. It is a catalog of everything we want to know about the nature of data within a system. It includes separate specifications for data process, data flows, data stores, and data elements. The need for each of these entries is derived from symbols in the data flow diagram.

Data processes ultimately must be translated to program code. Process logic can be described by using such tools as decision tables, decision trees, Structured English and structure charts. A decision table is a textual tool that lays out the logic of complex problems where there are multiple actions based on multiple conditions. A decision tree is a graphic representation of a decision structure. It is a graphic alternative for decision structures that are not too complex. Structured English and structure charts will be discussed in more detail in Chapter 17.

The design tool structure described in this chapter can be enhanced by use of CASE software. Nevertheless, it is the human system analyst that ultimately must make design decisions, not structured design software.

CONCEPTS LEARNED

- Difference in emphasis between analysis and design tools
- Structured use of design tools
- Composition and use of data dictionary
- How to construct decision tables

- How to construct decision trees
- What is Structured English?
- What is a structure chart?
- The role of CASE in using design tools

KEY TERMS

actions
action entries
aliases
conditions
data dictionary
decision rules
decision table
decision tree

entry type
label
mutual exclusivity
project root
shadow entries
structure chart
Structured English

REVIEW QUESTIONS

1. Who is the audience for analysis tools? Design tools?
2. How is the hierarchy chart related to the data dictionary?
3. What is a data dictionary?
4. What is a repository?
5. What is an alias, and how is it handled in Visible Analyst?
6. When is a data structure specification required?
7. Which data dictionary specifications are transformed to COBOL DATA DIVISION entries? PROCEDURE DIVISION entries?

8. What is the organization of a decision table?
9. Give an example of two mutually exclusive events.
10. How can you simplify a decision table?
11. How does a decision tree differ from a decision table?
12. What is the role of Structured English in a data dictionary?
13. How can CASE enhance use of design tools?

CRITICAL THINKING OPPORTUNITIES

1. Draw a diagram to show how this chapter is organized.
2. Compare and contrast a process entry with a data store entry in a data dictionary.
3. Given the data flow diagram shown in Figure 11–19:

a) What data store specifications will be required?
b) What data flow specifications will be required?
c) What data structure specifications will be required?
d) What process specifications will be required?
e) What data element specifications will be required?

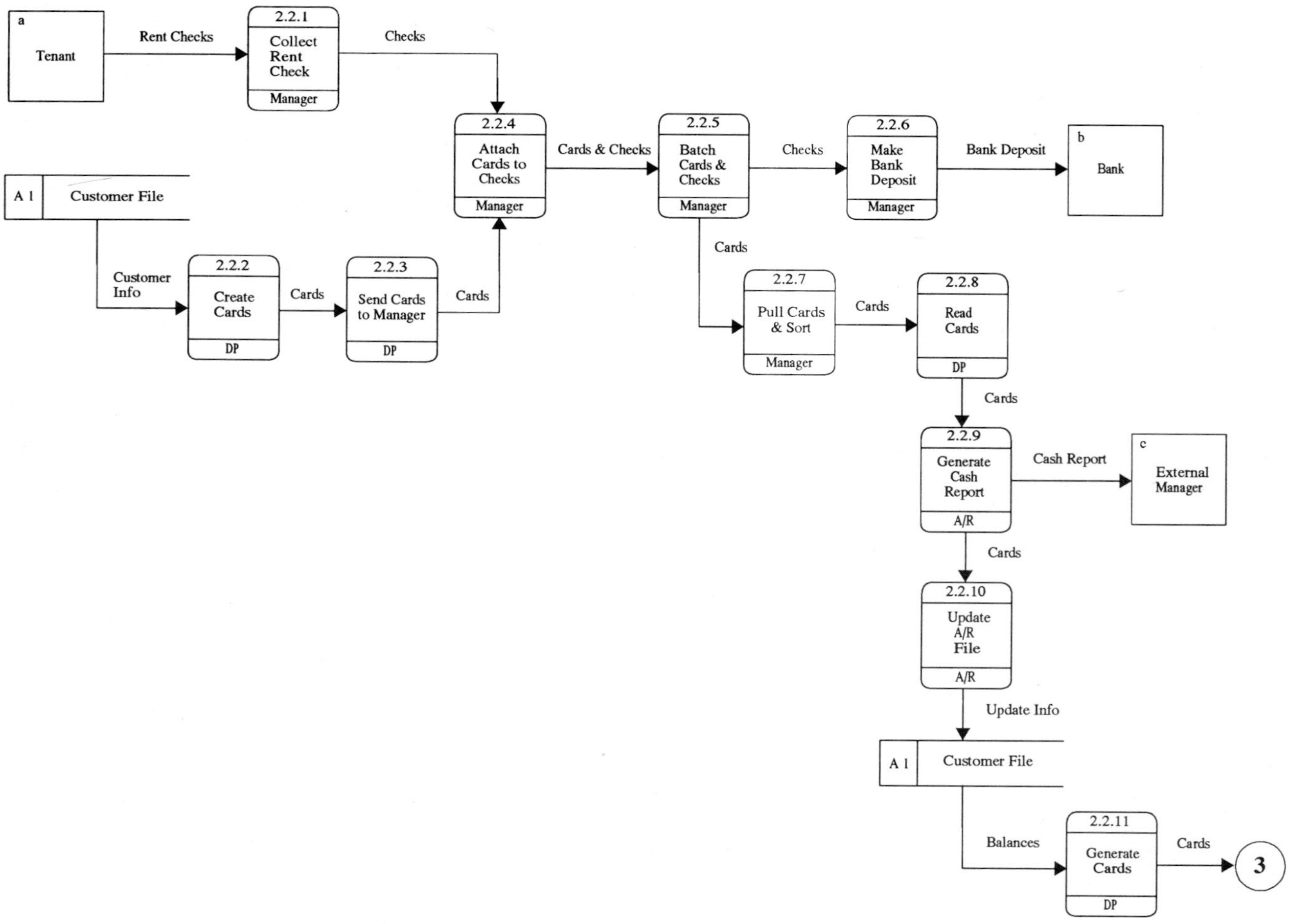

FIGURE 11–19   DFD for Collection of Rent Checks

4. Design a simplified decision table for the attached description.

A minimum of 5 percent discount applies for all purchases. If the retailer maintains an average monthly purchase volume of at least $100,000, a 15 percent discount applies, provided the retailer is an AGA member. When the retailer's purchase volume is under $100,000, the discount rate is 12 percent for AGA members and 7 percent for nonmembers. Retailers who are not AGA members, but who maintain a $100,000 monthly purchase volume, qualify for a 10 percent discount, unless the purchase totals less than $35,000.

5. Convert the decision table of Exercise 4 into a decision tree.

6. An additional notation that can be used in decision tables is the NOT symbol. By placing a dash above an entry, the entry can be read as "Every condition but this one." In the Mega Video credit policy (Figure 11–11), an entry of "1" for Amount of Charge could be read as category one. Placing a dash above this one would cause the entry to be read "Not 1," or "Every other Amount of Charge Category Except 1." Simplify Figure 11–11 further by use of this new symbol.

7. Convert the decision table resulting from Exercise 6 into a paragraph of COBOL PROCEDURE DIVISION code.

OBJECTIVES

In this chapter you will learn about:

WHAT: (Concepts) Design of information system output, primarily reports.

WHY: Output has the most direct impact upon end-users.

WHEN: This is the first stage in the design phase of the SDLC.

WHO: System analyst in coordination with end-users.

WHERE: Information systems department and user work areas.

HOW: (Techniques) Reports requirement document
                      Print layout sheet
                      Output design rules

OUTLINE

- Setting
- A Total Quality Approach
- A Structured Approach
- Output Media
- Document Design
- Report Design
- Output Design Tactics
- Profile of a Poorly Designed Report
- Inquiry-Based Systems
- Human Aspects

OUTPUT DESIGN

Farmer's Law on Junk:
What goes in, comes out.
Corollary 1:
He who sees what comes out, and why, gains
wisdom.

—RICHARD N. FARMER, 1975

SETTING

Design of output is critical. Output from an information system is the main reason the system was developed. Even when input data are stored, they are done so in anticipation that they will be output at some later time. That is why output design occurs *before* the design of input and files.

   As an overview to this chapter, it is important to review the process by which output is produced in a business information system. Figure 12–1 shows this process graphically. A typical output process occurs as follows:

1. Data (transactions) are input to information systems to update resource files.
2. Action documents (for example, purchase orders) are produced for each incident of a transaction updating a record. These documents are produced immediately so the actions they initiate (for example, ordering supplies from vendors) are not delayed.
3. At the end of the update cycle (either at the end of some time period or when there are no more transactions), batch reports are produced. These reports are delayed,

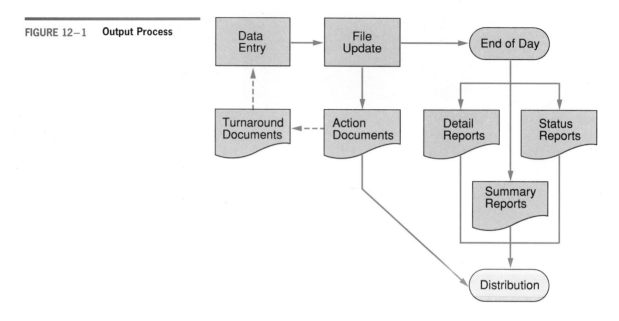

FIGURE 12–1   **Output Process**

rather than produced immediately, for two reasons: printers are dedicated to producing action documents and reports are not always immediately needed.

Several problems are characteristic of this typical output process.

Information Delay. End-users and IS personnel become used to end-of-period, batch production reports. This routine becomes a barrier to producing quick information when rapid decisions are required.

Information Overload. Often reports are compromise lists of all possible information that could be included. The erroneous philosophy of "more is better" dominates. As a result, bulky reports are produced. Users find the reports almost impossible to analyze in the limited time before they receive the next report.

The classic example of information overload is the twenty-five page report that a sales manager receives on a monthly basis reporting sales by region. The scope of the report is too detailed for this manager, so she or he pulls totals from four different pages and files the rest of the report, never to be used again.

Paper Domination. Not only do we produce miles of reports, but we produce them on paper. It is still uncommon for reports to be produced electronically or in efficient media such as microfilm (which was introduced in the 1960s). Even rarer are the reports produced on secondary storage devices where they can be viewed at a workstation at the user's leisure. We kill a lot of trees in this business.

Excessive Distribution. Businesspeople associate an element of organizational power with being on the distribution list of information systems reports. Many reports are sent to people and offices with only a marginal need for the information. Information overload and paper-dominated problems multiply.

Nontailoring. The typical business report is a compromise among several parties. As a result, it is not entirely satisfactory to any one party. The technology exists to produce reports specifically tailored to each interested party. Perhaps habit has prevented tailored reports from becoming a matter of course rather than an exception.

The delivery of the Friday afternoon summary report at Sandman Manufacturing regional headquarters is crucial to four functional area managers. The report contains all the sales, accounting, financial, and production activities for the week. From the report, the four managers extract the information they need to assess the status of the organization and to make schedules and procurements for the upcoming week. The extractions can take up to two hours and preparation of the derived report can take up to four additional hours. For years, the managers have complained about the extraction problem, which is severely compounded if the report is delivered late. They often spend much of Friday evening working on items that could be handled more efficiently by a properly designed computer system. These problems do not have to exist. Rather than discussing the design of systems output as it is done now, this chapter focuses on how it will be done tomorrow.

A TOTAL QUALITY APPROACH

In designing information system output, we must remember the nine information system characteristics we have established as our total quality checklist.

1. *Relevancy:* Output should be relevant to user needs in detecting and solving problems. Output should include only those fields required by users. Extraneous data obscure required information.
2. *Completeness:* Output should be complete in that *all* user-required fields are included.
3. *Correctness:* No incorrect information should be included on output. Accuracy is always important. It is particularly important in output design because people tend to trust computer reports. Users feel betrayed when they discover output errors. Output from newly designed reports must be audited carefully before the first copy reaches the user community. Most end-user impressions of the information processing department rest on the quality of output products.
4. *Security:* Distribution of output should be only to those users whose tasks depend on it. This is particularly important when information is sensitive, such as that about market strategies.
5. *Timeliness:* Delivery of output products must be scheduled to user needs rather than to the convenience of the information systems department. The IS department is responsible for being aware of current and changing user needs so it can produce timely output.

6. *Economy:* Given two or more options for providing proper output, the least costly is preferable.
7. *Efficiency:* Ratios such as Timeliness per Dollar or Errors per Dollar should be minimized.
8. *Reliability:* All the first seven characteristics on this list should be delivered to the user with minimum variances. For example, variances should be minimized around average report delivery time. Reductions of variances results in dependable output products.
9. *Usability:* Output should be easily and effectively used by nontechnically trained end-users. Quality of information is only as good as users perceive it to be. Regardless of potential usefulness, information distrusted by end-users is useless. Balanced, attractive reports elicit user confidence.

A STRUCTURED APPROACH

The structured approach to output design proceeds in four stages: data flow diagram, data flow specification, data structure specification, and data element specification.

Data Flow Diagram. The output report or action document first appears as an exit data flow from a DFD process. Thus, Figure 12–2 shows the purchase order action document as an exit data flow from the purchasing process.

Data Flow Specification. The overall characteristics of the output data flow are described in a data flow specification template. This template includes such characteristics as volume, medium (e.g., paper), and distribution. Figure 12–3 is a data flow specification for the purchase order.

Data Structure Specification. The group output description must now be broken down into its individual data elements and their sequence. Figure 12–4 shows the **data structure specification** for the purchase order.

Data Element Specification. Each field in the data structure specification is described in detail in a **data element specification.** Figure 12–5 is such a specification for the vendor code field of the purchase order.

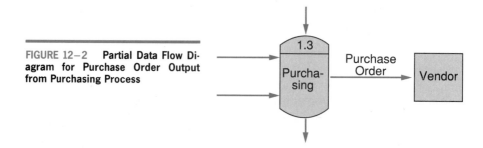

FIGURE 12–2   **Partial Data Flow Diagram for Purchase Order Output from Purchasing Process**

```
┌══════════════════════════════════ PROJECT:  MAIN ═┐
│                                                     │
│  LABEL:        Purchase-Order                       │
│                                                     │
│  ENTRY TYPE:  DATA FLOW                             │
│                                                     │
│  DESCRIPTION: Form sent from purchasing to vendor to order │
│               replenishment stock.                  │
│                                                     │
│  ALIAS:       Form # MAT132                         │
│                                                     │
│  COMPOSITION: Frequency: 200 per day plus or minus 75 │
│                                                     │
│                                                     │
│                                                     │
│                                                     │
│  NOTES:       Flows from purchasing to vendor       │
│                                                     │
│                                                     │
│                                                     │
│  LOCATIONS:  0, 1.3, 1.3.1, 1.3.1.1, 1.3.1.2        │
│                                                     │
│                 Press <Esc> key for option line     │
│ F2=SET SEARCH   F3=EXPAND    F4=FILE                │
└─────────────────────────────────────────────────────┘
```

FIGURE 12-3   Output Data Flow Specification for Purchase Order

```
┌══════════════════════════════════ PROJECT:  MAIN ═┐
│                                                     │
│  LABEL:        Purchase-Order                       │
│                                                     │
│  ENTRY TYPE:  DATA STRUCTURE                        │
│                                                     │
│  COMPOSITION:  DATA ELEMENT        TYPE      LENGTH  │
│               ───────────────────────────────────── │
│                Vendor-Code         A/N         6     │
│                Vendor-Name         A/N        30     │
│                Vendor-Address      A/N        40     │
│                1(Order-Item)10                       │
│                  Stock-Number      A/N         8     │
│                  Description       A/N        15     │
│                  Quantity          NUM         5     │
│                  Unit-Price        NUM         4.2   │
│                  Extended-Price    NUM         9.2   │
│                Total-Price         NUM        11.2   │
│                                                     │
│                                                     │
│                                                     │
│          Edit  eRase  Save  Delete  Next  Prior  eXit │
│ F2=SET SEARCH   F3=CONTRACT   F4=FILE        SEARCH:   /    / DS │
└─────────────────────────────────────────────────────┘
```

FIGURE 12-4   Input Data Structure Specification for Purchase Order

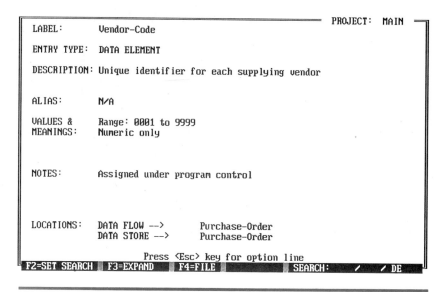

FIGURE 12–5   Data Element Specification for Vendor Code Field

OUTPUT MEDIA

You probably have been introduced to hardware characteristics of computer systems, including output media and devices. For purposes of continuity, the topic is treated briefly here, but with an emphasis on design factors that influence selection of appropriate output media. The communication media that produce systems output are hard copy (physical output), electronic display, and other media such as voice.

Hard-Copy Devices

Printers, plotters, and microform equipment are hard-copy devices. Most output is still produced by line printers.

Printers. Printers are classified by speed: high speed (15,000 to 20,000 lines per minute), medium speed (1,000 to 3,000 lines per minute), and low speed (20 to 750 lines per minute). High-speed printers achieve their speed through laser beam or photographic technologies.

Medium-speed printers are impact printers. Impact can be in the form of chain, train, belt, or drum. Medium-speed printers require hammer strokes, thereby reducing print speed. Yet, as might be expected, impact printers are less expensive than high-speed, nonimpact printers.

Low-speed printers are referred to as remote site printers; they allow presentation of information closer to the end-user. The number of remote printers in an organization often is quite large, because there are so many end-users. The amount of information printed at remote stations is considerably less than at centralized, mainframe computer sites. Accordingly, end-user emphasis is on slow, but low-cost, remote site printers.

Figure 12–6 shows a typical disbursement of printers. The centralized mainframe site produces volumes of reports and uses a few expensive high-speed printers. Intermediate centers use medium-speed printers. Low-speed printers are attached to end-user workstations.

At State University, the centralized, high-speed printers are primarily dedicated to central administrative output (that is, student rosters, payroll, disbursements, accounts receivable) where there is great volume. The medium-speed, decentralized, dot-matrix and letter-quality printers are used for word processing, statistical reports for individual faculty research, and college and departmental administrative output. Each faculty and staff member with a computer has a low-speed, dot-matrix printer for output purposes. Any output that requires letter-quality form is uploaded to the decentralized, medium-speed, letter-quality printers.

Plotters. Plotters produce paper versions of charts, graphs, and pictures. Graphics can be produced on VDT screens or even dot-matrix printers. However, plotters are

FIGURE 12–6   **Printer Mix within an Organization**

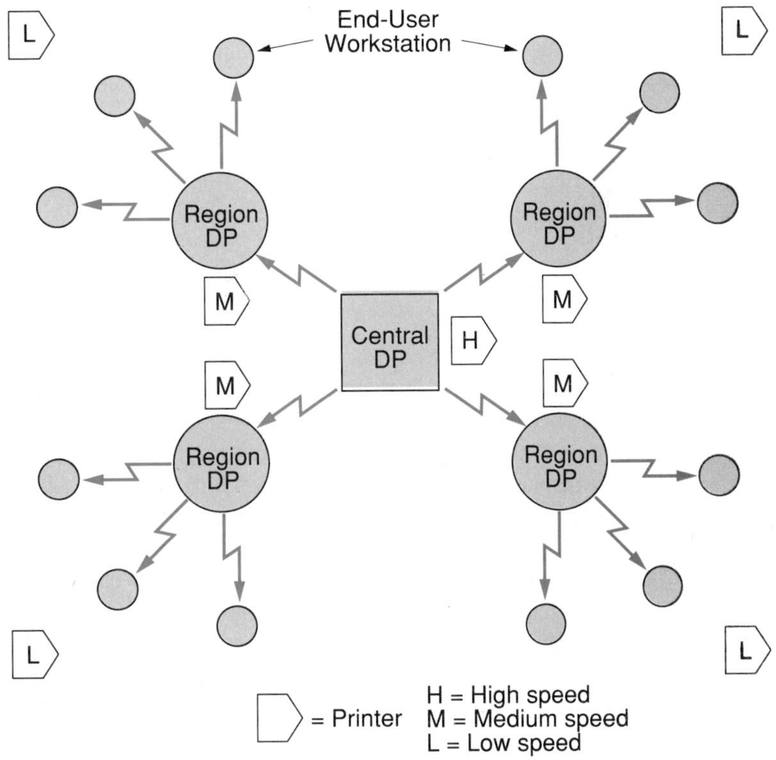

required to produce graphics in high-resolution color for publications such as annual reports. While plotters have been expensive, less expensive desktop plotters are now available. They do not have the capabilities of the larger plotters, but they can satisfy 70 to 80 percent of business graphic requirements, at reduced costs.

A new advance in graphics capability is the camera that films VDT screens with high resolution. The camera can capture computer graphics quickly, with reasonable quality. Costs are decreasing and resolution quality is increasing for these cameras. Eventually, they will eliminate mechanical plotters.

Taylor Consulting relies heavily on graphics for marketing and proposal presentations. The company produces overhead transparencies on a color plotter for in-house presentations and also takes pictures of VDT screens for client presentations. The time and cost factors limit the use of camera-produced slides in-house.

Microform Equipment. Microfilming of documents to save storage space has been an established office procedure for many years. For information systems, the output medium is called computer output microfilm (COM). COM is as fast as nonimpact printers. Storage of information on microfilm is more compact than on traditional paper media, and storage and paper costs are reduced.

Currently, COM equipment is expensive. Its use has been restricted to high-volume reports for which later retrieval is infrequent (for example, historical data). A firm can reduce COM equipment costs by working with an outside vendor. As microform develops as an input medium—computer input microfilm (CIM)—microfilm will become more extensive in information systems.

Bondwell, a CPA firm, does year-end and tax processing for several hundred clients. Bondwell stores all active client files on disk, all inactive historical files that are two to three years old on magnetic tape, and all inactive files older than three years on microfilm.

Electronic Display

The most common electronic display unit is the video display terminal. A VDT is an example of a dual input/output medium—one used for both input and output. VDT workstations have been used for data entry for years.

An overlooked electronic output device is the television. Only computer output is displayed, but in a larger screen format than available on a VDT workstation. Use of TV display has been directed to calendar applications such as airline departures and arrivals at an airport, events scheduled at a hotel or convention center, and course status, open or closed, at registration for university classes. This inexpensive medium could be applied more imaginatively in industrial settings such as production control or inspection. Have you noticed the use of this medium for customer service in such fast-food chains as Taco Bell? Counter clerks enter orders to a microcomputer. Orders are then displayed on a television screen for food preparers in the order in which they were entered.

Other Output Media

Voice response units are fairly common now. Technological advances have made this medium more versatile, inexpensive, and popular. (Do not confuse voice response with voice input, which is discussed in the next chapter on input design.)

Voice response units are limited to a vocabulary of hundreds of words; however, they are used in situations where the number of response situations is also limited. You need preprogram only a few words or phrases to provide response to a telephone inquiry for a savings account balance. Similarly, voice response units at a supermarket checkout counter need handle only product name, dollar price figures, and cents price figures.

As the number of vocabulary words that can be processed by voice response units increases, the technology will encompass a greater range of applications. The greatest advantage of this medium is its link to our most widespread technological unit—the common telephone.

Another use of voice output is on some manufacturing assembly lines. The hands and eyes of workers are busy performing tasks. Voice output allows the computer to communicate with the workers without interrupting the work flow. Such information as line speed, lack of raw materials, quality control, and emergency situations can be conveyed whenever appropriate.

One final output medium is mentioned primarily because it is not thought of in this perspective. This is secondary storage, most commonly magnetic disk. Rarely are reports produced directly from computer to printer. Instead, as shown on Figure 12–7, reports are first placed on a disk record and then printed *if needed*. Placement of reports on disk also allows information referral to be done electronically rather than by paper.

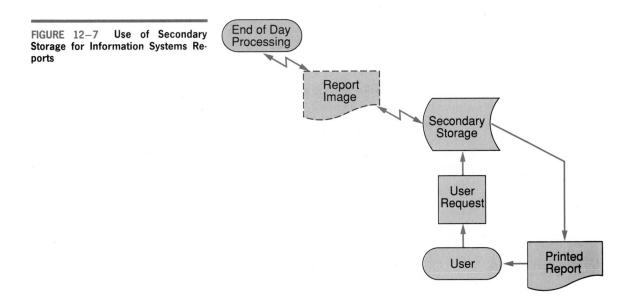

FIGURE 12–7   Use of Secondary Storage for Information Systems Reports

INTERACTIVE VISUAL DECISION MAKING

B usiness graphics is one of the fastest growing and technically complex areas of computer output. Graphics support financial analysis, marketing analysis, production planning and support, and other functional business activities. Turban and Carlson (1989) feel that visual graphics can bridge the gap between computer-based quantitative analysis tools and end-users. Graphics make information available to end-users in a form that they can understand. Businesses are spending millions of dollars on graphics-based software packages.

An emerging area in business graphics is interactive visual decision making (IVDM). Complex decision situations can be created and modified using IVDM. What-if analysis comes to life when the outcomes are depicted graphically rather than represented numerically. Managers who use IVDM seem to value it more highly than other computer dialogue options.

IVDM graphics can be summaries of data (bar charts, pie charts, histograms, and so forth) or iconic displays of processes or systems (e.g., parts, tools, machines, persons used in simulation situations). Manual visual representations have been around for a long time; maps used in routing decisions are a good example. Computerizing visual representations enables faster experimentation, analysis, and final solutions. Advanced IVDM uses artificial intelligence techniques for faster learning of experimental results and searching for possible solutions. IVDM can represent static or dynamic systems. Flickering techniques indicate changing states and animation moves iconic images around in the display.

The following characteristics of IVDM make it valuable and viable:

■ It provides a believable representation of the decision-making environment.
■ It provides immediate feedback on input.
■ It is easy to use and requires minimal training.

One of the systems designer's primary development tasks is to select from among these output media. Obviously, the choice of output medium constrains the design of documents produced by a business information system.

DOCUMENT DESIGN

Design of output documents follows the same guidelines that are appropriate for other documents, whether or not the documents are used with a computer system. This is also true whether the document is produced on paper or sent to a VDT screen.

Systems designers try to transform action documents into turnaround documents. A turnaround document is an output document that subsequently can be used as input. Turnaround documents eliminate the time-consuming and error-prone data input functions of coding, validation, and entry. Producing output in the form of a turnaround document can be expensive because it requires special output equipment that produces data in machine-readable format. Still, benefits gained in saved time and reduced entry errors often are worth extra equipment costs.

Another factor related to output design is compatibility with other systems, both within and outside the firm. Two positive results occur when output is designed to be compatible with other systems within the firm. First, the overall goals of the firm are enhanced, although there may be more costs for the new information system. Second, the costs of machine-readable output equipment can be shared among several systems, rather than entirely assigned to the new system.

A design opportunity also exists in making a firm's output compatible with systems outside the firm. For example, Hebert Pharmaceutical produces purchase orders that are compatible with the computer systems of several of its hospital supply vendors' computer systems. These vendors then grant concessions such as lower prices to Hebert Pharmaceutical. One vendor even provides use of its computer facilities when Hebert's computer is down.

Despite technological advances, there still exists a widespread bias in favor of producing action and turnaround documents on paper. Production of action documents by one system, and the transmission of those documents as inputs to another system, can be done electronically. The most noted example of paperless transfer is **electronic funds transfer (EFT).** In this process, financial documents are transferred electronically between systems with no use of paper. Many company paychecks are now transferred electronically to local banks **(automatic deposit).**

Systems designers must focus on the future, when paper documents will be rare and when business systems (within or outside the firm) will be linked. In the remainder of this chapter, design of paperless reports is emphasized.

REPORT DESIGN

How do systems designers know what reports to generate in a business information system? For a new system, they ask users what reports they need. Often, users do not really know. To play it safe they request all possible information. When the existing computer system is replaced, the same reports are generated as were previously produced. Yet poor-quality reports may have been one of the underlying reasons why the system was replaced.

Too often, designers decide what reports to produce in a sporadic, unstructured manner. This leads to report duplication, exclusion of important information, and mounds of paper on busy managers' desks. A structure is presented here for systematic design of reports produced by business information systems. It includes report characteristics, report types, and structure of typical business reports. This framework is applicable to both structured paper reports and unstructured inquiry-based reports.

Report Characteristics

An information systems report is described by when it is produced (frequency), who receives it (distribution), and its contents (format). One other dimension is used to classify reports: Why is the report being produced? The latter is discussed in the next part of this chapter on output design tactics.

Frequency has two aspects: reports can be produced on a periodic basis or only as required (ad hoc).

Periodic reports have set frequencies such as daily, weekly, monthly, or semi-annually. **Ad hoc reports** (sometimes referred to as demand reports) are produced at irregular intervals upon user demand. An example of a routine daily report is a daily sales summary report. An example of an ad hoc report is a detailed sales report for a salesperson who is on a route and asks for year-to-date figures on three clients who are in different regions but in the same industry.

The characteristic of **distribution** also has two subcategories. Reports are distributed internally or externally. **Internal distribution** is to persons or offices within the application producing the report. These reports are detailed in nature and are intended for those interested in the mechanics (for example, auditing) of the system. **External distribution** includes persons or functions outside the established boundary of the application. This group includes management, customers, and vendors. Reports for external distribution are less detailed in nature than those for internal distribution. A quarterly summary payroll report for the IRS is an example of a routine external report. A daily sales report is an example of a routine internal report.

The **format** of a report is fixed (structured) or user designed (unstructured). A **fixed report** is like an off-the-shelf suit from a department store. The suit can be changed slightly, but its format is largely predetermined. On a fixed report, the fields of information, their sequence, and how they appear are preset. **User-designed reports,** on the other hand, are similar to tailor-made suits. The user has almost complete control over how the reports look. User-designed reports allow choice of fields to be included, field sequence, and how fields are printed on reports.

Information systems reports can be described as a combination of these three characteristics. One report may be periodic, internal, and fixed. Another may be ad hoc, external, and user designed. Figure 12–8 gives you an idea of how these three characteristics are combined to describe different business information systems reports.

Report Types

The three types of reports produced by business information systems are detail, resource status, and summary (management).

Detail reports support the day-to-day, primarily clerical, operations of an organization. They are produced on a periodic schedule such as daily or weekly. They are distributed internally within the applications to which they apply. Detail reports are also very structured, rarely varying from the same predetermined format. Examples of detail reports are transaction listings, error listings, and summaries of action documents (e.g., purchase orders) for the day.

Resource status reports depict how one or many resource records appear at a specific point in time. They are produced on a periodic basis (e.g., once a month). They

Frequency	Periodic Reports		Ad Hoc Reports	
Distribution	Internal	External	Internal	External
Structured (Fixed)	Standard Detail	Standard Summary	Full Resource Status (On Request)	Full Summary (On Request)
	Standard Resource Status			
Unstructured (User Designed)	N/A	End-user Designed	Resource Status Inquiry	Summary (Management) Inquiry

(Format — left vertical label)

FIGURE 12—8   Characteristics of Reports and Associated Report Types

may also be requested as required. Distribution can be internal or external, depending on who needs the information. The format of a resource status report can be structured, but commonly it is unstructured to support on-line status inquiries. Examples of resource status reports are inventory zero balance, inactive customers, and outstanding purchase orders. These show the amount of a particular resource available at a specific point in time.

Summary (management) reports include statistics and ratios that managers use to gauge the health of a business. These reports can be either ad hoc or periodic. They are distributed externally to managers who are not intimately involved in the day-to-day operation of the application. While many summary reports are structured, fourth-generation languages are being used to produce summaries tailored to the particular person seeking the information. Examples of summary reports are customer order filling performance, vendor performance, and inventory turnover.

Detail, resource status, and summary reports have different characteristics of frequency, distribution, and format. However, there is a consistent structure underlying all of them.

Report Structure

An information systems report has three dimensions: page, column, and line (Figure 12–9). There is no physical limit to the number of pages. However, remember information overload. Information systems reports often are so large that users have little chance to digest them before the next version arrives. One tactic used to enhance the readability of multipage reports is to organize printouts in a manner allowing readers quick references, as in a telephone book. Output can be sorted into categories and page control breaks can be used on that field. In this way, readers can proceed quickly to the category containing a desired item. A page control break means that each new category

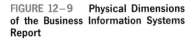

FIGURE 12–9   Physical Dimensions of the Business Information Systems Report

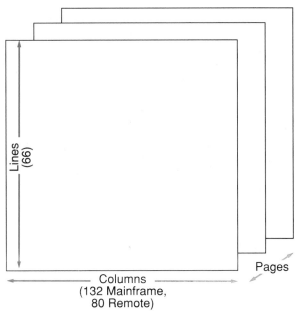

(for example, product type) begins printing at the top of a new page. In some phone books, listings start on a new page for each last name that begins with a new letter.

Typically, there are 132 columns in information systems reports; this size is dictated by mainframe line printers. Now, however, systems designers must begin thinking about how to condense traditional systems reports to fit 80 columns. This makes reports compatible with inexpensive printers at end-user workstations and personal computers. It also makes reports compatible for printout at user VDTs. More and more reports are being produced in the 80-column format.

These dimensions describe reports, and not necessarily action documents. Action documents are printed on specially printed, continuous forms. They are designed as a portion of a report page since they are of varying sizes (Figure 12–10).

The information systems report page has the following elements:

- *Title line:* From left to right, current date, report title, and page number
- *Headings:* Two or three lines that briefly but adequately describe fields printed on detail lines
- *Body:* Information the report imparts. For detail reports, there is one line for each transaction (business event). For resource status reports, there is one line for each resource item. For summary reports, there is one line for each statistic or ratio computed.

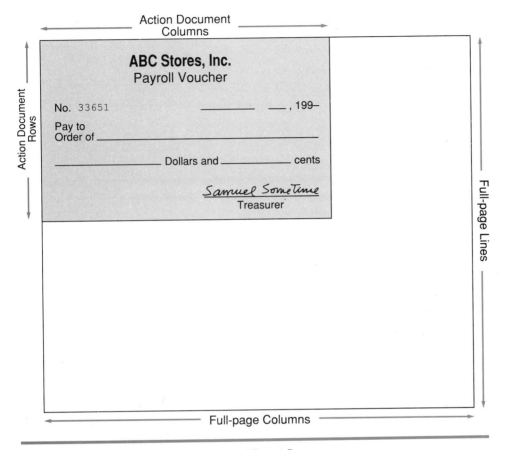

FIGURE 12–10   Action Document as Portion of Report Page

- *Footings:* A line of totals for fields printed in detail lines (e.g., the footing "total pay" at the bottom of a page under the column including the pay computation for each employee, or detail line)
- *Summary page:* At the end of the pages containing the aforementioned elements, a page containing totals for all preceding detail pages. Typical totals are total items (detail lines printed); total dollars, for monetary fields; and total units, for quantity fields.

Figure 12–11 shows the structure of the report page. Figure 12–12 is an example of a detail report. A resource status report is shown in Figure 12–13. Figure 12–14 is a summary report.

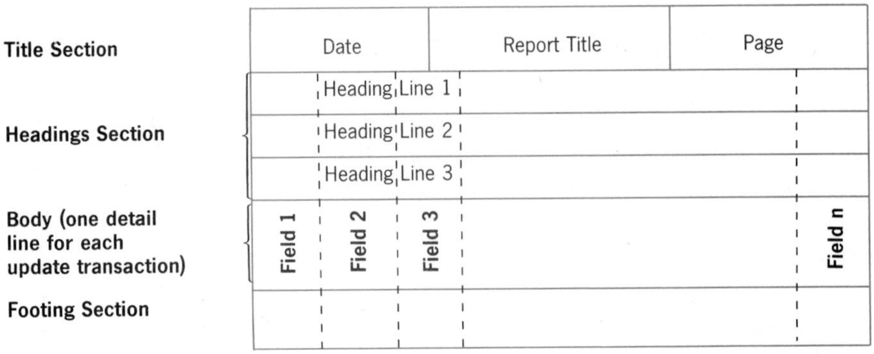

| | | Title Section | Date | Report Title | Page |
| | | | | | |

Headings Section
- Heading Line 1
- Heading Line 2
- Heading Line 3

Body (one detail line for each update transaction): Field 1 | Field 2 | Field 3 | ... | Field n

Footing Section

FIGURE 12-11   Organization of Report Page

    Accounts Receivable Register   **Page 13**

Trans. No.	Cust. No.	Trans. Type	Apply to Acct. No.	Check No.	Amount	Discount	New Balance
0096	16723	Pay	01	1623	327.23	0.00	0.00
0097	97277	Inv	05	—	222.37	0.00	1,673.77
0098	83111	Pay	01	1444	962.00	16.72	0.00
0099	43912	Inv	03	—	150.00	9.00	940.77
0100	34772	Crd	05	—	216.33	12.22	0.00
0101	75113	Pay	05	2123	55.99	0.00	14.61

Total Transactions	512	Beginning Receivables	$197,213.37
Total Invoices Processed	153	Add Invoices	49,121.22
Total Credits Processed	27	Net:	$246,334.59
Total Payments Processed	332	Less: Credits	616.15
		Payments	42,952.77
		Discounts	522.23
		Ending Receivables	$202,243.44

FIGURE 12-12   Detail Report for Accounts Receivable Register

Nov. 20, 1990		Inventory Report			Page 3
Stock Number	Class Code	Date Last Demand	Unit Price	Quantity on Hand	Whse. Location
15763	B1	7/12/88	9.97	1627	A16C12
24929	A3	12/13/87	16.23	9273	A23F3
66527	B2	5/17/86	32.60	627	306D4
93763	A2	6/16/85	12.15	75	C15A12

Summary by Class Code

A	22,573
B	16,172
C	41,213

FIGURE 12–13   Resource Status Report for Obsolete Inventory

Nov. 23, 1990		Customer Support Report				Page 1
Customer Number	Items Requested	Items Issued	Item Fill Rate	Units Requested	Units Issued	Unit Fill Rate
17325	1,290	1,109	86.0	43	39	90.7
24634	3,612	2,888	80.0	172	134	77.9*
36923	4,185	3,394	81.1	93	80	86.0
87923	682	512	75.1	19	16	84.2
95712	4,960	4117	83.0	124	105	84.7
Total	37,692	30,907	82.0	7,582	6,394	84.3

* Below Standard

FIGURE 12–14   Summary Report for Customer Support

REPORT REQUIREMENTS

Date 6 / 17 / 90   Department Purchasing   Report No. P-134-85

Report Title Inventory Status Report   Frequency Weekly

Files (1) Inventory   (2) Purch-Order   (3) 0

Field Group Description

Seq. No.	Field Name	Picture	Max. Size	From File	Headings 1	Headings 2	Headings 3	Total Field Group Size*
1	Inventory Number	X(5)	5	1	INVEN-	TORY	#	5
2	Description	X(20)	20	1			DESCRIPTION	20
3	Product Code	X	1	1	PRO-	DUCT	CODE	4
4	Vendor Code	X(4)	4	1	VEN-	DOR	CODE	4
5	Unit Price	2229.99	7	1		UNIT	PRICE	7
6	Balance-on-Hand	2(4)9	5	1	BALANCE	ON	HAND	7
7	Balance-on-Order	2(4)9	5	1	BALANCE	ON	ORDER	7
8	Date-Due-In	99/99/99	8	2	DATE	DUE	IN	8
9	Total-Investment	222,229.99	10	Comp	TOTAL	INVEST-	MENT	10
							Total	72

*Maximum of Headings or Field Size

FIGURE 12–15   **Report Requirements Document**

OUTPUT DESIGN TACTICS

Whether you are producing an action document or a report, there are ways to make it more effective. Remember to consider these six design principles: use of output design tools, aesthetics, strategic design, distribution testing, field selection, and design for change.

Output Design Tools

Two tools used to design output formats are the report requirements document and the print layout sheet. Figure 12–15 shows the **report requirements document;** note the following items:

1. General report information
2. Report title specifications
3. Field specifications
   - Field name
   - Maximum size of data (expressed as a COBOL picture description)
   - Field headings
   - Maximum size of field unit, which is the greater of the maximum field size and the maximum heading size

The report requirements document leads to the **print layout sheet** (Figure 12–16)—an important document because it presents a picture of what the report will look like. This picture is more communicative to end-users than the report requirements

| 99/99/99 | | | | Inventory Status Report | | | | | Page 99 |

Inventory #	Description	Product Code	Vendor Code	Unit Price	Balance on Hand	Balance on Order	Date Due In	Total Investment
XXXXX	XXXXXXXXXXXXXXXXXX	X	X	$9999.99	99999	99999	99/99/99	$999,999.99
XXXXX	XXXXXXXXXXXXXXXXXX	X	X	9999.99	99999	99999	99/99/99	999,999.99
XXXXX	XXXXXXXXXXXXXXXXXX	X	X	9999.99	99999	99999	99/99/99	999,999.99

| XXXXX | XXXXXXXXXXXXXXXXXX | X | X | 9999.99 | 99999 | 99999 | 99/99/99 | 999,999.99 |

FIGURE 12–16   Print Layout Sheet

document. It allows users to provide corrective comments before programming begins for the output report. The print layout sheet is also important because it indicates the aesthetics of the report.

Aesthetics

Users accept reports that look good. If you produce accurate output that appears untidy, users tend to distrust it. If you produce aesthetic output, even inaccurately, users tend to trust it. There are several aspects to aesthetic production. Many, including color, are more applicable to screen reports; these are discussed in Chapter 14. Three aesthetic tactics applicable to printed reports are selection of appropriate fields, symmetrical spacing, and page decoupling.

Many reports contain every possible field that can be printed within page column restraints. This approach, sometimes labeled "more is better," violates the principle of avoiding information overload. Information systems reports should be restricted to those information fields most needed. Judicious field selection is an important part of output design. The increased tendency toward 80-column, VDT-oriented reports forces system designers and users to decide which information fields *should not* be printed.

Reports should be symmetrical. Reports skewed to one side create an uneasy feeling for many users. Users unconsciously think, "There must be some reason for the imbalance. Why can't I understand that reason?" One key to providing symmetrical reports is even distribution of space. Separate fields by an even number of spaces and make the left and right margins equivalent. The same consideration applies to the vertical as well as the horizontal dimension. Place an equal number of spaces *before* printing at the top of the page and *after* printing the last line of the page. Headings should also be symmetrical. Reposition a heading such as

ITEM

DESCRIPTION

to a symmetrical one, as follows:

ITEM

DESCRIPTION

The final aesthetic tactic is page separation or decoupling. Separate pages into cohesive groups. The title printed at the top of the page should be applicable to the entire page. Follow these simple design rules:

1. Print all summary statistics on a separate page.
2. Start new sections of a report at the top of a new page.
3. Use control breaks on major fields. Include in the title the name of the **control break** variable. A **page control break** is a start of a new page and summary totals when there is a change in a key field. For example, a report is printed in vendor code sequence. When the program detects a change in the vendor code (for example,

from ABC to BAX), a new page is started for the new vendor code. New totals are also started.

Remember, users feel comfortable with reports that look good.

Strategic Design

Any action document or report that is distributed externally has strategic value. **Strategic value** is a condition increasing the profit potential of the firm. Increased profit potential is accomplished by increasing sales, decreasing costs, or both.

Designers sometimes seem as if they are wearing blinders when designing business information systems. It is easy to become so involved with the details of a system's inner world that you lose touch with the world outside the system. Remember that the action documents produced are the drivers of other systems, even systems outside a firm (for example, vendors' or customers' systems).

Strategic advantages are gained by making output compatible with processes outside the immediate scope of a system. By making shipping documents machine readable for customers' systems, you lock those customers into future sales with the firm. By making purchase order documents compatible with vendors' systems, you gain purchasing cost discounts or other benefits. By converting action documents to turnaround documents, you decrease costs of front-end information processing in your own firm.

Business information processing is no longer an experimental, research venture. Business information systems must show profit potential, either through real cost savings or by contributing to the firm's revenues. One way of realizing this potential is to design information systems output so it can be used by others within and outside the firm.

Distribution Testing

Several years ago I had the opportunity to participate in a team designing a state court's first judicial information system. We followed all the steps in the systems development life cycle, including determining user information needs and report requirements. We designed the system with a host of detail, status, and summary reports. Because the reports were to be distributed to every judge in the statewide system, we designed the reports according to what the judges wanted.

After four months of operation, we stopped sending out all reports. We did this to determine who would complain—who was really using these expensive reports? No one complained. We concluded that no one was using any of the reports, at least not on a recurring basis. We changed all these periodic reports to ad hoc (on-demand) reports, and this judicial system lived happily ever after.

The point of this personal experience is that report distribution is often too frequent when based entirely on user desires. Sometimes, the number of reports a person receives is perceived as a measure of that person's power. In other cases, decision makers request everything just in case they may need it. Systems designers must find the means to determine who really needs systems output and at what frequency. Otherwise, information systems will be submerged in paper.

Field Selection

What data items should be included on a report? Often, this question is sidestepped by trying to include all possible fields. This creates three problems:

1. The report becomes cluttered, appears unaesthetic, and is hard to read.
2. The report cannot be converted easily to the 80-column format required for end-user remote printers.
3. The end-user receives a mixture of essential, nice-to-have, and meaningless fields. Information overload occurs.

The tendency to include everything often is driven by programming efficiency. Programmers strive to use a few sections of code that will work for all output reports, regardless of the different needs of those end-users receiving the reports. Programming a new information system is a onetime process. Operation of the system is a day-after-day process. Therefore, it is wrong to optimize programming efficiency at the expense of everyday requirements.

Systems designers should select only fields pertinent for business reports. The fields best selected are:

- Key fields to access resource records (for example, stock number)
- Fields used for control breaks (for example, vendor code)
- Fields that change as a result of the transaction (for example, quantity on hand)
- Exception fields (e.g., field indicating customers who are 60 or more days behind on payments).

Design for Change

This final output design tactic—design for change—is one often ignored. We become so focused on finishing systems for today's users that we fail to focus on tomorrow's needs. Information systems that must constantly be changed become more of a liability than an asset. Systems must be designed to adapt to future change.

Consider these tactics for minimizing output changes:

- Emphasize unstructured reports over structured reports.
- Set field sizes to reflect future activity growth.
- Make field constants into variables (for example, change "high security" to "security status").
- Leave ample room in summary reports for added ratios and statistics. (New managers always seem to require new methods of analyzing problems.)

PROFILE OF A POORLY DESIGNED REPORT

The six design principles discussed are important for designing information systems output in general and report output in particular. Now let's look at these principles in a reverse perspective.

Glorfeld Industry has a materials control transaction processing system that, in part, produces a stock status report (Figure 12–17). The report shows balances of stock on order and on hand for each inventory item. Clerks use the report to determine what items to order from the fifteen vendors supplying Glorfeld Industry. The purchasing system is a batch update system rather than a real-time system.

The stock status report is always more than 150 pages long. It contains one detail line for each item in stock, regardless of that item's status (it is not an exception report). The report is not segregated by any control field such as vendor code; instead it is organized sequentially on stock identification number. The report is produced daily. Clerks find it impossible to study the entire report before they receive the next one.

Eight copies of the report are produced on paper and sent to (1) purchasing, (2) inventory control, (3) receiving, (4) auditing, (5) production, (6) marketing, (7) the vice president for manufacturing, and (8) the information systems department. No one in the information processing department can explain what all these offices do with the report.

The report is structured; there are no capabilities for the various users to select specific items, specific report fields, or summary statistics on items or fields selected. The report contains the first ten fields of each stock record in the same sequence as these fields occur on the record. It is designed for 132 columns and thus is incompatible with the numerous 80-column remote printers the company has recently purchased for the end-user community.

051288 **Stock Status Report**

Stk ID#	Vendor Code	Stock CD	Nomenclature	Bal O/H	Bal Ord	Bal Cmmt	Whse Loc	Security CD	Unit Price
11652	A	1	Blue Shirt	62	00052	000000	2022	N	0173.63
12963	A	5	Beard Trimmer		01651	000651	16A16	N	0009.99
12998	T	9	Sun Glasses	2542	00000	000000	1T19	H	0005.32
15117	V	1	Car Cover		00511	000500	7B6	M	0016.92
18832	M	3	Aquarium	175	00000	000000	32A32	N	0723.16
19963	L	1	Snooze Alarm	23	00127	000000	4C16	M	0025.00
	L	1	Ear Plug Set	1627			12A12		
		5	Chrome Hub						
		6	Slide Rule						
		9	Wet Bar						
		3	Hair Dye						
		1	Pet		00000	000000		N	0074.32
21617	T		Gold		01621	007000	27T16	H	0263.00
21379	V			16	00000	000000	12C6	M	1999.99
21792	A			1792	00000	000000	6B1	N	0157.63
22513	A			237	00100	000000	22A22	H	0016.92

FIGURE 12–17 Poorly Designed Report Format for Stock Status

When you look at the format of the report (see Figure 12–17), the following problems will be evident:

- Title line: The title is positioned unsymmetrically across the 132 columns. In addition, there is no field printed for page number. The date is printed without separation between month, day, and year; it looks more like a report number than a date.
- Heading lines: The pairs of lines containing field headings are not symmetrical. Headings contain jargon and abbreviations confusing to all but the most knowledgeable inventory user.
- Detail lines
  1. Codes are printed rather than clear text descriptions. This is a programmer convenience that is required due to the great number of fields that have to be squeezed onto the page.
  2. There are no lines separating the listing of stock items. It is difficult to separate one detail line from another or to make notes about possible purchasing actions.
  3. There are no dollar signs for monetary fields.
  4. The printed fields are not aligned symmetrically with appropriate field headings.
  5. The balance-on-order field does not use the zero-suppress option, thus making the field difficult to read.
  6. The balance-on-hand (BAL O/H) field does use the zero-suppress option, but zero balances are printed as blanks rather than as a single zero. The reader does not know if there is no stock on hand or if the programmer neglected to print the field.

An exercise at the end of this chapter asks you to redesign this stock status report to make it more useful.

INQUIRY-BASED SYSTEMS

Current business information systems are inundated with structured reports that are produced daily or weekly and distributed in multiple copies to every imaginable office. People do not use these reports in the manner envisioned during the output design phase. It is easy to understand why.

Fixed periodic reports, particularly those of wide dissemination, require the designer to predict far ahead of time who will be the *typical* report user. But often, there is a wide variety of users; additionally, firms experience turnover and the tastes of individual users change. In such cases, focusing on a single, typical user is a difficult task. It's like having to decide upon a single CD to stock in a music store visited by a diverse group of customers.

The secret to designing reports for a varied user group is not to design those reports at all. Let users design reports that fit their specific needs. **Inquiry-based systems** allow users to design reports on an ad hoc basis.

The advent of fourth-generation languages (4GLs) has made inquiry-based systems more popular. So has the drive toward distributed processing and end-user computing. Fourth-generation languages allow computer-naive users to extract rapidly from databases *only* the information they want, in the *exact format* they desire, and *exactly when* they need it. Structured query languages such as **SQL** allow users to submit commands in a natural, nonprocedural (no set sequence) format. Inquiry-based systems are more expensive than structured report systems because they require a database management system, many remote workstations and printers, and therefore, investment in telecommunications.

Current inquiry-based systems have three problems that keep them from being used more often. The first problem is increased cost; however, costs are expected to continue to decrease over the next several years.

The second problem is 4GL compatibility with end-user needs. This problem also seems solvable. Current 4GLs have become more understandable by computer-naive workers, but not completely. It is rare that an end-user can use a 4GL without some training. Most managers and top executives find little time for such training and try to operate through an intermediary.

Remember the court system discussed earlier. Recall that we suspended all periodic report distribution to find out which judges were really using the reports. When no judge complained, we stopped periodic distribution of structured reports. We substituted an ad hoc (as required) environment. However, court judges had little time or interest in learning a 4GL with which to generate tailored reports. So we set up a central, statewide clearinghouse where all parties needing judicial information could telephone or send an electronic message. Personnel at the clearinghouse (1) accepted telephone or message inquiries, (2) helped interested parties determine their needs, (3) entered structured inquiries to the judicial database, (4) mailed or faxed ad hoc reports to requesting parties, and (5) made sure that the information delivered was what the interested party really wanted.

The **information clearinghouse** concept became so popular that legislators, law-enforcement officials, attorneys, and others outside the court system requested permission to use the system. This system was relatively inexpensive, since distributed workstations, printers, and telecommunications links were not needed.

Sometimes this type of information clearinghouse operates in industry through an information center. An **information center** is a user-oriented service center that provides consultation, assistance, and documentation to encourage end-user development and use of applications.

The third problem with inquiry-based systems involves wider user access to important record fields. This can compromise file integrity because unauthorized access to restricted information can occur. Inquiry-based systems present more security problems than do traditional structured report systems. Nevertheless, these security problems can be handled.

Periodic, structured reports will become less important in tomorrow's business information systems. Inquiry-based systems, either direct or through an intermediary information center, are the mode of the future.

HUMAN ASPECTS

You hear about a new snack food called Margarita Chips. You go to the supermarket to buy some. You find two brands, both priced the same. One brand is in a plain white wrapper, with no window to see through. The other brand is in a multicolored, attractive wrapper which allows you to see the chips. Which brand would you buy?

Like snack food, information system output must be packaged to appeal to users. At the same time, make sure that the packaging does not hide a shoddy product. The packaging helps to garner initial user acceptance to a new information system. Nevertheless, it is the quality of what is inside that package that determines long-term user feelings about the system.

So, when designing information system output, think of Margarita Chips!

SUMMARY

Design of information systems output is an important task confronting systems designers. If systems output is designed ineffectively, excellent design of input and file processes becomes meaningless. The success of any information system is largely measured by the quality of output.

The usual output products are action documents and reports. Action documents can be transformed, however, into turnaround documents that save entry time and potential errors. Documents are produced in a real-time or batch mode; reports often are produced in a batch mode.

The typical output environment has several problems: (1) delays in distributing reports, (2) production of too much information (information overload), (3) emphasis on paper rather than on electronically produced reports, and (4) common rather than user-tailored reports.

Output media belong to the categories of hard copy, electronic display, and other. The latter category includes the old but newly popular medium of human voice. Emphasis in all media should be on transforming action documents to turnaround documents.

Three characteristics describe the typical business information systems report. These are frequency (when the report is produced), distribution (who receives the report), and format (what the report looks like). Frequency includes ad hoc (as required) and periodic reports. Distribution of reports is internal, external, or a combination of both. The format of a report is structured (fixed) or unstructured (tailored to the situation).

The three generic types of reports are detail, resource status, and summary. Detail reports often are periodic, fixed, and internally distributed. Resource status reports are periodic or ad hoc, fixed, and distributed internally and externally. Summary reports are ad hoc, user designed, and distributed externally.

A repetitive structure is characteristic of every report. It consists of the dimensions of page, line, and column. Page structure includes title, headings, body (detail lines), footings, and a summary page.

Any type of output will benefit if the designer considers six design principles:

1. Report requirements document and print layout sheet, which facilitate both action document and report design
2. Output aesthetics, particularly symmetrical spacing
3. Strategic values of output when used outside the system
4. Proper distribution
5. Inclusion of required fields only on action documents and reports
6. Design of output documents for future conditions, to facilitate change

The future of output design is in the direction of ad hoc, unstructured, tailored reports. The environment producing this type of output is called an inquiry-based system; it features fourth-generation languages. As an alternative, information centers serve as intermediaries for report tailoring. Such centers accept user requests, tailor them to a specific database, use a 4GL to process the requests, and distribute output to the inquiring user.

CONCEPTS LEARNED

- Problems with typical information systems output settings
- Typical types of output media, their advantages and disadvantages
- Why systems designers attempt to transform action documents to turnaround documents
- Report characteristics of frequency, distribution, and format
- Different characteristics of detail, resource status, and summary reports
- Basic page structure of a business information systems report
- Use of the report requirements document and the print layout sheet
- Importance of report aesthetics
- Importance of designing systems output for strategic objectives
- How to test report distribution specifications for authenticity
- Importance and means of selecting appropriate output fields
- How to design reports for change
- Tendency toward and importance of inquiry-based systems

KEY TERMS

ad hoc report
automatic deposit
control break
data element specification
data structure specification
detail report

distribution
electronic funds transfer (EFT)
external distribution
fixed report
format
frequency

information center
information clearinghouse
inquiry-based system
internal distribution
management report
page control break
periodic report

print layout sheet
report requirements document
resource status report
SQL
strategic value
summary reports
user-designed report

REVIEW QUESTIONS

1. Describe five problems often associated with business information output.

2. How do mainframe and remote site printers differ?

3. What is COM and how is it used?

4. What is the importance of transforming an action document into a turnaround document?

5. What is the difference between ad hoc and periodic distribution?

6. Describe the different characteristics of detail and summary reports.

7. What is the role of page control breaks in making bulky reports more readable?

8. What is the relationship between the report requirements document and the print layout sheet?

9. What is page decoupling?

10. Describe two ways to design output products for strategic purposes.

11. Why do people want to receive reports they really do not need?

12. Why should the information fields on information systems output be selected carefully?

13. What four types of fields should be considered for business output?

14. Describe three ways of designing output to aid future change.

15. Why can output now be more easily tailored to the needs of individual users?

16. Explain the role of an output intermediary.

17. What is an information clearinghouse?

18. What four structured specifications are needed to describe the output of any single system?

CRITICAL THINKING OPPORTUNITIES

1. Draw a diagram showing the outline of this chapter.

2. Compare and contrast 80 column and 132 column reports.

3. Visit a local firm with an automated processing system. Collect copies of five information action documents. Describe how to convert each document into a turnaround document.

4. For each of the action documents collected in Exercise 3, suggest how to use the document for strategic purposes.

5. Refer to the stock status report shown as Figure 12–17.

   a) How would you change the frequency characteristics?

b) How would you change the distribution characteristics?

c) Using a report requirements document and a print layout sheet, redesign the format of the stock status report.

d) How did you select which fields would be included in the report?

6. Refer to the report shown in Figure 12–12. Convert it to a data structure specification as shown in Figure 12–4.

In this chapter you will learn about:

WHAT: (Concepts) Designing information system input.

WHY: You cannot get anything good out of a system unless you put something good in.

WHEN: This is the second stage of the design phase of the SDLC.

WHO: Systems analyst in conjunction with end-users.

WHERE: Information systems department and end-user work area.

HOW: (Techniques) Coding methods
                 Error checking methods
                 Source document design methods

OUTLINE

- Setting
- A Total Quality Approach
- A Structured Approach
- Input Tactics
- Input Media
- Source Document Design
- Coding Considerations
- Error Checking (Validation)
- Human Aspects

INPUT DESIGN

To record some transaction as a sale when the customer is truly dissatisfied, or truly erratic, or truly dead, is to make a foolish decision.

—C. WEST CHURCHMAN, 1968

SETTING

Resource transactions update resource files. Transactions are changes to resource balances. Slow or inaccurate entry of these changes results in resource records that do not accurately portray how many units of a resource actually exist. You cannot sell something that apparently is not there. This chapter describes the design of input documents and processes to assure accurate and timely posting of files.

A TOTAL QUALITY APPROACH

Design of input is done according to the criteria of information characteristics used throughout this book.

1. *Relevancy:* The quote at the beginning of this chapter reminds us that unless input is relevant to management decision making, that input is misleading.
2. *Completeness:* All required input should be entered.
3. *Correctness:* This often is measured by the percentage of transactions entered without error.

4. *Security:* Records should be updated only by input entered by authorized personnel. Often this is accomplished by use of passwords.
5. *Timeliness:* This is measured by **throughput,** which is the number of errorfree transactions entered during a specified time.
6. *Economy:* All other things being equal, the cheapest input methodology should be used.
7. *Efficiency:* Ratios should be computed by dividing each of the measures 1 through 5 above by item 6 (e.g., Correctness per Dollar). These ratios should be maximized.
8. *Reliability:* For all of the above criteria, there should be consistency in computed rates (range of variance from time period to time period).
9. *Usability:* There are three considerations here:
   - *Boredom and fatigue:* How long data entry operators can perform without a decrease in quality of performance. (Most operator's performance deteriorates significantly after five hours of transaction entry per day.)
   - *Learning rates:* How fast untrained operators become productive
   - *Environmental conditions:* Effects of levels of noise, lighting, humidity, and so forth on operator performance

A STRUCTURED APPROACH

A structured development approach to input design calls for input description at four levels.

Data Flow Diagram. Inputs are data flows entering a process. For example, a customer order enters the order processing process (Figure 13–1).

Data Flow Specification. Each input data flow is described with an input data flow specification. Figure 13–2 shows this specification for the customer order.

Data Structure Specification. The **data input specification** is exploded into individual field sequence and characteristics. Figure 13–3 shows this explosion for customer order.

Data Element Specification. Each field on the data structure specification is described in detail in a data element specification. Figure 13–4 is such a specification for the customer category field of the customer order.

FIGURE 13–1 **Partial Data Flow Diagram for Customer Order Input into Order Process**

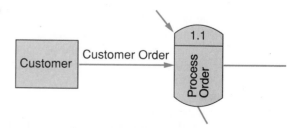

```
                                                        PROJECT:  MAIN
 ┌──────────────────────────────────────────────────────────────────┐
 │  LABEL:        Customer-Order                                      │
 │                                                                    │
 │  ENTRY TYPE:   DATA FLOW                                           │
 │                                                                    │
 │  DESCRIPTION:  Form containing product items ordered by customer   │
 │                                                                    │
 │                                                                    │
 │  ALIAS:        Form # MAT116                                       │
 │                                                                    │
 │  COMPOSITION:  Frequency: 2500 per day plus or minus 300           │
 │                                                                    │
 │                                                                    │
 │                                                                    │
 │                                                                    │
 │  NOTES:        Flows from customer to order-processing             │
 │                                                                    │
 │                                                                    │
 │                                                                    │
 │                                                                    │
 │  LOCATIONS:    0 , 1.1, 1.1.3                                      │
 │                                                                    │
 │                                                                    │
 │                   Press <Esc> key for option line                  │
 │ F2=SET SEARCH ║ F3=EXPAND ║ F4=FILE ║         ║ SEARCH:   /   / DF │
 └──────────────────────────────────────────────────────────────────┘
```

FIGURE 13-2   Input Data Flow Specification for Customer Order

```
                                                        PROJECT:  MAIN
 ┌──────────────────────────────────────────────────────────────────┐
 │  LABEL:        Customer-Order                                      │
 │                                                                    │
 │  ENTRY TYPE:   DATA STRUCTURE                                      │
 │ ─────────────────────────────────────────────────────────────────│
 │  COMPOSITION:  DATA ELEMENT           TYPE         LENGTH          │
 │               ──────────────────────────────────────────          │
 │                Date                   DATE         8               │
 │                Customer-Number        NUM          6               │
 │                Customer-Category      A/N          1               │
 │                1(Order-Number)10                                   │
 │                   Stock-Number        NUM          8               │
 │                   Description         A/N          15              │
 │                   Unit-Price          NUM          5.2             │
 │                   Extended-Price      NUM          10.2            │
 │                Total-Price            NUM          12.2            │
 │                Shipping-Code          A/N          2               │
 │                Back-Order-Code        A/N          1               │
 │                                                                    │
 │                                                                    │
 │                   Press <Esc> key for option line                  │
 │ F2=SET SEARCH ║ F3=CONTRACT ║ F4=FILE ║       ║ SEARCH:   /   / DS │
 └──────────────────────────────────────────────────────────────────┘
```

FIGURE 13-3   Data Structure Specification for Customer Order

```
                                                      PROJECT:  MAIN
   LABEL:        Customer-Category

   ENTRY TYPE:   DATA ELEMENT

   DESCRIPTION:  Group code to catagorize customer types


   ALIAS:        Customer-Type

   VALUES &      E=Educational; G=Government; R=Rental; W=Wholesale
   MEANINGS:



   NOTES:        Flows from customer to Order-Processing




   LOCATIONS:    DATA FLOW -->      Customer-Order
                 DATA STORE -->     Customer
                     Press <Esc> key for option line
  F2=SET SEARCH   F3=EXPAND    F4=FILE           SEARCH:       /    / DE
```

FIGURE 13–4   Data Element Specification for Customer Category Field

INPUT TACTICS

Clerical personnel record a business transaction on a form called the source document. The **source document** contains data that change the status of a resource. For example, a vendor shipment document tells a firm an item of material now has additional units in the warehouse. In the same manner, a vendor invoice document tells the firm that it must produce a check to pay the vendor. It also indicates that the firm must reduce the amount of funds it has collected (bank balance) by the amount of its check to the vendor.

The goal of this phase of the systems development life cycle is to design input documents and procedures so that transactions can be quickly and accurately brought into information systems. Input involves the processes shown in Figure 13–5. Systems designers must decide on several alternatives related to these processes.

Source versus Turnaround Document

The transaction originates from outside the designer's immediate control. For example, a vendor shipping document is produced in a format dictated by the vendor. The receiving firm has little control over what that document looks like. It must enter this source document as is, but in a way that fits its own needs.

If the transaction document can be designed to be machine readable by the firm's information system, much input preparation can be eliminated. This results in faster and more accurate transaction entry. Such a document is called a **turnaround document;** Figure 13–6 shows its flow. Examples of turnaround documents follow:

- Customer bills with account number and amount to be paid printed in machine-readable format (e.g., by optical scanning). In many retail situations 90 percent or

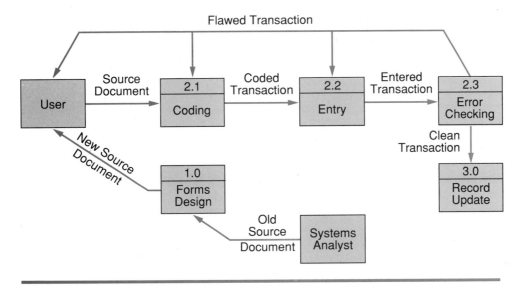

FIGURE 13−5   Transaction Input Processes

more of customers remit the exact amount billed. Therefore, little additional data entry is required when customers return their bills with payments.

- Tags on new clothing that allow stock identification and price to be scanned automatically by a laser reader
- Order sheets for record or tape companies with machine-readable selections
- Employee payroll checks with employee name, date of check, and amount of check in machine-readable form

Turnaround documents can be created in three ways. First, within the same system, output action documents can be designed so they are machine readable on input. Second, designers of other TPS applications in a firm can be requested to design their action documents to be compatible with another system's input requirements. For example, a purchasing system produces a vendor purchase order. When that order document is returned with the shipped material, it acts as the receipt for the receiving

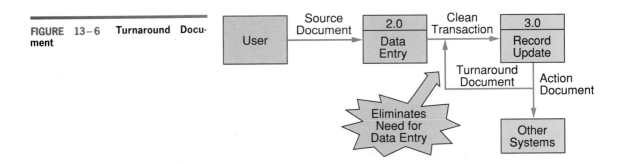

FIGURE   13−6   Turnaround Document

TPS. Third, suppliers or customers outside the firm's TPS environment can be encouraged to produce action documents compatible with the firm's input needs. Whichever options are chosen, use of turnaround documents results in cost savings. Each TPS source document represents an opportunity for design of a turnaround document.

Centralized versus Decentralized Entry

Transactions can be entered centrally or at remote workstations. Centralized entry slows down record updating because all source documents must be sent to one place. However, centralized entry makes most efficient use of data entry personnel. In addition, it reduces types and incidents of entry errors to a predictable and correctable range. It also allows proper sequencing of multiple types of transactions. For example, centralized entry allows all inventory receipts to be processed before customer orders. In this way, newly arrived stock is added to inventory balances before a customer order tries to draw from stock on hand.

On-line versus Off-line Entry

Transactions can be entered directly to computer systems or through intermediary, off-line devices such as key-to-disk. Off-line entry is less expensive. On-line entry allows immediate use of computer power to detect entry errors. Rapid and early detection of transaction errors is a major goal of systems design.

Batch versus Real-time Record Update

Use of on-line transaction entry does not mean that resource records are updated immediately (on a real-time basis). Transactions can be edited immediately on-line and then saved (batched) for later record update. Figure 13–7 shows the relationship between transaction entry and record update methods. Note the following paths:

- The path from 2.2 to 2.3 is on-line transaction entry, regardless of the method used to update the resource file.
- If record update is done in a *batch* (delayed) mode, then processing proceeds from 2.3 (error checking) to a batch transaction file (update delayed) and *then* to 3.0 (record update).
- If record update is *real time* then process 2.3 proceeds directly to process 3.0 without the intervening batch transaction file.

Multiple Source Documents

Often, one transaction entry station is responsible for input of multiple source documents. For example, one group of operators enters receipts, inventory adjustments, and order adjustments. It is more efficient to batch documents into similar types (e.g., all order adjustments) and to assign a particular type to a particular operator. In this way, there is a single warm-up time associated with a large group of transactions.

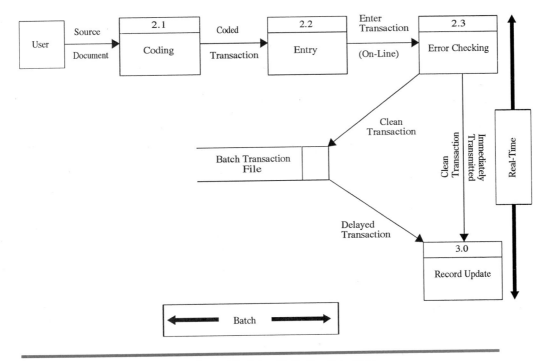

Conversely, an operator entering many different types of transactions will have many warm-up times, one for each change in type of transaction entered.

INPUT MEDIA

This chapter's material on the hardware of data entry systems provides the systems designer with a checklist for input options, and emphasizes the advantages and disadvantages of selecting specific input media or devices. In making selections, designers consider keystroke entry, automatic scanning entry, and voice.

Keystroke Entry

Keystroke entry requires a human user to enter data on a typewriterlike device. The device may be off-line (not directly connected to a computer) or on-line. A **key-to-tape system** is a method by which data are entered directly onto magnetic tape. The magnetic tape can then transfer entered data to a computer system at a later time. It is an old method but it is still in use.

The centralized mainframe computer at Trumbly's Manufacturing is running at close to processing capacity from 7 A.M. to 7 P.M. Sales data entry is performed during the 7–3 and 3–11 shifts; all records are stored on magnetic tape. A small minicomputer handles the processing. At midnight, when the two data entry shifts are concluded and the mainframe is less busy, the tapes are loaded and used to update the sales transactions and accounts receivable files that are stored on disk.

Often, magnetic tape is used as backup (off-line storage) for storing records from disk. This illustrates an important point in the selection of any computer resource. In a rapidly changing field such as information systems, a particular medium may seem like a dinosaur even though it's not. Never dismiss any input, output, or processing medium simply because of its age. Rate a medium on its merits (although its merits may be decreasing) versus its disadvantages. There is a valley near San Jose, California, where hundreds of windmills generate electrical power—a new use for an old medium.

Key-to-disk systems carry off-line data entry a step further. This medium allows access, retrieval, and change of individual records, since disk is not restricted to sequential processing as is magnetic tape. Operators enter data on small-capacity disks that are then sent to a centralized computer site. Key-to-disk processing is a more sophisticated method than key-to-tape processing, but it is also more expensive.

The accounts payable department at Trumbly's uses a different technique for data entry and updating than the accounts receivable department. For accounts payable, the volume of transactions is much lower, but tracking the status of an account is crucial. Therefore, key-to-disk processing is appropriate. A minicomputer with disk storage handles on-line updating of accounts payable files. At any time, an internal department can call up an accounts payable transaction and determine its status. On a bimonthly basis, checks are issued for accounts payable items, and an update of the general ledger system occurs. Emergency checks can be generated at other times.

THE DVORAK KEYBOARD

The standard American keyboard is called QWERTY. It takes its name from the six leftmost keys on the top row of the keyboard. Although this keyboard has been around for a century, many have questioned whether its particular arrangement of keys is the best possible.

A researcher named Dvorak conducted experiments in the late 1920s to determine the most effective layout of keyboard keys. He studied relative reach and strength of each finger on left and right hands. He also studied frequency of key usage (e is the most frequently used letter). He placed the most frequently used letters and letter combinations within immediate reach of the strongest fingers. The result was the Dvorak keyboard.

Today, the Dvorak keyboard is still used only rarely. Some microcomputers allow you to switch between QWERTY and Dvorak. Still, the optimally designed Dvorak keyboard has not taken hold. Habit and comfort often slow down technology. They have thwarted this country's attempt to convert to the metric system and also seem to have derailed the Dvorak keyboard.

Both key-to-tape and key-to-disk entry devices are off-line. Operators enter transactions individually, but resource records are updated in groups (batches) of transactions rather than one transaction at a time. A keystroke entry device that is more amenable to real-time updating of resource records is the VDT, now sometimes referred to as a **video display station (VDS).** Some people still call this device a CRT (cathode-ray terminal), but the terms *VDT* and *VDS* are more current and less tied to a specific technology.

A variety of VDTs are available in today's marketplace. Most have a standard typewriter keyboard, although a few have a **Dvorak keyboard** rather than the traditional **QWERTY keyboard** (see the box "The Dvorak Keyboard"). Virtually all VDTs have a ten-key numeric pad for entering numbers, and they all include a display screen to view information.

Another distinction is between so-called dumb terminals and intelligent terminals. **Dumb terminals** are merely communication devices to a central mainframe computer. **Intelligent terminals,** on the other hand, have local processing capabilities to store, edit, and verify data. In some cases, intelligent terminals can function as stand-alone computers.

Interactive terminals allow expansion of computer power early in the information processing process. Errors can be detected before transactions enter the computer system. Early error detection and correction are important requirements for a successful information system.

VDTs are more expensive than other types of keystroke entry devices. Business systems designers decide whether the additional error-correction capabilities are worth increased costs. However, VDT costs continue to decrease, and because of their benefits—earlier and more powerful error detection—they will become more popular as other keystroke entry devices (off-line) eventually become obsolete.

Finally, there are two older, yet revitalized, keystroke entry devices that firms are using increasingly in business information systems. The first is the telephone. In many banking systems, customers can use home telephones to access and change their bank accounts. The second familiar instrument is the cash register. It is now common in retail stores for clerks to use cash registers that automatically feed entered data into a computer system. The computer system, in turn, sends to cash registers pricing, sales, and other important retail information.

Automatic Scanning

All keystroke entry devices require human operators to select and press keys. Keystrokes take time and are susceptible to error. An excellent design tactic mentioned earlier is to allow computer output to double later as computer input. This is the turnaround document which reduces human keystrokes, thereby saving time and decreasing entry errors.

The computer produces turnaround documents in computer-readable format. A special device automatically scans documents and accepts data into the computer system. Common automatic scanning media are magnetic ink character recognition (MICR), optical character recognition (OCR), and point of sale (POS).

Magnetic ink character recognition (MICR) is the oldest of the automatic scanning media. It uses a restricted set of numbers to identify account numbers, amounts, and other information required to process personal checks. From a technological point of view, MICR is outdated. However, the banking industry has so much invested in MICR equipment and procedures that, for that industry, MICR is still a viable input alternative.

Optical character recognition (OCR) allows automatic recognition of more characters and font sizes than MICR. If an input character's pattern matches one stored in computer memory, the device accepts it; otherwise, the device rejects it. OCR is used in a wide variety of applications. The United States Postal Service uses OCR to automatically route correspondence. The Columbia Record and Tape Club uses OCR to automatically process orders from its members.

OCR equipment is expensive. In addition, entry rejection rates are high, since input character patterns must closely match those stored in computer memory. Despite a high rejection rate (e.g., 5 to 10 percent), OCR is valuable because of the great amount of human keystroke entry that is avoided. Therefore, firms can justify the increased speed and inaccuracy of OCR with even moderate levels of transaction volume.

Point-of-sale (POS) equipment allows laser scanning of specially prepared documents or codes. A shopper buys a pair of slacks at a Montgomery Ward store. The salesperson passes a light gun over a tag attached to the slacks. The stock identification and price of the slacks are automatically entered into the store's computer inventory system. An even more familiar example of the POS medium can be found in most large supermarkets where the **universal product code (UPC)** of each purchased item is scanned by laser to retrieve its price from central computer memory.

Voice

The most revolutionary input medium on the near horizon is the human voice. Current **voice entry systems (VES)** are expensive and limited in the number of words they recognize. They also require a warm-up period to adjust to an individual's voice. Soon these technical limitations will be resolved. Voice entry systems allow input to computers without any manual transcribing of data. In addition, voice is a medium that is completely natural and not threatening to end-users.

Fighter pilots have many tasks to perform that require the use of both hands and eyes. Experimental voice input systems are being explored as input devices for cockpit management. The pilot has a headset and can use a limited set of short, direct commands to control air speed, altitude, temperature, cabin pressure, and other variables. All of these voice-driven mechanisms can be overridden by traditional manual controls in case of emergency or computer problems.

Use of automatic scanning or voice input will eventually make keystroke transaction entry obsolete. For some time to come, however, keystroke transcription from paper source documents will exist for many business information systems. Therefore, the

VOICE RECOGNITION

Keystroke input is not a very efficient means of computer and human interaction. Keystrokes involve many steps of translation in order to communicate. The user must first decide what to say or do. Then the user must transcribe this thought into words. The words are typed into the keyboard. The words are echoed on the screen. Then some other key must be pressed in order for the computer to recognize that there is some input to be processed. The computer must store the keystrokes and then interpret them. Wouldn't you prefer to speak to the computer in natural language rather than to go through all these steps?

Speech recognition by computers, which has been in development for almost thirty years, has two levels: isolated word and continuous speech recognition. Isolated word systems with vocabularies of from 30 to 200 words exist and are fairly reliable. Continuous speech recognition is not as well perfected. Speech patterns vary from individual to individual and it is difficult to train the computer to understand a large vocabulary spoken by a large number of users.

Industrial applications of speech recognition include quality control, incoming inspection, part and serial number verification, and warehousing and sorting. In these situations, required vocabularies are small and the number of users is also small and consistent.

Speech input is advantageous when one or more of the following conditions apply:

- The worker's hands are busy.
- Mobility is required during data entry.
- The worker's eyes must remained fixed on some visual information other than the data to be entered (for example, air traffic control).
- The environment does not allow use of a keyboard (for example, the cockpit of an airplane).

business systems designer must know something about the design of such documents. Many principles of document design are also applicable to design of interactive screens.

SOURCE DOCUMENT DESIGN

Business systems designers are responsible for design of transaction source documents for several reasons. First, poor design of source documents leads to slow and inaccurate entry of transaction data. Second, because of changing technology, many source documents need to be replaced with automatically read turnaround documents. Third, few other persons in a firm have the necessary training, experience, and knowledge to create information instruments. When considering source documents as targets for redesign, elimination, or replacement, systems designers should be aware of standard requirements.

Document Requirements

Any well-designed document, or form, meets the following seven requirements:

- *Easy to use:* A form that is difficult to fill out will have a high rate of incomplete and erroneous fields.
- *Unique or specific:* Two forms that appear similar or two forms that are used for similar purposes are confusing. Forms should have different colors, different type styles, and so on, so that workers can quickly distinguish one from another.
- *Concise:* Only absolutely needed fields should be on the form. The greater the number of fields on a form, the longer it takes to complete the form. In addition, the more chance there is for entry personnel to make errors. Test each field on an existing or proposed document with this question: What would happen if we didn't collect these data?
- *Informative:* Clerks should be able to understand the form without the need for computer intervention. A form that is not informative to a clerk will not be completed adequately by that clerk.
- *Expandable:* Forms (at least well-designed forms) are costly. If they must be reprinted whenever someone makes a change, two things happen: (1) the inventory of old, unmodified forms becomes a lost investment; and (2) someone will confuse an old form with a new form, thus violating the uniqueness requirement. Leave room on the form for new or infrequently required fields. Design forms with ease of change in mind.
- *Amenable to computer data entry:* Designers should play the role of data entry clerk to determine what problems the existing or proposed form will present. Better yet, enlist the aid of data entry clerks when designing source documents.
- *Economical:* Note that this is the *last,* not the *first,* requirement. Costs should be reduced within the six described requirements. A form designed cheaply, at the expense of the other six requirements, is a form that may cause future problems. The resulting decrease in information systems quality (for example, error rates) is very expensive indeed.

Design Guidelines

In addition to the seven requirements for well-designed forms, several specific guidelines will help you design source documents. These rules of thumb are based on personal experience in designing forms that have ranged from workable to almost unusable.

Spacing. If the form uses either a typewriter or a computer printer, the spacing between lines must be consistent with spacing conventions of the standard typewriter. It is annoying to have to manually adjust the line spacing on a typewriter.

Color. Multiple-color forms are expensive, but they can be effective in highlighting important fields on source documents. Certain combinations of colors are counterproductive; they are either distracting or in the realm of human color deficiencies. An

Order of Legibility	Color of Printing	Color of Background
1	Black	Yellow
2	Green	White
3	Red	White
4	Blue	White
5	White	Blue
6	Black	White
7	Yellow	Black
8	White	Red
9	White	Green
10	White	Black
11	Red	Yellow
12	Green	Red
13	Red	Green

Reprinted, by permission, from M. Martin, "The Human Connection in Systems Design: Screen Design," *Journal of Systems Management* 37(October 1986):21.

FIGURE 13–8   Le Courier Color Legibility Table

accepted guideline for appropriate colorization of forms is the **Le Courier Chart,** shown as Figure 13–8.

Prompting and Labeling. Data entered on a form can have different formats. An example is a date field (see the box, "The Fuzzy Date Field"). Possible ambiguities can be reduced by using prompting and labeling (Figure 13–9).

Copies. Frequently, multiple copies of completed forms are sent to different places for different purposes. Follow these suggestions for dealing with the number and medium of multiple copies:

■ Clearly mark each separate copy with the name of the department or person to receive the copy.
■ Print separate copies on different-colored paper to ease routing.
■ Assign copies near the front of multipart forms to the most important users (those who do follow-up information processing). No matter how expensively produced, some loss of legibility occurs with each succeeding copy.

Eliminate as many copies as possible. Multipart forms are costly. The elimination of even one copy can result in significant cost savings.

FIGURE 13–9   Use of Prompting and Labeling on Forms

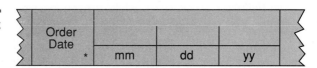

THE FUZZY DATE FIELD

You would think that a commonly used field such as date would have a standard format throughout information processing. Yet, each of the following date formats exists in business:

- mm/dd/yy
- yy/mm/dd
- dd/mm/yy
- Julian date, which has the following format:

  > 9   /   999
  > last digit   sequential day number of year
  > of year   /   (for example, February 28 equals 069)

- Month (spelled out), dd, 19yy
- dd/month (spelled out), 19yy

Which format will you choose when designing a system? Which format is most comfortable for the system's users?

Sequence. The sequence in which fields appear on a source document should be natural to those who must fill out the form. The sequence should not be a convenience to data entry operators. Yet, the data entry operator's job will be easier if data entry screens are designed to be in the same sequence as the source document (for form-filling screens), and if fields on the source document that require data entry are shaded. The transaction entry clerk can then easily skip nonshaded fields.

Costs. Source document costs can be reduced in one or more of the following ways:

- *Forms control:* Set up a central group to standardize versions of forms printed, stocked, and used.
- *Multiple copies:* Periodically review and justify all copies of forms. Reduction of even one copy of a multipart form can lead to considerable savings.
- *Length:* Restrict forms to 8 1/2-by-11-inch or 8 1/2-by-5 1/2-inch size. Other sizes are "off-sized." Off-sized paper costs more than standard paper. In addition, file folders to hold off-sized forms are more expensive than standard-sized folders.
- *Local printing:* Reproduce modestly designed forms at local facilities. Locally printed forms are less expensive than forms produced through contract printing.
- *Inventory systems:* Maintain a simple, automated, inventory system for forms. This can decrease stock costs while preventing work interruption due to out-of-stock forms.

Figure 13–10 is an example of a well-designed form. You do not have to be a form expert to design effective source documents. Many firms recognize that good form

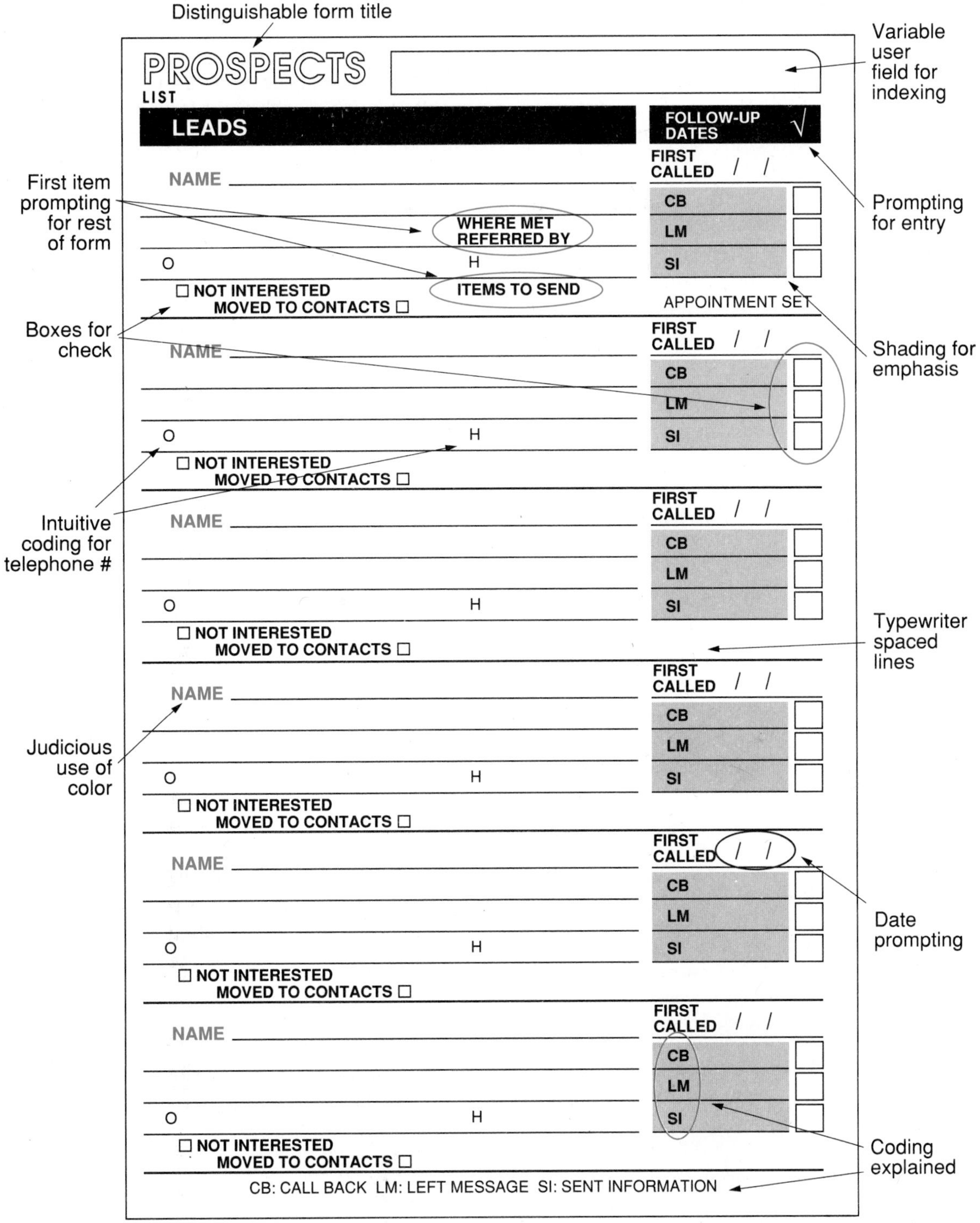

Distinguishable form title

PROSPECTS
LIST

LEADS

Variable user field for indexing

FOLLOW-UP DATES √

First item prompting for rest of form

NAME _____

WHERE MET
REFERRED BY

O   H

ITEMS TO SEND

☐ NOT INTERESTED
MOVED TO CONTACTS ☐

FIRST CALLED / /

CB
LM
SI

APPOINTMENT SET

Prompting for entry

Boxes for check

NAME _____

O   H

☐ NOT INTERESTED
MOVED TO CONTACTS ☐

FIRST CALLED / /

CB
LM
SI

Shading for emphasis

Intuitive coding for telephone #

NAME _____

O   H

☐ NOT INTERESTED
MOVED TO CONTACTS ☐

FIRST CALLED / /

CB
LM
SI

Typewriter spaced lines

Judicious use of color

NAME _____

O   H

☐ NOT INTERESTED
MOVED TO CONTACTS ☐

FIRST CALLED / /

CB
LM
SI

NAME _____

O   H

☐ NOT INTERESTED
MOVED TO CONTACTS ☐

FIRST CALLED / /

CB
LM
SI

Date prompting

NAME _____

O   H

☐ NOT INTERESTED
MOVED TO CONTACTS ☐

FIRST CALLED / /

CB
LM
SI

Coding explained

CB: CALL BACK   LM: LEFT MESSAGE   SI: SENT INFORMATION

FIGURE 13-10   Example of a Well-designed Form

design is hard to do and consequently use the outside services of a professional form designer. Still, systems designers must know enough about form design to select a good designer and evaluate his or her work.

CODING CONSIDERATIONS

A major task facing the systems designer during the input phase is when and how to code transaction data. Coding may be done by the end-user processing the source document. Alternatively, it may be done by the data entry operator. Wherever the coding is done, the business systems designer must determine specifics of coded fields.

Coding has five advantages:

1. Saves computer storage space
2. Reduces time-consuming keystrokes (e.g., the letter *F* requires less time to enter than the word *Female*)
3. With reduced keystrokes, decreases opportunities for keystroke errors
4. Allows grouping for later summarization (e.g., coding a student's class standing with the letters *SPH* for *sophomore* permits compilation of summary statistics for all sophomores *as a group*)
5. Satisfies external requirements that impose certain codes upon a system (e.g., zip code)

Coding of fields can be done in a decentralized or in a centralized mode. **Decentralized coding** is done by clerical personnel on source documents. Data entry personnel then enter codes directly from the source document. In **centralized coding**, clerks record transactions in their own language. Data entry personnel convert this language to codes at the time they enter transactions to the computer.

CENTRALIZED VERSUS DECENTRALIZED CODING

The Alaska Court System's first information system required clerks at the more than fifty state courts to code entries on source documents. They then sent the forms to Anchorage for data entry. The system became saturated with source documents that were incomplete, not coded (instead contained scribbled narrative entries), and miscoded. The information system was unreliable and quickly failed.

The second information system provided an uncoded form that, by state law, courts had to complete. Few fields were left incomplete because of the legal requirement. Courts sent the extra copy of the form to Anchorage, where clerks first coded certain fields, then entered the data. While centralized coding errors occurred, they were in a narrow range that could be countered with training.

The reason for this narrower error range was that only seven data entry clerks now did the coding. In the first system, hundreds of dispersed court clerks did the coding.

Decentralized coding allows data conversion at the transaction source, where personnel are more knowledgeable of the working environment, and thus, the coding required. Centralized coding, however, reduces the *range* of coding error, as shown in the box "Centralized Versus Decentralized Coding." Whichever mode is chosen, there are five types of codes from which to choose: numeric, block (category), serial, mnemonic, and self-checking.

Numeric

Numeric codes dominated the early stages of business information processing. Business computer languages (such as FORTRAN) had difficulty handling any other types of codes. Use of a number 1 to describe females and a number 2 to describe males is an example of a numeric coding. While this type of code saves some computer storage space, it is not directly readable by humans and so can result in more coding errors.

Block

Block, or **category, codes** contain special, unique numbers that identify separate resource units such as customers, employees, vendors, or inventory items. In a block identification code, each character has a specific meaning. Suppose, for example, you established an employee identification number of five characters with the following meaning:

	Identification Number Position and Meaning				
Code	1 Employee Type	2 Plant Location	3 Marital Status	4 Home Owner	5 Group Insurance
1	Engineer	New York	Married	Yes	Yes
2	Accountant	Chicago	Single	No	No
3	Foreman	Los Angeles	Divorced	—	—
4	Lawyer	—	Separated	—	—
5	Secretary	—	Widowed	—	—

In this structure, an employee number of 32412 indicates a foreman (3) in the Chicago plant (2) who is separated (4), is a home owner (1), and does not have group insurance (2). An employee identification number of 35412 is invalid since the character 5 is not listed under the second (plant location) identification number position.

Block codes are more inefficient than serial codes because block codes do not use all possible combinations for each position (see the plant location position). Thus, block codes take more record space than serial codes. However, block codes allow more rapid and structured retrieval of resource categories (blocks). They are particularly important for producing management reports. For example, using the block code structure, you can respond quickly to a request for payroll statistics dealing only with accountants in the New York plant (21XXX).

A serious problem with block codes is that two or more resources can end up with the same code. For example, there may be two foremen in Chicago who show the same characteristics of marital status, home ownership, and group insurance. For this reason, designers often add a serial code to the block code.

Serial

A **serial code** is a number that uniquely identifies a resource unit (for example, employee, customer, part). Unlike the block code, digits of the serial code have no meaning. They are merely used for identification, much as the number on a baseball player's uniform. The serial code combined with a block code provides a resource item with a unique identifier. For example, you might expand the employee identification code discussed to include a serial code portion as shown in Figure 13–11.

Mnemonic

All of the codes described so far have been numeric. Numeric codes require less computer storage space. A concentration on saving space dominated systems design in its early years. Now, with the end-user revolution, system designers and programmers must communicate in a human-oriented fashion rather than in computer language. This had led to an increased use of mnemonic codes.

A **mnemonic code** is the representation of information in a form that describes its condition more humanly than does a number. Most often, mnemonic codes are alphabetic in nature. The following example illustrates the difference. A numeric representation of an employee's gender might be done in this way:

$$1 = MALE$$
$$2 = FEMALE$$

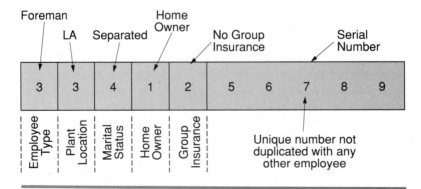

FIGURE 13–11   **Employee Identification with Block and Serial Codes**

On viewing an output report with such a coding structure, users would be confused about whether the number 1 represented male or female. The numbers 1 and 2 do not connote a natural relationship between the female and male conditions they attempt to represent. Suppose the following mnemonic coding structure were used instead:

```
M = MALE
F = FEMALE
```

Now the code is closer to English language, the domain of the end-users.

Mnemonic coding is more understandable to users. In that context, it has two advantages. First, those who are coding can visually catch errors. Second, programmers can catch erroneous combinations of coded characters more easily. For example, a unit-of-issue code of "EACH" might be required to begin with the letter E followed by a second character of A (for *ea*ch).

Mnemonic codes may be longer than numeric counterparts. The code of EA for unit-of-issue could be replaced with a numeric code of one digit. Designers must decide whether the advantages of mnemonic coding outweigh increased storage size and keystroke requirements.

Self-checking

A disruptive problem in any transaction-processing system is the inability to find the record to be updated by a transaction. Usually, an error has been caused by data entry transposition of numeric characters in a resource identification field. For example, a customer identification number is 6371473213. A data entry operator records it as 6371437213 in the input transaction screen. Now there is no way to match the customer ID number to the master record. This type of mismatch between a transaction and a record occurs with all resource master files.

Self-checking codes help to detect this type of error. A **check digit** is a code that traps transposition errors through the following computational sequence:

1. The numbers in the identification code are mathematically processed to arrive at a single digit. This digit is appended as an additional last digit to the original identification code.
2. Whenever an identification code is input by data entry operators, a verification program performs the same mathematical calculation used to create the original check digit.
3. If the computed value of this check digit matches the last digit of the code entered, the identification field is accepted. Otherwise, the field is rejected.

As with mnemonic codes, check-digit codes are redundant; they result in added keystrokes. The business systems designer must be sure that this type of code is reserved for those situations where errors produced without it are significant. The box "Check Digits" presents an example of the use of self-checking codes.

CHECK DIGITS

One of the more popular check-digit algorithms is MODULUS 11. It uses the following procedure to assign a check digit to a key field:

1. Number each digit in the field from right to left beginning with the number two:

$$\text{Customer number} = 999999$$
$$\text{Assigned digit} \quad = 765432$$

2. Multiply each digit in the key field by its assigned digit (weight). Assume a specific customer number of 731520.

Customer Number		Weight		Product
7	×	7	=	49
3	×	6	=	18
1	×	5	=	5
5	×	4	=	20
2	×	3	=	6
0	×	2	=	0

3. Sum the products: 49 + 18 + 5 + 20 + 6 + 0 = 98
4. Divide this sum by 11: 98/11 = 8, remainder 10
5. Subtract the remainder from 11: 11 − 10 = 1
6. Append the remainder to the key field: 731520 1 (check digit)

ERROR CHECKING (VALIDATION)

Once operators have entered transactions to computer systems, these transactions are checked for errors. The error-checking system involves error-checking methods, types of transaction errors, error messages, and error feedback.

Error-checking Methods

Three guidelines are essential for checking errors in a transaction-processing system. The first is, *Catch errors as early as possible.* The quicker an error is caught, the closer that error is to the person who generated it. The error then becomes easier to correct. In addition, the transaction has not aged appreciably before it is rejected. For example, in some batch-processing systems, the computer searches immediately for errors (on-line data entry) before file processing (batch record update). In this way, erroneous transactions are detected before they are placed in the batch file.

A second guideline is, *Reduce processing disruptions.* Transactional processing is a production environment that works best when there is a steady flow of transactions with a minimum of interruptions. Although transaction errors (production flaws) must be caught, error-checking procedures should be designed to maximize transaction through-put. Consider the following options:

1. Set aside rejected transactions for correction at another time or by another person. Data entry operators should not interrupt their throughput flow to perform time-consuming corrections.
2. When it is uncertain that a field is in error, use warnings rather than rejecting the transaction. Mark the transaction causing the warning for off-line research and correction.
3. Compare the results of any error against the impact that detecting that error has on continuous transaction throughput. For example, you might produce a warning for a larger-than-normal order quantity rather than an error. In such a case, the trans-action would be processed, reviewed, then reentered if necessary.

The third guideline is, *Provide frequent error feedback to end-users and data-entry personnel.* An **error feedback report** (Figure 13–12) allows correction of systems deficiencies, training of new personnel, and phasing out of personnel with error tendencies.

Types of Transaction Errors

The most common types of errors and some examples follow:

1. *Improper field type:* For example, alphabetic information is entered to a numeric field.
2. *Improper field size:* The data field entered is longer or shorter than the defined field.
3. *Unreasonable quantity:* The quantity field contains an abnormally large or small value for the typical business transaction.

Error Feedback Report		Date _____
Department XXX	Operator XXX	Period XXX to XXX

Error Code	Description	Number	Time to Clearance 1 2 3 · · · · ·
122	Incorrect Record ID	23	15 7 –
129	Unreasonable Quantity—Purchase Order	12	11 – 1
957	Incorrect Unit Issue	5	5 – –
	Total	127	92 16 12 · · ·

Average Errors per Day = XXX   Average Time to Clearance = XXX

FIGURE 13–12   Error Feedback Report

4. *Field not filled in:* For example, the customer billing address is missing.
5. *Field beyond logical range:* For example, the month field value is less than 1 or greater than 12.
6. *Negative balance:* The field is negative when it should never be less than zero.
7. *Illogical combinations:* Two or more conditions exist illogically; for example, a back-order code exists for a merchandise return.
8. *Record not found:* No resource record exists for the entered identification code.

When any of these errors occur, an error message should be displayed to alert data entry personnel that a problem exists. The nature of error messages is critical to timely and proper correction of error conditions.

Error Messages

Shneiderman (1987) suggests seven guidelines for designing and programming error messages.

1. Be as specific and precise as possible. General, ambiguous messages do not provide users with enough guidance to correct problems. Messages such as "syntax error" or "invalid data" merely frustrate users.
2. Be constructive. Show what needs to be done. For example, when detecting a record-not-found error, a program might display the following message: "No record found for this customer number. Make sure you did not transpose the customer number. Otherwise, forward transaction to new accounts clerk."
3. Use a positive tone. Avoid condemnation. Shneiderman gives this example of an inappropriate message: "Catastrophic error; logged with operator." Avoid negative terms such as *illegal, invalid,* or *bad.*
4. Choose user-centered phrasing. Design error messages that suggest that users control the system. Do not use imperative forms such as "enter date." Instead, use "ready for date."
5. Consider multiple levels of messages. Users should be able to demand a more detailed explanation of an error by choosing the help option. Yet, do not force this lengthier level of information on users if not needed.
6. Keep consistent grammatical form, terminology, and abbreviations. Surprise (inconsistency) interrupts the transaction throughput process.
7. Keep consistent visual format and placement. Display error messages on the same portion of the screen. Make them consistently flashing or nonflashing.

Shneiderman's seven guidelines are logical rules that you might subconsciously use when you communicate *verbally* with end-users.

Error Feedback

The purpose of error-detection systems is to discover errors so they can be corrected as quickly as possible. Effective systems report the rate and pattern of errors to management. Central to such a system is the **error suspense file** (Figure 13–13).

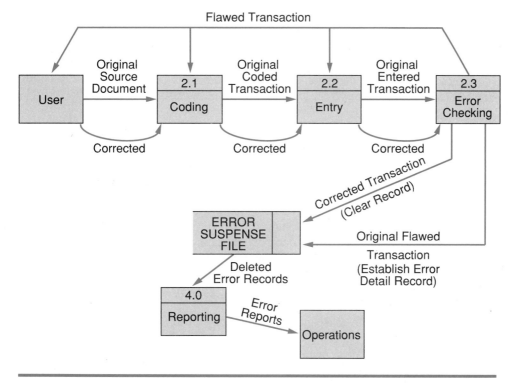

FIGURE 13-13   **Error Suspense File**

As the validation program detects an error, it sends the flawed transaction and error codes to an error suspense file on disk storage. When a clerk corrects the error and reenters the transaction to the computer, the program deletes the error suspense record for that transaction. The error suspense record has the following eight fields:

1. Data entry operator identification
2. Date of transaction entry
3. Time of entry
4. Transaction type
5. Transaction image (a replica of the transaction, character by character)
6. Fields in error
7. Error codes
8. Date transaction reentered successfully (in order to compute error correction time)

Collection of such data for each flawed transaction allows production of several error reports. Uncleared errors are reported with the oldest listed first (field 8 is empty). In another report, distributions of times to correct errors are listed (field 2 is subtracted from field 8). Error patterns are also reported by operator (field 1), by transaction type (field 4), by transaction field (field 6), by error type (field 7), and by time of day (field 3).

Most mainframe computer systems maintain entry logs to collect extensive transaction data for auditing and file recovery purposes. Much of the data required for error suspense files is already present in these logs. Therefore, design of an error feedback system does not represent a large investment.

Timely and accurate detection of transaction errors is critical to the health of any information system. Output from any system can be no better than its input.

HUMAN ASPECTS

There is an old saying in our field: "Garbage in, garbage out." No matter how clever systems analysts are in designing reports and files, the quality of the output is limited by the quality of what is input to the information system. And it is human beings who most often are responsible for that input.

Clerks fill out forms; errors can occur. Other persons enter data from these forms to the computer via VDT; errors can occur. Sometimes human input can be bypassed by design of turnaround documents. However, many information systems will continue to be reliant on human input in the years to come. We cannot ignore the human aspects to information system input.

Never forget this human aspect. Do not design your forms, input screens, or error correction procedures in isolation. Design them in partnership with the people who will be using them. Instill in these humans a sense of ownership. Then they will take more care in accepting and preparing only quality information.

SUMMARY

The goal of the input design phase of the SDLC is to design input documents so that transactions can be quickly and accurately brought into information systems. Input design includes selecting input media, designing source documents, coding data fields, and detecting data entry errors.

Before input design can begin, several decisions must be made:

- Can we transform source documents to turnaround (machine-readable) documents?
- Should we centralize or decentralize data entry?
- Should we make entry on-line or off-line?
- Should we make record update batch or real time?
- How should we organize data entry with multiple source documents?

Input media fall into the categories of keystroke entry, automatic scanning entry, and other means such as voice. Automatic scanning and voice will eventually make keystroke entry obsolete. However, for some time to come, keystroke transcription from paper source documents will exist in many business information systems. Therefore, design of such documents is important.

Design of source and other documents should be done with the following requirements in mind: easy to use, unique or specific, concise, informative, expandable, amenable to computer data entry, and economical. Considerations such as spacing, color, and prompting are also relevant.

Designers realize five advantages by coding data. Field coding saves computer storage space, reduces time-consuming keystrokes and thus reduces opportunities for keystroke errors, allows grouping for summary reports, and satisfies external requirements. Codes can be numeric, block (category), mnemonic, and self-checking (check digit).

All entered transactions undergo extensive checking (validation) to make sure that impure data do not enter an information system. Errors should be caught as early as possible. Error-detection methods are designed so there is minimum disruption to the data entry process. Error patterns should be reported to data entry personnel so they can improve entry.

The most common input errors are (1) improper field type, (2) improper field size, (3) unreasonable quantity, (4) incomplete field, (5) field beyond logical range, (6) improper negative balances, (7) illogical combinations, and (8) no resource record for the transaction. Systems designers need to couple identification of input errors with specific, constructive error messages. To improve data entry, the system collects incidents of error and timeliness of correction; error reports are produced for management.

An information system with faulty input can never produce effective output.

CONCEPTS LEARNED

- Relative advantages and disadvantages of centralized and decentralized data entry
- Structured approach to describing input
- Various input media options, characteristics, and relative use
- Seven requirements for a well-designed document, or form
- Six guidelines for designing forms
- Advantages of coding fields
- Types of coding structures and their relative advantages and disadvantages
- Concept of a self-checking code (check digit)
- Three guidelines for error checking
- Common types of transaction errors
- Guidelines for developing error messages
- Uses of error suspense records

KEY TERMS

block code
category code
centralized coding
check digit
data input specification
decentralized coding
dumb terminal

Dvorak keyboard
error-feedback report
error suspense file
intelligent terminal
key-to-disk system
key-to-tape system
Le Courier Chart

magnetic ink character recognition (MICR)
mnemonic code
numeric code
optical character recognition (OCR)
point of sale (POS)
QWERTY keyboard
self-checking code

serial code
source document
throughput
turnaround document
universal product code (UPC)
video display station (VDS)
voice entry system (VES)

REVIEW QUESTIONS

1. What is the difference between a source and a turnaround document?
2. What is transaction throughput?
3. Why should a document be concise?
4. What does the Le Courier Chart contribute to input design?
5. Explain the differences between numeric and mnemonic coding.
6. Why should entry errors be detected quickly?
7. Give an example of an illogical combination error for a payroll system.
8. What does Shneiderman mean by multiple levels of messages?
9. Describe an error suspense record.
10. What is a data input specification?

CRITICAL THINKING OPPORTUNITIES

1. Draw a diagram describing the organization of this chapter.
2. Compare and contrast a block code with a serial code.
3. Develop a mnemonic coding structure for a customer order (refer to Case 2.1).
4. Develop a self-checking code for a social security number. Demonstrate it with your own social security number.
5. Design the format of an error suspense record.
6. Refer to the formats shown in Figures 13–2 and 13–3. Complete a data input specification and data structure specification for a driver's license.

In this chapter you will learn about:

WHAT: (Concepts) Design of interactive information screens.

WHY: Interactive screens are a special type of input and output especially suited
           to real-time file update systems.

WHEN: Concurrent with design of other input and output.

WHO: Systems analyst in partnership with end-users.

WHERE: End-user work area.

HOW: (Techniques) Interactive screen menus
                        Form-filling screens
                        Adaptive systems

OUTLINE

- Setting
- A Total Quality Approach
- A Structured Approach
- The Psychology of Interactive Systems
- Interactive Structure
- Interactive Tactics
- Dialogue Modes
- Common Screen Considerations
- Screen Usability
- Human Factors Design Principles
- Human Factors Design Techniques

INTERACTIVE SCREEN DESIGN

"We are not amused!"

— QUEEN VICTORIA (1887)

(upon viewing an interactive screen
using five different colors)

SETTING

You have just learned how to design quality information input and output. However, there is a special type of input and output particularly relevant to on-line entry and real-time update of information systems. The input and output design principles and techniques you have learned so far still apply here. Nevertheless, there are additional concerns and techniques applicable to interactive screens that go beyond design of other input and output. That is because interactive screens, as the name implies, interact directly with mostly nontechnical human users.

When designing interactive screens, the systems analyst must step away from the technical world and journey into the realm of human relations. In addition, the systems analyst must wear a marketing hat to determine the proper type of "packaging" for the information system. This is because interactive screens are used by people with varying levels of computer knowledge, running the gamut from novice to experienced user.

431

A TOTAL QUALITY APPROACH

Interactive screens merely are a special form of information input and output. Hence, it is not surprising that the criteria for designing quality interactive screens follows the same nine information system characteristics. These include:

1. *Relevancy:* Is all data shown on a screen relevant to the task to be performed?
2. *Completeness:* Are all required fields shown?
3. *Correctness:* Is screen input checked for accuracy?
4. *Security:* Are passwords used so that only authorized personnel have access to the interactive screen?
5. *Timeliness:* Is the interactive system quickly responsive to user requests?
6. *Economy:* All other things being equal, is the cheapest method of user interaction being used? (Do you need interaction at all?)
7. *Efficiency:* Are the ratios of elements one through five above divided by Economy maximized (e.g., Are we getting the best Accuracy per Dollar we can expect?)
8. *Reliability:* Do all of the above criteria operate within a narrow range (variance)? This is particularly important for novice users.
9. *Usability:* Considerable knowledge has been accumulated on how to design interactive screens to maximize user effectiveness. Are we using these techniques?

A STRUCTURED APPROACH

On any data flow diagram, any data flow to or from a process is a candidate for an interactive screen. The data flow specification we use for interactive screens is similar to that used for output (Chapter 12) and input (Chapter 13).

THE PSYCHOLOGY OF INTERACTIVE SYSTEMS

Interactive systems are those that facilitate continuous communication between human users and computer systems. Interactive computer applications are often (but not always) synonymous with immediate, on-line entry of transaction data, which then updates records on a real-time basis. **On-line** refers to data entered directly to a computer system rather than through an intermediate data-entry device (e.g., key-to-disk). **Real-time update** means that each record is current as of the last transaction; there is no delay in record update.

Interactive systems are more than just another way to design an information system. Interactive systems require analysts and programmers to think differently about information systems. They require a mindset different from that required in designing batch applications. Interactive programming also requires a different approach—a different design organization.

A typical batch applications environment is found where: (1) transactions are collected into a batch over a period of time (batch period), (2) records are updated on a delayed basis by the batch of transactions, rather than by each transaction individually as it occurs, and (3) reports are produced simultaneously with the batch record update.

When the setting changes from a batch to an interactive environment, systems analyst thinking and styles must change. Following are some of the more important differences between interactive and batch environments that affect writing application programs.

Organization Prime-time: Batch processing generally is done after normal work hours (end-of-day) or on weekends. Interactive processing is done during a firm's prime work hours when most business is taking place. Thus users of interactive systems are subject to interrupting influences such as customer traffic, telephone calls, and coworker conversations. Interactive processing is similar to a student trying to study on the noisy floor of the New York Stock Exchange.

Multiuser Environment: Interactive applications often allow processing by more than one user at a time. Opening up an application to more than one user forces designers to pay more attention to such factors as (1) need for security to lock out unwanted users, (2) **simultaneous update,** when two users attempt to update the same record at the same time, and (3) increased **user response times** (the interval from user request to system response) due to multiple user demands on the applications system.

Breadth of User Experience: A batch processing environment generally is used by computer knowledgeable data entry operators keying in transactions, and technically trained operations personnel running record updates and producing output reports. Interactive applications typically are used by nontechnical applications clerks rather than information specialists. These clerical users will have computer experiences ranging from limited to extensive. Systems analysts must design interactive applications with a wide range of users in mind.

Emphasis on Communication: For all the foregoing reasons, there is more emphasis in an interactive system on analysts and programmers as effective verbal communicators. Error messages, requests for user responses, and help text are examples where interactive analysts must be more than good technicians; they must be effective communicators.

Interactive programming requires predicting who will be the user and what will be the best way to communicate with that user. In interactive applications, systems analysts must reach towards the user (the customer) in both style and technique.

INTERACTIVE STRUCTURE

Interactive systems include a series of workstation screens that allow users to select an appropriate path leading to specific tasks they wish to perform. Figure 14–1 shows the following series:

1. **Greeting screen:** This appears when the information system is first activated. The screen typically includes the company logo, name of the information system, and some sort of pleasant greeting.

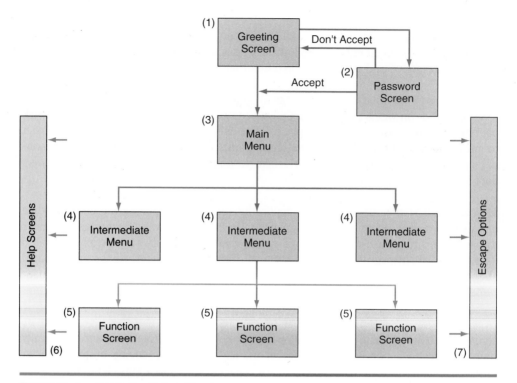

FIGURE 14-1 **Interactive System Structure**

2. **Password screen:** This screen prevents unauthorized users from entering the information system. The screen requires a user to enter an authorized password to continue processing.
3. **Main menu:** This interactive screen allows users to select one of several applications available in the information system.
4. **Intermediate menus:** These screens further delineate the user path towards the required information function.
5. **Function screens:** These screens allow users to perform functions such as updating or deleting records.
6. **Help (text) screens:** These instruct users how to use a particular screen or perform a specific task.
7. **Escape options:** These allow users to escape from a particular interactive screen or the entire information system.

There are several interactive tactics you can use to design the above structure.

INTERACTIVE TACTICS

Consider three tactics, regardless of the type of interactive system you design. The first tactic is, *Allow users to escape easily and quickly from any point in the transaction process.* Users must feel that they are in control of the computer system. They must know they can end the session at any point without being the captive of some programmer's escape maze.

The second tactic is, *Keep the user from getting lost.* The programmer of interactive sessions must adopt the mindset of a mall designer. Ensure that the user always knows where he or she has been, is now, and will be going. A common human fear is being disoriented or lost.

The third interactive tactic is, *Design interactive screens to ease transaction throughput.* Sometimes designers become so caught up in the artistry of their colorful and clever screen displays that they forget their goal. That goal is not to entertain but to produce more rapid throughput. The production nature of transaction entry should always be dominant in the mind of business systems analysts. An example of this type of thinking is to repeat screens automatically until the data entry operator signals a need to change. This allows continuous entry of volumes of the same type of transaction.

All three of these tactics are part of the underlying framework for the techniques that follow.

DIALOGUE MODES

Four common types of screen dialogue modes are form filling, inquiry, command language, and menus. Form-filling and menu screens are described in more detail after a brief discussion of the inquiry and command language modes.

An **inquiry mode** is a simple question for which users must provide a short response. Use this type of screen format when the situation is not suitable to a list (menu) or blocks of data (form filling). Inquiries often supplement other dialogue modes, particularly when you must alert users to possible shortcomings. Examples of such inquiry messages include:

- Do you want to end this session without saving your changes (y/n)?
- Are you sure you want to delete this file (y/n)?
- Would you like some help (y/n)?
- The quantity entered is larger than the typical maximum of XXX. Do you wish to correct your entry (y/n)? (This message is an example of using a warning instead of an error message when detecting a suspicious transaction entry.)

Some authors do not recommend use of the inquiry mode of dialogue for experienced users. For those who surely know what they are doing, continuous reminders are annoying. Yet, even experienced fighter pilots must follow an exhaustive checklist each time they fly. Hence, the inquiry mode should also be used for experienced users when the consequence of error is great.

Command languages are instructions that allow users to tell the applications program what to do without the intervention of menus or other interactive modes. Command languages should be restricted to sophisticated computer users. Command language consists of mnemonic codes such as Quit, Help, or Copy. This allows users to achieve objectives immediately.

Systems analysts direct screen interaction to the least common denominator — the new (novice) user. Command language then becomes merely a short cut convenience to experienced users. In this setting, command language systems rarely are visible to the novice end-user.

Form-Filling Screens

Form-filling screens are used routinely as function screens for data entry in a transaction processing system. Clerks complete manual source documents, then send them to a data entry operator. The operator enters specified fields from the document to the computer system. Transcription from manual to computer mode can be easy if data screens are compatible with (look like) the source document.

The typical user of a form-filling screen is a novice or an intermediate-level user. Thus, designers of form-filling screens assume users know only a little or nothing about computer systems. Figure 14–2 shows the format of a form-filling screen. Follow these directions when designing form-filling screens:

1. Make sure fields to be entered appear in the same sequence as on the source document and with the same labels. For example, a field labeled Customer Number on the form will be labeled the same on the screen. Do not change the screen to a variation such as Cust. #.

FIGURE 14–2   **Form-Filling Screen**

Reprinted by permission from M. Martin, "The Human Connection in Systems Design: Screen Design," *Journal of Systems Management* 37 (October 1986):16–17.

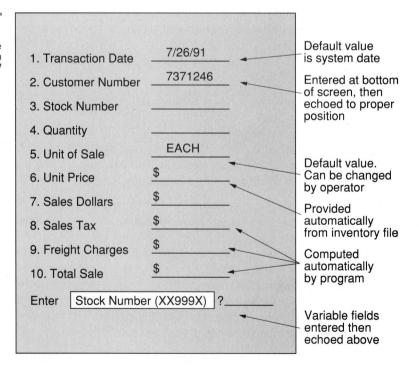

2. Use maximum cueing. **Cueing** provides users with field formats or other clues leading to faster, more accurate entry. If you require a particular date format, specify that format (for example, mm/dd/yy). Keep screen formats consistent with source document formats.

3. Provide default values whenever possible. A **default value** is a value automatically supplied by the applications program when the end-user has left a field blank. A default value allows users to skip entry fields and reduce keystrokes. Examples of default values are current (system) date for transaction date, an order unit of "Each," and an answer of "yes" to the question "Do you wish to continue?" Take care that default values represent options users choose most often. Also be aware that one danger of default values is that they may become habitual, and therefore may be used even when they should not be.

4. Edit all entry fields for transaction errors (refer to Chapter 13). Display and highlight error messages at the bottom of the screen to seize user attention.

5. Make sure that data entry operators rarely have to use a key to position the next field they must enter. Move the entry cursor automatically to the beginning of the next entry field **(Autoterminate)**.

6. Make sure that entry is free-form. For example, the program allows operators to enter data without leading zeros or left or right justification of fields.

7. Consider the entry option of entering data at the same place on the screen. The entered field is repeated (echoed) on an allotted space on the screen. This technique forces operators to exercise an eye movement that allows them to detect subtle data entry errors.

The entire process of manually completing and transcribing a source document can be replaced by point-of-sale techniques—bar coding, cash register terminals, and laser scanners. However, until such POS media become more economical, forms and form-filling screens will be common.

Interactive Screen Menus

The **menu** serves several purposes. First, it is a directory path to form-filling function screens. Second, it is a directory (memory aid) to command language instructions when the command set is large. Third, the menu is a training intermediary to command language. Fourth, the menu is a gentle means to support novice users. This discussion emphasizes novice support. Figure 14–3 shows one useful format of a screen menu for novices. Note these parts of the menu (numbers on the Figure correspond to the paragraph numbers below):

1. A short phrase serving as a user guide. Phrases such as "Payroll," "Inventory," or "New Customer" allow users to remember how they reached this particular menu screen.
2. A coded menu identification to allow experienced users to select a specific menu screen without having to follow the menu path for novices **(direct screen access)**.
3. A short title (for example, Report Choices) that quickly informs users of the screen's purpose.

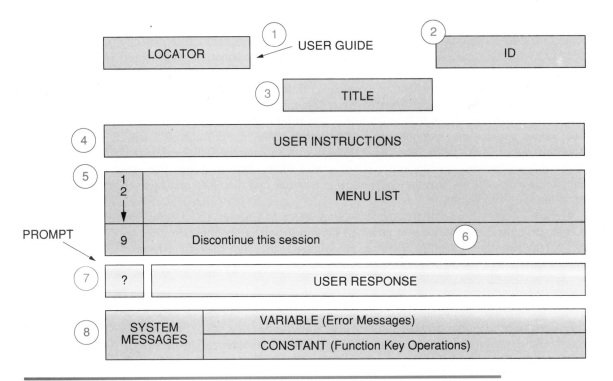

FIGURE 14-3   **Standard Menu Format**

Reprinted by permission from M. Martin, "The Human Connection in Systems Design: Screen Design," *Journal of Systems Management* 37(October 1986):18.

4. Brief user instructions such as "Select one of the following reports, then press Return." These instructions stand out by highlighting, underlining, or enclosure in asterisks.
5. A list of numbered options with brief descriptions of what the options represent. The number and sequence of options is important and will be discussed later.
6. A discontinue or escape option. This option should be listed last so frustrated users do not choose it too easily. Selection of the discontinue option can lead to a second chance menu (Figure 14-4).
7. A prompt to show where users type their selections. The program edits the selection for correctness. Users can correct out-of-range entries.
8. System messages of two types.
   ■ Variable: warnings or error messages. Highlight these to catch the user's attention.
   ■ Constant: user options common to many or all screens (for example, "H for Help"). The escape option can be placed here rather than in the menu list.

Two aspects of the menu screen warrant further discussion: option sequence and number of menu options. Option sequence should lessen user surprise. Accomplish this

FIGURE 14–4   **Second Chance Menu**

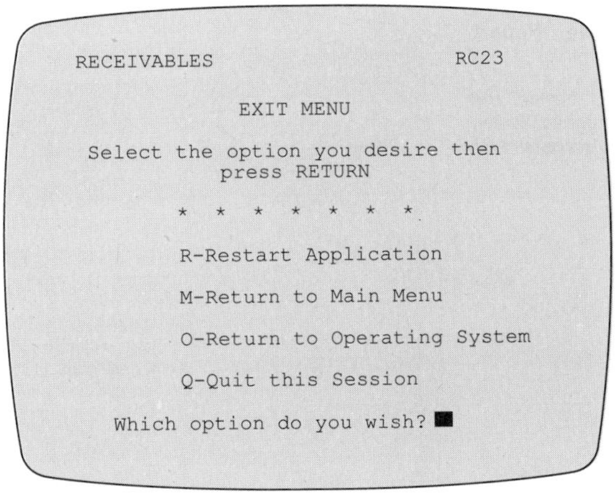

```
 RECEIVABLES                          RC23

                  EXIT MENU

    Select the option you desire then
               press RETURN

         *   *   *   *   *   *

         R-Restart Application

         M-Return to Main Menu

         O-Return to Operating System

         Q-Quit this Session

      Which option do you wish? ■
```

by a sequence that is (1) logical (for example, "Load new record" option precedes "Update record" option), (2) by expected frequency, where options selected most frequently are listed first, or (3) in alphabetic order.

Many experiments have tried to determine the optimum number of options to include on menu screens. Results tend toward a consensus of no more than eight choices. Many systems analysts use no more than six menu options per screen, not including the options for returning to the main menu and quitting the session. If the number of options must exceed six, consider two separate columns (**split screen**) of choices rather than one column. Figure 14–5 is an example of an interactive report menu.

Windows

Intermediate menu screens, help screens, and error messages can be designed as separate, full screens that fully replace the current interactive screen. For example, a data entry operator may be using a form-filling screen for updating an inventory record to reflect that material has been received by a vendor. While entering that transaction, the data entry operator needs help in determining which vendor code to use. He presses the "H" key, and a help screen appears, completely replacing the form-filling screen.

An alternate to complete screen replacement is the window. A window is a highlighted box that superimposes current screen text. The window contains additional user requested information such as acceptable Vendor codes. Figure 14–6 shows how the Vendor Code window might appear on a form-filling screen. This type of display is called a **pop-up window.**

Another type of window is used when there is a series of menus. The second in a series of menus is "pulled down" from the original menu. Figure 14–7 is an example of a **pull-down** menu.

FIGURE 14–5 **Interactive Report Menu**

Reprinted by permission from M. Martin, "The Human Connection in Systems Design: Screen Design," *Journal of Systems Management* 37 (October 1986):20.

```
┌─────────────────────────────────────────────────────────┐
│ ┌──────────────┐                          ┌───────────┐  │
│ │ Inventory    │                          │  IC 692   │  │
│ │ Control      │                          └───────────┘  │
│ └──────────────┘                                         │
│                      REPORT OPTIONS                       │
│                                                           │
│           Select the report you want to be               │
│           printed, then press 'return'                   │
│                                                           │
│           1. Warehouse Location                           │
│           2. Excess Inventory                             │
│           3. Vendor Shipments Overdue                     │
│           4. Inventory Investment                         │
│           5. Short Stock                                  │
│           6. Discontinue this session.                    │
│                                                           │
│                                                           │
│           Which report do you want? [ ]                   │
│                                                           │
│  ┌──────────────┐            ┌────────────────────┐       │
│  │ "H" for help │            │ "M" for Main Menu  │       │
│  └──────────────┘            └────────────────────┘       │
└─────────────────────────────────────────────────────────┘
```

```
┌─────────────────────────────────────────────────────────┐
│ INVENTORY                                        RECP     │
│                    RECEIPT ENTRY                          │
│ Date: │12│16│94│                                          │
│                            ┌──────────────────────┐       │
│ Vendor Code: [        ]    │    VENDOR CODES       │       │
│                            │ Able Industries   ABI │       │
│ Vendor Name: [           ] │ Casper Supply     CSP │       │
│                            │        •              │       │
│ Vendor Address: [        ] │        •              │       │
│                            │        •              │       │
│ Purchase Order No: [      ] │        •              │       │
│                            │        •              │       │
│ Inventory Item No: [      ] │ Zenith Supply     ZEN │       │
│                            └──────────────────────┘       │
│ Item Description: [                              ]        │
│                                                           │
│ Quantity Received: [  ]   Quantity Short: [  ]            │
│                                                           │
│    H-Help                              Q-Quit             │
└─────────────────────────────────────────────────────────┘
```

FIGURE 14–6   **Pop-up Window for Vendor Code**

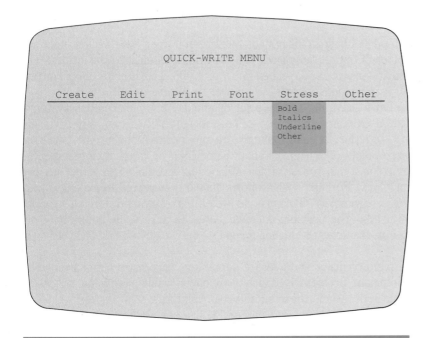

FIGURE 14–7   Pull-down Menu (When "Stress" option is selected, intermediate menu is shown.)

COMMON SCREEN CONSIDERATIONS

Regardless of the type of dialogue mode(s) you select, there are design considerations applicable to all interactive screens.

Highlighting

Highlighting means presentation of information in a mode that contrasts with other screen information. Since highlighting signals for attention, restrict it to critical information, unusual values, high-priority messages (for example, errors), or items the user must change. Also use highlighting for prompts to user entry and options in a menu list. In addition, you can use highlighting as a status indicator that the system is searching for a record.

Highlighting is done with flashing fields, change of color, or reverse images (for example, black on white message on a screen of white lettering on a black background). Reverse images are most noticeable. Some people have had bad personal experiences with flashing fields. They capture the user's attention, but also the attention of everyone else in the room.

Some recommend that highlighting be used for no more than 10 percent of the screen area. This makes sense. Highlighting should be a surprise to the user, and anything more common than 10 percent is not much of a surprise.

Color

Most microcomputers have color options for screen border, text background, and the text itself. For each option, users can choose from sixteen different colors. The screen color combinations are sixteen cubed (16^3), or 4,096. This is color out of control, and the number of combinations increases in newer monitors.

Art schools seem to have solved the color dilemma. As for information systems, there is no consistent evidence that three colors are better than two, any particular color combination is superior, or color monitors are superior to monochrome monitors. Still, there are three points of consensus about using color on interactive screens.

First, the way color stimulates is variable among human beings and within any one person at different times. Perhaps design efforts should be directed to making it easy for users to change screen colors. This may be preferable to trying to force a set color combination on all users. The problem is compounded because some colors have accepted meanings. For example, red means danger in the western world (but not so in Asia).

Second, 12 percent of males and a lesser percentage of females suffer from color deficiency. The dominant problem is difficulty in distinguishing between shades of greens, browns, and reds. Avoid these screen color mixtures.

Third, Le Courier's legibility table (Chapter 13) has been used for many years in forms design. It also applies to interactive screen design.

Remember, innovative color combinations are attractive but disruptive as well (See Victoria's quote at the beginning of this chapter). Your design goal is not to entertain users, but to allow them to have productive interactions with the computer system.

Information Density

There are two measures of screen clutter, or density. The first is **total screen density**—total characters printed divided by total character capacity of that screen. The second measure is **local screen density,** which measures average characters in close proximity to each character on the screen.

Overall density should be no more than 25 percent. Experienced users have more tolerance for cluttered screens than do novice users. You can give users the ability to drop part of a screen and then recall it if desired. This capability gives users some say in what screen densities they prefer. It also speaks against novice use of screens that lay windows over still partially exposed windows. A new window should completely block out all previous windows so screen density is minimized. The exception is the situation in which moving between several screen windows is important.

Figure 14–8 presents examples of low- and high-density screen formats.

Message Content

Follow these rules for constructing interactive messages:

1. Use active voice.
2. Use short, simple sentences.

FIGURE 14–8   **Screens with (a) Low and (b) High Density**

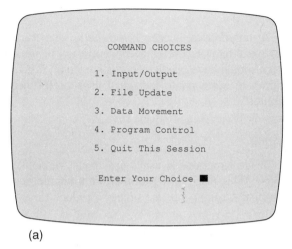

```
              COMMAND CHOICES

              1. Input/Output

              2. File Update

              3. Data Movement

              4. Program Control

              5. Quit This Session


          Enter Your Choice ■
```

(a)

```
      CHOOSE THE COMMAND YOU WANT

      1. MOVE          7. RETURN

      2. WRITE         8. UNLOCK

      3. READ          9. REWRITE

      4. DELETE       10. UPDATE

      5. MOVE CORR    11. ADD

      6. COPY         12. OPEN/CLOSE

        WHICH ONE DO YOU WANT?■
```

(b)

3. Use affirmative statements.
4. Avoid hyphenation and unnecessary punctuation.
5. Separate text paragraphs with at least one blank line (**local screen density**).
6. Keep field width within forty characters for reading ease.
7. Avoid word contractions and abbreviations.
8. Use nonthreatening language.
9. Avoid godlike language.
10. Do not patronize.
11. Provide a mixture of uppercase and lowercase letters.
12. Use humor carefully.

Symmetry

A symmetrical screen is aesthetic, and thus more comforting. However, users who wear bifocals prefer a concentration of messages at the bottom of the screen. Users should have profile records stored on disks. These profiles can be used to tailor interactive sessions to individual user preferences such as color or relative screen symmetry.

Timing

While experienced users prefer fast response, novice users prefer consistent response. This places programmers in a unique position. They may have to slow down individual screen response times to reduce time variances for novice users.

Help Functions

Help functions are text screens explaining in narrative detail how users might better use the particular model's capabilities. Disagreement exists about whether help functions should be provided automatically or upon request. A workable compromise is to include a constant cue at the bottom of the screen to remind users that help is available by pressing a certain key.

Input Verification

This technique is directed to novice users. It shows the results of the user's most recent entries. Verification occurs through such inquiry messages as, "Is this input correct?" or "Are you sure that you want to delete this file?" These types of messages are rather patronizing and wear thin. Use them only when results of improper user entries are serious.

SCREEN USABILITY

Design of interactive screens is complicated by the fact that there is such a wide variety of end-users interfacing with these screens. In addition, end-users are consistently changing in their levels of computer skills.

User Migration

Designers of business information systems must determine the characteristics of their users and then tailor interface techniques to match these user groups. This is difficult enough, but in addition, users rarely remain static; they change in several ways. Change occurs within user groups because the cast of users changes. Hence, the mix of novice and experienced users also changes. Migration occurs between user categories; novice users become experienced and experienced users become rusty. Finally, a single user in any category can change performance characteristics within a short time.

Within User Groups. When designers and users belonged to the same organization, they knew each other. The designer knew the users' characteristics. Now, even when users are known prior to the design of a system, many users eventually leave the specific applications arena and move to another. Some users leave the firm. Some are promoted to other levels of the firm. The places of these departing users are filled with new users who are not familiar with the nuances and history of the applications system.

It is ironic (but necessary) that so much emphasis is placed on early and constant user participation during the design process. Within two years after implementation of the new system, the cast of system users will have so changed that few who participated in the design remain on the scene.

Between User Groups. Users constantly migrate from one user category to another. This migration follows the pattern shown in Figure 14–9 and can be described as follows:

1. The novice user provided with model training becomes an intermediate user. The line between these two types of users slopes downward because it is difficult to use an applications system frequently without learning something about the application itself.

2. Typically, a clerk can execute adequately 70 to 80 percent of an applications system's capabilities without being totally knowledgeable of the application. The remaining capabilities require considerable applications expertise. The intermediate user who develops that expertise becomes an experienced user.

3. Experienced users who infrequently run the model move to casual, or rusty, user status. While there are many permutations of this path, perhaps the most important is that of promotion.

4. Casual users periodically refamiliarize themselves with an applications system. This transition path is difficult for the systems designer to handle because, during retraining, the designer first must treat the casual user as a novice. Then, after a relatively short warm-up period, the designer must treat the casual user as an experienced user.

FIGURE 14–9   User Migration between Categories

Reprinted by permission from M. Martin, "The Human Connection in Systems Design: User Categories," *Journal of Systems Management* 37(October 1986):10–14.

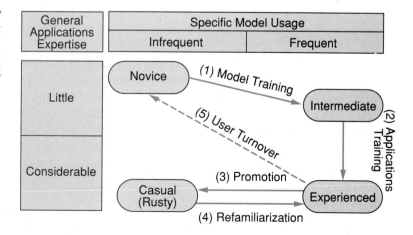

5. As experienced users become casual users or leave the applications area, user vacancies occur. Such vacancies often are filled by novice users who require both systems and applications training. The rate at which experienced users are replaced by novice users is referred to as **turnover rate.**

Within User Categories. The preceding types of user migration are difficult for the business systems designer to plan for. Perhaps even more difficult to predict are variations of individual users within any particular category of expertise. Such within-category variations can occur for several reasons. The most common are warm-up time, fatigue, boredom, environmental conditions, and extraneous events.

- *Warm-up*. Humans require time to ease up to optimal production rates. These warm-up periods generally occur at the beginning of a workday, after a lunch break, and after any other extended time when operation is disrupted (for example, an operator leaves the VDT to distribute reports).
- *Fatigue*. After time, fatigue erodes performance. Tasks such as data entry become counter-productive. For example, a common practice is to switch data entry operators to nonkeyboard tasks such as report distribution after five or six hours.
- *Boredom*. Repetitive activities cause humans to lose concentration—to begin dwelling on other, more exciting activities. Assignment of different tasks reduces risks of boredom, but it entails a new warm-up period for each newly assigned task.
- *Environmental Conditions*. Variance in environmental factors such as lighting, heat, and humidity affect human performance. Variations in noise levels are particularly disruptive.
- *Extraneous Events*. Individual performance deteriorates through unplanned, unpredictable happenings such as physical injury, an argument with one's spouse, or other traumatic events.

These within-category variations coupled with between-category transitions make any particular user a moving design target. It is difficult to program a fixed-factor model effective for all people and for all places. What is needed is a user interface that adapts to users as they change.

Adapting to Changing Users

It is feasible to construct business systems with a user interface that treats broad classes of users differently. For example, **adaptive models** might treat differently users in categories of novice, experienced, and casual.

Figure 14–10 shows the conceptual structure of an adaptive computer model. The numbers of the figure correspond with the numbers of the paragraphs that follow. The structure includes:

1. A **triggering question** or menu is posed to the user. The question differentiates among different degrees of applications knowledge, specific model experience, and even computer knowledge.

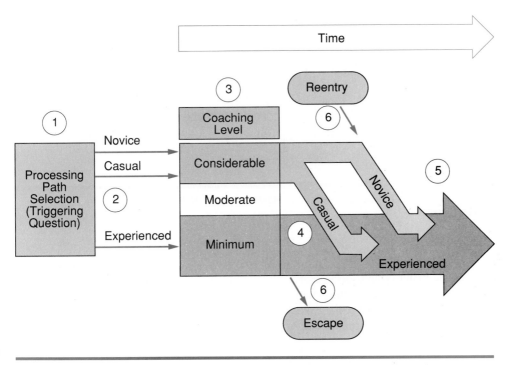

FIGURE 14—10 **Adaptive Model Structure**

Reprinted by permission from M. Martin, "The Human Connection in Systems Design: Adaptive Models," *Journal of Systems Management* 37(October 1986):26.

2. The triggering question differentiates among user categories of novice, experienced, and casual. (The category of intermediate user has been subsumed within the experienced category for the sake of simplicity.) A sample triggering question is shown in Figure 14–11. Sometimes the triggering question is replaced by a user profile record that resides on disk. This record automatically assigns the user path as well as other user-tailored features (Figure 14–12).

3. Alternative processing paths are established for different levels and are segregated by use of programmed coaching techniques such as automatic help functions, warnings, highlighting, and default values.

4. The casual (rusty) user begins with the processing path that involves a considerable amount of coaching. At some point in time, when this user is sufficiently warmed up, the level of coaching is decreased. The casual user eventually operates in the experienced processing path.

5. Novice users are also initially assigned to the processing path with considerable coaching. After a certain learning period, the level of coaching begins to be reduced and the novice user operates in the experienced track.

```
        Which of the following describes
your present level of computer knowledge?

1. I know a lot.
2. I know something about computers.
3. I know nothing about computers.
4. Please discontinue this session.

   Which option do you choose?
```

```
ID                        657323-5
NAME                      Merle P. Martin
STATUS                    Novice
COLOR PREFERENCES:        (1) RED ON YELLOW
                          (2) BLACK ON WHITE
INTENSITY:                MEDIUM
SYMMETRY:                 (HORIZONTAL) NORMAL
                          (VERTICAL) BOTTOM
```

FIGURE 14–11   **Triggering Question to Determine Computer Knowledge**

FIGURE 14–12   **User Profile Record (on Disk)**

6. Users may find themselves in a processing path too difficult for effective performance. Programmed progression of the user has gone too fast. This can occur for two reasons. First, the user may have moved too quickly from the novice to the experienced processing path. Second, the user may be experiencing one of the within-category variations described earlier—perhaps the user has a head cold.

An adaptive model has an escape mechanism that allows users to reenter the model at a point with increased coaching. Figure 14–13 shows such an escape mechanism.

HUMAN FACTORS DESIGN PRINCIPLES

Shneiderman (1987) has suggested eight "golden rules" for designing screens for human usability. The following nine principles are an enrichment of Shneiderman's list.

Keep It Simple. Recall from Chapter 2 that there is a critical limit to the size of short-term memory. When new chunks are received before old chunks are learned, the old chunks quickly are forgotten. Modularize complex tasks to the level where each task is simple and distinguishable from other tasks.

FIGURE 14–13   **Menu for Escape Mechanism**

```
Select one of the following options
 for changing the current pace of
       this computer program.

1. The pace is too fast.
2. The pace is too slow.
3. The pace is just right.
4. Return to main menu.
5. Discontinue this session.
   Which option do you choose?
```

AN EXAMPLE OF CLOSURE

This author had a problem compiling COBOL programs on a badly overloaded mini-computer. Compilation took a horrendously long time; however, compilation had been broken down into six complete subtasks. After each subtask was completed, a message would appear on the screen, "Phase X completed." Waiting became more tolerable because I could mark the compiler's progress toward its compilation goal. I could also leave the room, return with my cup of coffee, and see immediately on the screen where I was in the compilation process.

Be Consistent. Humans seek comfort zones and tolerate only limited (controlled) surprise. Consistency is particularly important for novice user learning.

Design Tasks for Closure. After breaking tasks into their smallest modules, provide feedback to users so they know when they have completed a task. In this way, users can use scarce short-term memory capacity to concentrate on the next task at hand.

Support Internal Locus of Control. Make users feel that *they* are in control of the user interface, not the computer or applications programmer. For example, avoid frequent warnings, patronizing messages, and use of the pronouns we or I in system response messages.

Provide User Shortcuts. The process of learning requires slow repetition. Once a user learns material, however, repetition is counterproductive to throughput goals. Provide experienced users with shortcut methods that bypass tactics suited to new users. Command language is an excellent means to implement shortcuts; so is direct screen access.

Handle Errors Civilly. Do not embarrass users. Do not make them guess what went wrong. Error messages should be clear, short, and positive. Remember, if you do not allow users to handle errors quickly, throughput suffers. Uncivilized error handling also inhibits learning.

Allow Easy Reversal of Actions. Ability to make changes relieves anxiety and encourages exploration. Exploration is particularly important for casual (rusty) users trying to reestablish long-term memory retrieval paths. Exploration is enhanced when one knows that errors are not cast in stone, that they can be "undone."

Use Surprise Effectively. Avoid surprise unless it is needed to distract a user from a consistent, but dangerous, pattern. Surprise is only surprise when it occurs infrequently. The following screen techniques are distracting; avoid them unless the situa-

Human Factors Principles	Organizational Goals						
	Time to Learn	Speed	Acceptable Error Rate	Efficiency	Reliability	User Satisfaction	Effectiveness
Keep It Simple.	X					X	X
Be Consistent.	X				X	X	X
Design for Closure.	X					X	X
Support Internal Locus of Control.						X	X
Provide User Shortcuts.		X		X		X	X
Handle Errors Civilly.			X			X	X
Allow Easy Reversal of Actions.	X	X	X	X		X	X
Use Surprise Effectively.				X	X	X	X
Do Not Lose the User.	X	X			X	X	X

Source: Adapted from Ben Shneiderman, *Designing the User Interface* (Reading Mass: Addison-Wesley, 1987).

FIGURE 14–14   Relationship of Human Factors Principles to Organizational Goals

Adapted from Ben Shneiderman, *Designing the User Interface* (Reading, Mass.: Addison-Wesley, 1987).

tion presents potentially disastrous results: highlighting, input verification, flashing messages, and auditory messages such as bells.

Do Not Lose the User. Long menu paths may be necessary to reduce clutter for any one screen. Often, however, such long paths cause users to become disoriented. Users should always know where they are and where they have been. Remember the "You Are Here" maps you've seen in large public places such as shopping malls? Use that concept when designing menu paths. Mall-like maps also can be programmed to be a part of Help functions.

These golden rules relate closely to organization computing goals (Figure 14–14).

HUMAN FACTORS DESIGN TECHNIQUES

The preceding human factors principles can be translated into design techniques that are programmable. Here is a checklist of tactics that implement the nine principles:

1. Keep it simple.
   - Simple screen displays
   - Minimal use of windows
   - Mnemonic coding (that is, codes that resemble what they represent—the letter *F* for female)
   - Hierarchy charts for task decomposition
2. Be consistent.
   - Same terminology throughout all screens
   - Similar screen formats

- Standard escape routes
- Consistent processing times (particularly important for novice users)
3. Design tasks for closure.
   - Modularity
   - Goal feedback ("Task successfully completed")
   - Current status feedback ("Now sorting")
   - Performance statistics (e.g., error rates and patterns)
4. Support internal locus of control.
   - Minimum number of warnings
   - No patronizing messages
   - Avoidance of pronouns *we* and *I*
   - User choices on coaching level (adaptive models)
5. Provide user shortcuts.
   - Command language alternatives
   - Function key alternatives
   - Shortened response times for experienced users
   - Direct screen access
6. Handle errors civilly.
   - Polite error messages
   - Specific messages suggesting cause of errors
   - Help functions providing detailed assistance when requested
7. Allow easy reversal of actions.
   - Erase commands
   - Escape menus
   - Allowance for reversal of a single action, a data entry, or a complete group of actions or transactions
   - Paging back to previous screens or entry fields
8. Use surprise effectively.
   - Minimal highlighting
   - Minimal input verification
   - Few flashing and auditory messages
   - Departures from consistency only when situation is threatening to performance
9. Do not lose the user.
   - Menu labels
   - Graphic directories of menu path in help function
   - Menus restricted to three levels (main menu to intermediate menu to function screen)

SUMMARY

Interactive systems have psychological characteristics different from batch systems. These include (1) operating during organizational prime-time, (2) including a multi-user environment, (3) wider breadth of user experience, and (4) emphasis on analyst communication skills. Interactive systems have a common structure that runs sequentially from greeting screen, to password screen, to main menu, to intermediate menus, to function screens. This sequence is supported by help screens and escape options.

Three interactive tactics should be used regardless of the type of interactive screen being designed. First, allow users to escape easily and quickly from any point in the transaction process. Second, keep the user from getting lost. Third, ease transaction throughput.

The four types of screen dialogue modes are form-filling, inquiry, command language, and menus. This chapter provides detailed guidance on design of menus and form-filling screens. Considerations common to both these screen types include (1) highlighting, (2) color, (3) information density, (4) message content, (5) symmetry, (6) timing, (7) help functions, and (8) input verification.

Business systems users are always in the process of change; therefore, predicting usage patterns is difficult. The cast of systems users changes. Some users leave the setting. Others remain but progress from the category of novice to the categories of intermediate and then experienced. Experienced users become rusty, or casual, users. Even within any given category, user performance varies because of warm-up, fatigue, boredom, environmental conditions, and extraneous factors.

One evolving tactic to counter user variability is the adaptive model. This model tests users to determine the category to which they belong, assigns users to separate processing paths dedicated to different levels of expertise, and moves users to other categories at user request or when sufficient training or warm-up is determined to have taken place.

This chapter concluded with nine principles of screen design. These principles were then translated into specific, programmable screen techniques.

CONCEPTS LEARNED

- Different characteristics associated with interactive systems
- Structure of interactive systems
- Four dialogue modes
- How to construct interactive menus
- How to construct form-filling screens
- Considerations common to all interactive screens
- Design of adaptive interactive models
- Nine human factors design principles
- Human factors design techniques

KEY TERMS

adaptive model
autoterminate
command language
cueing
default value
direct screen access
escape option
form-filling screen

function screen
greeting screen
help screen
highlighting
information density
input verification
inquiry mode
interactive systems

intermediate menu
internal locus of control
local screen density
main menu
menu
on-line
password screen
pop-up window

pull-down menu
real-time update
simultaneous update
split screen
total screen density
triggering question
turnover rate
user response time

REVIEW QUESTIONS

1. Describe four primary differences between an interactive and batch environment.

2. What is the seven-step path that marks the structure of an interactive system?

3. What is the difference between an intermediate menu and a function screen?

4. What is the difference between inquiry and command language screen dialogue modes?

5. Describe four directions for designing form-filling screens.

6. What is a default value?

7. Describe the eight parts of an interactive screen menu.

8. When should highlighting be used?

9. What are potential problems with overuse of color?

10. Why is information density important?

11. List six rules for designing message content.

12. Why is symmetry important to screen design?

13. What is input verification?

14. Why are adaptive models useful?

15. Describe four "Within User" sources of variation.

16. Describe the elements of an adaptive model.

17. How can you design interactive tasks for closure?

18. What is internal locus of control?

19. What are some distracting uses of surprise?

20. How can you keep from losing the interactive user?

21. What are some common user shortcuts?

CRITICAL THINKING OPPORTUNITIES

1. Draw a diagram to describe the organization of this chapter.

2. Compare and contrast the four types of interactive screen modes.

3. Select a software package that performs an application such as file management. Select from that package a menu, form-filling screen, help menu, and escape function. Critically evaluate these functions based on what you have learned in this chapter.

4. You have been asked to design an interactive information system for your professor to keep track of students, exam and homework scores, and grades. Use your course syllabus and knowledge of your class to design the following interactive screens.

a) Greeting screen

b) Password screen to allow only your program to access the system

c) Main menu

d) Function screen to allow initial student data including (but not restricted to) names, identification number, and class level

C A S E 14.1

GOODBYTE PIZZA: SCREEN DESIGN

SETTING

Linda Alvires' design team has to create the interactive screens for the new inventory system. The screens will service the system shown in Figure 14.1–1.

MENU MAP

The team creates the Menu Map shown in Figure 14.1–2. The items marked "Stubbed Outs" are screens that can be developed later.

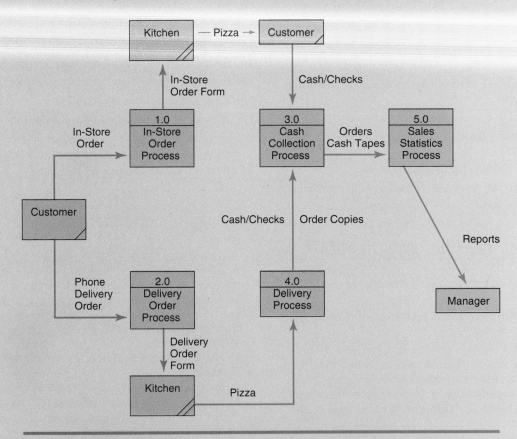

FIGURE 14.1–1   **Data Flow Diagram of Goodbyte Pizza Company Order Process**

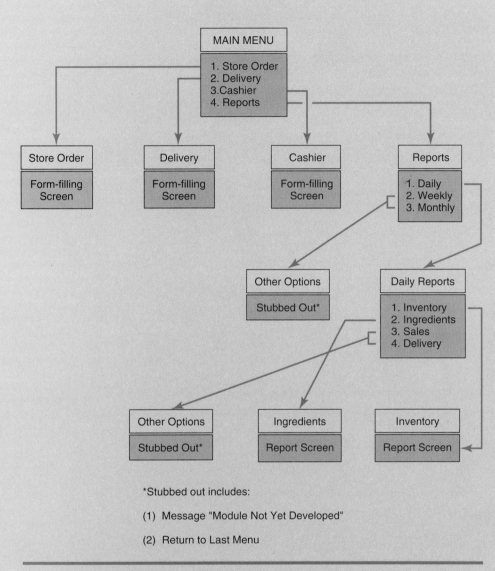

MAIN MENU

1. Store Order
2. Delivery
3. Cashier
4. Reports

Store Order

Form-filling Screen

Delivery

Form-filling Screen

Cashier

Form-filling Screen

Reports

1. Daily
2. Weekly
3. Monthly

Other Options

Stubbed Out*

Daily Reports

1. Inventory
2. Ingredients
3. Sales
4. Delivery

Other Options

Stubbed Out*

Ingredients

Report Screen

Inventory

Report Screen

*Stubbed out includes:

(1) Message "Module Not Yet Developed"

(2) Return to Last Menu

FIGURE 14.1–2   **Menu Map**

DATA DICTIONARY ENTRIES

Figures 14.1–3, 14.1–4, and 14.1–5 show Data Dictionary entries for three of the screens to be designed.

EXERCISE

Construct interactive screen layouts for:

1. Main menu
2. Store Order screen
3. Delivery screen
4. Cashier screen

```
Label:          Store Order Screen

Entry Type:     Data Structure

Description:    Form-filling Interactive Screen Used to Post In-Store
                Customer Orders

Alias:

Composition:    Order-Number + Date + Time +
                Customer-First-Name +
                1 (Order-Item) 5
                  = Quantity +
                    Description
```

FIGURE 14.1–3 **Store Order Screen**

```
Label:          Delivery Order Screen

Entry Type:     Data Structure
Description:    Form-filling Interactive Screen Used to Post In-Store
                Customer Orders

Alias:

Composition:    Order-Number + Date + Time +
                Customer-First-Name +
                1 (Order-Item) 5
                  = Quantity + Description
                + Phone-Number + Address +
                  Nearest-Cross-Street
```

FIGURE 14.1–4 **Delivery Order Screen**

```
Label:          Cashier Screen

Entry Type:     Data Structure

Description:    Form-filling Interactive Screen Used to Post Cashier
                Entries

Alias:

Composition:    Order-Number + Time +
                Customer-First-Name +
                1 (Order-Item) 5 =
                    Quantity + Description + Price
                + Total-Price + Delivery-Feet
                    Total-Due + Paid (Cash) (Check)
```

FIGURE 14.1–5   **Cashier Screen**

OBJECTIVES

In this chapter you will learn about:

WHAT: (Concepts) Designing information system files.

WHY: Files allow information to be stored for later use. Update of resource files
          is the primary function of most business information systems.

WHEN: Only after design of output and input can we accurately determine what
          needs to be stored.

WHO: Files are largely transparent to end-users; thus the systems analyst typ-
          ically designs files independently.

WHERE: Information systems department.

HOW: (Techniques) File space algorithm
                        File requirements document
                        File layout document
                        File relationship tables

OUTLINE

- Setting
- A Total Quality Approach
- A Structured Approach
- Database and Conventional Environments
- Reasons for Designing Files
- Record Structures
- Fixed-Length versus Variable-Length Records
- File Media Considerations
- File Access Methods
- Storage Requirements (File Space)
- File Retention and Recovery
- Designing Files for the Future
- File Design Tools
- Profile of a Poorly Designed File
- Human Aspects

DATA STORAGE DESIGN

The Sermon on the Mount is 2000 years old, and it's still relevant.

—INSTANT ANALYST, 1974

(on use of older technologies)

SETTING

At this point, the input and output for the business information system have been designed. It is rare, however, that what is input is immediately output. Data must be stored for future output. For example, customer order data entered today will be accumulated until the end of the month, when it will be used with other daily entries to produce monthly customer billings.

The form of data storage has two dimensions. The first is physical. Data may be stored in a steel file cabinet, on celluloid magnetic tape, or on rotating magnetic disk. This chapter briefly describes physical data storage media, but that is not the chapter's major thrust. The second dimension of data storage is logical—how data are organized in storage. This is the emphasis of the chapter. It is here that designers exercise most of their storage decisions. How should data be organized while they are being stored for future use?

This chapter describes design choices for each of these elements. Database design is described in more detail in the next chapter.

A TOTAL QUALITY APPROACH

Design of information systems files follows the same information system criteria used throughout this book.

1. *Relevancy:* How relevant is the stored information to future problem solving (decision making) opportunities? Is irrelevant data purged?
2. *Completeness:* Do files contain all information elements that will be needed?
3. *Correctness:* Can we depend upon the accuracy of file record fields?
4. *Security:* Are files accessible by only those people who have a legitimate need?
5. *Timeliness:* Are files updated in a timely manner?
6. *Economy:* All other things being equal, have we selected the least expensive file media and access method?
7. *Efficiency:* Have we optimized the ratios computed by dividing in turn items one through five above by item six (e.g., Correctness per Dollar)?
8. *Reliability:* Are the variances small for each of the above measures? Can we depend on constant performance for each of these measures?
9. *Usability:* Is it easy to update and retrieve from files?

A STRUCTURED APPROACH

In a structured environment, files are referred to as data stores. The levels of description are data flow diagram, data store specification, and data element specifications.

Data Flow Diagram. Figure 15–1 is a portion of a data flow diagram showing the purchase order store (file).

Data Store Specification. Figure 15–2 gives a specification for the purchase order data store.

Data Element Specification. Each of the fields in the data store specification is described in its own separate data element specification.

FIGURE 15–1   Partial Data Flow Diagram for Purchase Order Data Store

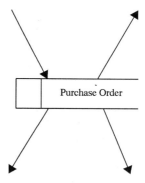

Purchase Order

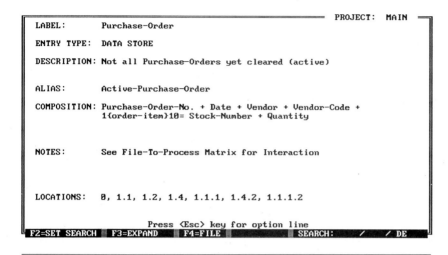

```
                                            PROJECT:  MAIN
  LABEL:        Purchase-Order

  ENTRY TYPE:   DATA STORE

  DESCRIPTION: Not all Purchase-Orders yet cleared (active)


  ALIAS:        Active-Purchase-Order

  COMPOSITION: Purchase-Order-No. + Date + Vendor + Vendor-Code +
               1{order-item}10= Stock-Number + Quantity



  NOTES:        See File-To-Process Matrix for Interaction




  LOCATIONS:    0, 1.1, 1.2, 1.4, 1.1.1, 1.4.2, 1.1.1.2


                     Press <Esc> key for option line
  F2=SET SEARCH   F3=EXPAND    F4=FILE           SEARCH:      /    / DE
```

FIGURE 15–2   Data Store (File) Specification for Purchase Order

DATABASE AND CONVENTIONAL ENVIRONMENTS

Not too many years ago, the topic of database management systems would be an afterthought in a textbook on systems analysis and design. Now, it not only commands a separate chapter (Chapter 16) but begins this chapter on data storage design. Database management systems have become an operational standard in the information field, particularly in the microcomputer realm.

A **database management system (DBMS)** is an organized collection of two or more resource files. Among other things, a DBMS reduces incidents of duplicate data fields. For example, in a non-DBMS environment, both a vendor file and an inventory file have a field containing a vendor code. Under a DBMS environment, that field would occur only once and would be used by receiving, purchasing, and inventory personnel.

A non-DBMS environment deals with conventional files. A **conventional file** is a data storage repository designed for a single business application. These are sometimes called "flat files," although we will see that this term is misleading. Hence, a vendor file would be used only by the purchasing department. The field vendor code would be contained in this and other independent resource files. Duplication is not a concern in a conventional file environment.

This chapter deals with conventional design. Why deal with conventional files, you might ask, if the DBMS is becoming a standard? There are two reasons. First, despite the rising popularity of the DBMS, many business firms also use conventional files. Second, most of the techniques and principles of conventional file design also apply to the design of database management systems. Design of a DBMS is typically done in a committee environment. Design of conventional files allows designers and end-users to make independent decisions about the structure of data storage.

REASONS FOR DESIGNING FILES

The need to design information systems files seems obvious. Still, a review of why files are required at all will be a reminder to limit files to proper data elements.

The underlying reason for the existence of any information system is production of information output—action documents and reports. That is why output is designed first, before imaginations are constrained by input and file limitations. There are three sources for information output. The first is input documents. For example, the information system may copy the order-date field from a customer order source document to the output customer invoice. Internal computer calculation is a second source of output information. Thus, the input fields of hours-worked and rate-of-pay are multiplied to create a new output field, gross-pay. In a different vein, by comparing today's-date-of-last-payment, an overdue statement can be generated on a customer invoice.

The third source of output information is stored data—the concern of this chapter. A system saves data in storage before they are used in output products. There are four reasons for storing data: generation of future output, historical reference, reduction of input keystrokes, and triggering of future actions.

Future Output. Systems often collect data over time to produce output products in the future. A W-2 form and a monthly activities report are two examples of such future products.

Historical Reference. Analysis of past data can lead to creation of future activities. A business information system stores historical data so decision makers can forecast future trends. For example, sales managers study customer demand for the past year to project future customer demand. Historical data are also valuable for determining patterns that require management intervention. For example, review of historical data on entry errors by type and operator may lead managers to focus their training efforts. Finally, historical data are essential for auditing the system.

Reduction of Keystrokes. Constant, lengthy data can be stored to avoid repeating entry at other times. For instance, operators enter a two-position product code instead of a twenty-character product description. The system uses the code to search a table for the right product description stored in memory and produces the description on output. Stored data reduce input keystrokes and thus lead to faster and more accurate output.

Triggering. Information systems store some data to trigger future management action. For example, a date-of-last-payment field on a customer file leads to follow-up (dunning) activity if that date is more than a certain number of days old. A reorder-point field leads to purchasing activity when the quantity of stock on hand falls below that reorder point.

These are common reasons why data are stored in files. Here is an interesting and practical exercise. Select a typical business record and judge if the fields it includes are justified by the reasons just discussed. By asking why the field is being stored, you will discover fields that need not be stored at all.

Given these reasons for storing data, systems designers must determine what fields to store in what records.

RECORD STRUCTURES

Business information is organized into a hierarchy. This hierarchy is changing, but it still dominates information systems. It begins with the basic character, proceeds to the field, then to the record, to the file, and finally to the database.

The **character** is the basic element of business information. It can be either numeric (used for computation), character (used for display and categorizing), or logical (either a condition is present or absent). An example of a logic field would be payment-overdue, which is set to Y if the customer payment is late and N if it is not.

One or more characters grouped together form a **field.** Field usage is either computational or display when described in a data element dictionary. Hence, thirty-five alphanumeric characters (not used for computation) can be grouped into an employee-name field. This field is used for display rather than computational purposes.

Fields are grouped into **records.** There are five types of business information records: master, detail, transaction, report, and table. Groups of related records are combined into a **file.** Thus, there will be a single employee record for each person working in a firm. When all employee records are grouped together, the new entity is an employee file.

A group of interrelated files is called a **database.** This chapter concentrates on design of individual information systems records which, when combined, become conventional information systems files.

Master Records

There is one **master record** for each resource item belonging to the firm. For example, there is one record for each of the firm's customers, vendors, and inventory items. Figure 15–3 shows the format of the master record. The master record contains several groupings.

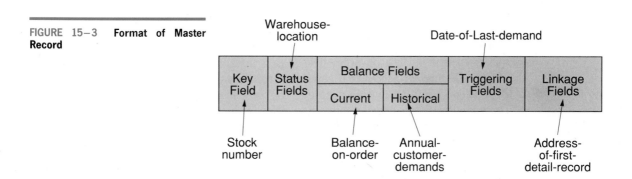

FIGURE 15–3 **Format of Master Record**

Key Field. The **key field** is the field by which different records are accessed for update of resource records. For example, the customer-number field is a key field in the customer record. Each transaction input to update this record includes customer-number so the correct record can be found and updated. Other examples of key fields are product-number, vendor-number, and purchase-order-number.

Status Fields. **Status fields** contain constant information identifying a resource item as different from others. Thus, item-description, warehouse-location, and unit-price are status fields that, as a combination, separate one inventory resource item from another.

Balance Fields. **Balance fields** are numeric fields reflecting current, future, or past availability of resource items. For inventory items, the fields might be called balance-on-hand, balance-on-order, and number-of-items-issued-during-current-year (past usage history for order quantity calculations).

Triggering Fields. **Triggering fields** initiate exception processing. These often are coded fields such as a code authorizing overtime paid to an employee. Sometimes, these are date fields triggering future time action (for example, date of follow-up on overdue balance notice).

Linkage Field. Often, one business record is linked to another; this is the case with master and detail records. **Linkage fields** contain addresses of where related records lie in storage. For example, the record for a particular inventory item may have a linkage field allowing access to another item. This other item may be used as a substitute when the first item is out of stock. Linkage fields are also used for record-access overflow conditions (discussed later in this chapter).

Detail Records

Master record balance fields contain totals. A common inventory record total is the balance-on-order at a future date. **Detail records** are explosions of master record balance fields (Figure 15–4). Here are two examples:

1. The master inventory record contains a balance-on-order field showing the total amount of an inventory item ordered from vendors. Upon receipt, the order will increase the balance-on-hand field. Separate detail records are set up for each separate vendor order. The quantity of each of the separate vendor orders adds to the total quantity in the balance-on-order field of the master inventory record.

2. The master accounts receivable record has a total-customer-balance-due field. In some accounts receivable systems, this field has many detail records. Each detail record reflects one specific customer order. Summation of the dollar amount for all detail records equals the total-balance-owed field on the master record.

The detail record is really a second dimension of the master record. Hence, the term "flat file," often used to describe conventional records, is not truly appropriate.

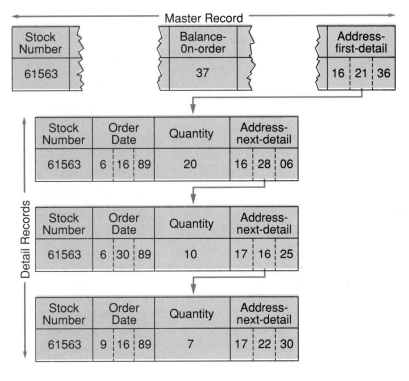

FIGURE 15–4   **Detail Records from Explosion of Master Record**

Transaction Records

As each input transaction is entered to update a resource record, the transaction is captured in the form of a **transaction record.** A collection of all such transaction records captured during a day or week is called a transaction file. The transaction record is an exact image of the transaction entered in the information system.

Report Records

A **report record** is written to disk for later retrieval by either VDT or line printer. One report record is equivalent to one report page.

Tables

A reference **table** allows access by many users and applications programs. A typical table is one containing freight rates (Figure 15–5). A reference table includes two elements. The first is a key field which allows search of the table to find the desired entry. Thus, the freight table is searched until the correct code in the freight-code field is found. The second segment contains fields to be retrieved from the table. For example, in Figure 15–5, once the correct freight code is found, other fields of that freight category (freight-rate and maximum-weight) are retrieved.

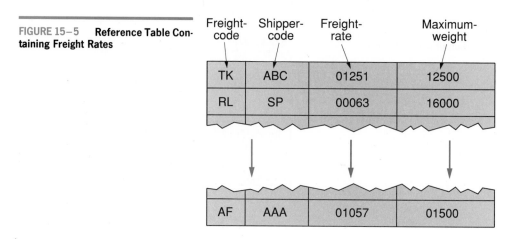

FIGURE 15–5   **Reference Table Containing Freight Rates**

Freight-code	Shipper-code	Freight-rate	Maximum-weight
TK	ABC	01251	12500
RL	SP	00063	16000

Freight-code	Shipper-code	Freight-rate	Maximum-weight
AF	AAA	01057	01500

FIXED-LENGTH VERSUS VARIABLE-LENGTH RECORDS

A final distinction concerning how to organize business information is whether fields are fixed or variable in length. In **fixed-length records,** all fields have the same length, regardless of the size of the data required for any particular resource item. Thus, you may set the last-name field for a customer record to twenty alphanumeric characters; that is the maximum size for the last name of any expected customer. You do this even though some of the customer names may be smaller.

Variable-length records have fields tailored to specific data items. The last-name field for the customer named Jones is five characters, while that for the customer named Christofeson is twelve characters. Variable-length records require less storage space than fixed-length records. However, they are more difficult to process than fixed-length records. This is so because the programmer cannot treat each record in a repetitive manner; rather, each record must be tested for its unique size.

Variable-length records also play a common role in describing records with a varying number of repeating items. For example, an inventory record has a field for prior months' usage. There are multiple subfields representing the item's usage for each of the months in the past. Some inventory items may have a fifty-month history; newer items may have only a two-month history. Accordingly, the number of subfields varies. Hence, the total size of the USAGE field will vary depending on the particular inventory item.

The systems designer must design a variety of records for business information systems. Implicit in design is selection of appropriate physical file media to hold these records.

FILE MEDIA CONSIDERATIONS

You probably have studied the specifics of data storage hardware media in a prerequisite course. A brief discussion is presented here for continuity and to emphasize functional rather than mechanical aspects. The file storage media reviewed next are magnetic disk, magnetic tape, microcomputer-oriented media, and other (future) media.

Magnetic Disk

Magnetic disk is the prevalent medium used today for data storage on mainframe computers. The hardware device consists of thin metal disks with read/write heads for each side of each disk, concentric circles around each disk side (tracks), and sectors contained within each track. Each sector contains a resource record that is accessed, read, changed, and rewritten to the same address. Resource records are accessed through an address such as the following one:

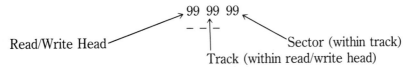

Magnetic disk has become the default medium for mainframe computer files. For several reasons, other primary memory media are compared to magnetic disk:

- Magnetic disk provides faster record access than the magnetic tape medium.
- Magnetic disk allows both sequential and random access to records.
- Magnetic disk contains more storage capacity at a lower cost than does prime memory.

Magnetic Tape

Magnetic tape is slower than magnetic disk. Also, since the costs of disk memory have steadily decreased, the initial cost advantage of magnetic tape has eroded. So the use of magnetic tape has decreased; however, magnetic tape has not disappeared. Businesses still use magnetic tape extensively for three reasons. First, magnetic tape is still cheaper than magnetic disk, and in certain types of file access situations, it is as efficient as magnetic disk. Second, magnetic tape is an excellent augmentation to magnetic disk. Magnetic tape allows high-capacity, inexpensive storage of data that are not retrieved often. One example is historical data—it is not needed often but must be stored just in case. Third, as an off-line storage device, magnetic tape provides a safeguard against disasters or other adverse contingencies. For example, the state of Alaska requires computer installations to store copies of magnetic disk data at least ten miles from the computer site as a precaution against earthquake damage. Magnetic tape is an excellent medium for such off-site storage.

Microcomputer-Oriented Media

The counterparts of magnetic disk and magnetic tape for microcomputers are random-access memory (**RAM**) and floppy disks. Capacities of these microcomputer-oriented storage media are sometimes less than media for mainframe counterparts. However, designs of file structures and update procedures are similar. The

MULTIMEDIA SYSTEMS

Conventional information systems use data that are record based (use numbers and other alphanumeric characters). There are other forms of information such as text (for example, documentation), graphics, images (for example, photographs), sound, and video. Although these forms have been around in paper and film media for a long time, they have not always been accessible to computer-based systems. Current computer systems incorporate these other media into what are called multimedia systems.

Problems exist in the computerization of each of these forms. Text storage takes a lot of capacity and is difficult to organize for search and retrieval. The words by themselves do not convey enough meaning. Images—whether graphic, still, or video—present retrieval problems also. Images are not self-identifying; some human must view the contents and write a meaningful description of the images contained on the film. Images take up even more storage capacity than do text forms.

Multimedia systems are useful in paper-intensive situations, reporting and analysis applications, sales systems, training situations, and decision analysis. Three planning guidelines for multimedia systems are offered by *IS Analyzer:*

1. Avoid islands of automation (uncoordinated use).
2. Plan for sufficient band width (channel capacity).
3. Follow national standards for electronic mail, optical storage, and document interchange.

Source: "Multimedia Systems," *IS Analyzer* 25 (October 1987):1–16.

floppy disk is not restricted to microcomputers; it also can be found in some mainframe environments.

Other (Future) Media

Other file storage media are available now or will be available in the future. Two examples are mass storage systems and optical disks. As such media become less expensive, they will replace magnetic disk as the typical business file medium. However, the structure or methods of accessing business files will not change drastically. The hardware aspects of business files play only a minor role in the design of logical files. Regardless of the physical medium, systems designers select from alternative means for logically accessing the resource records stored.

FILE ACCESS METHODS

If an organization has a centralized database system, the procedures discussed in this part of the chapter will not be as important as they are in other systems. There are, however, still a large number of firms that are not totally in a database environment.

The choice of physical file medium restricts how records can be accessed in the file. For example, magnetic tape dictates that record access be done sequentially. For the most part, choice of access method does not depend on the physical file but on the information needs of users. The four methods of accessing resource records are sequential, relative, direct, and indexed. Before discussing each of these methods, some basic definitions are needed.

Access Characteristics

Six characteristics are important to a discussion of file design: activity rate (hit rate), record access time, storage areas, collision rate, record density, and hashing routine. Many of these characteristics are not applicable to sequential processing.

Activity rate, or **hit rate,** is the percentage of resource records updated during any transaction processing run. For example, if you update 15,000 of 50,000 resource records each time you process transactions, your hit rate is 15,000 divided by 50,000, or 30 percent. Hit rate is an important factor in determining the appropriate access method.

Record access time is the interval it takes to search for, find, and transfer resource records. Figure 15–6 shows that record access time has the following intervals:

- Seek time: Specific disk read/write head is selected and positioned over track containing record sought.
- Wait time: Read/write head waits on selected track until desired sector (resource record) rotates to the head.
- Transfer time: Accessed record is transferred from storage media disk to prime memory.

The type of **storage area** depends on the access method chosen. The **index storage area** holds the indexes required for access when the indexed method is being used. The **prime record area,** which is common to all access methods, holds the resource records. The **overflow storage area** is applicable to all but sequential-access methods. One criterion for selecting among access alternatives is the amount of storage required.

Collision rate is the percentage of occasions when more than one resource record is assigned the same address (slot) in storage. A collision requires all but one of the colliding records be placed in the record overflow area. When this happens, access time increases significantly.

Record density is the percentage of record space occupied by resource records. For example, if there is space for 100,000 records (sectors), and 23,000 records are spread throughout that space, record density is 23,000 divided by 100,000, or 23 percent.

Lastly, a **hashing routine** is a programmed mathematical operation that converts a transaction input field into a specific storage location where a resource record is placed and retrieved. This routine applies to relative and direct file access.

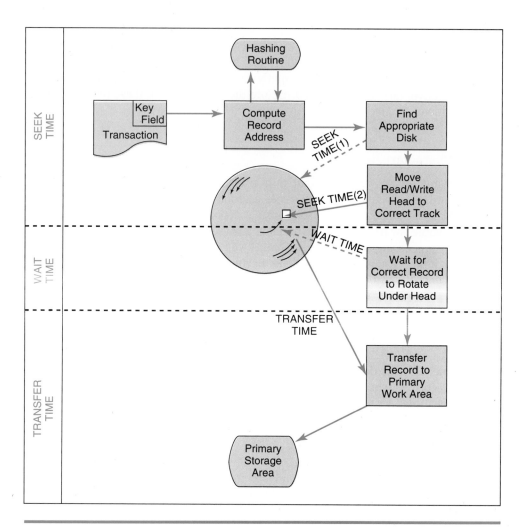

FIGURE 15-6   Record Access Time Elements

Sequential file access (Figure 15-7) processes each resource record one at a time in a given sequence. It is similar to using a phone book without the name indexes at the top of each page. Hence, to find the name Martin, you start on page 1. You then read each name on the page. You continue page by page in this manner until you find Martin.

Sequential file access is used when hit rates are high; that is, a large percentage of the records on the file is accessed on any single processing run. Two examples are payroll and file save applications. In a payroll application, most employee records must be accessed to produce payroll checks. The hit rate is high. In a file save operation, *all* resource records are copied to magnetic tape to cover the contingency that magnetic

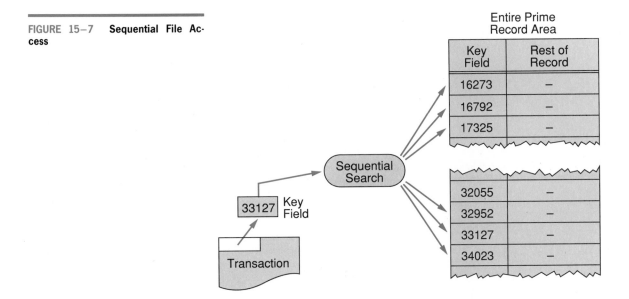

FIGURE 15–7   **Sequential File Access**

disk files are destroyed. The hit rate is 100 percent. Many times, however, an application's hit rate is low. Only a small percentage of stored records is accessed at one time. In such a situation, sequential file processing is inefficient, because the first record must be accessed before the second can be reached, the second record before the third, and so on until the desired record is found. When the hit rate is low, a preferable method is to access resource records directly.

The two methods for direct access are called **relative file access** and **direct file access.** These techniques (shown in Figure 15–8) access a resource record without

FIGURE 15–8   **Relative and Direct File Access**

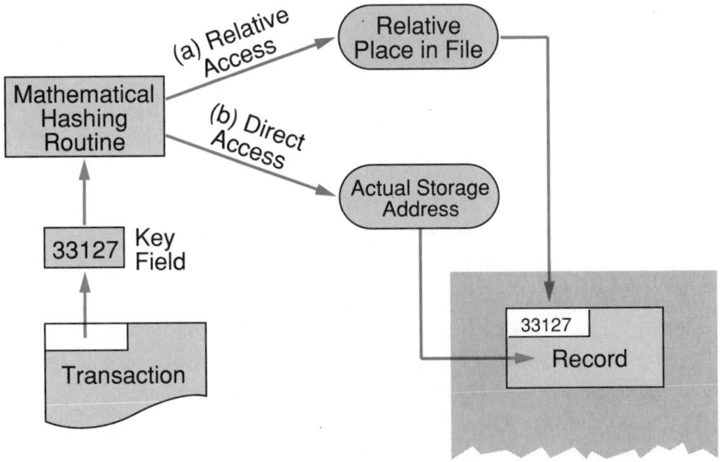

DIVIDE/REMAINDER HASHING ROUTINE

The following routine computes the relative slot number address of a resource record:

$$\text{Relative slot number} = 1 + \text{Remainder of } \frac{\text{Key Field}}{\text{Number record slots in file}}$$

Suppose we have an inventory file with 500 records. We need 500 record slots. Our key field is an inventory stock number which is *unique* for each inventory item in stock. For stock number 573259, the computation looks like this:

$$\text{Relative slot number} = 1 + \text{Remainder of } \frac{573259}{500} = 1 + 259 = 260$$

The record for stock number 573259 would be placed and could be found in relative slot 260. This computation occurs each time an inventory record needs to be accessed. The key field can be found on the transaction entered to update a particular inventory record.

---

having to process prior records in the file. Access is sometimes via a hashing routine. This routine uses an input transaction field to compute the place in memory where a particular record is located. The box "Divide/Remainder Hashing Routine" contains an example of how to convert input to record addresses.

Relative and direct access have several advantages over sequential access. First, for files with low or moderate hit rates, record access is faster. This is an important advantage for fast-changing files such as airline reservations and product inventories. Second, relative and direct access require only one file. Individual records are accessed, read into prime memory, changed, then rewritten to the same place in the file. Sequential file processing requires reading of an old master file and creation of a new master file. Two files are required, one for input and one for output.

Relative and direct access also have disadvantages in comparison to sequential access. First, storage is less efficient because storage density is lower. Second, there are overflow considerations in direct and relative access. The hashing routine may create a collision condition—two or more resource records having the same storage address; for example, the same remainder can occur in the division operation. Third, direct or relative access requires the magnetic disk medium, which is more expensive than the magnetic tape commonly used with sequential access.

Another commonly used access is indexed, often called **indexed sequential file access.** In IBM computer environments it is referred to as the **virtual storage access method (VSAM).** Indexed access (Figure 15–9) is a compromise between the advantages and disadvantages of sequential access and relative and direct access. In-

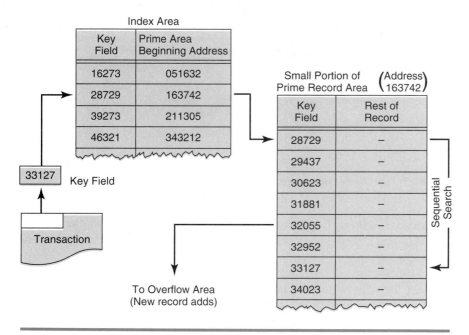

FIGURE 15–9   **Indexed Sequential File Access**

deed, one compelling aspect of indexed organization is that a file can be accessed directly (randomly) for one application, then sequentially for another. With the indexed access method, you can turn to a specific page in the phone book (for example, Mar), then sequentially step down that page until you find the name you are seeking (Martin). Indexed access enjoys advantages over sequential access. First, it is faster. You do not have to start at the very beginning of the file; instead, you can locate the start of a smaller area containing the record you are seeking. Second, indexed access allows you to use the same file for both reading and rewriting a resource record. Two files are required with sequential processing. Third, indexed files can be used to randomly access resource records. You need not enter update transactions in sequence as with sequential processing.

There also are disadvantages of using indexed rather than sequential access. First, indexes require additional storage area. Second, added resource records cannot be sequenced easily into the prime area; they must be placed in an overflow area. This increases record access time. Whenever there is a high rate of new resource records added to the file, the indexed file must be reorganized constantly (sorted sequentially with an adjustment to the indexes). Think of a phone book being reorganized frequently when there is a high rate of new subscribers.

The indexed access method also enjoys advantages over relative and direct access methods. First, file density is higher. Thus, storage is more efficient. Second, indexed files can be accessed *both* sequentially and randomly. This allows effective processing of

FIGURE 15–10 Choices among
Record Access Methods

Sequential	Indexed	Relative and Direct
High	Hit Rate	Low
Slow	Access Time	Fast
N/A	Collision Rate	High
High	Record Density	Low
Low	Cost	High

a range of applications varying from low to high hit rates. On the other hand, the indexed access method is much slower than the relative and direct access methods for applications with a low hit rate.

Figure 15–10 illustrates the choice between sequential, indexed, relative, and direct access for the different access characteristics discussed.

One final point is pertinent to file access methods. One method is not selected at the exclusion of all others. Magnetic disk space can be partitioned to allow allocation of different space for different access methods. For example, you want to access an inventory file on a real-time basis—as each transaction arrives. Obviously, such an update has a low hit rate (one record divided by total records). You can assign a portion of magnetic disk storage for the inventory file, which you then access either relatively or directly. Concurrently, you wish to process sequentially a payroll application once a month, when most of the records are updated (high hit rate). So, you assign a part of magnetic disk storage for a VSAM payroll file accessed sequentially.

Using a chart such as Figure 15–10, you can analyze each resource file and determine which access method is appropriate. Once you have selected the access method for each file, you can compute how much file space is required.

STORAGE REQUIREMENTS (FILE SPACE)

Storage requirements (file space) must be calculated for the following reasons:

- Required storage space needs to be matched to existing space to determine if the new system will require purchase of additional storage modules.
- The information systems department typically bills applications users for file space used. Such billing costs must be estimated before implementing the new system.
- Record sizes are matched with physical file media to limit record access time. For example, suppose you set the size of an inventory record at 246 characters. However, the physical hardware sector size is only 200 characters. Each record must occupy two hardware sectors. This will increase record access time, since each sector is read and written separately.

FIGURE   15–11   **Computing   File Space Requirements**

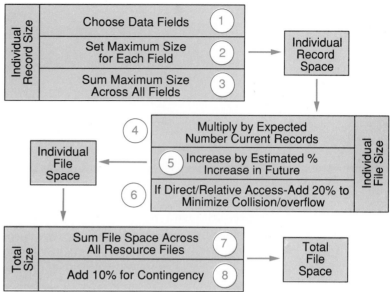

Computation of storage requirements (file space) includes the computation algorithm and techniques for reducing file requirements.

File Space Algorithm

A simple algorithm is available for computing file space. Figure 15–11 summarizes the following steps:

1. Determine which data fields will make up each individual resource record.
2. For each field in each resource record, set maximum size (that is, maximum number of characters).
3. Sum the maximum sizes across all fields to arrive at total individual record space.
4. Multiply the total resource record space by expected number of current records.
5. Increase the figure in step 4 for future increases in resource record activity.
6. If you use relative or direct access methods, increase the figure in step 5 above by another 20 percent to decrease the probabilities of collision and thus overflow conditions.
7. Sum results of step 6 across all resource files applicable to the system under design.
8. Increase the figure in step 7 by 10 percent for file processing overhead contingencies.

The box "Computing File Space" demonstrates this algorithm.

COMPUTING FILE SPACE

A purchase order has the following fields:

Field Name	Maximum Field Size
Purchase-order-number	6
Vendor-code	3
Order-quantity	5
Order-date	6
Total	20

So the total record space is twenty characters. A maximum of 750 outstanding purchase orders are expected. (Once material is received, the purchase order record is purged from the file.) Computation of file space is as follows:

Total record space:		20
× Maximum expected records:		750
= Required record space:	=	15,000
× 15 percent increase in future:	=	17,250
× 20 percent for relative file access:	=	20,700

Assume this is the only file. Add a 10 percent contingency factor. The total file space requirements are 20,700 + 2,070 or 22,770 characters.

Reducing File Requirements

The algorithm just described is a first-attempt method for computing optimal, or desired, file space. Often, computed space exceeds physical or logical design requirements. In such cases, a choice must be made to delete storage fields, reduce field storage requirements, or to do both. There are three techniques for reducing field storage requirements.

Packed Fields. Numeric fields can be stored in a packed, or binary format, rather than in numeric character format. This reduces storage space and speeds internal program calculations. However, all such packed fields have to be converted to character (display) format before printing output reports or action documents.

Exponential Smoothing. Historical quantity fields are usurpers of record space. For example, a primary triggering field in an inventory control system is economic-order-quantity (EOQ). This field requires an annual summation of customer demands for each stocked inventory item. There are twelve fields of data, one for each month. Assume each field is five characters long. The EOQ requirement dictates use of sixty (5 × 12) or more characters of record space.

USE OF EXPONENTIAL SMOOTHING TO REDUCE STORAGE SPACE

The exponential smoothing formula is:

New smoothed value = a × Current value + [(1 − a) × Old smoothed value]

where a = the smoothing constant between the values of 0 and 1.0,
Current value = latest input value for variable being smoothed, and
Old smoothed value = New smoothed value computed during last processing run.

Now, make these assumptions:

- This month's customer demands for inventory item 67923 is 11,233.
- Last month's computed new smoothed value was 9,763.
- The smoothing constant is 0.15. This means that this month's demand is weighted by 15 percent and last month's new smoothed value by 85 percent.

Calculate the formula with assumptions. The new smoothed value for this month equals:

$$(0.15 \times 11.233) + [(1 - 0.15) \times 9,763]$$

or $$1684.95 + 8298.55$$

or $$9983.50 \text{ rounded to } 9984.$$

This new smoothed value will become the old smoothed value next month.

The storage requirement for customer demands is five characters for the old smoothed value and five characters for the current month's customer demands. This sums to ten record characters. Storing twelve months' worth of customer demand data would take sixty characters of record space.

Exponential smoothing (see the box "Use of Exponential Smoothing to Reduce Storage Space") is a statistical technique that requires storage of only one smoothed demand field and smoothing constant. This is about a ten to one reduction in storage space.

Prioritizing. In one military information system, generals argued over the adding of new fields to an inventory record. The situation required that all fields in that record be ranked according to operational needs. The lower-ranked fields fell out of competition for storage in this situation of tight record space. Prioritizing requires an organizational decision about who prioritizes.

We have reached a critical point in designing business information systems files. We have determined record composition, access method, and file size. We have, it seems, an ideal file design. But there are two special considerations that bring "ideal" file design into a design that fits the real world of information processing: file retention and recovery, and design of files for the future.

FILE RETENTION AND RECOVERY

The subject of file retention and recovery may not seem to have much to do with *design* of business information systems files. Instead, the topic seems more germane to *maintenance* of files after design. This is a popular misconception. Considerations of file retention and recovery actually increase a design's scope. **File retention** is the separation of active and inactive records. **File recovery** is the contingency procedure to reestablish resource files destroyed or otherwise made ineffective.

File Retention

Resource records are classified as active or inactive. An **active record** is a record that has had a transaction update activity within a specified time. An **inactive record** is a record that has not had update activity within a specified time. Mixing of inactive and active resource records in the same file causes several problems:

- Inactive records use scarce space at the expense of active records.
- For sequential and indexed files, search and update routines must step through inactive records to find active records. This increases record access time.
- File save procedures (discussed later in this chapter) take longer, since there are more records to be saved.

Most information systems contain procedures to move inactive records to a separate history file. In such procedures, the time definition of what is an inactive record is critical. If the established time is too long (e.g., three years), the active file is cluttered with inactive records. If the cutoff time is too short (e.g., six months), a sizable proportion of inactive records will show new activity. These records will have to be moved back from the history file to the active file.

Select a cutoff date that yields a low probability that inactive records will again become active. Such a date might be, for instance, one year. In this case, when a resource record has shown no update activity for one year, move it to the history file.

File Recovery

If a business information resource file is destroyed or damaged, business will halt, or at least limp. If there are file recovery procedures, files can be restored quickly with minimum disruption of business activities. Files can be damaged or destroyed through earthquakes or fire, operator or programmer errors, and sabotage.

Information systems contingency planning calls for the following steps (shown graphically in Figure 15–12):

1. Periodically, copy the entire contents of the resource file to magnetic tape.

FIGURE 15–12   **File Recovery Process**

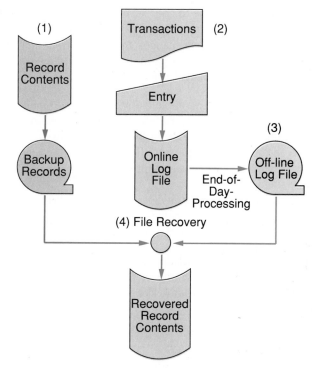

(4) File Recovery

2. During daily transaction processing, capture the images of each transaction entered on a **log file** maintained on magnetic disk. A log file contains all transactions entered to a computer during a working day.
3. During end-of-day processing, copy the on-line disk log file to off-line magnetic tape.
4. If the resource disk file is subsequently damaged, activate these file recovery procedures:
   ■ Copy to the new magnetic disk file the last-copied contents of the file (the magnetic tape created in step 1).
   ■ Sequentially update the recreated resource file from the magnetic tape log files produced in step 3.

   File recovery often is the responsibility of operations management. Nevertheless, it is part of a design because (1) users view the absence of an effective recovery system as a design failure, (2) the format of recovery files is a design issue, and (3) the format of the log file is a source of performance statistics required for quality measurement systems (described in Chapter 21).

DESIGNING FILES FOR THE FUTURE

Once a file design is in place, major changes to that design create havoc in day-to-day operations. All input and output documents using that file, and all programs controlling access and updates to the file, must be changed. Major changes to information systems files are a shock to orderly operation of a high-volume transaction throughput system.

Sometimes such changes cannot be avoided. Thus, it is best to prepare for them by designing files with an eye to the future. Follow these three tactics when designing files to ease future change:

1. Be sure there is ample file space to accommodate future increases in the number of resource records. Be aware of current record and transaction volumes and of increases forecast during the expected life of the new information system.
2. Extend record space to the end of the physical section, even if the natural record is shorter. This allows extra space for expansion of current fields and addition of new fields.
3. Include triggering fields for future use. Triggering fields most commonly added after systems implementation are date field (for example, date of last event), status code (for example, security code), and comment field.

Design of information systems files for the future goes beyond a list of tactics. Future design is a frame of mind that allows designers to visualize continually what resource files might look like several years from now.

FILE DESIGN TOOLS

Commonly used file design tools are the file requirements document, file layout document, and relationship table. These augment the Data Store Specification described earlier in this chapter.

File Requirements Document. The **file requirements document** (Figure 15–13) describes (1) fields included in each record, (2) how many records are in the file, including expected growth, (3) sequence of fields in the record, (4) size and format of each field, (5) record access method, (6) record and file size, and (7) relationship with other records and files. The document not only aids in the design of resource files, but it is also excellent file documentation.

File Layout Document. The **file layout document** (Figure 15–14) is a graphic complement to the file requirements document. It is an excellent means of communication between the designer and the programmer responsible for physical construction of the file.

Relationship Tables. Designers commonly construct tables showing the relationship of files to other entities such as input or output documents. There are three common types of **relationship tables:**

1. Input to file (Figure 15–15)
2. Output to file (Figure 15–16)
3. Data element to file (Figure 15–17)

Relationship tables allow designers, and later maintenance programmers, to determine the impact of a design change. For example, any format changes (for example, zip code expansion) for a data element can be traced to the files including that data element.

Relationship tables are amenable to automated production. For instance, a computer could search all files and list record fields. This would produce the data-element-to-file table. It would also produce a list of data element dictionary items not included in any file. These items could then be dropped from the system.

FILE NAME: _PURCHASE ORDER_   FILE NO. _P3_

DESCRIPTION: _All Active Purchase Orders_
DEVICE TYPE: _Disk_   ORGANIZATION: _VSAM_
RECORD SIZE: _283_   AVERAGE VOLUME: _1,250_
PEAK VOLUME: _2,000_   RECORD -KEY: _VENDOR-CODE_
RETENTION: _MOVE TO INACTIVE FILE ONE MONTH AFTER INACTIVE_
BACKUP: _WEEKLY, MONTHLY, AND YEAR-END_

FIELDS: (Continue on additional sheet if necessary)

#	Name	Picture
1.	DATE	X(06)
2.	VENDOR-CODE	9(05)
3.	VENDOR-NAME	X(20)
4.		
9.		
10.	TOTAL-PRICE	9(5)V99

ACCESSED BY:

PROGRAMS	UPDATE	PRIORITY
P1.3.1.1	YES	2
P1.3.1.2	NO	5

FIGURE 15–13   **File Requirements Document**

RECORD LAYOUT CHART FOR INVENTORY FILE DATE 12/07/90

Field Name	STOCK-NUMBER	NOMEN-CLATURE	UNIT ISSUE	STOCK-CODE	WAREHOUSE LOCATION	SECURITY CODE
Characteristics*	X (8)	X (20)	X (2)	XXX	X (6)	X
Position	1–8	9–28	29–30	31–33	34–39	40

Field name	VENDOR CODE	BALANCE-ON-HAND	BALANCE-ON-ORDER	BALANCE-COMMITTED	MONTHLY DEMANDS	ANNUAL DEMANDS
Characteristics	X (8)	X (20)	X (2)	XXX	X (6)	9 (6)
Position	41–43	44–48	49–54	55–60	61–66	67–72

Field name	DATE LAST DEMAND	DATE LAST ORDER	REORDER PRINT	REORDER QUANTITY	ADDRESS FIRST DETAIL	OVERFLOW ADDRESS
Characteristics	9 (6)	9 (6)	9 (6)	9 (6)	9 (6)	9 (6)
Position	73–78	79–84	85–90	91–96	97–102	103–108

*COBOL Picture

FIGURE 15–14 **File Layout Document**

FIGURE 15–15 **Input-to-File Table**

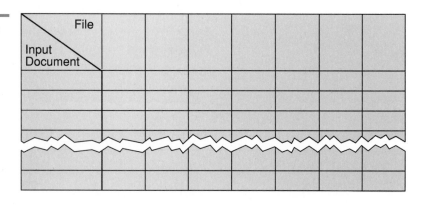

FIGURE 15–16   **Output-to-File Table**

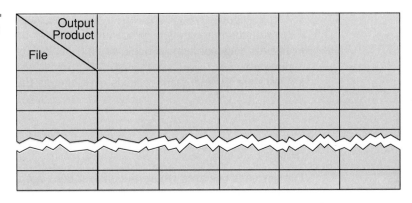

FIGURE 15–17   **Data-Element-to-File Table**

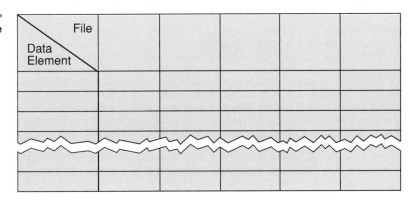

PROFILE OF A POORLY DESIGNED FILE

A review of a poorly designed file will help fix the principles of effective file design and serve as a checklist for testing current files. A poorly designed file has at least the following characteristics:

- It uses a file access method not chosen by assessment of hit rate, the percentage of new records added, collision rates, or hashing routine assumptions.
- There is no room for future record or file expansion.
- No triggering fields are available for exception management.
- Space is taken for historical data even though record space is scarce.

- Active and inactive records are in the same file.
- No retention or recovery procedures exist for the file.
- The file does not help reduce entry keystrokes by allowing code conversion to literal printouts.
- There are packed quantity fields even though there is no scarcity of record space.

HUMAN ASPECTS

File design is one area where the analyst does not require extensive coordination with end-users. This is because file formats generally are transparent to end-users. Files are a means for producing the ends of output reports and action documents. The analyst must be aware, however, that the designed file may be used later to produce reports tailored to specific end-users (inquiry-based systems). Therefore when designing files, the analyst must make such future retrieval as nontechnical, and as usable as possible, for end-users. Even with the relatively technical topic of designing information system files, the analyst must keep the human user in mind.

SUMMARY

Files are designed to generate future output, maintain historical references, reduce input keystrokes, and trigger future management actions. The structure of business information begins with the character and proceeds to fields, records, files, and databases. The five types of information systems records are master, detail, transaction, report, and table. Master records have the following fields:

- Key field, which is the basis for record access
- Status field, which specifies the uniqueness of each resource item
- Balance fields, which include past, current, and future resource quantities
- Triggering fields, which notify management of exceptional circumstances
- Linkage fields, which tie together different records such as one master to another or a master to a detail record

Detail records are explosions of master record fields. For example, there may be one detail record for each separate order to a vendor. Order quantities from individual detail records are summed to make the balance field of quantity-on-order in the master record. Transaction records are temporary collections of business transactions that later update master or detail records. Report records are an intermediary between the update process and output reports. Tables consist of data stored for access by several users or applications programs.

The most common physical media for business information files are magnetic disk, magnetic tape, microcomputer-oriented RAM and floppy disks. Technologies oriented toward the future are mass storage systems and optical disks.

Alternative methods for reaching (accessing) information systems records include sequential, relative, direct, and indexed. The most appropriate access method is chosen using performance indicators such as:

- *Hit rate:* Average percentage of master records updated during transaction processing runs
- *Record access time:* Interval it takes to search for, find, and transfer resource records
- *Storage areas:* Index area, prime record area, and overflow area
- *Collision rate:* Percentage of incidents where more than one resource record is assigned the same storage address
- *Record density:* Percentage of available record space actually occupied by resource records
- *Hashing routine:* A mathematical routine assigning records to a specified storage location while reducing collision rate and increasing record density.

Designers compute total file size so they can acquire sufficient file capacity. When there are constraints on record or file space, they can be relieved by packing fields in binary format, using exponential smoothing for historical balance fields, and prioritizing fields competing for space on resource records.

Two important aspects of file design are file retention and recovery. File retention is the separation of active resource records from inactive records. File recovery is a contingency procedure to reestablish destroyed or damaged resource files.

Major changes to operational files should be avoided. Nevertheless, sometimes changes must be made; so files should be designed with an eye to the future. Tactics recommended for file design that look toward the future include allowing space for an increase in the number of resource records, extending record space to the maximum physical size, and including space for more triggering fields.

Several tools are commonly used to design information systems files: file requirements document, file layout document, and relationship tables.

CONCEPTS LEARNED

- Structured approach to file design
- Database versus conventional file environments
- Why files are necessary
- Hierarchy of business information
- Five types of information systems records
- Structure of the master record
- Role of detail records

- Physical storage media commonly used
- Six criteria for selection among access methods
- Why and by what means file retention and file recovery are included in the file design stage of the SDLC
- Methods of designing files to accommodate future change
- Commonly used file design tools

KEY TERMS

active record
balance field
character
collision rate
conventional file
database
database management system (DBMS)
detail record
direct file access
exponential smoothing
field
file
file layout document
file recovery
file requirements document
file retention
fixed-length record
hashing routine
hit rate
inactive record
indexed sequential file access
index storage area
key field

linkage field
log file
magnetic disk
magnetic tape
master record
overflow storage area
packed field
prime record area
RAM
record
record access time
record density
relationship table
relative file access
report record
sequential file access
status field
storage area
table
transaction record
triggering field
variable-length record
virtual storage access method (VSAM)

REVIEW QUESTIONS

1. Why do we need to store business information?

2. How can input keystrokes be reduced through storage of data?

3. Explain the hierarchy of business information.

4. Describe the structure of a master record.

5. What are the differences and relationships between a master record and a detail record?

6. Describe two uses of master record triggering fields.

7. Describe the difference between fixed- and variable-length records.

8. What is the most common use of the magnetic tape medium?

9. What is the difference between hit rate and collision rate?

10. List the advantages and disadvantages of indexed access versus relative and direct access of resource records.

11. How can exponential smoothing help reduce record size?

12. Describe a method for computing file size.

13. What are the differences between file retention and file recovery?

14. Describe tactics used to design files for easy change.

15. What are the different relationship tables and why are they important in file design?

CRITICAL THINKING OPPORTUNITIES

1. Draw a diagram of how this chapter is organized.

2. Compare and contrast indexed access with real-time update of records.

3. Refer to the purchase order data store specification (Figure 15–2).
   a) Prepare a file requirements document (See Figure 15–13).
   b) Prepare a file layout document (See Figure 15–14).
   c) Prepare an estimate of file space requirements for an expected number of current records of 7,000.
   d) How would you change the purchase order file to reflect future requirements?

OBJECTIVES

In this chapter you will learn about:

WHAT: (Concepts) Designing files in a database environment.

WHY: Integrated databases play a growing role in business information, particularly in the personal computer world.

WHEN: Design of databases occurs at the same stage of the SDLC as design of traditional files.

WHO: Systems analyst.

WHERE: Information systems department.

HOW: (Techniques) Data modeling
                    Databases
                    Top-down modeling approach
                    Bottom-up modeling approach
                    Normalizing databases

OUTLINE

- Setting
- A Total Quality Approach
- A Structured Approach
- Database Concepts
- Database Structures
- Design Approaches
- Designing a Database
- Creating a Relational Database
- Integrity and Security Concerns
- Human Aspects

DATABASE DESIGN

First you figure out what is inevitable. Then you find a way to take advantage of it.

—RUSSELL ACKOFF, 1968

SETTING

Strategic decisions encompass all information systems. Top management's decision to buy computer hardware from a single vendor is strategic. It applies no matter which individual information system is being modified, enhanced, or redesigned. Tactical information decisions occur within a single information system. For example, an OCR input medium is selected for a purchasing system. This tactical decision is made independently of input media used by other systems. Management makes strategic decisions across *all* information systems; it makes tactical choices on a system-by-system basis.

In Chapter 15, file design was treated as a tactical decision. The analyst designed files for a specific information system with little regard to what was happening in other information systems. For example, one analyst designed a customer file for an accounts receivable function. She was not concerned with the composition of the vendor file for the purchasing application or the parts file for the inventory module. Chapter 15 assumed that all databases (files) were decentralized—under local department or application control. Hence, file design was largely a local rather than centralized decision.

This decentralized assumption does not fit the situation where consolidated databases are under central control rather than local control. Here, the individual systems designer has limited control over file composition and change. The tactical file design of

Chapter 15 is now constrained by management's strategic decision to use a centralized database, which becomes common to all individual information systems (Figure 16–1).

Database management systems provide firms with increased data integrity and data consistency. A DBMS also decreases data redundancy. **Data integrity** is the characteristic whereby stored data are changed or viewed only by persons formally authorized by the firm. **Data consistency** is the characteristic ensuring that multiple occurrences of the same stored data field have the same values. **Data redundancy** is multiple occurrences of the same stored data field. The following example places these characteristics in context.

The Alaska Justice Information System (AJIS) is an integrated computer system housing the criminal processing components of police, prosecutor, courts, and corrections operations. There is one common record for each criminal defendant. Prior to AJIS implementation, each criminal justice agency had its own defendant record. This created a condition of *data redundancy*. In addition, duplicate fields were not updated in a consistent manner. This author investigated the date-of-birth field in three agencies' records and discovered numerous instances where the different agencies had entered different dates of birth for the same criminal defendant. This was a violation of the principle of *data consistency*. AJIS allowed only the courts to update criminal history records and a few authorized individuals to view these records. Hence, the system had *data integrity*.

In a DBMS environment, files are not designed in a piecemeal manner. Instead, the totality of all organizational data—how it flows and interrelates—is considered. This panoramic approach is referred to as data modeling. **Data modeling** is the graphic representation of how data should *ideally* be *organized* and *flow* through an information system. Emphasis is on how data entities *relate* to one another. The data modeling approach has several advantages over the conventional approach described in Chapter 15. It is a structured (checklist) approach that provides (1) accurate, current, and nonredundant data; (2) fulfillment of current user information needs; and (3) ease of

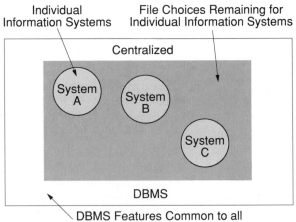

FIGURE 16–1   How the DBMS Constrains Choices about the File Design of Individual Information Systems

Individual Information Systems

File Choices Remaining for Individual Information Systems

Centralized

System A

System B

System C

DBMS

DBMS Features Common to all Information Systems

meeting changing user requirements. Data modeling is associated with, but not restricted to, a DBMS environment.

The topic of database design is complex, often requiring two or three database courses. Naturally, such coverage is beyond the scope of this book. Yet, neither can it be assumed that readers will have already taken even one database course. In addition, all systems designers must be literate in data modeling because it has an impact on conventional file design choices, and because data modeling concepts are used routinely in design of small systems. The following compromise has been reached to solve this dilemma. This chapter includes only a general approach to database design rather than specific details. You will find other specifics in "References and Further Readings" at the end of this section.

A TOTAL QUALITY APPROACH

A TQM approach to designing databases entails the same criteria as discussed in design of traditional files (Chapter 15). The difference is that the criteria for databases is established and evaluated from a total firm perspective rather than for each of the firm's separate tactical units. The following example will show the difference.

Walls Bottle Works previously had a materials control information system with traditional, independent files. There was a purchasing file which was the responsibility of the purchasing department. There was an inventory file which was the responsibility of the warehouse department. Finally, there was a vendor file which was the responsibility of the accounting department. Each of these departments was separately responsible for quality assurance pertaining to the individual file in their caretaking.

Walls Davis Bottle Works has established an integrated database replacing the traditional purchasing, inventory, and vendor files. In this new database environment, a central database administration is responsible for quality assurance of the integrated databases. File management has been moved from the tactical, department level to the strategic, firm level. Total quality management is still used, but it is done at a higher level in the firm.

A STRUCTURED APPROACH

As with tactical files, database design opportunities emanate from Data Store symbols on the data flow diagram. Nevertheless, there is an important difference. A traditional file is designed for *each* incident of a data store on the DFD. For database design, we first consolidate all separate data stores into a single, integrated data store. This then leads to the design of a single, integrated database. In addition, the entity-relationship diagram (ERD) is used for design of databases. The ERD was described in Chapter 9.

DATABASE CONCEPTS

A **database** is a structured collection of two or more data files. It has three principle dimensions: data location and control, data perspectives (views), and database components.

Data Location and Control

Databases can be classified by their physical location and where they are procedurally controlled. Figure 16–2 is a spectrum of database location and control.

Centralized. In a **centralized database,** all data are stored and controlled at one central site. The Bank of Amos Green has all its data stored on a centralized database located in central Sacramento. All the bank's branches access this data through telecommunications lines. Hence, this centralized database is a **distributed database** in that it is shared by different locations within the firm.

Replicated. In a **replicated database,** some of the centralized data are copied at another location in case central files are damaged or destroyed. The Bank of Amos Green replicates loan data at its Fair Oaks branch, and savings data at its Highlands branch. Should anything happen to the centralized database, the bank can restore it from the replicated data at the two branch locations.

Segmented. In a **segmented database,** any single data entity is stored in only one location. However, different data entities are stored in different locations. The Bank of Amos Green decides to separate its centralized database into three segmented databases:

1. All commercial loan and account data remain in the central office.
2. All customer savings data are moved to the Highlands branch.
3. All customer loan data are moved to the Fair Oaks branch.

Segmentation decreases centralized hardware, software, and processing requirements. It reduces adverse results from natural disasters such as fire. It also allows for specialization of efforts (for example, management transfers all customer loan officers to the Fair Oaks branch).

Decentralized. In a **decentralized database,** file location, composition, and control are established at the end-user departments. It is at this end of the spectrum that traditional file design (Chapter 15) comes into play. For example, the Bank of Amos

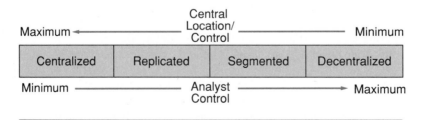

FIGURE 16–2   **Spectrum of Database Location and Control**

| Characteristic | Database Environment | | | |
	Centralized	Replicated	Segmented	Decentralized
Redundancy	Low	Moderate (Planned)	Low	High
Efficiency	High	Moderate	Moderately High	Low
Costs	Low	Moderate	Low	High
Local Control/Service	Low	Moderate	Moderate	High
Security	High	Moderate	Moderate	Low
Disaster Coverage	Low	High	Moderate	Moderate
Procedural Consistency	High	Moderate	Moderate	Low

FIGURE 16–3   **Characteristics of Different Database Environments**

Green could allow each branch to store its own data independent of all other branches. Of course, chaos would result if customers tried to cash checks at other branches.

Hybrid. The four parts of the database spectrum are not mutually exclusive. All or several parts can function in different combinations—a **hybrid database.** Take, for example, Amos Green's segmented database. The customer savings data located in the Highlands branch could be replicated at the West Sacramento branch.

Proceeding from left to right in Figure 16–2, the applications designer has more choices about file composition and control. Figure 16–3 lists characteristics of these different database environments.

Data Perspectives (Views)

A decentralized database presents end-users with a tailored use of stored data. In early centralized databases, a specific group of end-users might lose the privilege of tailored, unique data. That is not true now. A DBMS allows efficiencies from centralized storage, but it can tailor data to the needs of individual end-user groups. Figure 16–4 graphically shows how this is done.

Data are stored in a generic (overall) physical mode and sequence that optimize hardware and software considerations. For example, all data elements may be stored in a single sector record, despite the fact that most end-user groups will only use a quarter of the elements at any one time. The global arrangement of data is called a schema. Under a DBMS, the global **schema** is transparent to end-users. The DBMS transforms the overall record into a logical record tailored to individual end-user groups. From an end-user view, the logical record received *could* be how the record is stored. The end-user really does not care how the data is stored. Tailored records derived from a global schema are called **subschemas.** Thus, subschemas allow a centralized database to appear to end-users as tailored decentralized databases. The critical difference is in the extent of control the systems designer has over file design.

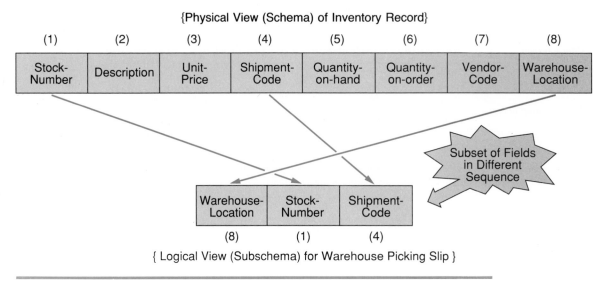

FIGURE 16–4   **Physical and Logical Views of a Database (Inventory System)**

Database Components

Databases include several elements (Figure 16–5).

Data Definition Language. The **data definition language (DDL)** sets up the record types, fields, and relationships making up the schema. It also sets up individual end-user logical views of the database (subschema). In microcomputer-based database systems, the data definitions are created by defining files or tables. In dBASE IV, for example, "Create" is one of the choices at the top-level menu of the ASSIST mode. No other function will work until a database file is created.

Data Manipulation Language. The **data manipulation language (DML)** manipulates and updates the database. It includes such functions as retrieving a specific record or group of records, appending new records, deleting old records, modifying current records, and sorting and merging files. In dBASE IV, once a file or files have been created, other ASSIST options (Set up, Update, Position, Organize, Modify, Tools) will function. These are data manipulation functions.

Inquiry Language. The **inquiry language (IQL)** allows tailored retrieval of screens or reports according to parameters provided by end-users. An example of an IQL for most mainframe environments is SQL (Structured Query Language). SQL has the capability of interfacing with many programming languages, including COBOL. The IQL for R:BASE is called CLOUT.

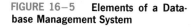

FIGURE 16–5   **Elements of a Data-base Management System**

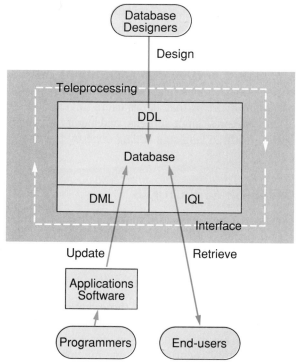

THE CASE OF FREDDY THE BAIL BONDSMAN

Freddy had been posting bail bonds for arrested criminal defendants for twelve years. His reputation was, at best, questionable. The chief judge convinced Freddy to get out of business in Icetown or face a criminal indictment for his shady dealings. Freddy eagerly agreed to leave.

The chief judge instructed Carla, the court clerk, to produce a billing for all outstanding bail amounts that Freddy owed the courts. These were bail amounts for cases in which the defendant deserted and never reappeared in court. The chief judge wanted the billing in one hour. Carla used an IQL called ENGLISH and inserted the following parameters:

File:	BAIL BOND
Bondsman:	FREDDY
City:	ICETOWN
Field:	ARREARS (bail amounts owed)
Function:	FIND, TOTAL

Within minutes, Carla produced a billing for Freddy. Within one hour, Freddy had paid the billing amount. That afternoon, Freddy was on a plane leaving Icetown.

Teleprocessing Interface. The **teleprocessing interface** controls access to databases via VDT workstations in a multiple-user DBMS environment. In R:BASE, the teleprocessing portion is called File Gateway.

Applications Interface. The **applications interface** allows database interface with business applications that use conventional languages such as COBOL. The name of the portion of R:BASE that allows users to generate applications is Application EXPRESS. Menus, reports, input screens, and inquiry screens can be generated into an integrated system with no language coding done by the user.

DATABASE STRUCTURES

Databases can be designed to one of three structures: (a) hierarchical, (b) network, and (c) relational.

Hierarchical Architecture

Figure 16–6 shows how three material control system files can be linked through a hierarchical structure. Each vendor has a single vendor record. Each vendor has multiple inventory records—one for each inventory item supplied by that vendor. For each inventory record, there are multiple occurrences of purchase order records. A particular inventory item may be ordered many times for many different customers and for stock replenishment.

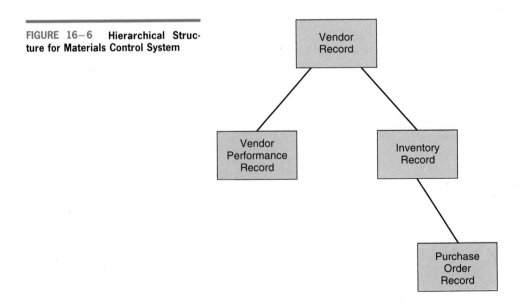

FIGURE 16–6   Hierarchical Structure for Materials Control System

FIGURE 16–7   **Hierarchical Linkage**
for Vendor to Inventory Records

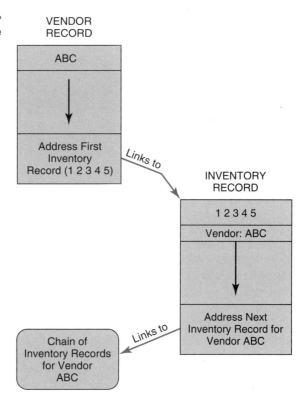

In a hierarchical system, each higher level is called a parent. Multiple incidents of records emanating from the parent at the next level are called children. The entity-relationship diagram described in Chapter 9 is ideal for describing a hierarchical structure. One additional characteristic completes this brief description of the hierarchical structure.

The contents of each record contains a field that links the record to its children and parents. For example, a record for vendor ABC may include a linkage field sharing the address of the first inventory record (12345) for that vendor. The contents of this first inventory record will contain a linkage field containing the address of the second inventory record for vendor ABC. Figure 16–7 shows this hierarchical linkage relationship.

Network Architecture

This structure is similar to the network structure except that a child can have more than one parent. Suppose we modify Figure 16–6 to allow a single inventory item to be ordered from more than one vendor. Now each vendor (parent) is linked to several inventory records (children). However, each inventory record (child) can be linked to more than one vendor. It is clear that the linkage structure required for a network structure is far more complex than that required for a hierarchical structure.

FIGURE 16–8   **Separate Files (Tables) Required for Relational Architecture**

Table 1	
Item Number	Vendor Code
1052	XY2
1123	ABC
1125	MPM
↓	↓
9763	ABC

Table 2	
Item Number	Shipping Code
1052	TKL
1123	MAL
1125	AIR
↓	↓
9763	TKL

Relational Architecture

The rich linkage structures required of the hierarchical and network structures make these approaches amenable only to complex, costly DBMS packages. These packages typically require use of large, mainframe environments serviced by highly technical database specialists. Such packages are difficult for nontechnical end-users to learn and operate.

The relational structure sacrifices record search efficiencies and speeds associated with the hierarchical and network structures. Instead, the relational structure emphasizes ease of database creation, update and retrieval. Hence, it brings database operation within the realm of everyday, nontechnical users. The relational database is more applicable to an environment where there is a relatively low level of database transactions; access speed is not as important. This is typically the realm of personal computers.

Figure 16–8 shows a simple relational structure for vendor code and shipping code as they relate to each inventory record. Here two separate tables are used rather than integrating the data into a single, flat record. Linkage fields are not required.

DESIGN APPROACHES

Data models can be constructed in two ways: the top-down approach and the bottom-up approach.

Basic Definitions

Definition of a few terms will make the following discussion easier. These terms were introduced briefly in Chapter 9, but need amplification here. **Entities** (records) are countable senders, collectors, and receivers of information. An entity represents something to which we give a name. This can be a person, a place, an agency, or any such thing. Examples include such common items as customers, inventory, cash, vendors, and amounts owed. From a design perspective, there is roughly a one-to-one correspondence between entities, traditional files, and data stores on a data flow diagram.

Attributes (fields) are individual data elements that aid the flow of documents and reports through the business information system. Hence, the attribute customer-address helps effective flow of shipping documents (an entity). The attribute employee-social-security-number is critical to annual production of W-2 forms. Attributes (fields) are assigned to entities (records). Traditional record formats contain a sequenced list of attributes. The DFD does not contain a list of attributes for each data store shown.

Relationships (pointers) describe how entities relate to each other. This can be done effectively with the entity-relationship diagram (ERD). Vendor-code in an inventory record relates vendor and inventory entities. Department-code in an employee record relates employee and organizational entities. Sometimes, a relationship between entities itself becomes an entity requiring establishment of a data file. For example, customer and inventory entities relate via the customer order. This is made a countable entity in the form of a pending customer order file. Figure 16–9 shows one structure of entities, attributes, and relationships.

Top-Down Design Approach

The top-down approach is used frequently in developing data models for transaction processing systems. The reason is that TPS applications are fairly standard; therefore, systems analysts know more about them. That is an important requirement for the top-down approach. In the top-down approach, analysts develop a **prior data model** of how they think the system should operate. They do so based on experience and

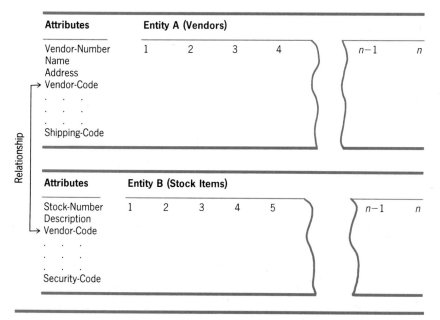

FIGURE 16–9   **Structure of Entities, Attributes, and Relationships**

intuition. Then they refine this model during the requirements analysis stage by discussing it with knowledgeable end-users.

Outside consultants often use the top-down approach to data modeling. They come into a firm with preconceived ideas of how a TPS such as accounts receivable works based on experience elsewhere. They assume it should work the same in this firm, so they adjust their prior data model for processes and circumstances unique to this specific firm. Figure 16–10 illustrates the top-down approach.

Bottom-Up Design Approach

In contrast, systems analysts often use the bottom-up method in designing decision support systems, expert systems, management information systems, and executive information systems. These advanced types of information systems are peculiar to a specific firm. Therefore, the analyst's experience and intuition are not as valuable as they are in TPS design. For similar reasons, bottom-up design is the preferred approach for inexperienced systems analysts.

The approach begins with collections of all forms and reports used in the information system. The physical data flow diagram is an excellent checklist of what forms and reports need to be collected. A list of attributes (fields) is then compiled. Attributes are combined or dropped when they are redundant, unused, or difficult to update. Figure 16–11 shows the bottom-up approach to data modeling.

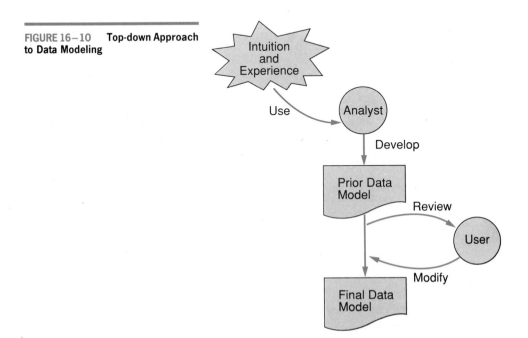

FIGURE 16–10   **Top-down Approach to Data Modeling**

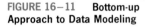

FIGURE 16–11   **Bottom-up**
Approach to Data Modeling

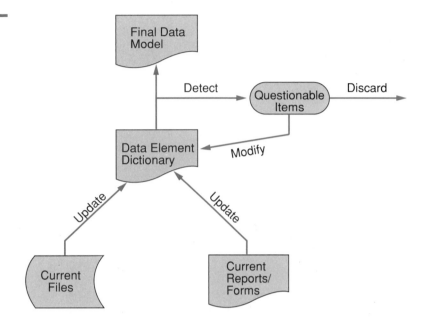

DESIGNING A DATABASE

If a firm has a **system plan,** a data model exists and the top-down design approach is preferable. A system plan is a structured blueprint for developing and modifying a firm's information systems within some future time frame. If there is no system plan and systems designers have little experience in the application, the top-down approach is risky.

The bottom-up approach has three advantages. First, it is appropriate when analysts do not have much experience or intuition. Second, it is a consistent approach that different analysts can replicate. This contrasts with the top-down approach, which is intuitive and tends to lack consistency among analysts. Third, the bottom-up approach is a natural by-product of the systems analysis phase of the SDLC.

The bottom-up approach is the basis for designing a data model and then a database in this book. Figure 16–12 illustrates this design approach. Following are the logical steps required to design a business database.

1. Examine each report and form. The physical DFD is an excellent checklist for determining which reports and forms to examine.
2. Create or update report and form fields in a preliminary data element dictionary.
3. Examine current files. These are data stores on the physical DFD.
4. Create or update file fields in the **Data Element Dictionary (DED).** In a structured design environment, the DED is that part of the Data Dictionary comprised only of data element specifications.

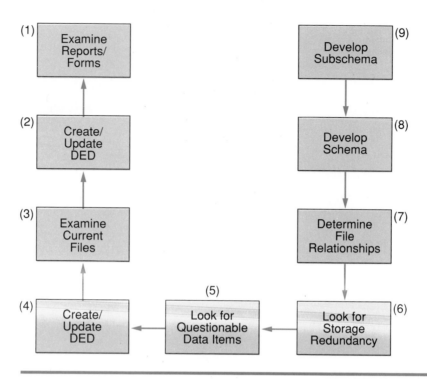

FIGURE 16—12   **Database Design Sequence Using Bottom-up Approach**

5. Look for questionable data fields. These are fields that are never output, hence probably never used, and not on daily input forms (transactions), and thus difficult to keep current. When appropriate, drop these fields and update the DED.

6. Look for storage redundancy. Do not include the same field in more than one file unless there is a documented reason. Suppose you discover that inventory field unit-price is in both the inventory and customer order file. Can you justify that redundancy? You may find that the inventory file contains *current* unit price. The customer order file contains unit price at the time a merchandise shipment was committed to the customer. The customer order is not subject to later price increases. In such a case, you can justify storage redundancy by creating two fields called "Current Unit Price" and "Committed Unit Price." In many cases, redundancies cannot be justified. In these cases, (1) select the file (entity) to which the data element (attribute) is most appropriate, (2) select the most appropriate of duplicate data names and formats, and (3) update the DED.

7. Determine file (entity) relationships. For each file, decide if and how that file relates to other files. Use an ERD for this purpose.

8. Develop the schema. This is the physical view of the data model. It is similar to the file format discussed in Chapter 15. The difference is that the schema includes all integrated file formats, including linkages between files. The conventional file format reflects a single independent file.

9. Develop end-user subschema. The subschema is a logical view of data tailored to specific end-user needs. The schema for an integrated database is extensive. It includes many times the number of data fields that any one end-user needs. Subschemas are constructed for each end-user group. To the end-users, the database *is* the subschema; it consists of only what end-users need. The subschema is also used to control and monitor access to the database. In many database software packages, the subschema is called a **view.**

CREATING A RELATIONAL DATABASE

Use of the relational database architecture entails four special design rules:

1. *Limit file to fixed-length records:* There are incidents where record length varies depending on individual item characteristics. For example, in a traditional file environment, inventory item A175 has 12 fields for past monthly usage. Item A275 has only 5 fields, since it is a more newly stocked item. In a relational database system, one table would be established with the fixed format shown in Figure 16–13.

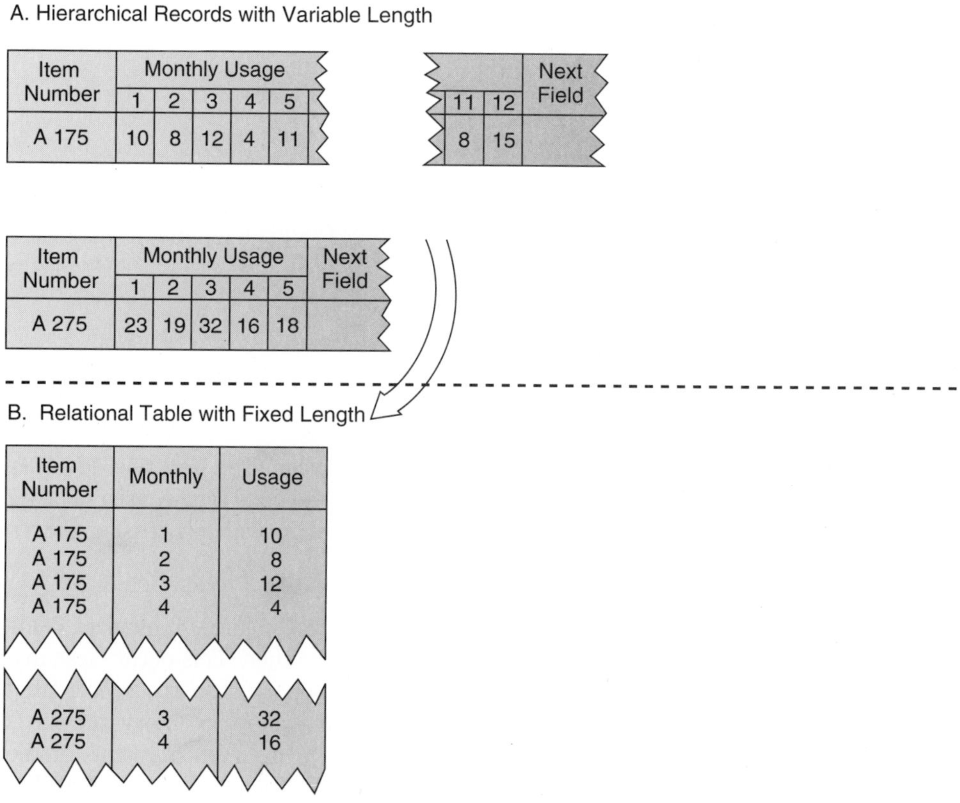

A. Hierarchical Records with Variable Length

B. Relational Table with Fixed Length

FIGURE 16–13   **Conversion of Hierarchical Variable-length Records to Relational Fixed-length Records**

2. *All repeating nonkey fields are eliminated from a record:* In the example just cited, the only way we could establish a fixed-length record was to eliminate all repeating nonkey items. A **nonkey field** is a field not used to access records, Monthly-Usage in this case. A **key field** is a field used to access records, such as Inventory-Item-Number in this case.

The process of eliminating all repeating nonkey groups is called **normalization.** Following normalization, all records will be of fixed length.

3. *A nonkey field must provide a fact about a key field:* If it does not, that field is not required.

4. *Storage is restricted to items that cannot be derived:* If items can be computed from other fields, they are not stored. Instead they are computed each time they are required.

The application of these rules is complex and beyond the scope of this book. More importantly, relational database software packages' use of these rules is transparent to the nontechnical user. As an analyst, you should know these rules and learn to apply them in the context of a database course. As a designer who uses commercial DBMS software, you can design, construct, and use your database without conscious application of the above rules.

INTEGRITY AND SECURITY CONCERNS

Data integrity and security are concerns with both traditional and integrated files. However, the concerns vary somewhat in the two environments.

Integrity

Concerns about integrity include processing errors, data inconsistencies, and simultaneous update.

Processing Errors. Two types of processing errors can occur. The first type involves data that are incomplete, lost, or not received on time. The second type consists of data entry errors. There are no essential differences in dealing with processing errors between a traditional and database file environment.

Data Inconsistencies. Data inconsistencies occur in two ways. First, redundant fields are updated independently and are inconsistent with one another. This occurs less in a DBMS environment, where redundancy is minimized. Second, records are treated independently rather than as a group. For example, a master inventory record is deleted while a purchase order detail record for stock replenishment remains for the same inventory item. When the item is received, there is no longer a master record to post the received quantity. A DBMS is less susceptible to this inconsistency because of its more extensive linkage between related records.

AJIS SECURITY

The Alaska Justice Information System includes statewide criminal history data. Only authorized end-users can access or update this important data (data integrity). To protect the data from unauthorized access and update, AJIS has a multilevel access code which includes (1) operator password, (2) workstation identification, (3) time of day, (4) files that can be accessed, and (5) operations performed on those files. For example, (1) operator password MELLOW (2) is authorized only for workstation CT01 (3) from 8 A.M. to 5 P.M. (4) and only for the criminal history file for which the operator (5) can read but not change that file.

Any departure from this multilevel access structure causes AJIS to lock out the user. AJIS also sends a security breach message to the state troopers. This author was almost arrested one Saturday for using his password on someone else's workstation.

Simultaneous Update. If two or more persons access the same record at the same time, processing discontinuities may result. For example, the system may lock out a data entry clerk posting a customer order while another clerk is deleting that customer record because of inactivity. Traditional batch-up-dated files do not have simultaneous update problems, since transactions are sorted into logical sequence before update.

Security

Security and privacy, though related, are different. **Security** is protection of data which, if wrongly disseminated, may damage organizational goals. **Privacy** refers to protection of data which, if wrongly disseminated, may damage individuals. Databases are more complex and accessed by many persons; therefore, security and privacy are more difficult than for traditional file environments. Consequently, DBMS environments include extensive security modules that protect against many security and privacy problems. Protection typically is by access codes (passwords). These codes allow users to reach only those portions of the DBMS for which they have been given clearance. End-user access codes are part of the DBMS subschemas.

HUMAN ASPECTS

The role of the systems analyst changes under a DBMS environment. Compared to conventional file design, a database environment presents the analyst with several constraints.

A DBMS optimizes a firm's total storage requirements, so the priorities of a specific end-user group are secondary to the firm's total requirements. Of course, design of subschemas allows tailoring of data to better fit local needs. Still, the analyst must perform file design within constraints imposed by the total database. This may be difficult to explain to local groups of end-users.

The systems analyst is only one voice in many who may be suggesting database changes. First there is a database administrator who is responsible for update, maintenance, and access control for the DBMS. Then there are companywide users. This group includes persons who lack ownership in the analyst's specific information system. It is difficult for any one analyst to effect significant changes in a DBMS environment. This also may be difficult to justify to local end-users.

Despite these constraints, there is a tendency toward integrated databases. Does this mean that traditional file design is a dead subject? No, this is not the case for several reasons. First, while the *approach* to database design is different, most techniques discussed in Chapter 15 still apply. Second, integrated databases are still expensive and complex. Sometimes they are beyond the realm of small- to medium-sized companies. Finally, many firms have considerable investment in conventional file environments which are working quite well. They intend to continue such settings for some time.

In conclusion, this chapter on database design is intended to bolster rather than replace the chapter on traditional file design. The systems analyst still has considerable control of file design, even in a database environment.

SUMMARY

Systems analysts are limited by strategic design choices. The DBMS is a strategic device within which all localized data storage specifications must be consistent.

Database design begins with a data model. Data modeling is the graphic representation of how data ideally should be organized and flow through an information system. A data modeling approach has several advantages over conventional file design: it provides (1) accurate, current, and nonredundant data, (2) fulfillment of current user information needs, and (3) adaptation to changes in user requirements. Data modeling is associated with, but not restricted to, database environments.

Database environments are categorized by their location and where they are controlled. They can be centralized (often distributed), replicated (duplicated), segmented (split apart), or decentralized. Decentralized databases involve traditional files.

There are two ways of viewing a database. The first is global, showing how the full database is organized. The second view is logical, tailoring portions of the physical database to suit individual end-user needs. The global view is called a schema and the logical view a subschema.

The three database architectures used are hierarchical, network, and relational. Relational databases sacrifice retrieval speed for ease of nontechnical user creation and use. Design of relational databases requires some special considerations explained in this chapter.

Databases include five elements: data definition language, data manipulation language, inquiry language, teleprocessing interface, and applications interfaces.

There are two approaches to designing the data model that leads to the database. The first is the top-down approach. Here, the analyst uses intuition and experience to develop the prior data model and then refines this model during the requirements analysis stage of the SDLC. The top-down approach is used frequently in design of transaction processing systems, since they are fairly standardized. The second is the bottom-up approach. The analyst builds the data model from current forms, reports, and files and then eliminates redundant and questionable data. The bottom-up approach is appropriate for nonstandard information systems such as MIS, DSS, or ES. It is also used when systems analysts are relatively inexperienced.

Design of a database using a bottom-up approach proceeds by logical steps:

1. Examine each report and form.
2. Create and update fields in a preliminary data element dictionary.
3. Examine current files.
4. Create or update storage fields in the DED.
5. Look for questionable data fields.
6. Look for storage redundancy.
7. Determine file relationships.
8. Develop the physical schema.
9. Develop logical end-user subschemas.

Data modeling and database design must account for several integrity and security concerns. Integrity concerns include processing errors, data inconsistencies, and simultaneous update. Security concerns also include individual privacy. Data are protected through multilevel access codes which are part of the end-user subschemas.

The systems analyst's role in file design changes in a database environment. In a traditional file environment, the analyst has a wide range of choices. Under a database environment, the analyst's choices are constrained by the companywide database organization led by the database administrator.

Although use of integrated databases is increasing, analysts still need to master the concepts and techniques of conventional file design. Data modeling and traditional file design exist concurrently in many firms.

CONCEPTS LEARNED

- Definition of data modeling
- Concepts of data integrity, data consistency, and data redundancy
- Characteristics of centralized, replicated, segmented, and decentralized databases
- Difference between schema and subschema
- Database components
- Different database architectures
- Definitions of entities, attributes, and relationships
- Top-down approach to database design
- Bottom-up approach to database design
- Design of relational databases
- Database integrity concerns
- Database security concerns
- Differences between the systems analyst's role in a conventional file environment and a database environment

KEY TERMS

applications interface
attribute
centralized database
database
data consistency
data definition language (DDL)
data element dictionary (DED)
data integrity
data manipulation language (DML)
data modeling
data redundancy
decentralized database
distributed database
entity
hierarchical architecture
hybrid database
inquiry language (IQL)

key field
network architecture
nonkey field
normalization
prior data model
privacy
relational architecture
relationship
replicated database
schema
security
segmented database
simultaneous update
subschema
system plan
teleprocessing interface
view

REVIEW QUESTIONS

1. Why are an analyst's file design choices constrained in a database environment?

2. What are the advantages of the data modeling approach over that of conventional file design?

3. Describe the difference between a replicated and segmented database.

4. What is a subschema?

5. What are the roles of the DDL and DML?

6. Define entity, attribute, and relationship.

7. Describe the three types of database architectures.

8. When would you use a top-down approach to database design?

9. What is a system plan?

10. Explain the steps in bottom-up design of databases.

11. How can you recognize questionable data fields?

12. What is storage redundancy?

13. What is simultaneous update?

14. What is normalization?

15. What are the four rules of relative database design?

16. Explain the difference between security and privacy.

17. How is security enforced in a DBMS environment?

18. Describe the role of the systems analyst in a database environment.

CRITICAL THINKING OPPORTUNITIES

1. Draw a diagram of the organization of this chapter.

2. Compare and contrast the three database architectures.

3. Select a business office. Collect a copy of all forms and reports. Manually simulate bottom-up design of an integrated office database.

C A S E   16.1

CSU SUTTER CREEK: FILE DESIGN

SETTING

Robert Gardner is a systems analyst employed by California State University (CSU) at Sutter Creek. He has been assigned to design an integrated database for classroom management. Robert analyzes the current system and selects three traditional files for consideration. The first is a faculty file (Figure 16.1–1). The second is a student file (Figure 16.1–2). The third is a course file (Figure 16.1–3).

Robert has been asked to produce the following class management products:

1. Student report showing all courses/instructors for which each student is enrolled for the current semester.
2. Faculty report showing all course/students for which each faculty member is responsible for the current semester.
3. Course report showing all faculty members/students assigned to each course for the current semester.

Robert Gardner tells his supervisor that he will need some help in completing this project. The supervisor assigns you to help Robert with this file design project. After only a week, Robert Gardner leaves CSU Sutter Creek to take another job. You are now totally responsible for completing this project.

ASSIGNMENTS

1. Combine the faculty, student and course files into a series of tables amenable to a relational database structure.

2. Recommend appropriate file media and access methods.

3. There are currently 5000 students, 150 faculty and 200 courses. How much file space is required now? How much file space will be required in a relational database system?

4. Prepare a plan for file retention and recovery.

FIGURE 16.1–1 **Faculty File Format**

Field Name	Picture
Last Name	X(15)
First Name	X(15)
Street Address	X(20)
City	X(15)
State	X(2)
Zip	X(9)
Telephone	X(10)
Social Security Number	X(9)
Salary	9(5) v99
Highest Education	XX (coded)
Office Number	X(7)
Office Telephone	X(10)
Department	X(4)

Field Name	Picture
Last Name	X(15)
First Name	X(15)
Street Address	X(20)
City	X(15)
State	X(2)
Zip	X(9)
Faculty Advisor Last Name	X(15)
Faculty Advisor First Name	X(15)
Major	X(4)
Class Standing	X(4)

Courses Taken This Semester
— First Course Code   X(8) ⎫
— Number Hours   99   ⎪
— Grade Received   XX   ⎬ Repeated for
                                         ⎪ 10 possible
— Second Course Code   X(8) ⎪ courses
— Number Hours   99   ⎪
— Grade Received   XX   ⎭

Courses Taken 1st Semester Past (See Last Description)
Courses Taken 2nd Semester Past (See Last Description)

•
• ←— Repeated for
•   20 possible semesters

FIGURE 16.1–2   Student File Format

FIGURE 16.1–3   Course File Format

Field Name	Picture
Course Code	X(8)
Course Name	X(20)
Course Description	X(100)
Number Hours	99
Department	X(4)
Maximum Number Students	999

OBJECTIVES

In this chapter you will learn about:

WHAT: (Concepts) Design of information system processes.

WHY: Quality of information system output is a result of how well data transformation processes are designed.

WHEN: After design of output, input, and files.

WHO: Systems analyst in conjunction with end-users.

WHERE: End-user work area (physical processes) and information systems department (information processes).

HOW: (Techniques) Principles of process design
Structured English
Structure charts

OUTLINE

- Setting
- A Total Quality Approach
- A Structured Approach
- Analyst Responsibilities in Process Design
- Principles of Process Design
- Profile of a Poorly Designed Process
- Structured English
- Structure Charts
- Reengineering
- Human Aspects

CHAPTER 17

PROCESS DESIGN/REENGINEERING

"I'm so busy squashing ants, that the elephants are stomping me to death."

—INSTANT ANALYST, 1975

SETTING

Information system processes convert input data to output information. Processes are what ultimately end up as computer programs. **Information processes** are those tasks which transform data; they are subject to automation. **Physical processes** are tasks that modify a physical product or flow; these generally are not amenable to computer programming. An important goal of this chapter will be to clarify the role of the information systems analyst in design and reengineering of physical as well as information processes.

This chapter relies heavily on process design principles described in total quality management (TQM) literature. These principles are directed to the specific goal of designing an effective business information system. One of the goals of this chapter is to expand analyst focus on process design beyond merely writing efficient computer programs. The chapter includes description of two commonly used tools for describing process logic—structured English and structure charts.

A TOTAL QUALITY APPROACH

As stated, this chapter uses a TQM framework. In addition, design of information system processes uses the same quality criteria as with other design tasks. These quality criteria follow:

1. *Relevancy:* Is the process necessary to producing quality information system products (output)?
2. *Completeness:* Does the process do all it is required to do?
3. *Correctness:* Does the process perform with a minimum level of errors?
4. *Security:* Can the process be activated only by authorized personnel?
5. *Timeliness:* Is process cycle-time within expectations/standards?
6. *Economy:* All other things being equal, is the process designed as inexpensively as possible?
7. *Efficiency:* Are ratios (e.g., Correctness per Dollar) maximized?
8. *Reliability:* Are variances minimized for process performance?
9. *Usability:* Is the process easy to understand and to learn?

A STRUCTURED APPROACH

Recall the structured sequence for transforming current system to proposed system specifications using data flow diagrams.

1. A hierarchy chart of the current system is translated into a leveled set of physical data flow diagrams for the current system.
2. This set of physical DFDs is stripped of (a) physical processes, and (b) implementation (HOW) considerations, resulting in a leveled set of logical DFDs for the current system.
3. Logical DFDs for the current system are transformed to a leveled set of logical DFDs for the proposed system.
4. New implementation (HOW) considerations are added to produce a leveled set of physical DFDs for the proposed system.
5. This last set of DFDs is translated in data dictionary entries.

It is step 3 of this sequence that is the emphasis of this chapter. How do we take existing information system processes and transform them, or add to them to produce a more effective set of processes for a new or improved information system?

ANALYST RESPONSIBILITIES IN PROCESS DESIGN

Structured design principles call for transforming from physical to logical DFDs by, in part, eliminating all physical processes from consideration. The implied message seems to be that information systems analysts should restrict their focus to information processes; physical processes and considerations should be ignored. This message is of questionable validity.

Concentration on information processes forces concentration on development of computer programs. Computer programs, however, are only one part of a total information system. A total information system (often called a **computer-based information system**) is comprised of hardware, software, database, telecommunications, people, and procedures (Stair, 1992). This list extends far beyond the consideration of only programming and establishment of databases. Focus on only information processes tends to restrict analyst attention to only a small part of the information system spectrum.

There is another reason why systems analysts must broaden their attention beyond merely information processes. The **industrial engineer** is the professional responsible for designing and improving physical processes. This includes such concerns as workplace layout, physical flow, and task efficiency. Industrial engineers, however, typically are found only in large organizations. Even there, their numbers have been dwindling. It is uncommon to find industrial engineers in small- and medium-sized business firms. Who then is responsible for physical process design in such firms?

By default, it is the systems analyst who is responsible for physical flow design in small- to medium-sized organizations. Recall that the same default situation occurred with forms design. If this seems unfair, it really is not. There is nothing so frustrating as designing an outstanding software system only to see its effectiveness blunted by poor personnel execution, inadequate training, and unreadable documentation. The systems analyst who is by heart a computer programmer rarely implements a successful information system of more than limited scope.

Therefore, this chapter concentrates on information process design and redesign, but not at the exclusion of physical process design.

PRINCIPLES OF PROCESS DESIGN

Harrington (1991) describes 12 cornerstones to streamlining processes. A few of these cornerstones are not relevant to our discussion in this chapter. Hence, we can refocus this list to the principles of process design noted below. These are:

1. Eliminate duplicate processes.
2. Eliminate processes that are not value-added.
3. Simplify processes.
4. Reduce process cycle-time.
5. Simplify language.
6. Standardize processes.

Error-proofing processes have been discussed throughout this chapter. Each of the remaining principles will now be discussed in detail.

Eliminate Duplicate Processes

Look for processes where the same activity is being performed in different places, by different individuals, or both. Duplicate processes increase costs. In addition, such duplication can lead to conflicting information. An example would be two different law enforcement people ascertaining the birth date of a defendant. The two dates collected may not agree. This is, of course one of the reasons we establish integrated databases—to prevent conflicting information in separate files.

From a software perspective, you may discover two programs performing the same task. You then can produce a single subprogram to perform this task. This subprogram then can be called by each of the separate programs when the task is to be performed. This is the underlying rationale for object-oriented programming (OOP) and object-oriented analysis and design (OOAD).

Eliminate Processes That Are Not Value-Added

Some activities exist because processes are not well designed. Processes and process activities should be value-added. A **value-added process** is one which clearly adds value (quality) to information system output. You can ask these questions of each process: Could this process be eliminated without adversely affecting output? Would end-users pay us to perform these processes?

Look for processes that do not alter the nature of the information or physical product. These processes often involve activities such as *moving, waiting, setup, storing,* or doing work over *(rework)*. Also look for questionable control activities such as *logging in* of documents, *control totals,* and *routing slips.* The italicized words in this paragraph provide you with a checklist by which to analyze data flow diagrams to spot processes that are not value-added.

RECOGNIZING INFORMATION BOTTLENECKS

The data flow diagram can be enhanced by adding to the data flows leading into all processes flow statistics. Refer to Figure 17–1. Note that, for each data flow leading into a process, there are three numbers within parentheses. These numbers are measures of the number of documents flowing to that process per chosen time period. The left number is the minimum, the right number is the maximum, and the middle number is the average. For example, Sales Orders flow from the Customer to the Order Verification process. The flow of these orders per week is:

MINIMUM   –   175
AVERAGE   –   250
MAXIMUM   –   400

Compare the volumes of documents flowing into and out of each process. Look for these processing abnormalities.

- BLACK HOLE: More comes in than goes out. This is either a political power center or people in the process are having problems doing the work.
- MIRACLES: More goes out than comes in. How can this happen? These are generally work centers that saturate the system with questionable data.
- LABORATORIES: Input and output are balanced, but it takes a long time to get anything out. What are they doing with those documents?

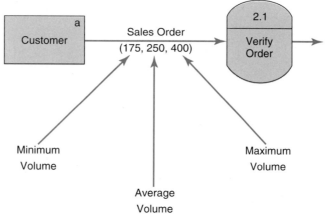

FIGURE 17–1   **Annotating Transac-tion Volume Statistics on a Data Flow Diagram**

Simplify Processes

The simpler the process, the easier it is to learn and the fewer errors are made. From a software perspective, the simpler the process (module), the easier it is to maintain and change. There are six things to look for when simplifying processes.

1. *Duplicate or fragmented tasks:* These should be combined or eliminated. For example, suppose there are three separate program modules writing three parts of the Purchasing Report. Combine these into one cohesive module that produces the entire report.
2. *Complex flows or bottlenecks:* These will act like clogging cholesterol in the blood-stream. Change the sequence of tasks, combine or separate tasks, or balance the workload so all tasks are approximately the same size. See the boxed item for recognition of information bottlenecks using the data flow diagram.
3. *Similar activities:* Combine, especially if they are consecutive in the flow sequence.
4. *Excessive handling with no alteration:* Reduce or eliminate handling tasks.
5. *Unused data:* Eliminate. Recall the Chapter 2 tests for separating data from information.
6. *Nonstandard reports:* Standardize.

Reduce Process Cycle Time

There are six techniques for reducing the time it takes to perform tasks.

1. *Convert serial to parallel activities.* Two tasks done at the same time take less time than two tasks done one after another. Refer to Figure 17–2a. This shows two serial tasks. The second cannot begin until the first is completed. Suppose however, that we were to make the Customer Order data flow a two-part form, with a separate copy sent separately to both the Order Verification and Credit Check processes. Now these two processes are parallel as shown in Figure 17–2b. Process cycle-time is reduced.

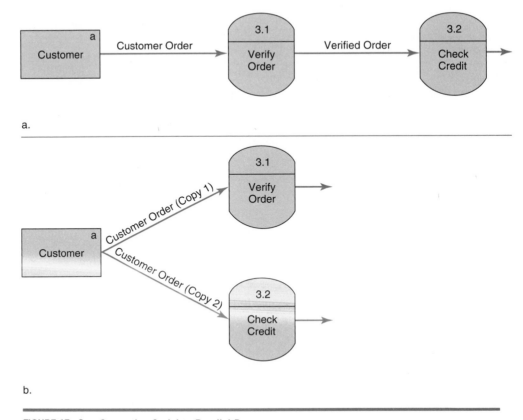

a.

b.

FIGURE 17–2   Converting Serial to Parallel Processes

2. *Change activity sequence.* Refer to Figure 17–3a. Process 1 output is sent to building B where process 2 is completed. Process 2 output is sent back to building A for process 3. Let us change the sequence so that the first two activities are done in building A (Figure 17–3b). Now process cycle-time is reduced because physical handling is minimized. The same tactic will work if we are dealing with two different people or two different computer programs instead of two different buildings.

3. *Decoupling.* Sometimes processes cannot be made parallel but must be sequential. Customer Order edit checks must be completed *before* shipping the product to the customer (Figure 17–4a). In such cases, it often is beneficial to decouple the processes from one another. **Decoupling processes** is reducing the dependence of one upon another. Decoupling means that each process can work at its own speed and not be affected by different speeds of the other process. This is shown in Figure 17–4b. Here output from the Edit Order process is sent, not directly to the Ship Product process, but to a buffer data store (file) called Pending Orders. Now the Ship Product process

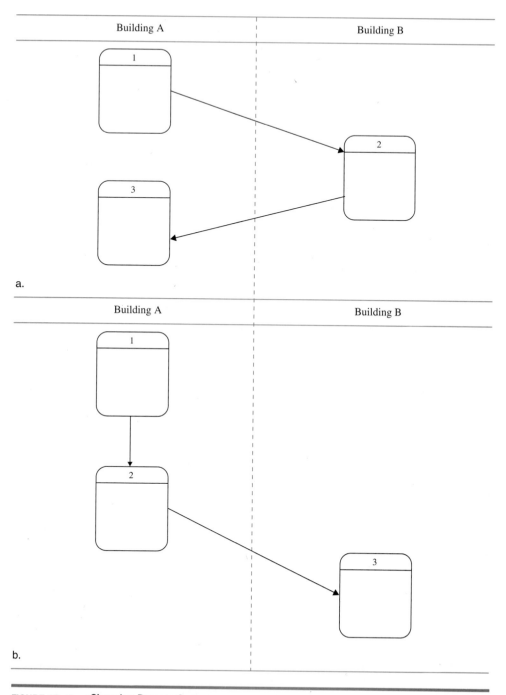

FIGURE 17–3   Changing Process Sequence

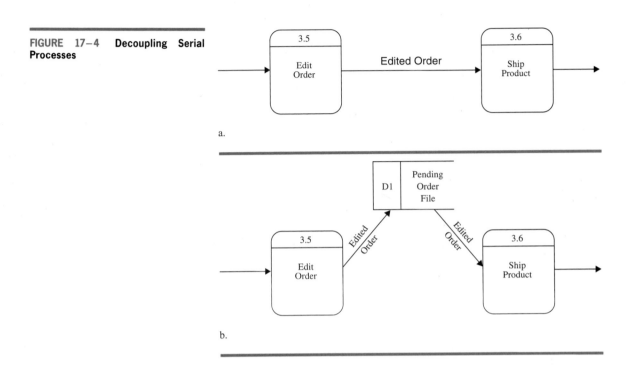

FIGURE 17–4   Decoupling Serial Processes

can draw from the buffer file at its own speed and when it desires (e.g., weekends). Temporary files are an excellent medium for decoupling sequential processes.

4. *Reduce interruptions.* This is particularly relevant with data entry operations. Place these operations in quiet areas where there is minimum traffic and minimum environmental disruptions. Would you be comfortable studying for an examination on the floor of the New York Stock Exchange?

5. *Reduce output movement.* Consider electronic movement of output (workstation screen reports) rather than physical movement to paper reports. In addition, position sequential activities physically close so output from one process does not have to move far.

6. *Set priorities.* Some processes and process tasks are more important than others. Some transactions require more expeditious handling than others. Set processing priorities to recognize more important events and handle them first.

Simplify Language

This pertains to operating procedures and interactive screen design. Simple language reduces inconsistencies (increases reliability) and decreases learning times (increases usability). Know the reading and comprehension level of your workforce. Use abbreviations and acronyms with care.

Standardize Processes

Look for similar activities and algorithms and standardize them. Interactive screen layouts are one example. The header and footer information should be similar for all screens. Standardization of software modules allows you to take advantage of reusable code.

PROFILE OF A POORLY DESIGNED PROCESS

Tim Stafford is a systems analyst for Walls Stationary Company. Tim has been asked to design an automatic version of the current manual warehousing system. He starts by constructing a physical data flow diagram of the current system. Tim's first draft of this diagram is shown in Figure 17–5. Tim uses this diagram and an inspection of the actual work area to list the following opportunities for improving this warehousing process.

1. In processes 1 and 2, the salesperson and the sales clerk have to record similar sales data onto a form (duplicate activities).

2. Processes 2 and 4 are not value-added. They do not add to the nature of the information or to the value of the system output. (Would customers pay to have orders sorted?)

3. The returned order data flow (from process 2 back to process 1) and returned order form data flow (from process 3 back to process 2) are the result of errors. Therefore, a portion of the tasks performed at processes 1 and 2 are rework. This should be eliminated or minimized (value-added).

4. Processes 5 and 6 can be consolidated since they are done by the same person in consecutive activities. Files B1 and B3 can also be consolidated (simplification).

5. Process 1 can be eliminated by allowing customers to communicate sales directly to the sales clerk (simplification).

6. Credit limit processes (5 and 6) can be done at the same time (parallel) with determining warehouse location (process 8). Tim Stafford finds that only 10 percent of the output from process 6 goes to process 7. Hence, 90 percent of the time process 8 is performed in any case. Therefore, there is no reason processes 6 and 8 cannot be done at the same time, thus reducing process cycle times.

7. The record order task (process 2) can be automated with an extensive error-checking routine to prevent flawed customer orders from reaching process 3 (error proofing).

8. Tim Stafford finds that documentation from the credit limit decision is dated and poorly written. Errors result and it is difficult to train people to make this decision when the credit supervisor is not available (simple language).

9. Tim also finds that there are several different versions of the customer order form, resulting in confusion and lack of complete data (standardization).

These are but a few of the problems, or opportunities, that can be determined from the DFD of Figure 17–5. A problem at the end of this chapter will allow you to detect more process design opportunities.

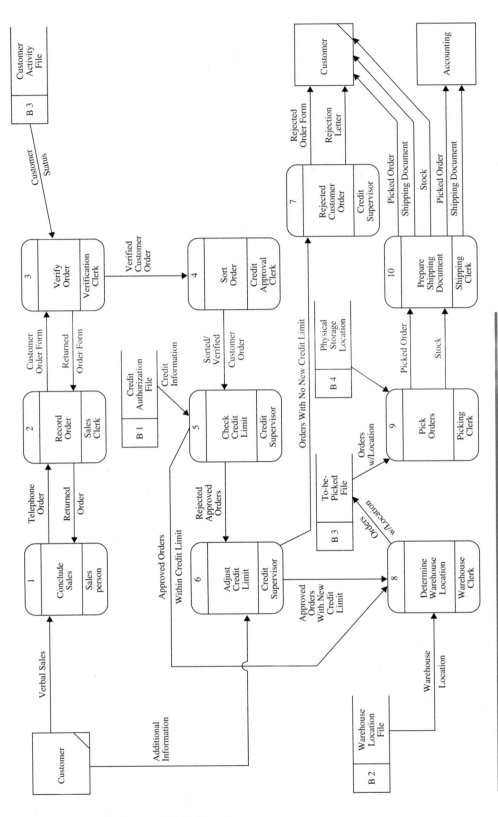

FIGURE 17–5 Physical DFD for Walls Stationary Manual Warehousing System

STRUCTURED ENGLISH

After processes have been designed, each remaining process must be specified in sufficient detail to allow translation to computer language code. Use of decision tables and decision trees was described in Chapter 11. Here we concentrate on use of **structured English,** an English-like, syntaxfree language used to describe process logic. Before we can describe structured English, however, we must first explore the background of structured programming. This is because our design information system will be constructed using structured programming methodologies.

Goals of Program Logic Tools

Every program logic tool has several goals:

To convey adequate logic detail to the programmer without overspecifying. Overspecification restricts the flexibility of the solution and is too time-consuming for the analyst. Remember, the programmer is not merely a coder, but an information expert trained to make detailed logic decisions.

To convey logic in a simple, easy-to-create, and understandable manner. Graphic-based tools lend clarity and simplicity to this task.

To confine logic control at the primitive level to the structured control constructs of sequences, iteration, and selection (see Figure 17–6). Primitive level is where there is a one-to-one translation between specification logic symbols and program language statements.

To convey logic in a generic, non-language-specific manner. Once the analyst specifies logic, the programmer is responsible for adding any language-specific details. The logic itself should translate into any programming language.

To create strongly cohesive modules loosely coupled to one another. The optimal approach is to create modules that perform only one task (that is, they are cohesive) and are only coupled to other modules by data. The strategy is to build subroutine drivers that call other modules down to the most primitive level of programming language statements. Once lower modules are completed, control returns to upper-level modules and finally rests at the topmost level. (This sequential process is explained in more detail later in this chapter.)

Structured Approaches to Programming

In the early days of programming, the approach to coding was bottom-up. Once the systems design specification phase was completed, the lead analyst divided primitive-level tasks (lowest level of hierarchy chart) and distributed them among programmers. The programmers went off on their own and spent an allotted amount of time coding their own modules. They were responsible for creating and testing each module in an isolated manner. At the end of the specified time, the programmers delivered their modules to the team. Now the upper-level modules were written and all modules were tested together (systems test). This approach left the difficult task of testing interfaces

FIGURE 17–6 **Nonoverlapping Blocks in Structured Logic**

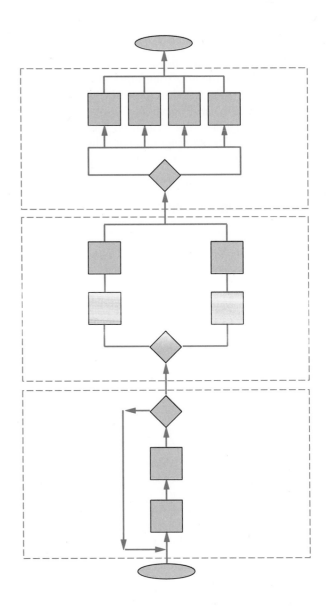

between modules until last. In addition, none of the lower-level modules could function without the upper-level modules. Therefore, no part of the system could function until the entire system operated as one unit. No lower-level module could be tested until the entire system was put together.

Contrast this with the top-down approach in which the upper-level modules are coded and tested first and the lower-level modules are tested last. With the top-down approach, the system can function on a partial basis and debugging can be done incrementally. This approach allows partial delivery of a functioning system as opposed to late delivery because of the need to wait until the entire system is functional.

As systems grew larger and more complex, the bottom-up approach in combination with tricky, undocumented code became unacceptable. This gave rise to the "structured revolution." The first phase of structured methodology was dedicated to straightening out the programming mess. Liberal use of GOTOs was identified as the chief problem. Logic control, it was determined, should be confined to three structures that increase the modularity of program code, namely, sequence, iteration, and selection. GOTOs were discouraged and sometimes banned.

Structured Programming Constructs. Today, the three control structures of structured programming are in common use.

The **sequence construct** involves sequential progression from one module into another (or from one statement into another) with no branches or GOTOs. Figure 17–6 shows sequence in a segment of a program flowchart.

The **iteration construct** is repetition of logic. Structured iteration without GOTOs means use of logic such as DO WHILE, REPEAT UNTIL, or PERFORM UNTIL. Figure 17–6 shows these types of iteration.

The **selection construct** is branching, which is difficult to accomplish without GOTOs. The structured approach adds IF/THEN/ELSE and CASE logic to programming languages; they allow more controlled selection. See Figure 17–6 for a visual representation of these two structures.

Benefits of Structured Techniques. Over 50 percent of programming effort over the life of an information system is devoted to maintenance (Yourdon, 1988). Some estimate this figure to be as high as 85 percent. Soon after system delivery, most programming effort is aimed at debugging and fixing. As time goes on, efforts are directed to adapting the system to fulfill changing needs of the organization. Maintenance effort translates into labor, money, and wasted time. Structured techniques help to simplify the maintenance effort by enforcing straightforward logic and modularity. Structured techniques also emphasize documentation.

When a system is decomposed into many cohesive, loosely coupled modules, code is much easier to maintain. The maintenance programmer can identify the correct module for alteration and can change that module without fear that those changes will cause problems in other modules or that other modules may be causing this module's problems.

The structured approach also enhances the productivity of novice programmers. Even though it takes longer to train them in structured methodology, the results are worthwhile. Novice programmers start by coding several simple modules rather than just one or two complex modules. The tools used to convey logic from analyst to programmer are fairly simple to learn and lessen the programmer's work. Perhaps the structured approach takes the art out of programming and reduces it to a fairly routine task. This is unfortunate. Yet, the trade-off is substantial: newly developed systems that are functionally correct and easy to maintain.

Structured English

Structured English is a form of pseudocode. **Pseudocode** is a technique for specifying primitive-level logic, and it has been in use for many years. Structured English is just what it sounds like. Each operation or task is stated in an English-like, syntaxfree phrase. These phrases use verb-object combinations to state the logic of a program. Objects are confined to data elements that are in the data dictionary. Verbs are confined to operations that are generic to most programming languages. No undefined adverbs or adjectives are permitted. The goal is to lay out the logic of a program module in an algorithmic manner while avoiding language specificity. Programmers can take a structured English module and from it write code in any programming language.

Pseudocode resembles specific programming languages such as FORTRAN and BASIC. Structured English is programming-language independent. Another difference between pseudocode and structured English is that structured English is confined to the three control structures just described. Conversely, pseudocode can use GOTOs and IF/THENs or any other command logic. Structured English includes END DO and END IF phrases to close the logic of program segments. Including the exact identification of segment endings avoids confusion on the part of maintenance programmers.

Now let's look at structured English in the context of two of its control structures.

Sequence. Sequence is merely a sequential set of commands that do not require branching or iteration. When one command is finished executing, the next is executed, and so forth. An example follows:

```
Heading
Read MEMBER NAME, MEMBER ID, BALANCE DUE
Calculate NEWBALANCE using the formula:
NEWBALANCE = BALANCE DUE + TRANSACTION TOTAL
Print MEMBER NAME, MEMBER ID, NEWBALANCE
Replace BALANCE DUE with NEWBALANCE in MEMBER ACCOUNT
```

Note that the nouns and objects found in the data dictionary are capitalized.

Iteration. There are several permissible structured constructs for repetition, or iteration. The key is that each construct is self-contained; that is, it begins and ends in one local, contiguous set of commands. The following generic set of formats illustrates the options available:

- While [condition], do [instruction/s]
- Repeat [instruction/s] until [condition]
- Do the following [X (some number)] times:

Three examples of structured English iteration follow:

Example 1

```
Read MEMBER NAME, MEMBER ID, BALANCE DUE
While BALANCE DUE not equal to zero, do:
  Print MEMBER NAME, MEMBER ID, BALANCE DUE
  Accumulate TOTAL BALANCE
  Increment COUNTER
  Read MEMBER NAME, MEMBER ID, BALANCE DUE
End while
```

Example 2

```
Repeat:
  Read BOWLER, GAME1, GAME2, GAME3
  Calculate TOTAL SCORE using the formula:
  TOTAL SCORE = GAME1 + GAME2 + GAME3
  Calculate AVERAGE using the formula:
 AVERAGE = TOTAL SCORE/3
  Accumulate TEAM TOTAL
  Increment COUNTER
  Print BOWLER, TOTAL SCORE
Until End of File
Print TEAM TOTAL
```

Example 3

```
Do the following 10 times:
  Read STUDENT NAME, EXAM SCORE
  Accumulate TOTAL POINTS
  Print STUDENT NAME, EXAM SCORE
End do
Calculate AVERAGE using the formula:
AVERAGE = TOTAL POINTS/10
Print AVERAGE
```

Structured English is particularly suited for the logic summary portion of the process entry in the data dictionary. Figure 17–7 shows a data dictionary entry for end-of-month processing for an inventory system.

STRUCTURE CHARTS

Another structured design tool for describing process logic is the structure chart. A **structure chart** is a graphic tool that shows the hierarchy of program modules and

LABEL:	4.1.1
ENTRY TYPE:	PROCESS
DESCRIPTION:	END OF MONTH PROCESSING
ALIAS:	NONE

VALUES AND
MEANINGS:
(COMPOSITION
AND LOGIC
SUMMARY)

```
DO FOR EACH INVENTORY ITEM
        COUNT STOCK IN STOCK ROOM
        ENTER COUNT ON INVENTORY SHEET
END DO

DO FOR EACH INVENTORY ITEM
        COUNT STOCK IN DISPLAY ROOM
        ENTER COUNT ON INVENTORY SHEET
END DO

DO FOR EACH INVENTORY ITEM
        READ ITEM FROM INVENTORY FILE
        ADD DISPLAY ROOM COUNT TO STOCK ROOM COUNT
        ENTER AMOUNT IN RECORD
END DO

SELECT CASE
CASE 1:       (CONDITION 1-CALCULATE WHOLESALE)
                INITIALIZE TOTALWSVALUE
                DO FOR EACH INVENTORY ITEM
                        READ PHYSCOUNT, WSPRICE
                        MULTIPLY PHYSCOUNT TIMES WSPRICE
                                GIVING WSVALUE
                        ACCUMULATE TOTALWSVALUE
                END DO
                        WRITE TOTALWSVALUE
END CASE 1

CASE 2:       (CONDITION 2-CALCULATE RETAIL)
                INITIALIZE TOTALRETAIL
                DO FOR EACH INVENTORY ITEM
                        READ PHYSCOUNT, WSPRICE, MARKON
                        MULTIPLY PHYSCOUNT TIMES WSPRICE
                                TIMES MARKON GIVING RETAIL
                        ACCUMULATE TOTALRETAIL
                END DO
                        WRITE TOTALRETAIL
END CASE 2

CASE 3:       (CONDITION 3-CALCULATE SHRINK)
                INITIALIZE TOTALAUTOCOUNT
                        AND TOTALPHYSCOUNT
                DO FOR EACH INVENTORY ITEM
                        READ PHYSCOUNT, AUTOCOUNT
                        ACCUMULATE TOTALPHYSCOUNT
                        ACCUMULATE TOTALAUTOCOUNT
                END DO
                SUBTRACT TOTALPHYSCOUNT FROM
                        TOTALAUTOCOUNT GIVING SHRINKCOUNT
                        WRITE SHRINKCOUNT
                DO FOR EACH INVENTORY ITEM
```

FIGURE 17–7   **Data Dictionary Entry for End-of-Month Inventory Processing**

```
                                    READ AUTOCOUNT, PHYSCOUNT, WSPRICE
                                    TOTAL SHRINKBUCKS = TOTAL
                                              SHRINKBUCKS + (AUTOCOUNT *
                                                   WSPRICE) − (PHYSCOUNT *
                                                        WSPRICE))
                              END DO
                              WRITE TOTALSHRINKBUCKS
            END CASE 3

            CASE 4:      (CONDITION 4 − BEGINNING BALANCE)
                              DO FOR EACH INVENTORY ITEM
                                    READ RECORD
                                    PLACE AUTOCOUNT WITH PHYSCOUNT
                                    SET PHYSCOUNT TO ZERO
                              END DO
            END CASE 4

                                    DO FOR EACH INVENTORY ITEM
                                    READ PHYSCOUNT, WSPRICE
                                    MULTIPLY PHYSCOUNT TIMES WSPRICE
                                              GIVING WSVALUE
                                    ACCUMULATE TOTALWSVALUE
                              END DO
                                    WRITE TOTALWSVALUE
            END
```

NOTES:

LOCATIONS: THIRD LEVEL EXPLOSION OF INVENTORY PROCESSING

FIGURE 17–7   (continued)

interfaces between them. The structure chart is similar to a hierarchy chart. However, the structure chart adds annotations for data flowing between modules. Figure 17–8 shows structure chart symbols. Figure 17–9 is an example of a structure chart produced by the Visible Analyst CASE tool.

REENGINEERING

This chapter so far has described design of information system processes as a part of the system development life cycle—as a part of *new* system development. However, one of the frameworks of total quality management is continuous quality improvement. **Continuous quality improvement (CQI)** is the ongoing effort to improve business processes. In an information systems context, this means we must continue to improve our processes even when we are not in the midst of an SDLC. We call this reengineering.

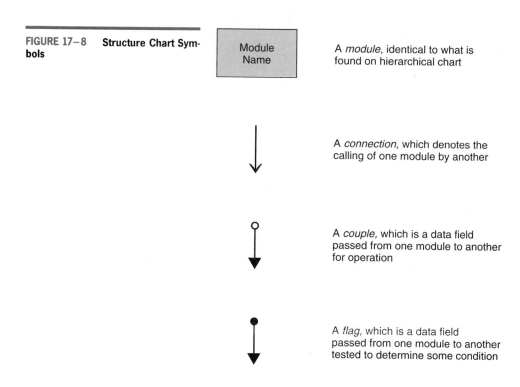

FIGURE 17–8   Structure Chart Symbols

A *module*, identical to what is found on hierarchical chart

A *connection*, which denotes the calling of one module by another

A *couple*, which is a data field passed from one module to another for operation

A *flag*, which is a data field passed from one module to another tested to determine some condition

Reengineering is improvement of information processes after the system is operational. Reengineering of information system processes includes the following functions:

1. Redesign of program code to make it more structured. Some automated products reorganize computer code and eliminate nonstructured code such as GOTO or ALTER.
2. Elimination of logic branches that will not be executed.
3. Production of specifications such as hierarchy charts from program code.
4. Analysis of frequency of use of differing program logic paths.
5. Analysis of operating times by program logic paths.
6. Analysis of storage allocation.

Sometimes problems with information systems can be alleviated through reengineering, thereby eliminating the need to begin the expensive and timely SDLC. Reengineering is considered a part of maintenance, rather than development of information systems.

HUMAN ASPECTS

There is a danger to using the structured approach to system development. This danger is that the analyst tends to concentrate on the process symbol of the data flow diagram, and to play with this symbol as if it were an animate object. Information processes are,

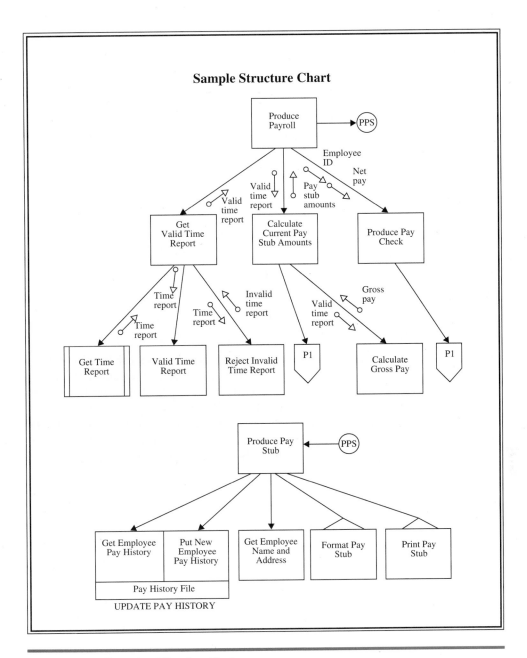

FIGURE 17–9 **Example of Structure Chart**

Reprinted with permission of Visible Systems Corporation, Waltham, Mass.

however, most often a geographic location filled with people. Even when the process is completely automated (a module in a computer program), humans feed data into the process and use the information output from that process.

Information system processes cannot be designed adequately in the isolated office of an analyst or a programmer. Information system processes must be designed, at least partially, in the user work-area. So, throw aside your DFDs for the moment. Go out into the user work-area and see how human the information system process really is.

SUMMARY

The principles of information system process design are:

- Eliminate duplicate processes.
- Eliminate processes that are not value-added.
- Simplify processes.
- Reduce process cycle-time.
- Simplify language.
- Standardize processes.

This chapter presented numerous ways in which these principles can be applied.

Process logic must be described in sufficient detail to allow translation to program language code. Two structured tools for this description are structured English and structure charts. Both of these tools were described.

Reengineering is improvement of information processes after the system is operational. Sometimes problems with information systems can be alleviated through reengineering, thereby eliminating the need to begin the expensive and timely SDLC.

CONCEPTS LEARNED

- Analyst responsibilities in process design
- Seven principles of process design
- How to use structured English
- What structure charts are
- The principle of reengineering

KEY TERMS

computer-based information system
continuous quality improvement (CQI)
decoupling processes
industrial engineer
information processes
iteration construct
physical processes

pseudocode
reengineering
selection construct
sequence construct
structure chart
structured English
value-added process

REVIEW QUESTIONS

1. What is the responsibility of an industrial engineer?

2. Why is the systems analyst concerned with physical processes?

3. List the seven principles of process design.

4. Why do we wish to eliminate duplicate processes?

5. What is a value-added process? Give three examples of non-value-added processes.

6. Describe three methods for simplifying processes.

7. Describe four ways to decrease process cycletime.

8. Why must we simplify process language?

9. What are the three structured programming constructs?

10. What are the differences between pseudocode and structured English?

11. What are the goals of program logic tools?

12. Describe differences between the top-down and bottom-up approaches to programming.

13. What are the benefits of structured techniques?

14. Describe a structure chart.

15. Where does reengineering fit in the design of information systems?

CRITICAL THINKING OPPORTUNITIES

1. Draw a diagram of the organization of this chapter.

2. Compare and contrast pseudocode, structured English, and structure charts.

3. Reference Figure 17–5:
   a) Detect problems other than those described in the textbook.
   b) Redraw the DFD for the redesigned process.

4. Read the following description of the Stuffit Ticket Company and do the following exercises.
   a) Select two of the processes and describe the logic in structured English.
   b) Reengineer the system by using the principles of process design.

STUFFIT TICKET COMPANY*

The Stuffit Ticket Company operates eighteen ticket-selling outlets in selected Sears stores in the Sacramento Valley between Modesto and Chico. The company is in business to sell theater, concert, sporting events, and other tickets to persons interested in attending such events.

A ticket outlet consists of a counter, the Stuffit Ticket sign, one telephone, and two to three ticket clerks assigned to ticket booths located behind the counter.

The Stuffit operation works as follows: Stuffit's owner, Mr. Yormy Mark, enters into an agreement with event promoters to buy a designated number of tickets (unsold tickets are not refundable). Customers desiring tickets to an event go to the nearest Stuffit Ticket location and queue up. When it is his or her turn, the customer requests a ticket (or tickets) for an event on a specified date. The ticket clerk checks availability of the desired ticket from a master ticket inventory prepared each night by Mr. Mark at Stuffit's headquarters. If the ticket is shown available on the master ticket inventory, the clerk prepares a ticket voucher, calculates the ticket price (equal to face value of the ticket plus $.50 per ticket commission), and collects payment from the customer.

One copy of the ticket voucher is given to the customer; one copy is sent to the event's box office; and the last copy is sent at day's end to Stuffit headquarters. (The customer presents his or her copy of the ticket voucher at the "will call" window of the event's box office to redeem the ticket on the day of the event.) The ticket clerk also posts the number of tickets sold to the master ticket inventory, and computes a new balance of available tickets for the event.

If the ticket desired by the customer is shown as unavailable, the ticket clerk tries to persuade the customer to buy a ticket for an alternative date or event. If that fails, the ticket clerk is instructed to call Stuffit headquarters to see if additional tickets have been purchased that day by Stuffit that might be available for sale.

Each evening, Mr. Mark receives the just concluded day's ticket vouchers from the ticket outlets. He subtracts the number of tickets sold from the event and event-date available counts shown on the master ticket inventory, and produces a new ticket inventory for the next day.

Mr. Mark believes that, perhaps, a means is required to improve ticket order processing. Several incidents have given rise to this concern. First, one customer threatened to reconfigure Mr. Mark's nose because the customer's tickets were gone when he presented his ticket voucher to the box office on the day of the event. Apparently, this has happened more than once, resulting in a rash of lawsuits.

Also, ticket clerks report that customers seem to take exception to waiting in long lines and then finding that no more tickets are available. In fact, Mr. Mark has noticed that customers often have to wait up to two hours to buy tickets at some ticket outlets; many potential customers just walk away angry.

*This case was prepared by Professor David Schultz, MIS Department, California State University, Sacramento.

MCKRAKLIN AEROSPACE: DESIGN PHASE

SETTING

Last month Dave Costner presented the design proposal for a new inventory/receiving system to top management. The oral presentation lasted one hour. Dave used a prototype as part of his presentation. The management group agreed that the proposed new system had investment potential and that design should begin.

Dave added four systems persons to the team of Susan Willebe and Ron Sauter. Dave appointed Susan project leader. The team completed the logical design phase of the project. Now it is time to enter the physical (detail) design stage of the life cycle.

RECEIVING SUBSYSTEM

Concentration will be on the receiving portion of the total inventory system (Figure 17.1–1). The products completed during logical design include:

- Physical data flow diagram (Figure 17.1–2)
- Data dictionary entry for the receiving screen (Figure 17.1–3)
- Data dictionary entry for the receiving slip (Figure 17.1–4)

- Data dictionary entry for purchase order file (Figure 17.1–5)
- Decision table for receiving logic (Figure 17.1–6)

REVIEW QUESTIONS

1. Why did Dave Costner (IS manager) present the design proposal rather than the analysis team (Susan Willebe and Ron Sauter)?
2. What is the difference between the logical and physical stages of the systems development life cycle?

EXERCISES

1. Design the receiving screen.
2. Design the receiving slip.
3. Design the purchase order file (including coding of appropriate data elements).
4. Convert the decision table to structured English.
5. Use pseudocode, structured English, or decision tables to describe the editing logic for fields entered to the receiving screen.

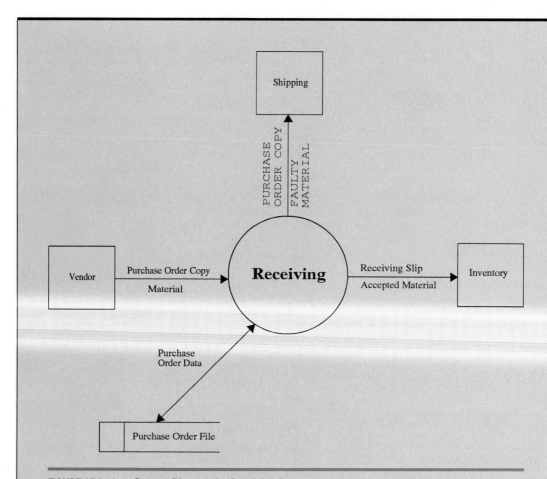

FIGURE 17.1–1   **Context Diagram for Receiving Process**

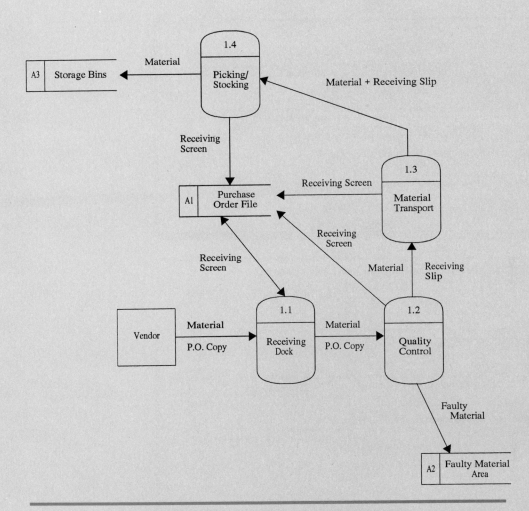

FIGURE 17.1−2   **Physical Data Flow Diagram for Proposed Receiving Subsystem**

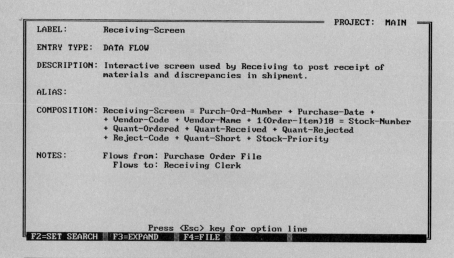

```
                                              PROJECT:  MAIN
LABEL:        Receiving-Screen

ENTRY TYPE:   DATA FLOW

DESCRIPTION:  Interactive screen used by Receiving to post receipt of
              materials and discrepancies in shipment.

ALIAS:

COMPOSITION:  Receiving-Screen = Purch-Ord-Number + Purchase-Date +
              + Vendor-Code + Vendor-Name + 1{Order-Item}10 = Stock-Number
              + Quant-Ordered + Quant-Received + Quant-Rejected
              + Reject-Code + Quant-Short + Stock-Priority

NOTES:        Flows from: Purchase Order File
                  Flows to: Receiving Clerk




                     Press <Esc> key for option line
 F2=SET SEARCH    F3=EXPAND      F4=FILE
```

FIGURE 17.1-3   Data Dictionary Entry for Receiving Screen

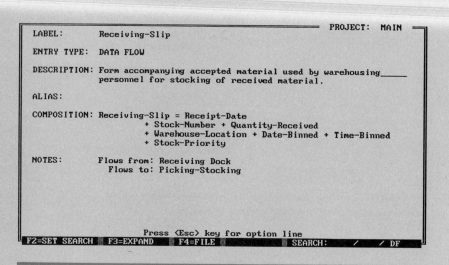

```
                                              PROJECT:  MAIN
LABEL:        Receiving-Slip

ENTRY TYPE:   DATA FLOW

DESCRIPTION:  Form accompanying accepted material used by warehousing_____
              personnel for stocking of received material.

ALIAS:

COMPOSITION:  Receiving-Slip = Receipt-Date
                          + Stock-Number + Quantity-Received
                          + Warehouse-Location + Date-Binned + Time-Binned
                          + Stock-Priority

NOTES:        Flows from: Receiving Dock
                  Flows to: Picking-Stocking




                     Press <Esc> key for option line
 F2=SET SEARCH    F3=EXPAND      F4=FILE                    SEARCH:    /    / DF
```

FIGURE 17.1-4   Data Dictionary Entry for Receiving Slip

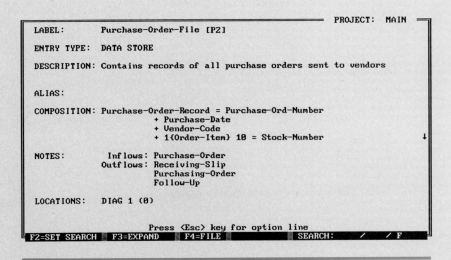

```
                                                          PROJECT:  MAIN
  LABEL:        Purchase-Order-File [P2]

  ENTRY TYPE:  DATA STORE

  DESCRIPTION: Contains records of all purchase orders sent to vendors


  ALIAS:

  COMPOSITION: Purchase-Order-Record = Purchase-Ord-Number
                          + Purchase-Date
                          + Vendor-Code
                          + 1{Order-Item} 10 = Stock-Number            ↓

  NOTES:        Inflows: Purchase-Order
               Outflows: Receiving-Slip
                         Purchasing-Order
                         Follow-Up

  LOCATIONS:   DIAG 1 (0)


                    Press <Esc> key for option line
 F2=SET SEARCH   F3=EXPAND   F4=FILE            SEARCH:     /     / F
```

FIGURE 17.1−5   Data Dictionary Entry for Purchase Order File

		Rules						
Conditions		1	2	3	4	5	6	7
Priority Shipment?		Y	N	N	N	N	N	N
Obvious Physical Damage?		—	Y	N	N	N	N	N
Every 5th Container?		—	—	N	Y	Y	Y	Y
Parts Damaged?		—	—	—	N	Y	N	N
Parts Short?		—	—	—	N	—	N	Y
Actions								
Send Container to Warehouse		*		*	*		*	*
Open and Inspect					*		*	
Complete Discrepancy Report			*			*		*
Return Shipment to Vendor			*			*		

FIGURE 17.1−6   Decision Table for Receiving Logic

CLASS DESIGN PROJECT: DESIGN PHASE

SETTING

In this phase of your class design project, you will be responsible for the following deliverable

P7 System Report

The contents of this report include the following:

A. Organization
   1. Cover letter
   2. Title page
   3. Table of contents
B. Output
   1. Layouts
   2. Run frequencies
C. Input
   1. Layouts
      2. Input validation rules
      3. Description of error messages
D. Interactive screens
   1. Screen flow (menu map)
   2. Screen layouts
   3. Description of error messages
E. File structures
   1. Schema
   2. Subschema
   3. Layout
   4. Access method
   5. Storage requirements
   6. Retention/recovery procedures
F. Process design
   1. Leveled set physical DFDs for new system
   2. Process frequencies/timing
G. Data dictionary

REFERENCES AND FURTHER READINGS

Bailey, R. W. *Human Performance Engineering: A Guide for System Designers.* Englewood Cliffs, N.J.: Prentice-Hall, 1982.

Benham, Harry, Leon Price, and Jennifer Wagner. "Comparisons of Structured Development Methodologies." *Information Executive* 24(Spring 1989):18–23.

Buckler, G. "DPs Told They Need New Programming Methods." *Computing Canada* 13(April 1987):1, 7.

Flaatten, Per, et al. *Foundations of Business Systems.* Chicago: Dryden Press, 1989.

Galitz, Wilbert. *Handbook of Screen Format Design,* 2nd ed. Wellesley Hills, Mass.: QED Information Sciences, 1985.

Gane, C., and T. Sarson. *Structured Systems Analysis: Tools and Techniques.* Englewood Cliffs, N.J.: Prentice-Hall, 1979.

Gore, Marvin, and John Stubbe. *Elements of System Analysis.* Dubuque, Ia.: William C. Brown, 1983.

Grief, R., and S. Sarin. "Data Sharing in Group Work." In *Proceedings of the Conference on Computer-Supported Cooperative Work.* Austin, Texas, 1986, pp. 175–183.

Hare, Van Court. *Systems Analysis: A Diagnostic Approach.* New York: Harcourt, Brace & World, 1967.

Harrington, James. *Business Process Improvement.* New York: McGraw-Hill, 1991.

Joint Application Design. GUIDE Publication GPP-147. Chicago: GUIDE International, 1986.

Martin, Merle. "The Human Connection in Systems Design: Adaptive Models." *Journal of Systems Management* 37(October 1986):23–29.

Martin, Merle. "The Human Connection in Systems Design: Screen Design." *Journal of Systems Management* 37(October 1986):15–22.

Martin, Merle. "The Human Connection in Systems Design: User Categories." *Journal of Systems Management* 37(October 1986):8–14.

"Multi-media Systems." *IS Analyzer* 25(October 1987):1–16.

Shneiderman, Ben. *Designing the User Interface.* Reading, Mass.: Addison-Wesley, 1987.

Stair, Ralph. *Principles of Information Systems.* Boston: boyd & fraser, 1992.

Sullivan, William, and W. Wayne Claycomb. *Fundamentals of Forecasting.* Reston, Va.: Reston Publishing, 1977.

Turban, E., and J. E. Carlson. "Interactive Visual Decision Making." In *Decision Support Systems: Putting Theory into Practice,* edited by R. H. Sprague and H. J. Watson. Englewood Cliffs, N.J.: Prentice-Hall, 1989.

Yourdon, E. *Managing the Structured Techniques.* New York: Yourdon Press, 1988.

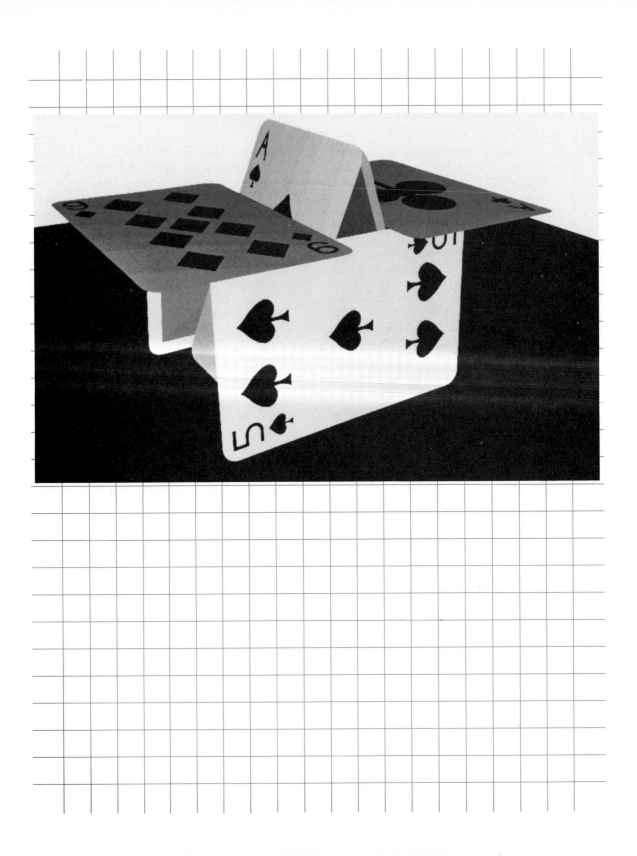

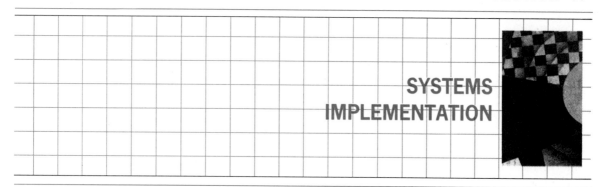

SYSTEMS IMPLEMENTATION

Design of business information systems often borders on the artistic. After creating the logical system, the systems analyst may show little patience for the construction phase (systems implementation). However, poor construction of a well-conceived system leads to failure. Therefore, a critical portion of the SDLC is that of implementation.

Chapter 18, "Program Construction and Testing," stresses the need for programming control, standardization, and documentation. The primary goal of programming is ease in making future changes in programs. Structured, comprehensive testing is critical to successful implementation of information systems.

Chapter 19, "System Changeover," discusses several options for moving from the old to the new information system. Emphasis is placed on causes and manifestations of user resistance and what can be done to reduce that resistance.

Chapter 20, "System Evaluation," stresses the need to establish system goals and measurements, and to monitor them continually. The chapter describes a structured approach to designing a quality evaluation system.

In this chapter you will learn about:

WHAT: (Concepts) Construction and testing of information system computer programs.

WHY: A well-designed system is useless unless it is programmed correctly.

WHEN: First stage of implementation phase of SDLC.

WHO: Programmer in coordination with systems analyst.

WHERE: Information systems department.

HOW: (Techniques) Programming standards
                       Programming documentation tools
                       Testing methods

OUTLINE

- Setting
- A Total Quality Approach
- A Structured Approach
- Coordinating the Programming Effort
- Programming Standards
- Construction of Test Data
- Testing Control
- Automated Testing Support
- Profile of a Poorly Programmed System
- Human Aspects

C H A P T E R 18

PROGRAM CONSTRUCTION AND TESTING

If builders built buildings the way programmers wrote programs, then the first woodpecker that came along would destroy civilization.

— GERALD WEINBERG

SETTING

The systems blueprint is now complete. It is time for physical construction of the new business information system. The major task in construction is converting inputs, outputs, files, processes, and their interactions into program code that drives the operational system. This chapter describes the programming process. Many organizations purchase applications software rather than building it internally. In such cases, the contents of this chapter can be used to evaluate purchase of software rather than as a means to construct it.

Physical design of a business information system is guided as much by the principles of the well-designed system (Chapter 10) as is logical design. The principles of modularity and cohesion are particularly important.

As shown in Figure 18–1, the major percentage of programming dollars is spent on systems maintenance, not on systems design. Therefore, it is foolish to optimize design programming at the expense of maintenance programming. Indeed, it is sometimes wise to design programs less efficiently, if this will ease future maintenance programming. Figure 18–2 illustrates this rather startling concept. Programming costs include development (one-time) costs and maintenance (recurring) costs. In Figure 18–2(b) costs of development programming have been increased so ensuing maintenance programming costs can operate at a lower level.

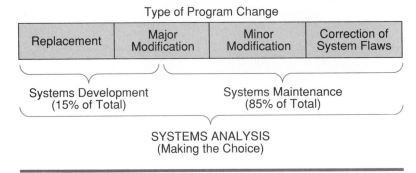

Type of Program Change			
Replacement	Major Modification	Minor Modification	Correction of System Flaws

Systems Development
(15% of Total)

Systems Maintenance
(85% of Total)

SYSTEMS ANALYSIS
(Making the Choice)

FIGURE 18–1   Spectrum of Business Programming

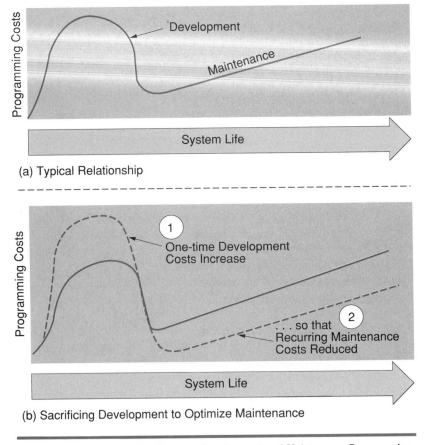

(a) Typical Relationship

(b) Sacrificing Development to Optimize Maintenance

FIGURE 18–2   Relationships between Development and Maintenance Programming

This chapter is devoted to the often-ignored principle that programming design and testing should be accomplished with an eye to the future. This is true even though a future focus may add to programming costs in the short run.

A TOTAL QUALITY APPROACH

Programming quality can be assessed by using the same nine information tests as described in the preceding chapters. Here is a checklist that can be used.

1. *Relevancy:* Have priorities been established for program modules so that the most important are begun and finished first?
2. *Completeness:* Have all logical specifications been programmed?
3. *Correctness:* Have you conducted a specification walkthrough to ensure that all functions have been correctly translated to program code?
4. *Security:* Have programs been made secure so that unauthorized personnel cannot make changes?
5. *Timeliness:* Will the tested program code be delivered on schedule?
6. *Economy:* All things being equal, is the programming being done as inexpensively as possible?
7. *Efficiency:* Are all relevant ratios optimized? For example, what is our performance as it relates to Program Steps Produced per Day?
8. *Reliability:* Is the day-to-day variance low for each of the above seven measures?
9. *Usability:* Is the resulting program code usable to maintenance programmers?

A STRUCTURED APPROACH

A structured development approach develops process specifications to further and further detail until processes have been broken down to the level of primitive code.

Primitive code is a one-to-one transaction from pseudocode or structured English code to lines of a production programming language code. The approach follows a systematic sequence using the data flow diagram and process specification.

Data Flow Diagram. Figure 18–3 shows a lower level DFD process for a payroll system. Note the inputs to the process, outputs from the process, and interactions between the process and data stores.

Process Specification. Processes are exploded to further detail in the next level of DFD. When the last level of detail is reached, the process is specified in primitive code. Figure 18–4 is a process specification for overtime processing of a payroll system. The primitive code used here is structured English. Structured English includes these seven rules:

1. Each process (operation) is stated in an English-like, syntaxfree phrase.
2. Phrases are verb-object combinations (for example, GET PAYROLL-RECORD).
3. Verbs are confined to operations generic to most programming languages.

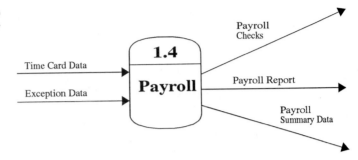

FIGURE 18–3   Partial Data Flow for Payroll Process

4. Objects are data elements contained in the data dictionary.
5. Logic is confined to the three control structures of sequence, iteration, and selection.
6. END DO and END IF phrases are used to close logic of program segments.
7. No undefined adverbs or adjectives are permitted.

COORDINATING THE PROGRAMMING EFFORT

The complexity of programming effort is considerable for all but the smallest business information systems. Complexity comes from several sources:

1. Often several programmers are involved.
2. Time constraints are frequently placed on the total programming effort in general and on specific programming modules in particular.
3. Modules are interdependent even when loosely coupled. Success or failure in one module may significantly affect success or failure in other modules. Outputs from one

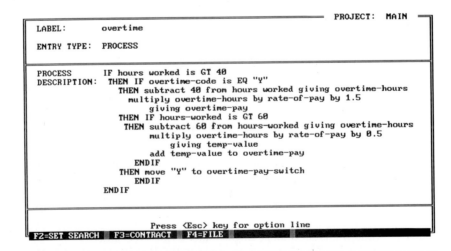

FIGURE 18–4   Process Specification for Overtime Pay

module become inputs to other modules. Delayed testing in one module may cause delayed testing in other modules.

4. Programming standards must be established and enforced to ensure efficiency of future changes.

5. User contacts must be structured and minimized. It is unsettling for a user to have visits from twelve programmers, each with questions about his or her specific module.

6. Testing of programs can interfere with the operational information system.

American Express is involved in a programming effort that is extremely complex. The company is rewriting almost all of its basic transaction processing systems. This project is called Genesis. Over one hundred programmers and many hundreds of thousands of lines of code are involved. The current code is structured poorly and the goals of this effort are to create well-structured modules that will be easy to maintain and that will interface with DB2 databases rather than the current IMS databases. Much effort has to be placed on the initial organization of this project.

Three tactics help to reduce programming complexity: the hierarchy chart, project leader assignment, and use of a common programming terminology.

Hierarchy Chart

The hierarchy chart is a tool of the top-down approach. It breaks complex programming problems into small modules (tasks). The modules can be assigned to a single programmer or a small team of programmers. Figure 18–5 is a hierarchy chart for a purchasing application. The hierarchy chart becomes the organizing tool for the programming effort. It has the following characteristics:

▪ The project is broken into small, cohesive tasks assigned to single programmers or groups of programmers.

FIGURE 18–5   **Hierarchy Chart for Purchasing Application**

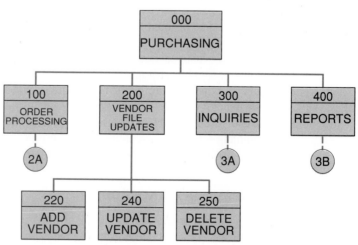

- Module dependencies follow a left-to-right structure. For example, in Figure 18–5, you must test the ADD VENDOR module successfully before the UPDATE VENDOR and DELETE VENDOR modules, since you cannot update or cancel a purchase order that does not exist. The hierarchy sets up module dependencies used in development of the programming project schedule and the test plan (both discussed later in this chapter).
- Unit modules are organized into group modules. For example, VENDOR FILE UPDATES (a group module) is not tested fully until the ADD, UPDATE, and DELETE modules are complete. This is important for testing purposes and for assignment of project responsibilities (e.g., one person is assigned completion of a group module).

The hierarchy chart serves two purposes. It provides documentation (circuitry diagram) for future changes in a system, and it is a means for organizing programming efforts.

Lead Programmer

One person from the programming staff is selected to be **lead programmer,** or project leader. For small projects, this leadership may be no more than additional duties added to regular programming duties. In large-scale projects, the project leader may be a full-time position. The duties of the project leader include (1) coordinating the several programmers working on the project, (2) interacting with users, (3) making sure enough resources (people, funds) are available to complete the programming project, and (4) reporting to management on progress of the project. You can expect that all but the smallest system development project will result in team, rather than individual, programming.

Common Programming Terminology

Programmers working on separate programming modules must work with a common terminology. Otherwise, chaos follows. It is not enough to use a common programming language such as COBOL. Additionally, commonly used data names and subroutines must be standardized. This is done by use of the data dictionary, which forces use of consistent terminology by the entire programming team.

Often, the data dictionary is transformed to a COBOL data division placed in a commonly accessible storage area. The first task for any programmer is to copy this common data division into his or her program. Not only does this standardize programming terminology, it also saves coding steps.

These three techniques to reduce programming complexity help coordinate the programming effort. Coordination, which creates a cohesive programming product, is enhanced further by use of strict programming standards.

PROGRAMMING STANDARDS

In the rush and pressure of making the new system work, it is easy to forget the overall goals of that system. One important business goal is design of the system to ease future programming changes. This goal may call for sacrificing the efficiency of design programming to optimize maintenance programming.

The most effective means of emphasizing future programming considerations is to set up and enforce strict programming standards. Too often, this subject is missing from discussions on systems development. Case 18.1 contains detailed descriptions of programming standards that optimize maintenance programming. In this chapter, standardization is briefly summarized in regard to coding, internal program documentation, and external program documentation.

Coding

A modular structure using the hierarchy chart and sections within individual programs is essential for coding. This allows changes to small program sections with minimum interruption of the rest of the system. Similarly, automobile engines are designed for modular repair. Avoid program code that is contrary to the concept of ease of future repair. Discourage use of such programming tactics as GOTOs, ALTERs, COMPUTEs, or use of special arithmetic logic symbols.

Internal Program Documentation

Narrative explanations of program functions should be emphasized in **internal program documentation.** Case 18.1 explains that even self-documenting languages such as COBOL require narrative augmentations so maintenance programmers can quickly and fully understand the logic used by design programmers. Languages such as FORTRAN, C, PL/1, and dBASE require even more internal program documentation than does COBOL. Refer to Figure 18–6 for examples of internal program documentation.

External Program Documentation

Maintaining a program is much like repairing a television set. The repairperson must first isolate where in the TV system the problem is occurring. Only then does he or she start digging into the television set to remove, test, and replace components. The key to the repairperson's search is the circuitry diagram. It is the same with program maintenance. The programmer searches for the module that needs repair, then steps through the code. The key to the programmer's search is **external program documentation.** This documentation includes such tools as the program hierarchy chart, the input-process-output chart, the structured detail flowchart, the Nassi-Shneiderman diagram, and the macro flowchart.

Detailed discussion of program documentation belongs in a book on programming. Many systems analysts, to their later regret, pay little attention to the programming stage of the systems development life cycle. What a huge mistake! Would the architect of a building ignore how engineers were constructing that building, or whether the building might crumble after it is finished? This analogy is not farfetched. Good design

```
BASIC program
110 REM T$ IS THE TOP MARKER
120 REM B$ IS THE BOTTOM MARKER
130 REM W$ IS THE WORD READ
140 REM C  IS THE NUMBER OF WORDS TO READ
150
200    READ T$
210    READ B$
220    READ C
300    FOR I = 1 TO C STEP 1
310       READ W$
320       IF WS< "N" THEN 400
330          PRINT T$
340          PRINT W$
350          PRINT B$
400       NEXT I
500
800 DATA ...
990 END


COBOL program

PROCEDURE DIVISION.

TAX-COMPUTATION.
     MULTIPLY AMOUNT BY0.07 GIVING TAX ROUNDED.
     NOTE       *** OUTPUT IS NOW ACCOMPLISHED ***
                *** BY USING THE DISPLAY VERB   ***
     DISPLAY AMOUNT, "TAX IS," TAX.  NOTE
                *** TEST TO DETERMINE WHETHER ***
                *** AMOUNT HAS EXCEEDED $100  ***
     IF AMOUNT IS LESS THAN 100.25 GO TO TAX-COMPUTATION.
     STOP RUN.


PASCAL program

PROGRAM COMPUTE;
{THIS PROGRAM COMPUTES 3 TIMES 4 AND
 PRINT THE PRODUCT.}
VAR
     RESULT : INTEGER;
BEGIN
     RESULT : = 3 * 4;
     WRITELN ('PRODUCT IS ', RESULT)
END.
```

FIGURE 18–6   Examples of Internal Program Documentation

coupled with poor construction equals a poor system, whether that system is a building or a business information system. Therefore, this book includes techniques of programming documentation.

CONSTRUCTION OF TEST DATA

It is unsettling to users of a new system when the system operates improperly because of flaws. No matter how careful the design effort, some flaws generally occur. It is the designer's responsibility to reduce these flaws to a level where they do not erode user confidence. One means of reducing flaws is to insist upon stringent program testing before the system is implemented. A stringent testing program includes constructing test data, establishing testing control, and using automated test support.

Constructing test data is a structured, complex process that is more germane to a book on programming. Since this subject is so critical to successful implementation of information systems, however, it is summarized here. This summary includes a review of (1) benefits of structured development of test data, (2) goal of test data construction, (3) testing construction techniques, (4) user-provided test data, (5) when to stop testing, and (6) the politics of testing.

Benefits of Structured Development of Test Data

Structured development of program test data has three benefits. First, it allows standardized testing by all programmers involved in the project. This helps ensure a consistent product. Second, structured development of test data allows for blanket testing—assessment of all possible conditions that can cause errors in the system. Third, structured development can be heuristic; that is, test data can be improved over time by learning from the system's failures. Each time a flaw occurs, the condition creating that flaw is added to the test data. Then, the revised and larger collection of test data is used to test all future program changes. Figure 18–7 illustrates development of **heuristic test data.**

Goal of Test Data Construction

The goal of constructing test data is to limit the number of tests. Each additional program test takes time and money. Yet, a minimum number of tests is necessary to ensure software quality. How many tests are required? Without using testing techniques described in the next section, the answer to this question is "too many!" Consider a program with fifteen branches (fifteen IF/THEN/ELSE statements). The number of tests required to exercise all possible combinations of these fifteen branches is 2^{15}, or $32,768$ separate tests. This number of software tests for a single program would exceed project completion time and resource constraints. The key to successful software testing is to break the branches into cohesive groups and to test groups independently.

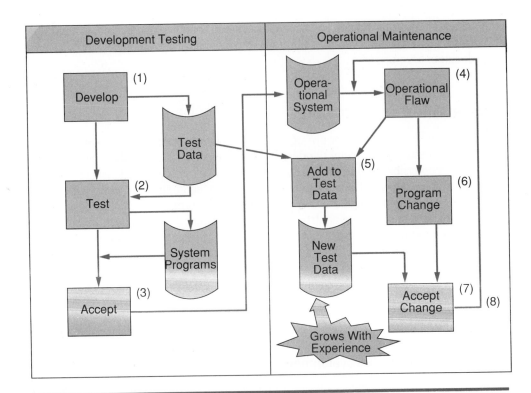

FIGURE 18–7   Heuristic Approach to Developing Program Test Data

Testing Techniques

Five techniques are available to reduce the number of testing possibilities and still ensure a comprehensive testing structure. These techniques are equivalency classes, dependency islands, risk assessment, seam testing, and specification walkthroughs.

Equivalency Classes. Two items handled by the same series of branches are in the same **equivalency class.** For example, if an input value is in the range of 1 to 100, then the 100 possible input values are in the same equivalency class. A test of one of these values will suffice instead of tests for all equivalency class values.

Dependency Islands. The technique of dependency islands separates the testing process into different output products. It is based on the common phenomenon that any one product from a system is not dependent on all the input. Look at Figure 18–8. Output 1 depends on inputs F1, F2, and F3. Output 2 depends on inputs F4 and F5. Finally, output 3 depends only on input F6. These three output **dependency islands** are independent of each other (this is where the term *island* arises). The three dependency islands can be tested independently of each other. As explained in the box "The Math-

FIGURE 18–8   **Dependency Islands**

Adapted from Bob Stahl, "The Ins and Outs of Software Testing," *Computerworld* (October 24, 1988).

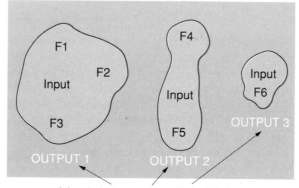

Software to Be Tested

Islands Independent of Each Other

THE MATHEMATICS OF DEPENDENCY ISLANDS

Refer to Figure 18–8. You are testing a software module with the six inputs F1 through F6. When the module is successful, it produces outputs 1 through 3. If all the outputs depended on all the inputs, there would be too many combinations of inputs with which to deal. However, this is rarely the case. Most information systems outputs do not depend on all possible inputs.

Assume each of the six inputs have five equivalency classes. This means that you can cover all the possible input values for each of the inputs (for example, 1 to 100) using only five tests. In this case, given six inputs, the number of tests required is 5^6, or 15,625. When each output depends only on some (not all) of the inputs, you can simplify testing. Figure 18–8 shows that output 1 is dependent only on inputs F1, F2, and F3; output 2 is dependent only upon inputs F4 and F5; and output 3 is dependent only on input F6. Since these three output dependency islands are not related to each other, you can test them separately and reduce the number of tests needed.

Output 1 depends only on F1, F2, and F3. Hence, you can step through those input fields with just 5^3, or 125 equivalence class combinations. You can leave F4, F5, and F6 at constant values during each of the 125 tests. In the same way, since output 2 depends only on inputs F4 and F5, you can test output 2 independently with 5^2, or 25 tests. Output 3 is dependent only on F6, so you can test it by itself with only five tests.

The total number of tests is now 125 plus 25 plus 5, or 155. This represents a more than 100-to-1 reduction in the number of tests required without consideration of dependency islands. The key is to focus testing tactics on output products rather than on possible input values.

SOURCE: Adapted from Bob Stahl, "The Ins and Outs of Software Testing," *Computerworld* (October 24, 1988).

ematics of Dependency Islands," this reduces the number of possible test runs from 15,625 to 155—a reduction of over 100 to 1.

Risk Assessment. The most important possible errors are tested first, then the next most important, and so on. In this way, if testing has to be stopped due to lack of resources, the most important tests will have been completed. How can you judge which of the many possible tests are more important?

One tactic is to use **risk assessment.** This technique classifies each possible error by its likelihood and its impact. Since likelihood is hard to judge, complexity of the program module is substituted. Consider Figure 18–9. Program module D is quite complex. It has tens of thousands of lines of code. Also, its failure is judged to have a high impact upon users. Module B, on the other hand, is a simple module with low impact on users. The other program modules fall somewhere in between. The testing strategy is to schedule program module tests in the sequence D, C, A, E, B. Assignment of module complexity and impact is done by a panel of systems analysts and users.

Seam Testing. When you buy an article of clothing, where does it suffer its first failure? The first flaw most likely will be at one of the seams. Software is similar to clothing. Many errors occur at module seams, where one function interfaces with another. **Seam testing** includes concentration of testing efforts on the following points:

- Extremes: Test high and low variable ranges. For example, if the range of values for input F1 is 1 to 100, test the values 1 *and* 100. In programming loops (e.g., PERFORM UNTIL or FOR statements), test the low and high values of the loop.

FIGURE 18–9   **Risk Assessment**

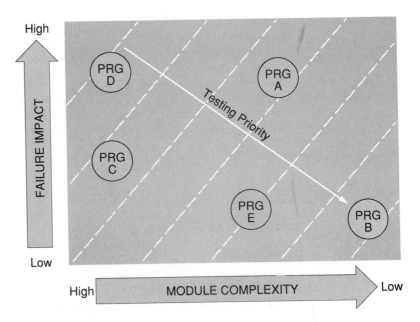

- Value zero: Have you ever tried to run a program where you divide by zero? This is only one of the many problems that the strange value zero can cause. For any input variable, always test the value of zero.
- Exceptions: These are conditions that cannot (should not) occur. Test software modules to be sure that impossible conditions cannot happen. For example, in a customer order processing system, include in your testing cancellation of a customer order that does not exist and an attempt to enter the same customer order a second time.

Specification Walkthroughs. Many systems errors are traced to accurate programming of poor specifications. These errors can be reduced by holding meetings early in the programming stage between blueprint designers (systems analysts) and construction programmers to step through the blueprint specifications together to see if they are correct. Such **specification walkthroughs** held early in the programming process help to reduce programming false starts and operational errors.

User-Provided Test Data

If users provide test data, they achieve a sense of ownership for the system. This procedure also ensures that unique circumstances will be tested. If **user-provided test data** are not comprehensive, however, the analyst may have to add data.

When to Stop Testing

Structured testing has one inherent flaw. It becomes infinite until all possible errors are found and corrected. Given systems constraints on time and money, such perfection in testing cannot be tolerated. The question then becomes when to stop testing.

The key to answering this question is to plot the number of errors found in a module against the testing effort (Figure 18–10). When the resulting curve flattens out, it is time to stop testing that module. This tactic implies some collection of test data, a topic covered in the next part of this chapter.

There are two dangers to this necessary approach. First, it allows implementation of systems with minor flaws. Second, this approach does not distinguish between high-impact and low-impact systems. For a system with a high impact on users, you probably will decide to test further than you would with a low-impact system.

Politics of Testing

You do not make a friend when you reveal his or her errors. The success indicator for an effective software testing strategy is the number of program errors discovered *before* implementation of the system. Yet, discovery of such errors may be embarrassing to some. In addition, discovery of errors seems counterproductive to the attitude of, "Let's be finished with this system. Let's get it going!" Therefore, there will always be some pressure to suppress rather than report testing errors.

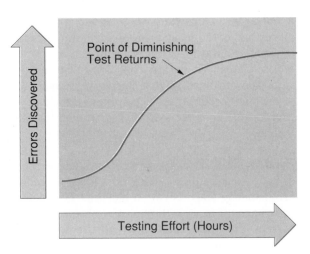

FIGURE 18–10   When to Stop Testing

Point of Diminishing Test Returns

Errors Discovered

Testing Effort (Hours)

One solution to this dilemma is to assign overall testing responsibilities to senior analysts. These analysts will prefer to do actual design and programming. However, they must be convinced that overall objectivity and rigorousness demand that testing be placed in the hands of professionals who are respected by those whose errors will be revealed.

TESTING CONTROL

Management of testing techniques is a difficult process that requires stringent control. Testing of a new system's programs is not done in isolation. Testing is done on the mainframe computers used to process the operational system. Therefore, program testing competes with and often gets in the way of day-to-day information processing. Cost and time constraints aside, systems analysts must control testing to reduce its impact on operations.

Good software testing is structured, standardized, comprehensive, and efficient. Such demanding and competing goals must have a testing control function, and that function should be the responsibility of a senior analyst. Testing control involves sequencing, documentation, responsibility, and a testing plan.

Testing Sequence

The sequencing of software testing involves traversing the hierarchy chart (Figure 18–5) in reverse. The sequence then becomes as follows:

1. **Elementary testing:** The lower-level modules (for example, DELETE VENDOR) are tested independently to ensure that they operate effectively by themselves.
2. **Group testing:** Elementary modules already tested are combined into logical groups. Each group (for example, VENDOR FILE UPDATES) is then tested to ensure that elementary modules interact properly.

3. **Function testing:** Consolidation of subsidiary modules continues to level 2 of the hierarchy chart. Here, function groups are tested for intragroup interaction accuracy.
4. **System testing:** The entire system is tested to assess interactions between individual system functions.

Testing Documentation

Knowing when to stop testing involves plotting the number of errors discovered versus the amount of testing effort put forth. This information must be collected so that each testing effort is documented to include the following items:

- Software module tested
- Number of conditions (inputs) used in test
- Specific conditions tested
- Length of test in computer time
- Number of errors detected by type

INTEGRATED TESTING FACILITIES

Integrated testing facilities (ITFs) enable test data to be employed while transactions are being processed by on-line systems. The test data usually consist of transactions that contain the attributes of "live" data but are hypothetical, since both valid and erroneous data must be included. Test results are printed in a routine output summary with detected errors listed on an exception report. The errors should conform to what were expected results. The following conditions should be met when ITFs are used:

1. Every conceivable input error, logical processing error, and irregularity must be included.
2. A test database master file should be used so that the actual database does not become contaminated by test runs.
3. Careful procedures must be followed to ensure testing validity.

In the ITF technique, test transactions are entered into the computer system concurrently with live transactions. The test transactions undergo the same processing and programmed checks as the actual transactions. Test transactions are identified using a code. The code causes the test transactions to be shunted into a special test facility (a collection of files).

The ITF technique has several advantages over other testing techniques:

1. Testing simulates live transaction processing more closely.
2. Because actual and test data are entered together, the tester is assured that the production programs are processing both the same way.
3. On-line processing programs may be tested without contaminating the database.
4. On-line testing occurs in an integrated manner.

Testing Responsibility

For convenience, the programmer responsible for coding is often the one responsible for testing the code. This is similar to students grading their own test papers. Many companies add objectivity and a future orientation to their testing process by having maintenance programmers test new development programs.

Testing Plan

Sequencing of testing, composition of test data, and documentation of test results are set forth in a **testing plan.** This plan is developed with the hierarchy chart used to organize programming efforts. The plan is actually developed in the analysis phase and used during implementation. The testing plan becomes a subset of the project management plan used to control the entire systems development life cycle.

AUTOMATED TESTING SUPPORT

Development of automated aids for software testing has been slow. While several sophisticated packages exist, they are still too costly for small- to medium-sized information processing operations. In the next several years, more automated testing support packages will become available at affordable costs. Currently, automated testing support exists in the areas of utilities, debug functions, on-line editors, and software development and maintenance tools.

Utilities. **Utilities** packages accompany the computer operating systems. They include sorts, merges, screen and printer listings, and interactive compilers.

Debug Functions. **Debug functions** are often part of the specific language compiler. They include such aids as:

- **Memory map**—snapshots of what data are in memory at a specific point in time
- **Trace**—pictures of what logic paths are used and what values are changed as a program executes
- **Trap**—automatic program halts or prints when particular variables are modified or specific values occur
- **Step**—programmer-slowed, instruction-by-instruction step-through in a computer program. It allows the programmer to see the results of each program operation at that programmer's selected speed.
- **Watch**—halts the program whenever a specified data name value changes. The previous and current value of the data name and line location are displayed.

On-line Editors. **On-line editors** are either page or line editors which allow programmers to change code easily.

Development and Maintenance Tools. Several stand-alone development and maintenance tools are now on the market. They are expensive, but their price is decreasing with increased purchases. One example is **TEST-XPERT.** It marks all COBOL program paths and reports whether these paths were or were not executed. A second such product is **XPEDITER,** which allows testing and correction of COBOL programs in on-line rather than batch mode. This product speeds COBOL testing and correction functions.

Program testing and maintenance will be the subject of further development of automated tools. However, the safest guarantee of an effective and comprehensive testing program is not in the tools that are available. The guarantee lies in a structured testing strategy and on stringent testing control.

PROFILE OF A POORLY PROGRAMMED SYSTEM

Now that you know the characteristics of proper programming and testing, you can ask, "What would a poorly programmed system look like?" A poorly programmed information system has the following characteristics:

- No hierarchical organization is in place for programming responsibility and reporting. Everyone is "doing their thing."
- Enforced programming standards are lacking. Each programmer is operating as an independent artist.
- There is no view of the future. The main goal is to "get the system going" rather than to make programs easier to change in the future.
- No structured test plan shows date, methods, and documentation of testing efforts.
- Construction of structured test data is absent. Testing of the program is an afterthought rather than a rigorously planned process.
- Pressure is exerted to suppress test-discovered errors so that systems development efforts remain on schedule.
- The programmers responsible for systems development and testing are not the same persons who will have to make changes when the system is implemented.
- No automated program support tools are used. Program testing and documentation are done poorly by hand or not at all.
- Program documentation is done after rather than before program testing.
- A new or junior analyst or programmer is in charge of the program-testing effort.

HUMAN ASPECTS

Programming too often is viewed as a mental rather than a social process, much like doing crossword puzzles. The programmer must, however, keep two different people in mind when deriving and testing code. The first person is the nontechnical end-user, whose everyday world will be spoiled by the flaws resulting from poorly coded and poorly tested programs. The second person is the maintenance programmer who will be responsible for fixing any mess you create. Think of your program, not as a game, but as a product designed for human customers.

SUMMARY

The major task in the physical construction of the new information system is converting input, output, files, and their interactions into actual programming code. This programming effort must be done with an eye to easing future maintenance programming.

The programming effort must be closely coordinated because (1) often many programmers are involved, (2) time and fund constraints are placed on the programming effort, (3) program modules are interrelated, (4) programming standards need to be enforced, (5) user contact needs to be structured and minimized, and (6) program testing can interfere with day-to-day information systems operations. Three tactics for programming coordination are the hierarchy chart, assignment of a project leader, and use of common programming terminology (the data element dictionary).

Testing of programs is too often given a low priority. Structured development of test data allows standardized testing by all programmers involved in the project. It guarantees a consistent product. In addition, structured development allows for blanket testing—assessment of all possible conditions that can cause errors in the system. Finally, creation of structured test data can be heuristic; discovered errors can be added to the test bank over a period of time.

The goal of constructing test data is to limit the number of tests while still being comprehensive. Testing techniques available to do this include equivalency classes, dependency islands, risk assessment, seam testing, and specification walkthroughs.

An essential question in software testing is when to stop. You determine this by plotting the number of errors found in a module against the testing effort. When the resulting curve flattens out, it is probably time to stop testing that module.

Control of program testing includes proper sequencing, documentation (reporting), assignment of responsibilities, and a testing plan. Some automated testing support packages are available, but many are still quite expensive. Costs will likely decrease with extended usage.

The topics of programming and testing are often skimmed over in books dealing with systems analysis and design. This probably reflects the real-world attitude of many systems analysts to stay at arm's length from the programming process. As with negligent architects, however, designers who turn their backs on the programming and testing phases will likely end up with systems that quickly collapse.

CONCEPTS LEARNED

- Designing computer programs to optimize future maintenance
- Why coordination of the programming effort is essential and how to effect such coordination
- Reasons for and elements of programming standards
- Goals and benefits of structured test data
- Testing techniques, including equivalency classes, dependency islands, risk assessment, seam testing, and specification walkthroughs
- When to stop program testing
- Politics of the test environment and how to counter it
- Process of testing control—sequencing, documentation, assignment of responsibilities, and the test plan
- Automated testing support packages

KEY TERMS

debug function	risk assessment
dependency islands	seam testing
elementary testing	specification walkthrough
equivalency class	step
external program documentation	system testing
function testing	TEST-XPERT
group testing	testing plan
heuristic test data	trace
Integrated Testing Facilities (ITF)	trap
internal program documentation	user-provided test data
lead programmer	utilities
memory map	watch
on-line editor	XPEDITER
primitive code	

REVIEW QUESTIONS

1. What is the relationship of programming dollars spent for systems development versus systems maintenance?

2. Why must the systems analyst closely coordinate the programming effort?

3. Describe how the hierarchy chart coordinates the programming process.

4. Why is it important that programming terminology be standardized? How can this be done?

5. Why are programming standards important to the development of a business information system?

6. List the benefits of structured development of test data.

7. What is heuristic test data?

8. Give an example of an equivalency class.

9. Describe dependency islands.

10. How does risk assessment fit into structured development of test data?

11. Describe three types of seam testing.

12. How do you know when to stop testing?

13. Describe the testing sequence.

14. What does a testing plan include?

15. What is the difference between a trace and a trap debug function?

16. How does testing a new system affect the operational information system?

CRITICAL THINKING OPPORTUNITIES

1. Draw a diagram of the organization of this chapter.

2. The hierarchy chart for an on-line student registration system (SRS) is shown in Figure 18–11.

   a) Develop a skeleton testing plan that includes program testing sequence and type of test data required.

   b) Interview your registrar (an in-class interview might be appropriate). From the results of the interview, develop a risk/impact priority schedule for program testing of the SRS.

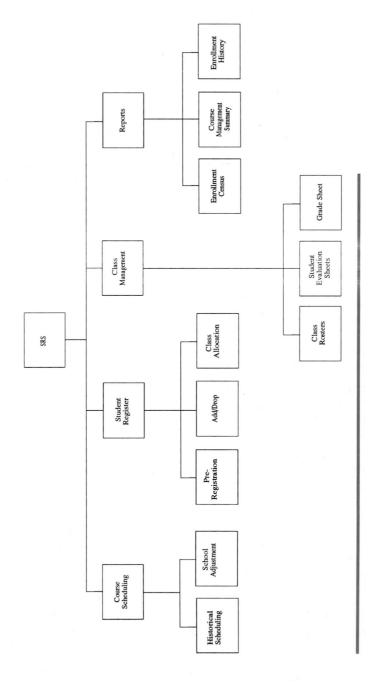

FIGURE 18–11 Hierarchy Chart for Student Registration System (SRS)

CASE 18.1

PROGRAMMING STANDARDS

SETTING

It may seem unusual to include information on programming standards in a book on systems analysis and design. However, the programming stage is often the least monitored and most inconsistently accomplished stage in the systems development life cycle.

One of the principles of well-designed systems is a design to ease change. It is a shame to design a system with an eye to the future and then have that design translated into spaghetti program code that defies future programming change. Programming standards are thus necessary to (1) optimize systems change and maintenance programming in the future, (2) coordinate efforts of the many individual programmers working on the development project, and (3) facilitate program testing where, beyond the elementary level, different modules are combined to test interactions.

The three types of standardization discussed here are coding, internal documentation, and external documentation. For brevity's sake, only examples in the COBOL language are provided; however, examples are transferable to other production languages such as C or PL/1.

CODING STANDARDS

Coding standards include the basic structure of the program and specific coding conventions that should be avoided. Program structure should follow five standards:

1. It should be modular, with no more than fifty lines of code for any one module, to allow repair of a module without disturbing the remainder of the program. Modular programs also allow the maintenance programmer to better understand program logic.
2. It should use top-down design, so each module has logical, cohesive, and loosely coupled submodules.
3. It should have one entry and one exit point for each module, to enhance the maintenance programmer's understanding.
4. It should follow sequential program flow, so the program executes in the same sequence as it appears in the program listing. To do otherwise would complicate the maintenance programmer's task of understanding the design programmer's logic.
5. It should include one statement per line to enhance understanding.

Some coding conventions should be avoided because they tend to decrease rather than enhance the maintenance programmer's understanding. Avoid the following conventions:

- ALTER allows the programmer to change transfer points in PERFORM and GOTO statements. This is an example of a program changing itself and it is difficult for a maintenance programmer to understand the situation.
- GOTO tangles processing paths by violating the structured principle of sequential program flow.
- Nested IF statements complicate program logic.
- COMPUTE violates the structured principle of one statement per line and rewards short rather than descriptive variable names.

INTERNAL DOCUMENTATION

Even a supposedly self-documenting language such as COBOL must be augmented to provide enough documentation. Remember that the program you design will likely have to be modified by another person six months or more later. Follow these six techniques for providing internal documentation:

1. Use meaningful user-defined names. For example, instead of CUSN, use CUSTOMER-NUMBER.
2. Align all PICTURE, VALUE, and USAGE clauses for easy reference and comparison.
3. Indent subordinate clauses.

```
READ INPUT-FILE INTO INPUT-IMAGE
     AT END MOVE ''Y'' TO END-OF-FILE
SELECT OUTPUT-FILE
     ASSIGN TO LINE-PRINTER
```

4. Use 88 levels to better document logic in the PROCEDURE DIVISION, and explain coding structures in the WORKING-STORAGE SECTION.
5. Place blank lines between divisions, sections, and paragraphs to enhance program readability.
6. Use comments to enhance understanding of program logic. The sample COBOL program at the end of this case (see Figure 18.1-3) shows the use of comments.

EXTERNAL DOCUMENTATION

Graphic documentation outside the program is the maintenance programmer's circuitry diagram. The maintenance programmer uses external documentation to search for the module most likely causing a problem. Once the programmer isolates that module (COBOL paragraph), the self-documenting, English-like language within the module allows further problem detection.

The keys to problem detection are that (1) all external documentation media must be consistent with each other and (2) all external documentation media must be consistent with the organization of the COBOL program. The

external documentation media that best fill these consistency requirements are the hierarchy chart and the macro flowchart.

The hierarchy chart has been discussed in several places in this textbook. Figure 18.1-1 is a chart for a typical business program. The program hierarchy chart has three features that tie it to the actual COBOL program.

1. It is a top-down design structure. The main program is divided into modules, the modules are divided into submodules, and so on. The hierarchy chart is not merely a picture of how the COBOL program has been organized, but a design aid determining how the program should be organized.

2. Each module block of the hierarchy chart is equivalent in name and sequence to a COBOL paragraph. The sequence is top to bottom within left to right. For example, in Figure 18.1-1, the hierarchy chart dictates that paragraphs in the actual COBOL program must be in the following sequence:

```
000--CONTROL
    100--SETUP
    300--PROCESS-CONTROL
        310--READ-MASTER
        320--READ-TRANSACTION
        400--PROCESS-TRANSACTION
            410--EDIT-TRANS
            430--TRANS-ERROR
                440--WRITE-ERROR
            450--UPDATE
                455--CHANGE-MASTER
                460--PRINT-DETAIL-LIN
            470--MASTER-DONE
                480--WRITE-NEW-MASTER
    500--RUNOFF
        530--TRANSACTION-RUNOFF
        550--MASTER-RUNOFF
```

3. Listing of the COBOL program in this sequence allows isolation of specific modules on the hierarchy chart. The programmer then can search sequentially through the program listing to find a paragraph of COBOL code.

Figure 18.1-2 is a sample macro flowchart. Use of this chart assumes the following maintenance programming conditions:

■ Maintenance programmers do not need flowcharts that explain the logic of most

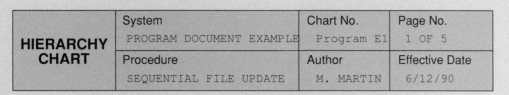

HIERARCHY CHART	System PROGRAM DOCUMENT EXAMPLE	Chart No. Program E1	Page No. 1 OF 5
	Procedure SEQUENTIAL FILE UPDATE	Author M. MARTIN	Effective Date 6/12/90

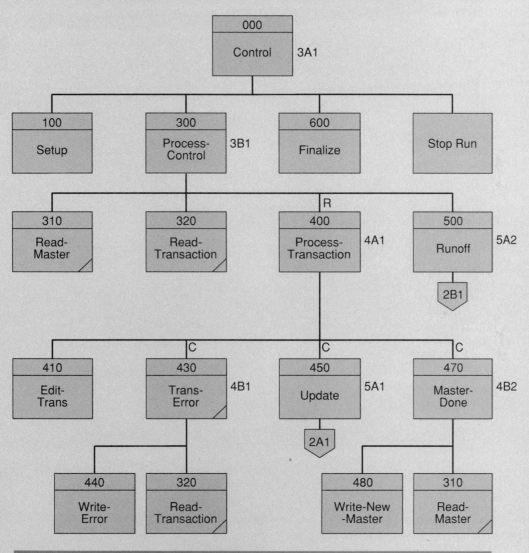

FIGURE 18.1–1 **Hierarchy Chart for a Typical Business Program**

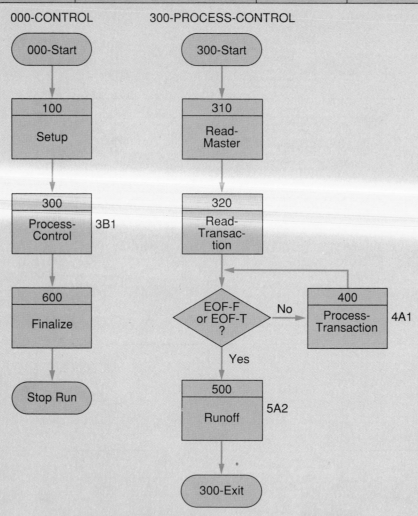

FLOWCHART	System		Chart No.		Page No.	
	PROGRAM DOCUMENT EXAMPLE		Program E2		3 OF 5	
	Procedure		Author		Effective Date	
	SEQUENTIAL FILE UPDATE		M. MARTIN		6/12/90	

000-CONTROL

300-PROCESS-CONTROL

000-Start

100
Setup

300
Process-Control 3B1

600
Finalize

Stop Run

300-Start

310
Read-Master

320
Read-Transac-tion

EOF-F or EOF-T ?

No → 400 Process-Transaction 4A1

Yes

500
Runoff 5A2

300-Exit

FIGURE 18.1−2 **Macro Flowchart for a Typical Business Program**

business programs. For example, a payroll maintenance programmer does not need to study a flowchart to see how payroll is calculated.

- Maintenance programmers need flowcharts that operate as a map to trace processing paths to the paragraph containing the code to be modified.
- If the program listing is in the same sequence as both the hierarchy chart and macro flowchart, then the programmer can scan the program listing to find the paragraph identified on the macro flowchart.
- Once the programmer finds the paragraph, English-like COBOL coding allows the maintenance programmer to understand the paragraph's logic without having to resort to detailed flowchart symbols.

The difference between macro and detailed flowcharts is that the macro flowchart does not include symbols describing the logic within closed paragraphs. A closed COBOL paragraph is one that does not have calls (PERFORMs) to other COBOL paragraphs; it is self-contained. By omitting closed paragraph logic symbols, the macro flowchart reduces the number of symbols by a factor of about five to one.

When you use these two external documentation media, be sure that (1) the hierarchy chart and the macro flowchart agree in paragraph sequence numbers, paragraph names, and processing sequence; and (2) the COBOL program listing corresponds in sequence and specifications to both the hierarchy chart and the macro flowchart.

SUMMARY

It is a mistake for business sytems designers to ignore the programming stage of the systems development life cycle. Particularly important in this stage are programming standards, because they relate directly to how easily programs (and thus the designed system) can be changed in the future. The systems designer can use the standards briefly discussed here as a checklist to ensure that the system designed for the future actually is constructed for the future. Figure 18.1–3 is an example of a documented program. Note how it follows programming standards.

```
001200* * * * * * * * * * *
001300 IDENTIFICATION DIVISION.
001400* * * * * * * * * * *
001500
001600 PROGRAM-ID. MIS102-1.
001700 AUTHOR. (YOUR NAME).
001800 DATE-WRITTEN. (ACTUAL DATE).
001900 DATE-COMPILED. (ACTUAL DATE).
002000*SECTION.  (YOUR SECTION).
002100
002200*REMARKS. THIS PROGRAM
002300
002400*    (1) READS A FILE OF INVOICE RECORDS
002500*    (2) CALCULATES ACCOUNTS RECEIVABLE AMOUNT FOR EACH RECORD
002600*    (3) COMPUTES GRAND TOTALS FOR ACCOUNTS RECEIVABLE,
002700*        DISCOUNT ALLOWED, AND AMOUNT PAID
002800*    (4) PRINTS AN ACCOUNTS RECEIVABLE REGISTER
002900/
003000* * * * * * * * * * *
003100 ENVIRONMENT DIVISION.
003200* * * * * * * * * * *
003300
003400* * * * * * * * * * *
003500 CONFIGURATION SECTION.
003600* * * * * * * * * * *
003700
003800 SOURCE-COMPUTER. VAX 11.
003900 OBJECT-COMPUTER. VAX 11.
004000
004100* * * * * * * * * *
004200 INPUT-OUTPUT SECTION.
004300* * * * * * * * * *
004400
004500 SELECT FILE-IN
004600    ASSIGN TO ``PROG1.DAT''.
004700 SELECT FILE-OUT
004800    ASSIGN TO ``PROG1.RPT''.
004900/
005000* * * * * * * *
005100 DATA DIVISION.
005200* * * * * * * *
005300
005400
```

1. CHANGE EACH PROGRAM

2. SEPARATION OF MAJOR DIVISIONS

3. CLAUSES INDENTED

FIGURE 18.1–3   **Example of a Documented Program (Cobol)**

In this chapter you will learn about:

WHAT: (Concepts) Preparation for changeover to the new information system.

WHY: A well-designed system that is poorly implemented is an unsuccessful system.

WHEN: Next-to-last stage of the SDLC.

WHO: Systems analyst in close cooperation with system end-users.

WHERE: End-user area.

HOW: (Techniques) Training checklist
                        Operating instruction checklist
                        Site preparation checklist
                        Hardware/software acceptance checklist
                        Vendor contract checklist
                        System changeover options

- Setting
- A Total Quality Approach
- Training
- Other Conversion Preparations
- System Changeover Tactics
- The Changeover Process
- User Resistance
- Profile of a Poorly Implemented System
- Human Aspects

SYSTEM CHANGEOVER

The most thoroughly planned Christmas Eve ends up in a chaos of Scotch Tape and Super Glue. But the toys are always ready on Christmas morning.

—INSTANT ANALYST, 1990

SETTING

We are nearing the end of the system development life cycle. The new information system has been designed and tested. Now users must be trained, equipment and software must be accepted and installed, and system operating instructions must be prepared. Then we must begin changeover of responsibility from the design team to end-users.

Changeover to the new system is a critical stage. The method and style of this changeover largely will determine user attitudes toward the new system. As stressed in previous chapters, user attitudes perhaps are the most important predictors of system success. The physical design phase of the SDLC was too technical for extensive and consistent user involvement. Hence, the sense of user ownership built up during the analysis and logical design stages eroded—despite the best intentions of the designer. If changeover is done well, user sense of ownership and confidence in the new system revitalizes.

The chapter begins with consideration of varied operating tasks such as training, preparing operating instructions, site preparation, hardware and software acceptance, and preparation of vendor contracts. Then the chapter focuses on changeover from the old to the new information system.

A TOTAL QUALITY APPROACH

This chapter includes several different tasks. They range from training, to site preparation, to system cutover. For each of these separate tasks, keep in mind the quality objectives that we have employed consistently throughout this book.

1. Is the task relevant to system success?
2. Is the task complete?
3. Has the task been done correctly?
4. Are only authorized personnel involved in the task?
5. Was the task done in a timely manner?
6. Was the task done as cheaply as possible?
7. Was the task done as efficiently as possible, where efficiency is defined as results divided by resources used?
8. Was the task completed in a reliable manner (low variance)?
9. Did the task stress human usability (e.g., was training geared to end-users, or were operating instructions geared to the correct reading level)?

TRAINING

Information systems professionals have a history of being reluctant trainers. We have improved a lot in recent years, but we will always have certain natural forces working against us:

- Fighter pilots hate to leave the cockpit to train new aviators. Designers hate to abandon design and implementation to perform training. Training is not in the trenches of systems development.
- Designers often are introspective; they prefer personal problem solving to group interaction. Even structured walkthroughs scare many of us. We do not greet eagerly the prospect of explaining the "obvious" to a group of nontechnical users.
- Until recently, information systems educational programs have not had courses on oral communication. In addition, the technical nature of the curricula often discourage such communication. For example, it is difficult to structure an oral presentation in a beginning COBOL course.
- We are trained to think in logical chains of how input is transformed to output. We are excited more by process than result. Therefore, the graphic tools we use—flowcharts, hierarchy charts—are difficult for users to understand. Users think in terms such as "What tools do I need, or what buttons do I push, to make sure this document never crosses my desk again?"

As a result, information people sometimes deemphasize training in the systems development life cycle.

Whether we actually conduct new systems training, or merely oversee it, we must pay more attention to our training effectiveness. Information systems training is discussed here by asking the following five questions:

1. Who is the audience?
2. What level of detail should be imparted to this audience?
3. Who should conduct the training?
4. Where should training be conducted?
5. When should training be conducted?

Who Is the Audience?

There are three quite different audiences to which new systems training is directed. The first and most critical audience is prospective end-users. This group must learn to use the new system *before* it is operational. The second training audience is the group of information-processing specialists who will operate the new system. They are called operations personnel. The third audience includes managers and executives who require only an overview of the new system. The level of delivery detail is much less for this audience than for the other two audiences.

It is a mistake to conduct omnibus training sessions aimed toward two or all three of these audiences. The needs of the audiences are quite different and means must be tailored to effectively reach them.

What Level of Detail Should Be Imparted?

Shneiderman (1987) classifies computer knowledge into the following categories:

- **Syntactic knowledge**—machine-dependent rules of how to use a specific application on a particular computer. An example of syntactic knowledge is what function keys do in a particular word-processing package.
- **Task semantic knowledge**—conceptual knowledge of how a particular application operates. For example, in a purchasing application semantic knowledge is knowing how a purchasing system works. In contrast, syntactic knowledge would be knowing how a particular automated purchasing package works on a specific computer configuration.
- **Computer semantic knowledge**—conceptual knowledge of how computers work in general. Sometimes this is referred to as computer concepts. An example of this type of knowledge is knowing how computer input/output buffers affect computer response time for user requests.

The three audiences described require different amounts of these three types of detail (Figure 19–1).

It is foolish to try to include more than one target audience in a single training session. The knowledge levels required are too varied. Even at the syntactic level, where both end-users and operations personnel require extensive knowledge, the type of syntactic knowledge differs. Syntactic knowledge for end-users includes how to use the keyboard and how to traverse a particular menu path. Syntactic knowledge for operations personnel more likely includes such subjects as report frequencies, program abort procedures, start-of-day procedures, and restart specifics.

FIGURE 19-1   **Levels of Training De-tail for Different Audiences**

Training Audience	Knowledge Level		
	Syntactic (Systems Mechanics)	Task Semantic (Applications)	Computer Semantic (Computer Concepts)
End-Users	E	N	M
Operations Personnel	E	M	N
Managers and Executives	L	L	L*

Legend: E = extensive, M = moderate, L = limited, N = none.
*If this is the first automated system

Who Should Conduct Training?

Training can be conducted by users, by the design team, or by training specialists. The advantage of user-conducted training is that the trainer-user speaks the same day-to-day language as user-trainees. This is particularly important when user-trainees ask questions specific to the applications area. Disadvantages of user-conducted training are that the user-trainer has only limited knowledge of computer syntax and semantics and few users have any experience in training.

Use of design team members as trainers provides syntactic and computer semantic knowledge. There may be even a moderate amount of task semantic knowledge. However, training by the design team has four disadvantages:

1. Systems people are sometimes untrained in oral and written communication skills.
2. Members of the design team are busy with other SDLC tasks.
3. Some systems people do not consider training to be as important as other SDLC tasks.
4. Systems people talk in a different language than the training audience. A common ground of communication is essential for effective training.

Training specialists are experienced trainers, while users and designers often are not. More importantly, training specialists are not as immersed in the details of the system or the application. Therefore, they tend to have a better view of the concepts and generalities of the situation. Humans have a difficult time pushing details into long-term memory without first having these details surrounded by a conceptual framework. Use of training specialists for systems education also has its disadvantages:

1. Except for large companies, such specialists will not be a part of staff. Contracting them from outside the firm can be expensive.
2. Training specialists may know little of the applications area.
3. Unless training specialists are intimately involved in design of the new system, they will not know enough of the syntactic details. This lack can be countered by first training the training specialists, but this further complicates the situation.

A mixed training team is recommended. A training specialist, a member of the design team, and an end-user should be included. If the team is involved in analysis and design efforts in the earlier stages of the SDLC, it can assume control of all new systems training. Then the abilities and attitudes of the training specialist, designer, and end-user can be matched to the needs of any specific training audience.

Where Should Training Be Conducted?

Training can be conducted in the actual working area, in on-site training facilities, or in off-site facilities. Training for syntactic knowledge often is conducted in the users' working areas with the workstations already located there. This allows training in a nonthreatening environment, but the press of everyday business often causes interruptions or distractions to training efforts.

Removal of trainees from the work environment eliminates operational distractions. However, reduced availability of workstations outside the immediate working area often limits the number of end-users who can be trained at any one time. In addition, supervisors are reluctant to release personnel to on-site or off-site training facilities for any length of time.

Off-site training facilities often are used for management training to reduce operational interruptions. Such off-site training is expensive. Costs may limit the size of the audience and length of training sessions.

Arthur Andersen Consulting Company (Andersen Consulting) conducts most of its training in St. Charles, Illinois. The company sends new employees there to receive training in methodology and also in advanced COBOL concepts. Initial training takes three weeks. Periodically, throughout their career paths, all employees spend time in training at St. Charles. The trainers at the St. Charles facility are a combination of educational and technical professionals.

Training can be conducted in a mix of locations. End-user training can be started in large groups in on-site training facilities. Then it can be moved to the work area for small, intensive one-on-one sessions. Short, intensive management training can be conducted off-site with short follow-up sessions scheduled for on-site training facilities.

Operational training is frequently conducted in on-site training facilities. As in the case of Arthur Andersen, however, some sessions might be conducted at an off-site computer installation to reduce operational interruptions and to provide insights into how other systems professionals work on similar systems.

The mix must be chosen according to the specifics of each training situation. Constraints on facilities, training personnel, workstations, and available time are too specific to allow recommendation of a rigid strategy on where to conduct training.

When Should Training Be Conducted?

Many times training is the last task performed before changeover to the new system. This is so because until then, a new system has not been developed fully enough to provide effective training, and because training has a lower priority than it deserves. Nevertheless, there are three strong arguments for beginning the training stage as early as possible in the systems development life cycle. First, time is essential for selling users on the new system so they feel a sense of ownership. Second, time is needed for users to feed criticisms back to the design process. Third, length of training can be increased, which is important since forcing knowledge to long-term memory often requires repetitive training.

Despite the desirability of early training, the problem remains that the new system may not be developed to a degree adequate to permit early training. Here is where automated training aids help. Such aids do not require *full* development of a new information system in order for training to begin.

Automated Training Systems

Systems training too often is dominated by the idea that the new information system must be fully operational, or very close to it, before training can begin. As a result, training is delayed to the last moment. It then becomes too intensive and ends too quickly. Systems training can begin early with only a partially completed system.

Remember, 20 percent of business transaction types represent 80 percent of transaction volume. In an inventory system, sales, receipts and returns are only three of many transaction types. However, they represent most of the transaction volume for a typical business day. Consequently, systems design and programming activities can be planned so that the most common transaction applications are developed and tested first. With a partial system in place, training can begin earlier in the SDLC and as a result last longer. One key to earlier systems training is use of automated training systems, which take one of two forms.

The first form is a **system with training wheels.** Such a system operates on a small subset of full systems options. For example, an inventory system with training wheels may fully process sales, receipts, and returns. It may also provide a small set of the most used reports and inquiries. By developing this system early in the design process, designers can use it as the skeleton for later design efforts and as a medium for early systems training.

The second form of automated training system is the **prototype**—a small simulation of the system being designed. The only difference between a prototype and a system with training wheels is the underlying purpose. A prototype allows user involvement so potential flaws in the system can be discovered early. A secondary use of prototypes is user training. The system with training wheels, on the other hand, is designed primarily for both training on the new system and everyday training after the system becomes operational. Of course, a prototype could be used as a system with training wheels. Whichever path is selected, development of such automated training systems has the following advantages:

- Systems training can begin earlier in the SDLC.
- Systems training can last longer.
- Training is hands-on so users can relate better to it than to artificial classroom media.
- Users can discover flaws early in the design process, thereby allowing correction before systems implementation.

Several other implementation preparations are coordinated by the systems designer.

OTHER CONVERSION PREPARATIONS

Operating Instructions

Operating instructions are procedures that tell users how to operate an information system. Instructions are necessary to train new users outside the classroom, reacquaint old users who have not used the system for a while, and provide guidance to uncommon system occurrences and capabilities not covered in formal training.

Operating instructions can be provided by members of the design team or by technical writers. Only at large firms are technical writers employees; elsewhere, they are contracted from outside the firm. Free-lance technical writers can be expensive and they probably will not be familiar enough with the specifics of the new business information system. So, the systems designer commonly is responsible for creating operating instructions.

There are three sets of instructions to prepare. User instructions allow end-users to learn and discover precise means to operate the information system. Technical instructions allow information systems workers to learn how to handle the technical aspects of the system—hardware, software, communications. Executive overviews are intended for managers and executives as summaries of how the system operates. Emphasis is on output products and their management uses. Figure 19–2 provides a checklist for design of operating procedures.

1. Since audiences for instructions are the same as those for training, use whatever worked for training to develop user instructions.
2. Consider on-line documentation (help functions) as an alternative or adjunct to written instructions.
3. Have members of the user community review the instructions before you publish them. This guideline is applicable even to executive instructions.
4. Make sure instructions are designed aesthetically; they are easier to read and inspire user confidence. Whether written or on-line, design instructions using interactive screen guidelines.
5. Organize instructions so that they begin with an overview, narrow down to specifics, and finish with another overview. Detailed information is hard to push into long-term memory unless accompanied by a map that shows where the details belong.
6. Write instructions as if they did not involve a computer. Assume persons following instructions must do so manually. This decreases reliance upon computer aids that may be threatening to novice users.
7. Once instructions are written, actually try to follow them on a step-by-step basis.

FIGURE 19–2   Checklist for Design of Operating Procedures

Site Preparation

Systems designers are responsible for completing **site preparation**. If this stage is not completed on time, the entire project may be delayed. "References and Further Readings" at the end of this section of the book suggests sources for detailed information on site preparation.

Preparation of computer sites varies in complexity. If a new system is the firm's first computer application, a computer site must be constructed from scratch. If a new system is one more in a long list of automated systems and does not require new hardware, site preparation is unnecessary. If a new system involves microcomputers, few site considerations are involved. The site preparation checklist presented in Figure 19–3 is general in nature. Designers must tailor it to fit a firm's specific computer situation.

Systems designers are not expected to know the technical details involved in preparation of a computer site. They should, however, consult a checklist to make sure that major considerations are addressed by the technicians who construct the computer site.

Hardware and Software Acceptance

Selection of a specific brand and type of hardware or software is a complex process that involves extensive testing before deciding to buy or lease. Because of that extensive process, when it comes to *acceptance,* you might ask, "Why not automatically accept the product since we tested it before we bought it?" There are several answers to this question.

First, the product must be transported and it can be damaged in the transportation process. While this situation is more applicable to hardware than to software products, software can also be damaged during shipment. For example, floppy disks can be demagnetized.

The second reason for testing hardware or software products before acceptance is that the serial number of the product tested before purchase may not be the serial number of the product delivered. You may not have been sent the actual product that you tested. Ninety-nine of a hundred units may work as specified, but you may have been shipped the one defective product.

Third, a product may have been changed between the time of the purchase test and delivery. Software may have undergone diagnostic changes, while hardware may have been enhanced.

For these reasons, a period of acceptance testing is critical. This period should be specified in the delivery contract. For hardware items, such acceptance testing is often a normal part of the vendor's delivery procedures. For software items, it is often not a part of these procedures. Designers must coordinate with systems technicians early in the design process to determine (1) how to conduct tests, (2) length of the test period, (3) criteria for a successful acceptance run, and (4) procedures to follow if hardware or software fails the tests.

Alpha testing is the testing of a unit and system independently from the operating system. **Beta testing** occurs in an operational environment and is usually done as a

1. Are security provisions adequate for access to physical computer sites?
2. Is wiring covered so no one will trip?
3. Are air-conditioning and heating requirements suitable? In low-humidity geographical areas, humidifiers may be required to raise room humidity to a level that prevents static electricity.
4. Have environmental monitoring and control devices been included so computer equipment can be shut down when specifications are exceeded?
5. Are fire- and smoke-detection systems located appropriately throughout the site to meet safety requirements? Sprinkler systems should be deactivated to prevent damage to computer equipment. Fire protection of computer installations is a complex issue and must be tailored to the specific installation. Fire inspectors and engineering specialists should be consulted.
6. Are additional power supplies available to handle new computer requirements?
7. Has equipment been placed with an eye to human safety and reducing human work movement?
8. Has a backup computer site been selected for off-line storage of tapes and operation if disasters occur?
9. Is there adequate telecommunications linkage for current and projected message requirements?
10. Have plans been made for separate storage areas for off-line magnetic tape storage and off-line systems documentation?
11. Do security provisions include badges for both identification and physical entry to locked facilities and locked machines?
12. Are floors raised with removable tiles to allow wiring and cables to be run from machine to machine with ease, no visibility, and no obstruction?
13. Have appropriate temperatures been considered? Most equipment vendors recommend an ideal temperature of around 70 degrees with a lower limit of 55 degrees and an upper limit of 85 degrees.
14. Do monitoring devices use analog input that is converted to digital information?
15. Is halon gas available instead of water to smother fires? Halon does not damage sensitive computer components.
16. Have arrangements been made for backup power generators that can take over in case of a power outage? If batteries are required, is a working supply available?
17. Has use of multiple-window and multiple-task console monitors been considered to allow operators to run and monitor several jobs from one location?
18. Have arrangements been made with a third party for off-site storage and disaster recovery?

FIGURE 19–3   **Site Preparation Checklist**

pilot test within a limited department or region. Conduct of hardware and software acceptance testing is related closely to vendor contracts.

Vendor Contracts

Here, again, is an area of expertise beyond that expected of a business systems designer. Designers must act merely as coordinators, and rely on legal staff or outside legal advice on contractual matters. An important ground rule for designers is not to accept vendor contracts as written. Such contracts too often have provisions favoring the vendor rather than the purchasing party. An example follows.

The Alaska Court System bought a minicomputer from a company based in Southern California. Staff attorneys were startled that the delivery contract specified that the court system would assume full responsibility for the minicomputer once it was loaded on the aircraft in Los Angeles. Obviously, the vendor contract was not signed. Indeed, it was two months after the minicomputer had been delivered and was operating before the parties finally signed a negotiated delivery and acceptance contract.

A court system has attorneys who can review contracts of this sort. On the other hand, small- to medium-sized firms probably do not have such a legal staff. Systems designers must be sure that, whatever the cost, a legal expert reviews vendor contracts. There are three areas of vendor contracts in the systems development life cycle: **delivery, acceptance,** and **maintenance.** Figure 19–4 includes broad guidelines for dealing with vendor contract provisions.

SYSTEM CHANGEOVER TACTICS

Now all preparations have been completed. It is time to deactivate the old system and start using the new information system. Four alternatives are available for changing from the old to the new business information system:

1. **Crash changeover:** The old system is discontinued and the new system is started simultaneously.
2. **Parallel changeover:** The old and new systems are operated concurrently for a specified period.
3. **Staged changeover:** The old system is replaced in stages.
4. **Day-one changeover:** After a given date, all new business is processed on the new system.

Figure 19–5 compares the four changeover tactics. Systems designers must select the most appropriate one for a given situation.

Crash

Crash changeover involves a cutoff date. On that date, the old system is halted and the new system becomes the only one in operation. Crash changeover is the least costly method because only one system is in operation at any one time. Redundant personnel hours, forms, and reports are not necessary.

Delivery Contracts.

1. At what point does responsibility transfer from vendor to purchaser? Beware of provisions such as "FOB Plant," where the buyer takes responsibility when the product leaves the manufacturer's shipping dock.
2. Are there specific dates and late penalties built into clauses on delivery time?
3. What provisions are there for products damaged in shipment?
4. Is there a specific person and telephone number to contact about delivery problems?
5. Is all required setup equipment (for example, cables) shipped with the product? If not, when will the missing equipment arrive?
6. Will vendor personnel be on hand to help install the product?
7. Who pays for shipment charges?

Acceptance Contracts.

1. How long will acceptance tests run?
2. How intensively will the product be operated during that time (for example, twelve hours each day)?
3. What are the performance criteria for acceptance (for example, 95 percent uptime)?
4. Will acceptance be by part (for example, printer) or for the entire system?
5. What provisions are there for replacement of product components that fail acceptance tests? What are delivery times for replacement components?

Maintenance Contracts.
1. For what period are maintenance costs fixed without increase?
2. Are there limits to increases in maintenance costs?
3. How quickly will vendor personnel respond to maintenance problems?
4. How quickly will vendors ship replacement parts?
5. What parts will be stocked in the immediate vicinity of the product?

FIGURE 19−4   Guidelines for Dealing with Vendor Contract Provisions

Another advantage of the crash tactic is that it forces users to abandon the old, comfortable system. They must dedicate their efforts and loyalties to the new system. This dedication may border on panic, but the dedication is always intense. The new system succeeds in part because there is no old system to fall back on.

There is another, more subtle, advantage to the crash tactic. Design and testing of a new system tend to be more thorough when designers know that the new system

FIGURE 19–5   **Four Systems Chan-**
geover Tactics

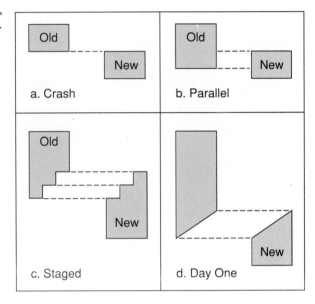

must work effectively. No old system can save them from design errors. Of course, the design and testing thoroughness called for may cost additional design time and dollars.

Two disadvantages are inherent in the crash approach. First, if the new system operates poorly, there is no old system on which to fall back. Several years ago, the U.S. Air Force used the crash approach to implement a new worldwide inventory control system. The pilot site was Andrews Air Force Base in Maryland. The new system failed. Since the old system had been dismantled, the base had to operate a slow, inaccurate manual inventory system for over a month. Andrews Air Force Base provides the parts required for maintenance of the aircraft of the President of the United States. Air Force officials were not impressed with the crash changeover tactic.

The second disadvantage of the crash tactic is that it often scares users, who immediately lose their comfort zones. This can be perilous for users new to automated systems. Systems literature maligns the crash changeover tactic. Even the name for the tactic implies doom; yet, there are times when it is appropriate.

Parallel

Parallel changeover is the safest of the changeover tactics. It includes a period when both old and new systems operate concurrently. If the new system fails, the old system is still there for uninterrupted operation. Parallel changeover also allows a comparison of output between the two systems. In addition, this type of changeover is less traumatic to end-users.

There are several disadvantages to parallel changeover. It is expensive to operate two systems simultaneously. End-users have less incentive to commit to the new system. In addition, operation of two systems may exceed available personnel resources. Even if funds are available, there may not be enough personnel hours available to operate two systems.

Most textbooks recommend the parallel changeover tactic. However, the method can be unacceptably expensive and can become a crutch for end-users who are unwilling to change. Parallel conversion was the option taken at one university computing site. Both the new system and the old system were allowed to run parallel until the old system physically broke down. New users were only allowed accounts on the new system. Experienced users migrated to the new system voluntarily. When the old system finally failed and could not be brought up again, several users of the old system were not prepared to make the change and became frustrated. They did not lose any data because of tape backup. However, they were not mentally ready or experienced enough on the new system to make an easy transition.

Staged

Staged changeover is a compromise between crash and parallel tactics. The new system is implemented and the old system is discarded one stage at a time. There are two types of staged approaches: pilot and phased. A **pilot conversion** is implementation of a complete new system at one of many possible locations. Conversion lessons learned at the pilot location are used when converting all other sites. A **phased conversion** is a situation in which portions of the entire new system are implemented in stages. Thus, a materials control system may be converted in the following phases: inventory, purchasing, receiving, and order entry. The two types of staged changeovers may be mixed. For example, phased conversion may be selected for the materials control system. Yet, a pilot site may be selected to convert the first phase (inventory). So both the *pilot* and *phased* methods have been selected to be part of the generic *staged* method.

The staged changeover tactic requires that the designer divide the systems project into natural dimensions that can be completed in portions. Some common dimensions are geographical divisions, offices within a single firm, and applications tasks. Each of these portions can be implemented one at a time. The lessons learned from the last implementation are applied to the new one. The staged tactic shares all the advantages and disadvantages of both the crash and parallel tactics, but to a lesser degree. It is a middle-of-the-road approach favored by many firms.

A microcomputer-based grant management and personnel system was constructed for an electrical engineering department at a major university. The system, which contained 220 separate modules, was introduced about two months before the end of a fiscal year. A decision was made to load personnel data and bring the personnel functions up first. Two months later, the grant management portion was brought up with many of the year-to-date figures loaded at zero. This was a much easier process than determining and loading the year-to-date amounts that would have been required at the earlier date. It also gave the operators a chance to learn the system with the less critical modules that were contained in the personnel functions.

All three of the changeover methods described fail to consider the efforts required to convert old system files to the revised formats demanded by the new system. File conversion efforts can be extensive, particularly for organizations changing to their first computer system. The approach that directly addresses **file conversion** is day-one changeover.

Day-One

Three paths can be followed to convert old files to revised formats required by the new information system. Figure 19–6 illustrates these paths. If the old system's files are in a manual format, they must be converted off-line to the new format (path 1). On the other hand, file formats for the new system are sometimes similar to old automated formats. In this case, programs can be coded to convert files automatically from the old to the new format (path 2). The third path is a hybrid of the first two paths. Even when converting from one computer information system to another, often there is a portion that cannot be converted automatically. Most likely, the new file designs include additional record fields, new coding structures, and richer linkage between associated records. Therefore, in most systems development projects, some nonprogrammable file conversion is necessary. This conversion can be expensive.

Assume a case of converting from a small, manual personnel system of 5,000 records to a new, automated system. Further assume the new system record format includes 300 characters (not large by personnel standards). Conversion would require the entry of one and a half million characters of data. At a traditional data entry rate of 1,200 errorfree keystrokes per hour, this equals 1,250 keystroke hours. At an average of 6 data entry hours per day, the result is 208 days, or 41.6 work weeks. This is the time for data entry only. It does not include other tasks such as researching missing fields on existing records, correcting data entry errors, and auditing the finished conversion effort.

For large applications, the investment in even partial, nonprogrammed file conversion can be substantial. The three traditional changeover tactics discussed require that all or a large percentage of records be converted to the new format before operating the

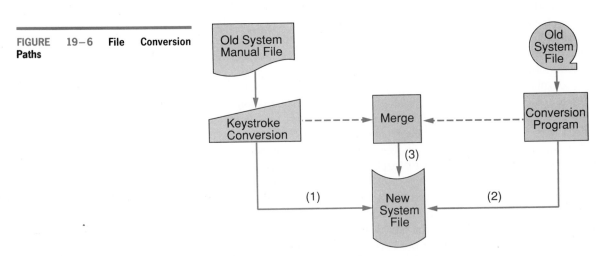

FIGURE   19–6   File   Conversion Paths

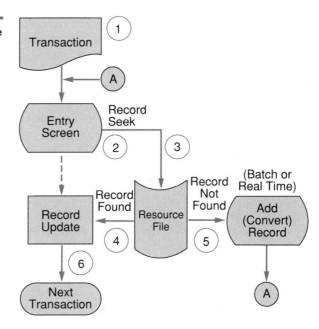

FIGURE 19–7   Sequence of Day-One Changeover Tactic

new system. The fourth changeover tactic—day-one changeover—softens the impact of the file conversion problem because old files are converted gradually. Records are converted only when they show transaction activity. In this way, the first and perhaps only records converted to new file formats are those that are active. Inactive records are the last of the old records to be converted. If resources are scarce, they may not be converted at all. The day-one changeover tactic follows this sequence (shown graphically in Figure 19–7):

1. A new business transaction is received.
2. The transaction is entered into the transaction processing system.
3. The transaction entry program searches resource files for the proper record.
4. If the proper resource record is found (has already been converted from the old system), the record is updated with data contained in the transaction.
5. If the proper resource record is not found, the record from the old system is retrieved and added to the new system. The transaction is then reentered (symbol A in Figure 19–7).
6. A new transaction is readied and the process begins at the first step.

Follow this example of day-one changeover. A small credit collection agency was changing from a manual system to a local-area-network microcomputer system. The office culture deemphasized clerical work; management placed the predominant effort on collection and legal tasks. No funds were available for one-time conversion of manual files to the new computer format. Therefore, the day-one changeover tactic was adopted.

When a transaction was ready for entry, the computer program sought the record from the newly automated creditor file. If the record had already been converted, the data entry clerk completed record update. If the record had not yet been added to the new system, the clerk passed the transaction to a second data entry workstation. The manual record was retrieved and converted to the new format. The second clerk entered the delayed transaction as a part of the task of adding the record.

At the end of one month, most of the active accounts had been added to the new file. File conversion had dwindled to the point where a second data entry workstation was not required. Inactive creditor records were not converted to the new format. Inactive records represented almost three-quarters of total record volume. The day-one changeover approach significantly decreased file conversion efforts that would have been required with crash, parallel, or phased changeover tactics.

Despite its success in this example, the day-one approach has disadvantages. First, file conversion efforts are extended over time, thereby creating a confusing environment. Second, additional data entry is required while the new system is in operation.

Third, the approach may be difficult in an environment that requires periodic reports. For example, if only half of the receivable accounts have been converted at the end of the month, the receivable total will not be accurate.

Choice of Methods

Which changeover method should be selected? That decision depends on several criteria.

Costs. If there are severe cost constraints associated with the new system, then parallel processing may not be a viable choice.

Systems Criticality. If a system failure would be disastrous, the safest approach should be selected regardless of the costs. That approach is parallel changeover.

User Computer Experience. The more computer experience users have, the less necessary it is to delay changeover to the new system, such as with the parallel and staged approaches. Crash changeover becomes attractive.

Systems Complexity. The more complex the design of the new system, the greater the chance of flaws upon implementation. Complex systems call for use of the parallel or staged changeover tactics.

User Resistance. The more resistant users are toward the new system, the more compelling is the crash changeover tactic, in which users are forced to live with the new system. Of course, the new system had better be relatively free of problems. Otherwise, resistance may increase.

Figure 19–8 displays these criteria as they relate to choosing among the four changeover tactics. Whichever tactic is selected, certain steps are required to perform the changeover from the old to new business information system.

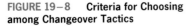

FIGURE 19–8   **Criteria for Choosing among Changeover Tactics**

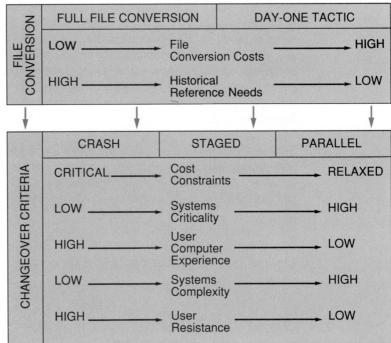

THE CHANGEOVER PROCESS

The process of changing over from the old to new information system includes changeover scheduling, user notification, activity phasedown, file conversion, systems cutover, new system priming, and activity resumption.

Changeover Scheduling. Many persons will be performing tasks during the changeover process. In addition, since changeover will be done during a phasedown in transaction activity, it must be done quickly. This is the "Scotch Tape and Super Glue" phase of the SDLC. Many things can and will go wrong. For these reasons, a tight and clear **changeover schedule** must be formulated and distributed widely.

User Notification. The changeover process is disruptive to normal clerical operations. All users should be told that a changeover is imminent, when and for how long the changeover will last, and how they will be affected. **User notification** should be far enough in advance to allow orderly planning on the part of users.

Activity Phasedown. It is not wise to accomplish a changeover while an application is in full operation. Transaction activity should be phased down (**activity phasedown**) so that only priority matters are processed during the changeover.

File Conversion. As you saw earlier, conversion to a new system entails some degree of **file conversion.** This activity transforms the file formats from the old system to those required for the new system. It often includes some off-line efforts that add to the new files elements not found in the old files. File conversion includes (1) generating off-line file augmentations, (2) developing programs for automatic conversion from the old to the new file formats, (3) downloading old files onto an off-line medium (for example, magnetic tape), and (4) using these three products to upload the new file formats onto the computer system. Figure 19–9 illustrates the process.

Systems Cutover. Specific dates and times are set for discontinuance of the old system and operational use of the new system. The process is referred to as **systems cutover.** If the crash changeover tactic has been selected, the dates and times for discontinuance of the old system and operational use of the new system are the same.

New System Priming. The newly operational system is carefully fed with transactions during activity phasedown. This activity is called **new system priming.** Control is ready to be returned quickly to the old system if the new system begins to sputter with these transactions.

FIGURE   19–9   File   Conversion Tasks

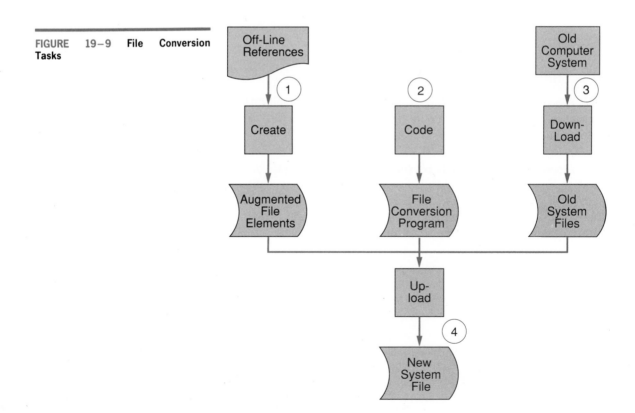

Activity Resumption. The application is returned to its full level of transaction activity **(activity resumption).**

At this point, the new business information system is in operation. However, the system will have to be fine-tuned before it can be turned over to the end-user community. One of the critical factors determining the success of the new system is the level of user resistance.

USER RESISTANCE

The success of any business information system is determined by how well users accept that system. The most carefully designed system will fail if it is poorly received by users. Thus, the designer's role cannot rest on technical analysis and design alone. That role must be expanded to include people skills. Designers must sell the new information system to users.

Why would users resist implementation of new, presumably better, information systems? Often, users perceive a new information system as a threat. One user may fear losing a job. Another may fear losing control to a computer. Others may fear that, with a system new to everyone, users with longevity will lose their knowledge edge over less tenured workers. In short, many users will be afraid of losing the comfort zone of the old information system.

Reluctance to change can lead to resistance in the following forms:

- **Avoidance**—Users pretend the new system does not exist; they maintain informal and redundant record-keeping systems rather than use the newly implemented system.
- **Projection**—Users blame all application problems on the new system.
- **Hostility**—Users display antagonism, particularly against those advocating the new system.
- **Sabotage**—Users actively try to make the new system fail.

Designers begin selling the new information system early in the systems development life cycle. They can reduce changeover resistance by honest use of the following methods:

- User involvement and participation in all phases of the SDLC
- Prototyping
- Training
- User feedback on systems problems and successes

When user resistance is high, the systems designer should consider the crash changeover tactic which forces all users to abandon the old system and work with the new one. In such cases, however, the new system had better be well designed and tested, with a minimum of fine-tuning required. Otherwise, there could be a palace revolt.

The manager of an established department store in a small Mississippi town decided to introduce computers to the bookkeeping process. He purchased a system that was relatively turnkey (needed no expertise to operate). All that had to be done to get started was to load initial general ledger account values. The two bookkeepers had been with the store for forty-five and fifty years respectively. They were entrenched in the manual process and did not understand or trust the new computerized system. They were forced to use the system, but they maintained their old manual procedures at the same time. Consequently, the new computer system made their work more burdensome rather than easier. They reacted by avoiding the use of the new system until absolutely necessary. They also blamed all inaccuracies on the new system. Actually, mistakes were due to deliberate sabotage (entering of misinformation) and lack of proper training.

COMBATING RESISTANCE TO CHANGE

A study conducted by Carey (1988) explored acceptance of a new information system in a university environment. Results indicated that individual rigidity, commitment to the status quo, knowledge of the status quo, exposure to the new system, preparation for the new system, and previous experience with the new system in a different environment all had an impact on acceptance of the new system.

What implications do these findings have for managers who are involved in information systems change and are charged with the task of acting as agents of change?

1. Rigidity is measured by behavioral rigidity scores in a personality test. It is a variable that is difficult to control since managers have other considerations when hiring personnel. To offset a rigid mindset within a work force, change could be introduced by stages (e.g., departmentally). The logical approach would be to measure the rigidity of all departments and introduce change first into those departments whose flexibility is at a higher level than other departments. Once the change has been introduced to these departments, the acceptance level of more rigid departments may increase.

2. Commitment to the status quo includes preference for the status quo over change and continued use of the status quo when change is available and encouraged. It may be advantageous to make the status quo unattractive in some manner. In the case of changing computer systems, some restrictions could be placed on use of the operational system. At the same time, efforts might be undertaken to make the new system more attractive to users. By using techniques that enhance the image of the new system and increase the status of those who use the new system, commitment to the old system could be lessened.

3. Knowledge of the status quo includes length of time spent with the status quo and familiarity with it. There is little a manager can do to alter this variable. The longer the status quo has been in force, the more resistance there will be to change. Understanding this relationship can alert the information systems manager to the difficulties inherent in changing systems and allow determination of a plan of action.

4. The longer a user is exposed to a change, the more positive his or her attitude will be toward that change. The IS manager should make every effort to encourage

adoption of the new system by users as soon as possible. Time and money incentives could be offered. Approaches such as offering hands-on instruction or team exercises could painlessly expose users to the new system. Since this variable was the most important in Carey's study, any effort to encourage early use ought to have a large payoff in terms of making the transition smooth and moving from a stressful situation to a more relaxed one. This speaks well to including end-users as early as possible in the SDLC.

5. To prepare for change, training seminars may be initiated for users. An additional or alternative preparation could be psychological. The IS manager may decide to try breaking down psychological barriers against change by distributing positive memorandums and using other media to promote the advantages of the new system.

6. Exposure to the new system in a different setting prior to its introduction in the current setting has a positive relationship to acceptance of the new system. It might be possible to exchange employees with another department so users experience the new system prior to its actual implementation.

The IS manager can alleviate resistance to a new information system by understanding the relationship among these key variables and acceptance of change. A new information system must be technically sound, but it also must be accepted by the users or it will fail.

PROFILE OF A POORLY IMPLEMENTED SYSTEM

Unfortunately, this profile of a poorly implemented system is not fictitious. It comes from personal experience. The system was a statewide traffic citation processing operation in a state court system. Federal grant money was used to design a replacement system, despite the fact that clerical personnel had few complaints with the old, manual system with which they had been working for years. Therefore, the new traffic system became immediately *their* rather than *our* system in users' eyes. User resistance began to swell.

Training was conducted too late in the SDLC. It was conducted by systems personnel who had never done such training before. Operating procedures were completed at the last minute. They were too complex; they looked like instructions for building a nuclear bomb.

The changeover tactic selected (without much thought) was parallel, even though (1) the courts were already short of clerical resources and really could not operate two systems effectively and (2) continuation of the old traffic citation system provided the means for clerical personnel to hold onto a system with which they were quite comfortable. The new traffic citation system operated miserably, and users blamed every problem in the courts on the new system (projection).

Traffic judges merely ignored the new system (avoidance) and requested their clerks to present to them information from the old system. Fancy reports from the new system mysteriously disappeared (sabotage). When visiting clerical offices, designers were greeted with hostility. Finally, the chief designer threatened to drop the new system and return to the old one. The traffic judges, perhaps feeling a twinge of professional guilt, met with the designer and drafted a new, joint implementation plan for a revised traffic citation system. The revised system started successfully two months later and operated several years before being replaced by another zealous designer.

HUMAN ASPECTS

If you have proceeded through the SDLC with the end-user consistently in mind, then conversion to the new information system should proceed rather smoothly. There will be rough points, but they probably can be smoothed out easily. If, on the other hand, you have proceeded through the SDLC with a strictly technical perspective, paying little attention to human aspects, the conversion stage will be entirely frustrating and unsuccessful. Information systems are not art. They are not intended to be looked at and admired. They are intended to be used—by humans.

SUMMARY

Important systems implementation tasks are performed by specialists outside the information systems field. The tasks all require expertise not expected of the typical systems designer. Designers act as the coordinators rather than supervisors. Published project schedules provide effective means to be sure that professional personnel in the other areas perform as directed.

The most important of these auxiliary areas is training. Information systems professionals traditionally have been less than adequate trainers for various reasons. This condition is improving, but there's still a long way to go.

Each of three training audiences—end-users, operations personnel, and managers and executives—requires a different mix of technical (syntactic) and conceptual (semantic) knowledge. Training can be conducted by end-users, members of the design team, or training specialists. A training team of members from all three groups is recommended. Training can be conducted in the work area, in on-site training facilities, or off-site. Training should be conducted as early as possible in the SDLC.

Use of automated training systems encourages early training. These training aids include systems with training wheels and prototypes. An SDLC emphasizing training gives priority to those tasks that allow early construction of automated training systems.

Systems designers also are responsible for writing three types of operating instructions: user instructions, technical instructions, and executive overviews. Several tasks lie outside the immediate information systems area. These include site preparation, hardware and software acquisition, and vendor contracts. Systems designers are responsible for coordinating efforts in these areas.

A striking feature that sets implementation aside from other SDLC stages is that systems designers must exert influence outside their realms of expertise.

Systems changeover is the final stage of the systems development life cycle. It is the most critical stage, since user attitudes toward the new system are crystallized here.

There are four ways to change from the old to a new business information system: crash, parallel, staged, and day one. The day-one changeover tactic is particularly important, since it addresses the common problem of converting files from the old to the new format.

The choice of which changeover tactic to use is based on criteria of costs, systems criticality, user computer experience, systems complexity, and user resistance. There is no "best" changeover tactic; the specific changeover situation dictates which approach to use.

The changeover process includes changeover scheduling, user notification, activity phasedown, file conversion, systems cutover, new system priming, and activity resumption.

Success of the new system depends on how well users accept it. Systems designers must sell new systems to overcome possible user resistance. Resistance arises from user fears such as losing jobs, losing control to the computer, and losing experience edges over newer workers. Resistance manifests itself in avoidance of the system, projection of all problems to the new system, hostility, and sabotage. Systems designers must be aware of and combat user resistance throughout the entire SDLC. Tactics to help reduce user resistance include user involvement and participation, prototyping, training, and user feedback.

CONCEPTS LEARNED

- System training tactics
- Guidelines for miscellaneous conversion tasks
- Four systems changeover tactics—crash, parallel, staged, and day one
- Criteria for choosing among changeover tactics

- Tasks involved in the changeover process
- Reasons for and forms of user resistance to the new information system
- Methods by which the systems designer reduces user resistance

KEY TERMS

acceptance contract
activity phasedown
activity resumption
alpha testing
avoidance
beta testing
changeover scheduling
computer semantic knowledge

crash changeover
day-one changeover
delivery contract
file conversion
hostility
maintenance contract
new system priming
operating instructions

parallel changeover
phased conversion
pilot conversion
projection
prototype
sabotage
site preparation

staged changeover
syntactic knowledge
systems cutover
systems with training wheels
task semantic knowledge
user notification

REVIEW QUESTIONS

1. What are the three audiences for systems training?

2. How do syntactic and semantic knowledge differ?

3. What are the advantages and disadvantages of specialists conducting systems training?

4. Why should systems training be conducted as early as possible in the SDLC?

5. Describe a system with training wheels.

6. What are the three types of operating instructions?

7. Why is hardware and software acceptance testing important?

8. What are the relative advantages and disadvantages of the crash versus parallel changeover approach?

9. Name some common dimensions used to separate a system into the modules necessary for use of the staged changeover tactic.

10. Describe how the day-one changeover tactic works.

11. What criteria are used to choose among changeover tactics?

12. Describe the seven tasks of the changeover process.

13. What is activity phasedown? Why is it important to the changeover effort?

14. Why might users resist implementation of a new business information system?

15. What forms of action might user resistance take?

16. How can the systems designer reduce user resistance?

CRITICAL THINKING OPPORTUNITIES

1. Draw a diagram of the organization of this chapter.

2. Compare and contrast the parallel and phased changeover approach.

3. Read the Mega Video example in Case 6.1. Develop a training plan for this system. Include who receives and who conducts the training, what the training materials should be, when in the SDLC training should take place, and where the training is conducted.

4. Refer to the Mega Video example in Case 6.1. Develop a plan for conversion to the new computer system. Include a changeover approach, tell why this approach was chosen, and give a conversion schedule.

SMALL SYSTEM DESIGN:
BULLDOG COLLECTION AGENCY

SETTING

This book presents analysis and design principles that are germane to most information systems. There are certain systems settings, however, where designers must tailor design techniques. The first type of setting involves specialized systems such as MISs, DSSs, ESs, and EISs. A second type of setting is design of information systems for small organizations. Several differences are apparent in the information setting of a small company compared to that of a larger firm:

1. Ratio of clerical to other types of personnel: In a small company, most employees are sales oriented first and clerically oriented second. There are fewer clerical specialists. Many accounting and other clerical functions are farmed out (out-sourcing). Some personnel double up. For example, the assistant manager of a clothing store may spend 60 percent of his or her time selling and the other 40 percent doing accounting, advertising, and personnel tasks. In a small company, clerical work is often viewed as tasks that must be done but get in the way of selling.

2. Microcomputer: Most small firms use microcomputers rather than mainframes. Some firms use local area networks (LANs), but many do not.

3. Software packages: The transaction processing systems of most small firms are fairly standard. There is little use of higher-level systems such as DSSs or EISs. Therefore, there is greater use of purchased software packages.

4. Lack of computer knowledge: Small companies frequently are at the lower end of the evolutionary scale of computer usage. Often the system to be-developed is the firm's first automated system. Personnel working for small firms rarely have much or any computer experience. New systems training becomes even more critical in such situations.

5. Limited physical resources: Microcomputer resources are shared. Few workstations are available. Most personnel work in a large common area with little work privacy or noise protection.

6. Lack of design expertise: Rarely is there enough work for or money to hire a full-time systems person; new systems development usually is contracted to outside consultants.

Of course, these are general characteristics. Many small firms may not have one or two of these traits; however, most small firms will demonstrate most of them. One such firm is the Bulldog Collection Agency, the subject of the case study that follows. In this case, the name of the small firm and some of the facts have been changed to preserve confidentiality, but most of what follows actually occurred. This author knows, since he was the principal designer involved in this development effort.

THE OLD SYSTEM

The Bulldog Collection Agency is located in Columbus, Mississippi. The agency employs fifteen people: one manager who also functions as a credit collector; one assistant manager who is in charge of all personnel, financing, and accounting tasks; eight credit collectors, two secretaries, and three miscellaneous clerical workers. Notice that the ratio of clerical (including secretaries) to other personnel is one to two—a low clerical ratio.

The Bulldog Collection Agency receives delinquent customer accounts from Columbus retail firms (e.g., department stores). The agency attempts to collect delinquent accounts through letter and telephone contact and legal action. The agency's income is a percentage (25 to 50) of monies collected from delinquent accounts. The collection procedure follows seven steps.

1. The retail firm assigns a delinquent account to the Bulldog Collection Agency through a legal letter of agreement.
2. The retail customer account is added to the agency's delinquent file. This file includes one record for each account assigned. If a person has delinquent accounts for two or more retail firms, there is a separate record for each delinquent incident. The delinquent file is a manual index card file.
3. A record is added to the customer file for the retail firm assigning the delinquent account. There is one record in the file for each assignment contract. Hence, if ABC Trucking has assigned thirty contracts for thirty different delinquent customer accounts, there are thirty separate records in the customer file. Customer records are kept in a manual card file.
4. A credit collector is assigned to each active delinquent file record. The collector contacts the debtor to try to collect some or all of the delinquent account. Collector contacts are recorded on the delinquent record.
5. When cash or checks are received from contacted debtors, the payment is entered to a payment register. The payment is also recorded on the delinquent record.
6. Once a month the assistant manager searches the payment register. For every entry, she (1) determines what percentage of the payment is to be returned to the customer (assigning firm), (2) writes a check for that amount, and (3) posts the payment to the customer record.
7. The manager, on the advice of a credit collector, pulls overdue delinquent records from the file and initiates legal action.

Several problems are evident with this manual system:

- There is no linkage for persons with several records in the delinquent file. Although the records are in alphabetical order, the cards are often misfiled.
- A three-day backlog is routine for posting entries to the delinquent file, customer file, and payment register.
- Posting of credit collection actions to the delinquent file is erratic. Twice this proved embarrassing in court when the debtor was sued for nonpayment and actually had paid.
- The manager has to rely on the advice of credit collectors to press legal action. A onetime search of the delinquent file revealed eighty-five incidents where legal action should have been taken but was not recommended by credit collectors.
- Assigning firms (customers) complain that the checks they receive are not always for the correct amount and that they would prefer one check every two weeks rather than several checks once a month.
- Turnover of clerical personnel is high. Thus, the assistant manager is spending a large part of her time training new employees to learn the manual card system.

Because of these problems, the manager decided to automate the record-keeping process.

THE NEW SYSTEM

The manager contracted two information systems consultants to design, program, and implement an automated collection system. The consultants observed the current system and interviewed the manager, assistant manager, and three of the credit collectors. The consultants decided not to use a structured development approach since it might seem too technical for the computer-naive agency people.

After three weeks, the consultants presented the manager and assistant manager with a conceptual design that included the following eight features:

1. The new system would be a microcomputer environment utilizing a secondhand microcomputer that the manager had purchased at an auction.

2. Initially, the system would be batch processing using the single workstation and daily status reports. Personnel would use the reports for manual file inquiries.

3. When more development funds became available, the system would be upgraded to real time with multiple workstations and a local area network.

4. The delinquent, customer, and payment register files would be automated. Any entry to the payment register file would automatically update the other files.

5. Data entry screens designed according to human factors considerations would allow relatively untrained operators to update records more quickly than making manual entries.

6. Customer checks would be generated automatically every two weeks. The amount of the check would be computed automatically and consolidated from separate entries on the payment register.

7. The delinquent file would be scanned automatically once a month to produce a report of cases recommended for legal action.

8. One problem *would not* be solved. Without multiple workstations and a LAN, the proposed new system could not promise better posting of credit collection contacts. However, daily reports tailored by individual collectors would allow manual entry of actions. These entries could then be entered the next day by clerical personnel. This would help, but not fully solve, the problem.

The manager accepted the proposed system. A letter of agreement was signed by the manager and the consultants relating to conceptual design, payment schedule, delivery schedule, and postchangeover responsibilities of the consultants. The consultants then began design of this not overly complex system. Problems began to occur almost immediately.

DESIGN PROBLEMS

Most of the problems encountered could exist in a large systems environment. Most often, however, they are found in smaller systems settings. Some of the problems were quite serious.

1. Workstation competition: Clerical personnel had started to use the microcomputer for word processing tasks (e.g., letters and contracts). There was not always sufficient time during the day to enter and test programs. This was not a workstation that was compatible with others available to the consultants. A partial resolution was reached by the consultants using the workstation at night and on weekends.

2. Change of scope: Almost daily, the manager and the assistant manager requested changes to the proposed system to address some point they had forgotten. These changes to the proposed system slowed down development.

3. Lack of file integrity: The manager hired a part-time programmer to develop a small dBASE customer and delinquent file to generate mailing labels. The consultants would return to find part of their programs and test files missing or modified. They decided to take a complete dump of their work whenever they left the agency. They then had to reload their system whenever they returned.

4. Disruptive setting: Credit collection is an emotional business. Credit collectors threaten and shout at debtors; debtors shout back. The atmosphere in a credit collection firm is angry and tense. Managers and credit collectors took out their frustrations on the young and underpaid clerical personnel. The consultants, working in a tension-charged atmosphere, became tense and made more than the expected number of logic errors. It was like a student trying to take an examination on the floor of the stock exchange.

5. Impatience: The manager became impatient with development progress although the project never was more than a week behind schedule. Even when the system was implemented, the manager's impatience grew. The consultants decided that there were not enough clerical hours available to convert all of

the old customer, delinquent, and payment register manual card files to the new automated format. So they decided to use the day-one changeover method. It would take about one month for all active records to be converted to the new system. When the consultants tried to explain this to the computer-naive manager, he ranted and raved and started to treat them as he treated the clerical personnel.

RESULTS

The manager withheld the next-scheduled payment to the consultants and they refused to continue working on the system until the payment was received. The manager threatened to sue and refused to meet with the consultants. The consultants abandoned the project. The new system was never fully implemented. The consultants were never fully paid.

REVIEW QUESTIONS

1. What circumstances differentiate this setting from that of a large system?
2. For each of the design problems described, point out mistakes the consultants made and suggest how these mistakes could have been avoided.
3. Why did the consultants abandon the development effort so quickly? What would you have done differently?
4. Suppose the system had been implemented. Would you expect user resistance? In what form?
5. Develop an alternate proposal for a new system.

In this chapter you will learn about:

WHAT: (Concepts) Continuous evaluation of information systems.

WHY: Information systems must be evaluated continually to detect problems as early as possible.

WHEN: This is the last stage of the SDLC; it continues into system operation and leads to problem detection.

WHO: Systems manager.

WHERE: Information systems department.

HOW: (Techniques) Changeover contract
                        Quality measurement system
                        Performance matrix
                        Daily transaction log

OUTLINE

- Setting
- A Total Quality Approach
- Systems Fine-Tuning
- Postimplementation Review
- The Changeover Contract
- Measurement Principles
- Quality Measurement Systems (QMS)
- Necco Farm Products QMS
- Profile of a Poorly Measured System
- Human Aspects

SYSTEM EVALUATION

"Measurement" is one of those terms which has attained a social prestige. Apparently—all other things being equal—it is better to measure than not to measure.

—C. WEST CHURCHMAN (1959)

SETTING

The new information system has been installed and is working, perhaps only in a so-so manner. Nevertheless, it is still working. There now is a period of evaluation and fine-tuning before (1) the new system can be turned over to end-users, and (2) the new system becomes part of the firm's operational inventory of day-to-day information systems. This is shown in Figure 20–1.

Yet, the development process technically does not end here. The SDLC is a cycle, not a serial process that just stops. This is shown in Figure 20–2. An information system is constantly evaluated in an effort to detect problems early enough to allow orderly repair. When major problems are detected, a new SDLC begins. This is a cycle that is fed by continuous evaluation systems.

Continuous evaluation of information systems is the topic of this chapter. First, however, we are concerned with finishing up the system development life cycle for the new information system.

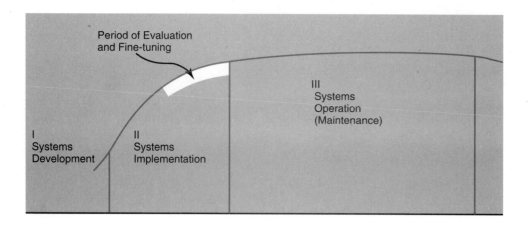

FIGURE 20–1   **Period of Evaluation and Fine-tuning in Information Systems Life Cycle**

FIGURE 20–2   **Continuous System Evaluation as a Part of the System Development Life Cycle**

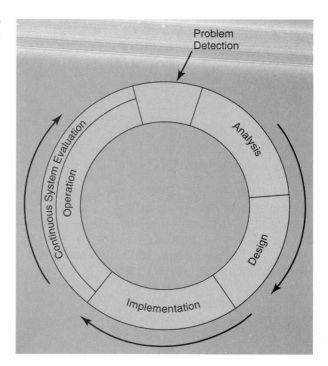

A TOTAL QUALITY APPROACH

Harrington (1991) describes evaluation of a process (system) to ensure it is effective. He states:

> To ensure that the process is effective, you must define the customer needs and expectations and then meet those needs and expectations. The first step should be to determine

what your customer's needs and expectations are. The second step should be to specifically describe those needs and expectations in measurable terms. The third step is to define the way the measurement data are collected and used. (Harrington, 1991, p. 75)

Harrington cites the need for measurable characteristics that can be (1) evaluated *before* the output is delivered to the customer, (2) documented in a specification so that employees have a standard, and (3) agreed to by both the supplier and the customer.

In the context of this book, the supplier is the information systems department and the system analyst responsible for developing the specific information system. The customer is the group of end-users who will be providing the input to and receiving the output from the new information systems. As information analysts, our task is to define what about the information system must be measured and how that measurement is to take place. In doing so, we will revisit the familiar characteristics of information, namely (1) relevancy, (2) completeness, (3) correctness, (4) security, (5) timeliness, (6) economy, (7) efficiency, (8) reliability, and (9) usability.

SYSTEMS FINE-TUNING

Before we develop a formal information system evaluation structure, let us first complete the SDLC for the new information system by describing three post-conversion evaluation activities. The first is system fine-tuning, the second is postimplementation review, and the third is the changeover contract. Systems fine-tuning involves the rapid fixing of minor system flaws always associated with the introduction of any new technology.

Types of flaws that occur in a system can be classified by seriousness of impact on users and by whether they were anticipated or not. As Figure 20–3 shows, there are three categories of flaws that can occur during the systems changeover stage (the category of anticipated/minor is considered an empty set): major anticipated, major unanticipated, and minor unanticipated.

Major anticipated flaws are features of the system that were excluded deliberately from design because of lack of time, funds, or other resources. Users should be notified of these omissions long before systems changeover. In that way user expectations are conditioned and a minimum of frustration results. The missing, but desired, features should be kept in a future file for later development when conditions are more favorable.

Major unanticipated flaws are major design errors. Extensive systems testing will make the chances low that such flaws will occur; however, a contingency plan should be in place (e.g., return to the old system) in case something major goes wrong.

Minor unanticipated flaws are not fatal to successful operation of the new information system. However, they do erode user confidence in the system if they are not handled effectively.

The process of handling minor unanticipated flaws is called **systems fine-tuning.** It must be done in an efficient, structured process. Otherwise, users lose confidence in

FIGURE 20—3   **Methods for Dealing with Systems Flaws According to Impact on Users and Predicted Occurrence**

Impact on Users	Predicted Occurrence	
	Unanticipated	Anticipated
Minor	Fine-tuning	(Empty Set)
Major	Contingency Plan	Future File

the new information system. They may even resist it. There are five elements in fine-tuning a system in a structured way:

1. Management of user expectations: Users expect perfect business information systems, as they expect their new cars and their toaster ovens to be perfect. Design of business information systems is too complex to expect perfection. Yet, IS professionals seem afraid to tell users that their Mona Lisa may have a flaw or two. As a result, users expect a quality level that cannot be delivered. All new information systems will have some flaws. Users must be conditioned to understand that new information systems will have minor flaws that can be quickly fixed. When users expect such minor flaws, they still retain confidence in the system when flaws occur.

2. Problem discovery: Systems designers need to set up a detection mechanism so users can discover minor flaws and report them quickly.

3. Rapid correction: User confidence during changeover correlates highly to how quickly reported discrepancies are corrected. If a problem-tracking system has not been established for program maintenance, it must be established during systems changeover.

4. New system priority: Correcting flaws in the new system must have priority over fixing flaws in operational systems (program maintenance). Users of new systems expect immediate action. They do not appreciate being placed at the end of a long line of program maintenance changes.

5. Status reports: Remember the supply officer's dilemma? The officer delivers 999 parts on time but is chastised for the one part delivered late. The same is true for new information systems. Users of new systems remember only failures unless reminded of the successes. Systems designers should produce frequent changeover status reports that include minor flaws, flaws corrected, correction times, parts of the system that have been operating with no flaws, and **systems success rate,** which is defined as:

$$\frac{\text{Number of transactions processed without systems flaws}}{\text{Total transactions processed}}$$

Status reports also should include trends to show that the new system is operating better over time.

After a period of fine-tuning, it is time to begin the process of turning over responsibility for operating this new system. The first step in this transfer of responsibility is the postimplementation review.

POSTIMPLEMENTATION REVIEW

A **postimplementation review** is done at a specific date, say six months after changeover to the new system. Alternatively, the review can be initiated when all parties agree that the newly implemented system has settled down; that is, it has been fine-tuned to eliminate most initial flaws.

The purpose of the postimplementation review is to show that the new information system is operating according to specifications. It is ready to be turned over to the end-user community. Participants in the review include designers, users, and an auditor. The report they produce includes the following items:

- Specification goals of the new system
- Current performance of the new system compared to specification goals
- Specific areas where the new system has not yet met specification goals
- Actions required to bring the new system up to full performance
- Estimated dates when the actions will be complete
- Date for final review of the postimplementation plan

Once the new information system has reached the standards set in the postimplementation review, responsibility for the system can be transferred from the design team to the user organization. The means for this transfer of responsibility is the changeover contract.

THE CHANGEOVER CONTRACT

You would not consider purchasing even a medium-priced appliance without first studying the product's specifications and warranty. Yet, it is common for users to accept an expensive information system without knowing what it is supposed to do, and with no guarantee of performance.

The final step of a systems development life cycle is the **changeover contract.** Often it is drafted before the design project is started, as a **scope of work agreement.** Since the scope of work can change, it is best to rewrite the agreement at this time into a changeover contract. The contract tells users exactly what to expect from the new information system. The changeover contract has five elements:

1. Performance goals—how the system is expected to perform in terms of VDT response time, computer downtime, report distribution time, and so on
2. Tolerances—how far performance can vary from goals before the system should be judged to be in trouble
3. Estimated system life—when enhancement or replacement is likely to be needed
4. Maintenance expectations—how long it takes from detection to correction of a problem with the system
5. Future changes—establishment of a future file for user-suggested enhancements and changes to the new system

After information systems personnel and users sign the contract, the new system belongs to the user community. The systems development life cycle is complete.

The remainder of this chapter is devoted to the building and use of a quality measurement system (QMS) for continuous evaluation of information systems. It is recognized that existence of a QMS would facilitate postimplementation review and the design of the changeover contract. While we discuss QMS at the *end* of the SDLC, it is clear that it is this type of measurement process that will detect information system problems—that will lead to beginning the SDLC. Quality measurement systems are discussed *here* as a presentation convenience, not as a recommended sequence.

There are four parts to the discussion of QMS. First, measurement principles are discussed. Secondly, a QMS structure is derived. Thirdly, a case study is presented. Finally, an example is given of a poorly evaluated system.

MEASUREMENT PRINCIPLES

Two models are used in this book to develop the framework for a quality measurement system. The second model is the problem structure model first discussed in Chapter 2.

The Kircher Model

Paul Kircher (1955) established seven elements for designing any measurement process, regardless of what is being measured.

1. Determine the system's objective, the purpose that is to be served.
2. Determine the types of factors that might serve to attain this objective.
3. Divide the types of factors into key aspects, the aspects that are to be measured.
4. Choose a measuring method and unit.
5. Apply the measuring unit to the key aspects.
6. Analyze the measurement to relate it to other measurements (e.g., in time or in kind).
7. Evaluate the effectiveness of the measurement system (steps 2 through 6) to determine how it assisted in attaining the system objective of step 1.

This process is similar to the total quality structure we established in chapters 1 through 3. This is not surprising, since TQM is essentially a measurement activity. There is also a similarity between the Kircher structure and that of critical success factors, discussed in Chapter 1.

Kircher's fourth step, choose a measuring method and unit, is too general. We will need to focus this step more precisely in order to fashion a workable quality measurement system. We use the problem structure model to add this precision.

Problem Structure

Figure 20–4 shows the structure of a typical business problem. We continually have stated that the goal of any information system is to help managers detect and solve problems. Therefore, a quality measurement system for a business information system must include the same elements as does the business problem.

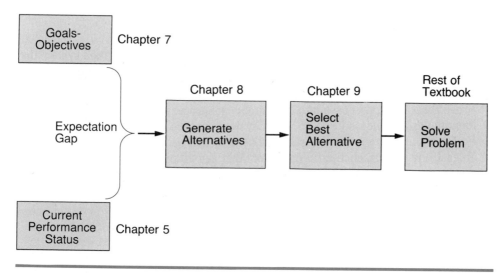

FIGURE 20—4   Structure of a Typical Business Problem

- *Goals/performance objectives:* Goals are established for each information system area (factor) to be addressed: For example the goal for data entry throughput may be set at 20,000 transactions per day.
- *Current performance status:* Periodically, each evaluation area is measured to determine current performance. For example, a data entry program may include tallies of how many transactions are processed successfully each day.
- *Performance tolerances:* An allowable tolerance is established for each evaluation area. Tolerance describes how far current status can deviate from performance objectives before we consider the situation to be a potential problem. For example, remember that data entry throughput was assigned a goal of 20,000 transactions per day. Suppose we establish a tolerance of 2,000 transactions. This means that as long as throughput remains above 18,000 transactions per day, any deviation between goals and current status will not be considered a significant problem.
- *Trend analysis:* Deviations between goals and performance are plotted over time to see if there is a trend of deteriorating performance. Performance may be increasing to the extent that it will become a problem six months from now. Trend analysis allows us the lead time necessary to start working on a potential problem *before* it has a large impact on information system operations.
- *Problem notification:* The existence of a potential, current, or future problem is communicated to the information systems department for further analysis.

This problem structure model has been the underlying framework for the organization of this book, and for the SDLC that has marked progression from one chapter to another. It should not be surprising, therefore, to see that this problem structure, in combination with the Kircher model, is the basis for constructing a quality measurement system.

QUALITY MEASUREMENT SYSTEMS (QMS)

A **quality measurement system (QMS)** is a formal problem notification system that allows management to detect system problems. It requires six construction steps:

1. Identify key processes.
2. Break these key processes into measurable subprocesses.
3. Identify performance criteria by which system success is judged.
4. For each combination of measurable subprocess and performance criterion, develop at least one performance ratio (indicator) that can be measured.
5. For each performance ratio establish the amount of measurement, tolerance, and trend period.
6. Establish a continuous measurement system.

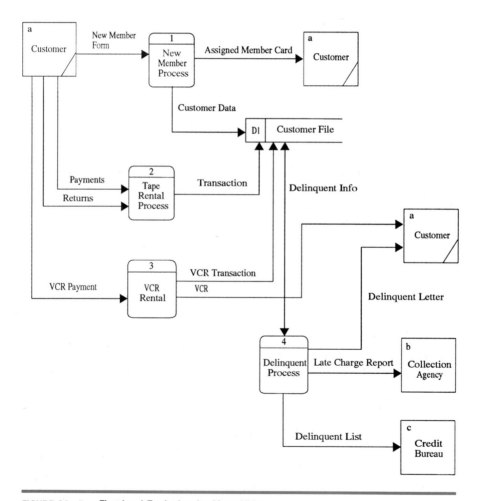

FIGURE 20–5   **First-level Explosion for Mega Video**

Following is a more detailed description of these construction steps:

Identify key processes: If the firm used a structured development strategy, the processes are simply those shown with the process symbol on the first-level explosion of the physical data flow diagram for the information system. In Figure 20–5, for example, the key processes are (1) new rental process, (2) tape rental process, (3) VCR rental, and (4) delinquent process.

   This does not mean that DFDs are the only means for identifying processes. As you will see, Necco Farm Products used a different means for identifying key processes.

Break Key Processes into Measurable Subprocesses: The DFD again can be used to identify relevant subprocesses. Figure 20–6 is an explosion of the VCR rental process for the DFD in Figure 20–5. Figure 20–7 is a further explosion of process 3.1, VCR checkout process. We can use the DFD explosion process to break a key process into measurable subprocesses. We need only decide to what level of detail (and thus complexity) we wish to go. Again, the DFD need not be used for identifying subprocesses. This is shown in the Necco Farm Products example.

Identify Performance Criteria: This has been done consistently throughout this book. Our criteria here are our old friends, the characteristics of information: relevancy, completeness, correctness, security, timeliness, economy, efficiency, reliability, and usability.

Develop Performance Ratio: Ratios are a convenient form of measurement because they can be compared over time and in kind. By *in kind,* we mean that an analyst can compare the same ratio between two different processes, even though the measurement quantities may vary. An example is shown in the box "Use of Ratios."

FIGURE 20–6   Second-level Explosion of Process 3 (VCR Rental Process)—Current Physical DFD

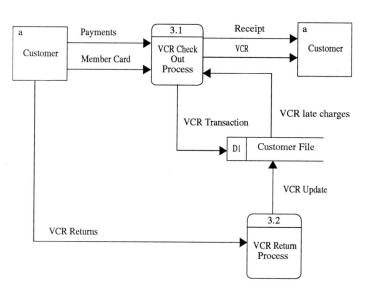

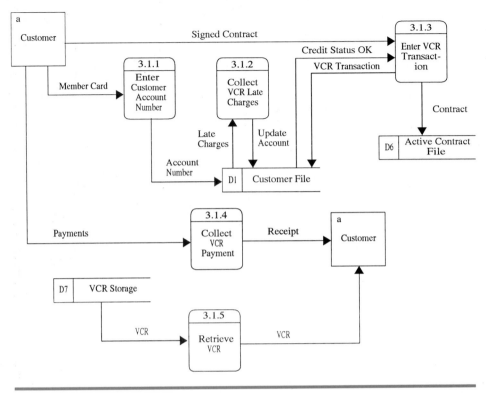

FIGURE 20-7   Third-level Explosion of Process 3 (VCR Rental Process)—Current Physical DFD

USE OF RATIOS

Process A produces an average of 200 errors per day. Process B produces an average of 400 errors per day. It would seem that process B is twice as incorrect as process A. However, process A handles 2,000 transactions per day while process B handles 8,000 transactions per day. Suppose we compute a performance ratio as follows.

$$\frac{\text{Transaction}}{\text{Error rate}} = \frac{\text{Number error transactions per day}}{\text{Total transactions per day}}$$

In this case:

$$\frac{\text{Process A}}{\text{Transaction}} = \frac{200}{2,000} = 10\%$$

$$\frac{\text{Process B}}{\text{Transaction}} = \frac{400}{8,000} = 5\%$$

It is process A that is twice as inaccurate.

FIGURE 20–8   **Performance Matrix Structure**

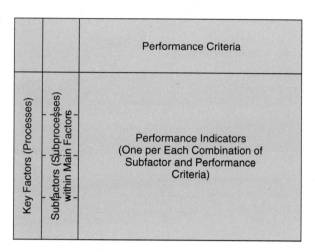

A useful method for developing performance ratios is the performance matrix as shown in Figure 20–8. A **performance matrix** is an inventory of indicators used to gauge system performance. The rows of the matrix are the key factors (processes) and subfactors (subprocesses) defined in the preceding stages. The columns are the performance criteria selected (e.g., correctness). For each matrix cell (row/column combination), at least one performance indicator (ratio) is described.

For each performance indicator so specified, a performance indicator profile is established. A **performance indicator profile** is a record that includes for each indicator:

- Name of indicator
- How it is computed (formula of ratio)
- Method of measurement (e.g., end user survey)
- Performance goal
- Performance tolerance
- Reporting mechanism (e.g., name of report)
- Trend period (e.g., compute trend over 6 months)

Create Continuous Measurement System: Various means can be used to measure the current performance status of an information system.

Some of these are user surveys, audits, program problem log sheets (Figure 20–9) and daily transaction logs. All of these measurement sources normally are part of any structured information systems department. Therefore, the costs of designing a quality measurement system need not be substantial for a business firm.

Often, the daily transaction log is overlooked as a source of performance management. The **daily transaction log** is a computer-stored record of all transactions that have been processed by the computer each day. Figure 20–10 shows a typical format

Systems Problem Log

Control
Number _____

Date Received: ___ / ___ / ___   Received By: _____

Time Received: _____

How Received: Telephone Correspondence Site Visit Other _____

Who Reported: _____   Ext.: _____

Position: _____

Application System: _____   Component: _____

Problem Description: _____

_____

_____

_____

(Use Other Side if Necessary)

FIGURE 20–9   **Form for Logging Information Systems Problems Reported to the IS Department**

from a daily transaction by file. From this we can glean several performance measures from this limited entry.

- Transaction processing time (End time minus Begin time)
- Error rate (Percent transactions with "E" conclusion code)
- False start rate (Percent transactions with "A" conclusion code)
- Operation statistics (Transactions, errors, false starts, etc. by Operation ID)
- Error type frequency (Error code)

These are the steps required to construct a quality measurement system. The Necco Farm Products examples shows this process.

FIGURE 20–10   **Daily Transaction Log in Tape Format**

Date:	062589
Operator ID:	Mellow
Workstation ID:	CRT01
Transaction ID:	ARUPT
Begin Time:	101637
*Conclusion Code:	E
**Error Code:	F102
End Time:	101703

*(E=Error: S=Successful; A=Abort)
**(e.g., F102="Invalid Unit Price Field Type")

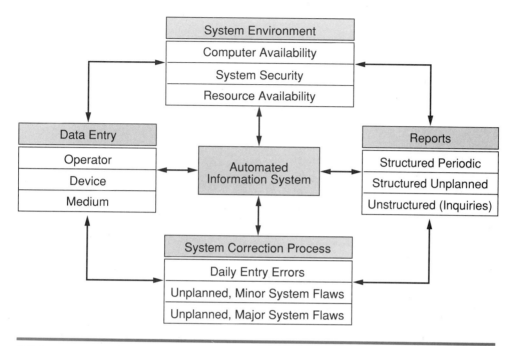

FIGURE 20–11   Key Factors and Subfactors in the Information System of Necco Farm Products

Reprinted by permission from M. Martin and J. Trumbly, "Measuring Performance of Computer Systems," *Journal of Systems Management* 37(February 1986):14.

NECCO FARM PRODUCTS QMS

David Martin is the chief information systems officer (CIO) for Necco Farm Products Company. Necco Farm Products is a medium size company located in California's Imperial Valley. David decided to design a quality management system for a typical Necco information system. He was trained in college to describe systems in terms of data flow diagrams. However, structured development had not yet been introduced at Necco Farm Products. Hence end-users were not familiar with the DFD charting technique.

David then chose to use a less technical approach to *identify key processes.* He described information systems as having the four key factors (processes) of data entry, system correction, reports, and system environment. He then *broke the key processes into measurable subprocesses* as shown in Figure 20–11. He next showed his diagram to his information system staff to see if he had left anything out.

David then *identified performance criteria.* He referenced a textbook he used in college to choose the criteria of accuracy, response rate, efficiency, and user accommodation. For each combination of measurable subprocesses and performance criteria, David Martin *developed a performance ratio.*

The performance matrix for David's work so far is shown in Figure 20–12. For each of these ratios, David created a performance indicator profile. Figure 20–13 is the

Factors		Criteria			
Key Factors	Subfactors	Accuracy	Response Rate	Efficiency	User Accommodation
Data Entry	Operator	Entry Error Rate	Transaction/Hour	Errorless Transactions/Hour	Operator Assessment of Environment
	Device	Downtime Rate	Transaction Response Rate	Avg. (Overall Operators) Transactions/Hour	Rate of Physical Discomfort (Illness, Complaints, etc.)
	Medium (e.g., form)	Inaccurate Recording Rate	Mediums Received per Hour	Errorless Mediums Received per Hour	Mediums Rejected per Hour
Report Processing	Structured Periodic	Report Accuracy Rate	Meeting Schedule Rate	Accurate Reports per Day	Report Use Rate
	Structured Unplanned	Report Accuracy Rate	Report Turnaround Rate	Unplanned/Planned Report Ratio	Report Use Rate
	Unstructured	Report Accuracy Rate	System Turnaround Rate	Unstructured Requests per Day	Attitudes toward Inquiry Capabilities
System Change Process	Data Entry Errors	Uncorrected Error Rate	Avg. Time to Correct Error	Uncorrected Errors per Day	Attitudes toward Error Messages
	Unplanned Minor System Flaws	Errors per Month	Avg. Time to Correct Error	Errors Corrected per Month	Attitudes toward Change Environment
	Unplanned Major System Flaws	Occurrences per Year	Avg. Time to Correct Error	Recorrections per Year	Attitudes toward Correction of Error
System Environment	Computer Availability	Downtime Hours per Month	Avg. Recovery Time	Uptime per Month	Perceived Impact of Downtime
	System Security	Incidents of Violations per Month	React/Adjust Time	Incidents per Number of Users	Attitudes on Safety of Information
	Resource Availability	Ratio of Funds Allocated to Funds Requested	Time to Handle Resource Request	Funds Issued to Requested Funds	Attitudes toward the Distribution of Funds

FIGURE 20–12   Necco's Performance Matrix with Indicators for Gauging System Performance

Reprinted by permission from M. Martin and J. Trumbly, "Measuring Performance of Computer Systems," *Journal of Systems Management* 37(February 1986):16.

FIGURE 20–13   **Performance Indicator Profile**

Indicator Name: Date Entry Operator Error Rate
How Computed: Number Transaction Errors / Number Transactions Entered
Unit of Measurement: Transaction
Method of Measurement: Transaction Log File
Performance Goal: <10%
Performance Tolerance: 6%
Reporting Mechanism: Monthly Performance Management Report

Necco Farm   10/16/95

Monthly Performance Report
Purchasing System

Process	Indicator	Goal	This Month	Trend
Data Entry Operator	Entry Error Rate	10%	12%	Up
Data Entry Device	Downtime Rate	5%	3%	None
Data Entry Medium	Inaccurate Recording	10%	8%	Down
Report Processing Structured	Accuracy Rate	5%	5%	None
Report Processing Unstructured	Accuracy Rate	5%	6%	None

Total Ratios: 16	No. Met Goals: 12	% Met 75%
	Unfavorable Trends: 4	% Unfavorable 25%

FIGURE 20–14   **Sample Quality Measurement Report for Necco Farm Products**

profile for entry operator error rate. David chose performance goals and tolerances after careful consultation with information system users.

Finally, David wrote the necessary procedures to *create a continuous measurement system*. He used the already existing daily transaction log to furnish much of the data needed to feed his QMS. He also designed a series of QMS reports, including the one shown in Figure 20–14.

David Martin's QMS is not perfect, but it is a meaningful start for measuring information system performance at Necco Farm Products. One of the critical thinking opportunities at the end of this chapter will give you the opportunity to expand on David's efforts. Yet, even as it stands, the new QMS is a major improvement over the poorly evaluated systems approach used by Necco Farm Products before David Martin arrived at the firm.

PROFILE OF A POORLY MEASURED SYSTEM

Prior to David Martin's QMS efforts, information system management at Necco Farm Products was characterized by the following conditions:

1. There was no consistent measurement of information system performance. For example, no one knew what were the current transaction error rate or the frequency of error types. Hence, there was no emphasis on focused operator training.
2. There was disagreement on what were performance objectives. Was a 10 percent error rate acceptable? Was a 10 percent error rate too much? No one knew.
3. There was no formal means of reporting alleged system problems to the information systems department.
4. No history was kept of information system problems. Thus, there was no awareness of adverse trends in information system performance.

HUMAN ASPECTS

There is a difference between alleged and real problems. A QMS is comprised of only problem *indicators*. When one of the indicators is "out of control," this merely means that we must look further into the situation to find if a real problem exists. An analogy is a call to a police station. The desk sergeant receiving the call records the incident as an *alleged* crime problem. Officers then are sent to the scene to verify if the phone call (indicator) represents a true crime problem, or is a false lead.

This is important from a human aspect. If we judge an information system purely on its statistics, we ignore the essential human role in these systems. If, instead, we use performance indicators as arrows guiding us to the most probable trouble spots, then we will journey into the world of the human user. Only there can real information system truths be found.

SUMMARY

The last portion of the system development life cycle is evaluation of the new information system after it has started operation. This involves the three steps of (1) system fine-tuning, (2) postimplementation review, and (3) preparation of the changeover contract.

A quality measurement system (QMS) is based upon the measurement model described in Chapter 2. The five steps required to design a QMS are (1) identify key processes; (2) break these key processes into measurable subprocesses; (3) identify performance criteria by which system success is judged; (4) for each combination of measurable subprocess and performance criterion, develop at least one performance ratio that can be measured; (5) for each performance ratio, establish the amount of measurement, method of measurement, performance goal, performance tolerance, and trend period; and (6) establish a continuous measurement system.

Two tools used in this process are the performance matrix and the performance indicator profile. The performance matrix is an inventory of indicators used to gauge system performance. A performance indicator profile is a record that includes for each indicator (1) name, (2) how computed, (3) method of measurement, (4) performance goal, (5) performance tolerance, (6) reporting mechanism, and (7) trend period.

One of the primary sources of quality measurement data is the daily transaction log, which is a computer-stored record of all transactions that have been processed by the computer each day.

CONCEPTS LEARNED

- Types of system flaws found in system fine-tuning
- Elements of postimplementation review
- What the changeover contract is
- How to build a quality measurement system
- Why ratios should be used for measurement
- How to construct a performance matrix
- What the performance indicator profile is

KEY TERMS

changeover contract
daily transaction log
major anticipated flaw
major unanticipated flaw
minor unanticipated flaw
performance indicator profile

performance matrix
postimplementation review
quality measurement system (QMS)
scope of work agreement
systems fine-tuning
systems success rate

REVIEW QUESTIONS

1. What is the difference between a major anticipated flaw and a major unanticipated flaw?
2. What is system fine-tuning?
3. What are the five elements in fine-tuning a system?
4. What are the elements of a postimplementation report?
5. List the five elements of the changeover contract.
6. List the seven steps of the Kircher model.
7. What are the elements of the problem structure?
8. Describe the six steps for constructing a QMS.
9. Draw a picture of a performance matrix.
10. What are the elements of a performance indicator profile?
11. What is the importance of the daily transaction log in a QMS?

CRITICAL THINKING OPPORTUNITIES

1. Draw a chart of the organization of this chapter.
2. Compare and contrast the Kircher model with the problem structure model.
3. Reference the QMS developed for Necco Farm Products.

a) Draw a leveled set of DFDs for a Necco Farm Products information system.
b) Was David Martin's set of performance criteria complete? What should have been the criteria?
c) Modify the performance matrix to include:

   (1) the new performance criteria
   (2) performance indicators for the expanded matrix

d) Select five performance indicators in your new matrix. Complete performance indicator profiles for these indicators.
e) Explain how a daily transaction log can be used to provide data for the new performance indicators shown in your performance matrix.

CASE 20.1

MCKRAKLIN AEROSPACE: IMPLEMENTATION PHASE

SETTING

The project team led by Susan Willebe has completed the design of the new inventory/receiving system. The new system is in the construction phase of the SDLC. A maintenance programmer has been added to Susan's team. This programmer and three other team members are programming the system's specifications. Soon they will be testing the individual programs and the entire coded system.

Susan has already scheduled training sessions for the new system. She plans to use the prototype for a portion of this training. The team built the prototype during the analysis phase of the SDLC. Dave Costner, the IS manager, used the prototype as a part of his presentation to management.

Susan's real concern is how to handle the changeover from the current system to the new system. This changeover is scheduled for sometime in November. Susan knows she should have thought more about the changeover earlier in the development process, but the subject just got lost in the complexity of the development process. Susan has two primary concerns about the changeover process. The first is whether users will cooperate in implementing the new inventory/receiving system. The second is the critical need for the system in McKraklin's day-to-day operations.

USER COOPERATION

Susan sensed there would be some user resistance to the new system. Ron Sauter, her coworker, said to her just the other day, "I'm sure getting some surly looks and icy talk whenever I visit the warehouse and receiving

areas." Susan wondered why that resistance had been building in the user community. She and Dave Costner had met earlier in the new system's life to decide how to involve users in the inventory project. They had decided on the following tactics:

- Development of a prototype during the requirements analysis stage. (They did build and use this prototype. It was abandoned for any further development after Dave's successful presentation to management.)
- Establishment of a user steering group for the inventory project. This group would include key supervisors in the receiving and warehouse sections. (The group did meet once a month and did sign off on all of Susan's recommendations.)
- Request for addition of a key receiving clerk and a key inventory clerk to the project team. (Supervisors of the receiving and inventory sections denied Dave's request because they were shorthanded and key personnel were needed for training of new clerks.)
- Publication of a monthly project status report distributed to top management, IS personnel, and the two managers of the receiving and inventory sections. (They did produce the reports.)

Susan's thoughts returned to last month's user steering committee meeting. Several observations seemed to stand out. First, three of the supervisors who had attended the first group meeting were no longer in the receiving or inventory sections. Two had transferred and one had retired. Second, two supervisors had sent clerical personnel to represent them at the meeting. Their excuse had been that the steering group meeting conflicted with other meetings.

Susan also recalled some characteristics of the user community that would influence her decision on the type of changeover. The annual clerical turnover rate is 85 percent and there is a 12 percent vacancy rate in authorized positions. Twenty percent of receiving and inventory personnel are due to retire within four years. A large percentage of the new hires at McKraklin have some educational experience in computer systems. The current system has been in place for eight years.

CRITICALITY OF THE SYSTEM

Adding to Susan's changeover concerns is the critical nature of the inventory/receiving system to day-to-day operations at McKraklin. She reviewed the following documentation on the current systems operations: processing priorities (Figure 20.1–1), changeover requirements (Figure 20.1–2), and hours of operation (Figure 20.1–3).

Susan walked to Dave's office. During the next hour they would make several initial decisions about how to implement the new system.

REVIEW QUESTIONS

1. Why did Susan add a maintenance programmer to the design team?
2. What type of training programs should Susan schedule?
3. When in the SDLC should Susan have made the changeover decision?
4. What went wrong in the plan to involve users in the development project?
5. What changeover method would you recommend? Why?

CRITICAL THINKING OPPORTUNITIES

1. Develop a calendar for the changeover process.
2. Write user procedures for implementing this changeover calendar.

FIGURE 20.1–1 **Warehouse Processing Priorities**

Stock Priority	Stock Class	Transaction Type
1	A	Receipt (Bin)
2	A	Order (Pick)
3	B	Order (Pick)
4	B	Receipt (Bin)
5	A	Adjustment (Count)
6	C	Order (Pick)
7	C	Receipt (Bin)

FIGURE 20.1–2 **Systems Changeover Requirements**

Date	Day of Week	Number of Days	Activity
11/15	Wed.	N/A	Finish New System Testing
11/15	Wed.	N/A	Finish File Conversion
?	?	7 Hours	Load New System Files
?	?	N/A	Start Operation of New System
?	?	N/A	Discontinue Old System

Stock Priority	Days and Times Open				
	Weekdays			Weekends	
	8 A.M.–5 P.M.	5 P.M.–12 A.M.	12 A.M.–8 A.M.	10 A.M.–5 P.M.	Other
A	X	X	X	X	Emergency Only
B	X	X			
C ·	X				

FIGURE 20.1–3   **Warehouse Hours of Operation**

C A S E   20.2

CLASS DESIGN PROJECT: IMPLEMENTATION PHASE

SETTING

You will be responsible for the following deliverable in this phase of your class design project.

- P8 Test plan
- P9 Training plan
- P10 Implementation plan
- P11 Operating procedures

A. P8 Test Plan

1. Introduction
   a) System test objectives
   b) Assumptions
   c) Philosophy and approach
   d) Success criteria
   e) Test criteria
   f) Test schedule
2. System test criteria
   a) Criteria description (input validation, output validation, and data integrity)
   b) Performance
   c) Human factors considerations

B. P9 Training Plan

1. Audience/type training
2. Training schedule
3. Training lesson plans

C. P10 Implementation Plan

1. Schedule
2. File conversion procedures
3. System cutover procedures
4. Postimplementation review schedule/checklists

D. P11 Operating Procedures

1. User instructions
2. Technical instructions
3. Executive overview

REFERENCES AND FURTHER READINGS

Carey, Jane. "Understanding Resistance to System Change: An Empirical Study." In *Human Factors in Management Information Systems,* edited by J. M. Carey. Norwood, N.J.: Ablex, 1988, pp. 195–206.

Dunn, Robert. *Software Defect Removal.* New York: McGraw-Hill, 1984.

Fowler, George. *Structured Programming Techniques for Solving Problems.* Boston: boyd & fraser, 1990.

Harrington, H. James. *Business Process Improvement.* New York: McGraw-Hill, 1991.

Kircher, Paul. "Fundamentals of Measurement." *Advanced Management* 4 (October 1955):5–8.

Martin, Merle. "The Human Connection in Systems Design: Prototypes for User Training." *Journal of Systems Management* 38(July 1987):19–22.

Martin, Merle. "The Day-One Implementation Tactic." *Journal of Systems Management* 40 (October 1989):12–16.

Martin, Merle, and James Trumbly. "Measuring Performance of Computer Systems." *Journal of Systems Management* 37 (February 1986):7–17.

Metzgar, Philip. *Managing a Programming Project,* 2nd ed. Englewood Cliffs, N.J.: Prentice-Hall, 1981.

Shneiderman, B. *Designing the User Interface.* Reading, Mass.: Addison-Wesley, 1987.

Sprague, R., and B. McNurlin. *Information Systems Management in Practice.* Englewood Cliffs, N.J.: Prentice-Hall, 1986.

Stahl, Bob. "The Ins and Outs of Software Testing." *Computerworld* (October 24, 1988):63.

Wilkinson, J. W. *Accounting Information Systems: Essential Concepts and Applications.* New York: Wiley, 1989.

Zmud, Robert, and J. F. Cox. "The Implementation Process: A Change Approach." *MIS Quarterly* 3(Spring 1979):35–44.

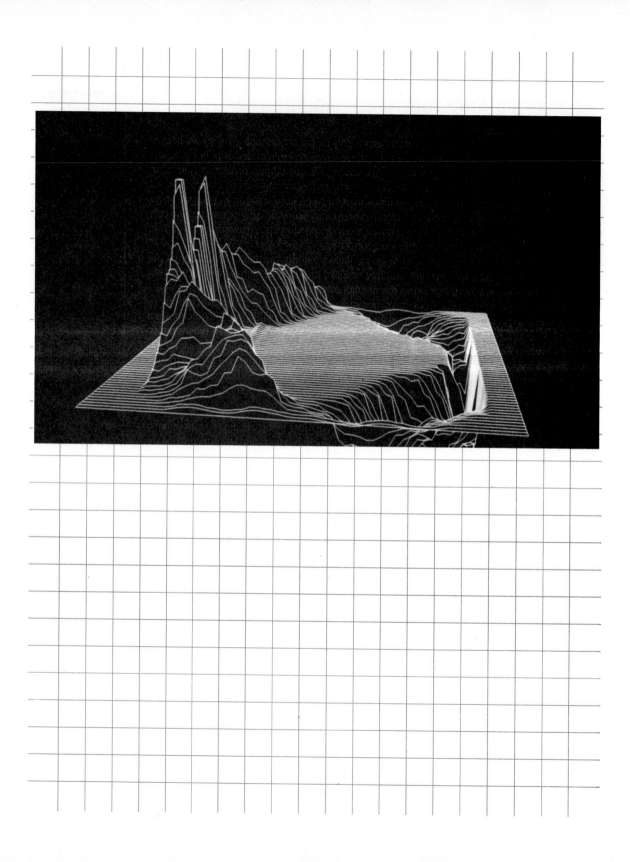

ADVANCED TOPICS

The last section of this book includes topics of two types. The first type are subjects that do not fit conveniently in the system development life cycle (SDLC) used to organize the book. Hence, prototyping and CASE can (a) fit in different parts of the SDLC, (b) not be used at all, or (c) be used throughout the SDLC. It is up to the instructor and student to place these topics in the correct perspective.

The second type is future oriented. It focuses on what may be rather than what is.

In this chapter you will learn about:

WHAT: (Concepts) Prototyping as a development approach.

WHY: Prototyping is end-user focused; it gives the customers a sense of ownership in the new information system.

WHEN: From the middle of the analysis stage through the implementation stage of the SDLC.

WHO: Systems analyst in teamwork with end-user community.

WHERE: End-user work area.

HOW: (Techniques) Prototyping tactics
                     Prototyping tools

OUTLINE

- Setting
- What Is Prototyping?
- Why Prototyping Now?
- Prototyping Environments
- Prototyping Approaches
- When to Use Prototyping
- Prototyping Methodology
- Use of Prototyping for User Training
- Transition from the Prototype to the Operational Environment
- Human Aspects

RAPID PROTOTYPING

It is better to understand a little than to misunderstand a lot.

—ANATOLE FRANCE, 1881

SETTING

Prototyping is not a new idea. Prototype aircraft were flown in wind tunnels in the 1920s. Architects have built scaled-down models of buildings for centuries. Yet the prototyping methodology is relatively new to the information systems field. It is an idea that had to wait for its proper time. That time has come.

Use of prototyping has increased dramatically over the past several years. The rise of fourth-generation languages, the microcomputer, and other sophisticated techniques have increased the use of prototyping as an approach to systems analysis and design. In fact, some software houses and information systems groups have replaced many traditional design techniques with some version of prototyping.

WHAT IS PROTOTYPING?

Definitions of prototyping vary considerably from software house to data-processing shop to individual systems analysts. Prototyping has taken on a variety of meanings and uses. The definitions focus on three major ideas. First, prototyping builds a model of the final system. A familiar use of prototyping is in the automobile industry, where prototype cars are built and tested before full-scale production. In prototyping software systems, only parts of a system are developed. Emphasis is on user interfaces such as menus, screens, reports, and source documents. The prototype, with its limited calculations and data handling, is a shell of the final system. The final system is either built from scratch using the prototype as a model or evolved from the prototype.

The second focus is emphasis on user involvement in the software development process. In the traditional systems development life cycle, analysts spend time interviewing users early in the life cycle to determine their information needs. Analysts then go off in isolation to develop the system. Users seldom are contacted again until the new system is delivered. Often, the resulting system does not satisfy users, which is not surprising, since users had little to say about most of the development process. Prototyping provides a hands-on communication tool that allows analysts to determine user needs and ensure communication throughout the development process. Prototyping is a joining tool.

The third focus is building prototypes faster than full-blown systems using the traditional SDLC. This is called "rapid prototyping" by proponents and "quick and dirty" by opponents.

Taking the various definitions into consideration, this chapter has its own definition of prototyping:

> **Prototyping** is the process of *quickly* building a *model* of the final software system; it is used as a *communication* tool to assess and meet user information needs.

WHY PROTOTYPING NOW?

Prototyping is an attempt to solve several problems that grew out of traditional software development approaches:

- For some systems, it was difficult for users to know what they needed before they had hands-on use of some version of the information system.
- Narrative descriptions of an information system (as found in the traditional functional specification) and static graphic techniques (such as system flowcharts) did not adequately communicate the reality and dynamics of an information system to users.
- The larger the development team, the more difficult the task of communication becomes. Language barriers and sheer lack of time inhibited the ability of all members of the team to have a common understanding of the system being developed.
- Systems developed in the traditional manner may have functioned correctly, but often they were difficult to learn and use.
- The traditional approach emphasized documentation, which was time-consuming and seldom decreased communication problems.
- Because of their scope and complexity, information systems required many months to complete. The traditional approach did not shorten delivery time. In fact, it may have lengthened time required because of its emphasis on documentation.
- Traditional approaches delivered systems that were not pleasing to users. Systems were also costly.
- Development backlogs existed in most large companies. A long line of projects waited project initiation. Users who requested these projects were frustrated and disillusioned.

Such problems suggested the need for some revolutionary technique. Prototyping was available to address many of these problems and provide possible solutions. However, technologies and attitudes to support prototyping did not come together until the 1980s; they included the following three developments.

Microcomputers. The microcomputer is important to prototyping because it provides an isolated, nonmainframe environment for experimentation. Thus, the prototype can be modified without interfering with the production setting of information systems. Conversely, end-users can interact with the prototype without the intimidation of the operating environment.

Fourth-Generation Languages. Production languages such as COBOL or PL/1 require too much overhead (structured) coding to achieve prototype objectives of quickness and ease of change. Newer, less procedure-oriented, more user-natural languages have surfaced and they are more conducive to prototyping. The languages are referred to as fourth-generation languages. One such language is R:BASE, which is used for the prototyping example included in Case 21.1.

End-User Computing. The microcomputer and other organizational factors led to a revolution in which information power transferred from information managers to decentralized end-users. It has become politically essential for the designer to include the end-user actively in the design process. Prototyping is an excellent means for such inclusion.

For all of these reasons, prototyping has burst onto the scene as an exciting idea for design of business information systems.

PROTOTYPING ENVIRONMENTS

Two major types of prototyping environments are common. The first is a complete capability to quickly generate business applications. It produces integrated menus, reports, and screens tied to a database. An example for the microcomputer is R:BASE.

The other environment is a prototyping tool kit, which is a collection of unlinked tools that aid rapid building of the separate pieces of a system. These tools include screen painters, data dictionaries, and report generators. Together, these tools are referred to as an **analyst's** or **programmer's workbench.**

The following list specifies workbench tools used in the prototyping process:

- Text editors
- Screen generators
- Report generators
- Relational databases
- Fourth-generation languages
- Spreadsheets

- Data dictionaries coupled to database management systems
- Ad hoc query languages (e.g., SQL)
- Security
- Statistical packages
- Backup routines
- Documentation generators
- On-line help
- Interactive testing systems

Many of these tools are available with full-function databases. They are, however, expensive when compared with traditional coding in a third-generation language such as COBOL. Also, they require training for both the development team and users.

The appropriate setting for a prototype is created by thorough training of staff and users. A systematic methodology for prototype use must also be established to ensure that the system resulting from the prototype is both usable and correct. Daniel E. Klinger, manager of laboratory systems and programming at Ortho Pharmaceutical Corporation, suggests (personal communication) five steps to ensure prototyping success:

1. Assess each application on an individual basis. Would prototyping provide gains?
2. Look at your environment and then develop and document a formal prototyping life cycle that fits that environment.
3. Acquire proper software tools and train your staff to use these tools.
4. Decide how you will manage and control the software development process.
5. Train end-users in procedures to follow during the prototyping life cycle.

The analyst faces a dilemma. The prototype should not become so structured that it is merely another inflexible sequence such as the SDLC techniques prototyping seeks to replace. On the other hand, if the environment is too loose, the prototype will seem more like a game than a serious systems development effort.

PROTOTYPING APPROACHES

There are two approaches to prototyping. The **Type I prototype** is an **iterative model** and the **Type II prototype** is a **throwaway model.** The iterative approach uses the prototype as the final system after a series of evolutionary changes based on user feedback. The throwaway approach uses the 4GL prototype as a model for the final system. The final system is coded in a third-generation language such as COBOL.

In the Type II approach, some iteration occurs; the steps of analysis, design, coding, testing, and modification may be repeated many times until all users' requirements are identified and met. Once this prototyping phase is complete, the prototype serves as a model for the final production system. Then the prototype is discarded, or used for other purposes. This throwaway approach to prototyping reverts to the traditional SDLC once the prototype has been developed. Figure 21–1 illustrates the SDLC incorporating Type II prototyping.

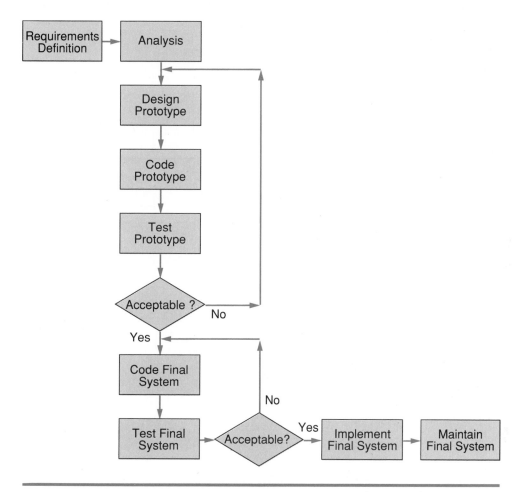

Requirements Definition → Analysis

Design Prototype

Code Prototype

Test Prototype

Acceptable ?   No

Yes

Code Final System

Test Final System   Acceptable?   No   Yes   Implement Final System   Maintain Final System

FIGURE 21–1   **Traditional Systems Development Life Cycle with Type II (Throwaway) Prototyping**

INSURECO is a large, multistate insurance company. The majority of the company's systems involve claims and new policies. The volume per day of claims is around 200,000 and new policies issued per day is about 600,000. INSURECO uses Type II prototyping for development of new systems and for development of significant enhancements to old systems. Prototyping is done in a 4GL that is integrated with a database and is separate from the production system. When users and developers are pleased with the prototype, it is used as a model for development in COBOL with a database to be run on a mainframe environment.

In the Type I approach, the life cycle consists of the following stages: training, project planning, rapid analysis, database design, prototype iteration (design, generate, and test), implementation, and maintenance. Inclusion of training and project planning is

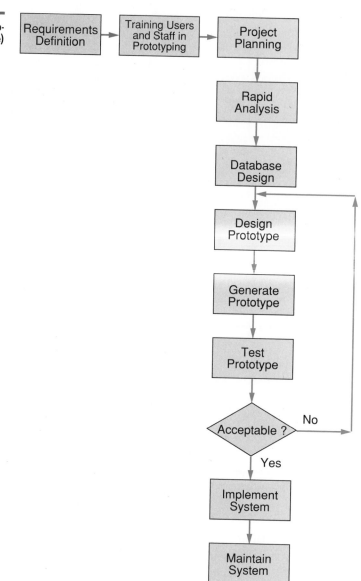

FIGURE 21–2   Systems Development Life Cycle with Type I (Iterative)
Prototyping

different from the traditional life cycle. See Figure 21–2 for an illustration of the SDLC incorporating Type I prototyping.

INVESTCO is a small financial analysis and investment firm. Most of the systems the company uses are based on external databases where searches are done on profitability and other variables that determine feasibility of investment. When new systems are developed by INVESTCO, frequently Type I prototyping is used with a 4GL package containing database capabilities. Much of the work can be done through an iterative query language. Occasionally, a formal, menu-driven system is needed. After analysis and design take place, the initial system is developed in a fourth-generation language. That system is tested and refined and remains as the production system. Because of the flexibility of 4GLs, the system can be modified quite easily; it never needs to be recoded in a third-generation language. The prototype evolves into the production system.

Regardless of the approach taken, the prototyping effort proceeds through three levels.

Level 1 (Input/Output). **Level 1 prototyping,** or **input/output prototyping,** is the generation of printed reports and on-line screens. Emphasis is on screen flow sequence and the method for sequencing screen options. A menu map (Figure 21–3) is programmed so users become familiar with basic systems inputs and outputs. The primary purpose of level 1 prototyping is to set up a means of communication between users and designers. This level of prototyping is a substitute for screen and report layouts.

Level 2 (Heuristic, or Learning). **Level 2 prototyping,** also called **heuristic proto-typing,** proceeds a step further by including important systems functions, particularly those related to updating of a database. These functions include collecting data and loading it into a database, investigating database interactions and data manipulations, and introducing the basic transactions that drive the system. This level of prototyping is similar to tutorials provided in most software packages; however, the prototype is designed before, not after, the rest of the system. The aim of level 2 prototyping is to help clarify information requirements and to increase user confidence by emphasizing rapid turnaround of systems change requests.

Edit and file update capabilities are not included—not because they are unimportant functions, but because they are too expensive and time-consuming for the objectives at this level.

Level 3 (Adaptive). **Level 3 prototyping, adaptive prototyping,** is a working model of the system. Often this level of prototyping is referred to as a system with training wheels. It can operate as an audit of the new system. The goal of this level is to provide a means for fine-tuning the final, deliverable product.

Figure 21–4 shows relationships among prototype types and levels.

WHEN TO USE PROTOTYPING

Since there are distinct advantages and disadvantages of prototyping, its use must be considered carefully.

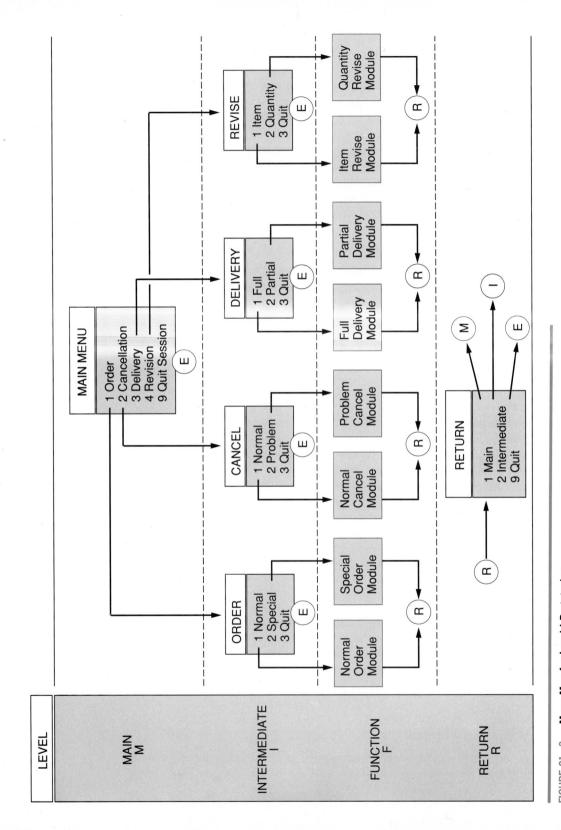

FIGURE 21–3   Menu Map for Level I Prototyping

Reprinted by permission from Merle Martin, "The Human Connection in Systems Design: Prototypes for User Training," *Journal of Systems Management* 38(July 1987):20.

Prototype Level	Prototype Type	
	I—Iterative	II—Throwaway
1—Input/Output	Sometimes (First Stage)	Often
2—Heuristic	Sometimes (Second Stage)	Rarely
3—Adaptive	Always	Never

FIGURE 21—4   **Relationships among Prototype Types and Levels**

Advantages

Proponents of prototyping cite the following attributes:

- Systems are developed faster through use of 4GLs and microcomputers isolated from the mainframe production environment.
- Systems are easier for end-users to learn and use. A rule of thumb is that 20 percent of business transaction types represent 80 percent of daily throughput volume. By restricting the prototype model to the 20 percent, the model becomes easier to develop but remains important to the end-user.
- Less programming and analysis effort are involved because fewer changes are needed when the system is implemented and fewer changes are requested by users late in the SDLC.
- Development backlogs are decreased, because SDLC time is decreased by as much as a third.
- End-user involvement is encouraged.
- System implementation is easier because users know what to expect. The system becomes their system, and they are more tolerant of minor system flaws.
- User-analyst communication is enhanced, since that communication is in the user's terms rather than the analyst's.
- User requirements are easier to determine, because users are allowed to experiment to find out what their requirements really are.
- Development costs are reduced for all these reasons.

These attributes make prototyping sound glorious and long overdue. Prototyping appears to answer every analyst's problems. Indeed, many organizations have adapted some prototyping within their development life cycle. There are, however, drawbacks to prototyping.

Disadvantages

Critics of prototyping cite the following problems:

- The ability of the systems group to develop a prototype so quickly may raise user expectations about delivery times for the real system. Users see the shell and do not understand that it is not the finished system. They may have been waiting for this system for some time and be anxious to get something in place. Being so close and yet so far frustrates them even more.

- If the prototype is a throwaway, the finally developed system may not be exactly like the prototype. What the user sees may not be what the user gets. It is up to the analyst to communicate and justify any differences between the prototype and the final system. If the user is forewarned, negative reactions are lessened. More importantly, an implemented information system should be as close to the prototype as possible to avoid user expectation problems.

- Availability of prototyping software may encourage end-users to develop their own systems when their needs are not met by the IS staff. While end-user involvement should be encouraged, *end-user development* may have negative ramifications for systems integration and database integrity.

- Large, complex systems may not be good candidates for the iterative prototyping technique. The 4GLs have a reputation for generating less than optimal code in terms of efficiency and throughput. Take care to determine whether the new system should be written with an applications generator as a prototyping tool, or coded in a third-generation language for maximum efficiency.

- Use of applications generators as prototyping tools does not guarantee that resulting systems will adhere to human factors principles. In fact, many applications generators have rather rigid screen and menu formats which inhibit use of good human factors techniques. They require additional background code to be written, defeating the purpose of applications generators.

- Prototyping applications generators are relatively easy to use and produce quick results. Analysts are tempted to go directly to prototyping before sufficient analysis is done. This results in systems that look good, with adequate user interfaces, but which are not truly functional. Thus the reputation of "quick and dirty" prototypes has come about. To avoid this pitfall, have a well-defined methodology that stipulates prototyping stages and does not short change analysis.

Effectiveness

Some form of prototyping may be used in development of large, complex systems and small, simple systems. Determination of whether to use the iterative prototyping technique or the throwaway type depends on several variables.

If the system has the following characteristics, it is a candidate for iterative prototyping: dynamic (always changing), based on decision support, based on dialogue, small versus large, poorly defined, on-line, and *about* the business rather than directly involved in transaction processing (e.g., decision support and expert systems).

On the other hand, if the system exhibits the following characteristics, it is unlikely that iterative prototyping will enhance the final system: stable, based on transaction processing, containing ad hoc retrieval and reporting, well defined, batch, making little use of user dialogues, large and complex, including extensive number crunching, and is the business (e.g., billing, record management, transaction driven, predetermined structure).

THE NEW JERSEY DIVISION OF MOTOR VEHICLES:
A PROTOTYPING FAILURE

From 1983 to 1985, the state of New Jersey's Division of Motor Vehicles contracted a nationally known consulting firm to build its primary information system. A new 4GL named Ideal from Applied Data Research, Inc. (ADR) was used to develop the system. When the system was delivered, the response times were so slow that the backlogs generated from using the system resulted in thousands of motorists driving with invalid registrations or licenses. Overtime pay to employees amounted to hundreds of thousands of dollars. In short, at delivery time, the system was declared a total disaster.

Why was Ideal chosen as the language for this development project? Time pressures dictated speedy completion of the project. The systems and communications division (SAC) of the state of New Jersey had already acquired ADR's Datacom/DB which supported Ideal as a 4GL. The consulting firm decided to use Ideal against the recommendations of several members of SAC. Robert Moybohm, SAC's deputy director, had earlier evaluated Ideal for possible use in other, smaller projects and determined:

1. Ideal would not be able to handle the development of large systems. He ran some benchmark tests against COBOL programs and Ideal ran three times slower on very simple processing.
2. Ideal did not offer index processing, a performance-related feature that had been the initial reason that SAC purchased the Datacom/DB system.
3. Ideal did not allow computer-to-computer interfacing. The large system would need to interface with fifty-nine other computers. This fact alone should have precluded the selection of Ideal.

Why did the consulting company choose Ideal? What went wrong? From the beginning, poor decisions were made regarding the systems development process. Ideal was a new product and was not well tested. The development staff had no experience using any 4GL and much time was spent learning and making mistakes. All along the development cycle, it was apparent that the system was not going to meet performance requirements. Yet, no one was able to stop the process and change to a third-generation language or determine how to combat the performance problems. It seems that one of the driving forces was the fact that the development team was locked into a fixed-cost contract and delivery date. Every month's delay of the delivery date would incur a stiff financial penalty. So a decision was made to deliver a nonperforming system within the deadline rather than a late but functional system.

After failed implementation of the new system and after the resultant flurry of irate users died down, an attempt was made to rectify the problem. It was determined that only about 58 of the 800 program modules needed to be converted to COBOL in order to meet acceptable response-time criteria. Eight of the modules were responsible for the nightly batch updates. The other fifty modules were on-line programs that were handling 85 percent of the system's transaction volume. Conversion was not a simple line-by-line process—many of the modules had to be redesigned to achieve performance requirements.

The impact of a failed system on the motorists of New Jersey could have been avoided by running the old system parallel with the new system until the problems were rectified. Instead, due primarily to costs and inadequate hardware resources, crash implementation was used as a tactic. Consequently, the failure of the new system was evident to everyone in the state of New Jersey.

Was Type I (iterative) prototyping with a 4GL the wrong choice for the New Jersey Division of Motor Vehicles? Given the volume of transactions, and the development team's inexperience, the answer must be yes. A more effective approach would have been to use the Type II (throwaway) approach using the 4GL to model the system. Then, the modeled system could have been converted to a 3GL (COBOL) operating system.

Source: David Kull, "Anatomy of a 4GL Disaster," *Computer Decisions* 18(1966):58–65.

PROTOTYPING METHODOLOGY

The key to prototyping success is to carefully determine which prototype level to use. Methodology should include thorough definition of requirements and identification of design stages before any prototyping is attempted. Next, the prototype should be defined, coded, tested, and used to refine requirements and design. Then it should be employed as a Type I or Type II prototype. During the refinement process, user comments and responses should be solicited and used to alter unsatisfactory features of the prototype. Once users and analysts are satisfied with the prototype, it can be retained and expanded to become the final system; or, it can be used as a model for the final system developed in a production language such as COBOL.

There are four phases to the development and completion of a prototype. The first phase is determination of the key aspects of the prototype system. The user interface, uncertain or vague system functions, and time and memory requirements all need prototypes.

- The user interface is the most common area that needs a prototype. Many prototyping tools are specifically aimed at rapid development of menus, screens, and reports.
- Development of a new system includes some tasks that are not understood by the systems designer. Any uncertain area is a probable candidate for prototyping. Development of a working model allows designers to make sure that proposed solutions satisfy user requirements. User involvement is not as heavy for this type of prototype as for the user interface, because the user may not fully understand the task's calculations and output. The user may, however, be able to provide both test input and output data to verify the model.
- The prototype related to time and memory requirements may more appropriately be termed a *simulation*. Many systems have huge volumes of transactions and data manipulations. Standards for interactive response times and memory use are estab-

lished and the prototype, or simulation, is exercised to ensure that the system can accomplish functional tasks within the standards range.

The second phase of development is building the prototype with the many tools available. Initially, the prototype is built rapidly using one or more of the prototyping tools described earlier.

The third phase is testing the prototype. The prototype is tested and fine-tuned based on user and performance feedback.

The fourth phase of prototype development is using the prototype as a model for the final system (Type II) or as the basis for the final system (Type I).

Adherence to a strict methodology helps the systems designer ensure the success of the prototyping approach. It also combats the "quick and dirty" reputation that sometimes results from prototyping done in a haphazard manner.

USE OF PROTOTYPING FOR USER TRAINING

Once a prototype is developed, it can be used for training end-users. This is true even when the prototype is a Type I (throwaway) model; such a prototype may be discarded for design purposes but retained for training tasks.

Systems specialists often find user training difficult. Sometimes user training conducted by systems specialists is deficient for several reasons:

- Historically, the communication between systems specialists and end-users has been faulty.
- Systems specialists sometimes are impatient to return to the front lines of analysis, design, and implementation.
- Users often cannot conceptualize the flowcharts, file layouts, and written instructions discussed by systems specialists in training sessions. (Data flow diagrams help, but they are not a panacea.)
- Training is not real enough because it occurs before the system is implemented. Can you teach someone to swim on a chalkboard?
- The system is so far into the design and implementation stages that user suggestions spurred by training cannot be incorporated.

Prototyping can provide an alternate training method that reduces the role of the systems specialist, if it is done in terms the user understands, is hands-on, and is done earlier in the SDLC. Figure 21–5 shows the sequence for using prototyping to train users:

1. A level 1 prototype is developed in the requirements analysis phase. The prototype is used as a means to elicit better identification of needs from users. It is also used as a demonstration to management of the essence of the proposed new system. Cost-benefit analyses typically include only graphs and figures; use of a working prototype adds realism to the system proposal.

The level 1 prototype often is done on a microcomputer, even if the operational system will be on a mainframe. Microcomputer models are cheaper and quicker to

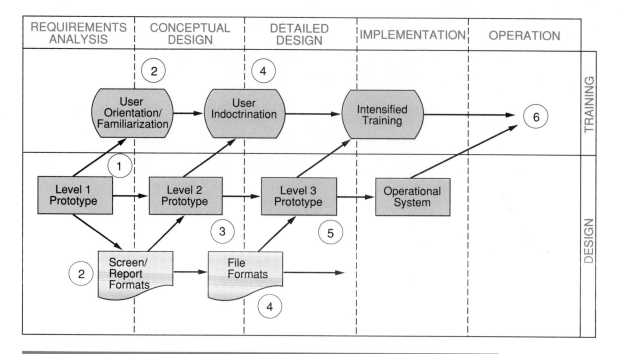

FIGURE 21−5   **Prototyping Training Sequence for Users**

Reprinted by permission from Merle Martin, "The Human Connection in Systems Design: Prototypes for User Training," *Journal of Systems Management* 38(July 1987):21.

develop using 4GL tools. In addition, microcomputer models are more portable and thus more amenable to demonstration before management. Finally, the microcomputer environment is isolated from the production tension of the mainframe operating environment.

2. Feedback from the use of the level 1 prototype enables development of screen and report formats during the conceptual design phase. These formats apply not only to the real system being designed but to the level 2 prototype as well. The level 1 prototype need not be abandoned, however; it can be used for user orientation and familiarization sessions.

3. The level 2 prototype is developed in the conceptual design phase using a skeleton DBMS environment. It may be helpful to develop this prototype in two stages. In the first stage, a microcomputer and a simple database language such as dBASE or R:BASE are used. In the second stage, user feedback from the first stage is used to develop a more costly, more permanent mainframe prototype. After systems implementation, the microcomputer prototype developed in the first stage can be used as a stand-alone model for demonstration and novice training.

Please note that with development of the level 2 prototype, user training can begin at the conceptual design phase of the SDLC. This is much earlier than training is traditionally done in systems development.

FIGURE 21–6   **Prototyping Training by User Category**

Reprinted by permission from Merle Martin, "The Human Connection in Systems Design: Prototypes for User Training," *Journal of Systems Management* 38(July 1987):22.

4. Users provide feedback from the phase 2 prototype model for the detail design phase of the SDLC. User indoctrination is intensified at this time.

5. The level 3 mainframe prototype is developed during the detailed design phase of the SDLC. Development includes the use of such prototype tools as FOCUS, MAP-PER, ISPF, and RAMIS II or other DBMS facilitators. The level 3 prototype is a workable system but without the infrequently used, frill features of the total system. The level 3 prototype still allows room for fine-tuning by users, and more importantly, it becomes the vehicle for intensive, in-depth user training.

6. Once the newly designed system is implemented, level 2 and level 3 prototypes become training models for novice users. Figure 21–6 shows the sequence for such training.

TRANSITION FROM THE PROTOTYPE TO THE OPERATIONAL ENVIRONMENT

An often ignored truth is that you cannot be cost efficient and quick in *both* the design and operation of a business system. A quick and cheap design will lead to a working system that often needs and is difficult to repair. A system designed to optimize operational efficiency requires a sacrifice of design speed and cost.

However, the very concept of prototyping is based upon its low cost and rapid development. The prototype then can lead to an ineffective working environment. This will be the case unless the systems designer's emphasis is switched from design to operational optimization somewhere in the prototyping life cycle. This is not a simple process because several differences are apparent between prototypes and operational systems.

Language. Ideally, the operational language is a self-documenting one such as COBOL. The prototype language is a macroprocedural language such as FOCUS or R:BASE. The macro language has functions not available in the operational language (e.g., date handling and automatic indexing). The macro language may not have the self-documenting functions required of an operational language (e.g., extended variable names).

Range of Transactions. A rule of thumb already mentioned is that 20 percent of all TPS transaction codes represent 80 percent of transaction volume. The 20 percent is the domain of the prototype; the prototype shows users what typically will happen, rather than what always will happen. An operational system, on the other hand, must cover all contingencies. The 20 percent prototype of transactions must be expanded fully to meet operational requirements.

Documentation Requirements. At times, both the prototype and the operational system need to be changed. Prototype changes occur in a relatively short time span, and changes typically are made by the original prototype designer. Therefore, documentation is not so important for the prototype, and too often it is neglected. An effective operational system, on the other hand, cannot tolerate shoddy documentation, since changes often are made at a later time by a different person.

Computer Architecture. A prototype model typically is designed for a microcomputer because the microcomputer is portable and the microcomputer prototype is isolated from, and thus less disruptive to, the operational environment. While a decision support or expert system model may reside on a microcomputer, most transaction-processing system prototypes will have to be transformed from a microcomputer to a mainframe environment.

Access Control. Isolation of the microcomputer prototype, coupled with its frequent use of simulated rather than real data, makes use of access control (for example, passwords) unimportant. Access control must be added in the transition to the operational model, because it is necessary in fully operational systems.

Procedures. The operational system is not merely a collection of hardware and software. Procedures tie together all systems components, including human operators. Development of such procedures is exhausting and time-consuming. Procedures rarely are developed for prototypes, but they *must* be developed before the operational system is implemented.

Transition from prototypes to the operational system is not a trivial process. There are, however, tactics that minimize transition efforts.

Structured Programming. Structured programming in a 4GL is not as easy as it is in COBOL; however, it can be done and it allows easier understanding of the algorithms of the macroprocedural language. Structured programming also eases conversion between prototype and operational languages.

Data Dictionary. The data dictionary should be initiated at the beginning of the prototyping effort. As prototype file structures are developed, dictionary entries should be required with *both* prototype and operational language specifications. For example, we can place a dBASE data element name of 'CUSTNO' in the 'ALIASES' portion of a data element specification while we place the COBOL name of 'CUSTOMER-NUMBER' in the 'DATA-NAME' portion. Such dual data dictionary design saves conversion time. In addition, and more importantly, it fosters an atmosphere of keeping the future operational system in mind.

Minimum "Gimmicks." Prototype languages often have convenient features (e.g., graphics, date functions, and automatic editing) that are not readily available in operational languages. Such special functions often falsely feed user expectations at the beginning. Prominent among these false expectations is overuse of color, which often cannot be delivered in a mainframe environment.

Minimum Documentation. Require at least program hierarchy charts, menu maps, and macro program flowcharts for the prototype.

These design tactics may slow prototype development and add to its costs. At the same time, the tactics ease the transition between the prototype and operational system. They also create an atmosphere of awareness that prototype and operational system are totally different entities.

HUMAN ASPECTS

Prototyping is about human beings. The most important reason for developing prototypes is to communicate with human users on their terms, rather than in technical terms. You cannot build a prototype without active participation of end-users. If you try to do so, the resulting product may be called a prototype, but it is not. It is merely an expensive model of the system analysts' thinking process. When you think prototyping, think people. When you build prototypes, include end-users.

SUMMARY

Prototyping is the process of *quickly* building a *model* of the final software system. It is used primarily as a *communication* tool to access and meet the information needs of the user.

Prototyping surfaced with fourth-generation languages, which allow application or code generation. Prototyping has been successful because it attempts to solve the problems involved in the traditional development of software systems using third-generation languages.

Two types of prototyping environment are common: complete applications generator environments, and tool kit, or workbench, environments.

The two types of prototyping are iterative (Type I) and throwaway (Type II). With the iterative approach, the prototype is changed and modified according to user requirements until it evolves into the final system. In the throwaway approach, the prototype serves as a model for the final system, which is coded eventually in a third-generation, or procedural, language. Both types of prototyping are designed through three succeeding stages: level 1—input/output, level 2—heuristic, and level 3—adaptive.

Advantages of prototyping include faster development time, easier end-user learning and use, less human power needed to develop systems, decreased backlogs, and enhanced user-analyst communication. Disadvantages of prototyping include fostering of undue expectations on the part of users, providing users with something initially that may not be what they get finally, and encouraging end-user computing through availability of applications generator software. Not all systems are candidates for prototyping. The designer should determine whether the system in question exhibits characteristics that make prototyping viable.

Prototypes enhance user training. They provide a hands-on environment expressed in the user's natural terms. In addition, prototypes allow training to occur earlier in the SDLC; this provides opportunities to change designs based on user feedback.

The transition from prototyping to the operational environment is extensive. This is because the prototype and the operational system differ in dimensions such as programming language used, range of transactions included, documentation requirements, computer architecture, access control, and presence of procedures. Several design tactics can ease the transition between prototypes and operational systems.

Prototyping is a powerful approach to development of business information systems. Systems built using prototypes can be highly successful if designers adhere to a strict methodology, perform a thorough analysis and requirements definition, and keep in mind the efforts required to change the prototype into an operational information system.

CONCEPTS LEARNED

- Meaning of prototyping
- Why prototyping has suddenly become a viable systems design tool
- Prototyping environments
- Types of prototyping models
- Levels of prototyping development
- Advantages and disadvantages of prototyping
- When prototyping is effective
- Prototyping methodology
- Use of prototyping for systems training
- Problems in the transition from prototypes to operational systems
- Tactics for easing the transition from prototypes to operational systems

KEY TERMS

analyst's workbench
adaptive prototyping
heuristic prototyping
input/output prototyping
iterative model
level 1 prototyping
level 2 prototyping

level 3 prototyping
programmer's workbench
prototyping
throwaway model
Type I prototype
Type II prototype

REVIEW QUESTIONS

1. Using the definitions cited in the chapter, develop a consensus definition of prototyping of your own.
2. Why is prototyping such a popular means of systems development today?
3. What are some of the advantages of prototyping?
4. What are some of the disadvantages of prototyping?
5. What two types of environments support prototyping?
6. What are the two basic types of prototyping approaches?
7. Explain the main differences between the three levels of prototyping development.
8. What characteristics should a system exhibit to make it suitable for the prototyping approach?
9. When should prototyping be avoided?
10. Draw a diagram that illustrates the SDLC with Type I prototyping.
11. Draw a diagram that illustrates the SDLC with Type II prototyping.
12. How can level 2 prototyping be used for user training?
13. Suggest ways to make the transition from the prototype to the operational computer setting easier.

CRITICAL THINKING OPPORTUNITIES

1. Draw a diagram of the organization of this chapter.
2. Compare and contrast the traditional SDLC that you learned about earlier in this book with the prototyping approach found in this chapter.

Refer to Mega Video example in Case 6.1.

3. Develop input screens and output reports for a level 1 prototype.
4. Convert the specifications to a working level 1 prototype using an applications development package such as R:BASE 5000 or dBASE III PLUS.

C A S E   21.1

USING R:BASE 5000 AS A PROTOTYPING TOOL[*]

SETTING

R:BASE 5000 (Microrim, Inc., Redmond, Washington) is a database management package. It allows users to create a relational database and manage the design, creation, deletion, editing, and altering of data for applications. Microrim has released several upgraded versions of R:BASE, including System V and R:BASE for DOS. This version increases the power of R:BASE as a prototyping tool. However, the specific system used here to illustrate prototyping was developed with R:BASE 5000. The portion of R:BASE 5000 that makes it useful as a prototyping tool is called Application Express. Application Express includes the following options:

- Define a new database.
- Change an existing database definition.
- Define a new application.
- Change an existing application.
- Display file directory.
- Exit.

All of these tasks also may be performed from the R:BASE command level (R>prompt); however, using the command level requires the user to write R:BASE code. In contrast, Application Express is a code generator. The user specifies certain aspects about the database, menus, screens, and reports desired. Application Express then generates the code automatically.

The advantages of using Application Express include:

- Reduction of development time.
- Convenience of not having to learn a new language to develop an application.

*The author acknowledges the work done by Mark D. Rines in the preparation of this R:BASE sample system.

- Ease of change for databases.
- Use of existing macro command files for new applications.

Some limitations of Application Express include:

- A maximum of only 40 columns can be defined for a database.
- Only three of these columns (or fields) may be sorted.
- Reports are limited to a width of 80 characters.
- Entry forms are limited to 20 columns.

The basic format of all Application Express development screens is the same. There are three functional areas. The top portion of the screen displays a menu or single prompt that informs the analyst/programmer of the options available. The middle area of the screen is the work area. Here, Application Express prompts the analyst or programmer to fill in blanks, choose a menu option, or respond to a question. The bottom of the screen is a status area displaying the database, table, and column in use. In addition to these three functional areas, Application Express has other features that make it easy to use: on-line help (F10), and display of all defined tables and columns in the open database (F3).

A list of some of the tasks that can be performed with Application Express follows:

- Naming a database
- Defining a new table
- Defining a new column
- Redefining a column data type
- Adding a column to a table
- Renaming a column
- Renaming a table
- Removing a column from a table
- Removing a table

- Defining screens
- Defining command modules
- Defining report modules
- Defining menu modules
- Defining optional files
- Linking custom files built using RBEDIT and called as subroutines

All of these options are easy to use because R:BASE Application Express walks the analyst, programmer, or user through the tasks. You do not have to memorize command statements or learn how to put them together to build the application desired.

PROTOTYPING EXAMPLE

The system used here to illustrate the use of R:BASE 5000 as a prototyping tool is a membership management system for a university honor society. The purpose of the system is to manage the application, induction, and processes of membership. The number of members in the organization grew from 10 in 1971 to more than 600 in 1987. This growth resulted in the obsolescence of the manual system, which was time-consuming and often inaccurate. A new system was developed to automate many functions such as keeping track of member addresses, generating mailing lists and reports, and keeping track of dues.

The first step was to determine user needs and the scope of the system. The second step was to analyze data flows. The third step was to design a menu hierarchy and a database. Once these steps were completed and users verified them as acceptable, the next step was to use Application Express to build the application. Then the system had to be tested thoroughly. The final step was to implement the system and maintain it through feedback from users. Figure 21.1–1 shows the flow of data through the proposed system.

Figure 21.1–1 is a context-level data flow diagram. Drawing the context-level DFD and subsequent explosions allows the analyst to conceptualize the full system and the environment in which the system must operate. Many of the components of the existing system will remain manual. The analyst must determine which processes are viable candidates for automation. The analyst bases the determination on both logical rationale and expressed user needs and desires. Often, there is a period of negotiation before this determination is made.

Once processes have been selected, a hierarchy chart is drawn to illustrate components and their relationships. Figure 21.1–2 shows the hierarchy chart of the proposed system. Note that it includes three levels of menus. This may not be the best way to segment the system, but R:BASE 5000 Application Express has a limit of a three-menu depth. There are three main tasks in this system: the application process, the induction process, and ongoing member management. This hierarchy chart can be easily translated into menus and options using Application Express.

The first step in using Application Express is to define the database. Do this by entering table names and their respective fields (Figure 21.1–3). After completing this step, you can generate menus, screens, and reports.

Figure 21.1–4 (a-c) illustrates three of the ten menus that drive the system. Application Express generated these menus. The level of each menu is included in the title and its options are listed. Note there is no message area to explain to the user what action to take. This drawback to system use can be overcome partially by addition of help screens. Nevertheless, human factors guidelines suggest that every screen should indicate to the user how to escape, where the user will end up after escaping, and how to choose the desired action. R:BASE 5000 Application Express does not allow these messages on the menu screen.

All menus generated by Application Express behave in the same manner. Selection occurs by using up or down arrows or pressing the appropriate numeric key to highlight the desired option. The enter key is then pressed to register user choice. Escape is selected by either choosing the exit option in the menu or by pressing the escape key.

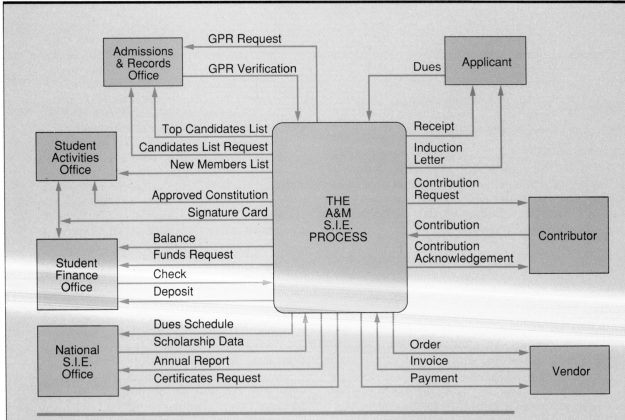

FIGURE 21.1−1   Data Flow Diagram of Proposed System

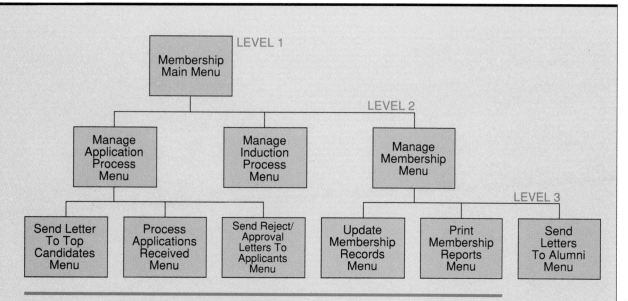

FIGURE 21.1–2 **Hierarchy Chart of Proposed System**

FIGURE 21.1–3 **Tables in the Database**

NAME	COLUMNS	ROWS
1. GRLUDESC	2	6
2. FORMS	2	130
3. ADDRESS	8	697
4. STATUS	3	404
5. DUES	4	15
6. STATDESC	2	15
7. REPORTS	2	533
8. NAMES	4	658
9. APPLICTN	10	45
10. RULES	8	0

FIGURE 21.1—4a **Level 1 Menu of Proposed System**

```
┌─────────────────────────────────────────────────────────┐
│                                                         │
│  ─────── SIE -- MEMBERSHIP MAIN MENU -- LVL 1 ───────    │
│                                                         │
│                                                         │
│             (1)  Manage Application Process             │
│                                                         │
│             (2)  Manage Induction Process               │
│                                                         │
│             (3)  Manage Membership                      │
│                                                         │
│             (4)  EXIT FROM THE SYSTEM                    │
│                                                         │
│                                                         │
│  ─────────────────────────────────────────────────     │
│                                                         │
└─────────────────────────────────────────────────────────┘
```

FIGURE 21.1—4b **Level 2 Menu of Proposed System**

```
┌─────────────────────────────────────────────────────────┐
│                                                         │
│ ──SIE --- MANAGE APPLICATION PROCESS --- LVL 2──         │
│                                                         │
│                                                         │
│ (1) Send Letter to Top Candidates  (3.0+ GPR MGMT Majors)│
│                                                         │
│ (2) Process Applications Received                       │
│                                                         │
│ (3) Send Reject or Approval Letters to Applicants       │
│                                                         │
│ (4) EXIT                                                │
│                                                         │
│  ─────────────────────────────────────────────────     │
│                                                         │
└─────────────────────────────────────────────────────────┘
```

FIGURE 21.1-4c **Level 3 Menu of Proposed System**

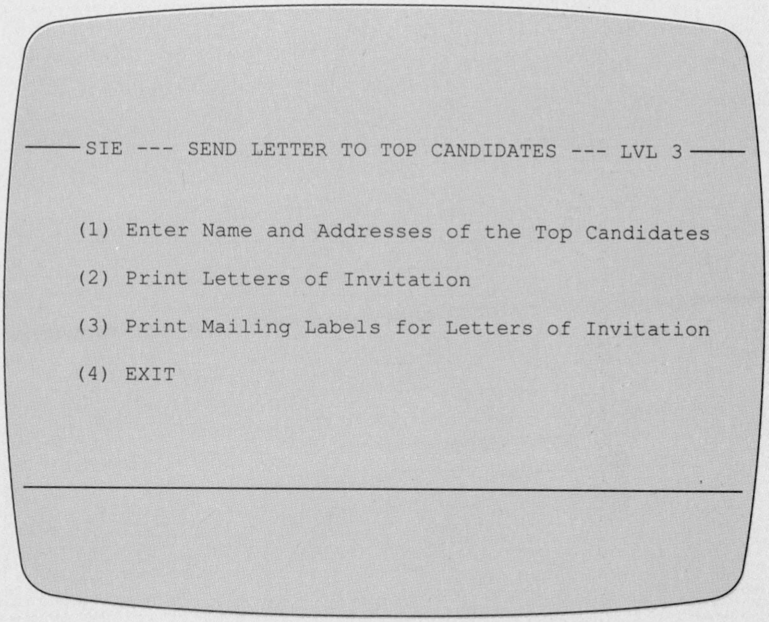

```
 ──── SIE ─── SEND LETTER TO TOP CANDIDATES ─── LVL 3 ────

     (1) Enter Name and Addresses of the Top Candidates

     (2) Print Letters of Invitation

     (3) Print Mailing Labels for Letters of Invitation

     (4) EXIT
```

When a user selects choice 1 in the "Send Letter to Top Candidates" menu (Figure 21.1–4 b), Figure 21.1–5 appears—the data entry screen for candidate names and addresses. This is how the user adds data values to the corresponding tables and fields. The user could also go through the R:BASE 5000 command language to add data values; however, using the data entry screen is easier. Figure 21.1–5 was created with Application Express.

Arrangement of fields can be altered easily. The boxes into which the user enters the data values are automatically defined by their field lengths. The message area at the bottom of the screen also is created automatically by Application Express. In general, screens created by Application Express are easy to use and understand and quick to create. Another advantage is that additional rules or conditions can be imposed on the various fields to ensure data validity.

Figure 21.1–6 consists of sample reports created using Application Express. These reports can be printed on the screen or the printer.

Report headings and repeating fields are defined and totals calculated (although no totals are contained in either of the reports shown here). One major drawback of R:BASE 5000 Application Express is that data for a single report can be pulled from only one table. (System V corrects this limitation.) Many reports need to draw data from multiple tables. To do this in R:BASE 5000 Application Express, custom code must be created and tied into the system by call insertions in the generated code.

This proposed system could be classified as a combination of iterative (Type I) and throwaway (Type II) prototyping. The initial system was generated by using Application Express. Changes based on user feedback were made to the system using Application Express where possible. Some portions that needed change could not be handled with Application Express; they were coded in R:BASE command language (a third-generation procedural language) and they replaced the generated code. About one-fourth of the final system was custom coded; the rest was generated by Application Express.

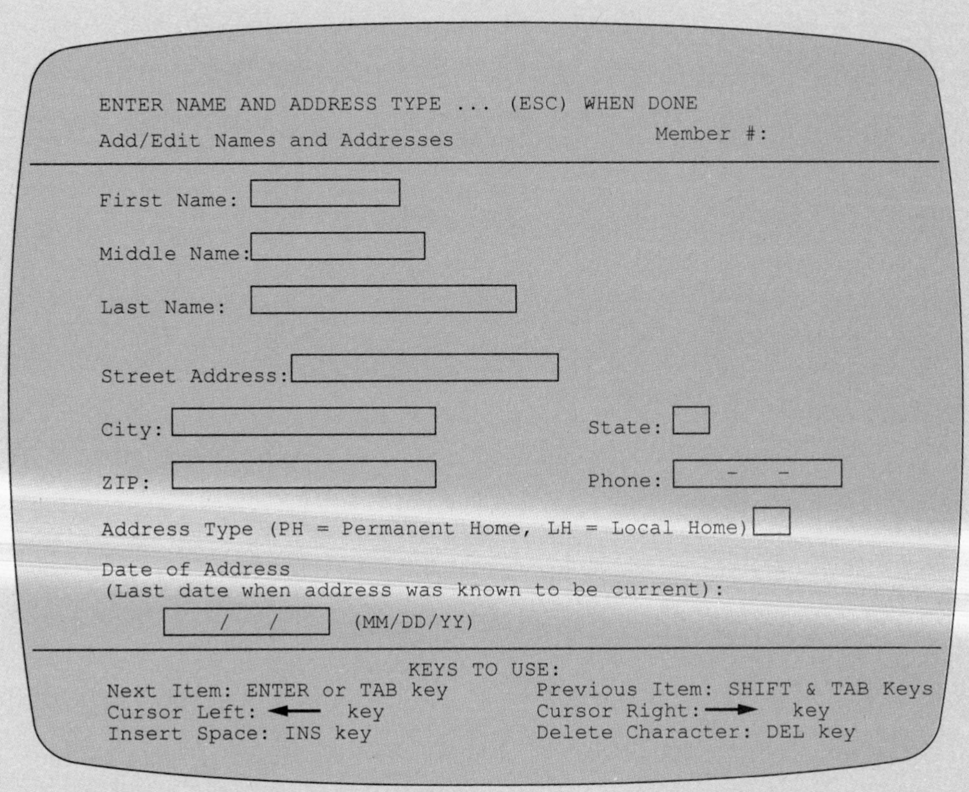

```
ENTER NAME AND ADDRESS TYPE ... (ESC) WHEN DONE
Add/Edit Names and Addresses                  Member #:
_____

First Name:  [          ]

Middle Name:[            ]

Last Name:   [                ]


Street Address:[                  ]

City: [                ]           State: [   ]

ZIP:  [              ]            Phone: [   -    -    ]

Address Type (PH = Permanent Home, LH = Local Home) [   ]

Date of Address
(Last date when address was known to be current):
        [    /    /    ]  (MM/DD/YY)
_____
                      KEYS TO USE:
Next Item: ENTER or TAB key       Previous Item: SHIFT & TAB Keys
Cursor Left: ◀━━  key             Cursor Right: ━━▶  key
Insert Space: INS key             Delete Character: DEL key
```

FIGURE 21.1–5   **Screen for Proposed System**

FIGURE 21.1–6   **Sample Report for Proposed System**

SIGMA IOTA PHONE LIST

LIST DATE: 05/10/88

KELLY DAWN SWAZE	409-696-1122
DARLA KAY SMITH	409-764-3344
ANTHONY JAMES ANDERSON	409-693-1123
ETC.	

SUMMARY

R:BASE 5000 Application Express is useful as a prototyping tool. It has many of the advantages and disadvantages of typical prototyping tools. The speed of generated code is machine dependent, but it can be slow when compared to custom coding. The most important advantage is that users get hands-on experience with the proposed system early in the development process and provide valuable feedback to be sure the final system meets their needs.

CASE 21.2

MCKRAKLIN AEROSPACE: PROTOTYPING

SETTING

Susan Willebe, senior analyst and a member of the development team, wishes to develop a prototype of an interactive inventory/receiving system. Figure 21.2–1 shows the data flow diagram on which the prototype will be based. Susan must decide both the nature and specifications of the prototype.

NATURE OF THE PROTOTYPE

Susan decided upon the following characteristics for the prototype:

1. It will be developed on a microcomputer so there will be no interference with the operating mainframe computer environment.
2. It will be a level 1 (input/output) prototype.

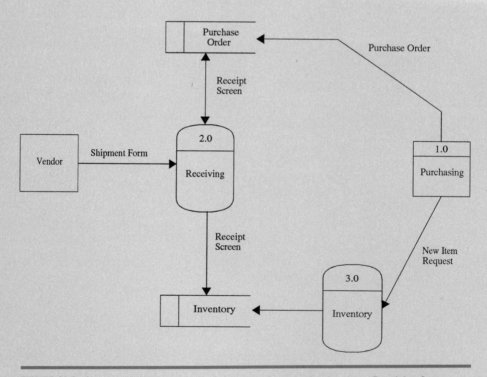

FIGURE 21.2–1   **Data Flow Diagram for Prototype of Interactive Inventory Receiving System**

3. The prototype will be used *only* to (1) refine user requirements, (2) enhance presentation of the system study before top management, and (3) conduct user training on the new inventory system.

PROTOTYPE SPECIFICATIONS

Susan chose the following design tools as specifications for the prototype:

- Menu map (Figure 21.2–2)
- Data dictionary entry for receiving form-filling screen (Figure 21.2–3)
- Data dictionary entry for inventory form-filling screen (Figure 21.2–4)

Susan then asked Dave Costner (the manager of the Informations Systems Department) to assign a programmer to design and code the inventory/receiving prototype model. (You are that programmer.)

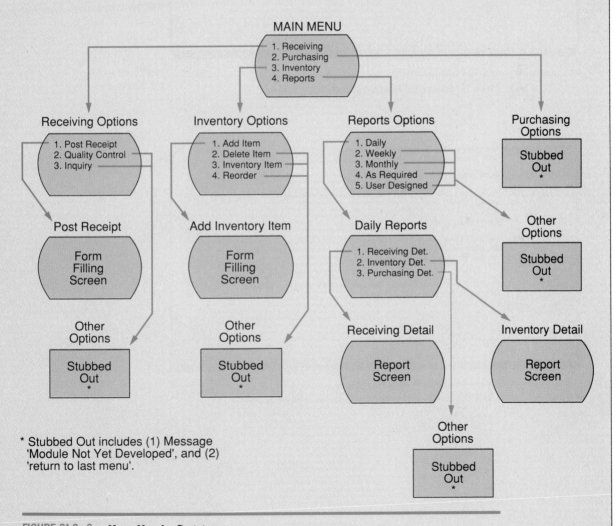

* Stubbed Out includes (1) Message 'Module Not Yet Developed', and (2) 'return to last menu'.

FIGURE 21.2–2   **Menu Map for Prototype**

```
                                                    ==== PROJECT:  MAIN ==
   LABEL:        Post Receipt Screen

   ENTRY TYPE:   DATA STRUCTURE

   DESCRIPTION:  Form-Filling Interactive Screen  used to Post Material
                 Receipts

   ALIAS:        Receiving Screen

   COMPOSITION:  Date + Purch-Ord-No + Vendor-Code + 1{items-recvd}10
                    = Stock-Number + Stock-Type + Post Receipt Screen +
                    .Quantity-Damaged + Inspector


   NOTES:        As many fields as possible from purchase order file upon
                 input of Purch-Ord-No.




                       Press <Esc> key for option line
  F2=SET SEARCH   F3=EXPAND    F4=FILE             SEARCH:      /     / DS
```

FIGURE 21.2-3   **Data Dictionary for Receiving Form-filling Screen**

```
                                                    ==== PROJECT:  MAIN ==
   LABEL:        Add Inventory Item Screen

   ENTRY TYPE:   DATA STRUCTURE

   DESCRIPTION:  Form Filling Interactive Screen for Adding New Inventory
                 Item

   ALIAS:        Inventory Screen

   COMPOSITION:  Date-Establish + Stock-Number + Stock-Type + Vendor-Code +
                 Reorder-Point + Reorder-Quantity + Warehouse-Location +
                 Security-Code + Unit-Price


   NOTES:        Fields of Current-Year-Demand and Last-Year-Demand
                 set to 0 by program center




                       Press <Esc> key for option line
  F2=SET SEARCH   F3=EXPAND    F4=FILE             SEARCH:      /     / DS
```

FIGURE 21.2-4   **Data Dictionary Entry for Inventory Form-filling Screen**

1. Is Susan Willebe's prototype a throwaway or an iterative model? Justify your answer.
2. Why has Susan chosen to abandon (for development purposes) the prototype after the management presentation?
3. Why did Susan need a programmer to develop the prototype?

1. Construct screen layouts for the prototype.
2. Convert these layouts to a computer format using a package such as R:BASE 5000, dBASE applications generator, or Visible Prototyper.

C A S E   21.3

GOODBYTE PIZZA COMPANY: PROTOTYPE

SETTING

Linda Alvires wished to develop a prototype for the Goodbyte order process using an application generator such as found in dBASE IV. Figure 21.3–1 shows the data flow diagram on which the prototype will be based. Linda must decide both the nature and specification of the prototype.

NATURE OF THE PROTOTYPE

Linda and her student design team decided upon the following prototype characteristics:

1. It will be developed on a microcomputer.
2. It will be a Level I (input/output) prototype.
3. The prototype will be continually expanded until it becomes the operational system.

PROTOTYPE SPECIFICATIONS

Linda and her team chose the following design tools as specifications for the prototype:

1. Menu Map (Figure 21.3–2).

2. Data dictionary entry for store order screen (Figure 21.3–3).
3. Data dictionary entry for cashier screen (Figure 21.3–4).

Linda was concerned about the programming skills required to complete the prototype. She and the rest of her team members had taken one or more COBOL courses and one of her team colleagues had taken a PASCAL course. Linda was not sure what should be the proper programming language for the prototype.

DISCUSSION QUESTIONS AND EXERCISES

1. Is Linda Alvires' prototype a throwaway or iterative model? Justify your answer.
2. Has Linda made the correct choice between throwaway and iterative models? Why?
3. What prototype language would you suggest that Linda and her team use? Why?
4. Construct screen layouts for the prototype.
5. Convert the prototype specifications to a computer format using an applications generator or Visible Prototyper.

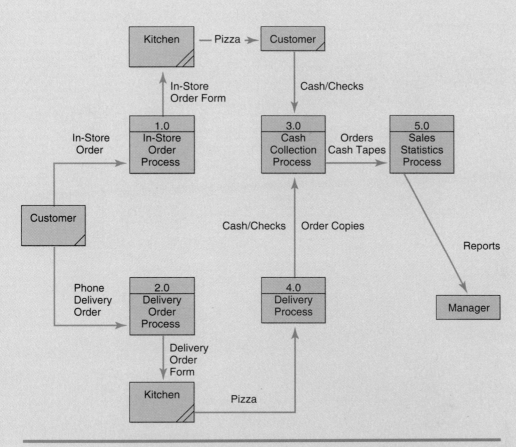

FIGURE 21.3—1   **Data Flow Diagram of Goodbyte Pizza Company Order Process**

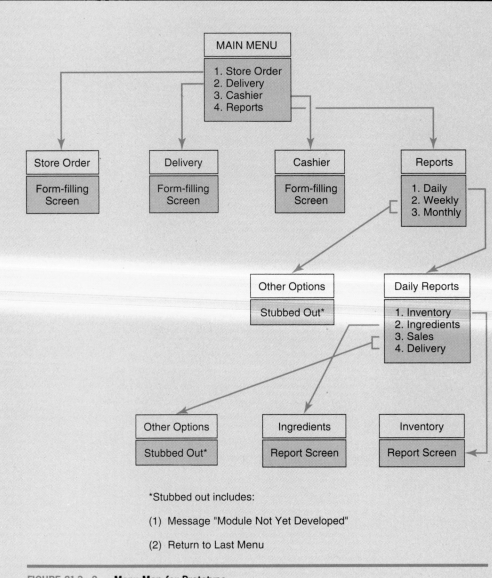

*Stubbed out includes:

(1) Message "Module Not Yet Developed"

(2) Return to Last Menu

FIGURE 21.3–2   **Menu Map for Prototype**

```
Label:          Store Order Screen

Entry Type:     Data Structure

Description:    Form-filling Interactive Screen Used to Post In-store
                Customer Orders

Alias:

Composition:    Order-Number + Date + Time +
                Customer-First-Name +
                1 (Order-Item) 5
                  = Quantity +
                      Description
```

FIGURE 21.3—3   **Store Order Screen**

```
Label:          Cashier Screen

Entry Type:     Data Structure

Description:    Form-filling Interactive Screen Used to Post Cashier
                Entries

Alias:

Composition:    Order-Number + Time +
                Customer-First-Name +
                1 (Order-Item) 5=
                    Quantity + Description + Price
                + Total-Price + Delivery-Feet
                    Total-Due + Paid (Cash) (Check)
```

FIGURE 21.3—4   **Cashier Screen**

CHAPTER 22

CASE AND OTHER AUTOMATED AIDS

If you're trying to eat an elephant, take one bite at a time.

— INSTANT ANALYST, 1974

SETTING

Systems analysts have a large toolbox containing many tools and techniques. There are two noteworthy aspects to this large collection. First, no agreed upon structure ties these techniques together. Several structured development approaches have been described in this book, and merit can be found in all these approaches. The particular approach chosen is not really important, as long as it is consistently and correctly used by everyone in the firm and deliverable products separate the SDLC stages.

The second noteworthy aspect is that, until recently, this volume of charts, notes, layouts, and dictionaries was produced by hand. We computer masters were still using quill pens. This created several problems:

- Systems analysts produced documentation on *paper* using *pencil* while fifth graders were using PCs to draw pictures and maps.
- Diagrams were *not integrated.* Consider the hierarchy and program flowcharts described throughout this textbook. Often these charts were produced manually and separately by different design team members. Integration of the charts was difficult.
- Different analysts produced the same types of products in a different, *nonstandard* manner.
- Using paper and pencil to produce system documentation required considerable analyst effort. Therefore, analysts often generated this documentation *after designing*

the system. Development tools can aid in the design process; they should be generated before, not after, systems design.

■ Because of these factors, systems documentation too often was disorganized. Hence, the documentation was *difficult to use for fixing the system at a later date.*

A new generation of automated development tools now exists to ease these problems. These tools provide automated help to analysts in deriving development aids, gathering reams of text, and integrating both into a tight, structured systems project. These automated aids have six goals:

1. Increase analyst productivity. Analyst productivity is difficult to measure because it is qualitative as well as quantitative. Some measures include completing specific milestones, meeting deadlines, meeting cost constraints, preparing documentation, meeting project management guidelines, and eliciting user acceptance of outputs.

2. Increase quality of systems product deliverables. Deliverables include current system data flow diagrams, entity-relationship diagrams, data dictionaries, definition of human-machine boundaries, detailed logic definitions, code, test plans, and implementation plans.

3. Ensure cohesion among the many tools and procedures. All data types must be consistent across modules. Modules must work together without being tightly coupled to each other. Changes should be easy to make so that a change in one module does not require a change in another module. Any data changes should ripple throughout the system and be self-correcting, whereas logic changes should be confined to a single module.

4. Standardize the efforts of several systems team members. The automated aid provides an on-line repository for the storage of all team work, including data definitions and a map of how the system fits together.

5. Enhance systems development team communication. An automated aid provides an up-to-date snapshot of the entire project. Completed work is stored on-line so that all team members have access to the work of others. A hands-on working model of the system allows all team members (users and IS professionals alike) an opportunity to see the system as it is developed.

6. Develop a systems documentation project that allows easier maintenance of that system. Documentation should be as easy to generate as possible; in some cases, the documentation can be self-generating. In other cases, particularly graphic-oriented documentation, generation and changing of graphic tools such as data flow diagrams should be simple and easy to execute and draw.

Automated development products carry a variety of names. Among these are CASE, applications generators, code generators, and prototype generators.

COMPUTER-AIDED SYSTEMS ENGINEERING (CASE)

Systems people have transformed the acronym CASE. It began as an abbreviation for *computer-aided software engineering,* a computer science term restricted to development of computer programs. Programs, however, are only a portion of total business information systems.

The systems field borrowed the concept, applied it to total systems design, and renamed the acronym *computer-aided systems engineering.* Now some have suggested changing the acronym to CASD—*computer-aided systems development.* As the immortal bard explained, "A rose by any other name would smell as sweet."

Computer-aided systems engineering (CASE) is the collection and integration of automated tools and procedures to help the systems development process. A discussion of the generic composition of CASE tools will be followed by an analysis of a specific product—the Visible Analyst WORKBENCH.

Five types of modules are partially or completely found in CASE products (Figure 22–1).

Repository (Data Dictionary)

The repository is the axis that ties together all other systems modules; it provides product integration. Two content types are included:

1. Systems specifications, including data flow diagrams, entity-relationship diagrams, hierarchy charts, and database schema (file layouts)
2. Text definitions, including screen and dialogue sessions, report and form images, and process descriptions

The data dictionary included in CASE products differs in scope from that found in a typical database management system. In the DBMS, the dictionary contains only stored variable descriptions, including record layouts and the data element dictionary. A CASE data dictionary includes these items: however, it also includes graphic items such as diagrams (for example, DFDs).

Repository					
Life Cycle Support					Reengineering
Strategic Planning	Analysis	Logical Design	Physical Design	Construction	
Project Support					
Continuous Quality Improvement (CQI)					
Life of System					

FIGURE 22–1   **Typical CASE Components**

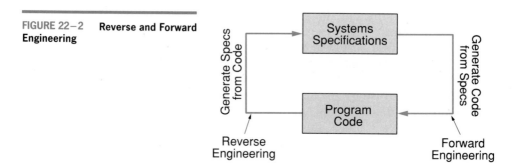

FIGURE 22–2   Reverse and Forward Engineering

Reengineering

Reengineering is concerned with maintenance of the new information system after it is operational. This concept has been borrowed (and not changed) from the software engineering discipline. There are two stages to reengineering: reverse engineering and forward engineering. **Reverse engineering** is modification of systems specifications from program code. Several commercial products analyze program code and develop graphic specifications such as hierarchy charts and program flow charts. **Forward engineering** is development of program code from design specifications. This development is done with code generators. Tools used for forward engineering include structured English and decision tables.

Figure 22–2 shows the relationship between reverse and forward engineering. Faulty code is discovered in the program code module. Reverse engineering traces the path to the specifications generating the code. Specifications are changed. Then forward engineering translates the new specifications into modified code. Reengineering refers to CASE products that have both reverse and forward engineering capabilities.

Life Cycle Support

CASE products have a special life cycle that includes the stages of strategic planning, analysis, logical design, physical design, and construction. Figure 22–3 compares the CASE life cycle to the SDLC used in the organization of this book.

Strategic planning analyzes systems requirements at a high level and prioritizes development activities. Some tools used are entity-relationship diagrams, data flow diagrams, and business strategic planning. The context-level (level-0) DFDs are particularly pertinent.

Analysis identifies specific application system objectives and collects information pertinent to both current and proposed systems. Three types of CASE tools support this stage of the life cycle. The first type includes graphic tools for structured analysis— entity-relationship diagrams, DFDs, and data dictionary structures. The second type of support is word-processor capabilities for collection and creation of text material such as interview notes, problem lists, proposals, and specifications (for example, screens or processes). The third type of support includes miscellaneous tools such as cost-benefit (feasibility) analysis, project planning, and presentation generators.

Textbook Life Cycle	CASE Life Cycle
No Counterpart	1. Strategic Planning
1. Problem Detection	No Counterpart
2. Initial Investigation	No Counterpart
3. Requirements Analysis	2. Analysis
4. Generating Systems Alternatives	No Counterpart
5. Selecting Proper System	No Counterpart
6. Output Design	3. Logical Design
7. Input Design	4. Physical Design
8. File Design	
9. Programming and Testing	5. Construction
10. Training and Other Preparations	No Counterpart
11. System Changeover	No Counterpart

FIGURE 22–3   **Comparison of Systems Development Life Cycle with CASE Life Cycle**

Logical design is the design of systems at a high level. It emphasizes the *what* rather than the *how* of doing things—general program logic. CASE products supporting this stage use such tools as program structure (hierarchy) charts, Warnier/Orr diagrams, structured English, and decision tables.

Physical design describes *how* the new system will operate. It identifies system logic at a detailed level. CASE products supporting this stage use tools such as database schema, program code, screen and report painting, and prototype capabilities.

Construction is development of a functioning system from physical design specifications. CASE provides programming support here, including translation of screen layouts to screen maps, translation of report layouts to report-generating programs, and testing and debugging of computer programs.

CASE manufacturers differentiate their products by how extensively they support the CASE life cycle. Vendors speak of CASE products being front end, back end, full life cycle, and integrated. **Front-end CASE** (sometimes called **upper CASE**) is analysis oriented. It includes the CASE life cycle phases of strategic planning, analysis, and logical design. **Back-end CASE** (sometimes called **lower CASE**) is design oriented. It includes the CASE life cycle phases of physical design and construction. A **full life cycle CASE** product has both front-end and back-end capabilities. An **integrated CASE (ICASE)** product is one which adds to the full life cycle the capabilities of reengineering and project support.

New CASE products are being introduced each day. Many CASE vendors are striving to quickly reach the ICASE development stage where (1) front-end, back-end, and full life cycle products are subsumed within an ICASE environment, and (2) ICASE products include the full spectrum of the SDLC. For example, current products do not fully address problem detection, feasibility analysis, system testing, or system changeover. ICASE promises to be exciting as it becomes more comprehensive, detailed, and cost-effective.

Figure 22–4 illustrates CASE product differentiation.

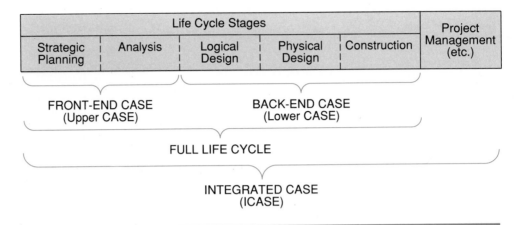

FIGURE 22–4   **CASE Product Differentiation**

Project Support

Often, business information systems are developed in teams rather than individually. Hence, there is a need for a work-sharing environment. CASE products provide such an environment through:

- Common repository of work done by other team members
- Project documentation tools
- Team communications including messaging, calendaring, and electronic mail
- Personal tools such as outliners, personal schedulers, and spreadsheets
- Miscellaneous project stage tools including resource estimating, security control, and audit control

Continuous Quality Improvement

One capability of CASE that is a still evolving is continuous quality improvement (CQI). It stresses fault removal from structured systems development and it pinpoints errors or inefficiencies in operating systems. CQI is dynamic. We continuously are striving to improve the effectiveness of existing information systems. CASE is more about improving quality than productivity.

VISIBLE ANALYST WORKBENCH

All current or developing CASE products cannot be described within the confines of a single book. One representative CASE product has been chosen for this book. It is a product that will give you the flavor of products used in business and the public sector. Remember that the inventory of available CASE products is increasing rapidly.

The Visible Analyst WORKBENCH is a full life cycle CASE product developed by the Visible Systems Corporation of Waltham, Massachusetts. The WORKBENCH is a complex system of software. Yet, once learned, it saves analyst time, integrates multiple analyst efforts, and increases total project quality. Two important aspects of the WORKBENCH are that it can be shared by several analysts (a team), and it can be used on a microcomputer.

WORKBENCH includes four separate but integrated modules. The first is the Visible Analyst, which allows analysts to create and edit all types of structured development diagrams. For example, WORKBENCH allows a complete development of DFD explosions. The second module is Visible Rules, which validates the accuracy and consistency of diagrams created in the first module.

The third module is Visible Dictionary. This module is the spine of the entire WORKBENCH software package. It allows analysts to maintain automatically a central definition catalog, or repository. The catalog ties together all WORKBENCH modules and includes graphic as well as narrative entries.

The fourth module is Visible Prototyper, which allows the analyst to simulate a prototyped design in a manner emulating the final product.

The following discussion of the first three modules concentrates on the timesaving and quality-generating features of this representative CASE product. Illustrations are from the actual Visible Analyst WORKBENCH.

Visible Analyst

Visible Analyst is the graphics module of this CASE product. Its capabilities are many:

1. Symbols, lines, and text drawings (Figure 22–5)
2. Text editing using different word processing protocols: For example, the data dictionary can be changed using such common packages as WordStar or WordPerfect.
3. Boilerplating capabilities: **Boilerplating** is the borrowing of features from other systems for the current system. In the programming arena, the term used is **reusable code**. The Visible Analyst package can set up constant screens, logos, dates, and so on.

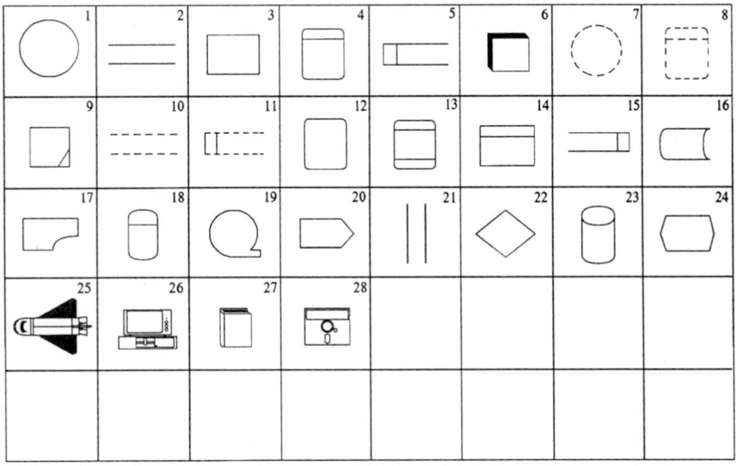

FIGURE 22–5   Visible Analyst Symbols

Reprinted by permission of Visible Systems Corporation, Waltham, Mass.

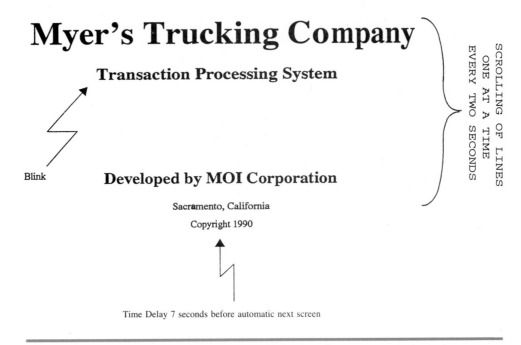

FIGURE 22–6   **Boilerplate Logo for Myer's Trucking Company (Done with Visible Analyst)**

These can be copied to separate diagrams and forms that are being generated. For example, Figure 22–6 shows a standard greeting screen logo for Myer's Trucking Company; this screen was done using Visible Analyst.

4. Custom symbol generator: Several custom symbols associated with Yourdon, Gane and Sarson, and Constantine versions of structured design are allowed. With the Visible Analyst, analysts can add individual or sets of tailored symbols.

5. Scales functions: Scales functions include horizontal and vertical screen rulers, a screen grid for aesthetically positioning symbols, and a zoom function. The zoom function allows the analyst to view the diagram in its full scope and then zoom in on an enlargement of any portion of the diagram.

6. Nesting: The Visible Analyst contains a hierarchy (nesting) tool called Treefile, which treats each diagram as a separate file. Each file can have child or parent relationships. For example, Figure 22–7 shows a level-1 data flow diagram which is a child of the level-0 context diagram. The level-1 DFD is also the parent of the level-2 explosion DFD. Nesting allows linking of separate diagrams into a total project shared among the several members of a design team.

7. Variable environment: Visible Analyst allows interfacing with a large list of different monitors, printers, mice, and local area networks.

The Visible Analyst allows analysts to generate virtually every type of design diagram either through custom or tailored means. These diagrams are linked in a project structure and are networked between design team members.

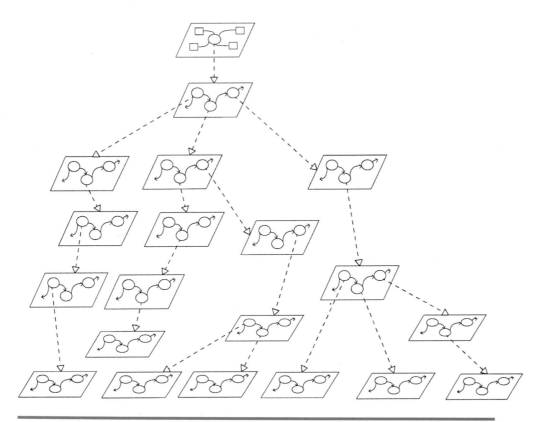

FIGURE 22–7   **Nesting—The Hierarchy of Diagrams**

Reprinted by permission of Visible Systems Corporation, Waltham, Mass.

Visible Rules

The Visible Rules module checks the accuracy of the diagrams created with Visible Analyst. The systems analyst must first indicate the structured design methodology that was used to prepare the diagram; the choice is between Yourdon and DeMarco and Gane and Sarson.

Typical errors detected are unlabeled symbols and data flows, unnumbered processes, unused data flows, and input/output flows that are inconsistent at different DFD explosion levels (e.g., input at level 1 not present at level 2). Several error reports are produced, including the one shown in Figure 22–8.

Visible Dictionary

The Visible Dictionary module is the spine of WORKBENCH. It is a repository for all parts of the diagrams created using Visible Analyst and edited using Visible Rules. This module allows the analyst to save, catalogue, and link data store files, data elements, data flows, and processes. Descriptions are saved in a text mode and can be edited using various word-processing packages.

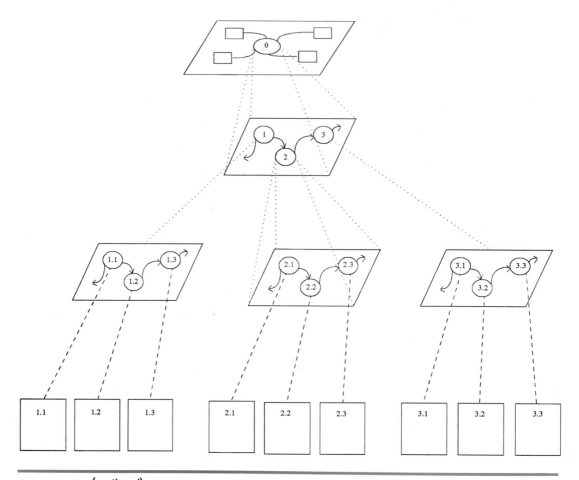

FIGURE 22-7   (continued)

Figure 22–9 shows a Visible Dictionary entry for a data element. Figure 22–10 shows a data flow entry. Finally, Figure 22–11 shows a dictionary entry for a DFD process.

Entries to Visible Dictionary are created automatically. The analyst creates and saves a diagram (by Visible Analyst and Visible Rules). Dictionary items then are created automatically for all data elements, data flows, and processes placed on the diagram. The items are created as shadow entries, which means the analyst must furnish entry details not included on the DFD. All data required by the Visible Dictionary format can be entered directly. If the automatically created dictionary item is not completed, an omission appears in error reports.

Visible Dictionary allows a search of specific items or groups of items. The module generates several structured reports, including the cross-reference report shown in Figure 22–12.

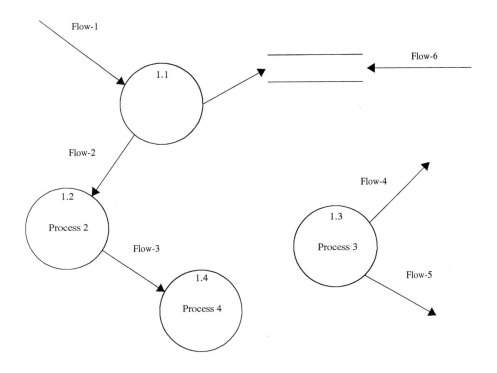

```
ERROR:    There are 1 unnamed Process(es).

ERROR:    There are 1 unnamed File(s).

WARNING: Data flow attached to file labeled '' is unnamed.

ERROR:    Data flow labeled 'Flow-6' is not attached to a
          process.

ERROR:    'Flow-5' should be shown as a net Input data
          flow.

ERROR:    Net Output data flow 'Flow-5' is not shown
          attached to parent process.

ERROR:    Net Input data flow 'Flow-1' is not shown
          attached to parent process.

ERROR:    Net Output data flow 'Flow-4' is not shown
          attached to parent process.

ERROR:    Net Output data flow '' is not shown attached to
          parent process.

ERROR:    Process labeled 'Process 3' is an output process
          only.

ERROR:    Process labeled 'Process 4' is an input process
          only.
```

FIGURE 22–8   **Visible Rules Error Report**

Reprinted by permission of Visible Systems Corporation, Waltham, Mass.

FIGURE 22-9   **Visible Dictionary Entry for Data Element**

Reprinted by permission of Visible Systems Corporation, Waltham, Mass.

Order Item	DATA ELEMENT
CONSULTANT-ORDER	DATA FLOW
ORDER PROCESSING (7)	
CONSULTANT ADMINISTRATION (2)	
BATCH ORDERS (7.4)	
ORDER-FILE	FILE
BATCH ORDERS (7.4)	
ORDER-DETAIL	FILE
ORDER PROCESSING (7)	
INVOICE ORDERS (7.10)	
RETURNED-PRODUCTS	DATA FLOW
CONSULTANT ADMINISTRATION (2)	
VISI LEVEL 0 DIAGRAM (0)	
INVENTORY (3)	
KITS	DATA FLOW
VISI CONTEXT DIAGRAM (CONTEXT)	
VISI CONTEXT DIAGRAM (CONTEXT)	
VISI LEVEL 0 DIAGRAM (0)	
INVENTORY (3)	
EUROPAK-SHIPMENT	DATA FLOW
VISI CONTEXT DIAGRAM (CONTEXT)	
VISI LEVEL 0 DIAGRAM (0)	
INVENTORY (3)	
DATA FLOW — VISIBLE-SHIPMENT	
VISI-JOURNAL	FILE
VISI LEVEL 0 DIAGRAM (0)	
KIT-DEBIT-NOTE	DATA FLOW
ORDER PROCESSING (7)	
CONSULTANT ADMINISTRATION (2)	
BATCH ORDERS (7.4)	

```
PURCHASES                                          DATA FLOW

    Description:

        Repeating structure that can contain multiple item types
        with varying prices and purchase conditions.

    Alias:

        PURCH-ITEMS
        BOUGHT-ITEMS
        PO-LINE-ITEMS

    Composition:

        ITEM PURCHASED
        ITEM PRICE
        APPLICABLE TAXES
        SPECIAL DISCOUNTS

    Notes:

        Current purchase conditions include a sale for item
        numbers B4515-B4595 with discounts of 20% on all
        remaining inventory. At end of sale, inventory of
        numbers will be reassigned to new items.
```

FIGURE 22-10   **Visible Dictionary Data Flow Description**

Reprinted by permission of Visible Systems Corporation, Waltham, Mass.

CHECK INDEPENDENT CREDIT SOURCES   PROCESS

Description:

    THIS ACTIVITY EVALUATES LARGE ORDERS WHERE CREDIT TERMS
    ARE REQUESTED, USING AN INDEPENDENT CREDIT SOURCE.

Process #   0.2

Process Description:

FOR EACH COMPANY APPROVED CREDIT ORDER
IF ORDER IS >= $ 10,000.00
    GET CO-REC-OK
    GET DUN'S-CREDIT-REPORT ON CUSTOMER
*NOTE*DUN'S-CREDIT-REPORT IS EQUAL TO DEBTSCAN REPORT
    IF DEBTSCAN INDICATES CREDIT PROBLEMS
    THEN IND-CREDIT-REPORT SHOULD BE SENT TO PROCESS
        "UPDATE BAD CREDIT LIST"
    ELSE DEBTSCAN INDICATES NO PROBLEMS AND CREDIT-GOOD
        SHOULD BE SENT TO PROCESS "SHIP TO CREDIT WORTHY
        CUSTOMERS"

ELSE IF ORDER < $ 10,000.00
THEN PASS CO-REC-OK TO PROCESS "SHIP TO CREDIT WORTHY
    CUSTOMERS" AS CREDIT-GOOD

Notes:

    THE DEBTSCAN SERVICE FROM DUN & BRADSTREET IS RELATIVELY
    COSTLY. PERIODIC CHECKS SHOULD BE MADE CONCERNING CREDIT
    SIZE AND NEED FOR DEBTSCAN REPORTING. TO BE CERTAIN WE ARE
    USING THE APPROPRIATE AMOUNT AS A DEBTSCAN TRIGGER.
    NOTE DEBTSCAN TRIGGER INFORMATION SHOULD BE COLLECTED FROM
        ACCOUNTS RECEIVABLE MANAGER AT CORPORATE FINANCE.

Location:

    EXAMPLE LEVEL 0 DIAGRAM (0)
        Input flows:
            CO-REC-OK
            DUN'S-CREDIT-REPORT
        Output flows:
            IND-CREDIT-REPORT
            CREDIT-GOOD

FIGURE 22–11   Visible Dictionary Process Description

Reprinted by permission of Visible Systems Corporation, Waltham, Mass.

ACCOUNT STATUS   DATA ELEMENT
    DUN'S-CREDIT-REPORT   DATA FLOW
        YOURDON CONTEXT DIAGRAM (CONTEXT)
        EXAMPLE LEVEL 0 DIAGRAM (0)
        INDEPENDENT CREDIT CHECK (0.2)
    APPROVALS FILE   FILE

AMOUNT-OF-ORDER   DATA ELEMENT
    PURCHASE-INFO   DATA FLOW
        EXAMPLE LEVEL 0 DIAGRAM (0)
        NEW CUSTOMER ORDER (0.1)
        SEPARATE NEW AND OLD CUSTOMERS (0.1.1)
        DATA FLOW   --> CUSTOMER-PO

BAD CREDIT DESIGNATION   DATA ELEMENT
    CURRENT-CUST-CREDIT-BAD   DATA FLOW
        CHECK COMPANY RECORDS (0.3)
    BAD-CREDIT   DATA FLOW
        EXAMPLE LEVEL 0 DIAGRAM (0)
        UPDATE BAD CREDIT FILE (0.5)
        DATA FLOW   --> UPDATE-CUSTOMER-DATA

BAD CREDIT REASON   DATA ELEMENT
    BAD-CREDIT-LIST   DATA FLOW
        EXAMPLE LEVEL 0 DIAGRAM (0)
        NEW CUSTOMER ORDER (0.1)
        SEPARATE NEW AND OLD CUSTOMERS (0.1.1)
        SEPARATE NEW AND OLD CUSTOMERS (0.1.1)
        DATA FLOW   --> COMPANY-INFO-FROM-FILES

BANK APPROVAL   DATA ELEMENT
    CREDIT-HISTORY   --> CREDIT-GOOD
        DATA FLOW   DATA FLOW

CHECK   DATA ELEMENT
    ORDER-PREPAID   DATA FLOW

FIGURE 22–12   Visible Dictionary Cross-Reference Report

Reprinted by permission of Visible Systems Corporation, Waltham, Mass.

FLORIDA CRIMINAL JUSTICE INFORMATION SYSTEM

The Visible Analyst WORKBENCH was used recently to provide structured development of the criminal justice activities in Hillsborough County, Florida (the county in which Tampa is located). The Criminal Justice Information System (CJIS) is described as the context diagram of Figure 22–13. The entire CJIS has not been developed; if it had, the total system would be too large for our discussion. Now discussion can concentrate on the processes shown in the partial hierarchy chart of Figure 22–14.

Criminal Justice Information System

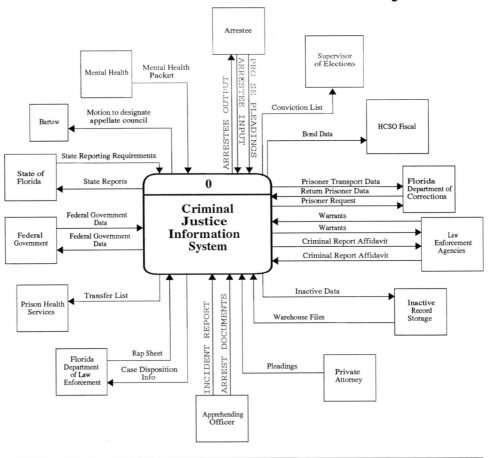

FIGURE 22–13   Context Diagram for CJIS of Hillsborough County, Florida

Reprinted by permission of Hillsborough County, Florida, and SCS of Tampa, Florida.

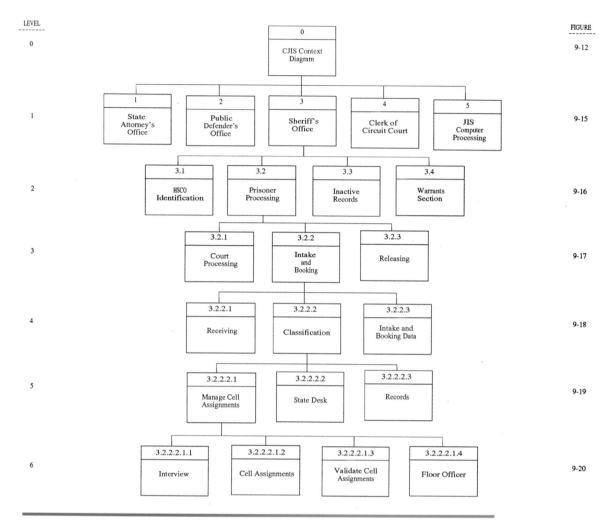

FIGURE 22–14   **Partial Hierarchy Chart of CJIS**

Figure 22–14 is the only figure not produced by CJIS designers using WORK-BENCH. That package could have produced the figure; however, CJIS designers started with the context diagram (Figure 22–13) and exploded the data flow diagram from there. They did not start with a hierarchy chart, as recommended in this book. Instead of a hierarchy chart, CJIS designers used Treefile and produced Figure 22–15.

A portion of the CJIS is seen in the partial hierarchy chart of Figure 22–14 and the boxed portion of Figure 22–15. In order, the context diagram in Figure 22–14 was automatically exploded as follows:

DFD Level	Figure	Process Number
1	22–16	0
2	22–17	3.0
3	22–18	3.2
4	22–19	3.2.2
5	22–20	3.2.2.2
6	22–21	3.2.2.2.1

After the DFD is exploded beyond levels 2 or 3, it may lose its communicative power with end-users. It then becomes more of a diagram for communication with other designers, analysts, and programmers. The degree of detail in this CJIS explosion allows a programmer to begin coding the process at the primitive level. The trade-off here is between user communication (less detail) and programmer communication.

```
Date:   09-06-1990              Project:  CJIS              Page:   1
Time:   00:35:13

            PROJECT TREEFILE - DIAGRAM DESCRIPTIONS

    1.CJIS CONTEXT DIAGRAM
        2.CJIS DEPARTMENTAL BREAKDOWN
            3.SHERIFF'S OFFICE
                4.PRISONER PROCESSING
                    5.RELEASING
                    5.COURT PROCESSING
                    5.INTAKE AND BOOKING
                        6.CLASSIFICATION
                            7.MANAGE CELL ASSIGNMENTS
                            7.RECORDS
                            7.STATE DESK
                        6.RECEIVING
            3.STATE ATTORNEY'S OFFICE
                4.CASE PROCESSING
                    5.FELONY PROCESSING
                    5.MISDEMEANOR PROCESSING
                    5.TRAFFIC PROCESSING
                    5.JUVENILE PROCESSING
            3.PUBLIC DEFENDER'S OFFICE
                4.PD INTERVIEW
                4.PD FELONY
                4.PD MISDEMEANOR/TRAFFIC
                4.PD JUVENILE
                4.PD APPEALS
            3.JIS COMPUTER PROCESSING
                4.JIS-HCSO PROCESSING
            3.CLERK'S OFFICE
                4.CLERK'S FELONY PROCESSING
                    5.CLERK'S COMPUTER ENTRY
                    5.CLERK'S FELONY INTAKE
                    5.COMMITMENT PROCESSING
```

FIGURE 22–15   **CJIS Project Treefile Description**

Reprinted by permission of Hillsborough County, Florida, and SCS of Tampa, Florida.

Departmental Breakdown

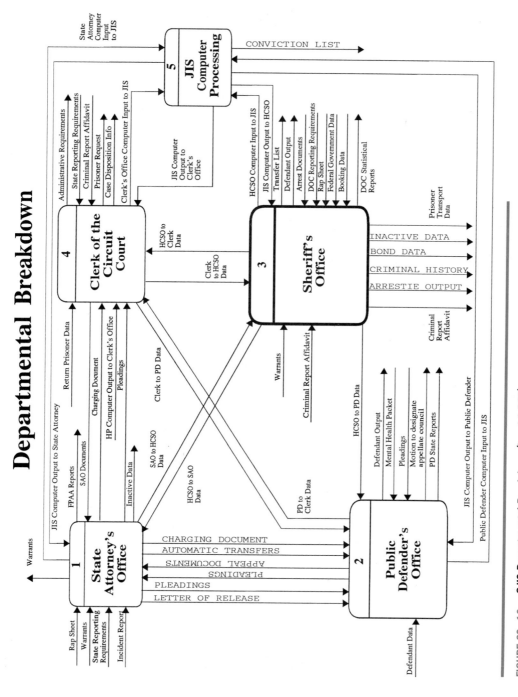

FIGURE 22–16 CJIS Departmental Breakdown (Level 1 DFD)

Reprinted by permission of Hillsborough County, Florida, and SCS of Tampa, Florida.

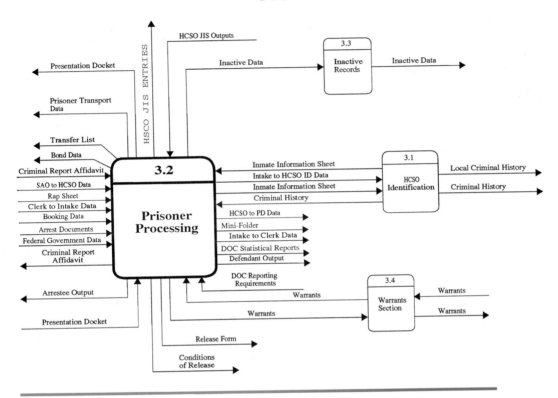

FIGURE 22–17   **CJIS—Level 2 DFD Explosion**

Reprinted by permission of Hillsborough County, Florida, and SCS of Tampa, Florida.

The Visible Analyst allows automatic integration between different explosion levels. For example, consider Figure 22–18. Once the DFD is complete, the mouse can be positioned within process 3.2.2. As a result, the shell for Figure 22–19 comes on the screen. Once the exploded DFD is completed (Figure 22–19), the two DFD levels are automatically linked together in the repository and can be accessed through Visible Dictionary.

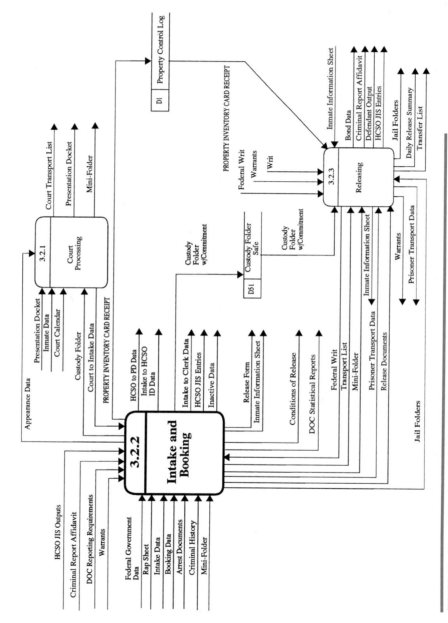

Prisoner Processing
3.2

FIGURE 22—18   CJIS— Level 3 DFD Explosion

Reprinted by permission of Hillsborough County, Florida, and SCS of Tampa, Florida.

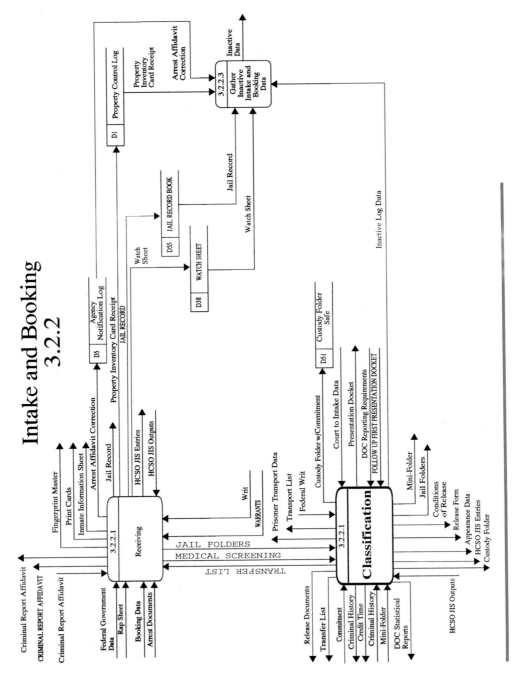

FIGURE 22–19   CJIS—Level 4 DFD Explosion

Reprinted by permission of Hillsborough County, Florida, and SCS of Tampa, Florida.

Classification
3.2.2.2

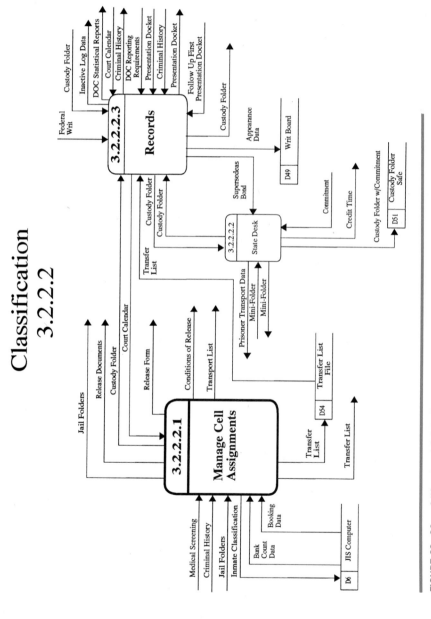

FIGURE 22–20   CJIS— Level 5 DFD Explosion

Reprinted by permission of Hillsborough County, Florida, and SCS of Tampa, Florida.

Manage Cell Assignments
3.2.2.2.1

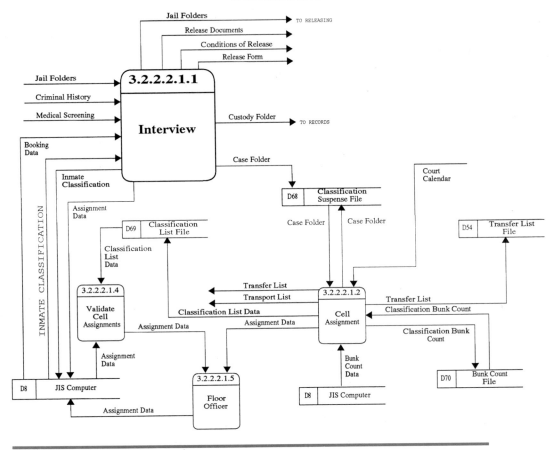

FIGURE 22–21   **CJIS—Level 6 DFD Explosion**

Reprinted by permission of Hillsborough County, Florida, and SCS of Tampa, Florida.

Figure 22–22 shows a process description produced by Visible Dictionary. It describes in detail process 3.2.2.2.1.1—screen inmate for housing assignments, which is the lowest level of detail reached in the CJIS. Presumably, programmers can begin coding from this primitive level. Note that the entry is structured English and thus is amenable to program coding.

Figure 22–23 is a data flow description produced by Visible Dictionary for a form called Charging Document. This profile has five parts:

1. Name of entity: Charging Document
2. Type of entity: Data flow rather than process or data store
3. Description

Interview   PROCESS

Description:

    Screen inmate for Housing assignments.

Process #   3.2.2.1.1

Process Description:

    Receive Jail Folders from Booking.
    Receive Criminal History from HCSO ID.
    Receive Medical Screening from Intake Nurse.
    Review File Material for :
        Release Eligibility
        Classification Custody Assignment
        Housing Assignment
    If Eligible for release:
        Complete: Intake Info sheet
                  Score sheet
                  ROR Paperwork
        Verification by Classification staff for satisfaction
            of eligibility requirements.
        Send Custody Folder to Records.
        Send Case Folder to Classification.
        Enter Custody into computer.
        Enter temp housing into computer.
        ROR Packet put in ROR file binder
            for presentation next AM.
    If not eligible for release:
        Folders split -
                    Custody Folder to Records
                    Case Folder to Classification
        Enter classification assignment into computer
        stamp Card 3X5
        Return Card 3X5 to Bull Pen Deputy for placement in
            pre-court holding cell
        Direct Housing Assignments
            By Classification Specialists :
                - Medical
                - Sentenced
                - Juvenile
                - Federals
                - Return from other County
                - Special Housing Requirements

FIGURE 22–22   CJIS Process Description

Reprinted by permission of Hillsborough County, Florida, and SCS of Tampa, Florida.

Charging Document   DATA FLOW

Description:

    Document used for filing formal charges.

Composition:

    [Information |
    Notice to Appear |
    Misdemeanor Affidavit |
    Petition |
    Direct Filed Information |
    Writ] +
    FELONY INFORMATION

Location:

    CJIS DEPARTMENTAL BREAKDOWN (0)

        Source: STATE ATTORNEY'S OFFICE (PROCESS)
        Dest.:   CLERK OF THE CIRCUIT COURT (PROCESS)

        Source: STATE ATTORNEY'S OFFICE (PROCESS)
        Dest.:   PUBLIC DEFENDER'S OFFICE (PROCESS)

        DATA FLOW   -->   SAO Documents

        DATA FLOW   -->   SAO Case File

FIGURE 22–23   CJIS Data Flow Description

Reprinted by permission of Hillsborough County, Florida, and SCS of Tampa,
Florida.

4. Composition: Other data flows included in this data flow are listed. These other data flows may be group data flows (forms) made up of elementary data elements. For example, the Notice to Appear will have a separate data flow entry within the repository (Figure 22–24).
5. Location: This is where this data flow appears in the hierarchy (tree) of data flow diagrams. There are three entries for each appearance of the data flow.
   - Chart name (for example, CJIS Departmental Breakdown)
   - Source (for example, State Attorney's Office, which is a process)
   - Destination (for example, Clerk of the Circuit Court, which is a process)

It is important to understand how the repository (created by Visible Dictionary) and the diagrams (created by Visible Analyst) are linked together. Consider the first incidence of location shown in Figure 22–23.

```
CJIS DEPARTMENTAL BREAKDOWN (0)
Source: STATE ATTORNEY'S OFFICE (PROCESS)
Dest.: CLERK OF THE CIRCUIT COURT (PROCESS)
```

Refer to Figure 22–16, which shows the CJIS Departmental Breakdown DFD. The State Attorney's Office (source) is the process symbol in the upper left corner. The Clerk of the Circuit Court (destination) is the process symbol at the top and middle of the figure. There are several data flows (lines) connecting these two processes. The

FIGURE 22–24   Appearance in Data Dictionary (Repository) of Data Flow as Group Then Elementary Data Element

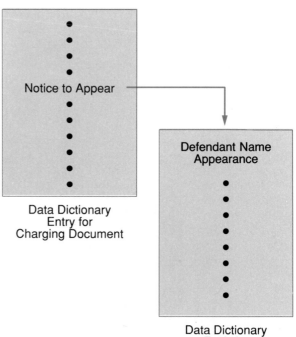

Notice to Appear

Data Dictionary
Entry for
Charging Document

Defendant Name
Appearance

Data Dictionary
Entry for
Notice to Appear

middle line is labeled Charging Document. It flows from the State Attorney's Office to the Clerk of the Circuit Court. This is how Visible Dictionary links the DFDs created by Visible Analyst to the CASE repository managed by Visible Dictionary. Errors in creating the diagrams or linking them to the repository are found by Visible Rules.

Finally, the repository managed by Visible Dictionary feeds into Visible Prototyper, where actual form, screen, and report pictures can be developed and a prototype can be developed. This criminal justice example is specialized and complex. Do not try to master its terminology and processing nuances. Rather, try to get a taste for the types of diagrams generated, the explosion from one level diagram to another, and how these explosions are controlled by a central information repository.

The Visible Analyst WORKBENCH is only one of many CASE products available. Most of products have similar processing methodologies, if not always the same capabilities. Another important CASE product is IBM's AD/Cycle.

SAA AND AD/CYCLE

A major deficiency of many current CASE products is their lack of integration. Front-end tools are not linked to back-end tools. Microcomputers are not linked to mainframes. We need applications development tools that encompass the entire SDLC. Efforts under way to correct this CASE deficiency include IBM's Systems Application Architecture (SAA), IBM's Application Development/Cycle (AD/Cycle), and international efforts in Japan and Western Europe.

Systems Application Architecture

Systems application architecture (SAA) is a full set of applications and application enablers that spans the entire IBM product line from the smallest intelligent workstation to the largest mainframe. SAA provides consistency across disparate systems by providing three specifications that allow user, programmer, and communications access to operating systems:

- Common user access (CUA): The CUA interface controls workstation interaction between the user and the applications program.
- Common communications support (CCS): This interface allows networks comprising different architectures to share information easily. CCS will conform to systems network architecture (SNA) and international standards; this will allow communication between IBM and other vendors' hardware.
- Common programming interface (CPI): The CPI allows programmers to write applications that are independent of computer hardware. High-level languages, applications generators, and expert systems are included.

AD/Cycle

Application development/cycle (AD/Cycle) is an extension of SAA; it provides integrated application development tools that encompass the entire SDLC. Some of the tools are being developed by IBM; others are being developed by independent vendors who become IBM partners. AD/Cycle is a full ICASE—one that may provide a beginning for industry-wide CASE standards.

AD/Cycle provides the following tools:

- Modeling tools to support business information planning
- Prototyping support
- Structured design tools
- Multiple applications languages
- Applications generators
- Expert systems
- Code generators
- Testing and maintenance tools
- Project management tools

Several independent vendors—Bachman Information Systems, Index Technology, Knowledge Ware, and Visible Systems, among others—have announced tools compatible with the AD/Cycle framework.

The IBM effort is not isolated. Two international projects are under way to develop a totally integrated CASE product.

International Efforts

The Japanese Ministry of International Trade and Industry has initiated a CASE integration project called Sigma. The project has a $200 million budget contributed to by its 187 members, which include manufacturers, software houses, banks, and the Japanese government. The objective of the project is to standardize the entire Japanese software development effort, with emphasis on CASE. Standardization is based on UNIX System V.

Several Western European countries have embarked on a project called European Strategic Program for Research in Information Technologies (ESPRIT). Participants in this project include twelve top European information technology firms from five countries. Several integrated CASE projects have been launched:

- Portable Common Tool Environment (PCTE)
- Automated Support for Software Engineering Technology (ASSET)
- Generation of Interactive Programming Environment for Software Configuration Reusing Components (KNOSOS)
- Integrated Frame Approach to Industrial Software Development (METEOR)

DERIVING MAXIMUM BENEFITS FROM CASE

CASE tools are impressive. Yet, some firms are still using pencil and paper for system development. Other firms have invested considerable funds in the CASE methodology but are disappointed in the results. For example, one large aerospace company invested hundreds of thousands of dollars in a popular CASE product. The investment included software purchase, hardware necessities such as mice and hard disks, and considerable amounts of training on the new design environment. Today the firm estimates that only 25 percent of its analysts use the CASE tool on a regular basis. The firm does not know if the CASE product is really paying off.

What has gone wrong with the CASE revolution? Nothing, really. Most reported failures are due to misplaced expectations, lack of training, or lack of patience. The following guidelines are recommended for deriving maximum benefits from CASE products:

1. Keep expectations realistic. Do not expect major productivity improvements for at least three years.

2. Measure performance. Keep track of short- and long-term costs and benefits of design and programming performance.

3. Move slowly and systematically. CASE represents a radical change from the way design has been done for 30 years. Make CASE implementation a slow, incremental process.

4. Introduce structured methodology. CASE products automate structured methodologies. Much resistance to and lack of success with CASE is as much frustration with the structured approach as with the CASE product itself. If design is not being done in a structured manner, do not expect miracles from CASE.

5. Expect operational expenses. Operational expenses for CASE products often run three times as high as initial costs.

6. Splurge on training. Training time will take about ten days to develop minimum CASE skills. It will take several months of training to develop full proficiency. Develop CASE coaches.

7. Use pilot teams. Give pilot teams the reign to explore *full* CASE usage. Members of pilot teams can double as coaches.

8. Be selective on initial CASE uses. Initially, choose implementations that have a high chance of success. A few successful CASE examples will build confidence and reduce resistance. An early, unsuccessful CASE experience may delay or even prevent widespread usage.

9. Make CASE improvement a strategic goal. Making CASE a strategic goal should not be difficult because of the extensive investment required to implement a CASE environment.

10. Do not forget program maintenance. CASE does not always increase design productivity. It almost always makes it easier to maintain applications.

11. Think quality, not quantity. Proper use of CASE technology will increase the quality of the design process. Any associated increase in productivity is a bonus.

Next, we'll consider several automated tools in use which, if not CASE, are cousins. They include applications generators, code generators, and prototype generators.

TOWN AND COUNTRY CREDIT LINE

In early 1988, Town and Country Credit Line (TCCL) decided to develop a system to enhance its competitive advantage over other banking cards. TCCL has long seen itself as the leader in banking card technology. (The actual nature of the system is proprietary at this time and the name of the company has been changed.)

TCCL decided to explore the costs and benefits of using CASE technology to enhance delivery time for new systems. It chose a service request system as an eight-week pilot project to accomplish this purpose. TCCL hired outside programmer consultants who had experience in the use of CASE technology and purchased **Information Engineering Facility (IEF)** from Texas Instruments.

The decision to develop the service request system as a pilot was based on the following four items:

1. The length of time required to deliver this product to the user community was estimated to be short. (It was perceived to be a system with a fairly narrow scope.)
2. The user community had been promised the system, with no delivery, for a long time.
3. It was felt that this system would give the development team the "biggest bang for the dollar" (quote from project manager).
4. It was felt that this system would provide the user community with dramatically enhanced productivity while simplifying complex choices.

Because CASE technology was new to the organization, the pilot project would additionally provide a knowledge base within the team to make accurate estimates for projects using a CASE tool, give each team member hands-on experience with all phases of a CASE tool, and so provide understanding of the limitations and capabilities of a CASE tool.

Two consultants were hired to provide support during the pilot project because the team had no prior experience with IEF. One consultant provided guidance on the methodology and project management. The other consultant provided guidance on IEF itself. Training of the resident staff members was limited. At the beginning of the pilot project, only two team members of nine had any training beyond IEF's business area analysis and business systems design. No team members had any training or experience with IEF technical design and construction. One team member had no training in CASE and IEF at all.

The system was developed by breaking it into its logical business components and then distributing one task to each group. The system was developed by the eight-week deadline and performed the required tasks efficiently and effectively with user acceptance. Some problems were encountered during the development process. One was related to the CASE technology and another was related to the nature of the system. Since the CASE technology was new to the organization, a learning curve was encountered. The competence of the team and a willingness to work additional hours helped to overcome the problem. The other problem was a lack of communication between groups. The groups sometimes went off on inconsistent tangents. Some work had to be redone. Once IEF became familiar to the team, and less time was spent on learning it, full-team meetings alleviated this problem.

IEF divides the development process into seven phases:

1. ISP (information strategy planning): Areas of concern are identified and directions are established.
2. BAA (business area analysis): Areas of concern are analyzed for entity relationship and process dependency.
3. BSD (business system design): Processes are packaged into procedures that are user interactive.
4. TD (technical design): BAA/BSD designs are converted into specific database tables (such as IBM's DB2), and COBOL II code.
5. Construction: Source and executable code and database definition and access statements are generated.
6. Transition: Data are loaded into databases and conversion strategies are determined.
7. Production: The system is implemented and used.

Throughout these phases, testing occurred. Unit or program testing was performed by individual team members. System testing occurred when the entire system was operational. User acceptance testing occurred at various points in the development process.

Some problems occurred with the interfaces between systems. Once these problems were solved, the end system performed adequately in terms of efficiency and effectiveness. Users were pleased with the system and it is functional at the present time.

Source: Adapted from a real-world organization whose name has been changed.

4GLS AND APPLICATIONS AND CODE GENERATORS

Analysts see an increasing need to develop applications quickly. **Applications** are systems with distinct boundaries and objectives. Examples are a purchasing TPS, insurance premium expert system, and resource acquisition decision support system. The need for quick application development stems from several sources:

- Prototyping is becoming an accepted part of the SDLC; the essence of prototyping is development speed.
- End-user design is increasing as the trend continues toward decentralization of design responsibilities.
- Application backlogs have been increasing dramatically; it is not unusual for a proposed project to wait in line for a year or more. Faster development decreases waiting time.
- There is growing demand for specialized, tailored systems: decision support systems, expert systems, management information systems, and executive information systems.

■ Analysts must sell to management the idea of developing a new or modified information system. A quickly developed, hands-on model of the proposed system is a better selling device than the detailed diagrams analysts have been trained to produce.

CASE products can contribute to more rapid development of applications. The primary goal of CASE, however, is increase of quality, not speed. Other software products, marketed outside the CASE realm, stress application development speed; these products are 4GLs, applications generators, and code generators.

Fourth-Generation Languages

The 4GLs are extensions of third-generation languages. Third-generation languages such as COBOL, PL1, and C are production languages. They are used to handle efficiently the huge volume of inputs and outputs of transaction-processing systems. Fourth-generation languages add the following characteristics to those of production languages:

■ Menu driven, therefore requiring fewer programming skills to operate
■ Database oriented, revolving around easy manipulation of stored information
■ Retrieval focused, emphasizing rapid and easy commands for answering user inquiries and writing structured and new reports
■ Human factors designed, making it easy and comfortable for nonprogrammers to learn the language (Features include help functions, tutorials, and tailoring to different user skill levels.)

Products such as FOCUS, dBASE IV, and NATURAL are 4GLs. They stretch toward end-user design rather than systems professional design and essentially are macro languages. A **macro** is a prewritten set of program code called and executed by a single command.

For example, consider the following dBASE statement:

```
DISPLAY ALL for Jobtype = Engineer
```

This command will display on the VDT screen all information for all records where the job type is engineer. Figure 22–25 shows in pseudocode a third-generation language logic required to execute this dBASE statement.

The 4GLs are the current rung on the ladder of business language evolution (Figure 22–26). The next rung may be voice input, procedure-free languages used by end-users without any programming training.

Applications Generators

Even the dBASE statement just described requires that the end-user memorize certain programming language syntax. An **applications generator** is a piece of software devoted to designing business applications while requiring no user programming.

```
ERASE SCREEN
WRITE Screen-headings
SET line-count to 4
READ first-record
DO UNTIL End-of-file
    IF Jobtype = 'ENGINEER'
        WRITE Record
        ADD 1 TO Line-count
        IF Line-count = 25
            WRITE Screen-headings
            SET line-count to 4
        ENDIF
    ENDIF
    READ next-record
ENDDO
```

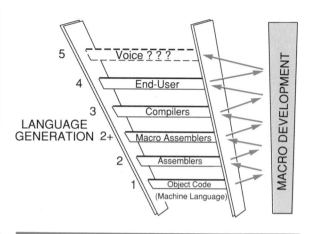

FIGURE 22–25 Pseudocode for dBASE Statement: DISPLAY ALL for Jobtype = Engineer

FIGURE 22–26 Fourth-generation Languages as the Current Rung on the Ladder of Language Development

Applications generators are menu and word processing oriented. Menus help users to select parts of the application they wish to develop. Word-processing features are used to paint screens, reports, and forms. In screen painting, the user places on the VDT screen an exact image of how the form, report, or interactive screen should look; the software then automatically converts that image to program code.

Let's look at the applications generator for dBASE III PLUS as an example. Figure 22–27 is a semblance of its menu and makes a convenient outline for discussing its capabilities:

1. Create database. The database (file) can either be designed and loaded here or transferred from previous dBASE projects.
2. Create screen form. The user paints the screen with the interactive image to be sent. Figure 22–28 is an example of screen painting.
3. Create report form. This option allows the user to paint forms or reports. The painting is automatically translated to dBASE program code.
4. Create label form. Mailing labels are a special type of report. Usage frequency is great enough that labels are treated as a separate menu class.
5. Set application color. Color can be set for screen borders, screen background, screen foreground, and boxes inside the screen.
6. Use applications generators (automatic and advanced). These options (numbers 6 and 8) allow the user to set up paths from one screen to another. For example, Figure 22–29 is a menu map for a purchasing system. The applications generator would allow the user to set up links between the screens and functions shown on the map.
7. Run application. Screens, reports, and databases are tied together using applications generator options. Now users can begin to operate the application.

FIGURE   22-27   **Semblance   of
dBASE III PLUS Applications Generator**

FIGURE   22-27   **Semblance   of
dBASE III PLUS Applications Generator**

```
                        dBASE III PLUS
                  APPLICATION GENERATOR MENU
    _____

        1.  CREATE DATABASE
        2.  CREATE SCREEN FORM
        3.  CREATE REPORT FORM
        4.  CREATE LABEL FORM
        5.  SET APPLICATION COLOR
        6.  USE AUTOMATIC APPLICATIONS GENERATOR
        7.  RUN APPLICATION
        8.  USE ADVANCED APPLICATIONS GENERATOR
        9.  MODIFY APPLICATION CODE

        0.  EXIT


    _____ select _____
```

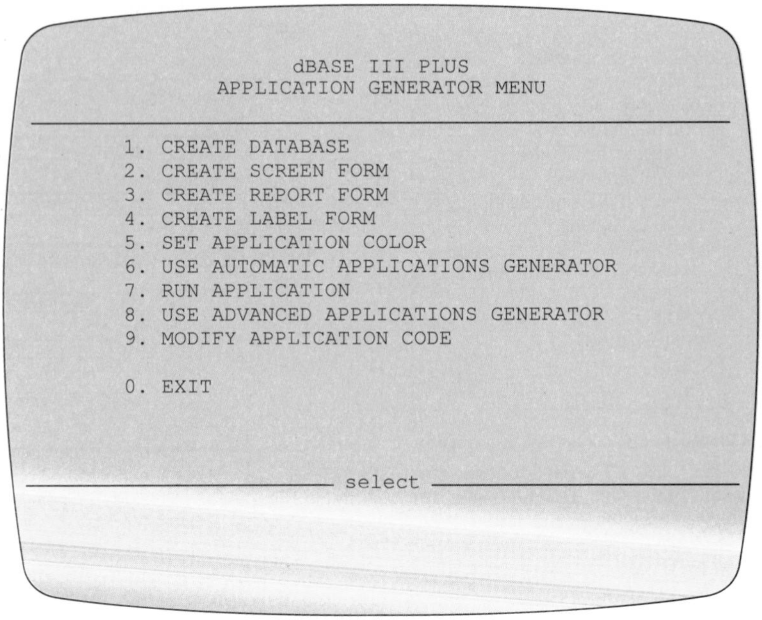

8. See number 6.
9. Modify application code. The software automatically generates the program code to execute user-designed applications. Professional programmers can then change this code to make it more efficient.

Applications generators perform three important functions. First, they allow end-users to develop applications with minimum help from systems personnel. This capability is consistent with the trend toward end-user computing. Second, applications generators can be used for rapid prototyping. Third, applications generators allow nonprogrammers to generate program code. As stated earlier in this chapter, some CASE products also generate program code.

Code Generators

There are three ways to generate program code for operating a business information system. The first way is to generate code automatically through CASE products and applications generators. The second way is traditional; that is, the programmer manually translates system specifications into operable code. The third method is to use **4GL code generators;** one such code generator is described later in this chapter.

Is automatically generated code more or less efficient than manually produced code? The answer to this question requires differentiation between microcomputer and mainframe environments. Microcomputer-based applications generators produce about the same 4GL code as programmers produce for microcomputers. This is so because microcomputer applications generators are written in the same language to which user

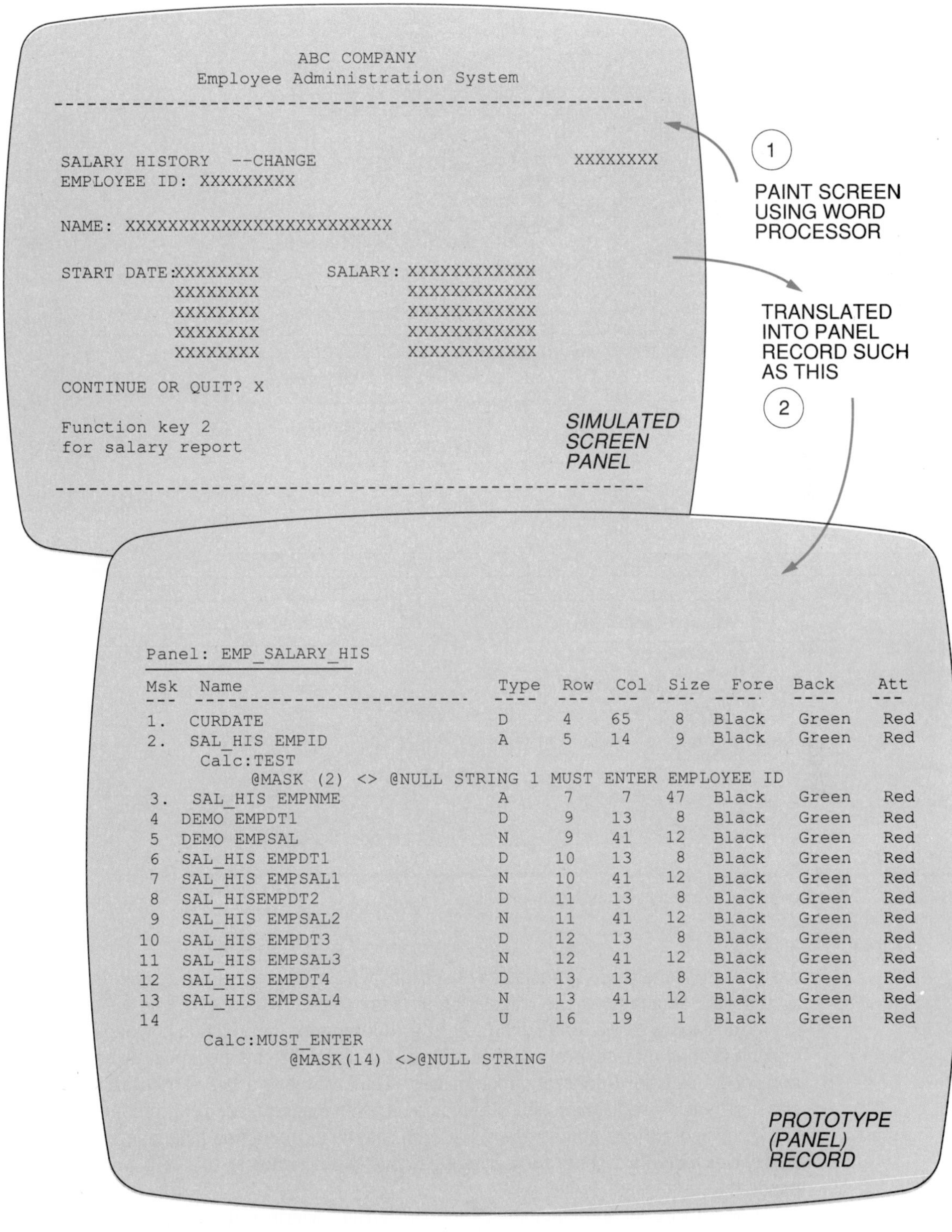

FIGURE 22-28 Example of Screen Painting

Reprinted by permission of Visible Systems Corporation, Waltham, Mass.

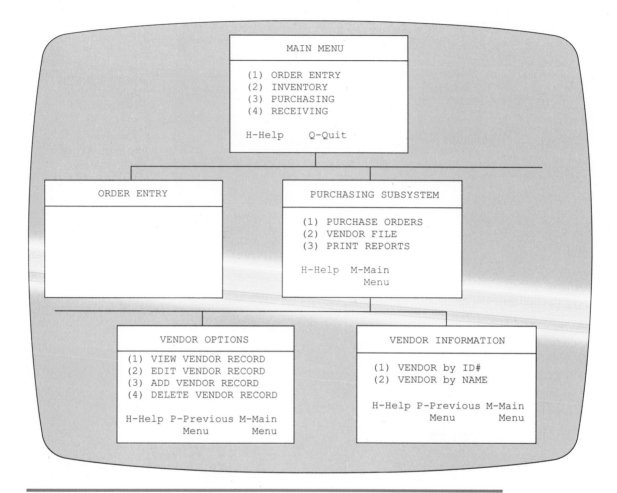

FIGURE 22—29   **Menu Map for Purchasing System**

designs are translated. Translation is reasonably efficient when the receiving language
is the same language as the translating system.

Translation of code to a mainframe, third-generation, production language is a more
difficult problem for several reasons. First, it is difficult to be an expert programmer in
both 4GLs and third-generation languages. Think of being a fan of both hard rock and
classical music—not impossible, but difficult. For mainframes, programmers of 4GL,
CASE or applications generators must translate to a production language such as CO-
BOL. Efficient third-generation language code often is not in the 4GL programmer's
mindset.

Second, production languages such as COBOL sacrifice design efficiency to make
system change more efficient. Thus, production programming in third-generation lan-

guages is more structured and naturally documented than it is in 4GLs. Computer-generated code often lacks this important documentation.

Third, production languages such as COBOL rely on copying (boilerplating) capabilities, which allow production programmers to reduce coding by copying reusable code. Reusable code is a programming segment that can be borrowed for future projects in lieu of developing new code. Systems such as IBM's **Customer Information Control System (CICS)** allow development of COBOL, PL/1, and RPG programs with a minimum of new code and a maximum of reusable code. Generation of third-generation language code by 4GLs often cannot take advantage of this copying feature.

Still, automatic code generation is important in two respects.

First, sometimes there is a need for system development where speed is more important than efficiently generated code. The aerospace company McDonnell Douglas uses COBOL code generators in this way: Rapidly generated code is used in emergency situations. Then it is modified by a COBOL programmer to make it more efficient for subsequent change. Second, automatically generated code can provide programmers with shells that they then can change. This can save a lot of initial programmer development time. Nevertheless, use of the COPY function does much the same thing.

One of the more exciting developments is code generators on PCs that generate mainframe computer (third-generation language) code. One such product is APS/PC Workstation, developed by Sage Software of Rockville, Maryland. With this product, PCs are used to generate COBOL programs that operate in mainframe production environments. The PCs can be used to (1) paint screens for interactive sessions and output forms and reports, (2) work with logic-creation tools (for example, decision tables), (3) select predefined macros (for example, file opening and closing), (4) generate mainframe-compatible COBOL code, and (5) allow users to test that code.

A McDonnell Douglas information executive recently proposed a future role for code generators. He stated, "COBOL won't disappear, but COBOL programmers might."

PROTOTYPE GENERATORS

Prototype generators are similar to applications generators. They differ primarily in purpose. The intended product of most applications generators is a working information system. The product of a prototype generator is a demonstration model for enhancing communication between analysts and users. Another difference is that prototype generators often are a part of CASE products. This is so with the Visible Prototyper—one of the modules in Visible Analyst WORKBENCH.

Visible Prototyper has six features: (1) prototype levels, (2) panel linking, (3) panel branching, (4) data selection, (5) data modification, and (6) generated reports.

Prototype Levels. Visible Prototyper includes four levels of sophistication. The panel is the element tying these four levels together. A panel is a separate VDT screen devoted to input (data entry), output (reports), or processing (file modification). Figure 22–30 shows how the panel threads throughout the following four levels of Visible Prototyper:

1. Panel creation and linking
2. Calculated branching from one panel to another
3. Selected database data display
4. Database modification and scenario looping

The last level is a full simulation of the suggested system.

Panel Linking. Panels are organized into scenarios, which are separate prototype situations. The analyst can design up to fifty panels per scenario and as many scenarios as desired. Once developed, panels can be linked together in a forward and backward sequence. Thus, panels (screens) A through E could be developed and then placed in the following forward scenario sequence:

$$A \longrightarrow E \longrightarrow C \longrightarrow B \longrightarrow D$$

or a backward sequence:

$$D \longrightarrow B \longrightarrow C \longrightarrow E \longrightarrow A$$

At this primary level, there is a fixed transition between one panel and another; sequence does not vary based on menu choices.

Panel Branching. In panel branching, transition between scenario patterns becomes dependent on user choices from a menu. These choices override the automatic forward/ backward sequencing set up at the first level.

Data Selection. This fourth part of Visible Prototyper allows users to search and select from a data file. The selected record fields then are displayed. The files were set up in the other modules of the Visible Analyst WORKBENCH and can be transferred to Visible Prototyper.

Data Modification. Data modification allows users to enter new data and change old database records. This final level of sophistication is a total simulation of the system under development.

Generated Reports. Visible Prototyper produces six different reports:

1. Panel/report displays
2. Panel link lists—how the panels were linked together
3. Panel records—a specification for each panel (This includes the processing flows needed to build the final prototype and design the actual information system. Figure 22–19 is an example of a panel record.)
4. Panel notes—commentary appended to each panel record

The Visible Prototyper

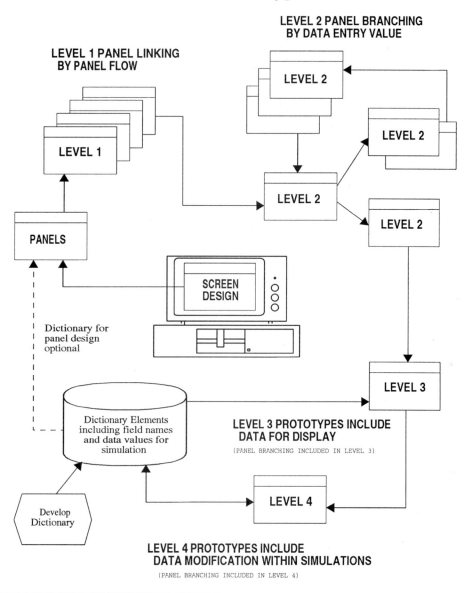

LEVEL 2 PANEL BRANCHING BY DATA ENTRY VALUE

LEVEL 1 PANEL LINKING BY PANEL FLOW

LEVEL 2

LEVEL 2

LEVEL 1

LEVEL 2

LEVEL 2

PANELS

SCREEN DESIGN

Dictionary for panel design optional

Dictionary Elements including field names and data values for simulation

LEVEL 3

LEVEL 3 PROTOTYPES INCLUDE DATA FOR DISPLAY

(PANEL BRANCHING INCLUDED IN LEVEL 3)

Develop Dictionary

LEVEL 4

LEVEL 4 PROTOTYPES INCLUDE DATA MODIFICATION WITHIN SIMULATIONS

(PANEL BRANCHING INCLUDED IN LEVEL 4)

FIGURE 22–30   **Four Levels of Visible Prototyper**

Reprinted by permission of Visible Systems Corporation, Waltham, Mass.

5. Panel flow report—a list of possible panels that can be displayed by branching from a particular panel
6. Dictionary report—a list of all database fields referenced in scenario panels

Visible Prototyper is only one example of a prototype generator. It is noteworthy because it can be used alone or with a full CASE product.

HUMAN ASPECTS

CASE is an acronym for computer-*aided* systems engineering. It will be a long time (if ever) before automated development tools replace system analysts or even programmers. Current tools are not comprehensive or precise enough to allow human replacement in this realm. Information systems typically are too complex to allow the structured definitions required for any computer to do it at all. Automated design is *not* about replacing or improving on the human analyst. Automated design is about helping the human analyst in those narrow areas where computers can perform better than humans. We will have more to say about this in the last chapter of this book.

SUMMARY

Until recently, systems analysts produced most of their designs with paper and pencil. The development of computer tools to aid them has been rapid.

The predominant automated development product has been computer-aided systems engineering (CASE)—a collection and integration of automated tools and procedures to aid the systems development process. Five types of components can be found, partially or completely, in CASE products: repository (data dictionary), reengineering, life cycle support, project support, and continuous quality improvement.

The repository, the axis of CASE, ties all other parts together. It holds definitions of screens, reports, forms, and information processes.

Reengineering is a synonym for systems maintenance. It combines reverse engineering and forward engineering, both of which involve a system's program code.

Life cycle support includes graphic aids for strategic planning, analysis, logical design, physical design, and construction. CASE products are differentiated by how they support the systems life cycle. Front-end (upper) CASE supports strategic planning, analysis, and logical design. Back-end (lower) CASE is design oriented; it supports the life cycle phases of physical design and construction. A CASE product that includes both front-end and back-end capabilities is called full life cycle. An integrated (ICASE) product adds the capabilities of reengineering and project support.

Visible Analyst WORKBENCH is one example of how a typical CASE product works. This product was used in a Florida Criminal Justice Information System and it illustrates how CASE works. To derive maximum benefits from CASE implementation, a firm should follow the guidelines recommended in this chapter.

In addition to CASE products, many applications generators are available. The generators address the need to develop applications quickly. Applications are systems with distinct boundaries and goals. The need for quick development stems from trends toward prototyping, end-user design, DSS/ES/MISs, and real rather than paper demonstration systems.

Another automated development aid is programming code generators. Sometimes these are part of a CASE product. Prototype generators are also automated development aids. They can be generated from applications generators (see Case 21.1). However, such prototypes are not as sophisticated as those generated by specialized prototype generators.

Two lessons emerge from CASE experience to date. The first is that CASE does not cure bad design. The second lesson is that CASE is more about quality than productivity. The key to successful use of CASE is realistic expectations.

CONCEPTS LEARNED

- Capabilities of automated systems development
- CASE components
- Role of the repository
- Reengineering
- CASE life cycle
- Difference between front-end, back-end, full life cycle, and integrated CASE
- SAA and AD/Cycle
- How to derive maximum benefits from CASE implementation
- Capabilities of 4GLs
- The role and examples of applications generators
- The role and examples of code generators
- The role and examples of prototype generators

KEY TERMS

application
Application Development/Cycle (AD/Cycle)
applications generator
back-end CASE
boilerplating
code generator
computer-aided systems engineering (CASE)
Customer Information Control System (CICS)
forward engineering
front-end CASE
full life cycle CASE

Information Engineering Facility (IEF)
integrated CASE (ICASE)
lower CASE
macro
prototype generator
reengineering
reusable code
reverse engineering
Systems Application Architecture (SAA)
upper CASE

REVIEW QUESTIONS

1. Describe goals of automated development aids.
2. Why have some suggested that the acronym CASE be changed to CASD?
3. Briefly describe each of the five components partially or completely found in CASE products.
4. What does the repository include?
5. What are the differences between reengineering, reverse engineering, and forward engineering?
6. Describe the stages of the CASE life cycle.

7. How does strategic planning differ from analysis in the CASE life cycle?

8. What are the three types of tools provided in the analysis stage of the CASE life cycle?

9. What is the difference between front-end and back-end CASE?

10. What is the difference between full life cycle and integrated CASE?

11. How does CASE enhance a design team environment?

12. What is boilerplating?

13. Explain the Visible Analyst nesting function—Treefile.

14. What are typical errors detected by Visible Rules?

15. Explain the following CASE guideline: Keep expectations realistic.

16. What is the expected ratio of CASE operational costs to initial costs?

17. Why do we need to build applications quickly?

18. Describe three characteristics of a 4GL.

19. What are applications generators?

20. What is screen painting?

21. In the dBASE III PLUS applications generator, explain how the option called "Modify application code" operates.

22. Give three reasons why it is difficult for 4GLs to generate third-generation language code.

23. Briefly describe the four levels of Visible Prototype.

CRITICAL THINKING OPPORTUNITIES

1. Draw a diagram of how this chapter is organized.

2. Compare and contrast CASE with 4GL. Why do CASE advocates think that CASE is 5GL?

3. Study a CASE product used at work or school.
   a) Is it front-end, back-end, full life cycle, or integrated?
   b) Describe aids provided for each of the CASE life cycle stages.
   c) Provide opinions about how the product could be improved to aid business systems development.

4. Refer to the Florida CJIS example in this chapter. An additional data dictionary (repository) entry from that system is shown below. Explain the meaning of this entry using Figures 22–13 through 22–24.

5. Use a CASE product to replicate Figure 22–13.

```
ARRESTEE Output        DATAFLOW
Composition:
        CRIMINAL REPORT AFFIDAVIT+
        PROPERTY INVENTORY CARD/RECEIPT+
        DEFENDANT OUTPUT
Location:
        CJIS CONTEXT DIAGRAM (CONTEXT)
        Source: CRIMINAL JUSTICE INFORMATION SYSTEM (PROCESS)
        Dest.: ARRESTEE (EXTERNAL ENTITY)
        CJIS DEPARTMENT BREAKDOWN (0)
        Source: SHERIFFS OFFICE (PROCESS)
        Dest.: Not on Diagram
```

C A S E   22.1

CLASS DESIGN PROJECT: CASE AND PROTOTYPING

SETTING

You are to convert your analysis and design specifications to prototype and CASE environments. While this part of the Class Design Project is described near the end of the book, it can be assigned by your instructor at any point in the semester. This is shown by Figure 22.1–1.

PROTOTYPING

Reference Case 9.2 Class Design Project:

Analysis Phase. Convert your preliminary design specifications into a level 1 prototype using a CASE tool or an application generator.

CASE

Reference Cases 9.2 and 17.2, Class Design Project: Design Phase. Convert these specifications to a CASE environment using an available CASE tool.

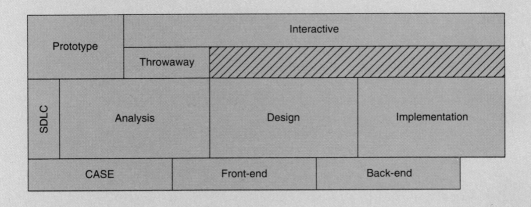

FIGURE 22.1–1   **Placement of Prototyping and CASE in System Development Life Cycle (SDLC)**

In this chapter you will learn about:

WHAT: (Concepts) Object-oriented approach to business systems development.

WHY: Object-oriented analysis and design (OOAD) promises to substantially reduce the time and costs of system development.

WHEN: OOAD encompasses (replaces) the conventional system development life cycle.

WHO: Systems analyst in conjunction with end-user community.

WHERE: Information systems department and end-user work area.

HOW: (Techniques) Object-oriented analysis
Object-oriented design

OUTLINE

- Setting
- A Structured Approach
- Objects
- Messages
- Classes
- Object-Oriented Development
- An Object-Oriented Approach to Mega Video
- Object-Oriented Differences
- Human Aspects

C H A P T E R **23**

OBJECT-ORIENTED ANALYSIS AND DESIGN

"I object to objects being treated so objectively."

— ANONYMOUS TRADITIONAL ANALYST

SETTING

There has been no more persistently nagging problem in our field than the **applications backlog.** This is the backlog of business applications waiting to be developed—to enter the systems development life cycle. It is estimated that the applications backlog for business in the United States may be as long as two-and-a-half to three years. Indeed, this may underestimate vastly the real applications backlog.

There is an unmeasurable but real **hidden applications backlog.** This includes applications where end-users refuse to join the line for applications waiting to be developed. They refuse to do so because the line is too long. This is similar to choosing not to see a movie in which you are interested because the line for the ticket window is a block long. The continued long length of the applications backlog, both visible and hidden, has given rise to the term **software development crisis.**

Advocates of structured development and CASE made early claims that their methodologies would cut substantially into this applications backlog. To date there is little evidence that either structured development or CASE has reduced significantly business system development times. Advocates seem now to be shifting to a position that these approaches are more about improving system quality than development speed. This author agrees.

It would seem that the key to decreasing significantly system development time is not to change HOW we develop. The key is to change WHAT we develop. Ideally, if we did not develop information systems at all, there would be no development time. Does this seem farfetched? It is not as crazy a statement as it appears to be. One of the causes of our long applications backlog is that we keep reinventing the wheel. We do not take enough advantage of work already done. Let us use COBOL as an example.

COBOL is the common business-oriented language predominately used in business applications. It was developed in the early 1960s. Since about 1980, detractors constantly have been crying that COBOL is a dead language—that it would soon be replaced by 4GL or other 3GL languages. Today COBOL still remains the most predominant programming language for business applications. There are two primary reasons for this. First COBOL is dynamic. New versions of the language give it new vitality. Second, there is a large amount of reusable COBOL code in the typical business firm. This allows applications to be programmed quickly using existing COBOL code, thus shortening programming time.

Currently, we design systems as if each one were totally distinguishable from all others. We rarely employ reusable systems specifications. Object-oriented analysis and design is about developing system modules that can be used over and over again. In this way (1) system development time ideally is reduced, and (2) the applications backlog is shortened. The primary goal of object-oriented analysis and design is to build reusable system modules much like a child's Leggo construction set.

OOAD represents a new way of thinking about business systems. In addition, no current charting technique or CASE product fully implements OOAD. Therefore, the material in this chapter is more conceptual—less technical—than other subjects discussed in this book. Nevertheless, most experts in business information systems agree that object-oriented analysis and design represents the future—the way we will be thinking about system development in the next century.

A STRUCTURED APPROACH

There is no doubt that, as OOAD is evolving, it will be a highly structured approach. OOAD represents, however, a drastic departure from current structured development approaches. There are two such current approaches—one process directed and the other data directed.

In the process-directed approach, attention is focused on system processes. These processes are also referred to as tasks, procedures, or decisions. A process decomposition diagram such as the hierarchy chart is used to explode the system into successfully refined data flow diagrams. This results in primitive level processes so well defined that they can easily be converted to programming code. A data dictionary is produced that describes all detail system processes along with all data entities feeding into and emanating from the processes.

In this data dictionary, data and processes are treated separately, much as COBOL does with its separated DATA DIVISION and PROCEDURE DIVISION. There is minimal linking between (a) one process and another, and (b) data and processes. In addition, each data element and structure is described only once, even though it may be applicable to several processes. This makes for efficient storage, but requires a complex, difficult-to-modify linkage between data and processes.

The data-directed approach proceeds in a similar manner. The primary difference between this and the process-directed approach is that the data approach uses the entity-relationship diagram for successive refinement. Emphasis is on data flows and data stores, here called entities, rather than the processes that manipulate that data. The resulting data dictionary is, hopefully, the same although it has been arrived at by a different path. There still exists the complex linkage between data and process.

Object-oriented analysis and design represents a high-level, philosophical trade-off between autonomy (independence) and efficiency. For example, rather than several processes sharing the same, single data specification, each process controls its own version of the data. This makes the processes more independent of each other. There is data redundancy here, but it is planned redundancy. Recall from Chapter 2 that planned redundancy is a desired system quality.

One analogy is that in Office A, there is one central appointment calendar on one workstation for all 15 salespersons. This is an efficient system because there are no duplicate entries. A meeting of six of the salespeople will only require one master entry. However, if the computer containing the master calendar is not operating, the entire office suffers. Moreover, addition of a new salesperson or deletion of a current salesperson will require system changes that will have a temporary effect upon all salespeople. Office A scheduling is analogous to traditional structured programming.

Office B, on the other hand, has a scheduling system whereby salespeople independently keep track of their individual calendars on their individual workstations. There is redundancy here. The meeting of the six salespeople will require six separate entries as opposed to only one in Office A. A LAN in Office B allows retrieval of individual calendars to create a master calendar. Despite its redundancy, Office B's system is more flexible. Addition or deletion of salespersons has no effect on continuing salespersons since their individual calendars are independent of each other.

In addition, these individual calendars are portable. Stan Taylor, one of Office B's salespeople, has just been reassigned to Office C. He can take his calendar with him to his new office. This might be termed *reusable calendaring*. Office B's calendaring approach is more analogous to an object-oriented system.

Essentially, OOAD represents a trade-off. System independence is gained at the cost of storage and processing efficiency. The result, however, are system units which (1) are less affected by system change, and (2) are reusable across a wide range of business applications. A structured approach remains, but it travels a far different path than does either current process or data-focused approaches.

OBJECTS

Object technology consists of three keys: objects, messages, and classes. The building block is the object. An **object** is a basic system element that combines data and processes to perform a unique system function. In an information system, the object is roughly equivalent to a software subprogram. The data elements within an object are called **variables;** the processes are called **methods.**

Both variables (data) and methods (processes) are embedded in the object. **Embedding** is the inclusion and protection of *all* variables and methods pertinent to the object. Figure 23–1 provides an example. The inventory object can be characterized as a shell where the method surrounds and protects the data. Objects are accessed by other objects only through methods. Objects do not interfere with data for other objects. In Figure 23–1, another object (subprogram) may "call" the inventory object by requesting the Inventory Report method. The data to be used by the Inventory Report is embedded within the object; the data is unavailable to the calling program.

This concept is called **information hiding,** the keeping of embedded object information away from access by other objects. Suppose you wish to change what data will be included in the Inventory Report. You can do so without affecting any other part (object) of the software system. You will not have to recode or retest any other software module *except* the inventory object module. This makes the inventory object independent of all other objects. Object (subprogram) autonomy is the key to understanding object methodology.

Identifying Objects: An object is something we wish to keep information about and interact with. In a data flow diagram, for example, we keep information about data flows and data stores. We also interact with external entities. In the DFD of Figure 23–2, for example, customer orders and picking slips can be considered system objects. Inventory is also an object. Finally, the Customer and Inventory Section are objects.

FIGURE 23–1   **Object Structure**

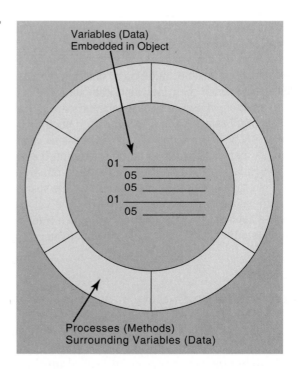

Variables (Data)
Embedded in Object

01 _____
05 _____
05 _____
01 _____
05 _____

Processes (Methods)
Surrounding Variables (Data)

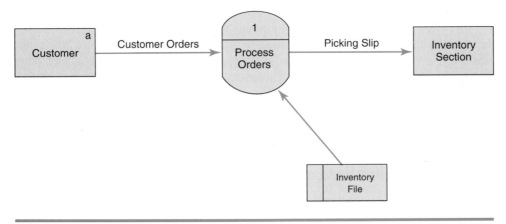

The five objects in this section have two common characteristics (1) each can be described by multiple data elements (fields), and (2) each is subject to certain processes (methods) such as adding, updating, deleting, and reporting. These each can become an object with data embedded within methods. Finally, note that for the DFD of Figure 23−2, processes are not objects; they are instead the methods that will be embedded around the data objects. This is illustrated in Figure 23−3.

FIGURE 23−3   **Purchase Order Object**

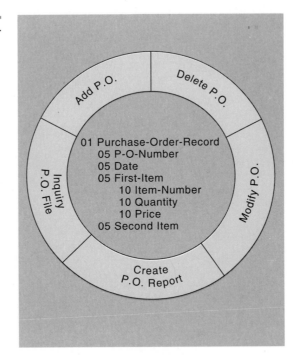

An object contains all the data that it needs to function. The data is surrounded by the methods (procedures) that will be used to manipulate the data. In Figure 23–3, for example, the embedded data are all the fields describing the purchase order object. The surrounding methods are the information functions that need to be performed on the data.

Relationship of Objects to Other Objects: Objects do not contain other objects. Instead, they refer to other objects through variables that contain the addresses of these objects. This is shown in Figure 23–4. Here the Shipping Document object refers to a particular Inventory Item object and to a specific Customer object. However, that same Customer object also can be referred to by another Shipping Document object.

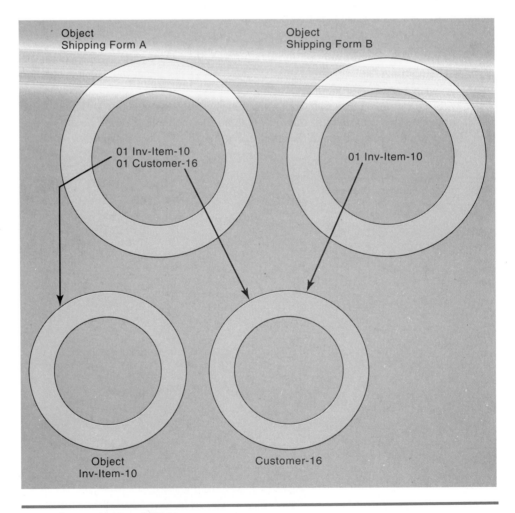

FIGURE 23–4   **Linking of Objects**

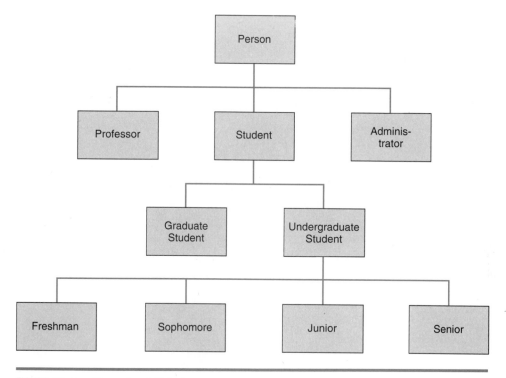

FIGURE 23–5   **Hierarchy of Objects**

There are several advantages to this method of relationship.

1. The referenced (called) object can change in size and composition without affecting the referencing (calling) object.
2. The referenced (called) object can participate in any number of referencing (calling) objects. This allows development of modules of reusable code.
3. A hierarchy of objects can be established (Figure 23–5). This allows us to implement the concept of inheritance described later in this chapter.

MESSAGES

Objects request services of other objects, just as main programs call subprograms. The object requesting services is the **sender.** The object performing the services is the **receiver.** The **message** sent has three parts.

1. identity of the receiver (e.g., subprogram name)
2. method (procedures) the receiver is to carry out (e.g., print report)
3. special information the receiver may need **(parameters)**

Figure 23–6 illustrates a message sent to a Customer Billing object.

There are several benefits to this message structure in object-oriented methodology.

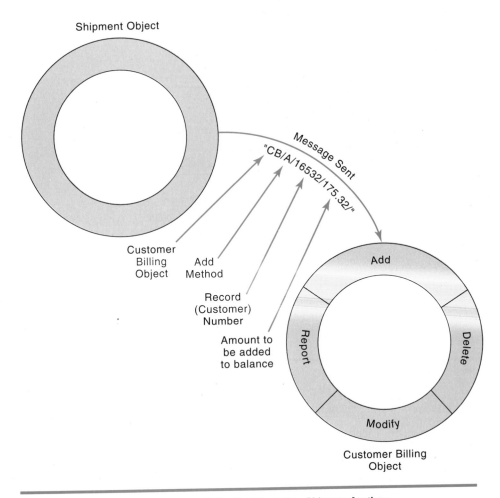

FIGURE 23–6   **Example of a Message Being Sent from One Object to Another**

- Object internal structures are protected from outside intrusion and inadvertent change.
- No other objects have to contain information about the structure of a called (receiver) object.
- It is easy to modify objects without affecting other objects.

This message structure allows use of polymorphism. **Polymorphism** is use of the same name for different methods in different objects. For example, the name ADD can be used to describe a method in a Purchase Order object and in an Inventory object. The ADD name would result in different procedures being executed depending on the object to which a message is sent.

CLASSES

Objects are grouped into classes. Figure 23–7 shows a class structure for Vehicles. Each lower level object of this class structure is an **incident** of the Vehicle class. The Piper Cub object inherits all the characteristics of the Small Plane object which inherited all the characteristics of the Airplane and Vehicle objects. All we need add in the Piper Cub object are those characteristics *unique* to this type of small airplane. **Inheritance** is the assumption of data from objects higher in the same class.

Inheritance proceeds as shown in Figure 23–8. Each object contains local data and variables that point to parent objects from which data can be inherited. Inheritance is a familiar concept when using subprograms in application programs. This is described in the box entitled "Inheritance in COBOL."

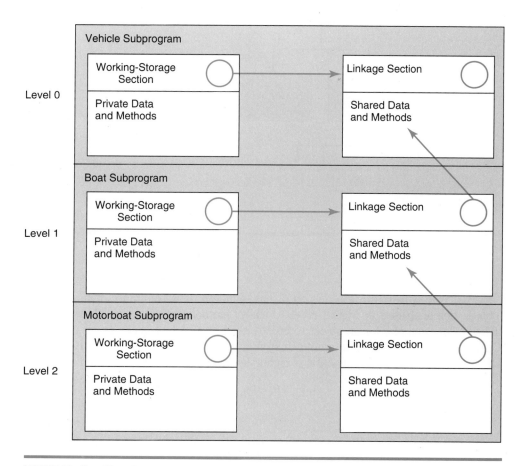

FIGURE 23–7   **Class Structure for Vehicles**

Adapted from E. Turbin, *Expert Systems and Applied Artificial Intelligence* (New York: Macmillan Publishing Company, 1992).

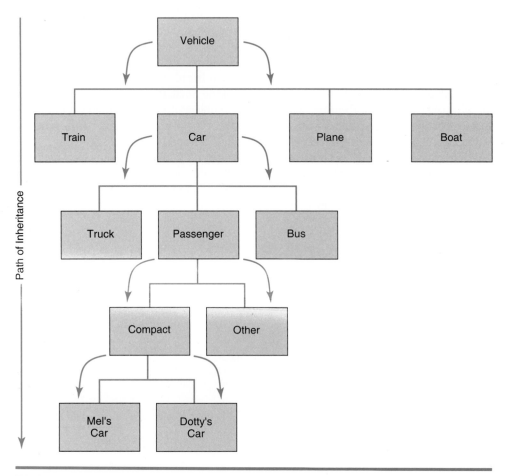

FIGURE 23–8   **Inheritance**

Multiple inheritance allows an object to inherit data from more than one class. This is demonstrated in Figure 23–9. Finally, methods can also be inherited. It is difficult, for example, for an object to create itself or to delete itself. To create a new Customer object or to delete an old Customer object requires that the CREATE and DELETE methods be contained in a higher level object. This is illustrated in Figure 23–10.

FIGURE 23–9 **Multiple Inheritance**

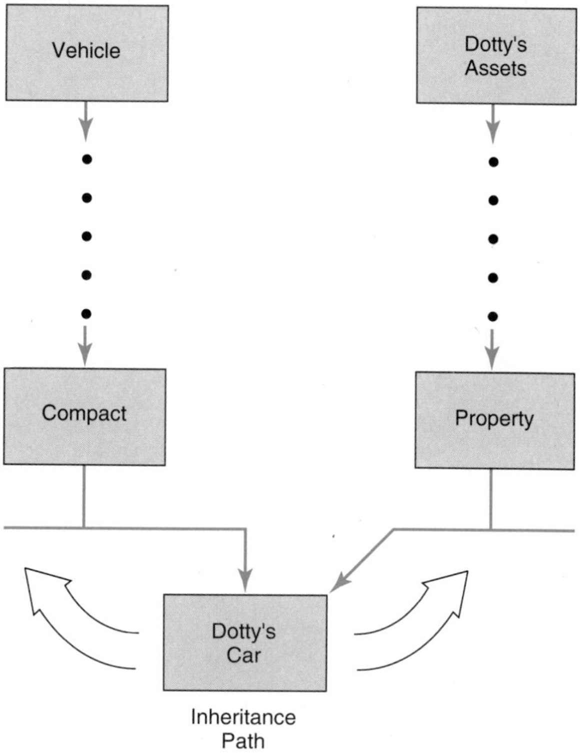

Vehicle

Dotty's
Assets

Compact

Property

Dotty's
Car

Inheritance
Path

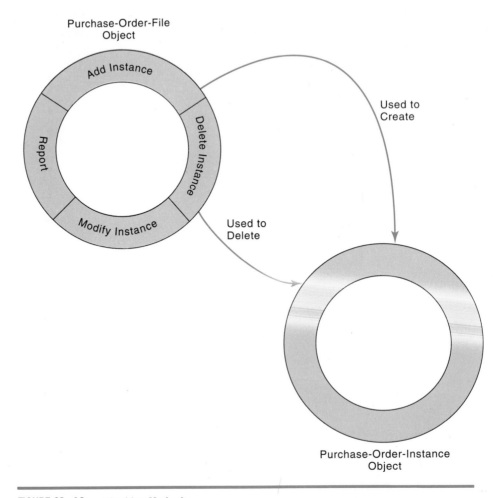

Purchase-Order-File
Object

Add Instance

Delete Instance

Report

Modify Instance

Used to
Create

Used to
Delete

Purchase-Order-Instance
Object

FIGURE 23–10   **Inheriting Methods**

INHERITANCE IN COBOL

In a COBOL subprogram, local data is contained in the WORKING-STORAGE SEC-TION of the subprogram. Data contained in this section is not available to (shared by) the calling program. Data passed by the calling program and shared by the subprogram is shown in the LINKAGE SECTION of the subprogram. The structure of the subprogram then becomes

```
DATA DIVISION.
WORKING-STORAGE SECTION.
     (local data)
LINKAGE SECTION.
     (inherited data)
PROCEDURE DIVISION USING (list of inherited data).
```

In a nested subprogram organization, the calling COBOL program would use a GLOBAL modifier for data to be shared, such as:

```
01 INVENTORY-RECORD IS GLOBAL.
```

In this case the subprogram would need no LINKAGE SECTION or USING statement. The GLOBAL data would be automatically inherited.

OBJECT-ORIENTED DEVELOPMENT

Development of object-oriented systems comprises **object-oriented analysis (OOA)** and **object-oriented design (OOD).** The specific steps within each one of these phases is adapted from Norman (1991).

Object-oriented Systems Analysis (OOA): This stage is done in five steps.

1. Determine objects and classes.
2. Identify class and object structures (inheritance paths).
3. Define object variables (attributes). These can be placed in an object diagram such as that shown in Figure 23–11.
4. Define object connections. This is done in a way similar to an entity-relationship diagram. One example is shown in Figure 23–12.
5. Define services (methods). These can be described using a diagram such as that shown in Figure 23–13.

The resulting OOA model can be used for building a rapid prototype of the problem domain. The OOA model also feeds into object-oriented design (OOD) described next.

FIGURE 23—11   **Recording Object Attributes**

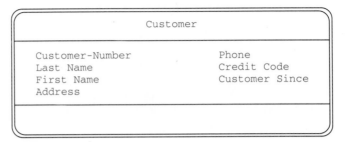

```
                        Customer

    Customer-Number            Phone
    Last Name                  Credit Code
    First Name                 Customer Since
    Address
```

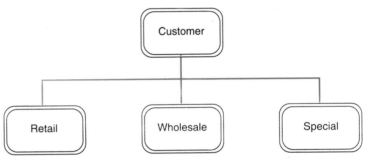

a. Generalization = Specializaton

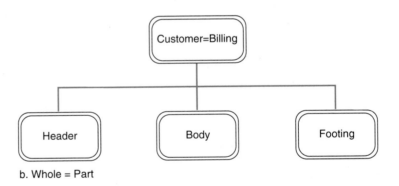

b. Whole = Part

FIGURE 23—13   **Defining Services (Object Methods)**

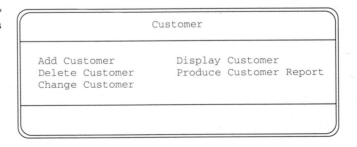

```
                        Customer

    Add Customer            Display Customer
    Delete Customer         Produce Customer Report
    Change Customer
```

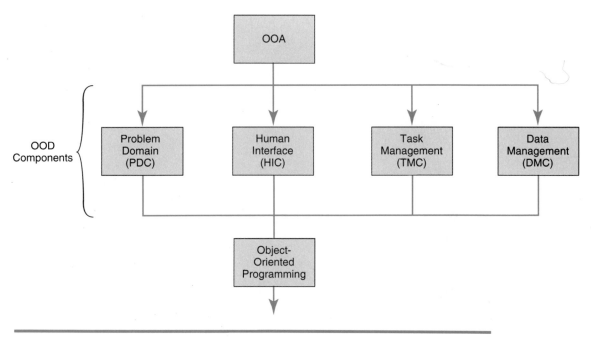

FIGURE 23–14 **Building Object-Oriented Design (OOD) on Object-Oriented Analysis (OOA)**

Object-oriented System Design (OOD): OOD builds upon the OOA model (see Figure 23–14) by adding the following components:

1. **Problem domain component (PDC):** This allows addition of specific criteria dealing with (a) existing reusable code, (b) application programming language to be used, (c) special user requirements not identified in the OOA phase.
2. **Human interactive component (HIC):** This primarily addresses interactive screen and other interface requirements.
3. **Task management component (TMC):** This component deals with external systems or devices. For example, it may deal with protocol interfaces in a telecommunication network.
4. **Data management component (DMC):** This provides protocol for storage, retrieval, and updating of objects within the database.

   Notice that OOD builds around OOA. There is no change in documentation medium or methodology when moving from analysis to design. The process just described is illustrated briefly using the Mega Video system described in Case 6.1.

AN OBJECT-ORIENTED APPROACH TO MEGA VIDEO

Figure 23–15 is an entity-relationship diagram (ERD) for the Mega Video system. It is easier to approach object-oriented methodologies from a data-oriented rather than a process-oriented perspective. Hence, the ERD is used instead of a data flow diagram.

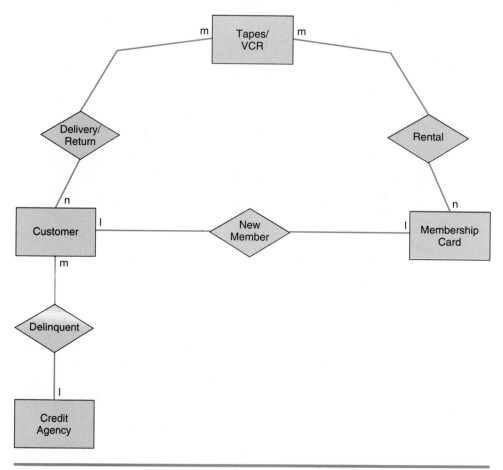

FIGURE 23–15   **Entity-Relationship Diagram (ERD) for Mega Video**

Object-oriented Analysis (OOA): Five steps are involved:

1. Determine objects and classes. The four objects shown here are the Customer, Credit Agencies, Membership Card, and Tapes/VCRs.
2. Identify class and object structures. Figures 23–16a, b, and c show class and object structures for the three classes of Credit Agency, Membership Card, and Rental Product. This latter class is a generalizable class which comprises tapes and VCRs.
3. Define object variables (attributes). Figure 23–17 shows this definition for the Customer object.
4. Define object connections. This is the ERD of Figure 23–15.
5. Define services (methods). Figure 23–18 shows what this will look like for the Rental Tape object.

Figures 23–17 and 23–18 would be done for all identified objects. At this point, (1) all objects have been identified, (2) these objects have been structured into classes to facilitate inheritance, (3) the objects have been related to each other, (4) all attributes

FIGURE 23–16 **Mega Video Object Structures**

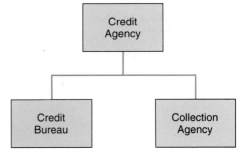

a. Credit Agency Object Structure

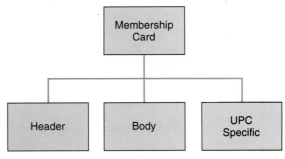

b. Membership Card Object Structure

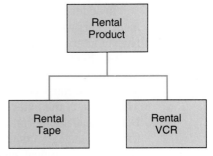

c. Rental Product Object Structure

FIGURE 23–17 **Attributes for Mega Video Customer Object**

```
                        Customer

   Customer-Number        Phone Number
   Last Name              Arrears Balance
   First Name             Arrears Status
   Address                Customer Since Date
```

FIGURE 23−18 **Services for Mega Video Rental Tape Object**

```
                        Rental Tape

    Add to Stock            Display Status
    Delete from Stock       Produce Outstanding Report
    Add to Backorder        Produce Usage Report


```

have been identified for each object, and (5) all methods (procedures) have been identified for each object. We now have a full object-oriented model of the Mega Video system. It is time to augment that model with the implementation means (the HOWs) required to make this an operational information system. This is done in the OOD phase.

Object-oriented Design (OOD): Four components are built here:

1. Problem domain component (PDC). Here we identify specific criteria. For example, we may decide to use the local Credit Bureau's delinquent processing system, which is available via modem for a monthly usage fee. This means we would not have to automate the Credit Agency object. (This is, in a sense, reusable code, since we will be using programs that already have been developed.)

    In addition, we may decide to use a microcomputer and laser-scanning environment. This would limit the automation options (e.g., languages) we can employ.
2. Human interactive component (HIC). Each object will be entered via an interactive screen. Figure 23−19 is the interactive screen for accessing the Customer object.
3. Task management component (TMC). In order to interface with the Credit Bureau system, we must define how to use the appropriate telecommunications network. This is one of the external interface specifications to be developed within the TMC.
4. Data management component (DMC). The Customer, Rental, Membership and Credit Agency objects will require database storage, retrieval and update. The DMC includes the protocol specification for this access.

Note OOD does not change the OOA model; it only specifies in more detail this model. There is complete compatibility of methodology when moving from analysis to design in an object-oriented approach.

Object-oriented Programming: The above specifications can then be translated into computer code using an object-oriented language such as C++. It is anticipated that there will soon be a new release of ANSI COBOL which will allow an object-oriented approach to be used in conjunction with that language.

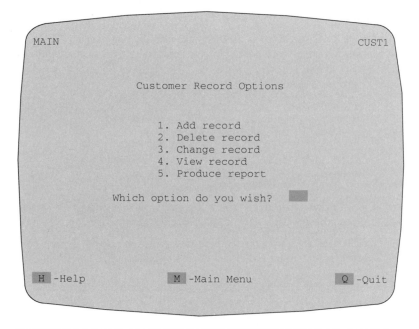

```
MAIN                                          CUST1


                Customer Record Options


                    1. Add record
                    2. Delete record
                    3. Change record
                    4. View record
                    5. Produce report

            Which option do you wish?   ▢



  H -Help            M -Main Menu            Q -Quit
```

FIGURE 23–19   Interactive Screen for Accessing Mega Video Customer Object

OBJECT-ORIENTED COBOL?

Object-oriented programming is implemented through the concept of a frame. A **frame** is a data structure that includes all knowledge about an object. It is similar to 01 record description in COBOL. A frame includes slots and facets. A **slot** is an attribute that describes the object represented by a frame. In COBOL terms, it is a 05 entry for a field comprising part of the 01 record. A COBOL "slot" for a Customer object might look like this:

```
01 CUSTOMER-OBJECT-RECORD            (frame)
      05 CUST-ID-NO-SLOT             (slot)
      05 CUST-NAME-SLOT              (slot)
      05 CUST-BALANCE-SLOT           (slot)
```

Each slot contains one or more facets. A **facet** describes data or procedures relating to the attribute (field) occupying the slot. Regard the following COBOL field description:

```
05 CUST-ID-NO-SLOT         PIC 9(5).
```

Here the slot contains the attribute which is the customer identification number. The PIC specification contains two facets: (a) the field is numeric, and (b) the field is five characters long.

Facets can take many forms, including the following:

- Values (e.g., initialize counter to 0)
- Default (what value to assume when none is entered for a transaction)
- Range of Values Allowable (e.g., 1 through 12 for Month slot)
- Field Size
- Field Type

Facets can also include methods. Two examples follow:

- If Added—actions to be taken when this is a new item (e.g., new customer)
- If Needed—how to compute a value if none is given (e.g., rate of pay)

COBOL'S DATA DIVISION is already comprised of frames, slots, and facets. Object-oriented COBOL is merely an extension and facilitation of its current frame structure.

OBJECT-ORIENTED DIFFERENCES

There is an old adage in the systems field. "When you gain, you lose. When you lose, you gain." This adage stresses that there never is a perfect choice. The best choice is that where the advantages more clearly outdistance the disadvantages. So it is with object-oriented analysis and design. There are several advantages and disadvantages associated with this methodology.

Advantages:

1. OOD handles *complexity,* including any kind of data—even multimedia.
2. It provides *flexibility* because objects have hidden data and methods. This allows adding, deleting, and modifying an object with minimum interference with other objects. (You can replace a spark plug in an engine without opening up the engine.)
3. It increases *responsiveness.* Autonomous objects lead to reusable module code. This means faster development of new applications since new programming is minimized. (Think of how you used to build things with Leggos.)
4. OOD enhances *quality.*
   a) It leads to *absence of defects* since it maximizes reusability of proven, reliable (already tested) software components.
   b) It provides *fitness of purpose* since applications are developed faster; this means the final system is closer to the initial (but changing) needs of end-users.
   c) It increases *usability,* since it encompasses a broader range of user needs including graphic interfaces, multimedia, etc.

Disadvantages:

1. An object-oriented approach to systems development is more closely aligned with data modeling than process modeling. This makes the learning curve even steeper for firms using a process modeling approach.
2. There is not yet much tool (CASE) support for OOD. Most current CASE tools do not group attributes in the Data Dictionary by objects. This can be done by allowing designers to construct Views of the Data Dictionary, much as users construct Views of integrated databases (Figure 23–20).

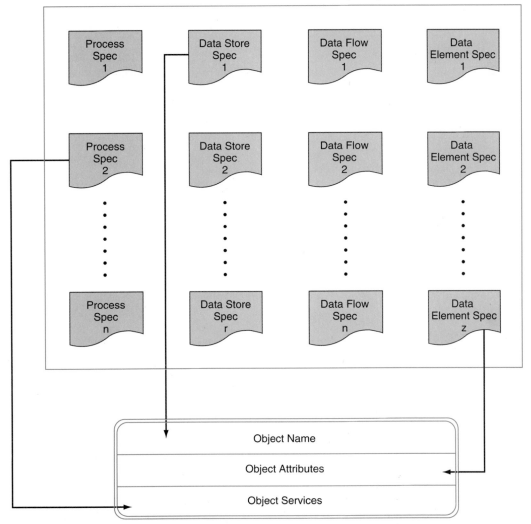

FIGURE 23–20   **Using a VIEW of the CASE Data Dictionary to Build an Object Description**

3. It is estimated that only some 25 percent of firms are using structured development approaches. Therefore, OOD represents a new revolution that must leapfrog another revolution that arguably has not taken hold yet.

4. It would not seem advisable for a firm to jump to OOD before becoming proficient with a structured development approach, preferably one stressing data modeling. You may recall that the same warning was issued for the use of CASE.

5. OOD concepts represent a new way of thinking for system specialists. Some question whether this approach will enhance or erode communication with end-users, particularly in the systems analysis phase of the SDLC. This point is stressed in the next section of this chapter.

HUMAN ASPECTS

This book has consistently stressed that a system developed without meaningful and continuous end-user involvement is a system doomed to ineffectiveness or failure. The primary purpose of Gane and Sarson's development of the Data Flow Diagram was to enhance communication between analyst and user. Enhancements to structured development methodologies arguably have deteriorated rather than enhanced analyst/user communication. CASE technology largely has been directed to technical specialists, rather than nontechnical end-users. Object-oriented methodologies do not promise to present a view of information systems that is compatible with the way typical end-users think. However, OOD's stress on rapid prototyping may well make this methodology more end-user oriented than typical structured development/CASE approaches.

Nevertheless, it is you—the systems analyst—that must be the interpreter between increasingly technical, engineering approaches to systems development and the largely nontechnical end-users of our information systems. Never forget the human aspects of the information system you are developing. You are the last hope for developing human information systems.

SUMMARY

Object-oriented Analysis and Design (OOAD) is designed to reduce the current application backlog. It attempts to do so by stressing use of predesigned, reusable modules of code. The basic element of OOAD is the object which combines data and processes (methods) to perform a unique system function.

Each object includes and protects all the data and processes it needs to perform its function. This is called embedding or encapsulation. Other objects can only deal with any one object by sending messages. Objects are grouped into classes from which they can borrow data and methods. This is called inheritance. An object can borrow data and methods from more than one parent (multiple inheritance).

Object-oriented analysis (OOA) entails five steps: (a) determine objects and classes, (b) identify class and object structures, (c) define object variables (attributes), (d) define object connections, and (e) define services.

Object-oriented design (OOD) builds on OOA by adding the components of (a) problem domain component (PDC), (b) human interactive component (HIC), (c) task management component (TMC), and (d) data management component (DMC). As with any new methodology, OOAD has advantages and disadvantages. It is clear that systems analysts employing the OOAD approach must be quite careful about retaining sufficient communication with the ultimate information system users.

CONCEPTS LEARNED

- Why the need for OOAD
- What an object is
- What a message is
- What a class is
- Steps in object-oriented analysis
- Steps in object-oriented design
- Advantages and disadvantages of OOAD

KEY TERMS

applications backlog
data management component (DMC)
embedding
facet
frame
hidden applications backlog
human interactive component (HIC)
incident
information hiding
inheritance
message
method
multiple inheritance

object
object-oriented analysis (OOA)
object-oriented design (OOD)
parameters
polymorphism
problem domain component (PDC)
receiver
sender
slot
software development crisis
task management component (TMC)
variables

REVIEW QUESTIONS

1. What is the software development crisis?

2. Define an object.

3. What are the differences between variables and methods?

4. Describe object embedding.

5. What is meant by information hiding?

6. How would you identify system objects?

7. How do objects relate to other objects?

8. What are the components of an object?

9. Describe polymorphism.

10. Describe inheritance; multiinheritance.

11. Describe the five steps of OOA.

12. What does the PDC do?

13. What does the HIC do?

14. What does the TMC do?

15. What does the DMC do?

16. What are the advantages of OOAD?

17. List the disadvantages of OOAD.

CRITICAL THINKING OPPORTUNITIES

1. Draw a diagram of how this chapter is organized.

2. Compare and contrast structured development with OOAD.

3. Reference Case 6.1, Mega Video: Structured Tools and the SDLC.

a) Determine all objects and classes.

b) Identify class and object structures.

c) Define object connectors by constructing an ERD.

d) Define object services (methods).

OBJECTIVES

In this chapter you will learn about:

WHAT: (Concepts) Future possibilities for systems development of business applications.

WHY: We and our systems must be adaptive to whatever future prevails.

WHEN: The future.

WHO: Systems analysts and end-user community.

WHERE: Information systems department and end-user work areas.

HOW: (Techniques) Who knows what techniques the future holds?

OUTLINE

- Setting
- A Total Quality Approach
- A Structured Approach
- System Development—Art or Robotics?
- Forces Driving the Future
- Three Scenarios of the Future
- The Systems Analyst as a Change Agent
- The Ethics of Information Systems
- Human Aspects

THE FUTURE

Daddy, what did you do during the computer revolution?

— BEN SHNEIDERMAN (1993)

SETTING

How does one forecast the future on a subject so intertwined with technology? It is said that the best long-range forecasters are those who die or leave the country before the year that they have forecast. This author has no plans to do either.

There are two keys to what follows in this chapter. The first is that no single view of the future of systems development is offered. Instead, alternate views (scenarios) of this future are presented. These are three paths on which this discipline may proceed— three paths in three different directions.

Second, the concern here is with the semantic rather than the syntactic. Recall that semantic knowledge is concerned with WHAT is being done. Syntactic knowledge, on the other hand, deals with HOW things are done. Specific computer hardware and software are examples of syntactic knowledge. It is difficult enough to predict WHAT systems analysts will be doing in the future (semantics). It is next to impossible to predict HOW (technology) changes, but the WHAT (methodology) is more permanent.

The one thing we can predict is that things will change. Therefore, the emphasis in this chapter is on anticipating, detecting, and managing change in business organizations in general, and in information system development in particular. The systems analyst must be an effective change agent. That is the only predictable way that our discipline will ride the waves of technology, rather than being drowned in its backwash.

A TOTAL QUALITY APPROACH

Whichever path system development takes, you can be sure that the path will emphasize total quality management (TQM). We have discovered that information system development is more about quality assurance than about development speed and costs. This lesson will not be unlearned. Another lesson we have learned is that the "trust me" days of business system development are gone. We must prove to our end-users that our information systems are operating effectively. This means that we must measure our system output and processes. Measurement is the underlying framework of TQM. Quality measurement systems, as described in Chapter 19, will become the framework of future business information systems.

A STRUCTURED APPROACH

A structured approach to business systems development means that everything required is done, and that nothing that is not required is done. Structured methodologies are systematic, top-down approaches that successively refine information problems into smaller and smaller chunks. The final chunks are the primitive level where they can be translated readily into specific programming language code. Structured approaches are necessary to ensure quality of information systems.

What specific structured approaches will be used? Process driven or data driven? OOAD? CASE driven? End-user driven? The answer is that all these approaches and more will play a role in the future. The relative mix of these approaches is uncertain, but the presence of these and various other approaches in some format is almost certain.

What also seems certain is that the early, artistic stage of system development is over. We must now be information engineers. Our artistic needs must be sacrificed to the overall good of the business firm. That overall good cries for predictable, easy-to-modify consistency, rather than creative flair. Structured development approaches lead us into engineering dependable information systems.

SYSTEM DEVELOPMENT—ART OR ROBOTICS

Forecasting the future of business systems development relies principally on the different capabilities of humans and computers. Any attempt to replace one with another will be fruitless unless we recognize that each has capabilities unmatched by the other. Render unto the computer what it does better than humans. Render unto humans everything else. Let us look then at differences in computer and human processing capabilities.

Computer Processing Capabilities

Computers are more effective than humans in several ways:

- Handling large volumes of complex data (remember Miller's 7 ± 2 rule)
- Sifting through such data and signaling for human intervention when unusual patterns arise
- Detecting signals in situations where unaided human observers detect only noise

Noise is data that show no detectable pattern. Keffler Lumber Company has shown a stable sales volume over the past four years. Computer analysis shows, however, that one large customer has significantly increased its purchases. All other Keffler customers have decreased their purchases. Increased sales from one large customer have hidden the state of general sales decrease. The sales increase by a single customer has been noise that prevents detecting overall sales patterns.

Humans have severe perceptual limitations. A relatively moderate volume of data received can create an information overload. New data then becomes noise that obscures important data problems. Computers do not share such perceptual limitations. Hence, they are more effective than humans in dealing with volumes of data. If we can free humans from these perceptual barriers, however, the computer suffers by comparison.

Human Processing Capabilities

Humans are more effective than computers in several information-processing capabilities:

- **Induction:** Humans can act on inconsistently formatted data to fill in gaps, recognize emerging patterns, and decipher trends. The human analyst is like the human detective: They both "smell" something in the data before them, although whatever it is does not show in the computer analysis.

  For example, during the requirements analysis phase of the SDLC, an analyst may note that clerks in one office often gather at the desks of either clerk A or clerk B. Those gathering at clerk A's desk never visit clerk B, and vice versa. Although this observation does not fit within any structured development methodology, it suggests to the analyst that there may be political dissension in this office. Such dissension would be an important barrier to arriving at a consensus about an information system and reducing clerical resistance to a new system.

- **Insight** (creativity): Humans are adept at using their inductive processes for creating alternatives to solving problems. Computers are not very good at generating alternatives. Why not? A problem-solving alternative is merely a combination of resources. A sales manager combines salesperson A with product X in sales territory Z to increase market share. More appropriately, a systems designer combines a unit product code with optical scanning technology and places it at a grocery counter. Voila! The computerized grocery checkout stand is born.

  Why is it so difficult for a computer to devise such unique combinations? Take the chessboard. There is a finite number of possible combinations of moves that a player can make. Yet, it is estimated that if the largest Cray computer had started searching the list of combinations at the beginning of the universe, the Cray computer would not be finished today. There are just too many combinations.

  Yet, the human mind can focus on a narrow but powerful subset of alternatives and then list the remaining possibilities. The feat is much like parachuting out of an aircraft into foggy San Francisco and landing within a few blocks of where you want to be. The magic of the human mind has not yet been explained.

■ **Adaptiveness:** Humans can adjust quickly to new and changing situations. Computers cannot adapt unless programmed by humans to do so.

In summary, humans have three information-processing capabilities not yet shared by computers. The first is induction, the ability to guess or reach a conclusion before all the data are in. The second is insight, or creativity, which allows generation of unique alternatives to solve information problems. The third capability is adaptivity; it allows humans to apply the first two capabilities to changing conditions. These capabilities do not yet exist in a meaningful manner in computers.

Automated Tools in Perspective

CASE and other automated tools cannot be used alone to design complex business information systems. Such design requires *insight* and *creativity,* both human rather than machine characteristics. Design of business systems requires zeroing in on a few potential information system alternatives.

In addition, design of business information systems requires a feel for the politics of system compromise and implementation. This is pure *induction.* Finally, nothing changes as fast as the business environment. If we design our systems for today, they will be obsolete when we implement them tomorrow. Design of business information systems requires an *adaptive* mindset. Adaptability, too, is a human rather than machine trait.

Then what role can computer-aided design assume? There are four ways computers can help analysts to design business information systems.

1. Computers reduce tedious tasks. The Visible Analyst WORKBENCH (VAW), for example, performs cross-checking that the analyst could do manually instead. However, the rigor and repetitiveness of this cross-checking would bore, tire, and distract most analysts, and errors would result.

2. Computers reduce requirements for human memory. Severe but natural limitations are characteristic of human perceptual ability. This is particularly true for short-term memory. In the VAW, the Visible Dictionary allows immediate storage of analyst tasks and observations. It becomes a surrogate analyst memory.

3. Computers enhance communication. Through central storage and telecommunications, the computer can enhance and make consistent communication between individual members of design teams. As an example, consider the central repository of Visible Dictionary. Local area network capabilities of products such as VAW are also relevant.

4. Computers reduce noise (validate). When combinations of conditions become complex, humans reach a condition of information overload. Computers can cut through the noise and point out the problem at hand.

It seems clear that computer technology will not replace the human in the near future, particularly not in the arena of business information system development. Nevertheless, there are forces that are rapidly changing. These forces will drive the field of systems development. They will change what systems analysts are, and how they go about designing business information systems.

FORCES DRIVING THE FUTURE

Eight driving forces are discussed briefly in this section: (1) hardware, (2) languages, (3) artificial intelligence, (4) end-user computing, (5) user interfaces, (6) structured methodologies, (7) automated design tools, and (8) society.

Hardware

Hardware costs continue to decrease at an exponential rate. Storage media continues to provide business users with greater capacity and quicker access speeds. Still, it is unclear whether the typical business end-user is trained and sufficiently conditioned to handle today's speeds and capacities. It may well be that technology may have to slow a little to allow human beings to catch up and to catch their breaths. This author remains unconvinced that most business people ever mastered 286 technology. How will we deal with more advanced technologies that seem to be evolving at the speed of light?

It is possible that we will see hardware advances become more functionally organized. It is difficult to justify increasing memory capacity just to show that we can do so. It is certainly justifiable to increase memory capacity for a specific purpose. Such a purpose might be use of multimedia methodologies, or video disk media.

Languages

Fifth-generation languages (5GL) and beyond will bring computer control closer to the natural realm of nontechnically trained end-users. This will include increased use of voice and optical scanning. Keyboarding will be deemphasized, but probably will not disappear. (Remember those windmills still operating outside San Jose, California.)

We will enter an era of programmerless programming. CASE–type software will automatically generate and revise the code required to operate business information applications. Human programmers will not disappear, but more and more system expertise will be focused on analysis of problems. We will have more systems architects, because the construction of the application system will be largely automatic. The future emphasis will be on object-oriented analysis and design (OOAD).

Artificial Intelligence

As more emphasis is placed on system architects rather than system construction workers, expert systems will be developed to aid the developer in the qualitative nature of analysis. This will include, but certainly not be limited to, alternative generation, user opinion consolidation, forecasting of system problems, and end-user training. In addition, heuristic models will be developed to adapt ES development models based upon past failures and successes. More and more, artificial intelligence methodologies such as Fuzzy Logic will be used to allow computers to handle non-numeric system design decisions. (See box on "Fuzzy Logic.")

End-user Computing

The advent of 5GL will bring system development more within the capabilities and interests of nontechnically trained end-users. There will be little end-user tolerance remaining for information system departments that produce late, low-quality systems that are not responsive to end-users' needs. Professional systems development will have competition and must improve accordingly. The systems analyst may become increasingly an end-user development consultant, rather than the one primarily responsible for systems development.

User Interfaces

More emphasis will be placed on the interfaces between information system programs and application users of these programs. Interactive screens, multimedia, and interfaces adaptive to different users will be stressed. **User Interface Management Systems (UIMS)** will allow analysts to use preestablished interface protocols. This is currently how technical interfaces with input/output peripherals are handled.

FUZZY LOGIC

Fuzzy set logic is an artificial intelligence technique that approximates human thinking by having the computer program behave less precisely (e.g., without relying on numbers) than traditional programs. Suppose, for example, a witness describes a male mugging assailant as being "tall and heavyset." These are qualitative terms. It is difficult to match these terms against a suspect file that includes specific heights and weights. Use of traditional computer programs is limited because we are trying to match qualitative describers (e.g., tall) against a file of largely quantitative data (e.g., height in inches).

Suppose we define two membership sets, one for "tall" and one for "heavyset." These are shown in Figures 24–1 and 24–2. Thus, a male with a height 6 feet (72 inches) can have a degree of membership of 0.75. There is a 75 percent chance that this male is "tall." The same type logic would apply to the "heavyset" membership.

Now suppose we search our suspect file and compute a total membership score for "tall" AND "heavyset." The results might look as shown in Figure 24–3. Suspect X would be the first person we would investigate. Next we would look at suspects V and U.

Fuzzy logic has been used to allow us to express qualitative logic in terms that can be used to match quantitative files.

FIGURE 24–1   **Tall Membership**

Height	Proportion of Males*	Membership Score (Cumulative Probability)
5'10"	0.05	0.05
5'11"	0.10	0.15
6' 0"	0.60	0.75
6' 1"	0.15	0.90
6' 2"	0.10	1.00

*Obtained by vote of expert panel.

FIGURE 24–2   **Heavy Membership**

Weight	Proportion of Males*	Membership Score (Cumulative Probability)
195	0.05	0.05
200	0.10	0.15
205	0.20	0.35
210	0.30	0.65
215	0.20	0.85
220	0.15	1.00

*Obtained by vote of expert panel.

(1)	(2)	(3)	(4)	(5)	(6)
Suspect	Height	Tall Membership Score	Weight	Heavy-Set Membership Score	Tall/Heavy-Set Membership Score (3) * (5)
X	6' 1"	.90	210	.65	.585
Y	5'10"	.05	215	.85	.004
Z	5' 6"	.00*	220	1.00	.000
U	6' 2"	1.00	195	.05	.050
V	5'11"	.15	205	.35	.053
W	6' 0"	.75	230	.00*	.000

*Not in membership group.

FIGURE 24–3   **Tall/Heavyset Membership Computation**

Structured Methodologies

Object-oriented analysis and design (OOAD) will (a) be simplified, (b) be made more compatible with end-user views of the world, (c) be made compatible with CASE, and (d) have a toolset with a quick learning curve. The result will be the development of a large group of predesigned (reusable) business application objects available for design of application systems. Quality business applications can then be quickly pieced together. Of particular importance, prototyping will become so easy that it will be considered as a traditional part of the SDLC.

Automated Design Tools

CASE and other automated development aids will continue to grow and thrive if they achieve certain conditions. First, they must continue to meld computer and human processing capabilities. This requires that CASE designers recognize the limit of computer replacement of human tasks.

Second, CASE products must become more integrated. Few firms can afford to buy a front-end package, a back-end package, and a project-management package. Firms want a single, integrated CASE product. IBM's AD/Cycle is an attempt to reach such integration, and similar efforts are under way in Western Europe (ESPRIT) and Japan (Sigma).

Third, packages must become affordable enough to be cost-effective to small- and medium-sized firms. This has happened with computer-aided manufacturing (CAM), but it is not yet a prevalent trend with CASE.

Fourth, CASE represents a revolutionary change in analyst culture and work habits. Emphasis must shift from software issues to implementation issues such as training and performance measurement. Emphasis must also shift from short- to long-term issues. CASE must be evolutionary, not revolutionary.

Fifth, CASE must become easier to use. Current long learning curves will not be tolerated.

Finally, CASE and other development aids must not be considered a design panacea—"the greatest thing since sliced bread." Two lessons have emerged from CASE experience to date. The first lesson is that CASE does not cure bad design. CASE employed in a nonstructured design environment merely speeds up and makes more visible design errors. The second lesson is that CASE is more about quality than productivity. Only expect from CASE what it can deliver. The setting of expectations is by far the most important step in CASE implementation.

Society

Business information system end-users are a part of society as a whole. Thus, these end-users will exhibit the same attitudes toward technology. Society will continue to become more reliant upon technology. The level of computer literacy will continue to rise. However, the most predominant societal trend may be a phenomenal increase in expectations about what computers can do. Consider the following scenario.

Cindra wants to buy two tickets for a concert to be held at the Redondo Beach Opera House. She dials into the ticket agency and, via her modem, her computer is connected with that of the agency. Cindra scans the list of available seats and the prices. She then puts on her virtual reality headset. Cindra finds herself walking into the auditorium and visualizes the two seating locations as if she were physically there. She finds that one of the locations is behind a post. Cindra takes off her virtual reality headset, tells the computer to order tickets for the other seating location, and then vocally orders the computer to rest for awhile.

As a systems analyst, how will you design tomorrow's Customer Order system to match the flair and reality of Cindra's experience? The above scenario soon will be commonplace. The business systems we design in the future will have built-in user interface expectations. These expectations will demand that we design business systems to be as exciting as systems users deal with in everyday life.

These are brief and highly personal reflections of how different forces will change the systems development environment. Whether our description of these forces is wholly or partially accurate, one fact is certain. Systems development will change in the future. The next section provides three different views (scenarios) of paths this change may take.

THREE SCENARIOS OF THE FUTURE

The following views of the future are designed to spur the imagination. It is not likely that any one of these scenarios will dominate. It is more likely that they will exist side by side. Smaller applications will tend toward one approach while larger applications will tend toward another. TPS applications will tend toward one scenario while EIS applications will tend toward another. This should not be surprising. Today, systems analysts must be conversant with multimedia while the outdated magnetic tape medium persists. As Blaah stated in an earlier chapter, "Old technology tends to persist in the face of new technology."

Robotic Design

Bill Ramos is a senior analyst for Moffett Entertainment Services, a large VCR and movie distributor located in Fresno, California. Bill has been asked to design a new accounts receivable system. He proceeds in the following manner:

1. From his home workstation, Bill brings to his large television screen the Integrated Robot Facility (IRF) program. This program automatically connects him with the Moffett west-coast integrated database.

2. Bill views the total Moffett information plan, which includes (a) the description of accounts receivable as an object, (b) the relationship of the accounts receivable object to other objects, (c) a short description of the methods (procedures) already coded for the accounts receivable object, and (d) a data dictionary view of the variables (data) contained in the accounts receivable object.

3. Bill uses the IRF Reengineering function to change the specifications for some of the data elements. He decides that current methods will still apply to the new system. However, he wants to (a) make the system interactive and real-time rather than batch, and (b) send customer billings directly to customers' computers via telecommunication channels.

4. Bill brings up on his home television screen the Human Interface Component (HIC). This component uses menus and questions to step Bill through the process of designing all the interactive screens. The HIC finds similar screen objects already in the reusable object program file. It then automatically makes Bill's new interactive screens *instances* of these existing objects. The Moffett total firm object hierarchy is changed automatically.

5. Bill then brings up the Data Management Component (DMC) of IRF. Again using questions and menus, DMC guides Bill towards designing the protocols necessary to update accounts receivable files (objects) on a real-time rather than batch basis.

6. Bill next brings up the Task Management Component (TMC) of IRF. This component guides him through the process of making the Customer Billing, Customer Statement, and Customer Inquiry methods produce output compatible with and directed to individual customer telecommunication channels.

7. Analyst Ramos then brings to the screen the Rapid Prototyping (RP) component. This component generates a prototype model of the new Accounts Receivable system. The prototype will be used for user training. However, Bill first steps through the prototype to simulate operation of the new system to see if he has left anything out.

8. Bill Ramos is satisfied now with his design of the new Accounts Receivable system. He brings to the screen the Program Design Component (PDC). PDC (a) automatically produces SAMTRAN language code, (b) produces all required Data Division documentation changes, and (c) replaces production scheduling calls for the old system with calls for the new system.

9. Finally, Bill calls up the Implementation Component (IC) of IRF. This component helps Bill (a) design and schedule multimedia training sessions for users of the Accounts Receivable system (which will take place at individual user workstations or via television at user homes), (b) send letters of notification to affected end-users, and (c) design and schedule user surveys to determine the relative success of the new Accounts Receivable system.

Bill Ramos, feeling very satisfied, tells his computer to "STOP PROCESSING." The computer shuts itself off after returning control to Bill's Home Environmental Control System.

The Artistic Toolkit

Victor Dossey is the chief information officer (CIO) for Floormart Department Stores. He has been with Floormart information processing for 22 years. Victor has been through the COBOL revolution, the structured programming revolution, the microcomputer revolution, the structured design revolution, the CASE revolution, and recently, the object-oriented analysis and design (OOAD) revolution. Victor has learned about, learned from, and been partially affected by all these revolutions. Nevertheless, his viewpoint has changed very little.

Victor believes that every design opportunity is a new experience with new people and new requirements. He is afraid of letting automated tools stand between him and his clientele, the end-users who request and use his designed systems. Victor believes his created information systems are as much a piece of art as poetry or symphonies. He is uncomfortable with reengineering, programmerless programming, and even most CASE products. He is uncomfortable because he believes that these approaches tend to limit (even eliminate) the role of human beings in the information development process.

He particularly is skeptical about the role of automated design products in the systems analysis phase of the SDLC. Victor believes there is no automated substitute for police-like "leg-work" where trained analysts go into end-user work areas and "smell out" information problems. Victor is particularly skeptical of reusable code, a basic framework of OOAD. His often cited comment on this subject is "Would you write a new piece of poetry by copying lines from other peoples' poetry?"

The typical process Victor Dossey uses for analyzing and designing a business information system is as follows:

1. When it is clear that a current information system is "in trouble," Victor sends out to the end-user area an investigative team comprised of a senior and junior analyst.

2. The team reports back to Victor on the extent of the problem. Victor and the investigative team decide whether or not to pursue the problem further.

3. Victor's analysts are encouraged to use data flow diagrams via a graphics design program (not CASE) for initial coordination with end-users. These DFDs never go beyond the first-level explosion. When it becomes necessary to explode the system into further detail, Victor encourages his analysts to use the graphics program to generate hierarchical, system flow, and eventually program flowcharts.

4. Victor encourages his analysts to develop prototype models using a dBASE-VI application generator. These prototypes are throwaway models, since the ultimate model will be programmed in COBOL.

5. Design specifications are developed in traditional paper rather than CASE technology. These paper specifications are turned over to human programmers after a series of intense, often inflammatory, structured walkthrough sessions.

6. Victor's programmers use stand-alone workstations to generate mainframe COBOL code from the design specifications. These PC workstations provide easy generation of code, easy and extensive editing, and automatic generation of internal and external program documentation. The workstation COBOL also facilitates use of Floormart's extensive inventory of reusable COBOL code.

Victor Dossey sometimes feels that his attitude toward and knowledge about system development are behind the times. Nevertheless, his position is secure and there are not too many complaints about how his department is run. At his age, Victor muses, he has become a *system philosopher* rather than a nonartistic technician.

Scotch Tape and Super Glue

Cathy Baugher is a senior analyst for Caremore Healthcare Products. After receiving her bachelors degree from California State University, San Jose, Cathy worked for four years as a systems analyst at Floormart Department Store in Victor Dossey's department. During the last two of these years, she studied for her M.S. degree in MIS at California State University, Sacramento. That curriculum emphasized structured development, CASE, object-oriented analysis and design, and automatic program generation. After receiving her degree, Cathy accepted her current, higher level position at Caremore.

Cathy always remembers one particular lecture she attended in a CASE course at CSU Sacramento. The professor told a little-known story of the first moon landing. Computers had calculated the route from Earth to the moon, the orbit around the moon, and the route from that orbit to the surface of the moon. The human astronauts had been primarily observers.

As the Lunar Entry Module (LEM) neared the surface of the moon, the excited astronauts peered out the small windows to see the landing area, a place no previous humans had ever been. Suddenly, one of the astronauts cried out in alarm. The LEM was heading towards a surface area littered with large rocks. The other astronaut quickly reacted and used human manual controls to bypass the computer steering system. The astronaut slightly varied the course and landed the LEM successfully.

The professor's moral to this true story had been, "Even the best-designed and best-planned information system project ends up with a last minute flurry of quick fixing—of Scotch tape and Super Glue."

Thus, Cathy Baugher had adopted a middle road between the robotic design approach of Bill Ramos and the artistic, toolbox approach of Victor Dossey. Cathy relies heavily on CASE technology, but she modifies the formal dance of the CASE approach as follows:

1. Cathy has so far rejected the object-oriented analysis and design (OOAD) approach because she feels it is not end-user oriented; it does not describe the real world in end-user terms. Cathy also prefers process-driven rather than data-driven CASE approaches because she feels that end-users are more comfortable with viewing and describing tasks—*what* task is done, rather than *with what* data the task is done.

2. Cathy halts the structured CASE approach at critical points to seek end-user consultation on their opinions about what has happened in the project so far. Unlike Bill Ramos, Cathy does not do any of her work at home. She does most of her work in the end-user work area.

3. Cathy exercises CASE's automatic generation of program language code (C++ in this instance), but she considers this output only as *skeleton code*. She sends this code to human programmers who make the CASE-generated code (a) more efficient, (b) more future (change) oriented, and (c) better documented.

4. Cathy considers her CASE tool similar to the astronauts Lunar Entry Module. She needs the CASE tool to produce quality information systems, but she refuses to

become an unprepared slave to that automated tool. She leaves room for scotch tape and super glue.

These are but three alternate scenarios concerning the future of business information system development. It is likely that all three scenarios will happen concurrently, along with various other scenarios not included here.

THE SYSTEMS ANALYST AS A CHANGE AGENT

Whichever of these future scenarios comes to pass, whether all three share the future, or if different scenarios emerge, one fact is clear. The systems analyst will be in the midst of organized change in the methodologies and techniques by which we design business information systems. Indeed, it is almost certain that the systems analyst will play an active role as a change agent. An **organization change agent** is one which identifies the need for, encourages, and helps implement change in an organization's culture.

Forigere (1991) describes seven roles of the systems analyst as a future change agent. Paraphrased somewhat, these rules are:

1. Develop a need for change.
2. Establish an information exchange relationship with end-users.
3. Assume an end-user perspective of problems.
4. Secure end-user commitment to change.
5. Use end-users to spread this commitment to other end-users.
6. Freeze positive user behavior toward change.
7. Shift from user reliance to self reliance.

Each of these roles will be briefly described.

Develop a Need For Change: The systems analyst should (a) point out to end-users alternatives to existing problems, (b) dramatize end-users' importance in the solution of these problems, and (c) convince these end-users that *they* are capable of solving the problems. This can be done by selling the concept of change. (See box on "Selling Change.")

Establish an Information-exchange Relationship: Establish with end-users creditability in competence, honesty, and empathy with their problems. You will recall that this role was stressed as a major objective in the systems analysis phase of the SDLC. Structured design methodologies that suggest we skip or curtail systems analysis miss a vital opportunity for systems analysts to sell themselves to end-users.

Assume an End-user Perspective: Do not analyze system problems in your office located in the information systems department. Get out into the end-users' work area. Utilize end-user related tools. This includes working prototypes rather than written specifications, and data flow diagrams that do not explode beyond the second level of detail.

SELLING CHANGE

End-users must sense (1) considerable advantages to them resulting from the change, (2) minimum disadvantages to them from the change, or (3) both, if they are to be convinced to support the change. Following are five areas of concern that the systems analyst must address in order to sell technological change in a business organization.

Relative advantage: What's in it for me? How will my relative position be enhanced as the result of this change?

Compatibility: What is the same in the new system as in the old system? What *won't* I have to learn?

Complexity: How long is the learning curve? Will I be able to learn the new system? How long will it take?

Try-ability: Can I try it out first before I am committed? (This speaks well for prototyping).

Observability: Can I see it in action? Who else is using it and how do they like it? (Most people are skeptical about being technological pioneers).

Any selling of change must address at least these five areas of concern.

Adapted from Kenneth Forigere, "The Future Role of the Systems Analyst as a Change Agent," *Journal of Systems Management.* November 1991.

When you write a letter or report addressed to the end-user community, use the following process:

1. Move the report to the opposite side of your desk.
2. Move a chair to that side of the desk.
3. Pretend you are an end-user (visualize an actual person).
4. Sit in the chair and read the report from an end-user perspective.

Secure End-user Commitment: This can only be done by integrating the social with the technical aspects of the system. There must be emphasis on building user competence to deal with the changing situation. This can be done in two directions (Figure 24–4). First, the change can be made easier by emphasizing system usability (human factors). Second, end-users can acquire additional knowledge and skills through early and consistent training. The key is to empower end-users so that they are aware of and can choose among the range of opportunities.

Use End-users to Spread Commitment: Identify and select opinion leaders among end-user groups (these are generally those persons who have many people visit their offices rather than the opposite). Use these opinion leaders to staff user steering groups. Temporarily assign one or more of these influential end-users to the project team during the length of the SDLC.

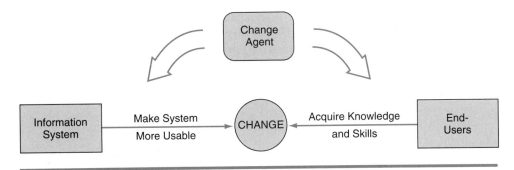

FIGURE 24–4   **Making Change Possible**

Freeze Positive Behavior: Provide rewards for change (e.g., recognition, promotion, bonuses, equipment, training). Make training for change a continuous rather than an ad-hoc process.

Shift from Reliance to Self-reliance: Slowly make end-users less reliant on you as the change agent. Build end-user ownership of the new system. Stay away from the end-user area for increasingly longer periods of time until they do not miss you. Here you must sacrifice your ego to the good of the organization.

The system analyst of the future will continue to be an organization change agent. This will be a difficult role. For, as a creator of change, the analyst must also be concerned with the ethics of such change.

THE ETHICS OF INFORMATION SYSTEMS

C. W. Churchman (1968) tells the following story:

> A famous management scientist, Professor Charnzig, . . . was on a lecture tour accompanied by a young and ambitious chauffeur. Near the end of the tour, the chauffeur remarked how marvelous it must be to stand up and give all those lectures and hear all the applause and praise. "Oh, I don't know," said Charnzig, immodestly, "it's really quite a bore." But the chauffeur insisted, until Charnzig said, "Well, see here; no one knows me at the next college, why don't you read the lecture? I'll even help you pronounce the difficult words."
> Thus it came about that the chauffeur read the lecture so bashfully titled, "A Few Fundamental Contributions to Generalized Network Flows." Then came the question period and an eager assistant professor arose from the rear and said, "Professor, we've been waiting a long time to ask you an important question. How do you compare out-of-kilter with the simplex method in semi-chance constrained networks?"
> The chauffeur, without a pause, replied, "I can't imagine why you'd ask such a simple question here. Why, it's the kind of thing my youngster has already mastered in his fifth-grade mathematics; and just to prove it, I'm going to ask my chauffeur to give you the answer!"
> (C. W. Churchman [1968]; pp. 137–138)

The moral to this story is that there are many different ways to view a situation—that what you think you see may not be what needs to be seen. Churchman proposes the following principle. "If you can't see a purposive activity in two different ways with different moods, you have failed to formulate the problem."

What has this to do with ethics? Ethics involves more than doing what you think is right. In a group setting, ethics is (a) discovering the different individual views of what is right or wrong, (b) attempting to reach a group consensus, and (c) living by that consensus as long as you remain a member of that group. To do otherwise may not be unethical, but neither is it totally ethical.

Applying this to business information systems means that we must seek out all end-user viewpoints of (a) what the system is, (b) what the system should be, and (c) what are the most important aspects of that system. To impose our own personal views, or those of a few select end-users, over that of the entire end-user community is, if not unethical, certainly unprofessional.

Our newspapers are filled with stories of doctors who have prescribed the wrong treatment because they did not perform the tests necessary to assess alternate diagnoses. Our newspapers are filled with stories of police who have sent the wrong person to prison because they did not do the analysis necessary to consider alternate possibilities of others who may have committed the crime. How many mediocre information systems have we implemented because we did not take the time to consider all reasonable alternatives.

A danger with our rush toward robotic design is that everything is locked in. We are limited in our choices. We are not encouraged to seek different viewpoints of the world. Too often, structured design methodologies are like the chauffeur of C. W. Churchman's story. He sure looked like a professor to us, because we were told he was a professor. In the same way, robotic design, carried to its extreme, tells us what should be a good information system. We are not encouraged to see if there is a better, off-the-wall approach.

Always look for different explanations for system problems. Play "what if" games. What if late reports is not the real problem at all? What if, instead, the complaining end-user doesn't know how to use the reports? Or, what if the complaining end-user is really rebelling against rude treatment by the information systems department? The ethics of information systems is that we present end-users with the range of opportunities and let them decide. This requires the systems analyst to look beyond the obvious—the automated development solution that some CASE product spits out.

This looking beyond the obvious has one more dimension. As technological change agents, we must look beyond the narrow scope of our immediate design project. We must use our scarce skills to do our part in improving the world in which we live.

Shneiderman (unpublished) speaks of "Community Beyond the Rapids." He equates the rapids as being the rush towards more and better technology. He believes that we should look beyond the rapids to see how technology can improve the world in which we live. Shneiderman suggests that systems analysts and other change agents should volunteer their skills to using technology to improve life in such areas as:

- Education (e.g., long-distance learning)
- Health (e.g., remote area health care)

- Connection with family and friends (e.g., E-mail)
- Home control/entertainment/shopping
- Community participation (e.g., bulletin boards, voting)
- Elderly (e.g., computer companions)

Shneiderman's concept of Community Beyond the Rapids is that we look beyond that technological task for which we are being paid, to the more general (and vital) use of technology in the world we live. The ethics of information systems, then, is that of actively seeking technological alternatives (opportunities) to solve societal problems in general, and business problems in particular. We must present technology users with choices and empower them to make those choices.

HUMAN ASPECTS

Relatively few people predicted the complete switch away from communism of the Soviet Union and eastern European countries. Even those who predicted that this event might occur were startled at how rapidly it happened. This is symbolic of what is happening in our modern world—of what will happen in the next century. The only thing that will likely remain certain is that things will change rapidly.

For systems analysts, it is critical to keep a future of change in mind. The key skill for the analyst of the next century will be adaptability. The analyst must be able to quickly, easily, and comfortably adjust methodologies to match changing technologies, organizations, and end-user expectations.

The emphasis will be upon semantic (conceptual) rather than syntactic (technical) skills. Much of our current syntactic responsibilities will be done by computers. As analysts we must concentrate on the *what* and *why*. We cannot become slaves of the *how* that dominates technological advances.

Only in this way will we be master of technology, rather than its slave.

SUMMARY

Events and technology are changing too rapidly to allow us to predict accurately the exact state of business systems development in the future. Nevertheless, this chapter has attempted to show trends and to prioritize issues. Of critical importance is the difference between what abilities humans possess that are superior to computers, and vice-versa.

Computers are more effective than humans in (a) handling large volumes of complex data, (b) recognizing unusual patterns, and (c) detecting signals in the midst of noise. Humans, on the other hand, are more effective than computers in induction, insight, and adaptiveness. Automated tools thus can help the human analyst by:

- Reducing tedious tasks
- Reducing requirements for human memory
- Enhancing communication
- Reducing noise

Forces driving the future of systems development include hardware advances, 5GL, artificial intelligence advances in the area of expert systems, increases in end-user computing (EUC), more emphasis on user interfaces, more emphasis on structured development (particularly OOAD), and a more computer literate and conditioned society.

Three possible scenarios of the future were presented. The first was automatic application design by computer software. The second was limited and reluctant use of computer design aids. The third was a middleground between the first two scenarios. Whichever future scenarios may prove to be accurate, one fact is certain. The business systems analyst will continue to function as an important organization change agent.

The analyst has seven roles as a change agent:

- Developing a need for change
- Establishing an information exchange relationship
- Assuming an end-user perspective of problems
- Securing end-user commitment to change
- Using end-users to spread commitment
- Freezing positive user behaviors towards change
- Shifting from user reliance to self reliance

The chapter concluded with a discussion of the ethics of information systems. Two points were stressed. The first was the need for the systems analyst to provide end-users with the full range of design opportunities and systems. The second point was the need for analysts to broaden this viewpoint beyond the immediate application problem. Business systems analysts must be concerned with the use of technology to better society in general—to concentrate on Shneiderman's Community Beyond the Rapids.

Finally, it was suggested that adaptability was the most important skill that the systems analyst can bring to the next century. Change is certain and the business systems analyst, above all, is an organization change agent.

CONCEPTS LEARNED

- Differences between computer and human information-processing capabilities
- Role of computer-aided design

- Forces driving the future
- Roles of the systems analyst as a change agent
- Ethics of information systems

KEY TERMS

adaptiveness
fuzzy set logic
induction
insight

noise
organization change agent
user interface management system (UIMS)

REVIEW QUESTIONS

1. Describe what a computer can do more effectively than humans.
2. What is "noise"?
3. Describe induction.
4. How does insight differ from induction?
5. Describe the four roles of computer-aided design.
6. Describe "programmerless programming."
7. What is "fuzzy logic"?
8. What seems to be the trend for EUC?
9. What is an interface management system?
10. How may CASE products evolve?
11. How may technology condition society in the future?
12. Describe the seven roles of the systems analyst as a change agent.
13. What is an "information-exchange relationship"?
14. What does Shneiderman mean by his "Community Beyond the Rapids"?
15. Why is adaptation so important for the future systems analyst?

CRITICAL THINKING OPPORTUNITIES

1. Draw a diagram to illustrate the organization of this chapter.
2. Compare and contrast human and computer information processing.
3. You are interviewed for a position by three companies as follows:

Company	Interviewer
Moffett Entertainment Services	Bill Ramos
Floormart Department Stores	Victor Dossey
Caremore Healthcare Products	Cathy Baugher

a) Prepare a list of questions you would ask of each interviewer (no more than six separate questions of each interviewer).
b) Based on the scanty information you have, which company would you prefer to work for? Why?

REFERENCES AND FURTHER READINGS

Carrol, J., and C. Carrithers. "Training Wheels in a User Interface." *Communications of the ACM* (August 1984):42–47.

Churchman, C. West. *Challenge to Reason*. New York: McGraw-Hill, 1968.

Forigere, Kenneth. "The Future Role of the Systems Analyst as a Change Agent." *Journal of Systems Management* 42(November 1991):6–9.

Kull, David. "Anatomy of a 4GL Disaster." *Computer Decisions* 18(1966):58–65.

Martin, Merle. "The Human Connection in Systems Design: Prototypes for User Training." *Journal of Systems Management* 38(July 1987):19–22.

Martin, M., and J. Carey. "Converting Prototypes to Operational Systems: Evidence from Preliminary Industrial Surveys." *Information and Software Technology* 33, 5(June 1991):351–356.

Norman, Ronald. "Object-oriented Systems Analysis: A Methodology for the 1990s." *Journal of Systems Management* 42(July 1991):32–40.

Norman, Ronald. "Object-oriented Systems Analysis: A Progressive Expansion of OOA." *Journal of Systems Management* 42(August 1991):13–16.

Taylor, David. *Object-oriented Information Systems*. New York: Wiley, 1992.

Turban, Efraim. *Expert Systems and Applied Artificial Intelligence*. New York: Macmillan, 1992.

GLOSSARY

A

accuracy: Information characteristic including completeness, correctness, and security.

action document: System output that later becomes input to the same or another system.

active record: Record that has had an update activity within a specified time.

activity phasedown: System changeover phase where only priority transactions are processed.

activity resumption: System changeover phase where the new system is returned to a full level of transaction activity.

adaptive (level 3) prototype: Working model of information system.

adaptiveness: Ability of humans to adjust quickly to new and changing situations.

alpha testing: Testing of a unit or system independently from the operating system.

application backlog: Business applications waiting to be developed.

application development/cycle (AD/cycle): IBM-provided integrated application tool that encompasses entire system life cycle.

application generator: Piece of software devoted to designing business applications while requiring no user programming.

attribute: Modification or description of both entities and relationships.

avoidance: User resistance by pretending that the new system does not exist.

B

back-end (lower) CASE: CASE product devoted to physical design and construction phases of the SDLC.

balance field: Numeric field reflecting current, future, or past availability of a resource item.

batch processing: Collection of transactions in a group before record update.

beta testing: Software testing done on a pilot basis within a limited department or region.

block (category) code: A code containing special, unique numbers that identify a specific resource item.

breakeven analysis: An alternative evaluation method that determines at what point cash flow turns from negative to positive.

breakeven point: The exact point in time when cash flow changes from negative to positive.

business data: An organization's description of resources and transactions.

business information: Business data that has been reorganized to allow managers to select future ways to fulfill goals.

C

centralized database: A database in which all data is stored and controlled at one site.

centralized coding: Coding done by centralized data entry personnel at the time transactions are entered to the computer.

changeover contract: A contract between developers and users including performance goals, tolerances, estimated system life, maintenance expectations, and future changes.

changeover scheduling: Formulation and distribution of schedule of system changeover activities.

checkoff group: User group convened as a fail-safe mechanism to prevent fatal design errors.

chief information officer (CIO):   A vice president–level director of all the firm's information resources and activities.

children nodes: Nodes having one higher level parent node.

closed questions: Structured questions with limited choice of responses.

closure: Completion of one task so the user can concentrate on the next task.

code generator: Software that translates system specifications to program code.

coding: Changing source data to a more suitable storage format.

cohesion: A state describing how well activities within a single program module are related to one another.

collision rate: The percentage of occurrences when more than one resource record is assigned the same address (slot) in memory.

command language: Instructions that allow users to tell the application program directly what to do.

completeness: An information characteristic describing the presence of all necessary message units.

Computer-Aided Systems Engineering (CASE):   The collection and integration of automated tools and procedures to help in the system development process.

computer semantic knowledge: Conceptual knowledge of how computers work in general.

confluence flow: The condition where one process receives input from two or more input files.

congruence: The distinction between separate sensual stimuli.

continuous quality improvement (CQI):   Stressing fault removal from the development process and detecting inefficiencies in operating systems.

control break: Starting a new page and summary totals on a report when there is a change in a key field.

convenience sampling: Selection of an easy to reach subset of a population.

conventional file: A repository designed for single business applications.

correctness: An information characteristic describing if message items are included accurately.

crash changeover tactic: A tactic where the old system is discontinued and the new system started simultaneously.

critical success factor (CSF):   An essential activity that must go right if the business is to succeed.

cueing: A screen technique providing users guidance as to how data is to be entered.

customer information control system (CICS):   An IBM software system providing a multiuser, interactive environment.

D

daily transaction log: A computer-stored record of all transactions processed each day.

data: The description of things and events we face.

database management system (DBMS):   An organized collection of two or more resource files.

data consistency: A characteristic ensuring that multiple occurrences of the same stored data field have the same values.

data dictionary: A repository for all data structures and elements within an information system.

data element: The lowest level of information on the basis of which a process can act.

data element dictionary: That part of the data dictionary comprised of data element specifications.

data definition language (DDL):   That part of a DBMS used to set up record types and schemas.

data flow: Data that is input or output to a process.

data flow diagram (DFD):   A graphic representation of the flow of data throughout a system.

data integrity: A characteristic whereby stored data are changed or reviewed only by persons formally authorized by the firm.

data management component (DMC):   Object-oriented design component that provides the protocol for storage, retrieval, and update of objects within a database.

data manipulation language (DML):   The language that manipulates and updates a database.

data modeling: Graphic representation of how data ideally should be organized and flow through an information system.

data packet: A data flow containing multiple data elements.

data processing: Changes performed on data to produce purposeful information.

data redundancy: Multiple occurrences of same stored data field.

data stores: Groups of data structures held temporarily as a file until needed.

data structure: A collection of data elements.

day-one changeover tactic: The tactic where, after a given date, all new business is processed on the new system.

decentralized coding: Transaction coding done by clerical personnel at decentralized locations.

decision support system (DSS):   A quantitative model to help managers solve semistructured problems.

decision table: A textual tool that lays out the logic of complex problems where there are multiple actions based upon multiple conditions.

decision tree: A graphic representation of a decision structure.

decoupling processes: Reducing the dependency of one process on another.

default value: A value automatically supplied by an applications program when the end-user has left the field blank.

demand (ad hoc) report: A report produced at irregular intervals based on user demand.

dependency island: The division of system inputs into independent classes (islands) relating to system output so as to facilitate system testing.

design freeze: The time after which no changes are allowed to design specifications.

detail record: Explosion of a master record's balance fields.

development programming: One-time programming of a new information system.

direct file access: Assignment of records to a specific storage location based on computations made by a hashing routine.

dispersion flow: The situation when one file flows into two or more processes.

distributed database: A database shared by different locations within the firm.

distributed data processing: The situation in which end-users decide equipment, implementation, and development priorities.

document review: An analysis tactic whereby existing documents are collected and evaluated.

E

economy: An information characteristic describing the level of resources needed to produce information.

efficiency: An information characteristic defined by the ratio of units of information output divided by units of resources expended.

electronic funds transfer (EFT):   The system where financial documents are transferred electronically between information systems with no use of paper.

elementary testing: Testing of lower level modules of the hierarchy chart.

entities: Objects making up data in a database.

entity-relationship diagram (ERD):   A graphic tool showing a data-oriented approach to describe system elements.

equivalency class: Two or more input values handled by the same series of logic branches.

error feedback report: A report providing error feedback to end-users and data entry personnel.

ESPRIT: A western European cooperative effort to develop an integrated CASE product.

executive information system (EIS):   A special management information system dedicated to strategic management and emphasizing use of information external to the firm.

expert system (ES):   A qualitative model that replaces managers on solution of structured problems.

explosion: Expansion of a higher level process into multiple lower level processes.

exponential costs: Costs that increase or decrease at an increasing rate of change.

exponential smoothing: A statistical technique that requires storage of one field rather than a series of historical data fields.

external entity: A group of people who interact with but are not an internal part of an information system.

external probe: Measurement conducted without the knowledge of operational units.

external program documentation: Logic aid outside program code.

F

feedback flow: Files output from one process and input to another process.

file conversion: Conversion from old to new system file format.

file layout document: Graphic representation of a file record.

file recovery: A contingency procedure to reestablish resource files that have been destroyed or otherwise made ineffective.

file requirements document: A textual description of a file.

file retention: Separation of active and inactive records.

fixed-length record: A record where all fields have the same length as all other records.

form-filling screen: A function screen that allows operators to enter data directly from source documents.

forward engineering: Development of program code from system specifications.

front-end (upper) CASE: A CASE product that includes the SDLC phases of strategic planning, analysis, and logical design.

full life-cycle CASE: A CASE product including both front-end and back-end capabilities.

functional cohesion: The condition where a module contains all and only those tasks contributing to the generation of a single information function or product.

functional discontinuity: The difficulty of operating several tasks that require different methods, procedures, and skills.

function testing: Testing of intergroup interaction accuracy.

future file: A file including enhancements that can be made to the system in the future.

G

general systems life cycle (GSLC):   A cycle of stages that occur in the life of any biological, social, or information system.

go/no-go decision: A management decision made at the end of the analysis phase of the SDLC as to whether or not the development project will be continued.

group data: A collection of data elements.

group testing: Testing of logical groups of elementary modules.

H

hashing routine: A programmed mathematical operation that converts an input key field into a specific storage location.

heuristic (level 2) prototype: An addition to a level 1 (I/O) prototype by including database updating.

heuristic test data: Test data continually being augmented based upon system experience.

hidden application backlog: A list of user-needed information applications where discouraged end-users have not requested development services.

hierarchy chart: A graphic tool that identifies all tasks and processes in a system by use of a hierarchical structure.

hierarchical database structure: A linking structure where each child node has only one parent node.

highlighting: Presentation of information in a mode that contrasts with other screen information.

HIPO chart: A graphic tool comprised of a hierarchy chart linked to input-process-output (IPO) charts.

hit rate: The percentage of resource records updated during a transaction processing run.

hostility: A form of user resistance where users display antagonism towards a new information system.

human factors: Study of the welfare, satisfaction, and performance of people working with an information system.

human interactive component (HIC):   Object-oriented design component dealing with interactive screens.

I

inactive record: A record that has not had update activity within a specified period of time.

incident: A lower level case of a parent object class.

index storage area: An area that holds the indexes required for record access when the index access method is used.

industrial engineer: A professional responsible for designing and improving physical work processes.

induction: The ability of humans to act on inconsistently formatted data to fill in gaps, recognize emerging patterns, and decipher trends.

information: Data organized to help managers choose a current or future action.

information center: A user-oriented service center that provides consultation, assistance, and documentation to encourage end-user development and use of information applications.

information clearinghouse: A central location where end-user information inquiries are serviced.

informational data: Values, characteristics, and labels associated with physical data.

information engineering facility (IEF):   A CASE tool developed by Texas Instruments.

information hiding: The keeping of embedded object information away from access by other objects.

information overload: The adverse effect from an entity receiving too much data.

information resource management (IRM):   A top-level management approach to organization computing.

information system life cycle: A special instance of the general systems life cycle dedicated to the life of an information system.

inheritance: The assumption of data from objects higher in the same class.

input-process-output (IPO) chart: A graphic tool delineating input files and output files or reports associated with tasks.

inquiry-based system: A system allowing users to design reports on an ad hoc basis.

inquiry dialogue mode: An interactive mode using simple questions to which the user must provide short responses.

inquiry language (IQL):   A database component that allows tailored retrieval of screens and reports according to parameters provided by end-users.

input/output (level 1) prototype: A model including only printed reports and interactive screens.

input verification: A question asking the user if the last field was entered correctly.

insight (creativity):   The ability of humans to use inductive processes for creating alternatives to solving problems.

integrated CASE (ICASE):   A CASE product including full life cycle support, re-engineering, and project support.

integrated testing facilities (ITC):   A testing tactic that enables test data to be employed while transactions are being processed on-line.

internal probe: Measuring a process directly with the knowledge of end-users.

internal program documentation: The narrative augmentation to code so that maintenance programmers can quickly and fully understand design programmer logic.

interview: A series of questions asked in person.

investment period: Period to the left of (before) the breakeven point where one-time development costs are expended.

iteration construct: A structured programming construct that describes repetition of the same program logic.

iterative (type I) prototype: A model that employs the prototype as the final system after a series of evolutionary changes based on user feedback.

J

Joint Application Design (JAD):   A session where users and analysts interact to develop higher level (logical) system specifications.

K

key field: A unique field that determines at what location a resource record will be stored.

L

learning: Moving information chunks from short-term to long-term memory.

Le Courier chart: A guideline for the appropriate colorization of forms and screens.

Likert scale: A closed question using a horizontal set of numbered responses.

linear costs: Straight line increases or decreases in costs.

linkage field: A field that contains the address of where a related record is stored.

loaded question: A question suggesting the desired response.

local screen density: The average number of nonblank characters surrounding a typical character on an interactive screen.

logical data flow diagram: A physical DFD stripped of information on *how* a process works.

logical design: The system blueprint for the new system.

long-term memory (LTM):   The human mind's permanent storage.

lowest cost strategy: The strategy where a firm creates products or services at a price lower than competitors.

M

macro flowchart: A flowchart without the lower (primitive) levels of the hierarchy chart.

maintenance planning stage: A stage in the planning spectrum where managers react to information system problems.

maintenance programming: The day-to-day correction of information system problems.

management information system (MIS):   A system providing information to meet problem-solving needs.

marginal costs: The actual additional out-of-pocket costs of implementing a new information system.

market barriers: A strategy where the firm uses technology to increase customer service to the point where it becomes prohibitively expensive for new firms to enter the market.

market niche: The strategy where a firm appeals to a specific segment of the market.

master record: A record containing information for a resource item.

memory capacity: The amount of human memory available.

memory map: A snapshot of what data are in computer memory at a specific point in time.

menu: An interactive screen presenting users with a list of processing options.

methods: Processes used to manipulate objects.

mission statement: The direction a firm wants to take.

mnemonic code: The representation of information in a form that describes conditions in a more human format.

modularity: Design of a system in relatively small chunks.

multiple inheritance: Ability of an object to inherit data from more than one object class.

mutual exclusivity: The state where the existence of one condition precludes the existence of another.

N

network database architecture: A two-way hierarchical structure where a child can have more than one parent.

new system priming: The part of implementation planning where the new system is fed a minimum number of transactions.

normalization: The process of eliminating all repeating nonkey data fields in a relational database.

O

object: A basic system element that combines data and processes to perform a unique system function.

off-line: The use of an intermediate stage between data entry and input to a computer.

on-line: Direct entry of data to a computer.

open question: A question with unlimited choice of responses.

operating instructions: Procedures that instruct users how to operate an information system.

operational management: Management of day-to-day decisions to keep the firm operating.

optimizing: Seeking the best possible choice.

overflow storage area: An area holding records that are synonyms of other resource records (randomize to same address).

overhead costs: The allocation of nondirect costs according to some measurable criterion.

P

parallel changeover tactic: A tactic where the old and new system are operated concurrently for a specified period.

parameter: Special message information that a receiver object may need.

parent node: A node having lower level children nodes.

payback period: The time when positive cash flow from operational savings matches the negative cash flow of one-time development costs.

periodic reports: Reports produced at a set frequency.

performance matrix: An inventory of indicators needed to measure system performance.

phased conversion tactic: Implementation of portions of the new system.

physical data: Resources that can be seen and counted.

physical data flow diagram: A graphic tool indicating *what* processes are in a system and *how* they operate.

physical design: Converting the system blueprint (logical design) into the specific detail required for programmers to construct program code.

pilot conversion tactic: Implementation of a system at a selected location in advance of other locations.

planned redundancy: Duplication of information deliberately to enhance communication or for protection.

polymorphism: Use of the same name for different methods in different objects.

postimplementation review: A review seeking agreement that the new system has settled down—that fine-tuning is complete.

preliminary design: Development of general system specifications in order to perform feasibility analysis and to determine whether or not to proceed with design.

preliminary problem report: A report containing the source, analysis, and recommendations for reported system problems.

present value: The present discounted value of a future cash receipt or outlay reflecting the time value of money.

prime record area: A storage area holding resource records.

primitive level (code):   The point where specifications can be translated on a one-per-one basis to lines of program code.

print layout sheet: Graphic representation of an output report.

prior data model: A model of how analysts think the information system operates.

privacy: Protection of data that, if wrongly used, may damage individuals.

probe: A follow-up question seeking more detail to a question already asked.

problem: The gap between what we expect and the current status.

problem domain component (PDC):   The object-oriented design component that identifies specific system criteria.

procedure flow: Analysis of operational procedures.

process specification: The definition of how a process works.

product differentiation: A strategy where the firm develops a product unique to the market.

program stub: An incomplete module that passes control back to the calling module.

programmer workbench: A collection of unlinked tools that aid rapid building of separate system pieces.

project management: An integrated collection of tools, techniques, and procedures that aid successful and timely completion of a system project.

projection: A form of user resistance by blaming applications problems on the new system.

programmer: A specialist who transfers analysis specifications into program language code.

prototype generator: Software designed to quickly and easily build prototypes.

prototyping: The process of quickly building a model of the final software system to be used as a communication tool to assess and meet user information needs.

pseudocode: A technique for specifying primitive-level program logic.

Q

quality measurement system (QMS):   A formal problem notification system that allows management to detect system problems.

questionnaire: A predesigned, printed instrument sent to many persons to solicit facts.

R

radical top-down approach: Completion of higher level modules first, then lower level modules on a priority basis.

real-time processing: Immediate posting of transactions to resource records.

receiver: An object performing services for another object.

record access: Use of a transaction key field to find a matching file record to change.

record access time: Interval for searching for, finding, and transferring a stored record.

record density: The percentage of file space occupied by resource records.

reengineering: Improvement of information processes after the system is operational.

relationship: A conceptual link that ties one entity to another.

relational database structure: A structure using two-dimensional tabular format rather than linkage between records.

relative file access: Assignment of a record to a particular file slot based on computations of a hashing routine.

relevancy: An information characteristic describing how a message is used for problem solving.

reliability: An information characteristic measuring how consistently a process performs.

replicated database: A database in which parts are copied to a central location.

report record: A record containing one report page.

report requirements document: A narrative description of an output report.

repository: The CASE axis that ties together all system modules.

requirements analysis document: A record of analysis efforts.

response rate: The percentage of questionnaires sent out that are returned.

return on investment (ROI):   The percentage profit the firm expects from investing its resources.

return period: The time (area) after the breakeven point when the new system is generating positive cash flow.

reusable code: Program code that can be extracted from other systems for use in a new system.

reverse engineering: The modification of system specifications from program code.

risk assessment: The classification of system errors by likelihood and impact.

S

sabotage: A form of user resistance where users actively try to make a new system fail.

sampling: Selection of an appropriate subset of a population for analysis in order to gauge the behavior of that population.

satisficing: Selection of an alternative that is better but not necessarily best.

schema: Global (physical) arrangement of data in a database.

seam testing: Concentration of testing at extremes, the value zero, and exceptional occurrences.

security: Protection of data that, if wrongly disseminated, could damage organizational goals.

security audit: A structured check to determine if sensitive information is being disseminated to unauthorized users.

segmented database: A database where parts are stored at different locations.

selection construct: A structured programming construct where there is branching to one of several processing paths.

selective perception: A human tendency to notice events that fit a preconceived notion.

self-checking code: A code with a computed check digit to detect inaccurate entry of data.

sender: An object requesting services from another object.

sequence construct: A structured programming construct where the process proceeds sequentially from one module to another.

sequential file access: The processing of resource records one at a time in a given sequence.

serial code: A code having no meaning but uniquely identifying a resource item.

short-term memory (STM):   The temporary, limited-capacity human memory that processes perceptual input.

sibling nodes: Nodes at the same level of the hierarchy chart having the same parent node.

SIGMA: The Japanese national effort to develop an ICASE tool.

simultaneous update: The situation in which two users attempt to update the same record at the same time.

sink: An external entity provided with output data from the system.

source: An external entity feeding data to a system.

specification walkthrough: A meeting with programmer peers to step through design specifications in order to reduce programming false starts and operational errors.

staged changeover tactic: An implementation tactic whereby the old system is replaced in stages.

standard information system: A system that is the same across different firms.

status field: A field differentiating one resource item from another.

steering committee: A committee of managers who have the power to stop implementation of the system.

step: A testing technique with a program-slowed, instruction-by-instruction stepthrough of a computer program.

step function costs: Costs that remain relatively stable until some event occurs that causes costs suddenly to rise sharply.

stimuli: Data detected by the human mind.

strategic computing: Computing designed to enhance the profit posture of the firm.

strategic level of management: Managers who make decisions about the overall goals and direction of the firm.

strategic value: A condition increasing the firm's profit potential.

strategy prioritizing planning stage: The business planning stage in which overall information technology goals are set on the basis of the firm's overall goals.

structure chart: A graphic tool showing the hierarchy of program modules and data interfaces between them.

structured English: A form of pseudocode not tied to specific program languages and using only structured programming structures.

structured walkthrough: A session in which the analyst presents design details before a group of peers.

subschema: A logical arrangement (view) of a database tailored to a specific user.

surround strategy: Use of telecommunications (UNIX) to let disparate systems communicate with one another.

syntactic computer knowledge: Machine-dependent rules for how to use specific applications on specific computers.

systematic random sampling: The selection of every Nth item from a population, where N is selected randomly.

system cutover: The date for discontinuance of the old system and operational use of the new system.

system fine tuning: The process of handling minor unanticipated flaws in a new system.

system flowchart: A graphic tool documenting physical (hardware) interfaces with a system.

system importation stage: A business planning stage where outside firms are searched for successful technological applications that can be imported to the firm.

system life: The length of time a new system can be expected to operate before it begins to become ineffective.

system maintenance: The fixing of minor system flaws.

system modification: The fixing of more than minor system flaws.

systems analyst: A problem solver who compares performance of the current system with performance it should deliver and determines how to solve any discrepancies.

systems application architecture (SAA): A full set of applications enablers that spans the entire IBM product line.

system study: A study including details gathered during the analysis stage and recommendations on the proposed system.

system success: The meeting of an established percentage of measurable system goals.

system success rate: The ratio of the number of transactions processed without flaws divided by total transactions processed.

system testing: Testing of the entire software system.

system with training wheels: A system that operates on a small subset of full system capabilities.

T

tactical management: Managers in charge of specific products, missions, or departments.

tactical prioritizing phase: The business planning phase in which technology priorities are established within each department.

tailored information system: An information system matched to the specific characteristics of a firm.

task management component (TMC): An object-oriented design component that defines external systems and devices.

task semantic computer knowledge: The conceptual knowledge of how a particular application (task) operates.

testing plan: A plan including the testing sequence, composition of test data, and documented test results.

throughput: The number of error-free transactions processed per unit of time.

throwaway (type II) prototype: A prototype used as a model for the final system.

timeliness: An information characteristic describing how fast input is transformed to output.

total screen density: A measure of interactive screen clutter computed by dividing the number of nonblank characters by total screen character capacity.

tolerance filter: A problem structure component that determines whether expectation gaps are large enough to require management attention.

top-down approach: A design approach in which definition starts at the general level, then undergoes successive refinement down to the specific, detailed level.

total quality management (TQM): Application of quality principles for the integration of all functions and processes of an organization.

trace: A diagnostic technique that provides a picture of how logic paths are used and what values are changed as the program executes.

transaction-processing system (TPS): An information system that keeps track of current and potential organization resources.

transaction record: A record containing a single transaction.

trap: A diagnostic technique that provides automatic program halts and stops when specified variables are modified.

triggering field: A field used to initiate exception processes.

turnaround document: A machine-read document that is input to the same system from which it was output.

U

usability: An information characteristic describing the usefulness of a system to humans.

user interface management system (UIMS):   Special software utilities that handle all screen interfaces.

utility package: Software accompanying a computer operating system and including sorts, merges, and the like.

V

value-added process: A process that clearly adds value (quality) to information system output.

variable: A data element embedded within an object.

variable-length record: A record where field size can vary.

virtual storage access method (VSAM):   An access method using indexes to direct a transaction to a storage area where its record is located.

W

watch: A diagnostic technique that halts a program whenever a specified data name changes.

waterfall model: An SDLC model that emphasizes that any stage can return to prior stages.

working memory: The part of the human mind that processes data, solves problems, and generates solutions.

INDEX

D